Frommer's®
Alaska

My Alaska

by Charles Wohlforth

MY FAMILY AND I HAVE LIVED IN ALASKA ALL OUR LIVES, BUT AT times, we feel like visitors. Our house in Anchorage is like a base camp, the place where we pack and prepare, peruse maps and dream, looking to the dark winter sky for inspiration for our next Alaska adventure. We live in this house all winter, working, going to school, and eating dinner around a table like anyone else. But even on school nights, when the sun sets at 3pm, the snow beckons us to strap on our skis. We follow the city's cross-country trails under electric lights, or simply glide in the moonlight, where the smooth landscape gleams a strange lunar color.

As spring nears and the sky lightens, my children strain at the bonds of the city like sled dogs, mad to run. It's not a specific place they want to visit. They yearn for the shock when a whale leaps high next to the boat. The sense of anticipation as a fish we just caught sizzles on the fire. They want to clamber to the top of a mountain in the morning and catch hermit crabs in a sand pail in the afternoon. Then, when we find ourselves awake past midnight under a bright sky, breathing crisp, immaculate air, surrounded by the life of the sea and by fragrant growth on the steep sides of the coastal mountains, we think: "Yes, we're home."

Any visitor can feel that visceral connection—and after looking through the photos in these pages, you'll begin to understand why.

© Charles Wohlforth

We took this **FAMILY PHOTO (left)** in Prince William Sound (South Culross Passage, to be exact) one night in July toward the end of a 16-day camping trip with our little boat. If you ask any of us what we do, who we are—even if you ask little Becky, 3 years old in this picture—you will hear about these summer boating trips in the wilderness. Thoughts of those moments carry us through exams, boring meetings, deadlines. It's all out there waiting.

When you're camping in the Sound, ice to refill the cooler is never too far away. Dozens of glaciers dump **CENTURIES-OLD ICE (above)** that is as clear and dense as crystal. It's this ice that carved the Sound's long fjords and sheer rock shores, and many extravagant landforms all along Alaska's southern coast.

Some **FISH (right)** for food, snagging big healthy salmon and grilling them over a fire. Others don't care if they catch anything, contented to feel the breeze and the sun and watch a fly dance over smooth water.

The view at **ALYESKA RESORT (below)**, an hour from our home in Anchorage, is a constant source of distraction: You want to stop your skis and gaze at the glistening water of Turnagain Arm stretching from just beyond the base of the mountain.

Ripples around the hull of the canoe. The scent of clean water. A circle of sky bounded by smoothly gliding shores. **CANOEING (above right)** is a favorite summer dream, a memory sustaining itself reliably beneath the ice of winter.

Even in gentle **PRINCE WILLIAM SOUND (below right),** being outdoors in Alaska requires a reliance on machines. You can't get way out there and be safe without them. Most visitors come on tour boats and cruise ships.

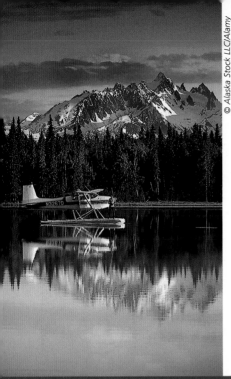

Among the unexpected wonders of the wilderness is the intense sense of privacy that befalls visitors to huge, empty places. A **FLOATPLANE (left)** is a portal to this aloneness. No visitor to Alaska should miss the opportunity to take a small plane either for a remote fishing trip, bear viewing experience, our mountain flightseeing outing. This image comes from the Alaska Range, south of Mt. McKinley.

You don't have to fly or have a boat. You can drive to the wilderness. If you can handle the dust, cracked windshields, and going hundreds of miles between crude services, you can be your own Arctic guide on the **DALTON HIGHWAY (below)**.

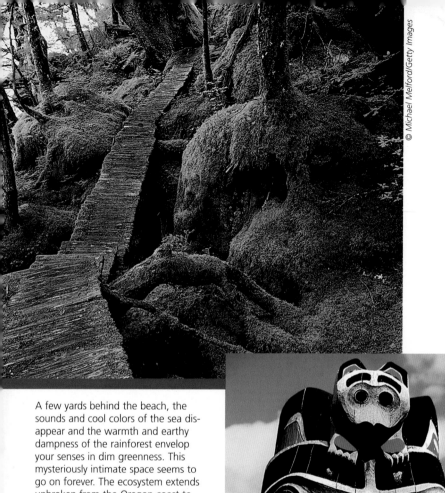

A few yards behind the beach, the sounds and cool colors of the sea disappear and the warmth and earthy dampness of the rainforest envelop your senses in dim greenness. This mysteriously intimate space seems to go on forever. The ecosystem extends unbroken from the Oregon coast to Prince William Sound, a distance greater than from Miami, Florida, to Portland, Maine. Often the land is so thick with mossy life that trails, like this one in **MISTY FJORDS NATIONAL MONUMENT** (above), can only be built on boardwalks.

The language of carved faces is not lost in Southeast Alaska. Master carvers still work among the huge trees of the rainforest. **TOTEM POLES** (right) were not meant to last; instead, old poles rotted away in the rainy woods over a century or so, inspiring new generations of carvers to follow. Today's carvers use traditional techniques and images, but also tell new stories, recording their peoples' ongoing history.

© Paul A. Souders/Corbis

Running into a bear can be an unwelcome thrill, but more and more visitors come to Alaska in search of bear encounters. The premier site is Katmai National Park's Brooks Camp, where, in season, huge **BROWN BEARS** (above) position themselves at the top of a waterfall to catch salmon heading upstream to spawn.

Children can become jaded by almost anything. I have examples—kids bored with huge waterfalls, spectacular sunsets, even s'mores. *Almost* anything. My children have seen **WHALES BREACHING** (right) often, but their jaws still drop every time.

Opposite page: © Leo Keeler/Alamy

© RO-MA Stock/Index Stock

In the fall (late Aug to Sept) it's not unusual to hear the crack and rattle of colliding antlers when **MOOSE FIGHT AT DENALI NATIONAL PARK.** Seeing a moose by design is hard, but it's a rare month that goes by our Anchorage home when we don't run across at least one. Rutting moose do show up in backyards during autumn in Anchorage and other towns.

MILEAGE CHART

Approximate driving distances in miles between cities.

	Anchorage	Circle	Dawson City	Eagle	Fairbanks	Haines	Homer	Prudhoe Bay	Seattle	Seward	Skagway	Tok	Valdez
Anchorage		520	494	501	358	775	226	847	2234	126	832	328	304
Circle	520		530	541	162	815	746	1972	2271	646	872	368	526
Dawson City	494	530		131	379	548	713	868	1843	619	430	189	428
Eagle	501	541	131		379	620	727	868	1974	627	579	173	427
Fairbanks	358	162	379	379		653	584	489	2121	484	710	206	364
Haines	775	815	548	620	653		1001	1142	1774	901	359	447	701
Homer	226	746	713	727	584	1001		1073	2455	173	1058	554	530
Prudhoe Bay	847	1972	868	868	489	1142	1073		2610	973	1199	695	853
Seattle	2243	2271	1843	1974	2121	1774	2455	2610		2493	1577	1931	2169
Seward	126	646	619	627	484	901	173	973	2493		958	454	430
Skagway	832	872	430	579	710	359	1058	1199	1577	958		504	758
Tok	328	368	189	173	206	447	554	695	1931	454	504		254
Valdez	304	526	428	427	364	701	530	853	2169	430	758	254	

Chukchi Sea

RUSSIA

Bering Strait

Little Diomede Island

Bering Land Bridge National Preserve

Nome

Norton Sound

Yukon Delta National Wildlife Refuge

Kuskokwim River

Bethel

Yukon Delta National Wildlife Refuge

Nunivak Island

Dillingham

Bering Sea

Pribilof Islands

Bristol Bay

Aniakchak National Monument and Preserve

Cape St. Stephen

Rat Islands

A L E U T I A N   I S L A N D S

Cold Bay

Unimak Island

ALASKA PENINSULA

Adak

Adak Island

Atka Island

Atka

Dutch Harbor

Unimák

Unalaska

PACIFIC OCEAN

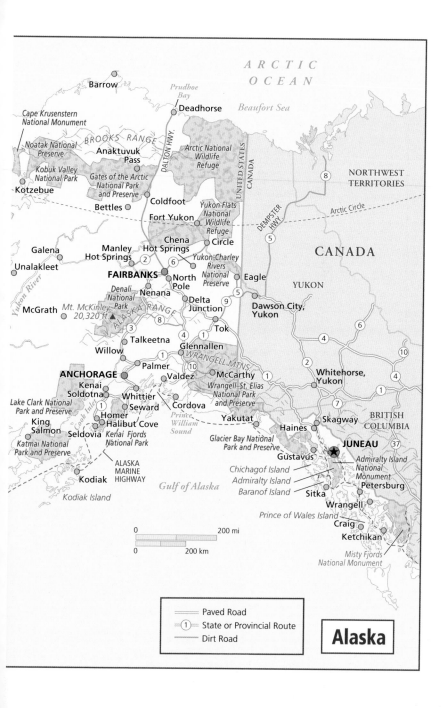

Alaska

ARCTIC OCEAN

Barrow

Prudhoe Bay

Deadhorse

Beaufort Sea

Cape Krusenstern National Monument

BROOKS RANGE

Noatak National Preserve

Anaktuvuk Pass

DALTON HWY.

Arctic National Wildlife Refuge

UNITED STATES
CANADA

8

NORTHWEST TERRITORIES

Kobuk Valley National Park

Gates of the Arctic National Park and Preserve

Kotzebue

Bettles

Coldfoot

Fort Yukon

Yukon Flats National Wildlife Refuge

DEMPSTER HWY.

Arctic Circle

5

CANADA

Galena

Manley Hot Springs

Chena Hot Springs

Circle

YUKON

Unalakleet

2

6

Yukon-Charley Rivers National Preserve

FAIRBANKS

North Pole

Eagle

5

Denali National Park

Nenana

Delta Junction

9

Dawson City, Yukon

6

McGrath

Mt. McKinley 20,320 ft.

ALASKA RANGE

8

Tok

4

Yukon River

3

Talkeetna

4

1

Willow

Glennallen

WRANGELL MTNS.

4

10

ANCHORAGE

Palmer

10

Valdez

McCarthy

2

Whitehorse, Yukon

4

Kenai

Whittier

Wrangell–St. Elias National Park and Preserve

1

Soldotna

Seward

Cordova

1

Lake Clark National Park and Preserve

Cook Inlet

Homer

Halibut Cove

Prince William Sound

Yakutat

7

BRITISH COLUMBIA

King Salmon

Seldovia

Kenai Fjords National Park

Glacier Bay National Park and Preserve

Haines

Skagway

37

Katmai National Park and Preserve

ALASKA MARINE HIGHWAY

Gulf of Alaska

Gustavus

JUNEAU

Admiralty Island National Monument

Kodiak

Chichagof Island

Admiralty Island

Petersburg

Kodiak Island

Baranof Island

Sitka

Wrangell

Prince of Wales Island

Craig

Ketchikan

Misty Fjords National Monument

0 ——— 200 mi

0 ——— 200 km

Paved Road

—1— State or Provincial Route

Dirt Road

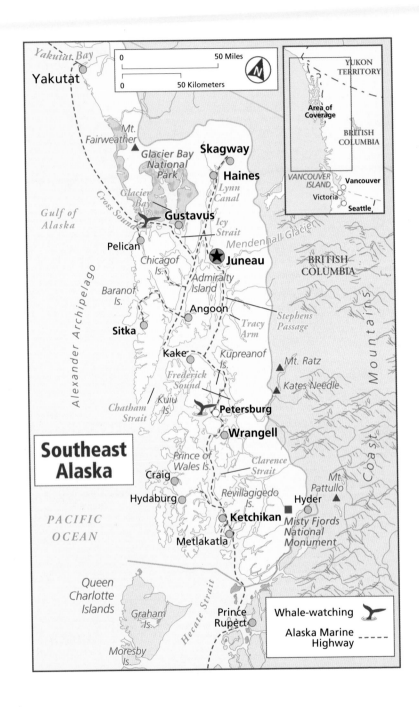

Southeast Alaska

Yakutat Bay
Yakutat

0 · · · · 50 Miles
0 · · · · 50 Kilometers
N

Mt. Fairweather
Glacier Bay National Park
Skagway
Haines
Lynn Canal
Glacier Bay
Cross Sound
Gulf of Alaska
Gustavus
Icy Strait
Mendenhall Glacier
Pelican
Chicagof Is.
Juneau
BRITISH COLUMBIA
Baranof Is.
Admiralty Island
Angoon
Tracy Arm
Stephens Passage
Sitka
Alexander Archipelago
Kake
Kupreanof Is.
Frederick Sound
Mt. Ratz
Kates Needle
Kuiu Is.
Chatham Strait
Petersburg
Wrangell
Prince of Wales Is.
Clarence Strait
Craig
Revillagigedo Is.
Mt. Pattullo
Hydaburg
Hyder
PACIFIC OCEAN
Ketchikan
Misty Fjords National Monument
Metlakatla
Coast Mountains

Queen Charlotte Islands
Graham Is.
Hecate Strait
Prince Rupert
Moresby Is.

YUKON TERRITORY
Area of Coverage
BRITISH COLUMBIA
VANCOUVER ISLAND
Vancouver
Victoria
Seattle

Whale-watching
Alaska Marine Highway - - - - -

The Kenai Peninsula & Prince William Sound

Alaska Marine Highway
Railway
Whale Watching

Alaska

Fairbanks
Anchorage
Kenai
Sitka Juneau
Ketchikan

CHUGACH MOUNTAINS
Valdez
Columbia Glacier
Cordova
Chugach National Forest
Prince William Sound
Montague Island
Gulf of Alaska
Sargeant Ice Field
Whittier
Portage
Moose Pass
Kenai Lake
Seward
Resurrection Bay
Harding Ice Field
KENAI FJORDS NATIONAL PARK
KENAI MOUNTAINS
ANCHORAGE
Turnagain Arm
Hope
Captain Cook State Recreation Area
KENAI NATIONAL
Cooper Landing
Sterling
Skilak Lake
WILDLIFE REFUGE
Tustumena Lake
Nikiski
Kenai
Soldotna
Kasilof
Clam Gulch
Sterling Highway
Ninilchik
Anchor Point
Homer
KENAI PENINSULA
Kachemak Bay
Halibut Cove
Kachemak Bay State Park
Seldovia
To Kodiak
Cook Inlet
Tyonek
LAKE CLARK NATIONAL PARK AND PRESERVE

0   20 Mi
0   20 Km

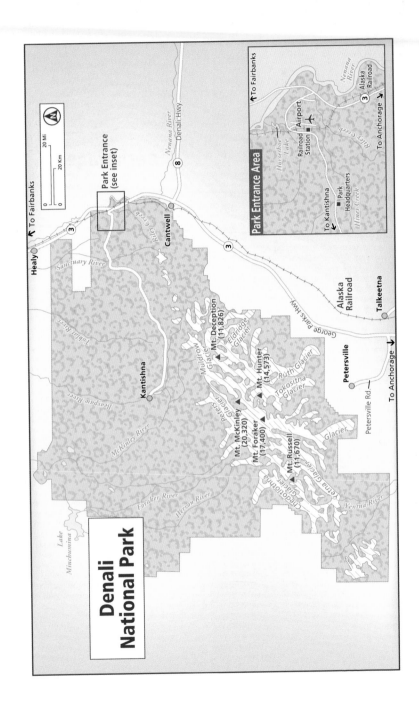

Frommer's®

Alaska

2008

by Charles Wohlforth

Here's what the critics say about Frommer's:

"Amazingly easy to use. Very portable, very complete."
—*Booklist*

"Detailed, accurate, and easy-to-read information for all price ranges."
—*Glamour Magazine*

"Hotel information is close to encyclopedic."
—*Des Moines Sunday Register*

"Frommer's Guides have a way of giving you a real feel for a place."
—*Knight Ridder Newspapers*

Wiley Publishing, Inc.

About the Author

Charles Wohlforth is a lifelong Alaskan who has been a writer and journalist since 1986. Wohlforth lives in Anchorage with his wife, Barbara, sons Robin and Joseph, and daughters Julia and Rebecca. His book about Eskimos experiencing warming in the Arctic is titled *The Whale and the Supercomputer: On the Northern Front of Climate Change* (North Point Press, $14). Wohlforth can be reached through his website, www.wohlforth.net.

Published by:

Wiley Publishing, Inc.

111 River St.
Hoboken, NJ 07030-5774

ISBN: 978-0-470-15288-1

Editor: Jamie Ehrlich
Production Editor: Michael Brumitt
Cartographer: Andrew Dolan
Photo Editor: Richard Fox
Anniversary Logo Design: Richard Pacifico
Production by Wiley Indianapolis Composition Services

Front cover photo: Juneau, Sawyer Glacier, Tracy Arm Wilderness Area: Group of people in boat watching calving glacier, rear view
Back cover photo: Katmai National Park: Brown Bears fishing in falls

For information on our other products and services or to obtain technical support, please contact our Customer Care Department within the U.S. at 800/762-2974, outside the U.S. at 317/572-3993 or fax 317/572-4002.

Wiley also publishes its books in a variety of electronic formats. Some content that appears in print may not be available in electronic formats.

Manufactured in the United States of America

5 4 3 2 1

Contents

4 Cruising Alaska's Coast   74

by Jerry Brown & Fran Wenograd Golden

5 Southeast Alaska   96

6 Anchorage & Environs   210

10 The Bush   434

Appendix: Alaska in Depth   466

Index   489

List of Maps

Acknowledgments

This is my eleventh edition of *Frommer's Alaska* and, more than ever, it is the product of team-work. From the very start I received enormous help from friends, colleagues, and my family. The size and diversity of Alaska would otherwise make the project impossible. I want to acknowledge them all, but I need to give special note to the remarkable professionals who assisted with this 2008 edition. Karen Datko is more than my right hand. She's my life preserver, too. Researchers and writers around the state contributed as well, bringing new life to the book and giving it the insider's insider information that I couldn't have produced alone, even as a life-long Alaskan. They include: Eric Troyer, Charlotte Glover, Kris Capps, Matt Hawthorne, Lisa Busch, Scott Christiansen, Carolyn Edelman, and Dan Zobrist.

An Invitation to the Reader

In researching this book, we discovered many wonderful places—hotels, restaurants, shops, and more. We're sure you'll find others. Please tell us about them, so we can share the information with your fellow travelers in upcoming editions. If you were disappointed with a recommendation, we'd love to know that, too. Please write to:

Frommer's Alaska 2008
Wiley Publishing, Inc. • 111 River St. • Hoboken, NJ 07030-5774

An Additional Note

Please be advised that travel information is subject to change at any time—and this is especially true of prices. We therefore suggest that you write or call ahead for confirmation when making your travel plans. The authors, editors, and publisher cannot be held responsible for the experiences of readers while traveling. Your safety is important to us, however, so we encourage you to stay alert and be aware of your surroundings. Keep a close eye on cameras, purses, and wallets, all favorite targets of thieves and pickpockets.

Other Great Guides for Your Trip:

Frommer's Alaska Cruises & Ports of Call
Alaska For Dummies
Pauline Frommer's Alaska

Frommer's Star Ratings, Icons & Abbreviations

Every hotel, restaurant, and attraction listing in this guide has been ranked for quality, value, service, amenities, and special features using a **star-rating system.** In country, state, and regional guides, we also rate towns and regions to help you narrow down your choices and budget your time accordingly. Hotels and restaurants are rated on a scale of zero (recommended) to three stars (exceptional). Attractions, shopping, nightlife, towns, and regions are rated according to the following scale: zero stars (recommended), one star (highly recommended), two stars (very highly recommended), and three stars (must-see).

In addition to the star-rating system, we also use **seven feature icons** that point you to the great deals, in-the-know advice, and unique experiences that separate travelers from tourists. Throughout the book, look for:

Finds	Special finds—those places only insiders know about
Fun Fact	Fun facts—details that make travelers more informed and their trips more fun
Kids	Best bets for kids and advice for the whole family
Moments	Special moments—those experiences that memories are made of
Overrated	Places or experiences not worth your time or money
Tips	Insider tips—great ways to save time and money
Value	Great values—where to get the best deals

The following **abbreviations** are used for credit cards:

AE	American Express	DISC	Discover	V	Visa
DC	Diners Club	MC	MasterCard		

Frommers.com

Now that you have this guidebook to help you plan a great trip, visit our website at **www. frommers.com** for additional travel information on more than 3,600 destinations. We update features regularly to give you instant access to the most current trip-planning information available. At Frommers.com, you'll find scoops on the best airfares, lodging rates, and car rental bargains. You can even book your travel online through our reliable travel booking partners. Other popular features include:

- Online updates of our most popular guidebooks
- Vacation sweepstakes and contest giveaways
- Newsletters highlighting the hottest travel trends
- Online travel message boards with featured travel discussions

What's New in Alaska

Here are some changes in Alaska travel since the last edition of *Frommer's Alaska*.

PLANNING YOUR TRIP For more planning information, see chapter 2.

Climate information shouldn't be showing up in the "What's New" section, but there's no doubt that Alaska is getting much warmer. Although it appears a 5-year warm spell may have broken, the long-term warming trend is evident and now is taken seriously by almost everyone, even politically conservative Alaskans. For visitors, global warming means more sunny days, more forest-fire smoke, and shorter, less predictable winters, among other things, but I'm not sure how you can make adjustments for that, since the weather in any particular year could be warm or cold. I've included a brief explanation of Arctic climate change in the appendix on p. 473. A discussion of how to avoid contributing to the problem is on p. 53.

Foreign travelers should prepare for more complicated procedures and delays setting up a visit and entering the United States. Visas now take weeks or months to obtain rather than the days that used to be required. In addition, U.S. citizens will be required to show a passport to reenter the country even from Canada and Mexico. Rules have changed as well for taking Alaska Native arts and crafts home. It has become essentially impossible to export items made from marine mammals unless they are antique. On the plus side, the government has relaxed draconian rules that used to discriminate against HIV/AIDS sufferers visiting the United States.

As I write this, the economy is strong, fuel prices are high, and visitor numbers are rising. Prices at hotels and for services and air tickets in Alaska have taken a significant jump over the last year, so much so that I've changed the categories for what I call an "expensive" hotel, a "moderate" one, and so on. A room for $135 to $174 might not be moderate other places, but that's the going rate in Alaska.

I've included a couple of fly-in wilderness lodges in chapter 2 that don't fit well anywhere else in the book, including a new addition, **Winter Lake Lodge** (© **907/274-2710;** www.withinthewild.com), which is northwest of Anchorage. I had a chance to visit over the winter and couldn't believe the quality of the food and service.

Touring Alaska's back roads became a bit more difficult with a change in policies at two car rental agencies in Anchorage. I can no longer recommend any Anchorage agencies that allow their vehicles to be used on gravel roads. Two Fairbanks companies with this service are listed in chapter 9.

THE SOUTHEAST For more, see chapter 5.

The proliferation of large **cruise ships** continues to grow well beyond the carrying capacity of the small-town ports the ships call on. Towns are now receiving more than 10,000 visitors in a day from cruise ships. The towns worst affected are Ketchikan, Juneau, and Skagway. In Skagway, less than 1,000 year-round residents get more than 900,000 visitors a summer. In sections on each place, I've given tips for avoiding the crowds where possible.

Alaskans remain hospitable to cruise visitors, but a backlash against the companies reached the ballot box in the form of a petition initiative late in 2006. Voters fed up with perceived abuses by the cruise industry approved new taxes, environmental regulations, and consumer disclosures on the cruise lines despite a massive media campaign in opposition funded by an industry association. For the visitor, the changes should be largely invisible except for one benefit: Cruise lines will be forced to disclose their commissions on shore tours. Business people in coastal communities have complained these charges can be as much as 50% of what the customer pays. Now clients will know and, perhaps, consider booking directly.

In **Ketchikan,** where the airport is on Gravina Island, across the water from town, the airport shuttle stopped operating. Most visitors will take a taxi to the airport ferry and then walk from the dock up to the terminal. But you can still take a water taxi that links the airport to downtown—in fact, that's currently one of the most economical options. A luxurious new inn opened in Ketchikan, on the waterfront, with its own beach: the **Black Bear Inn** (© **907/225-4343;** www.stayinalaska.com). The restaurant at the **New York Hotel** went out of business and now a coffee shop is expected to go in its place.

In **Wrangell,** the dining scene has improved a bit with a serviceable restaurant in the **Stikine Inn** (© **888/874-3388** or 907/874-3388; www.stikineinn.com);

the hotel itself has improved all over under new ownership. There's a great new B&B in town, too, **Zimovia Bed & Breakfast** (© **866/946-6842;** www.zimoviabnb.com).

In **Sitka,** the Native corporation has opened a good Tlingit-themed hotel, **Shee Atika Totem Square Inn** (© **866/300-1353** or 907/747-3693; www.totemsquareinn.com).

The **Wickersham House State Historic Site** in **Juneau** is reopening after several years of renovation. A new activity is offered on Douglas Island, a zip-line course that offers guests the chance to zoom through the treetops like Spiderman, by **Alaska Zipline Adventures** (© **907/790-2547;** www.alaskazip.com). The **Goldbelt Native Corporation** has sold off most of its tourism businesses; generally, they've been picked up by others, but the popular Tracy Arm tours now are offered only by a much smaller company, **Adventure Bound Alaska** (© **800/228-3875** or 907/463-2509; www.adventureboundalaska.com).

I have some new favorite restaurants in Juneau from a large crop of entries in the last year, including: **Zyphyr,** at 200 Seward St. (© **907/780-2221**) serving Mediterranean cuisine in a beautiful dining room, and **Wild Spice,** right across the street (© **907/523-0344;** www.thewildspice.com), where you can get Mongolian barbecue or many other international flavors.

Glacier Bay National Park and the nearby town of **Gustavus** will be easier to reach thanks to a new passenger ferry offered by the park concessionaire, **Glacier Bay Lodge and Tours** (© **888-BAY-TOUR;** www.visitglacierbay.com), connecting Juneau's Auke Bay harbor directly to Bartlett Cove three times a week. The boat will also be offering whale-watching tours. Given the frequent changes in this business, however, it's wise to call ahead for the latest information.

Alaska Discovery, the eco-tour guide operation, has dropped many of its lower-cost or day-trip offerings; at Glacier Bay, the wonderful Bartlett Cove sea kayaking outings now are led by **Glacier Bay Sea Kayaks,** based in Gustavus (© **907/697-2257;** www.glacierbayseakayaks.com).

The lineup of restaurants in **Skagway** always changes fast. Most recently, **Sabrosa's** closed and a good Thai place opened, **Starfire,** at 4th Avenue between Spring Street and Broadway (© **907/983-3663**).

ANCHORAGE & ENVIRONS For more, see chapter 6.

The area's biggest travel news was the acquisition, late in 2006, of **Alyeska Resort** in Girdwood (© **800/880-3880** or 907/754-1111; www.alyeskaresort.com) by a wealthy skiing enthusiast who plans to remake it with new facilities and expanded family skiing terrain. Among the announced plans is the complete demolition and reconstruction of the grim day-skiing building. The beautiful hotel has been renamed, simply, Hotel Alyeska. None of these exciting plans have come to fruition as of this writing, but some should be in place for the 2008–2009 ski season.

A couple of local celebrity chefs opened a fun new restaurant, **City Diner,** at 3000 Minnesota Dr. (© **907/277-CITY**), with chrome decor right out of a movie. Another favorite closed its doors, the socially-conscious **Noble's Diner.**

KENAI PENINSULA & PRINCE WILLIAM SOUND For more, see chapter 7.

The critical transportation link to Prince William Sound communities, the **Alaska Marine Highway System** (© **800/642-0066;** www.ferryalaska.com) has improved substantially with the operation of the fast ferry *Chenega*. Besides cutting running times in half, the ferry now provides much more frequent service to Cordova, making that fascinating community more convenient for visitors. The *Chenega* has been around for a couple of years, but at first the agency didn't establish a reliable pattern of operation.

There's a good new place to stay in Hope, for those visitors who make the detour to that sleepy wayside: **Bowman's Bear Creek Lodge** (© **907/782-3141;** www.bowmansbearcreeklodge.com). I've also added a wonderful inn on the Seward Highway, **Inn at Tern Lake** (© **907/288-3667;** www.ternlakeinn.com).

In **Seward,** I recommend a new operator for guided sea kayaking and rentals, **Kayak Adventures Worldwide** (© **907/224-3960;** www.kayakak.com). Also, be sure to see the new salmon exhibit at the **Alaska SeaLife Center** (© **888/378-2525** or 907/224-6300; www.alaskasealife.org), where live salmon in each stage of life are visible at any time you visit. I found a terrific family restaurant in Seward, **Christo's Palace,** at 133 4th Ave. (© **907/224-5255**).

Near **Cooper Landing,** we finally made it to **Kenai Backcountry Lodge** (© **800/478-4100** or 907/783-2928; www.alaskawildland.com), on Skilak Lake, and can report it is a terrific place for a natural outdoor vacation.

In **Valdez,** construction at the **Solomon Gulch Hatchery,** on Dayville Road (© **907/835-1329**), is expected to be complete for the 2008 season, allowing the fun self-guided tours to resume after a long hiatus. **Mike's Palace Ristorante,** 201 N. Harbor Dr. (© **907/835-2365**) has reopened. It's a good pizzeria and Greek restaurant.

DENALI NATIONAL PARK For more, see chapter 8.

The reconstruction of the **Eielson Visitor Center,** the destination of many Denali shuttle bus rides, is expected to be complete in 2008. These projects often are delayed, however, so I've included information for planning shuttle bus rides for either eventuality—that the work is complete, or that it is not.

THE INTERIOR For more, see chapter 9.

A new community museum opened in **Fairbanks.** The volunteer-operated **Historic Hall** at 825 First Ave. shows off the town's past in photographs and such.

THE BUSH For more, see chapter 10.

In **Kodiak,** a new **Kodiak National Wildlife Refuge Visitor Center** is under construction near the ferry terminal at Mission Road and Center Avenue (✆ **888/408-3514** or 907/487-2600; http://kodiak.fws.gov). The building isn't done yet, but is expected to be open for the 2008 season. At 8,000 square feet, it will be Kodiak's biggest indoor attraction. I recommend a new bed-and-breakfast that has some of the qualities of a good wilderness lodge: **Eider House Bed & Breakfast** (✆ **907/487-4315;** www.eiderhouse.com).

The Best of Alaska

As a child, when my family traveled outside Alaska for vacations, I often met other children who asked, "Wow, you live in Alaska? What's it like?" I never did well with that question. To me, the place I was visiting was far simpler and easier to describe than the one I was from. The Lower 48 seemed a fairly homogeneous land of freeways and fast food, a well-mapped network of established places. Alaska, on the other hand, wasn't even completely explored. Natural forces of vast scale and subtlety were still shaping the land in their own way, inscribing a different story on each of an infinite number of unexpected places. Each region, whether populated or not, was unique far beyond my ability to explain. Alaska was so large and new, so unconquered and exquisitely real, as to defy summation.

In contrast to many places you might choose to visit, it's Alaska's unformed newness that makes it so interesting and fun. Despite the best efforts of tour planners, the most memorable parts of a visit are unpredictable and often unexpected: a humpback whale leaping clear of the water, the face of a glacier releasing huge ice chunks, a bear feasting on salmon in a river, a huge salmon chomping onto your line. You can look at totem poles and see Alaska Native cultural demonstrations, and you can also get to know indigenous people who still live by traditional ways. And sometimes grand, quiet moments come, and those are the ones that endure most deeply.

As the writer of this guidebook, I aim to help you get to places where you may encounter what's new, real, and unexpected. Opening yourself to those experiences is your job, but it's an effort that's likely to pay off. Although I have lived here all my life, I often envy the stories visitors tell me about the Alaskan places they have gone to and what happened there. No one owns Alaska, and most of us are newcomers here. In all this immensity, a visitor fresh off the boat is just as likely as a lifelong resident to see or do something amazing.

1 The Best Views

- **A First Sight of Alaska:** Flying north from Seattle, you're in clouds, so you concentrate on a book. When you look up, the light from the window has changed. Down below, the clouds are gone, and under the wing, where you're used to seeing roads, cities, and farms on most flights, you see instead only high, snowy mountain peaks, without the slightest mark of human presence, stretching as far as the horizon. Welcome to Alaska.

- **Punchbowl Cove** (Misty Fjords National Monument): A sheer granite cliff rises smooth and implacable 3,150 feet straight up from the water. A pair of bald eagles wheels and soars across its face, providing the only sense of scale. They look the size of gnats. See p. 116

- **From the Chugach Mountains over Anchorage, at Sunset:** The city sparkles below, on the edge of an orange-reflecting Cook Inlet, far below the mountainside where you stand. Beyond the pink and purple silhouettes of mountains on the other side of the inlet, the sun is spraying warm, dying light into puffs of clouds. And yet it's midnight. See "Getting Outside" in chapter 6.

- **Mount McKinley from the Air** (Denali National Park): Your Bush pilot guides his plane up from the flatlands of Talkeetna into a realm of eternal white, where a profusion of insanely rugged peaks rises in higher relief than any other spot on Earth. After circling a 3-mile-high wall and slipping through a mile-deep canyon, you land on a glacier, get out of the plane, and for the first time realize the overwhelming scale of it all. See "Attractions & Activities outside the Park" and "Talkeetna: Back Door to Denali" in chapter 8.

- **The Northern Lights** (Alaska's Interior): Blue, purple, green, and red lines spin from the center of the sky, draping long tendrils of slow-moving light. Bright, flashing, sky-covering waves wash across the dome of stars like ripples driven by a gust of wind on a pond. Looking around, you see that your companions' faces are rosy in a silver, snowy night, all gazing straight up with their mouths open. See p. 391.

2 The Best Alaska Cruises

Cruises provide comfortable, leisurely access to the Inside Passage and the Gulf of Alaska. Here are some of the best bets. See chapter 4 for details.

- **Best Up-Close Alaska Experience:** Lindblad Expeditions is an expert at soft adventure cruising, and its Alaska cruises are no exception. The *Sea Bird* and *Sea Lion* each carry only 62 passengers and offer routes where the focus is clearly on wildlife viewing and exploring the wilderness, with no less than the National Geographic Society providing the expedition leaders.

- **Most Comfortable Small Ships:** Cruise West's *Spirit of Oceanis* offers a higher level of comfort than the other small ships in Alaska while still giving you an intimate, casual, up-close small-ship experience. And the yachts of American Safari Cruises are clearly in the high-end luxury category.

- **Most Luxurious Big Ships:** If you want a more casual kind of luxury, Radisson Seven Seas' *Seven Seas Mariner* offers just that. Meanwhile, Silversea Cruises' *Silver Shadow* offers pure luxury with an Italian edge. Among the mainstream cruise ships, Celebrity's *Infinity* and *Millennium* are the big winners, offering cutting-edge modern ships with great service, dining, and design. Also impressive are Princess' newest and biggest vessels in Alaska, the *Sapphire Princess* and *Diamond Princess*.

- **Best Cruise Tours:** Holland America Line and Princess are the leaders in linking cruises with land tours into the Interior, either before or after your cruise. They own their own hotels, deluxe motorcoaches, and railcars, and after many years in the business, they both really know what they're doing. Princess concentrates more on the Denali/Fairbanks and Kenai Peninsula routes, while Holland America has many itineraries that get you to the Yukon Territory. Royal Caribbean (which owns Royal Caribbean and Celebrity Cruises) has also made strides as the number three Alaska player, operating its own trains and motor coaches.

3 The Best Glaciers

More of Alaska—over 100 times more—is covered by glacier ice than is settled by human beings.

- **Grand Pacific Glacier** (Glacier Bay National Park): Two vast glaciers of deep blue meet at the top of an utterly barren fjord. They rubbed and creased the gray rock below for thousands of years before just recently releasing it to the air again. Three intimidating walls of ice surround boats that pull close to the glaciers. See "Glacier Bay National Park" in chapter 5.

- **Childs Glacier** (Cordova): Out the Copper River Highway from Cordova, this is a participatory glacier-viewing experience. The glacier is cut by the Copper River, which is ¼-mile broad; standing on the opposite shore (unless you're up in the viewing tower), you have to be ready to run like hell when the creaking, popping ice gives way and a huge berg falls into the river, potentially swamping the picnic area. Even when the glacier isn't calving, you can feel the ice groaning in your gut. See "Cordova: Hidden Treasure" in chapter 7.

- **Exit Glacier** (Seward): You can drive near the glacier and walk the rest of the way on a gravel path. It towers above like a huge blue sculpture, the spires of broken ice close enough to breathe a freezer-door chill down on watchers. See "Exit Glacier" in section 6 of chapter 7.

- **Western Prince William Sound:** On a boat from Whittier, you can see a couple dozen glaciers in a day. Some of these are the amazing tidewater glaciers that dump huge, office-building-size spires of ice into the ocean, each setting off a terrific splash and outward-radiating sea wave. See "Whittier: Dock on the Sound" in chapter 7.

4 The Most Beautiful Drives & Train Rides

You'll find a description of each road in "Alaska's Highways a la Carte" on p. 382. Here are some highlights:

- **White Pass and Yukon Route Railway** (Skagway to Summit): The narrow-gauge excursion train climbs a steep grade that was chiseled into the granite mountains by stampeders to the Klondike gold rush. The train is a sort of mechanical mountain goat, balancing on trestles and steep rock walls far above deep gorges. See p. 204.

- **Seward Highway/Alaska Railroad** (Anchorage to Seward): Just south of Anchorage, the highway and rail line have been chipped into the side of the Chugach Mountains over the surging gray water of Turnagain Arm. Above, Dall sheep and mountain goats pick their way along the cliffs, within easy sight. Below, white beluga whales chase salmon through the turbid water. Farther south, the route splits and climbs through the mountain passes of the Kenai Peninsula. See "Out from Anchorage: Turnagain Arm & Portage Glacier" in chapter 6 and "The Seward Highway: A Road Guide" in chapter 7 for information on the highway, and p. 251 for information on this Alaska Railroad route.

- **Denali Highway:** Leading east-west through the Alaska Range, the highway crosses terrain that could be another Denali National Park, full of wildlife and with views so huge and grand they seem impossible. See p. 346.

- **Richardson Highway:** Just out of Valdez heading north, the Richardson Highway rises quickly from sea level to more than 2,600 feet, switching back and forth on the side of a mountain. With each turn, the drop down the impassable slope becomes more amazing. North of Glennallen, the highway rises again, bursting through the tree line between a series of mountains and tracing the edges of long alpine lakes, before descending, parallel with the silver skein of the Alaska pipeline, to Delta Junction. See "The Richardson Highway & Copper Center," in chapter 9.

- **The Roads Around Nome:** You can't drive to Nome, but 250 miles of gravel roads radiate from the Arctic community into tundra that's populated only by musk oxen, bears, reindeer, birds, and other wildlife. See p. 456.

- **The Dalton Highway:** When you're ready for an expedition—a real wilderness trip by road—the Dalton Highway leads from Fairbanks across northern Alaska to the Arctic Ocean, a mind-blowing drive through 500 miles of spectacular virgin country. See "The Dalton Highway" in chapter 9.

5 The Best Fishing

The quality of salmon fishing in Alaska isn't so much a function of place as of time. See p. 33 for information on how to find the fish when you arrive.

- **Bristol Bay:** This is the world's richest salmon fishery; lodges on the remote rivers of the region are an angler's paradise. See p. 436.

- **Copper River Delta, Cordova:** The Copper itself is silty with glacial runoff, but feeder streams and rivers are rich with trout, Dolly Varden, and salmon, with few other anglers in evidence. See p. 335.

- **The Kenai River:** The biggest king salmon—up to 98 pounds—come from the swift Kenai River. Big fish are so common in the second run of kings that there's a special, higher standard for what makes a trophy. Silvers and reds add to a mad, summer-long fishing frenzy. See p. 297.

- **Homer:** Alaska's largest charter-fishing fleet goes for halibut ranging into the hundreds of pounds. See p. 314.

- **Unalaska:** Beyond the road system, Unalaska has the biggest halibut. See p. 449.

- **Kodiak Island:** The bears are so big here because they live on an island that's crammed with spawning salmon in the summer. Kodiak has the best roadside salmon fishing in Alaska, and the remote fishing, at lodges or fly-in stream banks, is legendary. See p. 441.

6 The Best Tips for Cooking Salmon

Now that you've caught a Pacific salmon, you need to know how to cook it—or order it in a restaurant—to avoid spoiling the rich flavor.

- **Freeze as Little as Possible:** It's a sad fact that salmon loses some of its richness and gets more "fishy" as soon as it's frozen. Eat as much as you can fresh because it'll never be better. Ask if the salmon is fresh when you order it in a restaurant. Don't overlook smoking, the traditional Native way of preserving fish for the winter. See p. 315 for information on getting your salmon frozen and smoked.

- **Choose the Best Fish:** The best restaurants advertise where their salmon comes from on the menu. In early summer, Copper River kings and reds are the richest in flavor; later in the summer, Yukon River salmon are best. The oil in the salmon gives it the rich, meaty flavor; the fish from the Copper and Yukon are high in oil content because the rivers are long and the fish need a lot of stored energy to swim upstream to spawn. King, red, and silver salmon are the only species you should find in a restaurant. Avoid farm-reared salmon, which is mushy and flavorless compared with wild Alaska salmon.
- **Keep It Simple:** When ordering salmon or halibut in a restaurant, avoid anything with cheese or heavy sauces. When salmon is fresh, it's best with light seasoning, perhaps just a little lemon, dill weed, and pepper and salt, or basted with soy sauce; or without anything on it at all, grilled over alder coals.

- **Don't Overcook It:** Salmon should be cooked just until the moment the meat changes color and becomes flaky through to the bone, or slightly before. A minute more, and some of the texture and flavor are lost. That's why those huge barbecue salmon bakes often are not as good as they should be—it's too hard to cook hundreds of pieces of fish just right and serve them all hot.
- **Fillets, Not Steaks:** Salmon is cut two ways in Alaska: lengthwise fillets or crosswise steaks. The fillet is cut with the grain of the flesh, keeping the oil and moisture in the fish. Do not remove the skin before cooking—it holds in the oils and will fall off easily when the fish is done. If you have a large group, consider cooking the salmon bone-in (sometimes called a roast), stuffing seasonings in the body cavity. When it's done, the skin easily peels off and, after eating the first side, you can effortlessly lift out the skeleton.

7 The Best Bear Viewing

There are many places to see bears in Alaska, but if your goal is to make *sure* you see a bear—and potentially lots of bears—these are the best places:

- **Anan Wildlife Observatory:** When the fish are running, you can see many dozens of black bears feeding in a salmon stream from close at hand. Access is easiest from Wrangell. See p. 126.
- **Pack Creek** (Admiralty Island): The brown bears of the island, which is more thickly populated with them than anywhere else on Earth, have learned to ignore the daily visitors who stand on the platforms at Pack Creek. Access is by air from Juneau. See p. 172.

- **Katmai National Park:** During the July and September salmon runs, dozens of giant brown bears congregate around Brooks Camp, where, from wooden platforms a few yards away, you can watch the full range of their behaviors. Flight services from Kodiak also bring guests at any time of the summer to see bears dig clams on the park's eastern seashore. See "Katmai National Park" and "Kodiak: Wild Island" in chapter 10.
- **Kodiak Island:** The island's incredible salmon runs nourish the world's largest bears, Kodiak brown bears; pilots know where to find them week to week, landing floatplanes as near as possible. See p. 437.

- **Denali National Park:** The park offers the best and least expensive wildlife-viewing safari in the state.

Passengers on the buses that drive the park road as far as mile 63 usually see at least some grizzlies. See chapter 8.

8 The Best Marine Mammal Viewing

You've got a good chance of seeing marine mammals almost anywhere you go boating in Alaska, but in some places it's almost guaranteed.

- **Frederick Sound** (Petersburg): A humpback jumped right into the boat with whale-watchers here in 1995. The whales show up reliably for feeding each summer. Small boats from Petersburg have no trouble finding them and watching in intimate circumstances. See p. 136.
- **Icy Strait** (Gustavus) and **Bartlett Cove** (Glacier Bay National Park): Humpback whales show up and often orcas are present off Point Adolphus, in Icy Strait, just a few miles from little Gustavus, a town of luxurious country inns, and in Bartlett Cove within Glacier Bay National Park. See "Glacier Bay National Park" and "Gustavus: Country Inns & Quiet" in chapter 5.

- **Sitka Sound:** Lots of otters and humpback whales show up in the waters near Sitka. In fall, when the town holds its Whale Fest, you can spot them from a city park built for the purpose. See "Sitka: Rich Prize of Russian Conquest" in chapter 5.
- **Kenai Fjords National Park** (near Seward): You don't have to go all the way into the park—you're pretty well assured of sea otters and sea lions in Resurrection Bay, near Seward, and humpbacks and killer whales are often seen in the summer, too. See "Kenai Fjords National Park" in chapter 7.
- **Prince William Sound:** Otters, seals, and sea lions are easy—you'll see them on most trips out of Valdez, Whittier, or Cordova—but you also have a chance of spotting both humpback and killer whales in the Sound. See chapter 7.

9 The Best Encounters with Native Culture

- **Ketchikan Totem Poles:** This Tlingit homeland has three unique places to see totem poles: historic poles indoors at the Totem Heritage Center, faithful reproductions outdoors in a natural setting at Totem Bight State Park, and brand-new poles as they are created in a workshop at the Saxman Native Village Totem Pole Park. See p. 109.
- **Sitka:** The Tlingits remain strong where they met Russian invaders in fierce battles 2 centuries ago. The totem poles and ancient Native art you can see here are second to none,

and the setting makes them only more impressive. See section 5 of chapter 5.
- **Alaska Native Heritage Center** (Anchorage): All of Alaska's Native groups joined together to build this grand living museum and gathering place, where dance and music performances, storytelling, art and craft demonstrations, and simple meetings of people happen every day. See p. 238.
- **Iñupiat Heritage Center** (Barrow): A living museum, this is a place to meet and enjoy performances by the

Native people who built it, and to see extraordinary artifacts they have made and recovered from digs in frozen ground. See p. 461.

10 The Best Museums & Historic Sites

- **Sitka National Historical Park:** The historic park, its buildings, and other structures in Sitka keep alive an alternate stream in history: one in which a Russian czar ruled Alaska and this little town was one of the most important on the west coast of North America. See p. 144.
- **The Alaska State Museum** (Juneau): This richly endowed museum doesn't just show off its wealth of objects—it also uses them to teach about the state. A visit will put Alaska's Native cultures and pioneer history in context. See p. 159.
- **Anchorage Museum at Rasmuson Center:** Alaska's largest museum has the room and expertise to tell the story of Native and white history in Alaska, and to showcase contemporary Alaskan art and culture. See p. 237.
- **The Pratt Museum** (Homer): The Pratt explains natural history (especially the life of the ocean) in a clear and intimate way you'll find nowhere else in Alaska. See p. 309.
- **UA Museum of the North** (Fairbanks): The spectacular renovation of this university museum includes a swooping new gallery to present Alaska's art. Its older gallery contains an extraordinary natural history collection, presented with the help of some of the world's top scientists on Alaskan subjects. See p. 392.

11 The Best Winter Destinations

- **Anchorage:** Anyone can enjoy the Fur Rendezvous and Iditarod sled dog races, which keep a winter-carnival atmosphere going through much of February and March, but winter sports enthusiasts get the most out of winter here. The city has some of the best Nordic skiing anywhere, close access to three downhill skiing areas, dog mushing, and groomed lake skating. See chapter 6.
- **Alyeska Resort** (Girdwood): Alaska's premier downhill skiing area has lots of snow over a long season, fantastic views, few lift lines, and a luxurious hotel. See "The Best Hotels," below, and p. 256.
- **Chena Hot Springs Resort:** A 90-minute ride from Fairbanks, and you're out in the country, where the northern lights are clear on a starry winter afternoon and night. The resort has lots of activities to get you out into the snowy countryside, or you can just relax in the hot mineral springs. See p. 410.
- **Homer:** In March, you can fish for king salmon in the morning and cross-country ski over a high ridge with limitless ocean views in the afternoon. In the evening, check out Alaska's best art galleries and eat in its best restaurants. See chapter 7, section 10.
- **Barrow:** Go to the shore of the frozen Arctic Ocean, and you have a chance to experience the most extreme winter conditions in the world. It's dark for 65 days except for the aurora blasting across the sky. There's not much to do, but you could run into a polar bear in the street. See "Barrow: Way North" in chapter 10.

12 The Strangest Community Events

- **Cordova Ice Worm Festival** (Cordova): The truth is, ice worms do exist. Really. This winter carnival celebrates them in February. The highlight is the traditional annual march of the ice worm (a costume with dozens of feet sticking out) down the main street. See p. 333.

- **Midnight Sun Baseball Game** (Fairbanks): For more than 100 years they have played a baseball game without lights that doesn't begin until 10:30pm on the longest day of the year. See p. 389.

- **Bering Sea Ice Golf Classic** (Nome): The greens are AstroTurf, as the sea ice won't support a decent lawn in mid-March. Hook a drive and you could end up spending hours wandering among the pressure ridges, but you must play the ball as it lies. See p. 455.

- **Polar Bear Swim** (Nome): This swim in the frigid Bering Sea takes place in late June, but only if the sea ice has opened up sufficiently to provide enough liquid water. See p. 455.

- **Piuraagiaqt** (Barrow): This spring festival, in April, includes lots of strange contests, such as the tea making race—contestants start with solid ice—and the white men versus Eskimo women tug-of-war contest, which the white men have yet to win after many years of trying. Or the community may have come up with some other silly contest this year. See p. 461.

- **Mountain Mother Contest** (Talkeetna): In this event in the July Moose Dropping Festival, mothers compete in a test of Bush skills, including splitting wood, carrying water, and diapering a baby. See p. 377.

- **Wild Cow Milking Contest** (Kodiak): The Labor Day Kodiak State Fair and Rodeo includes an event in which pairs of amateur cowboys and cowgirls pulled from the audience chase down and milk small cows unleashed in a ring. See p. 439.

13 The Best Hotels

- **Hotel Captain Cook** (Anchorage; ℃ **800/843-1950**): This is the grand old hotel of downtown Anchorage, with a heavy nautical theme, teak paneling, several terrific restaurants, and every possible amenity. It remains the state's standard of service and luxury. See p. 218.

- **Hotel Alyeska** (Girdwood; ℃ **800/880-3880**): The first sight of this ski resort hotel—designed in a château style and standing in an undeveloped mountain valley—will make you catch your breath. Wait till you get inside and see the starscape and polar bear diorama in the lobby atrium, or the saltwater swimming pool, with its high-beamed ceiling and windows, looking out on the mountain. A tram carries skiers and diners to the mountaintop. See p. 258.

- **Land's End Resort** (Homer; ℃ **800/478-0400**): It's the location: right on the end of Homer Spit, 5 miles out in the middle of Kachemak Bay, where you can fish for salmon from the beach right in front of your room, or watch otters drifting by. The hotel itself is excellent, too, with a tremendous variety of rooms, some extraordinarily luxurious, and a complete spa. See p. 316.

- **Westmark Fairbanks Hotel & Conference Center** (Fairbanks; ℂ **800/ 544-0970**): A tower rises over the flat river city of Fairbanks, a stylish and charming new wing of the city's oldest

modern hotel. The owners, the Holland America Line, demolished much of the original building, leaping decades from the past to just a little into the future. See p. 401.

14 The Best Websites

Many useful websites are listed throughout the book; some of the best are under "Visitor Information" near the beginning of each town section.

- **www.trollart.com.** Ketchikan artist Ray Troll has created a website that carries you deep into his mind, which is full of odd and resonant humor about the evolution of fish, man, and our common relations. His vibrantly colored art makes it an aesthetic journey.
- **www.adfg.state.ak.us.** The Alaska Department of Fish & Game posts valuable information for anyone interested in fishing, hunting, wildlife watching, or just learning about creatures. Everyone from children to wildlife biologists will find something at their level. Try **www.wildlife. alaska.gov** for information about where to go and how to see Alaska's wild animals.
- **www.awrta.org.** The Alaska Wilderness Recreation and Tourism Association unites hundreds of small eco-tourism operators. Authentic local guides and lodges can be hard to find, but they are listed here on a comprehensive and easy-to-use site.

- **www.gi.alaska.edu.** The Geophysical Institute at the University of Alaska Fairbanks maintains a fascinating and cool site filled with real-time earth science information about Alaska, such as aurora predictions, volcano watches, earthquake and tsunami updates, rocketry, and space science.
- **www.wohlforth.net.** A bit of self-promotion here, but readers can get something out of it. I've answered scores of reader questions, and supply links to many of the establishments listed in this book and some of my other writings on Alaska and other subjects. Other travelers have run into the same puzzles you have, and you'll find my advice here.
- **Favorite Small-Town Sites:** Small-town Alaska newspapers, and people in communities too small to have a newspaper, communicate through the Internet; visitors to these sites can vicariously experience the pleasures and pitfalls of remote living, which can be touching and hilarious. The best I've found are Seldovia's **www. seldovia.com,** Nome's **www.nome nugget.com,** and Kotzebue's **www. cityofkotzebue.com.**

2

Planning Your Trip to Alaska

Planning a trip to Alaska can be a bit more complicated than getting ready to travel in the rest of the United States. Aside from the vast distances and range of climatic conditions, the best places book up quickly for the high summer season. This chapter provides general orientation information, when to go, and how much it will cost. It then covers how to plan a trip to Alaska, including passport and visa information for international visitors, modes of travel, insurance, safety, and issues to watch out for. I will also point you to the best outdoor activities and places and the businesses to get you there. I've included primers on fishing and shopping for Alaska Native art as well.

1 The Regions in Brief

SOUTHEAST ALASKA The Southeast Panhandle is the relatively narrow strip of mountains and islands lying between Canada and the Gulf of Alaska. To Alaskans, it's Southeast, but to the rest of the country, it's more like the northernmost extension of the lush Pacific Northwest. This is a land of huge rainforest trees, glacier-garbed mountains, and countless islands ranging in size from the nation's third largest to tiny, one-tree islets strewn like confetti along the channels and fjords. The water is the highway of Southeast Alaska, as the land is generally too steep and rugged to build roads, but there are lots of towns and villages reachable by the ferry system or cruise ships. Southeast contains **Juneau,** Alaska's capital and third-largest city, and **Ketchikan,** next in size to Juneau. Southeast's towns are as quaint and historic as any in Alaska, especially **Sitka,** which preserves the story of Russian America and its conflict with the indigenous Native people. Alaska Native culture—here, Tlingit and Haida—is rich and close at hand. No other region offers more opportunities for boating or seeing marine wildlife. Likewise, no other region is as crowded with tourists. More than 800,000 visitors flood into Southeast annually aboard cruise ships, jamming the little towns all summer. The weather is wet and temperate.

SOUTHCENTRAL ALASKA As a region, Southcentral is something of a catchall. The area is roughly defined by the arc of the Gulf of Alaska from the Canadian border on the east to Cook Inlet and the end of the road network to the west. It's a microcosm of the state, containing **Prince William Sound,** which is similar to the wooded island habitat of Southeast; the **Kenai Peninsula,** a fishing, boating, and outdoor mecca with roads; **Anchorage,** the state's modern, major city; and the **Matanuska and Susitna valleys,** an agricultural and suburban region of broad flatlands between steep mountains. Southcentral dominates Alaska, with most of the state's population and a more highly developed transportation system than elsewhere, including a network of highways and the Alaska Railroad. The ocean influences Southcentral's weather, keeping it from

Alaska by the Numbers

This chart shows some comparative indicators for 16 of Alaska's most popular destinations. The third column is the best season to visit—months when, during at least part of which, there's enough going on and weather is suitable (that includes weather that's good for winter sports). The fourth column lists modes of transportation to each community—in Alaska you can't drive everywhere.

Place	Population	Season	Transportation	Precip. (in.)	Snow (in.)
Anchorage	274,003	May–Sept/ Jan–Mar	Road, air, rail	16	71
Barrow	4,417	June–Sept	Air	4.5	30
Cordova	2,372	May–Sept	Air, ferry	93	119
Denali National Park	133	June–Sept	Road, rail	15	83
Fairbanks	82,214	May–Sept/ Jan–Mar	Road, air, rail	11	68
Glacier Bay National Park	438	May–Sept	Air, ferry	70	117
Haines	1,715	May–Sept/ Nov	Road, air, ferry	48	123
Homer	4,893	May–Sept/ Mar	Road, air, ferry	25	55
Juneau	31,283	May–Sept	Air, ferry	56	99
Kenai	7,125	May–Sept	Road, air	19	61
Ketchikan	13,548	May–Sept	Air, ferry	151	37
Kodiak Island	13,811	May–Sept	Air, ferry	76	73
Nome	3,448	June–Aug/ Mar	Air	16	61
Petersburg	3,060	May–Sept	Air, ferry	110	67
Seward	2,733	May–Sept	Road, rail	66	81
Sitka	8,891	May–Sept/ Nov	Air, ferry	86	39
Skagway	845	May–Sept	Road, air, ferry	26	50
Unalaska/ Dutch Harbor	4,388	June–Sept	Air, ferry	60	88
Valdez	4,060	May–Sept	Road, air, ferry	62	304

being very hot or very cold. The coastal areas are wet, while just behind the coastal mountains the weather is drier.

THE INTERIOR   The vast central part of the state is crossed by highways and by rivers that act as highways. Big river valleys lie between great mountain ranges, the largest of which are the Alaska Range, which contains **Mount McKinley,** North America's tallest peak, and the Brooks Range, the northern end of the cordillera that includes the Rockies. McKinley is the centerpiece of **Denali National Park,** Alaska's premier road-accessible wildlife-viewing destination. The region's dominant city is **Fairbanks,** Alaska's second largest, which lies on the lazy Chena River, roughly in the middle of the state. The natural environment is drier and less abundant than that in Southeast or Southcentral. The Athabascans, the Interior's first people, still subsist on this sparse land in tiny villages and river fish camps. Summer days can be hot and winters very cold in the Interior, because of the distance from the ocean.

THE BUSH   Bush Alaska is linked by lifestyle rather than by geography. One good definition would be that the Bush is the part of the state that's closer to the wilderness than to civilization. It's also the only part of the state where Native people outnumber whites and other relative newcomers. In many Bush villages, readily accessible to the outside world only by small plane, people still live according to age-old subsistence hunting-and-gathering traditions. The Bush region includes the majority of Alaska outside the road and ferry networks, ranging from the north end of the Canadian border all the way around the coast, out to the Aleutians, and the Alaska Peninsula and Kodiak Island, south of Anchorage. But some towns in each of the other regions also could be called "Bush villages." The Bush contains many regions, including the Arctic, Northwest, and Southwest Alaska.

2 When to Go

This section covers some of the questions I am asked most frequently: "What's the best time to visit _____?" Alaska's vastness means the seasons change at different times in different parts of the state. Sports, cultural activities, and visitor facilities also happen different times in different places.

CLIMATE & SEASONS

The weather in Alaska can be extreme and unpredictable. The state is the first to get whatever Arctic Siberia or the void of the North Pacific have to throw at North America. The extremes of recorded temperatures are a high of 100°F (38°C) and low of –80°F (–62°C). At any time of year your vacation could be enlivened by weeks of unbroken sunny weather or weighed down by weeks of unbroken rain. All you can do is play the averages, hope for the best, and, if you do get bad weather, get out and have fun anyway—that's what Alaskans do. A statistical summary of weather probabilities in various Alaska places is found below in "Alaska's Climate, by Months & Regions." I've summarized the best visitor season in each destination in "Alaska by the Numbers," above.

JUNE, JULY & AUGUST   Summer in Alaska is a miraculous time, when the sun refuses to set, the salmon run upriver, and people are energized by limitless daylight. The sun dips below the horizon in Anchorage for only about 4 hours on June 21, the longest day of the year, and the sky is light all night. The state fills with people coming to visit and to work in the seasonal fishing, timber, and construction industries. Weather gets warmer, although how warm depends on where you go (see the chart below). June is the driest of the summer months, July the warmest, and August generally the rainiest month of the brief summer, but warmer than June. In most respects, June is the best summer month to make a visit, but it does have some drawbacks to consider: In the Arctic, snow can linger until

Alaska's Climate, by Months & Regions

	Jan	Feb	Mar	Apr	May	June	July	Aug	Sept	Oct	Nov	Dec
Anchorage: Southcentral Alaska												
Average high*•	21/-6	26/-3	33/1	44/7	55/13	62/17	65/18	63/17	55/13	40/4	28/-2	22/-6
Average low*•	8/-13	11/-12	17/-8	29/-2	39/4	47/8	51/11	49/9	41/5	28/-2	16/-9	10/-12
Hours of light•	6:53	9:41	12:22	15:20	18:00	19:22	18:00	15:15	12:19	9:29	6:46	5:27
Sunny days†	12	10	13	12	11	10	9	9	9	10	10	10
Rainy or snowy days	8	8	8	6	7	8	11	13	14	12	10	11
Precipitation‡	0.8	0.8	0.6	0.6	0.7	1.0	1.9	2.7	2.6	1.9	1.1	1.1
Barrow: Arctic Alaska												
Average high*•	8/-13	-12/-24	-8/-22	6/-14	25/-4	39/4	46/8	43/6	34/1	20/-7	5/-15	-6/-21
Average low*•	-20/-29	-24/-31	-21/-29	-8/-22	15/-9	30/-1	34/1	34/1	27/-3	10/-12	-6/-21	-17/-27
Hours of light•	0:00	8:05	12:33	17:43	24:00	24:00	24:00	17:34	12:30	7:46	0:00	0:00
Sunny days†	7	18	21	18	8	9	11	5	4	6	8	4
Rainy or snowy days	4	4	4	4	4	5	9	11	11	11	6	5
Precipitation‡	0.2	0.2	0.1	0.2	0.2	0.3	0.9	1.0	0.6	0.5	0.2	0.2
Cold Bay: Aleutian Archipelago												
Average high*•	33/1	32/0	35/2	38/3	45/7	50/10	55/13	56/13	52/11	44/7	39/4	35/2
Average low*•	24/-4	23/-5	25/-4	29/-2	35/2	41/5	46/8	47/8	43/6	35/2	30/-1	27/-3
Hours of light•	8:05	10:10	12:17	14:36	16:32	17:25	16:33	14:34	12:17	10:04	8:01	7:08
Sunny days†	8	6	8	4	3	3	3	2	4	6	6	7
Rainy or snowy days	19	17	18	16	17	16	17	20	21	23	22	21
Precipitation‡	2.8	2.5	2.3	2.0	2.5	2.3	2.4	3.7	4.3	4.2	4.2	3.3
Fairbanks: Interior Alaska												
Average high*•	-2/-18	8/-13	24/-4	42/6	60/16	71/22	73/23	66/19	55/13	32/0	11/-12	1/-17
Average low*•	-19/-28	-15/-26	-2/-19	20/-7	38/3	52/11	52/11	47/8	36/2	17/-8	-5/-21	-16/-27
Hours of light•	5:46	9:14	12:22	15:54	19:22	21:48	19:26	15:52	12:24	9:04	5:39	3:43
Sunny days†	15	14	17	14	16	13	12	10	10	9	12	12
Rainy or snowy days	8	7	6	5	7	11	12	12	10	11	11	9
Precipitation‡	0.6	0.4	0.4	0.2	0.6	1.4	1.8	1.8	1.1	0.8	0.7	0.8
Juneau: Southeast Alaska												
Average high*•	29/-2	34/1	39/4	48/9	55/13	62/17	64/18	63/17	56/13	47/8	37/3	32/0
Average low*•	18/-8	23/-5	27/-3	32/0	39/4	45/7	48/9	48/9	43/6	37/3	28/-2	23/-5
Hours of light•	7:31	9:55	12:18	14:55	17:11	18:17	17:13	14:54	12:20	9:49	7:27	6:22
Sunny days†	8	7	7	8	8	8	8	9	6	4	6	5
Rainy or snowy days	18	17	18	17	17	15	17	17	20	24	20	21
Precipitation‡	4.3	3.9	3.5	2.9	3.5	3.1	4.2	5.3	7.2	7.8	5.4	5.1
Valdez: Prince William Sound												
Average high*•	27/-3	30/-1	37/3	45/7	53/12	60/16	63/17	61/16	54/12	43/6	33/1	29/-2
Average low*•	18/-8	19/-7	24/-4	31/-1	39/4	45/7	48/9	46/8	41/5	33/1	23/-5	19/-7
Hours of light•	6:54	9:41	12:22	15:19	17:58	19:20	17:57	15:14	12:20	9:30	6:48	5:29
Sunny days†	9	9	11	11	9	8	8	10	8	8	10	7
Rainy or snowy days	17	14	16	14	17	15	17	17	20	20	16	18
Precipitation‡	5.7	5.5	4.7	3.2	3.2	2.8	3.6	6.5	9.3	7.9	5.7	7.6

*Hours of light is sunrise to sunset on the 21st day of each month.

**All temperatures are given in degrees Fahrenheit first, with degrees Celsius after the slash.

†Sunny days include the average observed clear and partly cloudy days per month.

‡Precipitation is the average water equivalent of rain or snow.

mid-June; in Southcentral Alaska, trails at high elevations or in the shade may be too muddy or snowy; and not all activities or facilities at Denali National Park open until late June. It's also the worst time for mosquitoes.

Summer also is the season of high prices. Most operators in the visitor industry have only these 90 days to make their year's income, and they charge whatever the market will bear. July is the absolute peak of the tourist season, when you must book well ahead and when crowds are most prevalent. (Of course, crowding depends on where you are. With a population density of roughly one person per square mile, Alaska is never *really* crowded.) Before June 15 and after August 15, the flow of visitors relaxes, providing occasional bargains and more elbow room. Real off-season prices show up before Memorial Day and after Labor Day. But the length and intensity of the visitor season varies widely in different areas: In cruise-ship ports, it's busy from chilly early May into stormy October.

MAY & SEPTEMBER More and more visitors are coming to Alaska during these "shoulder months" to take advantage of the lower prices, reduced crowds, and special beauty.

May is the drier of the 2 months and can be as warm as summer if you're lucky, but as you travel farther north and earlier in the month, your chances of finding cold, mud, and even snow increase. In Alaska, there is no spring—the melt of snow and resultant seas of mud are called **breakup.** Flowers show up with the start of summer. Many outdoor activities aren't possible during breakup, which can extend well into May. Except in cruise-ship towns, most tourist-oriented activities and facilities are still closed before May 15, and a few don't open until Memorial Day or June 1. Where visitor facilities are open, they often have significantly lower prices. Also, the first visitors

of the year usually receive an especially warm welcome. The very earliest salmon runs start in May, but for a fishing-oriented trip it's better to come later in the summer. Cruise ships begin calling May 1, and the towns they visit swing into action when they arrive.

Sometime between late August and mid-September, weather patterns change, bringing clouds, frequent rainstorms, and cooling weather, and signaling the trees and tundra to turn bright, vivid colors. For a week or two (what week it is depends on your latitude), the bright yellow birches of the boreal forest and the rich red of the heathery tundra make September the loveliest time of year. But the rain and the nip in the air, similar to late October or November in New England, mean you'll likely have to bundle up; and September is among the wettest months of the year. Most tourist-oriented businesses stay open, with lower prices, till September 15, except in the Arctic. After September 15, it's potluck. Some areas close up tight, but the silver salmon fishing is still active on the Kenai Peninsula, and the season there continues until the end of the month. A lucky visitor can come in September, hit a month of crisp, sunny, perfect weather, and have the state relatively to him- or herself. Or, it can be cold and rainy all month. Cruise ships continue to ply the Inside Passage well into October, while the sky dumps torrential rains: Ketchikan averages 22 inches and 24 rainy days in October.

OCTOBER, NOVEMBER, APRIL I always love Alaska, but I love it least during these transition months between winter and summer. From Southcentral Alaska northward, snow and ice arrive sometime in October; in Southeast Alaska, it is the month of cold, unending rain. Winter starts in November, but you can't count on being able to do winter sports and darkness is prevalent as the year's shortest day approaches. April is a month of waiting, as winter sports come to an end and summer activities are blocked by melt and mud (although spring skiing can still be great in high-snow years). In-town activities are down in these months, too; with few visitors, many facilities are closed.

DECEMBER THROUGH MARCH

Winter is the whole point of Alaska. For sightseeing, the scenery is at its best (although there are far fewer wildlife viewing opportunities). This is the time to see the aurora borealis. Communities get busy with activities such as sled dog and snowmobile races, theater, music and other performing arts, ice carving competitions and winter carnivals, and all the rest of the real local culture that takes a break in the summer, when most visitors come. If you enjoy winter and its outdoor activities, an Alaska visit is paradise, with superb downhill, cross-country, and back-country skiing; snowshoeing; snowmobiling; dog mushing; ice skating—anything that can be done on snow and ice.

By far the best time to come is late winter, February and March, when the sun is up longer and winter activities hit their peak. Anchorage's Fur Rendezvous is in late February, the Iditarod Trail Sled Dog Race is in early March. Visiting in late March could mean thin snow at lower elevations for cross-country skiing, but downhill skiing and skiing at back-country locations keep going strong. At Alyeska Resort, south of Anchorage, some skiing goes on through Memorial Day. In Homer, you can cross-country ski and go salmon fishing on the same day in March.

If you come in winter, you sacrifice some popular Alaska experiences. Some tourism-oriented towns such as Skagway close down almost completely. In places on the ocean, most activities and attractions are closed for the season, but services remain open for business travelers. Inland, where winter sports are better,

there is more to do. Hotel prices are often less than half of what you'd pay in the high season. Quite luxurious rooms sometimes go for the cost of a budget motel.

WHAT TO WEAR

You'll find little use for a tie or any formal attire anywhere in Alaska, but you do need to prepare for broad swings in weather.

SUMMER   You're not going to the North Pole, and you don't need a down parka or winter boots weighing down your luggage. But you do need to be ready for a variety of weather, from sunny, 80°F (27°C) days to windy, rainy 50°F (10°C) outings on the water. The way Alaskans prepare for such a range is with layers. The content of the layers depends on what you'll be doing, but everyone should bring at least this: warm-weather clothes, heavy long-sleeved shirts and pants, a wool sweater or fleece equivalent, a jacket, and a waterproof raincoat and rain pants. Gloves and wool hats are a good idea, too, especially for boating trips. If you'll be camping, add synthetic thermal long underwear and wool socks and make your jacket thick synthetic fleece. Combining these items, you'll be ready for any summer conditions. For hiking, bring sturdy shoes or cross trainers.

WINTER   You can be warm and comfortable no matter how cold it is. Once you know how to dress, winter is not a time of suffering, and the world of snow opens up to you. First, what not to wear: People don't wear heavy Arctic gear in town, even in the Arctic. To make the dash from car to heated building, all you need is an overcoat, sweater, hat, gloves, and wool socks. For outdoor pursuits, what to wear depends on how active you will be. The key to warmth and safety during vigorous outdoor activities is to wear layers of breathable clothing that will stay warm when wet, such as wool or

Moments   Only-in-Alaska Events

By the end of the winter, sports in Alaska can get extreme. The **Arctic Man Ski & Sno-Go Classic** (© **907/456-2626**; www.arcticman.com) sounds insane just in the description: A skier goes straight down a steep 1,700-foot slope, then grabs a rope to be pulled up the next slope by a snow machine going as fast as 88 mph, and then skis down the next, 1,200-foot slope. Thousands of spectators build a hard-partying city of RVs, snow machines, and a big tent for beer and rock 'n' roll in the remote, treeless hills of the Alaska Range near Summit Lake, 10 miles north of Paxson at mile 195 on the Richardson Highway. For a few days it's the fourth largest community in Alaska. Parking is $100. The event will be held from April 9 to 13, 2008 (race day the 11th).

Another kind of insanity occurs in the **Tesoro Iron Dog Snowmobile Race** (© **907/563-4414**; www.irondog.org). In mid-February, teams of two racers leave from Wasilla, near Anchorage, take the Iditarod Trail to Nome, then turn around and ride to Fairbanks, in the middle of the state. Racers cover a distance of about 2,000 miles of rugged, roadless wilderness at speeds often well in excess of highway driving. In 2007, the winning duo included Governor Sarah Palin's husband Todd, better known as the "First Dude." He covered the distance in just over 38 hours. The race is by far the longest and toughest in the world.

Muscle-powered sports also have big late winter events, including the 50km (31-mile) **Tour of Anchorage** Nordic ski race (www.tourofanchorage. com), which winds its way from one side of the city to the other on the first Sunday in March. With as many as 2,000 racers, it has become a major community happening and draws elite skiers, kids, and grandmothers. It is the second-largest race in the U.S. I ski it every year. Other towns around Alaska have started their own ski marathons during the following weeks, including Homer, Talkeetna, and Fairbanks. For a calendar of events and other Alaska cross-country skiing information, contact the **Nordic Ski Association of Anchorage** (© **907/276-7609**; www.anchoragenordicski.com).

And don't forget the various human-powered wilderness races that cross Alaska, winter and summer, often covering 100 miles or more on skis, snowshoes, bikes or foot, or a combination thereof. Sometimes these races have only a few competitors, and perhaps only one or two finishers. No one does it for glory, but somehow it makes sense where big, wild land is the dominant theme and trail sports are the primary form of recreation.

---

synthetics. With the following layers, you can be ready for temperatures well below zero (at which point you won't want to ski or skate anyway): synthetic thermal long underwear, synthetic fleece pants and coat, wool sweater, wind-resistant pants and jacket, wool socks and hat, warm boots with liners or covers, and lined mittens. Remove layers for warmer temperatures. For more sedentary outdoor activities, such as watching the aurora or riding a snowmobile or dog sled, you need warmer clothing. Likewise, drives on rural highways in winter require warm clothing in case of break-downs. On guided trips or at cold weather resorts they'll tell you what to bring or provide or rent it to you. A full cold weather outfit includes synthetic thermal long underwear, the stoutest Sorel-style or air force bunny boots, insulated snow pants, a heavy down or fur parka with a hood, thick insulated mittens (not gloves), a wool hat, a face-insulating mask, and ski goggles or quality sunglasses. You don't want any skin showing while riding a snowmobile or standing in a strong wind in below-zero (Fahrenheit) temperatures. Such a get-up costs more than $500. You can buy what you need in Anchorage at **Army Navy Store,** at 320 W. 4th Ave. (© **888/836-3535** or 907/279-2401; www.army-navy-store.com); or in Fairbanks at **Big Ray's Store,** at 507 2nd Ave. (© **800/478-3458** or 907/452-3458; www.bigrays.com).

ALASKA CALENDAR OF EVENTS

Here are some of the biggest community events of the year in Alaska's cities and towns. Event plans can change, so don't set up your vacation around any of these dates without checking for current details. I haven't listed fishing derbies, which go on in almost every coastal town in the summer and are listed in the sections on each town.

February

The Yukon Quest International Sled Dog Race (© **907/452-7954;** www.yukonquest.org). Mushers say this rugged 1,000-mile race is even tougher than the Iditarod. It runs between Fairbanks and Whitehorse, Yukon Territory, trading the direction each year. Starts February 9, 2008, in Fairbanks.

The Anchorage Fur Rendezvous Winter Festival (© **907/274-1177;** www.furrondy.net). The citywide winter celebration includes community events, fireworks, craft fairs, dog sled rides, and other fun. The main event has always been the **World Champion Sled Dog Race,** a 3-day sprint event of about 25 miles per heat. The Rondy's end coincides with the start of the Iditarod (see directly below). February 22 to March 2, 2008.

March

The Iditarod Trail Sled Dog Race (© **907/376-5155;** www.iditarod.com). The world's most famous sled dog race starts with fanfare from **Anchorage;** then the teams are loaded into trucks for the **Iditarod Restart,** north of the city, for the real beginning of the race, where the historic gold-rush trail becomes continuous for the dogs' 1,000-mile run to Nome. The start and the finish in Nome are the biggest sporting and cultural events of Alaska's year, drawing world media attention and turning Nome into a huge party for a few days (they even play golf out on the sea ice). Along the way, visitors can stay in remote lodges and fly bush planes to see the check points (with plenty of advance planning and a big budget). An animal-rights group opposes the race on the grounds that it's cruel to dogs. For more on the issue, see p. 482. In 2008 the race starts March 2.

The Nenana Ice Classic (© **907/ 832-5446;** www.nenanaakiceclassic.com), Nenana. This is a betting pool on the date of spring breakup that has happened every year for the last 9 decades. The kick-off is Tripod Days, when a "four-legged tripod" that will mark the ice going out on the Tanana River is erected during the first weekend in March, with a celebration of dance performances, dog mushing, and other activities. The ticket buyer who guesses the minute the tripod will move, usually about 2 months later, wins the jackpot, typically over $300,000.

The World Ice Art Championships (© 907/451-8250; www.icealaska. com), Fairbanks. Carvers from all over the world sculpt immense chunks of clear ice cut from a Fairbanks pond. Among ice carvers, Fairbanks's ice is famous for its clarity and the great size of the chunks. Some spectacular ice sculptures stand as tall as a two-story building. In 2008 carving will be February 27 to February 28 and March 2 to March 9, with the best viewing of finished works from March 8 to March 18.

April

The Alaska Folk Festival (© 907/463-3316; www.alaskafolkfestival.org), Juneau, April 7 to April 13, 2008. This is a communitywide celebration, drawing musicians, whether on the bill or not, from all over the state.

May

Copper River Delta Shorebird Festival (© 907/424-7260; www.cordova chamber.com), Cordova, May 8 to May 11, 2008. This festival revolves around the coming of dizzying swarms of millions of shorebirds that use the delta and beaches near the town as a migratory stopover. The whole community gets involved to host birdwatchers and put on a schedule of educational and outdoor activities for 3 days.

The Kachemak Bay Shorebird Festival (© 907/235-7740; http://homer alaska.org/shorebird.htm), Homer, May 8 to May 11. The festival includes guided bird-watching hikes and boat excursions, natural-history workshops, art shows, performances, and other events.

Little Norway Festival (© 907/772-3646; www.petersburg.org), Petersburg. This festival celebrates the May 17, 1814, declaration of the independence of Norway from Sweden. The town has several days of community

events. The festival takes place on the third full weekend in May.

Kodiak Crab Festival (© 907/486-5557; www.kodiak.org/crabfest.html), Kodiak, May 22 to May 26, 2008. This Memorial Day weekend event is the town's biggest of the year, including fun events, the solemn blessing of the fleet, and a memorial service for lost fishermen and other mariners.

June

The Sitka Summer Music Festival (© 907/277-4852; www.sitkamusic festival.org), Sitka. Since 1972, this chamber music series has drawn musicians from all over the world for most of June. Performances take place Tuesdays and Fridays, and other events all week, over 3 weeks in June.

Midnight Sun Baseball Game, Fairbanks. A century-old summer-solstice tradition: a game without artificial lights beginning at 10:30pm. The local semipro baseball team, the Alaska Goldpanners (© 907/451-0095; www. goldpanners.com), has hosted since 1960. Around June 21.

Midnight Sun Festival, Nome. Over the summer solstice, Nome gets more than 22 hours of direct sunlight, ample reason for a parade, softball tournament, raft race, and polar bear swim (so long as sea ice permits). Call © 907/443-5535 for information. Weekend closest to June 21.

The Last Frontier Theater Conference (© 907/834-1614; www.pwscc.edu), Valdez. The conference brings playwrights and directors from all over the nation to the community for a week of seminars and performances. June 14 to June 21, 2008.

July

Independence Day. Most of the small towns in Alaska make a big deal of the Fourth of July. Seward always has a huge celebration, exploding with visitors, primarily from Anchorage. Besides the parade and many small-town festivities, the main attraction is the **Mount Marathon Race,** which goes from the middle of town straight up rocky Mount Marathon to its 3,022-foot peak and down again. **Seldovia, Ketchikan, Skagway,** and **Juneau** also have exceptional Fourth of July events. See the individual town sections for more information.

The Southeast Alaska State Fair (© 907/766-2476; www.seakfair.org), Haines. Held for 4 days in late July, this is a regional small-town get-together music festival, with livestock, cooking, a logging show, a parade, and other entertainment.

August

The Alaska State Fair (© 907/745-4827; www.alaskastatefair.org), Palmer. The region's biggest event of the year is a typical state fair, except for the huge vegetables. The good soil and long Valley days produce cabbages the size of beanbag chairs. Try to imagine a 19-pound carrot. Held the 12 days before Labor Day.

October

Alaska Day Festival (© 907/747-8806), Sitka. Alaska Day, commemorating the Alaska purchase on October 18, 1867, is a big deal in this former Russian and U.S. territorial capital city.

November

Sitka WhaleFest (© 907/747-7964; www.sitkawhalefest.org), Sitka. Over a weekend in early November, during the fall and early winter period when humpback whales congregate in Sitka Sound, experts from around the world present a 3-day symposium, and there are whale-watching tours, concerts, an art show, a run, and community events.

The Alaska Bald Eagle Festival (© 907/766-3094; www.baldeagle festival.org), Haines. Seminars and special events mark an annual congregation of 3,000 eagles near Haines. Mid-November.

The Carrs/Safeway Great Alaska Shootout Men's Basketball Tournament (© 907/786-1250; www.gosea wolves.com), Anchorage. The University of Alaska Anchorage hosts top-ranked college teams at the Sullivan Arena over Thanksgiving weekend.

3 Cost & Money

Alaska is an expensive destination any way you slice it. With the exception of rural highway motels, standard motel rooms are rarely less than $140 in the high season. (I've rated them this way: inexpensive, under $135; moderate $135–$174; expensive $175–$250; very expensive over $250.) Airfare from Seattle to Anchorage fluctuates wildly with competition among the airlines, but a $350 round-trip, with 14-day advance purchase, is a good deal. (Flying is cheaper than the alternatives, driving or taking the ferry and bus.) You can easily pay twice that to fly to an Alaska Bush community. Even the train is expensive, with a one-way fare from Anchorage to Fairbanks (a 350-mile trip) costing $189. A couple ordering a good salmon dinner, appetizers, and wine will likely pay $100 in a fine restaurant, plus tip. One reason cruise ships have become such a popular way to visit Alaska is that, for the same quality level, they're less expensive on a daily basis than independent travel, and offer the chance to see remote coastal areas that can be quite costly to get to for land-based visitors. (See chapter 4 for details on cruising.)

To travel at a standard American comfort level, a couple should allow $150 per person, per day, for room and board. The

Native Art: Finding the Real Thing

In a gift shop in Southeast Alaska, I watched as a woman who said she was an artist's assistant sanded a Tlingit-style carving. When I asked who made the carving, the artist said, "It's my work." At the time, that seemed like an odd way of putting it. Only later did I learn from one of the artist's former assistants that his "work" involved ordering the carvings from Southeast Asia and shipping them to Alaska, where he hired locals to pretend to be working on them in the shop. Journalists have repeatedly documented shops fraudulently removing "Made in Taiwan" stickers and the like, and replacing them with "Made in Alaska." One journalist found a whole village in Bali carving Alaska Native designs out of ivory, whalebone, and other materials sent from Alaska.

Good estimates don't exist of the amount of counterfeit Alaska Native art sold annually, but authorities have put it close to $100 million. That's money taken from Alaska Bush economies where jobs in the cash economy are virtually nonexistent and prices for essentials such as fuel and housing are astronomical. Buying fake Native art is cultural and financial theft from subsistence hunters and fishermen who can least afford it. And besides, who wants to come home with an Eskimo mask made in Bali?

You can avoid being scammed if you pay attention. Ask questions before you buy. Any reputable art dealer will provide you with a biography of the artist who created an expensive work. Ask specifically if that artist actually carved the piece: Some Native artists have sold their names and designs to wholesalers who produce knockoffs. Price is another tip-off. An elaborate mask is more likely to cost $1,000 than $100. Another indicator is the choice of materials; most soapstone carvings are not made in Alaska. Even less expensive craftwork should bear the name of the person who made it, and the shop owner should be able to tell you how he or she acquired the item.

Another caution, for international visitors: do not buy products made from marine mammals, such as walrus ivory, whalebone, or sealskin. Except

cost of an activity such as flightseeing, wildlife cruises, or guided fishing typically is $90 to $350 per person. Add ground transportation: a car is the best way to see much of the state, and you won't do much better than $50 a day for an economy model from the major national firms. Weekly rentals generally cost the same as renting for 5 individual days. You also may need train and ferry tickets.

You can trim your costs, however, by cutting your demands. You'll learn more about the real Alaska staying in B&B accommodations than in a standard hotel room. Expect to pay $100 to $120 for a nice room with a shared bathroom, $120 to $150 for a private bathroom (much more in a luxury B&B inn). The free breakfast cuts down on food costs, too. And there are plenty of family restaurants where you can eat a modest dinner for two for $50, with a tip and a glass of beer. Traveling in that style will bring down the cost of room and board to about $100 per person, per day, for a couple.

You can save the most money by giving up a private room every night and cooking some of your own meals. Camping is a fun way to really see Alaska and costs only $10 to $20 a night in state and federal for antiques, export of these materials is illegal, so you won't be able to take your purchase home. (You may need a permit to export other wildlife items as well. See "What You Can Take Home," p. 43.)

The **Alaska State Council on the Arts** (ⓒ **907/269-6610**) authenticates Native arts and crafts with a **silver hand** label, which assures you it was made by the hands of an Alaska Native with Alaskan materials. But the program isn't universally used, so the absence of the label doesn't mean the work definitely isn't authentic. Other labels aren't worth much: An item could say ALASKA MADE even if only insignificant assembly work happened here. Of course, in Bush Alaska and in some urban shops, you can buy authentic work directly from craftspeople. Buying in Native-owned co-ops is also safe.

Another program covers any item made within the state, both Native and non-Native. The logo of a mother bear and cub (www.madeinalaska.org) indicates that a state contractor has determined that the product was made in Alaska, when possible with Alaskan materials. Non-Natives produce Alaskan crafts of ceramics, wood, or fabric, but not plastic—if it's plastic, it probably wasn't made here. Again, price is an indicator: As with anywhere else in the United States, the cheapest products come from Asia.

You can learn about and buy authentic work from the **Alaska Native Arts Foundation,** a nonprofit with online shopping at www.alaskanativearts.org and a brick-and-mortar gallery in Anchorage (p. 248). **Sealaska Heritage Foundation** offers a nonprofit website selling work by Southeast Alaska Natives at www.alaskanativeartists.com. Even if you don't buy anything from these sites, taking a look will give you an idea of what real Native art looks like and how much it should cost, so you can be a better shopper when you get to Alaska.

government campgrounds. Hostels are available in most towns for around $25 a night.

Don't economize, however, when it comes to activities. Unlike other destinations where relatively inexpensive museums or an interesting street scene take up much of your time, a trip to Alaska is all about getting outside and seeing nature. You can hike for nothing, but to go sea kayaking, whale-watching, or flying out to see bears or to fish in a remote stream, you have to pay. Cut those expenses and you cut much of the reason for going in the first place.

You can save on activities, however, by traveling in the shoulder season, before and after the peak summer season. Hotel and guided activity prices drop significantly, typically 25% or more. May and September are solidly in the shoulder season, and sometimes you can get bargains as late as June 15 or as early as August 15. Traveling in the winter is a whole different experience, but certainly saves a lot of money—where hotels are open, you'll find their rates typically running half of their high-season levels. For other considerations on off-season and shoulder-season travel, see "When to Go," earlier.

Carrying your money need not be a problem, regardless of your style of travel; those from the United States don't need to make any adjustments in their usual habits. Even Bush hub communities now have ATMs. The only places that don't usually have ATMs these days are remote outdoor destinations such as lodges or parks and tiny Native villages. In the "Fast Facts" section for each town in this book, I'll tell you where to find an ATM.

Every business you'd expect to take credit, charge, or debit cards at home will accept them here. Even bed-and-breakfasts and greasy-spoon diners take cards now. Few businesses of any kind will take an out-of-state personal check. Traveler's checks are good just about anywhere, but there's no longer any reason to go through the hassle and expense.

4 Getting There & Getting Around

BY PLANE

CARRIERS Anchorage is Alaska's main point of entry from the outside world (foreign and domestic) and is served by several major carriers to the rest of the United States. A few flights arrive in Anchorage from Japan, Korea, or Germany, but the vast majority of international travelers arrive in the U.S. in another major city in the contiguous states and then take a domestic flight to Anchorage. It's also possible to fly into Fairbanks or Southeast Alaska. Most passengers come into Anchorage through Seattle, but for a bit more you can fly nonstop to Anchorage from various major cities. There are far more choices in summer than in winter. **Alaska Airlines** (② 800/252-7522; www.alaskaair.com) has more flights than all other airlines combined, with as many as 20 a day to Seattle in summer and summer nonstops to many cities around the country. Alaska Airlines is the only jet carrier with more than token coverage anywhere in the state other than Anchorage and has arrangements with commuter lines that fan out from its network to smaller communities.

Here are the major airlines serving Anchorage as of this writing:

Air Canada ② 888/247-2262; www.aircanada.com

Alaska Airlines ② 800/252-7522; www.alaskaair.com

American Airlines ② 800/433-7300; www.aa.com

China Airlines ② 800/227-5118; www.china-airlines.com

Condor Airlines (German) ② 800/364-1664; www.condor.com

Continental Airlines ② 800/523-3273; www.continental.com

Delta Air Lines ② 800/221-1212; www.delta.com

Frontier Airlines ② 800/432-1359; www.frontierairlines.com

Northwest Airlines ② 800/225-2525; www.nwa.com

Sun Country Airlines ② 800/359-6786; www.suncountry.com

United Airlines ② 800/864-8331; www.ual.com

U.S. Airways ② 800-428-4322; www.usairways.com

The flight lineup (and the existence of the airlines) changes quickly, so all of this is subject to change.

FARES Alaskans fly so much we tend to talk about air fares the way New Yorkers talk about real estate. Fares vary wildly, so watching for sales can pay off. It's almost always cheapest to change planes in Seattle due to the competition on the Seattle-Anchorage route. The competition also makes these fares more volatile than the NASDAQ: You can easily pay more than $400, but it's not unusual to get a ticket for $350, and if

Travel in the Age of Bankruptcy

Airlines go bankrupt, so protect yourself by **buying your tickets with a credit card.** The Fair Credit Billing Act guarantees that you can get your money back from the credit card company if a travel supplier goes under (and if you request the refund within 60 days of the bankruptcy). **Travel insurance** can also help, but make sure it covers against "carrier default" for your specific travel provider (see "Travel & Rental Car Insurance," p. 44). If a U.S. airline goes bust midtrip, federal law requires other carriers to take you to your destination on a space-available basis for a fee of no more than $25, provided you rebook within 60 days of the cancellation.

you're really alert you can sometimes luck into one for $250. A website maintained by Anchorage travel consultant Scott McMurran (www.alaskatravelgram.com/airfares) monitors the current lowest fares from many cities. Use it for a reference, but don't expect to get those rock-bottom fares without a lot of flexibility and a skilled travel agent. Summer sales sometimes hit in April. If you can make a last-minute decision, sign up for Web specials on the Alaska Airlines website and other airline sites, as there often are bargains to be had you can't get any other way.

BUSH PILOTS   To fly to a roadless village, or to fly between most towns without returning to a hub, you will take a small, prop-driven plane with an Alaska bush pilot at the controls. Small air taxis also charter to fishing sites, lodges, remote cabins, or anywhere else you want to go—even a sand bar in the middle of a river. An authentic Alaskan adventure can be had by taking a Bush mail plane round-trip to a village and back. The ticket price is generally less than a flightseeing trip, and you'll have at least a brief chance to look around a Native village, although don't expect to find any visitor facilities without making arrangements in advance. It's cost effective to take these flights from towns that are relatively close to surrounding villages: Kodiak, Homer, Fairbanks, Nome, Kotzebue, and Barrow fit the bill. You will need to do some research; find the name of a

local flight service that carries mail from the town visitor center or on the Web, then call and explain what you have in mind. And wait for good weather.

BY SHIP

The most popular way to get to Alaska is on a **cruise ship.** (Chapter 4, "Cruising Alaska's Coast," provides an in-depth look at your options.)

For an affordable, independent trip by sea, with a chance to stop as long as you like along the way, take the **Alaska Marine Highway System** (© 800/642-0066; www.ferryalaska.com). It's my favorite form of public transportation. The big blue, white, and gold ferries ply the Inside Passage from Bellingham, Washington, and Prince Rupert, B.C., to the towns of Southeast Alaska, with road links to the rest of the state at Haines and Skagway. In summer, a ferry twice a month connects from that system across the Gulf of Alaska to the central part of the state. From there, smaller ferries connect towns in Prince William Sound and the Kenai Peninsula to Kodiak Island and the Aleutian Archipelago. For a complete discussion of the system and its intricacies, see "Getting Around by Ferry: The Alaska Marine Highway" in chapter 5.

BY RAIL

You can't get to Alaska by train, but you can get close. From the west coast of the U.S. you can take **Amtrak's** Cascades train

---

Value **The Cheapest Way to Alaska**

Flying is the cheapest and by far the simplest way to get to Alaska. Take other means only for the adventure, not for the savings. Round-trip train, ferry, and bus fare between Seattle and Anchorage costs several times as much as a good airfare between the same cities. Driving is expensive, too, when you count rooms, food, and wear and tear on your vehicle. Fuel alone for the 4,500-mile drive from Seattle to Anchorage and back would cost $675 in a car that gets 20 miles to the gallon—more than a plane ticket. (Okay, maybe a foursome can do it cheaper than flying if they drive a small car, camp every night, and eat rice and beans.)

(© **800/USA-RAIL;** www.amtrak.com) to Bellingham, Washington; the dock for the Alaska ferry is quite close to the railroad station. From the east, it makes more sense to use Canada's **Via Rail** (© **888/VIA-RAIL;** www.viarail.ca). The transcontinental route starts all the way back in Toronto; you change in Jasper to end up in Prince Rupert, B.C., where you can catch the Alaska ferry north. Of course, it's a long, weary journey, whichever way you go.

BY CAR

TIME & DISTANCE Figuring how long it takes to drive between various points in Alaska needn't be complicated, but don't trust your computer. A reader checked three different Internet map sites for one trip and came up with drive times ranging from 4 hours, 27 minutes to 8 hours, 45 minutes. I have included a description of the roads and average speeds you can expect ("Alaska's Highways a la Carte," p. 382). Get the mileage you plan to drive from the chart in this book's insert, or from www.maps.google. com, and then divide the distance by the expected speed to get the time it will take. Add some time for stops. For paved highways, you can count on averaging 50 mph. On some roads you can go faster than 50, but you can't often drive at freeway speeds on these two-lane highways. Even when the surface is smooth—not always a given—the roads aren't designed for high speeds and are often clogged in summer with lumbering RVs. Besides,

you need to be on the look-out for moose; hit one of those at 75 mph and you both die.

DRIVING TO ALASKA Driving from any of the other states to Alaska is a great adventure, but it requires thousands of miles on the road and plenty of time. Allow at least a week each way. By car, Anchorage is 2,250 miles from Seattle and 3,400 miles from Los Angeles. By comparison, New York to Los Angeles is 2,800 miles. Traveling at an average of 50 mph, few vacationers will want to cover more than 500 or 600 miles a day, and that's a long day of nothing but driving. On such a plan, Seattle is 4 or 5 days from Anchorage without breaks.

Some of the 1,400-mile **Alaska Highway** is dull, but there are spectacular sections of the route, too, and few experiences give you a better feel for the size and personality of Alaska (and B.C. and Yukon). Putting your car on the ferry cuts the length of the trip considerably, but raises the cost; you could rent a car for 2 weeks for the same price as carrying an economy car on the ferry one-way from Bellingham to Haines. I love riding the ferry up the Inside Passage, but I usually rent a car or bike to get around in the towns on the way. Details on the Alaska section of the Alaska Highway, and other highways, are contained in chapter 9. The ferry is described in chapter 5. *The Milepost* (Morris Communications; $28) contains good maps and mile-by-mile logs of all Alaska highways and Canadian approaches; however, it's not interesting to read and is clogged with advertising masquerading as editorial text.

THE RENTAL OPTION Renting a car is the easiest way to see the Interior and Southcentral parts of the state. All the major national car-rental companies are represented in Anchorage as well as many local operators, who may have lower prices for older cars. In smaller cities and towns, there is always at least one agency; the town descriptions throughout the book provide details on firms in each town. Base rates for major rental companies are in the range of $50 a day for an economy car. Weekly rentals equate roughly to 5 day's cost.

One-way rentals between Alaska towns are an attractive way to travel, but you generally pay steep drop-off charges, so a more popular plan is to fly into and out of Anchorage and pick up and return the car there. There are two popular circular routes from Anchorage: to Denali and Fairbanks on the Parks Highway and back on the Richardson and Glenn highways, or to Valdez by ferry from Whittier and back on another part of the Richardson Highway and the Glenn Highway. See chapter 3 for more on routes.

BY RV

Touring Alaska in an RV makes a good deal of sense. The home on wheels offers spontaneity by freeing you from hotel reservations (see "Car or RV Camping," p. 35), and it gets you out of town and into the countryside, closer to the natural Alaska most visitors come for. At the same time, an RV is more comfortable than a tent in cool, unpredictable weather conditions.

Many retirees drive to Alaska in their motor homes, park the RV by a salmon stream, and spend the summer fishing. Sounds nice, but for most of the rest of us, with limited time, it makes more sense to rent an RV after flying to Alaska. Rental agencies are listed in Skagway (p. 212) and Anchorage (p. 212). The option of shipping your own RV to Alaska is also covered in chapter 6. Unless you have a large family, an RV rental saves little over traveling with a rental car, staying in hotels, and eating in restaurants (RVs rent for around $1,500 a week, plus gas and possibly mileage charges), so you make this choice to gain advantages, not avoid costs.

Alaska Highway Cruises (© 800/323-5757; www.bestofalaskatravel.com) offers the unique option of traveling one-way on a Holland America cruise ship then picking up an RV for a land tour. You can choose a package that ends up back in Seattle by road or by air. The tours follow set itineraries with reservations along the way—the service is designed for first-time Alaska travelers and RV drivers who don't want to worry about the details—so some spontaneity is sacrificed. You get the security and simplicity of a package without being marched around in a group or cooped up in hotels. A cruise of a week followed by a week-long tour costs around $2,800 per person, double occupancy; a 3-week cruise to Alaska and drive back (or reverse) is around $4,100 per person. There are various discounts, including for third and fourth passengers. Simple one-way RV rentals to Alaska are available, too, with an added drop-off fee of $700 to well over $1,000. See p. 214.

5 Escorted Tour or Do-It-Yourself?

Hundreds of thousands of visitors come to Alaska each year on escorted package tours, leaving virtually all their travel arrangements in the hands of a single company that takes responsibility for ushering them through the state for a single,

lump-sum fee. Many others cut the apron strings and explore Alaska on their own, in the process discovering a more relaxed, spontaneous experience. Each approach has advantages and disadvantages, of course, and which way you choose to visit depends on how you value those pros and cons. Unfortunately, some people make the choice based on expectations that aren't valid, so it's important to know what you're getting into.

An escorted package tour provides security. You'll know in advance how much everything will cost, you don't have to worry about making hotel and ground-transportation reservations, you're guaranteed to see the highlights of each town you visit, and you'll have someone telling you what you're looking at. Often, a package price saves money over traveling at the same level of comfort independently. If there are weather delays or other travel problems, it's the tour company's problem, not yours. Everything happens on schedule, and you never have to touch your baggage other than to unpack when it magically shows up in your room. If you sometimes feel like you're a member of a herd on an escorted tour, you'll also meet new people, a big advantage if you're traveling on your own. Many passengers on these trips are retired, over age 65.

If you're short on time, escorted package tours make the most of it, as they often travel at an exhausting pace. Passengers get up early and cover a lot of ground, with sights and activities scheduled solidly through the day. Stops last only long enough to get a taste of what the sight is about, not to dig in and learn about a place you're especially interested in. On an escorted trip, you'll meet few if any Alaska residents, since most tour companies hire college students from "Outside" (a term Alaskans use to refer to any place other than Alaska) to fill summer jobs. You'll stay in only the largest hotels and eat in the largest, tourist-oriented restaurants—no small, quaint places loaded with local character. For visiting wilderness, such as Denali National Park, the quick and superficial approach can, in my opinion, spoil the whole point of going to a destination that's about an experience, not just seeing a particular object or place.

Studies by Alaska tourism experts have found that many people choose escorted packages to avoid risks that don't really exist. Alaska may still be untamed, but that doesn't mean it's a dangerous or uncomfortable place to travel. Visitors who sign up for a tour to avoid having to spend the night in an igloo or use an outhouse may wish they'd been a bit more adventurous when they arrive and find that Alaska has the same facilities found in any other state. Except for tiny Bush villages that you're unlikely to visit anyway, you'll come across the standard American hotel room almost anywhere you go. The tourism infrastructure is well developed even in small towns—you're never far from help unless you want to be.

It's also possible for an independent traveler to obtain some of the predictability a package tour provides. You can reserve accommodations and activities and control your expenses by using a good travel agent experienced in Alaska travel. Some even offer fixed-price itineraries that allow you to travel on your own (see "Independent Travel Planning," below). But independent travelers never have the complete security of those on group tours. Once you're on the road, you'll be on your own to take care of the details, and weather delays and other cancellations can confound the best-laid plans. If you can't relax and enjoy a trip knowing unforeseen difficulties could happen, then an escorted package tour is the way to go.

LARGE TOUR COMPANIES

A single cruise-ship company, Carnival, dominates the Alaska package-tour market operating under various brands. The "vertically integrated" operations allow the company to take care of everything you do while in Alaska with tight quality control. In some popular areas, cruise lines have bought everything in sight, even historic attractions. Holland America and Princess, both now owned by Carnival, developed independently as the primary competitors in Alaska and still operate separately. Each offers tours as short as a couple of hours to independent travelers who want to combine their own exploring with a more structured experience. All can be booked through any travel agent. Other cruise lines also offer land tours, but typically only for their own passengers. If you will cruise to Alaska and want to add an escorted land tour, check for deals with your own cruise line first.

Holland America Line Tours The Holland America cruise line is the giant of Alaska tourism and thousands of visitors do business with no one else when they come. The Alaska/Yukon operation employs more than 2,100 workers operating 225 buses, 14 railcars, and 2 day boats. Most clients arrive in the state on one of the company's ships (see chapter 4), but even within Alaska, chances are good that a tour you sign up for will put you on a Gray Line coach and exclusively in Westmark hotels, both owned by Holland America. The Westmark hotels are described in the appropriate sections of this book. Some are among the best in town, including those in Juneau (called the Baranof), Fairbanks, and Sitka, while others are unremarkable. But then, on a group tour you don't spend much time in the room, as schedules generally are tightly planned and daily departures are early. You'll find a description of the company's railcars on the Anchorage-Denali-Fairbanks run in chapter 8. The company goes more places than any other, with a catalog that covers just about anything in the state that could possibly be done with a group. Some of the tour excursions—on the Yukon River between Dawson City and Eagle, for example—are entirely unique. Prices depend on a variety of factors, but in general a tour of a week is about $1,400 per person.

300 Elliott Ave. W., Seattle, WA 98119. ⓒ 800/544-2206. www.graylineofalaska.com or www.holland america.com.

Princess Cruises and Tours Before its sale to Carnival (see above) Princess built its tour operation from the ground up, surpassing Holland America with the consistently outstanding quality of its smaller list of offerings. That advantage persists. The five Princess hotels are all among Alaska's best. Two are near Denali National Park, and one each are in Fairbanks, in Cooper Landing (on the Kenai Peninsula), and in Copper Center, near Wrangell–St. Elias National Park. Princess operates its own coaches and has superb railcars on the Alaska Railroad route to Denali. Descriptions of each hostelry can be found in the appropriate chapter. Most people on the tours come to Alaska on a cruise ship, but tours are for sale separately, too.

800 5th Ave., Suite 2600, Seattle, WA 98014. ⓒ 800/426-0550. www.princesslodges.com.

INDEPENDENT TRAVEL PLANNING

With this guidebook, you can book everything yourself, but for a long trip it can get quite complicated to keep track of all the dates and deposits. If you're using a trusted travel agency to make trip arrangements, our reviews can help you make informed decisions. Read through the book, make your selections, and approach the agent with as detailed a plan as possible, derived from your own research. Then let the agent make the bookings you have chosen. Most agents who don't specialize in Alaska are aware of only the biggest attractions and best-marketed companies. Another option is to use a travel agency or trip-planner based in Alaska. They'll know much more about the place and can help you more in picking out what you want to do. I've listed a few below.

Unfortunately, there are cautions to be offered in using the agencies. They work on commission, which means they're being paid by the establishments you're buying from. A good agent will disregard

Beware of Fraud

In 2003, one of the largest trip planners in Alaska went bankrupt, leaving many visitors with worthless vouchers for prepaid reservations. It turned out the owner was using clients' credit cards to keep her business afloat. She took her own trip to federal prison in 2005, but by then even worse rip-offs had cropped up on the Internet. Use caution. If you prepay large trip expenses to a planner or a provider directly, be certain to use a credit card that will protect you, and buy appropriate travel insurance. Do not buy the insurance from the same entity from whom you bought the trip (see "Travel & Rental Car Insurance," p. 44).

the size of the commission and really look out for you, but I've encountered too many visitors on poorly planned itineraries not to advise caution. Some travel agents book visitors on trips to far-flung corners of the state in quick succession, so they wind up staying only briefly in expensive places and then zoom off somewhere else, all with little concern for the visitors' true interests. Your best defense is to do enough research so you can actively participate in the planning.

Here I've gathered the names of some agencies that book Alaska trips. Expect to pay booking fees and to have the agent collect commissions from the businesses you use. My knowledge of these agencies is limited to contacting them as a journalist, so a mention here is no guarantee; however, all of these have been around for several years and I remove agencies from the list when I receive justified complaints.

Alaska Bound This Michigan-based agency is the only one I know of in the Lower 48 that specializes in Alaska with a staff of former Alaskans. It started as a cruise planner, working primarily with Holland America, but now plans many independent trips, too, charging a per person fee which depends on the length of the trip ($100 per person would not be exceptional).

116 Cass St., Traverse City, MI 49684. © 888/ALASKA-7 or 231/439-3000. www.alaskabound.com.

Alaska Tour & Travel Started in 1995 and steadily growing, this agency now claims to be the largest custom vacation company in Alaska. The same folks operate the Park Connection shuttle between Denali and Kenai Fjords national parks, and that central part of the state is what they know best and cover deeply. The website is remarkable, including a search tool that brings up preset itineraries based on criteria you specify, and a live availability-and-rate calendar for a range of Denali hotels.

P.O. Box 221011, Anchorage, AK 99522. © 800/208-0200. www.alaskatravel.com.

Alaska.org This is a deep and well-built website that allows users to shop and customize tour packages or design their own vacations in the Southcentral-to-Fairbanks region with as much or as little structure and guidance as they choose, and without surcharge. When you've seen enough, call the toll-free number for questions and booking. Or don't. Uniquely for this kind of site, you can use it just to get information and call the listed operators yourself.

507 E. St., Suite 206, Anchorage, AK 99508. © 888/ALASKA-8. www.alaska.org.

Ask Matt Alaskan Adventures & Tours Matthew Lowe is an energetic young concierge at the large Millennium Alaskan Hotel Anchorage who has turned his encyclopedic knowledge of Southcentral Alaska travel into his own business. His strength is in activities, but he happily books travelers into budget B&Bs as well as more expensive lodges and resorts and charges no upfront fee.

Millennium Alaskan Hotel Anchorage, 4800 Spenard Rd., Anchorage, AK 99517. © 888/355-6288. www.askmatt.com.

Sport Fishing Alaska Choose this company to plan a fishing vacation. The owners, former guides and float, charter, and air-taxi operators Larry and Sheary Suiter, know where the fish will be week to week. That means they book clients at fly-in fishing lodges when and where the fishing is hot—a critical piece of information that can be difficult to obtain on your own. They charge a $95 upfront fee. (See "Fishing," below.)

9310 Shorecrest Dr., Anchorage, AK 99502. ✆ 888/552-8674 or 907/344-8674. www.alaskatripplanners.com.

Viking Travel An entrepreneur in the small Southeast Alaska town of Petersburg built this agency, initially specializing in independent outdoor trips in their own area. Today, besides offering all the usual services of a travel agency, they plan trips for the whole state and book all the region's ferries without surcharge. Get on their list and they will book your cabins and vehicle reservations on the first day the system makes them available.

P.O. Box 787, Petersburg, AK 99833. ✆ 800/327-2571 or 907/772-3818. www.alaskaferry.com.

6 Planning an Outdoor Vacation

Most people visit Alaska to experience wilderness, so it's ironic that so many spend their time in crowded ships, buses, trains, and airplanes, the antithesis of a wilderness experience. You do need technology to get to the wilderness of Alaska, but unless you at least partly let loose of that umbilical cord, you'll never really arrive at your destination.

Every town in Alaska is a threshold to the wild. There's always a way to go hiking, biking, or sea kayaking, or to get on the bank of a stream or the deck of a boat to hook into a furiously fighting wild salmon—and end up in the evening back in a comfortable hotel room. Or take it a step further: Plan to go out overnight, perhaps with a friendly local guide at first, and then go out on your own. I've included lots of details on how to do this throughout the book. Scary? If it weren't a little scary, it would be Disneyland, and

that it definitely is not. It's real, and that's why it's worth doing.

Use this section to learn about activities, outfitters, and wilderness lodges. The destination chapters cover outdoor options and practicalities in particular places.

ACTIVITIES

BACKPACKING Alaska's best country for trail hikes is in **Chugach State Park** near Anchorage (see chapter 6), on Chena Hot Springs Road and on the Steese Highway near Fairbanks (see chapter 9), and in the **Chugach National Forest** on the Kenai Peninsula (see chapter 7). For hiking beyond trails, go to **Denali** or the **Denali Highway** (see chapter 8), **Wrangell–St. Elias National Park** or the **Dalton Highway** (see chapter 9). Alaska trail hikes require the same skills as backpacking anywhere else, plus preparation for cold and damp (see "What to Wear,"

⟨Value⟩ **For Coupon Clippers**

A coupon book called **The Great Alaskan Tour Saver** (✆ 907/278-7600; www.toursaver.com), which costs $100, is well worth the price if you plan on traveling as a couple, especially in the Southcentral region. The 150 coupons are freebies or two-for-one deals on some of the best activities, tours, train rides, flightseeing, and lodgings, valuable enough to pay for the book with just a couple of uses. Readers tell me they've saved a lot.

> **Tips A Guide to Guide Gratuities**
>
> As a general rule, tip fishing guides and outfitters $10 to $20 per person per day. For outings of less than a day, adjust the tip accordingly. At wilderness lodges, which normally have all-inclusive rates, it's often best to add the tip to your final payment when you leave and let the proprietor distribute it to the staff rather than try to do it at each meal. A blanket tip of $15 per person per day is acceptable.

earlier). Hiking beyond the trails is a glorious experience, but you need to know how to cross rivers and find your way—it's best if you have some outdoor experience. Or go with a guide; they're listed later. See section 9, later in this chapter, for some backcountry safety tips.

BIKING Most every town in Alaska has a bike-rental agency. There are excellent bike routes all over the state and few restrictions on where you can ride. A bike is a great way into Denali National Park (see chapter 8); Anchorage has an extensive network of paved trails and many mountain biking routes (see chapter 6); and guided biking is available in Haines and Skagway (see chapter 5). A couple that built an excellent reputation and a large business for over a decade offering bicycle tours on Alaska's long, rural highways now operates **Alaska Bicycle Adventures** (© 907/245-2175; www.alaskabike.com) on their own from a home office. These are terrific vacations for avid cyclists. The 8-day tour over the spectacular Richardson Highway costs $2,895, inclusive. The schedule includes bike and kayak tours, too.

BIRD-WATCHING In Alaska, birders can encounter birds in greater variety and greater numbers than they have seen before and add many new species to their life lists. I have listed birding groups and best places to go in many of the sections on destinations. Making a "best of" list is difficult, because good bird-watching is found in any Alaska town. For example, I could recommend you go to Haines for the eagle sanctuary, but since you are bound so see eagles in every coastal town, I hesitate to send you on a special trip for that purpose. Weeding out the excellent to mention only the truly exceptional, here are the places I would send birders. For marine birding, consider Sitka, Juneau, Seward (Kenai Fjords National Park), Unalaska, and the Pribilof Islands (chapters 5, 7, and 10, respectively). Migratory bird festivals happen in May in Homer and Cordova; Homer also has handy sea bird colonies, and Cordova has the wetlands Copper River Delta, an accessible bird paradise of immense proportions (see both in chapter 7). Alaska's two largest cities have parks dedicated to inland birding, and other bird resources as well: see the sections on Anchorage and Fairbanks for details (see chapters 6 and 9). For Arctic birding, Nome is probably the best choice thanks to the existence of roads that allow self-guided exploration (see chapter 10). The very best bird and wildlife destination in Alaska, and surely among the best in the world, is the Pribilof Islands. You can sign up directly with the island's own Aleut residents for a tour there, described in chapter 10. The Internet makes it easy to network with local birders all over Alaska before your trip to find out what they are seeing and get tips. Here's an active discussion board where you can get started: www.groups.yahoo.com/group/akbirding.

Serious birders with money to spend can dedicate an Alaska trip to some of the worlds' best and most famous remote bird-watching sites (those with a milder or budding interest might better choose a less ambitious destination first, or make bird-watching only a part of an Alaska vacation). Learn about trips in birding magazines. *Bird Watcher's Digest* (www.birdwatchersdigest.com) offers good, detailed advice on its website. Group trips are advertised in *Birders' World* (www.birdersworld.com) and *Birding* (www.americanbirding.org). Among the largest and most reputable operators coming to Alaska is Arizona-based **High Lonesome BirdTours** (© 800/743-2668 or 520/458-9446; www.hilonesome.com), priding itself on relaxed trips for small groups. All inclusive tours visit Kenai, Denali, Nome, Gambell, Barrow, Unalaska/Dutch Harbor, Adak, and the Pribilof Islands. Texas-based **Victor Emanuel Nature Tours** (© 800/328-8368; www.ventbird.com), counts well-known authors among its leaders.

CANOEING Paddling a canoe on a remote Alaska lake or river is the best way to get into the wilderness without a backpack, a guide, or a great deal of expense. For beginners, it's easy to rent a canoe in Fairbanks (see chapter 9) for a day trip. If you're ready to go overnight, the choices of routes are extraordinary, including the rivers of the Interior (see chapter 9), the bird-watching country of the Copper River Delta near Cordova, or the supreme lake canoe routes of the Kenai National Wildlife Refuge (see both in chapter 7).

CAR OR RV CAMPING Campgrounds are almost everywhere in Alaska, many in extraordinarily beautiful natural places. Public campgrounds outnumber commercial ones. They're usually located where they are because there's something special about the place: a great view or beach, an exceptional fishing stream or trail head. Rarely will you find running water or flush toilets; most are seasonal, with hand pumps for water. (When it's time to wash up, stay at a commercial campground, which I've noted in each

town section in the destination chapters throughout this book.) Alaska's public campgrounds fill up only in certain times and places (the Kenai River and Denali National Park campgrounds are among the exceptions), so campers have flexibility other travelers can't share, able to stop when and where they like.

Even if you don't usually consider camping, think about renting a comfortable RV for a tour. One company offers these rentals as add-ons with cruise vacations, taking care of all the details for clients (that and other rental options are under "Getting There & Getting Around," earlier in this chapter).

If you fly to Alaska, car camping can be a bit complicated. Carrying a camp stove on an airplane is forbidden unless there is no attached fuel canister and no odor of fuel (even in that case, keep the unit handy for inspection at check in). It often makes more sense to buy a new stove in Alaska and then give it away or ship it back to yourself at the end of the trip. Much car camping equipment is bulky and hard to fit into your limit of two checked bags. Consider renting some of your gear here: rental agencies are listed with large towns in this book. You can also use the mail, sending packages to yourself care of General Delivery at any post office, or simply invest in compact backpacking equipment that you can fit in your luggage.

I've mentioned some great campgrounds throughout the book, but there are many more than I had space to cover. A free map that lists all the public campgrounds along Alaska's highways is available from the Alaska Public Lands Information Centers (see "Fast Facts," later in this chapter). If you are planning to camp the whole way, get a copy of *Traveler's Guide to Alaskan Camping*, by Mike and Terri Church (Rolling Homes Press; $22), which contains detailed reviews of virtually every public and commercial campground in the state.

A Salmon Primer

In Alaska, it's not so much where you wet your line, but when. The primary catch, Pacific salmon, lives in salt water but spawns in freshwater, with each fish returning to the stream of its birth during a certain, narrow window of time called a "run." When the salmon are running, fishing is hot; when they're not running, it's dead. And the runs change from day to day, typically lasting only a few weeks. (Halibut, on the other hand, are bottom-dwelling ocean fish; you can fish them from a boat every day when the tide is right.) You can fish salmon all over the state in fresh- and salt water, but the closer you are to the ocean, the better the fish are. Salmon flesh softens in freshwater and the skin turns dull and red. Salmon right from salt water that haven't started their spawning cycle are called silver bright—when you see one, you'll understand why. No Pacific salmon feeds in freshwater, but kings and silvers, meat eaters at sea, strike out of habit even in the river.

There are five species of Pacific salmon, each preferring its own habitat, and, even when the habitat overlaps, each timing its run differently. Each species has two names.

King (or **chinook**) is the most coveted, best fighting fish, commonly growing to 30 pounds in 5 to 7 years at sea (the sport record, from the Kenai River, was 97 pounds, and the largest ever, taken by commercial fishermen near Petersburg, was 126 pounds). It takes a lot of effort to hook and land a big king, but it's the ultimate in Alaska fishing. You also need a special king stamp on your fishing license from the Alaska Department of Fish & Game, which you can buy at the same time you buy your license. King runs come mostly from late May to early July.

The **silver** (or **coho**) is smaller than the king, typically 6 to 9 pounds, but it fights and jumps ferociously, making it nearly as big a prize. Silvers run mostly in the fall, beginning in August and lasting into October in some streams.

FISHING Fishing in Alaska may spoil you for fishing anywhere else. The world's largest salmon and halibut were caught here in recent years, and Pacific salmon are so plentiful that catching and processing them still provides one of the state's largest sources of employment. Fly fishermen also come for thriving wild stocks of steelhead, cutthroat, and rainbow trout; Dolly Varden and Arctic char; and Arctic grayling.

There's no room here to tell you how to fish in Alaska—the best way is to pick it up from other anglers, most conveniently by going with a guide on your first outing. If you can afford it, a day of guided fly-in fishing to a remote stream is the ultimate

(you can do it from virtually any town listed in chapters 5, 6, or 7). You can also study with a book; several are available, the best of which focus on individual areas of the state or particular fishing techniques rather than trying to cover everything.

The best all-around source of information is the **Alaska Department of Fish & Game Sport Fish Division** (www.sf. adfg.state.ak.us). Browse the website for run timing information and hot spots updated weekly, to learn generally about fishing in Alaska, and to obtain particulars about where to wet a line in different parts of the state (click on "Publications" and then the region you are visiting). You

Red (or **sockeye**) salmon, so named for their tasty red flesh, are the trickiest to catch. They usually weigh 4 to 8 pounds and can run in any of the summer months, depending on the region and stream. Reds feed primarily on plankton at sea, and when they strike a fly, it's out of an instinct that no one really understands; you need perfect river conditions to catch reds legally, because snagging anywhere but the mouth generally is not allowed in freshwater.

Pinks (or **humpies**) grow to only a few pounds and aren't as tasty as the other three species; their flesh lacks the fat that makes salmon so meaty in flavor and it deteriorates quickly once the fish enter freshwater. Pinks are so plentiful that Alaska anglers usually view them as a nuisance to get off the line, but visitors often enjoy catching them: There's nothing wrong with a hard-fighting 4-pound fish, especially if you use light tackle, and a sliver-bright pink salmon is tasty if cooked right.

Chum (or **dog**) salmon return plentifully to streams over much of the state but are rarely targeted by anglers. Yet a typical 5- to 10-pound chum hits and fights hard. Chums aren't prized for the table and are mostly used for subsistence by Alaska Natives, who smoke or dry the fish for winter use or freeze it to feed dog teams.

The gear you use depends on the species you are after and the regulations for the area you're fishing. You have to catch the fish in the mouth; snagging is allowed only in special circumstances. On salt water, boats troll for kings and silvers with herring bait and gear to hold it down. Lures, salmon eggs, or flies will work on silvers and kings in the rivers, but regulations vary. Flies work best with reds. Most Alaska fishermen use spinning gear on the larger salmon species—landing such a large fish is iffy with a fly rod.

can even buy a fishing license online. If you lack Internet access, the agency also produces printed guides and fields questions from the public, and they record the weekly local updates on telephone hot lines. Contact the office nearest where you will fish: I have listed the phone number for each in the town sections.

If fishing is the primary goal of your trip, think about booking time at a fishing lodge. The remote rivers of the Bristol Bay region have Alaska's most prolific salmon fishing, and the only way out there is to take a floatplane to a remote site. You might find a stream jammed with salmon and few other anglers around to compete with. But you'll waste your money if you book a date that's not near the peak of the local salmon run (that does happen, as lodge owners hate to admit slow fishing). Consequently, I've listed few river-fishing lodges in this book. (The exceptions: on the Kenai River in Cooper Landing and Kenai-Soldotna, in chapter 8; and ocean fishing in Ketchikan in chapter 6.) Instead, I recommend booking through **Sport Fishing Alaska,** 9310 Shorecrest Dr., Anchorage, AK 99502 (© **888/552-8674** or 907/344-8674; www.alaska tripplanners.com). The business is run by a couple, Larry and Sheary Suiter, with years of experience on the Kenai River and in Southwest Alaska. After receiving a $95 advance fee, they plan a fishing vacation tailored to your budget that puts you right where fishing is hot at the time when you can travel.

FLIGHTSEEING No one should come to Alaska without seeing the scenery at least once from a small plane. The most spectacular rides of all are the Mount McKinley flights from Talkeetna (see chapter 8) and the Glacier Bay National Park flights from Haines or other surrounding communities (see chapter 5). But just about anywhere you go is worth seeing from the air; only then can you grasp how huge and complex the land is and how little changed it is by mankind. Fixed-wing flights give you the most time aloft for your money, with seats starting for around $100 for a brief flight. If you can't afford that, consider taking scheduled prop service between small communities on your itinerary for around the same price and see almost as much.

RAFTING Letting an Alaskan river pull you through untouched wild country in a raft provides a unique perspective without the sweat and toil of backpacking. Alaska has many great rivers, virtually all undeveloped and, with few exceptions, never crowded. White-water guides operate on rivers all over the state offering day trips in many towns. Outfitters also lead trips deep into Alaska, using the rivers to visit extraordinary places that can be reached no other way. Many companies offer floats; some are listed below and still others are in the destination chapters throughout this book.

SEA KAYAKING Just about every coastal town, from Kodiak east through Kachemak Bay, Prince William Sound, and the Southeast Panhandle has at least one kayak outfitter taking visitors on day trips or expeditions. I think it would be a shame for any fit person to come to Alaska and not take a sea-kayaking day trip. It is your best chance to get close

enough to really know the wilderness and see whales, sea otters, seabirds, and marine life in an intimate way. Local guides are listed in each town section. Outfitters offering longer trips to a variety of places are listed below.

OUTFITTERS & OUTDOOR PACKAGE TRIPS

Besides the outfitters and tour guides listed below, I've noted other operators in the destination chapters covering the towns where they are based. Browse through those chapters before deciding on a trip, as a trip with a small-town guide service can be wonderful. There are many other larger operators, too; increasingly, international adventure travel companies bring groups to Alaska, renting equipment or even hiring guides here. Although those trips may be excellent, I've listed mostly homegrown operators who know their territory intimately.

Alaska Discovery A local eco-tourism pioneer, Alaska Discovery was bought out by the famous Mountain Travel Sobek expedition company, but still keeps local staff in Juneau and offers some of the best guided sea-kayaking trips in Southeast Alaska (sales staff is now in California). Glacier Bay and Admiralty Island outings cater to both beginners and the truly rugged. Their inn-to-inn trips are essentially outdoor-oriented package tours, taking groups to the best spots for day activities like kayaking, rafting, or watching wildlife. Extended river trips float through the Arctic and on the Tatshenshini and Alsek rivers. They also offer outdoor packages for complete vacations. Check the website. A 3-day kayak expedition near Juneau is $1,090, while 10 days in the Arctic is around $4,400.

P.O. Box 35003, Juneau, AK 99803-5003. ⓒ 800/586-1911. www.akdiscovery.com.

Alaska Wildland Adventures This company specializes in outdoor vacations for those who want to be comfortable in the evening and aren't seeking strenuous physical challenges. Concentrating on the Kenai Peninsula, where they operate two wilderness lodges, but also going to Denali National Park, most of the company's trips link together a series of outdoor day activities, such as rafting, hiking, glacier cruises, or wildlife watching. Groups are small, and they also offer the lodges a la carte. A 10-day group safari is around $4,750; shorter trips, trips for families with kids, fishing trips, and other choices are available, too.

P.O. Box 389, Girdwood, AK 99587. ☎ 800/334-8730 or 907/783-2928. www.alaskawildland.com.

Equinox Wilderness Expeditions Karen Jettmar, author of *The Alaska River Guide,* the standard guidebook on floating Alaska's rivers (due out in a new edition in 2008), leads challenging rafting, sea-kayaking, and hiking trips and base-camp wildlife viewing each summer in some of the wildest and most exotic places around the state. Her groups are tiny, with five to eight members, and she offers co-ed, family and women's trips. A 10-day Arctic float trip costs around $4,000.

2440 E. Tudor Rd., Suite 1102, Anchorage, AK 99507. ☎ 604/222-1219. www.equinoxexpeditions.com.

Nova These guys started commercial rafting on Alaska's rivers in 1975, but as the industry developed, they expanded only slowly, keeping their base in a tiny village on the Matanuska River, northeast of Anchorage, and primarily employing Alaskan guides. I like the fact that they don't minimize the hazards: they make it clear that these fast, cold waters aren't Disneyland rides. Their catalog covers longer expeditions on some of the state's wildest rivers, but also includes more affordable itineraries of 2 or 3 days. Two days on the Matanuska costs $295; 3 days on the Talkeetna, including 14-mile-long, Class IV rapids of the Talkeetna Canyon, costs $1,150. Nova offers trips from Copper Center and Hope as well.

P.O. Box 1129, Chickaloon, AK 99674. ☎ 800/746-5753 or 907/745-5753. www.novalaska.com.

St. Elias Alpine Guides When you're ready for a real expedition, these are real professionals in real wilderness. Having given up on McKinley years ago as too crowded, they specialize in trekking, climbing, and floating the deep and rugged wilderness of Wrangell–St. Elias National Park. Theirs is the only trip catalog I know of that offers first ascents as part of the product line; so far, they've taken clients to the tops of previously unclimbed mountains more than 45 times. For details, see p. 431.

P.O. Box 92129, Anchorage, AK 99509. ☎ 888/933-5427 or 907/554-4445. www.steliasguides.com.

MULTIACTIVITY FLY-IN WILDERNESS LODGES

Any number of hotels use the word "lodge" in their names, but true wilderness lodges have unique qualities: they lie beyond the road system in places that are hard to get to but that are well worth spending some time in. These qualities also put wilderness lodges beyond most budgets. Getting there is expensive for guests and for operators; also, most lodges are small and have relatively large staffs to offer all-inclusive packages of rooms, meals, and guiding. For reasons explained elsewhere, I've generally excluded fishing lodges, concentrating instead on lodges that offer a variety of outdoor activities. Excellent lodges are described in the sections on Gustavus (p. 164), Homer (p. 317), and Denali National Park (p. 367). Here are two more that are so far from anywhere I had no other place in the book to put them.

Caribou Lodge ★★ South of Denali National Park, there's a lot to love about this place: the location above the tree line, on its own alpine lake, miles from any other structure; the unlimited dry tundra hiking and views along the rounded ridge tops; the wildlife and the quiet. But what I love best, and what I suspect will matter

---

Tips   Make Yourself Useful

You don't have to see Alaska only as an observer—you can be a participant. The **Iditarod Trail Sled Dog Race** (© 907/376-5155; www.iditarod.com), the 1,000-mile trek from Anchorage to Nome in March, uses volunteers at the start and finish and, for those who work their way up through the ranks, in the remote villages along the way. Visitors can be part of it and become a part of the real Alaska, contributing only their time and travel to the state. Find the application on the website and act early; they get more volunteers than they can use. Other races and events also use volunteers but don't have a formal program like the Iditarod's. (An animal rights group opposes sled dog racing. A discussion of that issue is on p. 482.)

Two facilities dedicated to study and rehabilitation of wildlife also take volunteers. You might not end up working directly with the creatures, but you can work behind the scenes and get much closer than a casual visitor—while contributing to a good cause. In Seward, the **Alaska SeaLife Center** (© 888/378-2525; www.alaskasealife.org) studies, exhibits, and heals marine mammals, birds, and other wildlife and makes extensive use of volunteers (p. 283). The **Alaska Raptor Center** in Sitka (© 800/643-9425; www.alaskaraptor.org) takes in injured eagles, owls, and other birds of prey and nurses them back to health in an impressive facility set along a rainforest stream. Volunteers work side by side with staff doing everything from selling T-shirts to working with birds (p. 146).

---

most to visitors, is that it's real. This is home to Mike and Pam Nickols, the couple who personally host just three parties at a time, and for a decade they've lived out here in true Bush style, year-round, far off the grid. They guide hiking, canoeing on the lake, and watching the wildlife; in the winter, they teach guests to drive a dog team over endlessly rolling hills of snow. Mainly, a visit is a chance to experience another way of life, one that exists in few places. The accommodations are simple but comfortable, each cabin with its own outhouse and a shared shower facility. Access is by small aircraft only, on skis in winter or floats in summer; in spring and fall, when the ice on the lake is soft, it's just about impossible to get there. For rough figuring, a plane from Talkeetna (p. 347) costs $145 to $180 per person, but inquire to get a more exact cost.

20 miles east of Talkeetna (P.O. Box 706), Talkeetna, AK 99676. ©/fax **907/733-2163**. www.cariboulodge alaska.com. 3 units. $285 per person per day. Rates include all meals and guiding and are based on double occupancy, 2-day minimum. No credit cards. **Amenities:** Restaurant (family style, included in rate); guided activities included in rate; sauna.

Winter Lake ✦✦✦ Among the best of Alaska's remote lodges, Winter Lake earned its fame—like other top lodges—thanks to a remarkable couple living there year-round, Carl and Kristen Dixon. Carl is a classic Alaskan outdoorsman: hearty, cheerful, and most at home when working or traveling on the land. Kristen is a meticulous innkeeper and a master chef and cookbook author, trained at Le Cordon Bleu, who turns out cuisine, using local ingredients, that is comparable to the best urban restaurants. The lodge faces a lake surrounded by mountains northwest of Anchorage and has the Iditarod Trail running through its grounds, near the Finger Lake checkpoint. A dog team is kept for guest instruction, and winter visitors also go snowmobiling and cross-country skiing. In the summer, they enjoy the lake, float a river, hike trails from the lodge, or use the helicopter that is kept on site for glacier or mountain top excursions or remote fishing. Yoga and cooking classes are offered every day. The accommodations are in five comfortable but authentic cabins—despite log construction and rustic furniture, they have oil heat and private bathrooms with showers and composting toilets. That's all part of the appealing contradictions of the place: remote, yet with fresh flowers everyday; offering Wi-Fi, but not when all the power is turned off at night. Visitors get to the lodge by air from Anchorage with Rust's Flying Service; the fare is included in the lodge rates listed below, which vary according to how long you stay. I've given just two examples; use of the helicopter is extra.

Hayes River Station (Mail: 2463 Cottonwood St., Anchorage, AK 99508). (℄ 907/274-2710. Fax 907/277-6256. www.withinthewild.com. 5 units. 2 nights $1,755 per person; 4 nights $3,120 per person. AE, MC, V. **Amenities:** Restaurant (family style, included in rate); some guided activities; massage, yoga, and cooking classes included in rate; hot tub; sauna.

7 Entry Requirements

Coming into the U.S. has become more difficult for almost everyone with new security measures. Even U.S. citizens who pass between the U.S. and Canada must make additional preparations. International visitors can learn of the latest requirements from a travel agent or airline. Another good place to look for help is the U.S. embassy or consulate nearest you, which can be found on the Internet through www.unitedstatesvisas.gov.

PASSPORTS

Under a new requirement, U.S. citizens need passports to reenter the United States even from other countries in the Western Hemisphere. The rule went into effect for 2007 for those coming in by air. Those coming in by land and sea— including drivers on the Alaska highway and cruise-ship passengers—will be subject to the same requirement. Implementation was planned for 2008, but could be delayed. For the latest, check the Department of State website, www.travel. state.gov.

For information on how to get a passport, go to **"Passports"** in the **"Fast Facts"** section of this chapter—the websites listed provide downloadable passport applications for each nation as well as the current fees for processing passport applications.

Note: Children are required to present a passport when entering the United States at airports. More information on obtaining a passport for a minor can be found at www.travel.state.gov.

VISAS

A visa is a permit allowing entry to foreign visitors. Many tourists coming to the United States do not need a visa. Canadian citizens never need visas to enter the U.S. In addition, the U.S. State Department's **Visa Waiver Program (VWP)** allows citizens of the following countries (at press time) to enter the United States without a visa for stays of up to 90 days: Andorra, Australia, Austria, Belgium, Brunei, Denmark, Finland, France, Germany, Iceland, Ireland, Italy, Japan, Liechtenstein, Luxembourg, Monaco, the Netherlands, New Zealand, Norway, Portugal, San Marino, Singapore, Slovenia, Spain, Sweden, Switzerland, and the United Kingdom. Citizens of these nations need only a valid passport and a round-trip air or cruise ticket upon arrival. If they first enter the United States, they may also visit Mexico, Canada, Bermuda, and/or the Caribbean islands and return to the United States without a visa.

Any passport issued on or after October 26, 2006, by a VWP country must be an

e-Passport for travelers to be eligible to enter the U.S. without a visa. E-Passports contain computer chips capable of storing biometric information, such as the required digital photograph of the holder. (You can identify an e-Passport by the symbol on the bottom center cover of your passport.) If your passport doesn't have this feature, you can still travel without a visa if it is a valid passport issued before October 26, 2005, and includes a machine-readable zone, or between October 26, 2005, and October 25, 2006, and includes a digital photograph. For more information, go to **www.travel.state.gov/visa** or contact any U.S. embassy or consulate.

Citizens of all other countries or any holder of a passport that is not machine readable must have (1) a valid passport that expires at least 6 months later than the scheduled end of their visit to the United States, and (2) a tourist visa, which may be obtained from any U.S. consulate. For information on how to get a Visa, go to **"Visas"** in the **"Fast Facts"** section of this chapter. Also check the U.S. State Department website, at www.travel.state.gov.

International visitors with visas must undergo an instant background check on arrival, be photographed, and have their fingerprints scanned. Exempt from the extra scrutiny are visitors entering from countries not required to have visas for short-term visits (p. 41). For more information, go to the Department of Homeland Security website at **www.dhs.gov/dhspublic** and look for "US-VISIT."

MEDICAL REQUIREMENTS

Unless you're arriving from an area known to be suffering from an epidemic (particularly cholera or yellow fever), inoculations or vaccinations are not required for entry into the United States. If you have a medical condition that requires syringe-administered medications, carry a signed prescription from your physician. Airline passengers cannot pack syringes in their carry-on baggage without documented proof of medical need. Pack any medication in its original, labeled containers. This is especially important if you need medication that contains narcotics. In that case, also carry documented proof of your need, such as a signed letter from your doctor, and carry no more than you reasonably could use yourself during your trip. Otherwise, you may risk being accused of smuggling.

A 1993 law barred people who are **HIV-positive or have AIDS** from entering the United States without a special waiver; however, late in 2006, President Bush directed a blanket waiver to be granted to anyone coming for a short stay, such as tourists.

CUSTOMS
WHAT FOREIGN VISITORS CAN BRING IN

Personal effects, which are items you use yourself, such as clothing, cameras, and fishing rods, are exempt from duties. In addition, every visitor over 21 years of age may bring in the following without paying duties: 1 liter of wine, beer, or hard liquor; 200 cigarettes, or 50 cigars for your own use and another 100 as gifts (but not from Cuba), or 2 kilograms (4.4 pounds) of smoking tobacco; and $100 worth of gifts. To claim these exemptions you must spend at least 72 hours in the United States and cannot have claimed them within the preceding 6 months. The duty on goods exceeding these exemptions is 3% of the value on the first $1,000 (the flat rate); above that amount, it depends on the item. The flat rate applies only to items for your own use or gifts and can be used only once in 30 days. Importation of most raw food and plant material is prohibited or requires a special license. Foreign visitors may bring in or take out up to $10,000 in U.S. or foreign currency, travelers checks, securities, and so forth, with no formalities; larger sums must be declared to U.S. Customs and

Border Protection (CBP) on entering or leaving and paperwork must be filed. A handy brochure called "Visiting the United States: U.S. Customs and Border Protection Regulations for Nonresidents" lays out the rules. It can be downloaded from U.S. Customs and Border Protection's website (www.cbp.gov) by typing the words "Visiting the United States publication" in the search window. Other avenues for information are your nearest U.S. consulate or embassy or CBP officials at the Anchorage airport (© **907/ 271-6309**).

It is exceedingly complicated for foreign visitors to bring **firearms** into the United States; don't even consider it except for a hunting trip. Unless you are a U.S. citizen or permanent resident alien, you cannot bring in, buy, or even possess a gun without a permit from the **Bureau of Alcohol, Tobacco, Firearms and Explosives** (ATF; © **304/616-4550**; www.atf.treas.gov); these take 2 months to acquire if everything goes well (the application is on the ATF website—search for "Form 6 NIA"). The application must be accompanied by a valid hunting license (there are a few narrow exceptions, such as athletes involved in shooting competitions). The **Alaska Department of Fish & Game** (© **907/ 465-6085**; www.alaska.gov/adfg) sells hunting licenses to nonresident aliens for $300 (tags are as much as $1,500 more); however, aliens can hunt only with a registered guide. First, find the guide and then let him or her help with all the paperwork, but start many months in advance and be ready to pay.

WHAT YOU CAN TAKE HOME

WILDLIFE PRODUCTS Authentic Alaska Native art and crafts made from protected marine mammals are perfectly legal to buy and own in the U.S, even though possessing marine mammal parts is not legal for non-Natives. Alaska Natives have used these materials for

thousands of years and their subsistence harvest is not a danger to the species. Generally, however, marine mammal products you buy made of any threatened or endangered species cannot be taken out of the country unless at least 100 years old. For those items that can legally be taken home, you need a wildlife export permit recognized by the Convention on International Trade in Endangered Species, known as CITES. These permits can be complicated and time-consuming to obtain. For international visitors, this means you should simply avoid buying anything made from marine mammals or any other species requiring a CITES permit, including brown or black bear, wolf, lynx, bobcat, or river otter. Before you buy an item, make sure you can legally take it home, then have the shop mail it to you insured, and have them take care of the paperwork. If you carry it with you in your baggage, perhaps because you bought it from someone who can't handle the paperwork, you'll need to get your own permits. U.S. residents transiting Canada with wildlife products requiring CITES permits can obtain a Personal Effects Exemption Certificate by calling the **U.S. Fish & Wildlife Service** in Anchorage (© **907/271-6198**; http:// alaska.fws.gov/law). Foreign visitors exporting wildlife may need to contact the agency's **Division of Management Authority** in Washington, D.C. (© **800/ 358-2104**; www.international.fws.gov) regarding permit requirements. Processing time for permits can take from 60 to 90 days.

OTHER GOODS Rules governing what you can bring back duty-free vary from country to country, and generally are posted on the Web. For a clear summary of **Canadian** rules, request the booklet *I Declare,* issued by the Canada Border Services Agency (© **800/461-9999** in Canada, or 204/983-3500; **www. cbsa-asfc.gc.ca** search for the phrase "I

Declare"). **U.K.** citizens should contact HM Customs & Excise at © **0845/010- 9000** (from outside the U.K., 020/8929- 0152), or consult their website at www. hmce.gov.uk. **Australians** can contact the Australian Customs Service (© **1300/ 363-263;** www.customs.gov.au). **New Zealand** citizens should contact New Zealand Customs (© **04/473-6099** or 0800/428-786; www.customs.govt.nz).

8 Travel & Rental Car Insurance

There are several kinds of travel insurance: for **trip cancellation or interruption,** for **medical costs,** and for **lost or delayed luggage.** Typically they are sold together in a per-trip or annual comprehensive plan. Insurance for trip cancellation or interruption is a must if you have paid the large cash deposits demanded by many Alaska outfitters, fishing guides, wilderness lodges, package tour operators, and cruise companies. A premium of 5% to 8% of the cost of the trip is well worth the protection against the uncertainty of Alaska weather (most deposits are lost in case of weather delays or cancellations) or unexpected crises that might prevent you from being able to depart as planned. Interruption insurance will get you home under covered circumstances. Major insurers such as those listed below offer policyholders access to 24-hour phone assistance to help handle crises. Read the policy carefully to find out when you are covered. Do not buy insurance through the operator holding your deposit, even though the insurer itself is a different entity. Policies often do not cover losses related to the company that originally solicited your business. Instead, buy your insurance directly from the insurance company without the involvement of anyone selling you travel products. Medical insurance is covered on p. 46.

Insurance on your **baggage** usually is included in most insurance plans; it may not be worthwhile as a stand-alone policy. Your baggage is often covered under your homeowners' policy or credit card benefits. If the airline loses or damages your bags, they are usually responsible for up to $2,500 per passenger on domestic flights or, on international flights up to approximately $635 per checked bag, excluding expensive items such as jewelry and cameras. You can pack those items in your baggage and cover them with travel insurance, but a simpler course is to carry them with you, insuring your baggage only if the worth you are able to prove is more than the airline's responsibility and the limits on your existing policies. That's unlikely, because to prove the value of your lost clothing and such you would need bills of sale or similar documentation for each item.

Various companies sell travel insurance online, including **AIG Travel Guard** (© **800-826-1300;** www.travelguard.com); **Travel Insured International** (© **800/ 243-3174;** www.travelinsured.com); and **Travelex Insurance Services** (© **888/ 457-4602;** www.travelex-insurance.com). Or look for the best deal around by going to **www.insuremytrip.com**. The site allows travelers to get instant quotes from many insurance companies at once by providing the dates of the trip, amount and type of coverage, and ages of the travelers.

With **rental cars** you face a whole different set of insurance considerations. Most of these are the same as renting a car anywhere, and a few simple preparations will get you through. Before you leave home, check your own auto policy for your liability coverage with a rented car (bringing proof of insurance along is a good idea), and check with your credit card issuer for coverage for damage to a rented car (make sure to use that card when you rent, too). Chances are, you are already covered and don't need to buy the unreasonably priced insurance offered by

(Tips **Using the Internet on the Road**

If you decide to bring your laptop, you'll find that many hotels and even B&Bs have wireless Internet access for guests, usually for free, and there are numerous other free hotspots all over the state. For a site that lists dozens of free hotspots in Alaska, with maps to get to them, check out www.tour saver.com/alaska-wireless.php. Getting online through dial-up is difficult for visitors to Alaska; national Internet service providers have access numbers only in the largest cities and dialing up long distance is slow and unreliable from many Alaska communities with antiquated phone connections.

If you leave the computer at home, you can stop in at an Internet cafe or the public library when you want to log on. Alaskans use the Internet heavily, even in tiny villages where people live largely by hunting and gathering, so you can always count on finding a way of getting online with a little effort. I have listed Internet access for each Alaska community in the appropriate sections of the book.

Coverage for wireless Internet technology, such as your BlackBerry or other Internet PDA, spread beyond Alaska's two or three largest cities only in 2006. The main provider is an Alaskan firm called ACS (check on roaming with your own provider). Voice cellular coverage has spread to smaller communities, but even that remains spotty or nonexistent beyond city limits. For more on wireless communication, see "Cellular Phone Coverage," p. 55, and "Getting Lost/Wilderness Communications" p. 48.

the rental car company when you rent, but if you are not covered, do buy it: the potential costs you face are even larger than having a crash at home, because they include the rental company's lost business.

One special Alaska consideration: ask the reservation agent or check the rental contract for rules about driving on **unpaved roads,** such as the Dalton, Denali or Steese highways. I have listed

two companies in Fairbanks that rent for use on unpaved highways (p. 395); very few allow it. Cars do get damaged on these roads, and you may be setting yourself up for a real headache if you violate the rental contract and that happens. I've suggested alternatives if you want to drive the Copper River Highway from Cordova (p. 332) or the McCarthy Road in Wrangell–St. Elias National Park (p. 428).

9 Health & Safety

CRIME & EMERGENCY SERVICES

CRIME Sadly, crime rates are not low in Alaska's larger cities, although muggings are rare. Take the normal precautions you'd take at home. You're safe in daylight hours anywhere tourists commonly go, less so late at night leaving a bar or walking in a lonely place. Women

need to be especially careful on their own, as Alaska has a disproportionately high rate of rape. This doesn't mean women shouldn't travel alone in Alaska, only that they should be cautious. Most women I know avoid walking by themselves at night, especially in wooded or out-of-the-way areas. The late-night sunlight can be deceiving—just because it's light out doesn't mean it's safe. Sexual assaults occur in towns big and small. Women should never hitchhike alone. If you are a victim of a crime, you can reach police almost anywhere by calling 911, or, if it is not an emergency, by using the numbers listed under "Fast Facts" in each community section.

MEDICAL EMERGENCIES You'll find modern, full-service hospitals in each of Alaska's larger cities, and even in some small towns that act as regional centers. There's some kind of clinic even in the smallest towns, although they often are staffed by physicians' assistants rather than medical doctors. I've listed the address and phone numbers for medical facilities in each destination under "Fast Facts." Call those numbers, too, for referrals to a dentist or other health professional. In an emergency, call 911.

If health is a particular concern, consider joining **MedicAlert** (© **888/633-4298;** www.medicalert.org) and wearing their engraved bracelet, which will inform emergency medical personnel of a primary preexisting medical condition and provide them with access to the organization's response center for your information on file, such as medications and physician and family contacts. The cost is $40 for the first year, then $25 per year thereafter.

HEALTH INSURANCE

Travelers from within the U.S. are often covered under their regular health insurance as long as they remain in the country. Take a minute to check your coverage, making sure it adequately covers emergency medical transportation and treatment, especially if you will be adventuring in remote areas. The cost of a medevac flight can easily be in the five figures. Check the coverage offered by your credit cards or buy a travel insurance policy to cover you just for the trip (p. 44).

International visitors should certainly make health insurance arrangements before traveling to the U.S. Doctors and hospitals are expensive and often require proof of coverage before they render services (in an emergency, of course, you'll always get quick treatment regardless of ability to pay). Good policies will cover the costs of an accident, repatriation, or death. Packages such as **Europ Assistance's "Worldwide Healthcare Plan"** are sold by European automobile clubs and travel agencies at attractive rates. **Worldwide Assistance Services, Inc.** (© **800/777-8710;** www.worldwide assistance.com) is the agent for Europ Assistance in the United States. **Canadians** should check with their provincial health plan offices or call **Health Canada** (© **866/225-0709;** www.hc-sc.gc.ca) to find out the extent of their coverage and what documentation and receipts they must take home in case they are treated in the United States.

OUTDOOR HEALTH & SAFETY

AVALANCHE When snow sliding down a mountain comes to a stop it hardens to a consistency that only metal tools can dig through. Avalanche survivors describe the terror of being helplessly locked in this unyielding material hoping for rescue. Understandably, survivors are in the minority. Victims die if not dug out quickly (well before emergency personnel can arrive at a remote slope). No one should go into the snowy backcountry without training in avalanche avoidance and recovery equipment, including locator beacons, probes, and shovels. Go with a guide if you are unsure.

BEARS & OTHER WILDLIFE Being eaten by a bear is probably the least likely way for your vacation to end. More people die from dog bites than bear attacks. But it's still wise to be prepared for bears and to know how to avoid being trampled by a moose, which can be fatal.

The first safety rule for bears is to avoid attracting them. Be tidy with your food and trash when you're camping, putting everything away in sealed containers.

When backpacking, you can protect your food by hanging it from a long tree branch or, above the tree line, storing it in a bear-resistant canister (for rent or loan in Anchorage or at Denali or Wrangell–St. Elias national parks; see chapters 6, 8, and 9). Be careful not to spread food odors when you're cooking and cleaning up. Clean fish away from your campsite. Never keep food, pungent items, or clothing that smells like fish in your tent.

Make noise when walking through brush or thick trees to avoid surprising a bear or moose. Call out, sing, or carry on a conversation. You might not scare a bear away this way, but at least you won't startle it. At all costs, avoid coming between a bear and its cubs or a bear and food (if a bear wants the fish you just caught, that's his food, too). Moose also are strongly defensive of their young, and a moose on its own can attack if it feels you're getting too close or if it previously has been stressed by contact with people or dogs. People are badly hurt every year trying to sneak by a moose on a trail. I see moose every day when I ski, bike, or run near my house in Anchorage; when the moose wants the trail I either find a way around or go back the other way.

If you see a bear, stop, wave your arms, make noise, and, if you're with others, group together so you look larger to the bear. Avoid running, tempting the bear to chase (unless, of course, you can run a few steps to your car); depart by slowly backing away, at an angle if possible. If the bear follows, stop. Once in a great while, the bear may bluff a charge; even less often, it may attack. If you're attacked, fall and play dead, rolling into a ball face down with your hands behind your neck. The bear should lose interest. In extremely rare instances, a bear may not lose interest, because it's planning to make a meal of you. If this happens, fight back for all you're worth.

Many Alaskans carry a gun for protection in bear country, but that's not practical for visitors or for anyone not practiced in shooting (a few years ago a greenhorn got flustered and threw his gun at a bear). A better alternative is a bear-deterrent spray. These are canisters that you fire to produce a burning fog of capsaicin pepper between you and a threatening bear. While less deadly than a gun, and with limited effectiveness in wind or rain, research shows they have a better overall track record against bear attacks than guns. The sprays also are legal in national parks and OK to carry across the Canadian border—two big advantages over firearms. However, you can't bring bear-deterrent spray on an airplane, even in your checked baggage, so if you fly you will have to buy it on arrival and get rid of it before you leave. The product is easily available at Alaska sporting goods stores for about $45, or order direct from **Counter Assault** (© 800/695-3394; www.counterassault.com). Be sure to get a holster, too, as the spray is of no use buried in your backpack. If you do take a gun, it had better be a big one, such as a .300-Magnum rifle or 12-gauge shotgun loaded with slugs. No handgun is big enough to stop a large bear bent on attacking.

BOATING SAFETY Because of the cool temperatures, unpredictable weather, and cold water, going out on the ocean or floating a fast river is more hazardous in Alaska than in most other places, and you should go only with an experienced, licensed operator unless you know what you're doing. There's little margin for error if you fall into the water or capsize in this cold water. Many boating deaths occur when good swimmers who are not wearing life jackets immediately sink—apparently, the shock of falling in is so intense they shut down and fail to swim. With a life jacket on, it takes a few seconds to get used to the cold water, and then you can concentrate on getting out. You have 15 minutes to half an hour before cold immobilizes you. Equally important, however, is getting warm and dry after you are out of the water. The body temperature of a wet, cold person can easily sink so far he or she cannot get warm without external heating, a deadly condition called hypothermia. If you're sea kayaking or canoeing, always wear a life jacket; stay close to shore; and use rubberized dry bags (also called float bags) to pack everything you need to quickly warm a person who gets wet (see "Hypothermia," below). Having a way to get help in an emergency is also important (see "Getting Lost/Wilderness Communications," p. 48).

DANGEROUS PLANTS Two shrubs common in Alaska can cause skin irritation, but there is nothing as bad as poison ivy or poison oak. **Cow parsnip,** also called pushki, is a large-leafed plant growing primarily in open areas, up to shoulder height by late summer, with white flowers. The celerylike stalks break easily, and the sap has the quality of intensifying the burning power of the sun on skin. Wash it off quickly to avoid a rash. **Devil's Club,** a more obviously dangerous plant, grows on steep slopes and has ferocious spines that can pierce through clothing. Also, don't eat anything you can't positively identify, as there are deadly poisonous mushrooms and plants.

DRINKING WATER Unpurified river or lake water may not be safe to drink. Hand-held filters available from sporting-goods stores for around $75 are the most practical way of dealing with the problem. Iodine kits and boiling also work. The danger is a protozoan cyst called *giardia lamblia,* which causes diarrhea and is present in thousands of water bodies all over the United States, even in remote areas, where it may have been carried by waterfowl. It may not show up until a couple of weeks after exposure and could become chronic. If symptoms show up after you get home, tell your doctor you may have been exposed so that you can get tested and cured.

GETTING   LOST/WILDERNESS COMMUNICATIONS Even experienced people get lost outdoors. Hiking off trail or voyaging in a canoe, raft, or kayak, you quickly find that one mountain looks a lot like another. If you are unsure of your navigational skills, maps, or equipment, don't go. Beyond those basics, the most important safety precautions are to go with another person and to make sure someone knows where to look for you if you don't come back. For extended trips (more than a day hike) leave a written trip plan with a person who will call rescuers if you are late. At the very least, leave a note in your car indicating where you are bound. Cell-phones sometimes work near towns and highways, but not reliably, and there is little coverage beyond those areas.

For serious outdoors people, technology can add an extra safety backup outdoors. Personal locator beacons with built-in GPS are the state-of-the-art solution. The beacon is a small device that, when activated, transmits a distress signal and your exact location to an orbiting satellite. Authorities receive the message and find out who you are from a database. After verifying you are really missing, they can then go to the exact spot where the beacon is broadcasting. ACR Electronics' Aquafix or Terrafix PLB (for marine or land use, respectively) cost from $550 from $700 at stores such as West Marine or REI.

If you don't want to shell out that much money, or if you want a device that also allows you to stay in touch in the wilderness, it is possible to rent an iridium satellite phone that will work outdoors anywhere on Earth. The drawback of this approach is that it is less useful in an emergency than a beacon: You need to know where you are and whom to call, and you have to be able to get the phone to work. I rented one for a 2-week wilderness trip and found it rather finicky; I was always able to make a call, but I wouldn't have wanted my life to depend on doing it quickly. I was happy with the customer service of the firm I rented from, a Canadian outfit called **RoadPost** (© **888/ 290-1616** or 905/272-5665; www.road post.com). Prices start at $79 for the first week, $7 for each additional day, plus around $2 a minute for calls, plus the $35 delivery fee. They send you the phone by DHL express.

HYPOTHERMIA A potentially fatal lowering of core body temperature can sneak up on you. It's most dangerous when you don't realize how cold you are, perhaps in 50°F (10°C) weather on a damp mountain hike or rainy boating trip. Dress in material (whether wool or synthetic) that keeps its warmth when wet, choosing layers to avoid chilling perspiration. (See "What to Wear," p. 19.) Eating well and avoiding exhaustion also are important. Among the symptoms of hypothermia are cold extremities, being uncommunicative, displaying poor judgment or coordination, and sleepiness. A shivering victim still has the ability to warm up if better dressed; a lack of shivering means the body has gone beyond that point and warmth must be added from the outside or from warm drinks. Get indoors, force hot liquids on the victim (except if not fully conscious, which could cause choking), and, if shelter is unavailable, apply body heat from another person, skin on skin, in a sleeping bag.

INSECT BITES The good news is that Alaska has no snakes or poisonous spiders. The bad news is that Alaska makes up for it with mosquitoes and other biting insects. West Nile virus has not arrived here as of this writing so the mosquitoes are not dangerous, but they can ruin a trip. Effective insect repellent is a necessity, as is having a place where you can get away from them. We use shirts with hoods of netting when the bugs are at their worst. Mosquitoes can bite through light fabric close to the skin, which is why people in the Bush wear heavy, baggy Carhart pants and jackets (made of canvas) even on the hottest days. Benadryl tablets or other antihistamines will often relieve swelling caused by mosquito bites.

RIVER CROSSINGS Hiking in Alaska's backcountry often requires crossing rivers without bridges. Use great caution: It's easy to get in trouble. Often, the water is glacial melt, barely above freezing and heavy with silt that makes it opaque. The silt can fill your pockets and drag you down. If in doubt, don't do it. If you do decide to cross, unbuckle your pack, keep your shoes on, face upstream, use a heavy walking stick if possible, and rig a safety line. Children should go in the eddy behind a larger person, or be carried.

SEASICKNESS Most summertime visits to Alaska involve boat rides for fishing or sightseeing. Seasickness probably ruins more of these outings than any other cause. Avoid seasickness by abstaining from alcohol the night before, eating a light breakfast, limiting coffee, and sitting low and near the middle of the boat, away from odors and with your eyes on the horizon—no reading. Some people use alternative medicine cures, such as ginger or acupressure, which have no proven benefits, but nonetheless work for many of those who believe in them—a placebo, such as a sugar pill, is 40% effective with seasickness if the patient has faith. My experience and the advice of experts suggests, however, that using seasickness drugs is worthwhile. The very best is the scopolamine skin patch, available only by prescription, which lasts up to 3 days. The main choices for over-the-counter drugs are meclizine (brand names Bonine, Antivert, or Dramamine II) and dimenhydrinate (original Dramamine). Both are drowsiness-inducing antihistamines, but there's less of that side effect with the newer meclizine. To be effective, the drugs need at least 2 hours to get through your digestive system, so you must take the pill well before you get on the boat. For best effectiveness, take a tablet before bed and another on the morning of the outing. If you've taken nothing and feel yourself getting seasick, there is a last-minute cure that sometimes works: chew up the tablets but don't swallow them, holding the mush under your tongue or against your cheek. The drug is partly absorbed through the lining of the mouth.

SHELLFISH Don't eat mussels, clams, or scallops you pick or dig from the seashore unless you know they're safe to eat. Generally, that means you need some specific and reliable local knowledge. There is a government program to assure that commercial shellfish areas are safe, but the only easily accessible beaches it affects are on the eastern shore of Kachemak Bay. The risk is paralytic shellfish poisoning, a potentially fatal malady caused by a naturally occurring toxin. It can cause total paralysis that includes your breathing. A victim may be kept alive with mouth-to-mouth resuscitation until medical help is obtained. For more information, check the **Alaska Department of Environmental Conservation** website at www.dec.state.ak.us/eh/fss/seafood/psphome.htm, or go to www.alaska.gov and search for "psp").

DRIVING SAFETY

ROAD REPORTS The Alaska Department of Transportation has centralized highway reports with a handy toll-free phone and Internet system (© **511;** http://511.alaska.gov). Even in dry summer conditions, it is worthwhile to make the call or check the site before heading on an inter-city drive, because road construction can cause long delays—at times, workers will close a major highway overnight for work. In winter, checking on conditions is a basic safety essential. Here are more seasonal tips.

SUMMER Alaska's highways are two lanes except close to Anchorage and Fairbanks. Keep your headlights on all the time to help oncoming vehicles see you. Drivers are required to pull over at the next pull out whenever five or more cars are trailing them on a two-lane highway, regardless of how fast they're going. This saves the lives of people who otherwise will try to pass. When passing a truck going the other way on a gravel highway, slow down or stop and pull as far as possible to the side of the road to avoid losing your windshield to a flying rock. Always think about the path of rocks you're kicking up toward others' vehicles. Make sure you've got a good, full-size spare tire and jack if you're driving a gravel highway. For remote driving, bring along a first-aid kit, emergency food, a tow rope, and jumper cables, and keep your gas tank full.

WINTER Drivers on Alaska's highways in winter should be prepared for cold-weather emergencies far from help. Take all the items listed for rural summer driving, plus a flashlight, matches and materials to light a fire, chains, a shovel, and an ice scraper. A camp stove to make hot beverages is also a good idea. If you're driving a remote highway (such as the Alaska Hwy.) between December and March, take along gear adequate to keep you safe from the cold even if you have to wait overnight with a dead car at –40°F (–40°C) (see "What to Wear," earlier in this chapter, and add blankets and sleeping bags). Never drive a road marked CLOSED or UNMAINTAINED IN WINTER. Even on maintained rural roads, other vehicles rarely come by in winter. All Alaska roads are icy all winter. Studded tires are a necessity. Also, never leave your car's engine stopped for more than 4 hours in temperatures of –10°F (–23°C) or colder. Virtually all vehicles in Alaska have electrical head-bolt heaters installed to keep the engine warm overnight; you'll find electrical outlets everywhere in cold, Interior Alaska areas.

10 Specialized Travel Resources

FOR TRAVELERS WITH DISABILITIES

Today it is rare to find a hotel without rooms accessible for travelers with disabilities, and many B&Bs have made the necessary adjustments as well. The results often are the best rooms in the house. Make sure to ask for the special rooms when making reservations, and question smaller establishments closely about exactly what accessible means to them. There are several Alaska agencies for travelers with disabilities. **Challenge Alaska,** 3350 Commercial Dr., Suite 208, Anchorage, AK 99501 (© **907/344-7399;** www.challengealaska.org), a nonprofit organization, offers therapeutic recreation and education, including outdoor adventures. They operate an adaptive ski school at Alyeska Resort in Girdwood (p. 256). Summer outings are inexpensive: A 4-day sea-kayaking outing was only $350. Get on the mailing list for current listings.

FOR SENIORS

People over age 65 get reduced admission prices to many Alaska attractions, and some accommodations have special senior rates. The National Park Service offers a senior free admission and discount program to those 62 or older under the ungainly name **America the Beautiful—National Park and Federal Recreational Lands Pass—Senior Pass** (formerly called the **Golden Age Passport**). The pass is good for lifetime free entrance to national parks, monuments, historic sites, recreation areas, and national wildlife refuges for a one-time processing fee of $10. Buy the pass in person at any park that charges an entrance fee. For more information, go to www.nps.gov/fees_passes.htm or call © **888/467-2757.**

Most towns have a senior center where you'll find activities and help with any special needs. The **Anchorage Senior Center** (© **907/258-7823;** www.anchorageseniorcenter.org) offers guidance for visitors, as well as use of the restaurant, a gift shop, and a fitness room and a chance to meet locals. Dances are held most Friday nights.

Elderhostel, 11 Avenue de Lafayette, Boston, MA 02111-1746 (© **877/426-8056;** 877/426-2167 TDD; from overseas, © **978/323-4141;** www.elderhostel.org), operates many weeklong Alaska learning vacations for groups of people 55 and older. The catalog of choices is on the website.

FOR GAY & LESBIAN TRAVELERS

Anchorage, Juneau, and Fairbanks have active gay and lesbian communities. In Anchorage, **Identity Inc.** (www.identityinc.org) offers referrals, publishes a newsletter called *Northview,* sponsors activities throughout the year, and operates a gay and lesbian help line (© **888/901-9876** or 907/258-4777). The June Pridefest includes a parade and picnic, among other events. Their Gay and Lesbian Community Center of Anchorage is at 333 E. Fifth Ave. (© **907/929-4528**).

Gays and lesbians can find some Alaska B&Bs and tours specifically marketing to them. For example, **Olivia Cruises and Resorts** (© **800/631-6277;** www.olivia.com) typically brings a lesbian cruise to Alaska each year, with well-known entertainers onboard. In Fairbanks, a small but growing company specializes in outdoor tours and backcountry trips for gays and lesbians. It's called **Out In Alaska** (© **877/347 9958;** www.outinalaska.com).

FOR STUDENTS

Many museums offer free or reduced admission for students and anyone under 18, although sometimes you have to ask. Make sure to bring a student ID card.

There are hostels in most towns in Alaska. Except for those in Anchorage, Fairbanks, and Juneau, they tend to be open in the summer only. I have described hostels in the text for each town. At present, none are affiliated with organizations such as **Hostelling International** that provide discounts to members. For a comprehensive listing of hostels, go to **www.hostels.com** and navigate to Alaska by clicking on the maps.

Many students travel to Alaska for summer work. It's usually possible to get a job in a fish cannery in most coastal towns. Work on the slime line is hard and unpleasant and the pay is low, but if the season is good and you work long hours, camping to keep your expenses low (most canneries have tent cities of summer workers nearby), you can take home more money for your summer's work than you would normally earn elsewhere. Hillary Rodham Clinton worked an Alaska slime line when she was in school, and you can, too (George W. Bush worked in Alaska as a young person as well at a politically connected air service and construction company). Offshore fish-processing ships hire many unskilled workers, too, but I wouldn't recommend that for a student; once you're on the ship, you are trapped there, and you may hate it. The work is hazardous (federal worker safety and minimum wage laws do not apply) and medical care may be inadequate. Also, don't come north expecting to make fabulous wages. The stories of college students making huge crew shares on fishing boats are legends—there are experienced deckhands to take lucrative jobs before boats hire raw hands they have to train. Go that way for the adventure (and danger and hard work) but not out of greed. Jobs are always available in the tourism industry, too, although without the extreme flexibility of fish processing. The **Alaska Department of Labor** posts a lot of useful information on its website, including job applications for seafood work and a live database of openings; start at **http://alexsys.labor.state.ak.us**.

FOR FAMILIES

When we researched our first edition of this book, my son, Robin, was 3, and my daughter, Julia, was 6 months. As I write this, Robin is 15, Julia is 12, Joseph is 8, and Becky is 6. You might run into us in a campground or on a boat dock anywhere in the state as we travel to research the next edition of "our Alaska book." Robin has surprised people carrying it and introduced himself. Yes, it's a great job, and bringing the family along is the best part.

Alaska's magnificent scenery is something even young children can understand and appreciate. Also, an Alaska vacation is largely spent outdoors, which is where kids like to be. The children never get enough ferry riding, and all four enjoy camping immensely. Our extensive experience camping with babies, even as young as 3 months, has been entirely positive. Having everyone sleep in a tent, at baby level, is an infant's idea of vacation paradise.

There are drawbacks to Alaska as a family destination. The primary one is the expense. We have never gotten a significant break on a child's airplane ticket on the Alaska route. Activities such as flightseeing and tour-boat cruises tend to have less-than-generous children's discounts and cost too much for most families. Often, bed-and-breakfast rooms are too small for a family. Hotel rooms and restaurant meals are expensive in Alaska. Car camping solves many of those problems, with stops in a hotel every few days to get everyone cleaned up. I wouldn't take kids over the Alaska Highway, however; instead, I'd fly to Anchorage and rent a car and any bulky camping gear there (see "Car or RV Camping," earlier in this chapter).

Be careful in choosing your itinerary and activities with children. The highways in Alaska are long and children will require a gradual approach to covering a lot of ground. They also need time to play, explore, and rest. Frankly, children often don't enjoy activities like wildlife watching. It takes a long time to find the animals, and when you do, they're usually off in the distance—kids younger than 8 often don't have the visual skills or patience to pick out the animals from the landscape. Don't overtax children with walks and hiking trips; we keep track of the longest hike we've managed without excessive whining and then try to extend that record just a little bit each time out. Short sea-kayaking excursions, on the other hand, are great for children who are old enough, riding in the front of a double-seat boat with a parent in back; we began with Joseph at age 5, and I have friends who have done it with a 3-year-old. In practice, the age limit depends on the outfitter and your child's level of responsibility.

If you're flawed mortals like us, you'll be getting on each other's nerves after a few weeks on the road. We survive by leaving time for low-key kid activities, such as beachcombing or playing in the park, while one grown-up splits off for a museum visit, shopping, or a special, more expensive activity. Of course, if you want to preserve your marriage, you'll have to be scrupulously fair about who gets to go flightseeing and who has to stay behind and change diapers, as you won't have my all-purpose excuse (research).

If you're interested in a package tour with your family, most of the companies listed in this chapter will take children, but research carefully to make sure you will have enough down time and not too much time on the road. **Alaska Wildland Adventures** (✆ **800/334-8730;** www.alaskawildland.com) has various trips for kids as young as 12 and can take children as young as 6 for a package of day activities based at their Kenai Riverside Lodge. The package, called the "Kenai Explorer," is flexible in length and geared to families, offering games and kid-oriented guides. The shortest, 2-night, 3-day version is $895 adults, $825 children.

11 Sustainable Tourism/Ecotourism

Climate change is affecting Alaska faster and more severely than anywhere else on the globe (see "The Warming Climate," p. 473). But even the most committed environmentalists in Alaska have a hard time reducing their carbon footprint—the amount of carbon dioxide each of us causes to be emitted to the atmosphere, which increases global warming. Getting to and around Alaska uses a lot of fuel. A single passenger flying from Seattle to Anchorage and back is responsible for about 1,700 pounds of carbon dioxide. Cruise ships emit twice as much carbon dioxide per passenger-mile as airliners. Driving to Alaska emits even more than taking a ship, partly because you have to go three times as far to cover the same distance.

Other than walking, rowing, or riding on horseback to Alaska, the only solution is to offset your carbon emissions by doing good somewhere else. To make that easy, a market has developed in carbon offsetting that allows buyers to fund a piece of a larger project that will cut emissions. The idea is that your purchase will offset the carbon you emit when taking your trip. This concept is still in its infancy, however, and there's work left to make it fully credible. Critics have pointed out that whether the offsets really reduce carbon emissions depends on the quality of the projects they fund and if those projects actually take place. Until the market matures, it's buyer beware. Make sure you're buying something real by reading up and checking that the seller is audited. U.S. companies selling carbon offsets include **Carbonfund.org** (www.carbonfund.org) and **TerraPass** (www.terrapass.org), and, in the U.K., **Climate Care** (www.climatecare.org). Best of all, reduce your own impact as much as possible—that's more important than offsetting.

Many other environmental issues affect Alaska and tourism has been on both sides—whom you choose to work with makes a difference. Ecotourism has had a significant role over the years in helping conservation. One of Alaska's best eco-tourism operators, **Alaska Discovery** (p. 38), started leading groups because its founders wanted to develop a constituency to save beautiful places by taking people there. The **Alaska Wilderness Recreation and Tourism Association** (www.awrta.org) is a large and effective coalition of ecotourism operators who communicate an environmental message to clients and use their political muscle to support conservation causes. The association's website makes it easy to find homegrown ecotourism operators in Alaska.

Information sources nationally include: **Responsible Travel** (www.responsibletravel.com), a source of sustainable travel ideas; the **International Ecotourism Society** (www.ecotourism.org), offering eco-friendly travel tips, statistics, and touring companies and associations; and **Ecotravel.com,** an online magazine and ecodirectory that lets you search for touring companies. In the U.K., **Tourism Concern** (www.tourismconcern.org.uk) works to reduce social and environmental problems connected to tourism.

FAST FACTS: Alaska

Area Code All of Alaska is in area code **907.** In the Yukon Territory, the area code is **867.** When placing a toll call within the state, you must dial 1, the area code, and the number.

Automobile Organizations Auto clubs will supply maps, suggested routes, guidebooks, accident and bail-bond insurance, and emergency road service. The **American Automobile Association (AAA)** is the major auto club in the United States. If you belong to an auto club in your home country, inquire about AAA reciprocity before you leave. You may be able to join AAA even if you're not a member of a reciprocal club; the Alaska branch is **AAA Mountain-West** (℗ 800/332-6119; www.aaa-mountainwest.com). AAA has a nationwide emergency road service telephone number (℗ 800/AAA-HELP).

Banks & ATMs There are banks and automated teller machines everywhere but tiny villages.

Business Hours In the larger cities, major grocery stores are open until late at night and carry a wide range of products (even fishing gear) in addition to food. At a minimum, **stores** are open Monday through Friday from 10am to 6pm, are open on Saturday afternoon, and are closed on Sunday, but many are open much longer hours, especially in summer. **Banks** may close an hour earlier and, if open on Saturday, hours are short. Under state law, **bars** don't have to close until 5am, but many communities have an earlier closing, generally around 2am.

Car Rentals See "Getting There & Getting Around," p. 26.

Cellular Phone Coverage Pretty much every town that can be reached by road or ferry has cellular voice coverage, as well as some of the paved highways. That means the great majority of the people are covered and the great majority of the land is not. The largest provider is an Alaska company called ACS, which posts maps of its coverage area at www.acsalaska.com (click on "wireless.") I've found usable coverage is often less than what the companies claim, so don't bet your life on being able to make a call. In any event, if you plan to use your cell-phone, check with your wireless provider to make sure it will work in Alaska and to find out just how badly you will be gouged on roaming charges.

Currency The most common bills are the $1 (a "buck"), $5, $10, and $20 denominations. There are also $2 bills (seldom encountered), $50 bills, and $100 bills (the last two are usually not welcome as payment for small purchases). Coins come in eight denominations: 1¢ (1 cent, or a penny); 5¢ (5 cents, or a nickel); 10¢ (10 cents, or a dime); 25¢ (25 cents, or a quarter); 50¢ (50 cents, or a half dollar); the gold-colored Sacagawea coin, worth $1; the presidential $1 coin; and the rare silver dollar.

Electricity As in Canada, the United States uses 110 to 120 volts AC (60 cycles), compared to 220 to 240 volts AC (50 cycles) in most of Europe, Australia, and New Zealand. Downward converters that change 220 to 240 volts to 110 to 120 volts are difficult to find in the United States, so bring one with you.

Embassies & Consulates All embassies are located in the nation's capital, Washington, D.C. Some consulates are located in major U.S. cities, and most nations have a mission to the United Nations in New York City. If your country isn't listed below, call for directory information in Washington, D.C. (© 202/555-1212) or log on to **www.embassy.org/embassies**.

Emergencies Generally, you can call © **911** for medical, police, or fire emergencies. On remote highways there sometimes are gaps in 911 coverage, but dialing 0 will generally get an operator who can connect you to emergency services.

Gasoline (Petrol) The cost of gasoline changes too quickly to make much sense to list in a book. You can find national and state price averages updated online daily at www.fuelgaugereport.com. Prices in Alaska vary by location: In Anchorage, they tend to be a little below the national average, while in rural areas they are well above it. As elsewhere in the U.S., taxes are already included in the price quoted or on the pump. One U.S. gallon equals 3.8 liters or .85 imperial gallons. Fill-up locations are known as gas or service stations.

Holidays Besides national holidays, banks and state and local government offices close on two state holidays: Seward's Day (the last Mon in Mar) and Alaska Day (Oct 18, or the nearest Fri or Mon if it falls on a weekend). National holidays, when many stores, restaurants, and museums close as well, include New Year's Day (January 1), Martin Luther King Day (3rd Mon in Jan), Presidents' Day (3rd Mon in Feb), Memorial Day (last Mon in May), Independence Day (July 4), Labor Day (the 1st Mon in Sept), Columbus Day (the 2nd Mon in

Oct), Veterans Day (November 11), Thanksgiving Day (the 4th Thurs in Nov), and Christmas Day (December 25).

Legal Aid If you are pulled over for a minor infraction (such as speeding), never attempt to pay the fine directly to a police officer; this could be construed as attempted bribery, a much more serious crime. Pay fines by mail, or directly into the hands of the clerk of the court. If accused of a more serious offense, say and do nothing before consulting a lawyer. Here the burden is on the state to prove a person's guilt beyond a reasonable doubt, and everyone has the right to remain silent, whether he or she is suspected of a crime or actually arrested. Once arrested, a person can make one telephone call to a party of his or her choice. International visitors should call their embassy or consulate.

Information Bureaus The **Alaska Travel Industry Association,** 2600 Cordova St., Suite 201, Anchorage, AK 99503 (© **907/929-2842;** www.travelalaska.com), is the state's official visitor agency. It sends out printed information, but refers questions to visitor bureaus in individual towns. The largest of these is the Anchorage Convention and Visitor Bureau (p. 215); otherwise, see the beginning of each town section in this book. For outdoor recreation, the **Alaska Public Lands Information Centers** are centralized sources of information on all government lands, which include some 85% of the state. The centers, located in Anchorage, Fairbanks, Ketchikan, and Tok, are operated cooperatively by many land agencies, including the National Park Service and U.S. Forest Service. The Anchorage center is at 605 W. 4th Ave., Suite 105, Anchorage, AK 99501 (© **907/271-2737;** www.nps.gov/aplic); the Fairbanks center is at 250 Cushman St., Suite 1A, Fairbanks, AK 99701 (© **907/456-0527**).

Liquor Laws The minimum drinking age in Alaska is 21 and ID is frequently checked. Most restaurants sell beer and wine, while some have full bars that serve hard liquor as well. Packaged alcohol, beer, and wine are sold only in licensed stores, not in grocery stores, but these are common and are open long hours every day. Open containers of alcohol are not allowed in your car or, with few exceptions, in any public place outside a bar or restaurant. Don't even think about driving while intoxicated, which in Alaska carries mandatory jail time for the first offense. More than 100 rural communities have laws prohibiting the importation and possession of alcohol (this is known as being "dry") or prohibiting the sale but not possession of alcohol (known as being "damp"). With a few exceptions, these are tiny Bush communities off the road network; urban areas are all "wet." Of the communities featured in this book, Kotzebue and Barrow are damp, and the rest are wet. Before flying into a Native village with alcohol, ask about the law or go to www.dps.state.ak.us/abc and click on "Local Option Restrictions." Bootlegging is a serious crime and serious bad manners in Alaska Native communities that are trying to address the damage of alcohol abuse.

Mail The locations of the post offices in each town in this book are listed in the appropriate "Fast Facts" sections. You can send mail from your hotel or the post office. Mail in the United States must have a five-digit postal code (or ZIP code), after the two-letter abbreviation of the state to which the mail is addressed. You can receive mail addressed to you at "General Delivery" at the post office.

Maps I've noted the best trail maps in each applicable section throughout this book. For most of the popular areas, I recommend the excellent trail maps published by **Trails Illustrated,** part of National Geographic (© **800/962-1643;** www.maps.nationalgeographic.com). They're sold in park visitor centers, too. The maps are printed on plastic, so they don't get spoiled by rain; however, they don't cover the whole state. For detailed topographic maps covering all of Alaska, the U.S. Geological Service is still the only place to go. Their maps sales office in Anchorage (a fascinating place for anyone interested in cartography) is on the campus of Alaska Pacific University, in the **Earth Science Information Center,** at 4230 University Dr. (© **907/786-7011**).

Newspapers The state's dominant newspaper is the *Anchorage Daily News* (www.adn.com); it's available everywhere but is not always easy to find in Southeast Alaska. Seattle newspapers and *USA Today* are often available, and in Anchorage you can get virtually any newspaper.

Passports **For Residents of Australia:** You can pick up an application from your local post office or any branch of Passports Australia, but you must schedule an interview at the passport office to present your application materials. Call the **Australian Passport Information Service** at © **131-232,** or visit the government website at www.passports.gov.au.

For Residents of Canada: Passport applications are available at travel agencies throughout Canada or from the central **Passport Office,** Department of Foreign Affairs and International Trade, Ottawa, ON K1A 0G3 (© **800/567-6868;** www.ppt.gc.ca). *Note:* Canadian children who travel must have their own passport. However, if you hold a valid Canadian passport issued before December 11, 2001, that bears the name of your child, the passport remains valid for you and your child until it expires.

For Residents of Ireland: You can apply for a 10-year passport at the **Passport Office,** Setanta Centre, Molesworth Street, Dublin 2 (© **01/671-1633;** www.irl gov.ie/iveagh). Those under age 18 and over 65 must apply for a 3-year passport. You can also apply at 1A South Mall, Cork (© **021/272-525**) or at most main post offices.

For Residents of New Zealand: You can pick up a passport application at any New Zealand Passports Office or download it from their website. Contact the **Passports Office** at © **0800/225-050** in New Zealand or 04/474-8100, or log on to www.passports.govt.nz.

For Residents of the United Kingdom: To pick up an application for a standard 10-year passport (5-yr. passport for children under 16), visit your nearest passport office, major post office, or travel agency or contact the **United Kingdom Passport Service** at © **0870/521-0410** or visit its website at www.ukpa.gov.uk.

For Residents of the United States: Starting in 2008, you will need a passport to reenter the U.S. from Canada, even by road. You can apply for a passport at many post offices. Before you go, get the requirements at the U.S. State Department website www.travel.state.gov/passport, or call their National Passport Information Center ((© **877/487-2778**).

Taxes As of this writing, there is no state sales tax, but most local governments have a sales tax and a bed tax on accommodations. The tax rates are listed in each town section throughout the book under "Fast Facts."

Telephone I am assured that all major U.S. calling cards will work in Alaska, but this certainly hasn't been the case in the past. To make sure, contact your long-distance company, or buy a by-the-minute card. They are sold in convenience stores and are often the cheapest way to call home for international visitors. **Local calls** made from public pay phones usually cost 25¢. In smaller Alaska communities, you may have to wait for the person you are calling to answer before quickly putting the money in the phone.

Time Zone Although the state naturally spans five time zones, in the 1980s Alaska's middle time zone was stretched so almost the entire state would lie all in one zone, known as Alaska time. It's 1 hour earlier than the U.S. West Coast's Pacific time, 4 hours earlier than Eastern time. Crossing over the border from Alaska to Canada adds an hour and puts you at the same time as the West Coast. As with almost everywhere else in the United States, daylight saving time is in effect from 2am on the second Sunday in March (turn your clocks ahead 1 hr.) until 2am on the first Sunday in November (turn clocks back again).

Tipping Tips make up a major part of the compensation for many service workers. To leave no tip in a restaurant is socially unacceptable and leaves your server unpaid. To leave a small tip is a powerful indication of displeasure for bad service; to leave no tip suggests you don't know any better.

In restaurants, bars, and nightclubs, tip your server 15% to 20% of the check, depending on the quality of service. Tip **bartenders** at least 10% to 15% (a dollar or more per drink is customary), tip **checkroom attendants** $1 per garment, and tip **valet-parking attendants** $1 each time you get your car. Tipping is not expected in cafeterias or fast-food restaurants where you order at a counter. In hotels, tip **bellhops** $1 per bag and tip the **housekeeper** at least $1 to $2 per day. Tip **cab drivers** 15% of the fare and tip **hairdressers** and **barbers** 15% to 20%. Do not tip gas-station attendants and ushers at movies and theaters.

See the box "A Guide to Guide Gratuities" on p. 34 for guidelines on tipping outdoor guides and outfitters.

Visas For information about U.S. Visas go to **www.travel.state.gov** and click on "Visas." Or go to one of the following websites:

Australian citizens can obtain up-to-date visa information from the **U.S. Embassy Canberra,** Moonah Place, Yarralumla, ACT 2600 ((© **02/6214-5600**) or by checking the U.S. Diplomatic Mission's website at **http://usembassy-australia.state.gov/consular**.

British subjects can obtain up-to-date visa information by calling the **U.S. Embassy Visa Information Line** ((© **0891/200-290**) or by visiting the "Visas to the U.S." section of the American Embassy London's website at **www.us embassy.org.uk**.

Irish citizens can obtain up-to-date visa information through the **Embassy of the USA Dublin,** 42 Elgin Rd., Dublin 4, Ireland (© **353/1-668-8777**) or by checking the "Consular Services" section of the website at **http://dublin.us embassy.gov.**

Citizens of **New Zealand** can obtain up-to-date visa information by contacting the **U.S. Embassy New Zealand,** 29 Fitzherbert Terrace, Thorndon, Wellington (© **644/472-2068**) or get the information directly from the website at **http://wellington.usembassy.gov.**

3

Suggested Alaska Itineraries

Readers ask me about how to fit together their itineraries more frequently than any other travel question. Alaska is unfamiliar territory and the transportation connections are different from those in most places. You can't get to the capital city of Juneau over land, for example, and the distances seem daunting between the towns that do have roads or rails. If you don't even know how to get around, it seems hard to know where to go or how much time to allow. But don't throw in the towel, like so many visitors who think the only way around these complications is to take a cruise or escorted tour. In fact, these travel issues aren't really that hard. Using a map and the list of transportation modes under "Alaska by the Numbers," on p. 15, you can get a good overview. The "Getting There" section for each destination in the book provides the details.

What's really challenging, and where visitors most commonly make mistakes, is in failing to define their interests and not limiting themselves to covering a reasonable area. Some feel compelled to try to see the entire state. Given that Alaska is defined in part by its enormous size, trying to go everywhere is a fool's errand. A version of the same thing is trying to "do" all the famous wilderness parks, which lie far apart in remote regions: You spend too much time and money getting from place to place. Each of Alaska's regions, by itself, has most of what you're

coming to Alaska for—wildlife, mountains, glaciers, historic sites, cute little towns—and you can have a better trip touring one or two regions than spending precious time going from region to region. To be specific, travelers with less than 10 days to spend should choose to tour either Southeast Alaska or Southcentral and Interior Alaska, but not both.

The other mistake some people make is to focus only on the largest and most famous destinations. Alaska isn't like Europe, with its cathedrals and monuments. Here a goal-oriented style of travel misses the fun and surprises—and may end up missing the whole point. Mount McKinley and Glacier Bay are certainly impressive, but it's perfectly allowed to skip them in favor of memorable places you find on your own that may be just as beautiful, if not as famous. More valuable—and more fundamentally Alaskan—are chance encounters with wildlife or interesting local people, or simply peaceful time alone in the woods.

Finally, remember why you are going to Alaska. Surely it's not to visit museums or tourist attractions, but instead to see one of the most beautiful unspoiled places on Earth. To do that, you need to get outside. There's only so much you can see and learn through glass. Take a chance on a sea-kayak excursion, a day hike, or a mountain bike ride. You may never have a better chance to try it.

(Tips Create Your Own Itinerary

If all travelers had the same interests, needs, abilities, and the same preferences in pacing, they could all follow the same itineraries. Of course, then only the limited number of places that fit on a sample itinerary would receive all the visitors, while the interesting and peculiar places off the beaten path would remain unknown. I hope you use the sample trip plans here as a starting point to design your own individual trip. Substitute different activities or towns, or extend the time in places that are more appealing to you. Do the trips in reverse order or cut and paste portions of two different plans together. Or simply use the itineraries to get a feel for the distances and places and then build your own plan from scratch after browsing through the rest of the book.

1 Southeast Alaska in a Week

This plan takes you to the Southeast's highlights, with whales, glaciers, mountains, totem poles, and Russian American history included. It's fast-paced yet still covers less than half of this diverse and fascinating region. If you have more time, this plan would make a much more relaxing 10-day trip. Add a day each in Sitka, Juneau, and Gustavus. There's plenty to do, or not do, in each town. You can extend this itinerary even more by beginning with a flight into **Petersburg** instead of Sitka. Spend a day or two there sea kayaking, hiking, fishing, or whale-watching before boarding an Alaska Marine Highway System ferry to Sitka and picking up on Day 1 of this plan.

Day ❶: Arrive in Sitka ⊛

Fly on an **Alaska Airlines** jet to the historic island city of Sitka, once the capital of Russian America. The town layout you see from the air is little changed from historic photographs and paintings. After settling in, take a walk along winding Lincoln Street, taking in the views from **Castle Hill** (p. 147), where the Russians handed over Alaska to the United States in 1867. Look into stately **St. Michael's Cathedral** (p. 146), and visit **The Russian Bishop's House** (p. 145), making sure to take a National Park Service tour of the extraordinary upstairs section.

Day ❷: Tlingit History & Sitka Wildlife ⊛⊛⊛

Start the day at the **Sitka National Historical Park** (p. 144) to see an extraordinary collection of historic and contemporary totem poles, meeting Tlingit artisans at

work, and learning about their culture and history. Now walk through the lovely forested totem park and battlefield sites before continuing to the **Alaska Raptor Center** (p. 146) to see eagles being rehabilitated and learning to fly again after injuries. After lunch, join any one of the half-day **wildlife cruises** that go from the boat harbor to see otters, sea lions, and possibly whales and, if conditions permit, the **sea bird colony** at St. Lazaria Island (p. 148).

Day ❸: Juneau by Ferry ⊛⊛

After a final goodbye to Sitka, board a ferry on the **Alaska Marine Highway System** (p. 97) for a spectacular ride to Juneau that will take most of the day. When you arrive, get a cab from the ferry dock to the airport and rent a car there. If you have time enough left in the day, you can now visit **Mendenhall Glacier**

Southeast Alaska in a Week

1 Arrive in Sitka
2 Tlingit History & Sitka Wildlife
3 Juneau by Ferry
4 Juneau
5 To Gustavus/Glacier Bay
6 Glacier Bay Tour
7 Sea Kayaking in Gustavus

(p. 166) and drive out the road (that's the common local phrase for it) for a lovely and moving walk to the tiny island of **The Shrine of St. Thérèse** (p. 167). Then move into your lodgings.

Day ❹: Juneau 👀👀

In the morning, take a **helicopter flight** to the **Juneau Icefield** (p. 170) for a walk or even a dog-sled ride and to get a feel for the immensity of the place and to touch glacier ice. If weather isn't promising for that, visit the **Alaska State Museum** (p. 159) or do the **walking tour** downtown (p. 160). In the afternoon, take a **hike** on one of Juneau's beautiful rainforest or mountain trails (p. 168). There are wonderful choices, such as the **Perseverance Trail** near

downtown, but since you have a car, you can hike anywhere and get away from any cruise-ship crowds that may wreck the solitude on some of the paths.

Day ❺: To Gustavus/Glacier Bay 👀👀

Fly a prop from Juneau to Gustavus, the gateway to **Glacier Bay National Park** (p. 180), to arrive early enough to orient yourself and take a walk on the trails around the park headquarters to enjoy the shoreline and mossy forest trails, or to go bicycling on the country roads or exploring the long sandy beaches in Gustavus. If you're more ambitious, the waters off Gustavus are among Alaska's best for watching humpback whales, and you'll have time today for a half-day viewing trip. You have two lodging choices here. Check in at the

Glacier Bay Lodge (p. 184), or stay at a wilderness lodge or country inn in Gustavus (your host will pick you up).

Day ❻: Glacier Bay Tour ⟨★★⟩

The all-day **boat tour ride** (p. 183) leaves from Bartlett Cove and passes through humpback whale areas and other marine mammal grounds far up the bay to where two large glaciers stand like walls at the edge of the water. Be sure to bring binoculars and warm clothing, as the glaciers produce frigid downdrafting winds, even in the height of summer.

Day ❼: Sea Kayaking in Gustavus ⟨★★★⟩

I've saved some of the best for last. Your Alaska Airlines jet doesn't leave Gustavus until the evening, so you have time today for a **sea-kayaking** outing in the lovely waters of **Bartlett Cove,** where whales frequently visit (p. 183), or, if you are staying in Gustavus, kayak from there (p. 183) into an area where whales are virtually always seen in the summer. You can connect the flight from Gustavus through Juneau onward to home.

2 Two National Parks in a Week

An itinerary connecting Kenai Fjords National Park, south of Anchorage, and Denali National Park, to the north, is probably Alaska's most popular land trip for first-time visitors. That's because these parks and the area in between offer so much of what visitors come to Alaska to see, and in spectacular places: at Kenai Fjords, waterways full of whales, marine birds, and glaciers; and at Denali, broad swaths of mountain tundra frequented by bears and caribou. This itinerary is set up to do without a car. To save money and have more flexibility, do the same tour with a car rented in Anchorage.

Day ❶: Arrive in Anchorage ★

Fly to Anchorage and move into a room in the walkable downtown area, which is near the train station, where you will be departing tomorrow. If the weather is nice, do the **walking tour** (p. 132) to find out what the area is like, or rent a bike and ride on the **Tony Knowles Coastal Trail** (p. 242) to see the waterfowl in West Chester Lagoon, the moose in Earthquake Park, and maybe even the beluga whales of Cook Inlet. You can go as far as you want: Anchorage's paved bike trails weave through the entire city on wooded greenbelts. In bad weather, or if you're not up to the exercise, spend your time at the **Anchorage Museum at Rasmuson Center** (p. 237), getting oriented to history and culture in the Alaska Gallery or checking out contemporary Alaskan art.

Day ❷: To Seward and in Kenai Fjords National Park ⟨★★★⟩

Board an **Alaska Railroad** (p. 251) train to Seward to enjoy some of Alaska's most spectacular scenery along the cliffs and surging ocean waters of Turnagain Arm and through the untouched mountains of the Kenai Peninsula; those who choose to drive get to see similar scenery on a slightly different route (see section 8 in chapter 6 and section 2 in chapter 7). In Seward, board a tour boat to **Kenai Fjords National Park** (see section 6 in chapter 7). Make sure to take a vessel headed all the way into the park so you see the best of the wildlife and get close to a tidewater glacier. Make sure also to take a seasickness remedy such as Dramamine or Bonine 2 hours before getting onboard. If the weather is bad, ask to be switched to a boat tomorrow and do tomorrow's activities instead.

Two National Parks in a Week

1 Arrive in Anchorage
2 To Seward & Kenai Fjords National Park
3 In Seward
4 Denali National Park
5 Exploring Denali National Park
6 Denali & Back to Anchorage
7 Anchorage Activities

Day ❸: In Seward ★★

After a couple of tiring days, this is a good day to relax in a charming little town. In the morning, join a half-day sea-kayaking paddle from Lowell Point with **Sunny Cove Sea Kayaking** (p. 281). You'll likely see sea otters, birds, intertidal creatures, and maybe spawning salmon. By going in the morning, your chances of smooth water are better. In the afternoon, see the marine life and seabirds you encountered yesterday, up close, at the **Alaska SeaLife Center** (p. 283). Consider joining one of their educational programs to get even closer to the animals.

Day ❹: Denali National Park

Take the comfortable and convenient **Park Connection Motorcoach Service** (p. 280) from Seward straight to Denali National Park, a journey of more than 360 miles. The driver does commentary on the highlights along the route. The bus ride takes almost 10 hours with a couple of long stops. If you drive instead, you can do it in under 7 hours. Arriving in Denali, check into your hotel and stretch your legs, but get to bed promptly to be ready for an early start tomorrow.

Day ❺: Exploring Denali National Park ★★★

This is the primary day to see Denali and the bears, caribou, and other wildlife there. The park shuttle bus system is the key to your visit. Reserve as far ahead as possible (the previous December is not too soon) to get a seat on the earliest bus

Tips Itinerary Add-Ons

This week-long itinerary to two national parks is fast-paced. You can have a more relaxing trip and allow for more spontaneity by adding days to the stops that are already planned.

If you've still got more time after slowing down the pace, extend your trip with a visit to **Fairbanks:** Instead of taking the train back to Anchorage on Day 6, take it northward to Fairbanks. There I recommend renting a car to see the sites and perhaps explore the surrounding rural highways for a few days. (See Days 1 and 2 of "A 2-Week Grand Loop," below.) When you're finished, fly home from Fairbanks.

Also consider adding on a **Southeast Alaska** sojourn. When you buy your ticket to Alaska, buy it from Seattle to Anchorage on Alaska Airlines and include a stopover, for a reasonable additional cost, in a Southeast Alaska town—Sitka would be my first choice. Spend time seeing the Russian American history and Tlingit culture there, and getting outdoors (see Days 1 and 2 of "Southeast Alaska in a Week," above), before flying on to Anchorage and beginning the itinerary listed at Day 1.

you can manage (reservation details are on p. 348). Wildlife tends to be more active in the morning. Ride deep into the park, taking along all your food and water, a warm jacket and raincoat, and good hiking shoes. Take a look at the suggestions for cross-country hiking in chapter 8, and then make your choice according to how the countryside looks to you. This is a remarkable chance for a low-stress, low-cost wilderness experience. When you're ready to head home, just catch another bus on the way back.

Day ❻: Denali and Back to Anchorage ⟨⋆⟩

Your train back to Anchorage doesn't leave until late afternoon, giving you most of the day to enjoy the Denali park entrance area. The **visitor center** (p. 361) and **Murie**

Science and Learning Center (p. 363) should not be missed: The exhibits and programs here will deepen your understanding of the natural places you have already seen. You also have time for a whitewater rafting ride on the Nenana River (p. 365) or a relaxing walk on the nature trails and hiking trails near the visitor center (p. 360). Your train arrives in Anchorage in the evening.

Day ❼: Anchorage Activities ⟨⋆⟩

If you can arrange for a flight home late in the day, you'll have time for one more activity in Anchorage. Take the free shuttle to the **Alaska Native Heritage Center** (p. 238) to meet indigenous people and learn about their cultures in a magnificent facility they built, own, and manage.

3 A 2-Week Grand Loop

This driving loop includes much of the best of the Interior, Prince William Sound, Anchorage, and Denali National Park. It allows you to end up where you started, saving money on plane tickets and car rental. And you'll see some remote and off-the-beaten-track places. Not many visitors make it to see Childs Glacier on the Copper

River Delta, but I think it's the most spectacular accessible glacier in Alaska. Likewise, a trip to Kennecott, in Wrangell–St. Elias National Park, takes you way off the grid, letting you see an amazing historical ghost town and a community of real, backwoods Alaskans.

Day ❶: Starting in Fairbanks ⍟

Fly to Fairbanks, rent a car, and then check into your hotel. (If you will drive the rented car on gravel roads, such as the McCarthy Road on Day 4 or the Copper River Highway on Day 8, you will need to rent from one of the few firms that allows this, listed on p. 395.) If time permits, visit the University of Alaska campus and see the magnificent **UA Museum of the North** and, if you are interested in such topics, the **Large Animal Research Station** or the **Georgeson Botanical Garden** (all p. 392).

Day ❷: Fairbanks ⍟

Take the car to explore the Chena Hot Springs Road and the boreal forest of the **Chena River State Recreation Area** (see section 3 of chapter 9). There are several wonderful trails here with varying difficulty levels. As an alternative, arrange for a canoeing paddle on the Chena. When you've finished hiking or paddling and start thinking about sore muscles, stop at the **Chena Hot Springs Resort** (p. 410) for a soak in the natural mineral springs pond there. At the end of the day, return to Fairbanks for dinner and bed.

Day ❸: The Richardson Highway to Copper Center ⍟⍟

Today you will drive approximately 260 miles (driving time: under 6 hr.) through some of Alaska's most spectacular scenery. Drive east from Fairbanks toward Delta Junction; stop there, after about 2 hours, to see the historical park at **Rika's Roadhouse and Landing** (p. 422), and for lunch in the town (see section 5 in chapter 9). Now drive south on the Richardson Highway. The best part of the drive is here, as the highway rises up and over the Alaska Range on open tundra country, along the silver Alaska pipeline, and at the edge of a series of alpine lakes. Stop for the night in the Athabascan village of Copper Center, where there is an exceptional hotel, **Copper River Princess Wilderness Lodge** (p. 426). Be sure to stop in at the **Wrangell–St. Elias National Park Visitor Center** (p. 429) to get oriented to the park before your visit tomorrow.

Day ❹: Kennecott ⍟⍟⍟

Get up early to drive east about 85 miles on the Edgerton Highway to Chitina, arriving there in time for the 8:30am **Backcountry Connection shuttle** (p. 428; reserve in advance) for a ride into the park. It's a rough road over an old railroad line deep into the wilderness park to a copper mine that was abandoned in the 1930s and the ghost town it left behind; by taking the van, you save yourself the driving and the planning necessary for that tough route, and you gain a guide to show you the way (you will have to cross a footbridge at one point). In Kennecott, check into one of two **wilderness lodges** (see section 8 of chapter 9) and join a guided walking tour through the enormous ghost-town buildings.

Day ❺: Kennecott to Valdez ⍟⍟

You have time in the morning to relax and wander in the friendly, quiet setting of Kennecott and its funky sister village of McCarthy. If you have the energy, take a half-day guided hike on the glacier that faces the ghost town. In the afternoon, take an air-taxi flight back to **Chitina** (p. 429) to get to your car (if you ride the van back, you will get in too late; besides,

1 Starting in Fairbanks
2 Fairbanks
3 The Richardson Highway to Copper Center
4 Kennecott
5 Kennecott to Valdez
6 Valdez to Cordova
7 Prince William Sound Sea Kayaking
8 Copper River Delta
9 Across the Sound to Whittier & Anchorage
10 Anchorage
11 Flying over Mt. McKinley
12 Exploring Denali National Park
13 Denali & Drive to Fairbanks
14 Fairbanks

the view from the plane will be fantastic). Drive back to the Richardson and then south to Valdez, about 190 miles total (4 hr.). The mountain scenery is spectacular through Thompson Pass nearing the town. Dine and check into lodgings in **Valdez** (see section 11 of chapter 7).

Day ❻: Valdez to Cordova Ferry ❀

Today you will be taking your car by ferry for a scenic trip across eastern Prince William Sound to the town of Cordova. Depending on when the ferry leaves, you may have time for a day hike, a museum visit, or another activity in Valdez. In the evening, walk around the quaint, forgotten town of Cordova; if time permits, take a look at the two small **community museums** (see section 12 of chapter 7).

Day ❼: Prince William Sound Sea Kayaking ❀❀❀

Join **Cordova Coastal Outfitters** (p. 338) for a sea-kayaking excursion, or, if you are staying at the **Orca Adventure Lodge** (p. 339), you can go with a guide there. Cordova is an exceptional spot for a day's sea kayaking because waters near town are protected and exceptionally rich in marine mammals. You're almost assured of seeing sea otters and sea lions, and very likely to see many other birds and animals as well (see section 12 of chapter 7).

Day ❽: Copper River Delta ❀❀

Drive your car east from Cordova over the gravel Copper River Highway through the Copper River Delta, an immense wetland teeming with wildlife, especially trumpeter swans and other waterfowl. (If your car rental agency doesn't allow this, you can rent a vehicle for the day in Cordova.) There are several excellent and little-used trails and bird-watching areas along the road. The destination at the far end is the Childs Glacier, an incredible wall of ice that is cut by the Copper River. From a viewing area on the other side of the river, you are remarkably close to the glacier, and in warm weather you can see huge chunks falling off and hear the groan of the moving ice (see section 12 of chapter 7). Spend a third night in Cordova.

Day ❾: Across the Sound to Whittier and Anchorage ✪

Get back on the ferry for a trip across the sound to Whittier. Again, the scenery is incomparable. Hopefully, you aren't too jaded yet! **Whittier** is a strange little port town built by the military during World War II that is reached only by boat or through a one-lane tunnel almost 3 miles long (p. 274). On the far side of the tunnel, you find yourself on Turnagain Arm about 80 miles from Anchorage. Time permitting, stop in Girdwood for a meal and perhaps a hike or visit to a **historic gold mine** (see section 9 of chapter 6). Finish the day in lodgings in Anchorage.

Day ❿: Anchorage ✪

Take in the **Alaska Native Heritage Center** (p. 238) in the morning to meet indigenous people and learn about their cultures in a magnificent facility they built, own, and manage. In the afternoon, visit the **Anchorage Museum at Rasmuson Center** (p. 237) or spend the day outdoors, hiking, mountain biking, fishing, or bird-watching (see section 5 of chapter 6). At the end of this fairly low-key day, eat in one of Alaska's best **restaurants**, of which Anchorage has the broadest selection (see section 3 of chapter 6).

Day ⓫: Flying over Mount McKinley ✪✪✪

Get an early start for the 112-mile drive to Talkeetna (less than 2 hr.) so you can be there in time for a morning flight over Mount McKinley before the clouds build up in the afternoon. The flight services that carry mountain climbers to the flanks of North America's tallest peak can also take you there for a landing on a high-elevation glacier (p. 377). This flight may provide the most memorable hours of your visit; I know I'll never forget any of the times I've done it. After lunch and a walk around hip and historic Talkeetna (see section 11 in chapter 8), drive about 150 miles (roughly 3 hours) to Denali National Park and check in to your lodgings. You should have time to take in the fascinating exhibits at the visitor center, too.

Day ⓬: Exploring Denali National Park ✪✪✪

This is the primary day to see Denali and the bears, caribou, and other wildlife there. The park shuttle bus system is the key to your visit. Reserve as far ahead as possible (the previous December is not too soon) to get a seat on the earliest bus you can manage. Wildlife tends to be more active in the morning. Ride deep into the park, taking along all your food and water, a warm jacket and raincoat, and good hiking shoes. Take a look at the suggestions for cross-country hiking in chapter 8, and then make your choice according to how the countryside looks to you. This is a remarkable chance for a low-stress, low-cost wilderness experience. When you're ready to head home, just catch another bus on the way back.

Day ⓭: Denali and Drive to Fairbanks ✪

The drive from Denali back to Fairbanks is only a couple of hours, so you can take your time at the park. A whitewater rafting ride in the Nenana River would be exciting; a nature walk in the woods from the visitor center might be calming. Also consider an educational program at the **Murie Science and Learning Center** (see chapter 8). Drive to your lodgings in Fairbanks in the afternoon.

Day ⑭: Fairbanks

Today you get on a plane and fly back home, but if you have time for a relaxing outing before that, stop off for a stroll in **Pioneer Park** (p. 390) to look at the historic paddle wheeler *Nenana* and the other museums and attractions, and to soak up the small-town ambience.

4 A Week in Alaska with Children

Traveling with children means limiting distances and increasing time for casual fun. The best place to do that is on the Kenai Peninsula south of Anchorage. Despite being a relatively contained area, the peninsula is a microcosm of the whole state, with glaciers, mountains, trails, and rugged coastline like that found over the vast span of the state. To make it even easier, I suggest renting an RV, which takes the stress out of having to keep children quiet in restaurants and hotel rooms. If you prefer to tent, rent a car instead; you can even rent most of your camping equipment in Anchorage. You'll have even more flexibility and opportunities for spontaneous fun. If you can, improve on this itinerary by adding days in Homer or on the Swan Lake Canoe Route.

Day ❶: Arrive in Anchorage

Fly to Anchorage and pick up your rented **RV** (p. 212), or pick up your car and rented **camping gear** (see "Equipment," p. 241). After buying your groceries, you can get on your way south on the Seward Highway, stopping at the **Bird Creek Campground** (p. 224) or the **Williwaw** or **Black Bear** campgrounds (p. 272). The children will need to burn off some energy after your flight and drive, and this stretch of the highway has some of Alaska's best hiking trails. They are all covered, along with other sites, in section 8 of chapter 6.

Day ❷: To Seward and Kenai Fjords National Park 𝄴𝄴𝄴

Drive the rest of the way to Seward on the Seward Highway and get on a tour boat to see **Kenai Fjords National Park** (see section 6 in chapter 7). Every kid enjoys a boat ride, and on this one you're likely to see whales, glaciers, and lots of seabirds. *Note:* These vessels go into the open ocean and seasickness is common.

Everyone in the family should take a seasickness remedy 2 hours in advance (see "Seasickness," on p. 49). Make sure to take a vessel headed all the way into the park so you see the best of the wildlife and get close to a tidewater glacier. After you get back on land, set up your camp: If in an RV, at **Waterfront Park** (p. 286) or, if tenting, drive out of Seward to the **Primrose Campground** (p. 273).

Day ❸: Seward 𝄴𝄴

You have three choices today, depending on the ages of your children and your interests (consider splitting up, as we often do, so everyone can choose what they enjoy most). (1) Visit the **Alaska SeaLife Center** (p. 283), where you can encounter the marine life and seabirds you saw in the fjords yesterday up close, and join in educational programs that get you even closer. Allow half a day. (2) Sea kayak for half the day or the whole day with **Sunny Cove Sea Kayaking** (p. 281). You'll likely see sea otters, birds, intertidal creatures, and maybe spawning

A Week in Alaska with Children

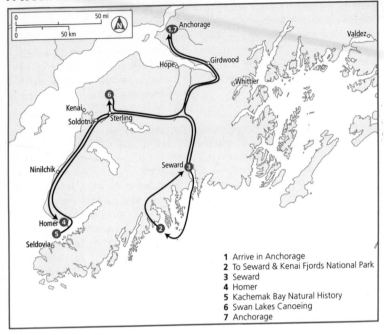

1 Arrive in Anchorage
2 To Seward & Kenai Fjords National Park
3 Seward
4 Homer
5 Kachemak Bay Natural History
6 Swan Lakes Canoeing
7 Anchorage

salmon. (3) Hike the **Caines Head State Recreation Area** (p. 282) to Fort McGilvray to explore the dark corridors of the abandoned World War II installation. (Bring a flashlight and go halfway by water taxi to make the hike more manageable.)

Day ❹: Homer ⍟
Today you'll drive 135 miles from Seward to the end of the road on the southern Kenai Peninsula and the town of **Homer** (see section 10 in chapter 7). Allow 4 hours, with traffic and some stops. In Homer, you can get hookups for the RV on Homer Spit—a fingerlike point into the middle of Kachemak Bay—or in the downtown part of Homer (still near the beach). Tenters have even more choices. Spend the afternoon beachcombing and enjoying relaxed time on the many miles of pebbled shoreline. If it's raining, take in the **Islands & Oceans Visitor Center** (p. 307) or the **Pratt Museum** (p. 308).

Day ❺: Kachemak Bay Natural History ⍟⍟⍟
Join the nonprofit **Center for Alaskan Coastal Studies** (p. 316) for a boat ride to the far side of Kachemak Bay. Their all-day natural history outings take visitors through tide pools to see strange little creatures, through a forest of big trees and wildflowers to learn about ecology, and to an ancient Native archaeological site. Even without the guides and all their knowledge, this would still be an enchanting place to visit, with wide beaches, caves, and plenty of space for a kid's energy and imagination to run free. Bring your own lunch.

Day ❻: Swan Lakes Canoeing ⍟
Now it's time to start heading back toward Anchorage. Drive about 90 miles to Sterling and stop at **Alaska Canoe & Campground** (p. 304) to rent a canoe you can take down the Swanson River Road to the Swan Lake Canoe Route in **Kenai**

National Wildlife Refuge (see section 9 in chapter 7). Spend the rest of the day paddling in this placid network of connected lakes, where you can fish and explore without seeing other people. There are numerous primitive campgrounds for the RV overnight, or, if you are tent camping, you may want to paddle to a campsite among the hundreds on the lakes. (If you're thinking this plan will leave you too far from the airport when it's time to fly home tomorrow, fair enough. Skip the canoeing and drive on. There are campgrounds all along the highway to Anchorage, so you can stop wherever you feel comfortable and explore there. See sections 2 and 3 of chapter 7.)

Day ❼: Anchorage

From Sterling to Anchorage is about 150 miles and will take more than 3 hours with traffic. You probably won't have extra time after returning the RV or camping equipment before your flight, but if you do, the best way to spend it is at the **Alaska Zoo** (p. 239), where you will be sure of seeing all the most popular Alaska wildlife.

Days ❽, ❾ & ❿ (Optional): Prince William Sound Loop

Another great trip for kids adds 2 or 3 extra days: Instead of returning to Anchorage on Day 7, drive to Whittier and take the Alaska Marine Highway ferry to Valdez. Drive north on the Richardson Highway to Glennallen and west on the Glenn Highway back to Anchorage. An overview of these roads is in "Alaska's Highways a la Carte" (p. 382), and details are included in chapters 7 and 9.

5 A Week of Alaska Winter Sports

Winter is when Alaska is at its best. The snow simplifies the scenery and makes it even more beautiful. The outdoor activities are superb: cross-country and downhill skiing, snowmobiling, ice skating, and dog mushing. The people are especially hospitable, since visitors are rare, and the towns are alive with festivals, sled dog races, and authentic cultural events—not just tourist stuff. There's also a very good chance you will see the northern lights. One proviso: It's impossible to make up a real itinerary for winter sports without knowing individual interests. Avid downhill skiers should spend most of their time on the slopes, for example. So take the list below as a starting point for ideas.

Day ❶: Anchorage Festivals & Sled Dog Races ⚝

To enjoy Anchorage fully, rent a car when you arrive. If you have planned your trip for late February or early March, you can be here when Anchorage is alive with the **Fur Rendezvous Winter Festival,** with its dozens of events and World Championship Sled Dog Race, and the **Iditarod Trail Sled Dog Race** (both p. 216), which starts its journey across Alaska to Nome right after the festival. Local cultural institutions will be busy, too: Visit the **Anchorage Museum at Rasmuson Center** (p. 237) during the day and catch a per-formance in the evening at the **Alaska Center for the Performing Arts** (p. 249).

Day ❷: Anchorage Cross-Country Skiing ⚝⚝

If you've never tried cross-country skiing, Anchorage is an excellent place to give it a go. If you do ski, you can enjoy some of the nation's best trails here in many settings and varying difficulty levels and with grooming that's world class—the ski club here sent its groomers to prepare the trails for the winter Olympics in Salt Lake City and Turin. There are no trail fees. The very best trail system is at **Kincaid Park** (p. 247). **Ski rental** is covered

A Week of Alaska Winter Sports

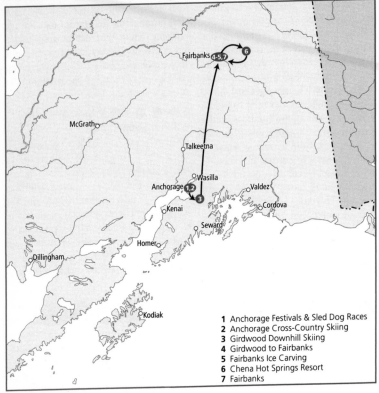

1 Anchorage Festivals & Sled Dog Races
2 Anchorage Cross-Country Skiing
3 Girdwood Downhill Skiing
4 Girdwood to Fairbanks
5 Fairbanks Ice Carving
6 Chena Hot Springs Resort
7 Fairbanks

under "Equipment," on p. 241. If you don't want to ski, Anchorage also has groomed ice-skating ponds; Westchester Lagoon has more than a kilometer of **skating trails** (p. 246). At the end of the day, drive 40 miles to the **Hotel Alyeska** (p. 258) in Girdwood for the night. You will find two of Alaska's best restaurants to choose from for dinner, the **Seven Glaciers** (p. 258) and **Double Musky Inn** (p. 258).

Day ❸: Girdwood Downhill Skiing ✦✦✦

Spend the day on the slopes of Alyeska Resort, skiing near sea level, but mostly above the tree line, and with extraordinary ocean views from the slopes and lifts. Those who don't want to ski have

enough to do: sliding at the tube park, swimming in the saltwater pool at the hotel, or skating on the outdoor rink at the base of the mountain.

Day ❹: Girdwood to Fairbanks ✦

Drive to Anchorage and return the car. Your next destination is Fairbanks, 360 miles north, and I don't recommend driving it unless you are experienced on icy highways and prepared for emergencies. The very best way to go is to take the Alaska Railroad, which runs a single-car train once a week from Anchorage to Fairbanks; it's a spectacular and uniquely Alaskan ride, one of America's last flag-stop trains, but it's unlikely that its infrequent schedule will match yours. The most practical route is to fly from

---

Tips   Doubling Up the Seasons

Here's a little-known approach to experiencing the best of Alaska: Arrive in late March and head to Homer, on the south end of the Kenai Peninsula, as an add-on to the above winter itinerary. The community has lengthy and spectacular cross-country ski trails that usually have plenty of snow all month. At the same time, salmon fishing gets started in March in the waters of Kachemak Bay—there's even a fishing derby joined by hundreds of boats. You can go salmon fishing in the morning and ski in the afternoon! (See "Late March Is Perfect," p. 310.)

Anchorage to Fairbanks and rent another car when you arrive. That will leave you with most of the day to explore the town. Be sure to stop at the **UA Museum of the North** (p. 392).

Day ❺: Fairbanks Ice Carving ⟨⟩

If you have timed your visit to see the Fur Rendezvous and Iditarod in Anchorage, you should also be able to see the **World Ice Art Championships** (p. 388) in Fairbanks. This amazing spectacle brings together the best ice carvers to create sculptures from enormous blocks of crystal-clear ice excavated from a Fairbanks pond. Some of the works are the size of a two-story building. Make a point of going for a dog-sled ride while you're here, too, with **Sun Dog Express Dog Sled Tours** (p. 397) or one of the many other operators giving rides; Fairbanks is a center for the sport, with limitless miles of trails in the hilly boreal forest that extends in every direction.

Day ❻: Chena Hot Springs Resort ⟨⟩⟨⟩

Drive a little over an hour into the Bush for a visit to the hot springs, a unique resort that includes them (unique, for example, in that one of the buildings is made entirely of ice), and the rounded mountains of winter in which the resort is nestled. **Chena Hot Springs Resort** (p. 410) has its flaws, but the experience of floating in a pond of hot artesian water on a day when the air around is below zero more than makes up for them. If you want to do more than soak, lots of activities are available, including snowmobiling and dog mushing. After dark, head out for unsurpassed aurora viewing out here, beyond city lights.

Day ❼: Fairbanks

Today you can take one more swim or ski before returning your car in Fairbanks and returning home by air.

4

Cruising Alaska's Coast

by Jerry Brown & Fran Wenograd Golden

Alaska's popularity as a top cruise destination is partly the result of its own natural splendor and partly because of its unavailability for most of the year. Inclement weather dictates that the 49th state is of interest to cruise lines and their passengers essentially only from mid-May to mid-September. Each year, this brief period sees more than 950,000 people take a cruise along its vast and rugged coastline (in fact, in 2008 the number could for the first time hit one million). Cruise passengers visit the towns and wilderness areas of the Southeast (the Inside Passage, also known as the Panhandle) or the Gulf of Alaska by day and burrow into their ships for effortless travel by night. The lack of roads between towns makes the waters of the Inside Passage the region's de facto highway. Your options are, basically, taking cruise ships or the Alaska Marine Highway System (the state ferries). You'd have to be willing to invest more time—both for the actual traveling and for the planning—to utilize the ferries. And you'd have to be willing to give up the comforts and diversions of the average cruise ship. (On the other hand, the ferry *does* give you unlimited stops along the way and a chance to meet Alaskan residents not only in major cruise ports but also in smaller, less-visited communities as well; see "Exploring Southeast Alaska," in chapter 5.) For most people, the luxury of cruise travel is preferable to the rough-and-ready nature of ferry transportation.

But no matter how much revenue cruise passengers (and ships' crews) generate for merchants in the ports visited, some locals aren't as welcoming as they might be. Alaskans are known for their hospitality, but they have their limits (don't we all?). The presence of too many cruise passengers has unquestionably spoiled some of Alaska's quaint places. Once-charming streets are transformed into virtual carnival midways jammed wall-to-wall with vacationers from simultaneous ship landings. As a result, no matter what residents may say, service standards suffer somewhat—especially toward the end of the season when Alaskans have been subjected to a steady stream of strange faces for several months and can get, ahem, a little grumpy.

Some communities feel that the cultural bulldozing brought by cruise ships is not worth the economic benefit and have placed limits on the number of ships that can come in to port or levied new taxes based on the number of people the ships bring. After years of fast growth, the industry, too, has begun talk of a "carrying capacity."

So strident has much of the opposition become that the state legislature last year—after a "yes" vote by the populace on a ballot sponsored by a citizen group called Responsible Cruising for Alaska—imposed a $50 head tax on every passenger carried by the cruise lines. The money is intended to offset the costs incurred by the ports in essential services used by visitors—police, sewage, roadways, and the like. It will be divvied up to the ports proportionately based on the number of ships visiting and passengers carried.

At the same time and as a direct result of the same ballot initiative, the state levied a 33% tax on shipboard casino profits (now *that* really hurts the cruise lines!) and insisted that each ship provide a cabin for a state employee to monitor the ship's pollution abatement practices. The initiative also contains a clause that requires cruise lines to disclose to passengers the commissions they earn from selling the shore excursions provided by local operators.

The initiative seemed to the sponsors—and apparently to the voters—to be a comprehensive "stick it to the cruise lines and make them pay for using our waterways" package. The whole thing has turned into a Pandora's box.

Many in the legislature are unhappy about having to enforce a new voter-written and voter-approved law which they perceive as unenforceable. Some argue that voters were swept up in the rhetoric of the Responsible Cruising for Alaska initiative and did not fully understand the law's impact on the state's economy. The cost of putting a state employee onboard every ship to monitor pollution practices, they say, would be prohibitive. It would require, they say, the addition of at least 80 new inspectors. And what about ports such as Juneau and Ketchikan, which already have their own local head tax on cruise visitors? Are they entitled to a share of the $50 a head as well? Or can they opt out of the local tax in favor of the state payout? Under what conditions? Nobody seems absolutely clear on subjects such as these.

In addition, the disclosure of commissions clause has led a group of tour companies that deal with the cruise lines to sue. Not surprisingly, they don't want their competitors to know how much they are paying to have their products promoted by the ship lines.

Clearly, it seems to some that the initiative needs amending. The trouble is, there's a question about just how much "tweaking" lawmakers are permitted to do. Alaska law states somewhat ambiguously that an independently promoted, voter-approved ballot initiative should be enacted into law—more or less as is. That, at any rate, is the position taken by the good folks at Responsible Cruising for Alaska. Minor amendments, they say, are okay. But the gist of the law must be maintained.

The legislature, of course, is left with the task of fitting all the pieces into the budget. Lawmakers are debating several bills that would soften the terms of the law. But nobody is certain how far they can go.

One move some of them favor is to have the pollution monitors inspect ships only when they dock, rather than traveling with them on every cruise. That would save much of the expense but, of course, doesn't satisfy the initiative's authors who argue that many environmental offences are committed at sea.

The Alaska government isn't all that hot and bothered about the commissions-for-tours disclosure clause. They are prepared to leave it to the courts to sort out. Local tour entrepreneurs not favored by the cruise companies want that part of the law enforced ASAP!

In a nutshell, the ballot proposal has created a bit of a mess. But nobody can deny that it reflects a growing attitude in Alaska—rightly or wrongly—that the cruise industry just isn't a particularly good neighbor.

Right or wrong, the cruise lines are taking the prevailing mood very seriously. Individual lines have appointed community affairs officers with orders to smarten up the public's perception of cruising and cruise operators. And the industry, as a whole, appointed Johne Binkley, a prominent lifelong political figure (he's a former state senator, gubernatorial candidate, chairman of the state-run Alaska Railroad, and much more) as a sort of super-lobbyist to liaise with both the elected officials in Juneau and with the voters who put them in power.

As a visitor, you can avoid much of the human congestion caused by ships by choosing a small-ship cruise that spends more time enjoying the wilderness and the small towns that big ships can't reach. On the small ships you can enjoy Haines, for instance, or Cordova or Metlakatla and a dozen other places the big guys don't (or, at least, seldom) go.

On the other hand, riding a megaship is a different kind of fun—the ship itself is an attraction, with far more amenities than any of the towns along the way. If you need to relax and leave all stresses of life at home behind—and if seeing Alaska wilderness isn't the most important part of your trip—a big ship is the way to go.

Another way to avoid some of the disadvantages of overcrowding and service problems is to choose an early season cruise—say, the last couple of weeks in May. One other option: You can always travel independently after the cruise to the real Alaska, inland from the cruise ports. (For more on the relative benefits of big versus small cruise ships, see "Weighing Your Cruise Options," below.)

In this chapter, we'll go through the cruise options available in the state, focusing primarily on those that provide a true in-depth experience. For even more information, pick up a copy of *Frommer's Alaska Cruises & Ports of Call* (Wiley Publishing, Inc.).

1 Weighing Your Cruise Options

Your three main questions in choosing a cruise in Alaska are "When should I go?" "Where do I want to go?" and "How big a ship?"

WHEN TO GO?

Alaska is very much a seasonal, as opposed to year-round, cruise destination, generally open to cruising from May through September (although some smaller ships start up in late Apr). May and September are considered the shoulder season, and lower brochure rates are offered during these months (and more aggressive discounts as well; watch your local newspaper and check the Internet). Cruising in May can be extremely pleasant—the real, near gridlock-inducing crowds have yet to arrive. Locals, coming off what is usually a fairly isolated winter, are friendlier than they are later in the season, when they're tired and, frankly, pretty much ready to see the tourists go home. There is also the statistical fact that May in the Inside Passage ports is one of the driest months in the season. Late September, though, also offers the advantage of fewer fellow tourists clogging the ports. The warmest months are June, July, and August, with temperatures generally around 50° to 80°F (10°–27°C) during the day, and cooler at night. In the past couple of years, the temperature soared even higher (when temperatures reached 90°F (32°C) in Juneau in the summer of 2004, there was much local speculation about global warming). You may not need a parka, but you will need to bring along some outerwear—a sweater or two, for instance, and maybe a rain slicker. June 21 is the longest day of the year, with the sky lit virtually all night. June tends to be drier than July and August, and April and May are drier than September (though in early Apr you may encounter freezing rain and other vestiges of winter). Somebody once said, "Everybody complains about the weather but nobody does anything about it." And that's very much the way it is in Alaska. The simple fact is that in Alaska, perhaps more than in many other states, the weather is going to do what it's going to do. We've both been forced to don a heavy coat and gloves on more than one occasion over the years in July and August—theoretically the months in which one might expect higher temperatures. On the other hand, we've also been comfortable in short sleeves on deck in Glacier Bay in September—when, again theoretically, it should be a little cooler. And Jerry once ran into such wind-driven rain in Skagway that you'd have thought the moisture was moving horizontally. A year or so later, in the same town, in the same month, he suffered a mild sunburn. In other words, be prepared for anything.

If you are considering traveling in a shoulder month, keep in mind that some shops don't open until Memorial Day, and the visitor season is generally considered over on Labor Day (although cruise lines operate well into Sept).

INSIDE PASSAGE OR THE GULF OF ALASKA?

The Inside Passage runs through the area of Alaska known as Southeast (which the locals also call "the Panhandle"), that narrow strip of the state—islands, mainland coastal communities, and mountains—that runs from the Canadian border in the south to the start of the Gulf in the north, just above the Juneau/Haines/Skagway area. The islands on the western side of the area afford cruise ships a welcome degree of protection from the sea and its attendant rough waters (hence the name "Inside Passage"). Because of that shelter, such ports as Ketchikan, Wrangell, Petersburg, and others are reached with less rocking and rolling, and thus less risk of seasickness. Sitka is not on the Inside Passage (it's on the ocean side of Baranof Island) but that beautiful little community, with its Russian heritage, is included in most Inside Passage cruise itineraries.

Southeast encompasses the capital city, **Juneau,** and townships influenced by the former Russian presence in the state (**Sitka,** for instance), the Tlingit and Haida Native cultures (**Ketchikan**), and the great gold rush of 1898 (**Skagway**). It is a land of rainforests, mountains, inlets, and glaciers (including Margerie, Johns Hopkins, Muir, and the others contained within the boundaries of **Glacier Bay National Park**). The region is rich in wildlife, especially of the marine variety. It is a scenic delight. But then, what part of Alaska isn't?

The other major cruising area is the **Southcentral** region's Gulf of Alaska, usually referred to by the cruise lines as the "Glacier Discovery Route" or the "Voyage of the Glaciers," or some such catchy title. "Gulf of Alaska," after all, sounds pretty bland.

The coastline of the Gulf is that arc of land from just north of Glacier Bay to the Kenai Peninsula. Southcentral also takes in the truly spectacular **Prince William Sound; the Cook Inlet,** on the northern side of the peninsula; **Anchorage,** Alaska's biggest city; the year-round **Alyeska Resort** at Girdwood, 40 miles from Anchorage; the **Matanuska** and **Susitna** valleys (the "Mat-Su"), a fertile agricultural region renowned for the record size of some of its produce; and part of the Alaska Mountain Range.

The principal Southcentral terminus ports are **Seward** or **Whittier** for Anchorage. No ships in regular Alaska pattern actually head for Anchorage proper, instead carrying passengers from Seward or Whittier to Anchorage by bus or train. (Getting all the way around the peninsula to Anchorage would add a day to the cruise.) Let us stress that going on a Gulf cruise does not mean that you don't visit any of the Inside Passage. The big difference is that, whereas the more popular Inside Passage cruise itineraries run round-trip to and from Vancouver or Seattle, the Gulf routing is one-way—northbound and southbound—between Vancouver and Seward or Vancouver and Whittier. A typical Gulf itinerary also visits such Inside Passage ports as **Ketchikan, Juneau, Sitka,** and/or **Skagway.**

The Gulf's glaciers are quite dazzling and every bit as spectacular as their counterparts to the south. **College Fjord,** for instance, is lined with glaciers—16 of them, each one grander than the last. On a 2005 cruise, Fran saw incredible calving at **Harvard Glacier** with chunks of 400- and 500-year-old ice falling off and crashing into the water with thunderous sounds every few minutes (worries about global warming aside, the sight was spectacular). Another favorite part of a Gulf cruise, though, is the visit to the gigantic **Hubbard Glacier**—at 6 miles, Alaska's longest—at the head of Yakutat Bay (our all-time favorite, by the way!).

Not to raise again the specter of global warming but, sadly, most of Alaska's glaciers are in retreat, some receding quite rapidly. On a visit to Sawyer Glacier last year, it appeared that the ice face had gone so far back that the ship was unable to get closer than a mile or so. Not the best way to view a glacier.

Cruisetours combine a cruise with a land tour, either before or after the cruise. Typical packages link the cruise with a 3- to 5-night Anchorage/Denali/Fairbanks tour, a 4- to 7-night Yukon tour (which visits Anchorage, Denali, and Fairbanks on the way), or a 5- to 7-night tour of the Canadian Rockies. Holland America, Princess, and Royal Caribbean/Celebrity lead the big-ship cruisetour market. Cruise West leads by a wide margin in the small-ship category. Even if you book with another cruise line, chances are that at least some portions of your land tour will be bought from one of these operators.

BIG SHIP OR SMALL?

Imagine an elephant. Now imagine your pet pug dog, Sparky. That's about the size difference between your options in the Alaska market: behemoth modern ships and small, more exploratory coastal vessels.

SMALL SHIPS Just as big cruise ships are mostly for people who want every resort amenity, **small** or **alternative ships** are best suited for people who prefer a casual, crowd-free cruise experience that gives passengers a chance to get up close and personal with Alaska's natural surroundings and wildlife. Small ships offer little in terms of amenities: They usually have small cabins, only one lounge/bar and dining room, and no exercise facilities, entertainment, or organized activities. There are little or no stabilizers on most of these smaller ships, and the ride can be bumpy in open water—which isn't much of a problem on Inside Passage itineraries, since most of the cruising area is protected from sea waves. They are also difficult for travelers with disabilities, as only three (Cruise West's *Spirit of '98* and *Spirit of Oceanus,* and Majestic America Line's *Empress of the North*) have elevators. Despite all of this, they're universally more expensive than the big ships and offer fewer discounts. That's the minus side.

But a big plus, thanks to their smaller size, is that these ships can go places that larger ships can't, such as narrow fjords, uninhabited islands, and smaller ports that cater mostly to small fishing vessels. Due to their shallow draft, they can nose right up to sheer cliff faces, bird rookeries, bobbing icebergs, and cascading waterfalls that you can literally reach out and touch. Also, sea animals are not as intimidated by these ships, so you might find yourself having a rather close encounter with a humpback whale, or watching other sea mammals bobbing in the ship's wake. The decks on these ships are closer to the waterline, too, giving passengers a more intimate view than they would get from the high decks of the large cruise ships. Some of these ships stop at ports on a daily basis, like the larger ships, while some avoid ports almost entirely, exploring natural areas instead. Small ships also have the flexibility to change direction

> ### *Tips* Sick Ships
>
> Every year, hundreds of cruise-ship passengers and plenty of visitors on shore come down with vomiting and diarrhea caused by a bug now known as the norovirus. The good news is it's rarer in summer than winter. Still, the illness is no fun. It lasts a day or two and is rarely serious, although some passengers do end up in the hospital because of dehydration. The virus is extremely contagious from the first symptoms until at least 3 days and up to 2 weeks after it clears up. Touching a contaminated handrail and then your face is enough to catch it. To minimize your chances of contracting the virus, wash your hands frequently, drink bottled water, and avoid eating raw food onboard, especially shellfish. The Centers for Disease Control and Prevention (CDC) also recommended in 1998 that passengers 65 and older or those with chronic illnesses check with their doctors before taking a cruise. The CDC website (www.cdc.gov/nceh/vsp) posts sanitation inspection scores for each ship. Type "norovirus" into their search page to find a fact sheet.

as opportunities arise—say, to go where whales have been sighted and to linger awhile once a sighting's been made.

Visitors aboard large ships may not see much of the real, natural Alaska unless they do some of the more remote shore excursions, such is the disjunction between the glitzy modern ships and the real world outside. Visitors aboard small ships will not have hotel-like accommodations and entertainment, but will get an experience that's many times more intimate, allowing them to really get in touch with the place they've come to see. Choose your ship accordingly.

BIG SHIPS   The **big ships** in the Alaska market fall generally into two categories: midsize ships and megaships. Carrying as many as 2,670 passengers, the **megaships** look and feel like floating resorts. Big on glitz, they offer loads of activities, attract many families and (especially in Alaska) seniors, offer a large number of public rooms (including fancy casinos and fully equipped gyms), and provide a wide variety of meal and entertainment options. And though they may feature 1 or 2 formal nights per trip, the ambience is generally casual. The Alaska vessels of the Carnival, Celebrity, Princess, and Royal Caribbean fleets all fit in this category, as does Norwegian Cruise Line's *Spirit, Sun, Star,* and *Pearl,* and Holland America's *Oosterdam* and *Westerdam.* **Midsize ships** in Alaska fall into two segments: the ultraluxurious, such as Regent Seven Seas' *Seven Seas Mariner* and *Silver Shadow,* and the modern midsize, such as the *Veendam, Ryndam, Amsterdam, Volendam, Zaandam,* and *Statendam* of Holland America Line, and the *Tahitian Princess* of Princess Cruises. In general, the size of these ships is less significant than the general onboard atmosphere. Both the midsize ships and the megaships have a great range of facilities for passengers. Cabins on these ships range from cubbyholes to large suites, depending on the ship and the type of cabin you book. Big dining rooms and a tremendous variety of cuisines are the norm. These ships carry a lot of people and can, at times, feel crowded.

The sizes of these big ships also come with **three major drawbacks** for passengers: (1) They can't sail into narrow passages or shallow-water ports, (2) their size and inflexible schedules limit their ability to stop or even slow down when wildlife is spotted, and

(3) when their passengers disembark in a town, they tend to overwhelm it, limiting your ability to get insight into the real Alaska communities. But on the plus side, they offer dozens of excursions at each port so you can get well out of town.

2 The Best Cruise Experiences in Alaska

Cruise lines are in the business of giving their guests a good time, so they've all got something going for them. Here are our picks for Alaska's best, in a few different categories.

- **The Best Ships for Luxury:** Luxury in Alaska is defined in 2008 by **Regent Seven Seas** and **Silversea.** If you want a more casual kind of luxury (a really nice ship with a no-tie-required policy), the *Seven Seas Mariner* offers just that on an all-suite vessel (most cabins have private balconies) with excellent cuisine. Silversea, on the other hand, represents a slick, Italian-influenced luxury experience with all the perks—big suite cabins and excellent food, linens, and companions. Both lines include fine wine and booze in their cruise fares. For the ultimate Alaska experience in a small-ship setting, check out the yachts of American Safari Cruises, where soft adventure comes with luxury accoutrements.
- **The Best of the Mainstream Ships:** Every line's most recent ships are beautiful, but **Celebrity's** *Infinity* is a true stunner, as is sister ship *Millennium.* These modern vessels, with their extensive art collections, cushy public rooms, and expanded spa areas, give Celebrity a formidable presence in Alaska. And the late-model *Sapphire Princess* and *Diamond Princess* have raised the art of building big ships to new heights. Both of these vessels will again be in Inside Passage service this year from Vancouver.
- **The Best of the Small Ships:** **Cruise West** is the most prominent small-ship player, now that Clipper and Glacier Bay Cruiseline have vanished from the scene. Our favorite of the fleet is the *Spirit of '98,* which has the cool hook of looking and feeling like a Victorian steamship (although it was built in 1984).
- **The Best Ships for Families:** All the major lines have well-established kids' programs. **Holland America** and **Norwegian Cruise Line** win points in Alaska for their special shore excursions for kids and teens, and **Carnival** gets a nod for offering shore excursions for teens.
- **The Best Ships for Pampering:** It's a toss-up—**Celebrity's** *Infinity* and *Millennium* offer wonderful AquaSpas complete with thalassotherapy pools and a wealth of soothing and beautifying treatments, and the solariums on **Royal Caribbean's** *Rhapsody of the Seas, Serenade of the Seas,* and *Radiance of the Seas* offer relaxing indoor-pool retreats.
- **The Best Shipboard Cuisine: Regent Seven Seas** is tops in this category. Of the mainstream lines, **Celebrity** is the best, though recently the line dropped its consulting French chef Michel Roux, so changes may be afoot. Dinner in the reservations-only specialty restaurants on both the *Infinity* and the *Millennium* ($30 service charge per person) is a world-class dining experience. And there are signs of a new and rather surprising challenger for the cuisine award: **Carnival,** which has upgraded both its main dining room and buffet offerings. The line's *Carnival Spirit* in Alaska boasts the Nouveau Supper Club ($30 service charge per person), where you can enjoy just about as fine a meal as you're likely to find anywhere. The expertly prepared and presented cuisine on **Silversea's** *Silver Shadow* must also come in for some props.

- **The Best Ships for Onboard Activities:** The ships operated by **Carnival** and **Royal Caribbean** offer a very full roster of onboard activities that range from the sublime (lectures) to the ridiculous (contests designed to get passengers to do or say outrageous things). **Princess's** ScholarShip@Sea program is a real winner, with excitingly packaged classes in such diverse subjects as photography, personal computers, cooking, and pottery (they even recently added scrapbooking to the roster).
- **The Best Ships for Entertainment:** Look to the big ships here. **Carnival** and **Royal Caribbean** are tops when it comes to an overall package of show productions, nightclub acts, lounge performances, and audience-participation entertainment. **Princess** also offers particularly well-done—if somewhat less lavishly staged—shows. **Holland America** has not, historically, been noted for its entertainment package, but the company has improved considerably in that department in recent years.
- **The Best Ships for Whale-Watching:** If the whales come close enough, you can see them from all the ships in Alaska. Smaller ships, though—such as those operated by **American Safari, Lindblad,** and **Cruise West**—might actually change course to follow a whale. Get your cameras ready!
- **The Best Ships for Cruisetours: Princess, Holland America,** and the twin-brand Royal Caribbean Cruises (which owns **Royal Caribbean International** and **Celebrity**) are the market leaders in getting you into the Interior of Alaska either before or after your cruise. They own their own deluxe motorcoaches and railcars. Princess and Holland America Line (HAL) also own lodges and hotels. After many years in the business, these two really know what they're doing. Royal Caribbean is a comparative latecomer but its land company, Royal Celebrity Tours, with some of the finest rolling stock (rail and road) around, has made huge strides. Most of the other lines actually buy their land product components from Princess or HAL. One of Holland America's strengths is its 3- and 4-night cruises combined with an Alaska/Yukon land package. The company offers exclusive entry into the Yukon's Kluane National Park, and they've added another Yukon gem—Tombstone Territorial Park, near Dawson City, a region of staggering wilderness beauty, Native architecture, stunning vistas, and wildlife. Princess is arguably stronger in 7-night Gulf of Alaska cruises in conjunction with Denali/Fairbanks or Kenai Peninsula land arrangements. Princess's Copper River Lodge is by the entrance to Wrangell–St. Elias National Park.
- **The Best Ports:** Juneau and Skagway are our favorites. Juneau is one of the most visually pleasing small cities anywhere and certainly the prettiest capital city in America. It's fronted by the Gastineau Channel and backed by Mount Juneau and Mount Roberts, offers the very accessible Mendenhall Glacier, and is otherwise surrounded by wilderness—and it's a really fun city to visit, too. As for Skagway, no town in Alaska is more historically significant, and the old buildings are so perfect you might think you stepped into a Disney version of what a gold-rush town should look like. If, that is, you can get over the decidedly turn-of-the-millennium Starbucks operation in the Mercantile Center and all the tourist shops (fortunately some of the jewelry stores including Little Switzerland that followed cruise passengers from the Caribbean have pulled up stakes and moved on). There are people who will tell you that Skagway is hokey and touristy—and it is. But if you can get yourself into the right frame of mind, and if you can recall the history of the place—the gold-rush frenzy that literally put the town on the map—it's easier to

capture the true spirit of Skagway. The residents have made every effort to retain as much as possible of the architecture and historic significance of their community, and they don't mind sharing it with visitors during the cruise season. For a more low-key Alaska experience, take the ferry from Skagway to Haines, which reminds us of the folksy, frontier Alaska depicted on the TV show *Northern Exposure,* and is a great place to spot eagles and other wildlife. Some ships also stop at Haines as a port of call, usually for a few hours after Skagway.

- **The Best Shore Excursions:** Flightseeing and helicopter trips in Alaska are absolutely unforgettable ways to check out the scenery if you can afford them. But airborne tours tend to be pretty pricey—sometimes approaching $600 a head. A helicopter trip to a dog-sled camp at the top of a glacier (usually the priciest of the offerings) affords both incredibly pretty views and a chance to try your hand at the truly Alaskan sport of dog sledding. (Yes, even in summer: The sleds are fitted with wheels.) It's a great way to earn bragging rights with the folks back home. For a less extravagant excursion, nothing beats a ride on a clear day on the White Pass and Yukon Route Railway out of Skagway to Canada—the route followed by the gold stampeders of '98. Last year the railway expanded its rail system to go not just to Fraser at the border but all the way to Carcross (also known as Caribou Cross) in the Yukon Territory (adding more than 30 miles by rebuilding old track). While you're riding the rails, try to imagine what it was like for those gold seekers crossing the same track on foot! And we also like to get active with kayak and mountain-biking excursions offered by most lines at most ports. In addition to affording a chance to work off those shipboard calories, these excursions typically provide optimum opportunities for spotting eagles, bears, seals, and other wildlife. Another, less hectic shore excursion that goes down well with many passengers is a float ride down one of the more placid stretches of Alaska's myriad rivers, such as the Kenai, the Mendenhall, or the Chilkat. These outings don't involve a lot of paddling—which can be hard work—but instead use the natural flow of the river to propel the four- to six-person rubber raft downstream. And they involve little or no whitewater. Generally, the group will stop for a picnic lunch en route and return to the staging area by motorcoach or automobile.

3 Booking Your Cruise

Every cruise line has a brochure full of beautiful glossy photos. You'll see low starting rates on the charts, but look further and you'll realize those are for tiny inside cubicles; most of the cabins sell for much more. Sometimes the brochures feature published rates that are nothing more than a pie-in-the-sky wish (most customers will pay less). We strongly suggest you look at the early-bird savings column and book your cruise early (by mid-Feb for average savings of 25%–30% and sometimes as much as 50%). In reality, you may be able to get the cruise for 40% or 50% off at the last minute. But here's the problem with waiting: Alaska right now is hot, hot, hot. Sure, you may be able to save by taking your chances, but if you don't reserve space early, you may also be left out in the cold. Keep in mind that the most expensive and the cheapest cabins tend to sell out first. The midrange rooms are by and large the last to go. Increasingly aggressive marketing by the cruise lines to previous passengers is adding to the increase in early bookings.

Most people still book their cruises through **travel agents** and, though the **Internet** has knocked some of those agents out of business, most traditional travel agencies have created their own websites in an effort to keep pace.

Shore Excursions: The What, When & Why

Shore excursions offered by the cruise lines provide a chance for you to get off the ship and explore the sights close up, taking in the history, nature, and culture of the region—from exploring gold-rush-era streets to experiencing Native Alaskan traditions such as totem carving.

Some excursions are of the walking-tour or bus-tour variety, but many others are activity oriented: Cruise passengers have the opportunity to go sea kayaking, mountain-biking, horseback riding, salmon fishing, and even rock climbing or zip-lining through the treetops, and to see the sights by seaplane or helicopter—and maybe even to land on a glacier and go for a walk. Occasionally, with some of the smaller cruise lines, you'll find quirky excursions, such as a visit with local artists in their studios. Some lines even offer scuba diving and snorkeling. The cruise lines vet the operators, so you do get assurance you're dealing with pros.

With some lines, shore excursions are included in your cruise fare, but with most lines they are an added (though very worthwhile) expense.

So which is the better way to book a cruise these days? The answer can be both. If you're computer savvy, have a good handle on all the elements that go into a cruise, and have narrowed down the choices to a few cruise lines that appeal to you, websites are a great way to trawl the seas at your own pace and check out last-minute deals, which can be dramatic. On the other hand, you'll barely get a stitch of personalized service searching for and booking a cruise online. If you need help getting a refund or arranging special meals or other matters, or deciding which cabin to choose, you're on your own. In addition, agents usually know about cruise and airfare discounts that the lines won't necessarily publicize on their websites. So the best bet, to our way of thinking, is to do your research electronically and, better informed, then visit a travel agent to make the reservation.

BOOKING A SMALL-SHIP CRUISE

The small-ship companies in Alaska—American Safari, Cruise West, Lindblad Expeditions, and Majestic America Line—all offer real niche-oriented cruise experiences, attracting passengers who have a very good idea of the kind of experience they want (usually educational and/or adventurous, and always casual and small scale). In many cases, a large percentage of passengers on any given cruise will have sailed with the line before. Because of all this, and because the passenger capacity of these small ships is so low (12–235), in general you're not going to find the kind of deep discounts you do with the large ships. Still, for the most part, these lines rely on agents to handle their bookings, taking very few reservations directly. All of the lines have a list of agents with whom they do considerable business, and they can hook you up with an agent if you call (or e-mail) and ask for an agent near you.

BOOKING A MAINSTREAM CRUISE

If you don't know a good travel agent already, try to find one through your friends, preferably those who have cruised before. For the most personal service, look for an agent in your local area, and for the most knowledgeable service, look for an agent who has cruising experience. It's perfectly okay to ask an agent questions about his or her personal knowledge of the product, such as whether he or she has ever cruised in

Alaska or with one of the lines you're considering. The easiest way to be sure the agent is experienced in booking cruises is to work with a **cruise-only agency** (meaning that the whole agency specializes in cruises) or to find somebody in a more conventional agency who is a **cruise specialist** (meaning he or she handles that agency's cruise business). If you are calling a full-service travel agency, ask for the **cruise desk,** which is where you'll find these specialists. If the agency doesn't have a cruise desk, per se, it might be wise to check elsewhere.

A good and easy rule of thumb to maximize your chances of finding an agent who has cruise experience and who won't rip you off is to book with agencies that are members of the **Cruise Lines International Association** (CLIA; ℂ **212/921-0066;** www.cruising.org) or the **National Association of Cruise Oriented Agencies** (NACOA; ℂ **305/663-5626;** www.nacoaonline.com/introduction.htm). Member agencies of both groups are comprised either entirely of cruise specialists, or employ at least some cruise specialists. Membership in the **American Society of Travel Agents** (ASTA; ℂ **800/275-2782;** www.astanet.com) assures that the agency is monitored for ethical practices, although it does not designate cruise experience.

You can tap into the Internet sites of these organizations for easy access to agents in your area.

THE COST: WHAT'S INCLUDED & WHAT'S NOT

However you arrange to buy your cruise, what you basically have in hand at the end is a contract for transportation, lodging, dining, entertainment, housekeeping, and assorted other miscellaneous services that will be provided to you over the course of your vacation. It's important, though, to remember what extras are *not* included in your cruise fare. Are you getting a price that includes port charges, taxes, fees, and insurance, or are you getting a cruise-only fare? Are airfare and airport transfers included, or do you have to book them separately (either as an add-on to the cruise fare or on your own)? Make sure you're comparing apples with apples when making price comparisons. Read the fine print!

Aside from **airfare,** which is usually not included in your cruise fare (see more on air arrangements below), the priciest addition to your cruise fare, particularly in Alaska, will likely be **shore excursions.** Ranging from about $30 for a bus tour to $299 and up (sometimes as high as $600) for a lengthy helicopter or seaplane flightseeing excursion, these sightseeing tours are designed to help cruise passengers make the most of their time at the ports the ship visits, but they can add a hefty sum to your vacation costs.

You'll also want to add to your calculations **tips for the ship's crew.** Tips are given at the end of the cruise, and passengers should reserve at least $10 per passenger per day for tips for the room steward, waiter, and busperson. (In practice, we find that most people tend to give a little more.) Additional tips to other personnel, such as the head waiter or maitre d', are at your discretion. On small ships, all tips often go into one pot, which the crew divides up after the cruise.

Most ships charge extra for **alcoholic beverages** (including wine at dinner) and for soda. Nonbubbly soft drinks, such as lemonade and iced tea, are included in your cruise fare. (Regent's *Seven Seas Mariner* and Silversea's *Silver Shadow* both include alcoholic beverages in the cruise price.) You'll also want to set some money aside for optional offerings such as spa treatments, fancy dinners in your ship's alternative dining room (which may carry a price tag of up to $30 per person), shipboard photos, Internet access, and other temptations.

MONEY-SAVING STRATEGIES

Cruise pricing is a fluid medium, and there are a number of strategies you can use to save money off the booking price.

EARLY & LATE BOOKING

The best way to save on an Alaska cruise is to **book in advance.** In a typical year, lines offer early-bird rates, usually 25% to 30% off the brochure rate, to those who book their Alaska cruise by mid- to late February of the year of the cruise. If the cabins do not fill up by the cutoff date, the early-bird rate may be extended, but it may be slightly lower—say, a 15% or 20% savings. Starting prices we've seen for 2008 are around $699 for an inside cabin on an early season weeklong cruise.

If the cabins are still not full as the cruise season begins, cruise lines typically start marketing special deals, usually through their top-producing travel agents. It's our feeling that in 2008, these last-minute discounts, which can run as high as 50%, will be less common than in some previous years. And keep in mind that last-minute deals are usually for a very limited selection of cabins. Planning your Alaska cruise vacation well in advance and taking advantage of early booking discounts is still the best way to go.

SHOULDER SEASON DISCOUNTS

You can save by booking a cruise in the **shoulder months of May or September,** when cruise pricing is lower than during the high summer months. Typically, Alaska cruises are divided into budget, low, economy, value, standard, and peak seasons, but since these overlap quite a bit from cruise line to cruise line, we can lump them into three basic periods:

1. **Budget/Low/Economy Season:** May and September
2. **Value/Standard Season:** Early June and late August
3. **Peak Season:** Late June, July, and early to mid-August

DISCOUNTS FOR THIRD & FOURTH PASSENGERS & GROUPS

Most ships offer highly discounted rates for third and fourth passengers sharing a cabin with two full-fare passengers, even if those two have booked at a discounted rate. It may mean a tight squeeze, but it'll save you a bundle. Some lines offer **special rates for kids,** usually on a seasonal or select-sailings basis, that may include free or discounted airfare.

One of the best ways to get a cruise deal is to book as a **group** of at least 16 people in at least eight cabins. The savings include a discounted rate, and at least the cruise portion of the 16th ticket will be free. Ask your travel agent about any group deals they may offer.

SENIOR DISCOUNTS

Seniors may be able to get extra savings on their cruise. Some lines will take 5% off the top for those 55 and up, and the senior rate applies even if the second person in the cabin is younger. Membership in groups such as AARP is not required, but such membership may bring additional savings.

BOOKING AIR TRAVEL THROUGH THE CRUISE LINE

Except during special promotions, airfare to the port of embarkation is rarely included in the cruise rates, so you'll have to purchase airfare on your own or take advantage of the cruise lines' air add-ons, which is usually a better option. Why? First of all, as frequent customers of the airlines, cruise lines tend to get decent (if not the best) discounts on airfare, which they pass on to their customers. Second, booking air with the cruise line allows the line to keep track of your whereabouts. If your plane is late, for instance, they may hold the boat, though not always. When you book air travel with your cruise line, most lines will include **transfers** from the airport to the ship, saving you the hassle of getting a cab. (If you do book the air travel on your own, you may still be able to get the transfers separately—ask your agent about this.) Be aware that once the air ticket is issued by the cruise line, you usually aren't allowed to make changes. The only times it may pay to book your own air transportation are if you are using frequent-flier miles and can get your air travel for free, or if you are particular about which carrier you fly or which route you take.

CHOOSING YOUR CABIN

Cruise-ship cabins run from tiny boxes with accordion doors and bunk beds to palatial multiroom suites with hot tubs on the balcony. Which is right for you? Price will likely be a big factor here, but so should the vacation style you prefer. If, for instance, you plan to spend a lot of quiet time in your cabin, you should probably consider booking the biggest room you can afford. If, conversely, you plan to be out on deck all the time checking out the glaciers and wildlife, you might be just as happy with a smaller (and cheaper) cabin to crash in at the end of the day. Cabins are either **inside** (without a window or porthole) or **outside** (with), the latter being more expensive. On the big ships, the more deluxe outside cabins may also come with **private verandas.** The cabins are usually described by price (highest to lowest), category (suite, deluxe, superior, standard, economy, and others), and furniture configuration ("sitting area with two lower beds," for example).

SPECIAL MENU REQUESTS

The cruise line should be informed at the time you make your reservations about any special dietary requests you have. Some lines offer kosher menus, and all will have vegetarian, low-fat, low-salt, vegan, and sugar-free options available.

4 The Small-Ship Cruise Lines

Small ships allow you to see Alaska from sea level, without the kind of distractions you get aboard the big ships—no glitzy interiors, no big shows or loud music, no casinos, no spas, and no crowds, as the largest of these ships carries only 235 passengers. You're immersed in the 49th state from the minute you wake up to the minute you fall asleep, and, for the most part, you're left alone to form your own opinions. Personally, we feel that despite these ships' higher cost, they provide, by far, the better cruise experience for those who really want to get the feel of Alaska.

Small-ship itineraries can be categorized as **port-to-port,** meaning they mimic the larger ships in simply sailing between port towns; **soft-adventure,** meaning they provide some outdoors experiences such as hiking and kayaking, while not requiring participants to be trained athletes; and **active-adventure,** meaning the hiking and kayaking will be the real focus of the trip, and may be strenuous.

On all of these types of cruises, the small-ship experience tends toward education rather than glitzy entertainment. You'll likely get **informal and informative lectures** and sometimes video presentations on Alaska wildlife, history, and Native culture. Meals are served in open seatings, so you can sit where and with whom you like, and time spent huddled on the outside decks scanning for whales fosters great camaraderie among passengers.

Cabins on these ships don't generally offer TVs or telephones, and they tend to be very small and sometimes spartan (see the individual reviews below for exceptions). There are no stabilizers on most of these smaller ships, so the ride can be bumpy in rough seas. Cruise West's *Spirit of '98* and *Spirit of Oceanus* and Majestic America Line's *Empress of the North* have elevators, but in general the small ships are not good choices for travelers who require the use of wheelchairs or have other mobility problems.

AMERICAN SAFARI CRUISES

19101 36th Ave. W., Suite 201, Lynnwood, WA 98036. ℭ 888/862-8881. Fax 425/776-8889. www.amsafari.com.

American Safari Cruises promises an intimate, all-inclusive yacht cruise to some of the more out-of-the-way stretches of the Inside Passage—and it succeeds admirably. The price is considerable—but so is the pampering. The vessels carry between 12 and 22 guests, guaranteeing unparalleled flexibility, intimacy, and privacy. Once passenger interests become apparent, the expedition leader shapes the cruise around them. Black-bear aficionados can chug off in a Zodiac boat for a better look, active adventurers can explore the shoreline in one of the yacht's four kayaks, and slacker travelers can relax aboard ship. A crew-to-passenger ratio of about one to two ensures that a cold drink, a good meal, or a sharp eagle-spotting eye is always nearby on the line's comfortable 120-foot ships. The ships offer 7- and 8-night Inside Passage itineraries.

PASSENGER PROFILE   Passengers, almost always couples, tend to be more than comfortably wealthy and range from 45 to 65 years of age. Most hope to get close to nature without sacrificing luxury. Dress is always casual, with comfort being the prime goal.

SHIPS   More private yachts than cruise ships, the 22-passenger *Safari Quest,* the 12-passenger *Safari Spirit,* and the 12-passenger *Safari Escape* look like Ferraris—all sleek, contoured lines and dark glass. Cabins are comfortable, and sitting rooms are intimate and luxurious, almost as if they had been transported whole from a spacious suburban home. A big-screen TV in the main lounge forms a natural center for impromptu lectures during the day and movie-watching at night. A shipboard chef assails guests with multiple-course meals and clever snacks, barters with nearby fishing boats for the catch of the day, and raids local markets for the freshest fruits and vegetables—say, strawberries the size of a cub's paw and potent strains of basil and cilantro. **Sample rates per person:** Lowest-price outside cabin from $612 per day for the *Safari Escape;* no inside cabins or suites.

CRUISE WEST

2301 5th Ave., Suite 401, Seattle, WA 98121. ℭ 800/426-7702 or 206/441-8687. Fax 206/441-4757. www.cruisewest.com.

Cruise West is the largest operator of small ships in Alaska, offering itineraries in various areas of Alaska, friendly service, and a casual onboard atmosphere. Like all small ships, Cruise West's ships can navigate in tight areas such as Misty Fjords and Desolation Sound, visit tiny ports such as Petersburg and Haines, and scoot up close to shore for wildlife-watching. But these are not adventure cruises. These vacations are for people who want to visit Alaska's coastal communities and see its wilderness areas up close and in a relaxed, comfortable, small-scale environment without big-ship distractions.

The operative words here are *casual, relaxed,* and *friendly.* At sea, the lack of organized activities on the line's port-to-port itineraries leaves you free to scan for wildlife, peruse the natural sights, or read a book. In port—whether one of the large, popular ports or a less-visited one—the line arranges some novel, intimate shore excursions, such as a visit with local artists at their homes outside Haines or an educational walking tour led by a Native guide in Ketchikan. All excursions are included in the price.

Ships sail a 4-night Glacier Bay cruise, between Juneau and Glacier Bay; a 3-night Prince William Sound cruise from Whittier; an 8-night Inside Passage cruise; an 11-night Coastal Odyssey cruise, between Vancouver and Whittier; and a 13-night Bering Sea cruise between Anchorage and Yanrakynnot (Russia).

PASSENGER PROFILE   Cruise West passengers tend to be older (typically around 60–75), financially stable, well educated, and independent minded—folks who want to visit Alaska's ports and see its natural wonders in a relaxed, dress-down atmosphere.

SHIPS   The 96-passenger *Spirit of '98,* a replica of a 19th-century steamship, carries its Victorian flavor so well that fully two-thirds of the people we met onboard thought the ship had been a private yacht at the turn of the 20th century. If you use a wheelchair or otherwise have mobility problems, note that the *'98* is one of only three small ships in Alaska that has an elevator. (The line's *Spirit of Oceanus* and Majestic America Line's *Empress of the North* being the others.) The 78-passenger *Spirit of Alaska* and *Spirit of Columbia* and 84-passenger *Spirit of Discovery* are all spartan ships, designed to get passengers into small ports and allow them to see the state up close. The 102-passenger *Spirit of Endeavour* and the recently added 128-passenger *Spirit of Yorktown* (formerly Yorktown Clipper), on the other hand, offer high levels of small-ship comfort among small ships in Alaska. The line's 114-passenger *Spirit of Oceanus,* the former *Renaissance V* of Renaissance Cruises, is the line's most luxurious ship, able to sail more far-flung itineraries. **Sample rates per person:** Lowest-price inside cabin $389 for a 4-night cruise; lowest-price outside cabin $563 for an 8-night cruise.

LINDBLAD EXPEDITIONS

96 Morton St., 9th Floor, New York, NY 10014. ℃ **800/397-3348** or 212/765-7740. Fax 212/265-3770. www. expeditions.com.

Lindblad Expeditions specializes in environmentally sensitive, soft-adventure vacations that are explorative and informal in nature, designed to appeal to the intellectually curious traveler seeking a cruise that's educational as well as relaxing. Days aboard are spent learning about the Alaskan outdoors from high-caliber expedition leaders trained in botany, anthropology, biology, and geology, and observing the world around you either from the ship or during shore excursions, which are included in the cruise package. Educational films and slide presentations aboard ship precede nature hikes and quick jaunts aboard Zodiac boats. Flexibility and spontaneity are keys to the experience, as the route may be altered at any time to follow a pod of whales or school of dolphins.

The ships cruise a 12-night itinerary between Juneau and Seattle and an 8-night trip between Juneau and Sitka.

PASSENGER PROFILE   Lindblad Expeditions tends to attract well-traveled and well-educated, professional, 55-and-older couples who have "been there, done that" and are looking for something completely different in a cruise experience.

SHIPS   The 62-passenger *Sea Lion* and *Sea Bird* (built in 1981 and 1982, respectively) are nearly identical and are, in fact, very similar to many of the other small ships in the Alaska market. All are basic vessels built to get you to beautiful spots and feature a minimum of public rooms and conveniences: one dining room, one bar/lounge, and lots of deck space for wildlife and glacier viewing. Cabins are small and functional. **Sample rates per person:** Lowest-price outside cabin $583 per day for a 12-night cruise; no inside cabins or suites.

MAJESTIC AMERICA LINE

2101 4th Ave., Suite 1150, Seattle, WA 98121. (✆) **800/434-1232** or 206/292-9606. Fax 206/340-0975. www.majestic americaline.com.

Carrying 235 passengers, this company's ship, *Empress of the North,* belongs in a whole new, separate category—stern-wheelers. Clearly, the appeal here is the nostalgia. Pure Americana—that's what the *Empress of the North* represents. The ship had a well-publicized accident (it ran aground near Juneau) but was expected to be back in service in 2008. There is not much in the way of organized fun and games. A lecturer accompanies each cruise, offering insights into the passing scenery and cultures. Shore excursions are included in the price, but don't look for kayaks off the back of the vessel, or scuba diving or anything of that nature. The line offers 7- and 11-night Inside Passage cruises.

PASSENGER PROFILE   Not necessarily filthy rich, but probably comfortably off. And they are experienced cruisers.

SHIPS   *Empress of the North,* built in 2003, carries 235 passengers. It has four decks, two lounges, and elevators. The cabins are large by small-ship standards, all have views of the ocean, and 105 out of 112 of the cabins have verandas. Elegance is the byword in public rooms. **Sample rates per person:** Outside cabin from $515 per day for a 7-night cruise; no inside cabins.

5 The Big-Ship Cruise Lines

The ships featured in this section vary in size, age, and offerings, but share the common thread of having more activities and entertainment options than any one person can possibly take in over the course of a cruise. You'll find swimming pools, health clubs, spas, nightclubs, movie theaters, shops, casinos, multiple restaurants, bars, and special kids' playrooms, and, in some cases, sports decks, virtual golf, computer rooms, martini bars, and cigar clubs, as well as quiet spaces where you can get away from it all. In most cases, you'll find lots and lots of onboard activities, including games, contests, classes, and lectures, plus a variety of entertainment options and show productions, some very sophisticated.

CARNIVAL CRUISE LINES

Carnival Place, 3655 NW 87th Ave., Miami, FL 33178-2428. (✆) **800/CARNIVAL.** Fax 305/471-4740. www.carnival.com.

Translating the line's warm-weather experience to Alaska has meant combining the "24-hour orgy of good times" philosophy to include the natural wonders, so you may find yourself bellying up to the rail with a multicolored party drink to gawk at a glacier. Drinking and R-rated comedians are part of the scene, as are "hairy-chest contests" and the like.

Entertainment is among the industry's best, with each ship boasting a dozen dancers, a 10-piece orchestra, comedians, jugglers, and numerous live bands, as well as a big casino. Activity is nonstop. Cocktails begin to flow before lunch, and through the course of the day you can learn to country line-dance or ballroom dance, take cooking lessons, learn to play bridge, watch first-run movies, practice your golf swing by smashing balls into a net, or just eat, drink, shop, and then eat again. Alaska-specific naturalist lectures are delivered daily. In port, Carnival offers **120 shore excursions,** divided into categories of easy, moderate, and adventure. For kids, the line offers Camp Carnival, an expertly run children's program with activities that include Native arts and crafts sessions, lectures conducted by wildlife experts, and special shore excursions for teens.

Carnival's ship in Alaska cruises the Gulf of Alaska route. In May and September, Inside Passage cruises that visit Glacier Bay are offered.

PASSENGER PROFILE   Overall, Carnival has some of the youngest demographics in the industry: mostly under 50, including couples, lots and lots of singles, and a good share of families. It's the same Middle America crowd that can be found in Las Vegas and Atlantic City and at Florida's megaresorts. This is not a sedate, bird-watching crowd. They may want to see whales and icebergs, but they will also dance the Macarena on cue.

SHIPS   The 2,124-passenger megaship *Carnival Spirit* returns to Alaska in 2008. It offers plenty of activities, great pool and hot-tub spaces (some covered for use in chillier weather), a big oceanview gym and spa, and more dining options than your doctor would say is advisable. **Sample rates per person:** Lowest-price inside cabin $115, lowest outside cabin $159, lowest suite $180 per day for an Inside Passage cruise.

CELEBRITY CRUISES
1050 Caribbean Way, Miami, FL 33132. (℅ **800/437-3111** or 305/262-8322. Fax 800/437-5111. www.celebrity cruises.com.

Celebrity Cruises offers a great combination: a classy, tasteful, and luxurious cruise experience at a moderate price—it's definitely the best in the midpriced category. The line's ships are real works of art; the cuisine is above the norm although the line has ended an agreement with famed French chef Michel Roux; the service first-class, friendly, and unobtrusive; and its spa facilities among the best in the business.

A typical day might offer bridge, darts, a culinary art demonstration, a trapshooting competition, a fitness-fashion show, an art auction, a volleyball tournament, and a not-too-shabby stage show. Resident experts give lectures on the various ports of call, the Alaskan environment, glaciers, and Alaskan culture. For children, Celebrity ships employ a group of counselors who direct and supervise a camp-style children's program. Activities are geared toward different age groups. There's an impressive kids' play area and a lounge area for teens.

Celebrity, like sister company Royal Caribbean, visits the tiny port of Icy Straight Point between Juneau and Glacier Bay; the port offers a prime vantage point for whale- and wildlife-watching and easier access to the Alaskan wilderness. The company offers 7-night Inside Passage and 7-night Gulf of Alaska itineraries.

PASSENGER PROFILE   The typical Celebrity guest is one who prefers to pursue his or her R&R at a relatively relaxed pace, with a minimum of aggressively promoted group activities. The overall impression leans more toward sophistication and less to the kind of orgiastic Technicolor whoopee that you'll find, say, aboard a Carnival ship. You'll find everyone from kids to retirees.

SHIPS   Sleek, modern, and stunningly designed, the 1,896-passenger *Mercury* and the larger, 1,950-passenger *Infinity* and *Millennium* have a lot of open deck space and lots of large windows that provide access to the wide skies and the grand Alaskan vistas. All the ships (but especially *Mercury*) feature incredible spas with hydrotherapy pools, steam rooms, and saunas, plus health and beauty services and exceptionally large fitness areas. **Sample rates per person:** Lowest-price inside cabin $115, lowest outside cabin $136, lowest suite $279 per day for a 7-night cruise.

HOLLAND AMERICA LINE

300 Elliott Ave. W., Seattle, WA 98119. ℂ **800/426-0327** or 206/281-3535. Fax 206/286-7110. www.holland america.com.

Holland America Line (HAL) can be summed up in one word: *tradition.* The company was formed way back in 1873 as the Netherlands-America Steamship Company, and its ships today strive to present an aura of history and dignity, like a European hotel where they never let rock stars register. And thanks to its acquisition over the years of numerous land-based tour operators, Holland America has positioned itself as Alaska's most experienced and comprehensive cruise company.

Though most of the line's Alaskan fleet is relatively young, the ships are designed with a decidedly "classic" feel—no flashing neon lights here. Similarly, Holland America's ships are heavy on more mature, less frenetic kinds of activities. You'll find good bridge programs and music to dance (or just listen) to in the bars and lounges, plus health spas and the other amenities found on most large ships. The line has improved its nightly show-lounge entertainment. Its Artists in Residence Program, arranged through the Alaska Native Heritage Center in Anchorage, has Alaska Native artists accompanying all 7-night cruises and demonstrating traditional art forms such as ivory and soapstone carving, basket weaving, and mask making. Club HAL is one of the industry's more creative children's programs, though the small children's playrooms are no match for what you find on the latest Princess or Celebrity megaships. Alaska itineraries include 7-night Inside Passage cruises and 7-night Gulf of Alaska cruises.

PASSENGER PROFILE   Holland America's passenger profile used to reflect a much older crowd. Now the average age is dropping, thanks to an increased emphasis on its Club HAL program for children and some updating of its onboard entertainment. Still, HAL's passengers in Alaska include a large percentage of middle-aged-and-up vacationers.

SHIPS   The 1,258-passenger *Ryndam, Statendam,* and *Veendam* are more or less identical. All cabins have a sitting area and lots of closet and drawer space, and even the least expensive inside cabins run almost 190 square feet, quite large by industry standards. Outside doubles have either picture windows or verandas. The striking dining rooms, two-tiered showrooms, and Crow's Nest forward bar/lounges are among these ships' best features. The newer, 1,432-passenger *Volendam* and *Zaandam,* and 1,380-passenger *Amsterdam,* are larger and fancier, with triple-decked oval atriums, nearly 200 suites and deluxe staterooms with private verandas, five showrooms and lounges, and an alternative restaurant designed as an artist's bistro, featuring drawings and etchings. The smallest cabin is a comfortable 190 square feet. The *Oosterdam* and *Westerdam,* the newest vessels in the fleet, weigh 85,000 tons and carry 1,848 passengers. These are sophisticated, spacious yet intimate ships well equipped to support HAL's position as a force in the Alaska market. **Sample rates per person:** Lowest-price inside cabin $114, lowest outside cabin $157, lowest suite $242 per day for a 7-night cruise.

NORWEGIAN CRUISE LINE

7665 Corporate Center Dr., Miami, FL 33126. ℂ **800/327-7030** or 305/436-4000. Fax 305/436-4120. www.ncl.com.

Norwegian Cruise Line (NCL) offers an informal and upbeat onboard atmosphere on the *Norwegian Sun,* sailing from Vancouver, and the *Norwegian Sky* and *Norwegian Star,* both sailing from Seattle. The line excels at activities, and its recreational and fitness programs are among the best in the industry. Though the onboard food has been described as unmemorable, NCL recently inaugurated what has become a very popular casual-dining policy that allows passengers to dine when they want pretty much any time between 5:30pm and midnight, with whomever they want, dressed however they want.

In Alaska, NCL offers an Alaskan lecturer, wine tastings, art auctions, trapshooting, cooking demonstrations, craft and dance classes, an incentive fitness program, and bingo, among other activities. Passengers can choose from a good selection of soft-adventure shore excursions, including hiking, biking, and kayaking. Entertainment is generally strong and includes Vegas-style musical productions. The top-notch kids' program includes an activity room, video games, an ice-cream bar, and guaranteed babysitting aboard, plus sessions with park rangers and escorted shore excursions. The line offers 7-night Inside Passage cruises.

PASSENGER PROFILE   In Alaska, the demographic tends more toward retirees than on the line's warmer-climate sailings, but you'll find families as well, including grandparents bringing along the grandkids.

SHIPS   The 2,050-passenger *Norwegian Sun* is the first ship built with NCL's new "freestyle" dining policy in mind, as evidenced by the nine separate onboard restaurants. An airy eight-story glass atrium welcomes visitors in the lobby. More than two-thirds of the guest rooms (about 650 in all) have ocean views, and closet space is more generous than on other NCL ships. The 2,240-passenger *Norwegian Star* has no fewer than 11 rooms in which people can eat—depending on the time of day. The *Star* is well equipped for the sports-minded and active vacationer—in addition to the fitness center, there are three heated pools, a jogging/walking track, and a wide array of sports facilities. The 2,466-passenger *Norwegian Pearl* is getting lots of attention from the company, and it shows. **Sample rates per person:** Lowest-price inside cabin $100, lowest outside cabin $122, lowest suite from $243 per day for a 7-night cruise.

PRINCESS CRUISES

24305 Town Center Dr., Santa Clarita, CA 91355. ℂ **800/LOVE-BOAT** or 661/753-0000. Fax 661/753-1535. www.princess.com.

Consistency is Princess's strength. With new ships joining its fleet like so many cars off a Detroit assembly line, you'd think that maintaining acceptable service standards could be a problem. All things considered, though, Princess accomplishes this rather well. Throughout the fleet, the service in all areas—dining room, lounge, cabin maintenance, and so on—tends to be of consistently high quality. Aboard Princess, you get a lot of bang for your buck, attractively packaged and well executed. Although its ships serve every corner of the globe, nowhere is the Princess presence more visible than in Alaska. Through its affiliate, Princess Tours, it owns wilderness lodges, motorcoaches, and railcars in the 49th state, making it one of the major players in the Alaska cruise market, alongside Holland America.

Princess passengers can expect enough onboard activities to keep them going morning to night, if they've a mind to, and enough nooks and crannies to allow them to do absolutely nothing, if that's their thing. Kids are well taken care of, with especially large children's playrooms. On shore, the line's shore-excursion staff gets big points for efficiency.

Princess offers 7-night Inside Passage cruises, 7-night Gulf of Alaska cruises, and 10-night Inside Passages cruises from San Francisco, and the new and smaller Tahitian Princess is doing 14-night cruises out of Vancouver to less-visited places including Kodiak and Valdez.

PASSENGER PROFILE   Typical Princess passengers are likely to be between 50 and 65, and are experienced cruisers who know what they want and are prepared to pay for it. Recent additional emphasis on its youth and children's facilities has begun to attract a bigger share of the family market.

SHIPS   Princess's diverse fleet in Alaska essentially comprises eight ships, five of which have entered service since the millennium. The fleet includes the *Diamond* and *Sapphire,* which were completed in 2004; the *Coral* and *Island,* of 2003 vintage and the *Golden* (2001) and *Star* (2002), not to mention the *Tahitian Princess,* which was built in 1999 and extensively refurbished in 2002 when it was purchased from Renaissance Cruises. The *Sun* (1995) completes Princess's Alaska fleet. The ships generally are pretty but not stunning, bright but not gaudy, spacious but not overwhelmingly so, and decorated in a comfortable, restrained style that's a combination of classic and modern. They're a great choice when you want a step up from Carnival, Royal Caribbean, and NCL but aren't interested in the slightly more chic ambience of Celebrity or the luxury of Regent Seven Seas. **Sample rates per person:** Lowest-price inside cabin $107, lowest outside cabin $122, lowest suite $207 per day for a 7-night cruise.

REGENT SEVEN SEAS CRUISES

1000 Corporate Dr., Suite 500, Fort Lauderdale, FL 33334. ℂ 800/285-1835. www.theregentexperience.com.

Regent's guests travel in style and extreme comfort. Its brand of luxury is casually elegant and subtle; its cuisine among the best in the industry. The line assumes, for the most part, that passengers want to entertain themselves onboard, so organized activities are limited, but they do include lectures by local experts, well-known authors, and the like, plus facilities for card and board games, blackjack and Ping-Pong tournaments, bingo, big-screen movies with popcorn, and instruction in the fine arts of pompom making, juggling, and such. Bridge instructors are onboard on select sailings. The line has a no-tipping policy and offers creative shore excursions. Room service is about the best you'll find on any ship, and the cuisine is excellent. As of January 1, 2007, Regent switched to a fleetwide liquor-inclusive policy on all departures. The *Seven Seas Mariner* sails a 7-night Gulf of Alaska itinerary.

PASSENGER PROFILE   Regent tends to attract passengers in their 40s to 60s who have a household income of more than $200,000 and don't like to flaunt their wealth. The typical passenger is well educated, well traveled, and inquisitive.

SHIPS   Cabins on the 700-passenger *Seven Seas Mariner* are all oceanview suites, and all have private verandas. The standard suite is a large 301 square feet; some suites can interconnect if you want to book two for additional space. The Constellation Theater is two-tiered and designed to resemble a 1930s nightclub. There are two additional lounges, plus a casino and the Connoisseur Club, a cushy venue for predinner drinks and after-dinner fine brandy and cigars. The ship's spa offers Judith Jackson European spa treatments using a variety of herbal and water-based therapies. **Sample rates per person:** Lowest-price suite $557 per day for a 7-night cruise; no inside or standard outside cabins.

ROYAL CARIBBEAN INTERNATIONAL

1050 Caribbean Way, Miami, FL 33132. ℂ 800/327-6700 or 305/379-2601. www.royalcaribbean.com.

Royal Caribbean sells a mass-market style of cruising that's reasonably priced and offered aboard informal, well-run ships with nearly every diversion imaginable—craft classes, horse racing, bingo, shuffleboard, deck games, line-dancing lessons, wine-and-cheese tastings, cooking demonstrations, art auctions, and the like—plus elaborate health clubs and spas, covered swimming pools, large open sun deck areas, and innumerable bars, lounges, and other entertainment centers. The Viking Crown Lounge and other glassed-in areas make excellent observation rooms from which to see the Alaska sights. Royal Caribbean spends big bucks on entertainment, which includes high-tech show productions. Headliners are often featured. Port lectures are offered on topics such as Alaska wildlife, and the line offers some 65 shore excursions. The line's children's activities are some of the most extensive afloat. The line offers 7-night Inside Passage and Gulf of Alaska cruises.

PASSENGER PROFILE   The crowd on Royal Caribbean ships, like the decor, rates pretty high on the party scale, though not quite at the Carnival level. Passengers represent an age mix from 30 to 60, and a good number of families are attracted by the line's well-established and fine-tuned kids' programs. In Alaska, Royal Caribbean is focusing more on international sales than the entrenched market leaders, Princess and Holland America, which often results in sailings populated by a good many international passengers, especially travelers from Asia and Europe.

SHIPS   Royal Caribbean owns the largest ships in the world: the new *Liberty of the Seas* at 160,000 tons, and four 142,000-ton voyager-class vessels. Although these 3,000-plus-passenger ships—which introduced such cruise-ship design features as ice-skating rinks, rock-climbing walls, and cabins overlooking interior atrium areas—are not in Alaska this year, Royal Caribbean does offer the very up-to-date 2,500-passenger *Radiance of the Seas.* The ship is joined in Alaska for the second year by its sister ship, the similarly dimensioned *Serenade of the Seas.* The *Radiance* is in Gulf of Alaska service between Vancouver, B.C., and Seward, the *Serenade* in Inside Passage service out of Vancouver. Also returning to Alaska in 2007 is the older (1997), but still up-to-date 2,435-passenger *Rhapsody of the Seas,* a vision-class ship. **Sample rates per person:** Lowest-price inside cabin on the *Rhapsody,* RCL's least expensive ship, is $95, lowest outside cabin $122, lowest suite $207 per day for a 7-night cruise.

SILVERSEA

110 E. Broward Blvd., Fort Lauderdale, FL 33301. ☎ **800/744-9966.** www.silversea.com.

Silversea left the Alaska market after the 2006 season in order, its management said, to give past passengers a greater variety of destinations to choose from. After a 1-year absence it is back this year, ready to give Regent Seven Seas a run for its money in search of the luxury trade. The other real luxury line ship is known for the quality of its service, its cuisine, and its all-suite accommodations. What it is not known for is its entertainment package, which, largely because of stage-size limitations, can't match the massive presentations of some of its larger competitors. That is a small sacrifice to make for all that the company offers—including free alcohol and a fine selection of complimentary wines at lunch and dinner. And probably at breakfast as well, if you're really interested. The line offers a 12-day rotation between San Francisco and Vancouver and reverse.

PASSENGER PROFILE   Look for the 60-something set, well heeled, well educated and knowing what to look for when they lay out the kind of money it takes to get a place on one of this company's ships.

SHIPS   Silversea has four; its representative in Alaska this year is the 382-passenger *Silver Shadow,* one of its two newer ships. (The other is the *Silver Whisper,* launched a year later, in 2000.) There are no rock-climbing facilities, but there are two alternative restaurants, one of which doubles as the breakfast and lunch buffet room, and there's a small casino—there is no children's program; it's not a ship for kids. **Sample rates per person:** Least expensive suite $533 per day.

Southeast Alaska

Rich, proud people have lived in Southeast Alaska for thousands of years, fishing the region's salmon and hunting in its primeval forests, where the tree trunks grow up to 10 feet thick. In canoes, they explored the hundreds of misty, mossy, enchanted islands where animals, trees, and even ice had living spirits. The salmon lived under the sea in human form, becoming fish in the summer to swim in seething masses up the rivers and streams as a gift of food to feed their kin, the people. In return, the people treated the salmon with respect and ceremony, allowing their spirits to return to human form under the sea to live another year. So blessed, the Tlingits and Haida built great, carved houses and poles, fought wars, owned slaves, traded with faraway tribes, and held rich contests of giving called potlatches, where they passed on the stories that still help explain their mysterious world. Even for a modern non-Native walking in the grand quiet of the old-growth rainforest, it's easy to find yourself listening for the spirits of the trees speaking their mysteries.

Discovery subsists on mystery, and Southeast Alaska is still being discovered. A honeycomb of limestone caves under Prince of Wales Island wasn't found until 1987. Explorers continue to map its endless miles of caverns, finding the bones of extinct animals, the artifacts of some of North America's earliest prehistoric people, bear dens, strange eyeless shrimp that live nowhere else, and even underground streams that host spawning salmon. The caves network at every step into passages that lead straight up or down or off to either side, some only wide enough to allow a cool wind to pass through. The unfathomable intricacy is exhilarating but also a bit disquieting, like a breath of the supernatural, for it is proof of the unknowable.

Southeast Alaska unfolds like this intricate, hidden world below the tree roots. On a map, this land of ice and forest may not look as large as other parts of Alaska, but the better you know it, the bigger it becomes, until you have to surrender to its immensity. You don't need to go underground to experience the sensation—you can feel it by gazing from a boat at the fractal geometry of the endlessly folded, rocky shoreline. On a cruise through the Inside Passage, you'll marvel at all the little beaches and rocky outcroppings you pass, hundreds of inviting spots each day. If you were to stop at random on any one of those uninhabited beaches in a skiff or kayak, you'd find you could spend a day surveying just a few acres of rocks, the overhanging forest, and the tiny pools of water left behind by the tide. And if you gazed down into any one of those pools, you'd find a complex world all its own, where tiny predators and prey live out their own drama of life in the space of a few square feet. The discoveries you make in Southeast Alaska depend only on how closely you look.

The region stands apart from the rest of Alaska, and not only because most of it can't be reached by road. No other part of the state shares the mysterious, spirit-laden quality of the coastal rainforest. No other area has such mild weather, more akin to the climate of the Pacific Northwest than to the heart of Alaska. Certainly no other area in Alaska gets as much rain, nor do many other places on earth. The traditional Native people here differed from other Alaska Natives, too: They were far richer and left behind more physical artifacts. The Tlingits, Haida, and Tsimshians exploited the wealth nature gave them and amplified it by successfully trading with tribes to the south and over the mountains in today's British Columbia and Yukon Territory. In their early contact, the Tlingits even briefly defeated the Russian invaders in the Battle of Sitka, and after white dominance was established, managed to save many of their cultural artifacts and stories.

Along with its other riches and complexities, Southeast Alaska also has many charming small towns and villages that seem to have grown organically from the mountainsides bordering the fjords and channels of the islands. With economies that predate Alaska's oil boom, they developed slowly, their fishermen building houses to hand down to their children. The smaller towns remain completely exempt from the American blight of corporate sameness. Real, old-fashioned main streets are prosperous with family businesses where the proprietors know their customers by first name.

1 Exploring Southeast Alaska

A unique and inviting aspect of travel in Southeast Alaska is that no roads connect most of the communities. People are forced to get out of their speeding cars and ride on boats, where they can meet their fellow travelers and see what's passing by—slowly. The islands of the region form a protected waterway called the **Inside Passage,** along which almost all of the region's towns are arrayed. Thanks to the **Alaska Marine Highway** ferry system, it's not too expensive to travel the entire passage, hopping from town to town and spending as much time in each place as you like. And if you're short on time, air service is frequent, with jets to the major towns and commuter planes to the villages.

GETTING AROUND BY FERRY: THE ALASKA MARINE HIGHWAY

The state-run **Alaska Marine Highway System** (© **800/642-0066** or 907/465-3941, TDD 800/764-3779; www.ferryalaska.com), is a subsidized fleet of big, blue-hulled ferries connecting many of Alaska's roadless coastal towns. Call for a free schedule or download it from the website.

PROS & CONS   The ferry system's strengths are its low cost, frequent summer sailings, inexpensive stopovers, exceptional safety, and the fact that kids love it. In the summer, Forest Service guides offer interpretive talks onboard in Southeast's Inside Passage and in Prince William Sound. The system's weaknesses are crowding during the July peak season, the fact that if they're late they can be many hours late (although they're usually on time), and a shortage of cabins, which means that most people have to camp on deck or in chairs during overnight passages.

ROUTES   The system mostly serves Southeast Alaska, though it does cover most of coastal Alaska, with two sailings a month (the *Kennicott*) connecting Southeast Alaska with the Southcentral region nearer Anchorage. The smaller Southcentral ferries link communities all the way out the Aleutian chain (see chapters 7 and 10).

Southeast Alaska

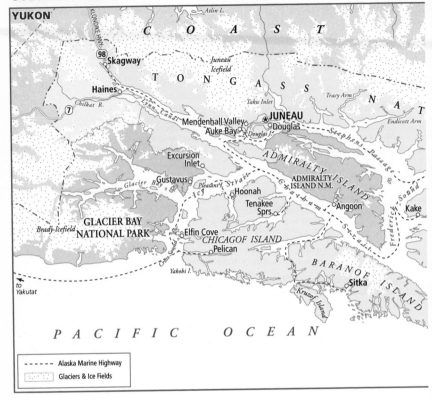

In the Southeast, five large, mainline ferries serve the Inside Passage. Two begin their run in British Columbia's Prince Rupert and travel about 30 hours north to Haines and Skagway. Two more start in Bellingham, Washington, travel 37 hours nonstop to Ketchikan, then continue up to Skagway and Haines. Each of these four towns is connected to the rest of the world by roads, but none of the towns in between are. In the summer, the large ships stop at least daily (although sometimes in the middle of the night) in Ketchikan, Wrangell, Petersburg, Juneau, Haines, and Skagway. Some make a side trip to Sitka on the way. Juneau is the hub, with many extra sailings north from Juneau on the Lynn Canal to Haines and Skagway. These are offered by a newer fast ferry, the *Fairweather,* which travels at up to 45 mph. It cuts travel times in half, connecting Juneau with Haines and Skagway several times a week and Sitka twice a week.

Smaller ferries connect the larger towns to tiny villages up and down the coast. They mostly take local residents back and forth to their villages, so they're rarely crowded. Those routes are definitely off the beaten track, offering the cheapest and easiest way to absorb the real wilderness of the Alaska Bush. The feeder ferries and fast ferry have food service but no cabins.

CONNECTING TO THE FERRY From the south: The appeal of taking the Alaskan Marine Highway ferry to Alaska from Bellingham, Washington, is obvious, but it is not cheaper than flying and it takes 2 days just to get to Ketchikan. The popular alternative is to board the ferry in Prince Rupert, B.C. You can get to Prince Rupert by rail or road (see "Getting There & Getting Around," in chapter 2). Another option is to get to Prince Rupert by riding the **BC Ferries** system, 1112 Fort St., Victoria, B.C., Canada V8V 4V2 (© **888/223-3779** or 250/386-3431; www.bcferries.bc.ca). This is quite a trek and requires you have a car. First you have to take a ferry to the southern end of British Columbia's Vancouver Island, then drive the island's length to its northern end, then take another ferry from Port Hardy to Prince Rupert. That ferry docks next to the Alaska ferry. You can get to Vancouver Island's southern end from the mainland from two directions. BC Ferries goes to Nanaimo from near the city of Vancouver. **Black Ball Transport** (© 360/457-4491; www.cohoferry.com) operates a ferry from Port Angeles, Washington, to Victoria.

To the north: The northern end of the Inside Passage Alaska ferry system rejoins the road system in Skagway and Haines. Haines is a bit closer to the rest of the state but is short on car rental options; Skagway has an Avis car rental outlet and an RV rental business (see sections 9 and 10 of this chapter). At times it is also possible to take a bus from Skagway to Whitehouse and there catch another bus to travel onward on the Alaska Highway. At the moment, these arrangements are up in the air, and it's never been a great way to spend a vacation.

By air: By flying to your starting point, you can save time and reduce the chance of having to spend the night sleeping in a chair onboard. Long hauls on the ferry can

---

Tips   Ferry System Booking

The **Alaska Marine Highway** (www.ferryalaska.com) has an online booking system that makes figuring out a trip far easier than using its inscrutable timetables. Just be sure to make vehicle and cabin reservations as early as possible. If you need to talk to a real person for advice or to change reservations, the system has a toll-free number (© **800/642-0066**), but it can be understaffed, with waits for an operator. One way around the state's reservation system is to call **Viking Travel,** in Petersburg (© **800/327-2571** or 907/772-3818; www.alaska ferry.com), which will accept your booking before the official reservation system opens, then reserve it the first day the system becomes available. They can also take care of all your air and tour connections, lodgings, activities, travel insurance, and so on.

You can sometimes avoid crowds on the boats with careful scheduling. Ferries are crowded northbound in June and southbound in August and both ways in July. If you're planning to fly one way and take the ferry the other, go against the flow.

---

be uncomfortable and don't save you much money over flying, but the ferry is much less expensive and more appealing for connecting nearby towns within the Southeast region. Fly into Juneau, Sitka, or another sizable town and plan a ferry trip from there, stopping at various places before catching a plane home.

STOPPING OVER   Buying ahead or booking round-trip tickets saves you nothing on the ferry, and stopovers of any length add little to the cost of your passage. Use the ferry system to explore the towns along the way, grabbing the next ferry through to continue your journey. If you travel without a vehicle, you generally don't need reservations (with the possible exceptions of the Bellingham sailings and passages across the Gulf of Alaska). Bring along a bike, or even a sea kayak, to have total freedom in exploring Southeast. Port calls usually are not long enough to see the towns; if the boat is running late, they may not let you off at all.

WALK-ON FARES   Fares change every year so don't count on these, but they may help for planning. The adult walk-on fare from Prince Rupert to Skagway is $184. Bellingham to Ketchikan is $239, Bellingham to Skagway $363. Juneau to Sitka is $45. All fares for children 6 to 11 and under are roughly half price and children 5 and under ride free. Off season only, October through April, the driver of a vehicle does not need a separate walk-on ticket and other fare sales sometimes go in effect.

BRINGING A VEHICLE   In the summer, you often need a reservation for any chance of taking your vehicle on the ferry, and reserving 3 to 6 months early is wise. The vehicle spots on the ferries from Bellingham and Prince Rupert are particularly coveted. Fares vary according to the size of the car as well as your destination; a passage from Prince Rupert to Haines for a typical 15-foot car is $395, the passage from Bellingham to Haines is $797. You also have to buy a separate ticket for each person on the ferry, including, in summer, the driver. Renting a car at your destination will probably save money and enhance your trip because you will have more flexibility in your stopovers. You can carry a kayak, canoe, or bike on the ferry (without a car) quite inexpensively.

CABIN RESERVATIONS   Sometimes you can snag a cabin from the standby list when you sail (board quickly and approach the purser immediately), but generally you must reserve ahead for the summer season. Cabins from Bellingham book many months ahead. A two-berth outside cabin (one with a window) with a bathroom is under $75 on most town-to-town hops, $178 from Prince Rupert to Haines, and $393 from Bellingham to Haines, plus the cost of your ticket. The great majority of the cabins are small and spartan, coming in two- and four-bunk configurations, but for a premium you can reserve a more comfortable sitting-room unit on some vessels. Most cabins have tiny private bathrooms with showers. Try to get an outside cabin so that you can watch the world go by. Cabins can be stuffy, and the windowless units can be claustrophobic as well.

DO YOU NEED A CABIN?   If you do a lot of layovers in Southeast's towns, you can arrange to do most of your ferry travel during the day, but you'll probably have to sleep onboard at least once (unless you make that hop by air). You can't sleep in your vehicle. One of the adventures of ferry travel is finding a chair to sleep in or setting up a tent on deck with everyone else. The patio-furniture lounge chairs on the covered outdoor solarium, on the top deck, are the best public sleeping spot onboard, in part because the noise of the ship covers other sounds. A camping pad will make it much more comfortable. If you're tenting, the best place is behind the solarium, where it's not too windy. On the *Columbia* that space is small, so grab it early. The *Kennicott* has very little outdoor deck space at all. Bring duct tape to secure your tent to the deck in case you can't find a sheltered spot, as the wind over the deck of a ship in motion blows like an endless gale. The recliner lounges are comfortable, too, but can be stuffy. Bring a pillow. If the ship looks crowded, grab your spot fast to get a choice location. **Showers** are available, although there may be lines. Lock any valuables and luggage you don't need in the **coin-operated lockers.** If all that sounds too rugged, or if you have small children and no tent, reserve a cabin. It offers a safe and private home base and a good night's rest, and there's a certain romance to having your own compartment on a public conveyance.

FERRY FOOD   If you can, bring at least some of your own food on the ferry. Ferry food can get boring after several meals in a row and, during peak season, lines are sometimes unreasonably long. We usually bring a cooler or picnic basket. Even if you're traveling light, you can pick up some bagels and deli sandwiches on a stopover or long port call.

THE BEST RUNS   Going to Sitka through **Peril Straits,** the ferry fits through extraordinarily narrow passages where no other vessel of its size ventures; the smooth, reflective water is lovely, and you may see deer along the shore. The **Wrangell Narrows,** between Petersburg and Wrangell, is also an incredible ride, day or night, as the ship accomplishes a slalom between shores that seem so close you could touch them, in water so shallow the schedules must be timed for high tide. **Frederick Sound,** between the Narrows and Wrangell, is prime for whale sightings. Approaching Skagway through the towering mountains of the **Lynn Canal** fjord also is impressive.

GETTING AROUND BY AIR & ROAD

BY AIR   Air travel is the primary link between Southeast's towns and the rest of the world. Several towns without road access have jet service, provided by **Alaska Airlines** (© **800/252-7522;** www.alaskaair.com), the region's only major airline. Juneau is Southeast Alaska's travel hub. Ketchikan and Sitka each have a few flights a day, while Wrangell, Petersburg, and Yakutat each have one flight going each direction daily. Gustavus is served from Juneau once daily during the summer. Some of these "milk runs" never get very far off the ground on hops between small towns: On the 31-mile Wrangell-to-Petersburg flight, the cabin attendants never have time to unbuckle. Haines and Skagway, which have highway connections, don't receive visits from jets, but all the towns and even the tiny villages have scheduled prop service.

Like the ferries, the planes can be quite late. Each of the airports in Southeast has its own challenges caused by the steep, mountainous terrain and the water. In bad weather, even jet flights are delayed or they "overhead"—they can't land at the intended destination and leave their passengers somewhere else. Your only protection against these contingencies are travel insurance, a schedule that allows plenty of slack in case you're significantly delayed, and low blood pressure.

BY ROAD   Three Southeast Alaska communities are accessible by road: Haines, Skagway, and the village of Hyder, which lies on the British Columbia border east of Ketchikan and is accessible from the gravel Cassiar Highway through Canada. If you're driving the Alaska Highway, passing through Haines and Skagway adds 160 miles of very scenic driving to the trip, as well as a 15-mile ferry ride between the two towns (they're separated by 362 road miles). This ferry route is not as heavily booked as the routes heading between either town and Juneau, but it's still a good idea to reserve ahead. You also can rent a car from Haines or Skagway for travel to the rest of the state at the end of a ferry journey (Haines saves just 60 miles over Skagway). If you're driving the highway in winter, you should be prepared for weather as cold as 40°F below zero (–40°C). Alaska winter driving information is under "Health & Safety" in chapter 2.

Bikes make a lot of sense for getting around Southeast's small towns, which tend to be compact. You can rent one almost anywhere you go, or bring your own on the ferry. The networks of abandoned or little-used logging roads on some islands offer limitless routes for mountain biking. Elsewhere, Forest Service hiking trails are often open for riding.

GETTING OUTSIDE IN THE TONGASS NATIONAL FOREST

Nearly all of Southeast Alaska, stretching 500 miles from Ketchikan to Yakutat, is in Tongass National Forest. The towns sit in small pockets of private land surrounded by 17 million acres of land controlled by the U.S. Forest Service—an area nearly as large as the state of Maine, and considerably larger than any other national forest or national park in the United States. The majority of this land has never been logged and the rate of logging has dropped dramatically in recent years, preserving one of the world's great temperate rainforests in its virgin state. It's an intact ecosystem full of wildlife, and mostly free of human development. Indeed, you quickly forget it *is* the Tongass National Forest. Since it always surrounds you when you're in this region, it's simply the land.

Tips Seeing Southeast from Above

If you can possibly afford it, take a **flightseeing** trip at some point during your trip. The poor man's way of doing this is to fly a small prop plane on a sched-uled run between two of your destinations instead of taking the ferry. If you ask, the pilot may even go out of his or her way to show you the sights; if not, you'll still gain an appreciation for the richness and extreme topography of the region. Each flight service also offers flightseeing tours in addition to sched-uled runs between destinations. Flightseeing costs as little as $100 for a brief spin. Flight services are listed in each town section.

> ### (Fun Fact Why There Are No Highways
>
> A tectonic plate under the Pacific Ocean brought the islands of the Southeast Alaska Panhandle from across the globe and squished them up against the plate that carries the landmass of Canada. Along the line of this glancing collision, large glacial mountains thrust up and islands were stretched and torn into the fractured geography that makes the area so interesting. In short, it has been too expensive to build roads through those icy mountains and across the steep, jumbled terrain of the islands. A plan to being a road from Juneau close to Skagway made some political headway, but the project is extremely controversial and may never make it off the drawing board.

FOREST SERVICE CABINS

One of the best ways to get into Southeast's wilderness is by staying at one of the scores of remote Forest Service Public Recreation Cabins. These are simple cabins without electricity or running water where you can lay your sleeping bag on a bunk and sit by a warm woodstove out of the rain. You need to bring everything with you, as if camping, but it's a good deal more comfortable than a tent. And you will probably find yourself in a stunningly beautiful spot, perhaps with your own lake and a boat for fishing. Cabins are located along canoe trails, on beaches best reached by sea kayak, on high mountain lakes accessible only by floatplane, and along hiking trails. We've done this many times with our family by boat or canoe or on foot. I've learned three critical lessons to pass on: Do your research, pack carefully (take all the essentials, but little more), and spend at least 3 nights, preferably a week, to make all the effort pay off with real relaxation.

GETTING CABIN INFORMATION   In this chapter, I've listed a few of the cabins in the sections devoted to the town that they're closest to, but for complete information check the Tongass website (**www.fs.fed.us/r10/tongass**) or contact the visitor centers and ranger offices listed with each town section in this chapter. The main contact point for recreation information for the whole forest is the **Southeast Alaska Discovery Center,** 50 Main St., Ketchikan, AK 99901 (© **907/228-6220**).

You'll need a good map to figure out where the cabins are, and an idea of how to get there and how much travel will cost—generally, the cost of transportation will be many times larger than the cabin rental fee of $25 to $45 a night. Few cabins can be reached without a boat or aircraft, and for all but large groups, flying is the economical way to go. A flight service can help you choose a cabin according to your interests and how far you can afford to fly. You may be able to rent the gear you need, but you'll have to reserve that ahead, too. The solution to these puzzles is different for each town; I've listed where to find help in the town sections later in this chapter.

RESERVING A CABIN OR CAMPSITE   The cabins and some campgrounds are reserved through a national system. Don't rely on the reservations operators or website for advice or cabin information—they're in upstate New York—instead, pose your questions to the ranger station nearest where you plan to go. The rangers are friendly and have probably stayed in the cabin you're interested in. When you're ready to book the easiest way is to use **www.recreation.gov**, where you can check availability dates at various places. By telephone, contact the **National Recreation Reservations Service** at

C **877/444-6777** or 518/885-3639 with toll from overseas. The phone lines are open March through October daily 10am to midnight eastern time, November through February 10am to 10pm. The system accepts payment only by bank card: American Express, Discover, MasterCard, or Visa. Cabins are available for reservation on a first-come, first-served basis, starting 180 days ahead, and campsites are available 240 days ahead. For the most popular cabins, you need to be online the minute reservations become available to have a chance.

2 Ketchikan: On the Waterfront

Had they known about it, the film noir directors of the 1950s would have chosen the Ketchikan (*ketch*-e-kan) waterfront for Humphrey Bogart to sleuth. The black-and-white montage: A pelting rain drains from the brim of his hat, suspicious figures dart through saloon doors and into the lobbies of concrete-faced hotels, a forest of workboat masts fades into the midsummer twilight along a shore where the sea and land seem to merge in miles of floating docks. Along Creek Street, salmon on their way to spawn swim under houses chaotically perched on pilings beside a narrow boardwalk; inside, men are spawning, too, in the arms of legal prostitutes. Meanwhile, the faces of totem poles gaze down on the scene disapprovingly, mute holders of their own ancient secrets.

Today, the director hoping to re-create that scene would have his work cut out for him removing the T-shirt shops and jewelry stores with bright street-front signs that seek to draw in throngs of cruise passengers to buy plastic gewgaws. Not so long ago, Ketchikan was a rugged and exotic intersection of cultures built on the profits of logging Southeast's rainforest, but in a decade it has transformed itself into a tourist center, softening its rough edges while selling it's charm to visitors. And the changes can only accelerate. More and bigger ships are coming, and Southeast Alaska's last major timber mill—the Louisiana Pacific–owned pulp plant in Ward Cove, north of town—closed in 1997 due, in part, to environmental concerns. A major portion of the mill was blown up in 1999; they sold tickets to see who would get to press the button on the explosives, but the occasion was less than festive, as former employees saw the scene of their work lives disappear into dust. The idea of a smaller, more labor-intensive operation, intended to replace the lost pulp mill jobs with jobs sawing lumber and making veneer, has had a rocky time getting off the ground. In the meantime, the economy had moved on.

On summer days, the white cruise ships tower above the town like huge new buildings on the dock facing Front Street, the downtown's main drag. Each morning their gangways disgorge thousands of visitors, clogging the streets and, for a few hours, transforming the town into a teeming carnival. On their short visits the passengers explore the closest of the twisting streets, see the museum at the Southeast Alaska Discovery Center, or take a tour to one of the totem pole parks. Then evening comes, the streets empty, and the cruise ships slide off quietly on the way to their next port.

That is when a sense of the old, misty, mysterious Ketchikan starts to return. Visitors with a little more time to spend, and the willingness to explore beyond the core tourist areas, can drink in the history and atmosphere of the place. Stay in a quaint old hotel, hike a boardwalk path through the primeval rainforest, and visit the museums, clan house replicas, and totem pole parks that make Ketchikan a center of Tlingit and Haida culture.

Ketchikan also makes a great jumping-off point for some spectacular outdoor experiences, including a trip to **Misty Fjords National Monument** (p. 118). As the state's fourth-largest city, Ketchikan is the transportation hub for the southern portion of

Ketchikan

ACCOMMODATIONS ■
Best Western Landing **1**
Cape Fox Lodge **15**
Captain's Quarters B&B **5**
Eagle Heights B&B **4**
Ketchikan Youth Hostel **8**
New York Hotel **18**

DINING ◆
Alaska Fish House **9**
Bar Harbor Restaurant **2**
Burger Queen **7**
Dai Sho Gun **6**
Diaz Café **19**
Good Fortune
  Chinese Restaurant **12**
Halibut Hole **13**
Ocean View Restaurante **3**

ATTRACTIONS ●
Cape Fox Hill–Creek Street
  Funicular **14**
City Park **22**
Creek Street boardwalk **16**
Deer Mountain Tribal Hatchery &
  Eagle Center **20**
Dolly's House **17**
Southeast Alaska
  Discovery Center **10**
Tongass Historical Museum **11**
Totem Heritage Center **21**

TONGASS
NATIONAL
FOREST

Tongass

Narrows

Pennock I.

Downtown Ketchikan

*Thomas
Basin*

Bar Harbor

Southeast Alaska. (The nicknames "Gateway City" and "First City" refer to its geographical location and transportation function.) Seaplanes based on docks along the waterfront are the taxis of the region, and a big interagency visitor center can get you started on your explorations of the area. Ketchikan is one of the wettest spots on Earth, with rain measured in the hundreds of inches; quality rain gear is requisite for any activity, in the wilds or in the streets of town.

ESSENTIALS
GETTING THERE
BY AIR   Alaska Airlines (© 800/252-7522; www.alaskaair.com) jet service connects Ketchikan south to Seattle nonstop and north to Petersburg, Wrangell, Sitka, Juneau, and Anchorage. Commuter lines run wheeled planes and floatplanes from Ketchikan to the neighboring communities, and also offer fishing packages and flightseeing.

The airport is on Gravina Island, to which there is no bridge (perhaps you've heard of the famous "Bridge to Nowhere" congressional scandal—the Ketchikan airport is its destination). A ferry runs each way every ½ hour (more frequently at peak times). Believe the airline when it tells you when to catch the ferry for your plane. The fare is $5 for adults, $2 for children ages 6 to 12, and free for children under 6. Returning the same day is free. The fare for cars is $6 each way, no matter how soon you come back. See "Getting Around," below, for how to get from the airport ferry dock to town and for a water taxi right from the airport (a fun option).

BY FERRY   The dock is 2½ miles north of downtown. **Alaska Marine Highway** ferries (© 800/642-0066; www.ferryalaska.com) run 6 hours north to Wrangell and 6 hours south to Prince Rupert, B.C. The walk-on fare from Prince Rupert is $60, from Wrangell it's $37. Call the local terminal at © **907/225-6182** or 907/225-6181 for a recording of updated arrival and departure times.

ORIENTATION
Ketchikan is on huge **Revillagigedo Island,** popularly known as **Revilla Island.** The downtown area, pretty much taken over by tourism, is quite compact and walkable, but the whole of Ketchikan, including a second commercial area used by locals, is long, strung out between the Tongass Narrows and the mountains. A waterfront road goes under various names through town (it's Water St. on our map), becoming North Tongass Highway as it stretches about 16 miles to the north. Saxman is 2½ miles to the south of downtown on the 14-mile South Tongass Highway.

GETTING AROUND
You can spend a day seeing the downtown sights on foot, but you will need transportation to get to the totem pole parks or airport.

BY TAXI   The local taxis, mostly minivans, are convenient and usually easy to flag down on the single main road through town. Try **Sourdough Cab** (© **907/225-5544**). **Alaska Cab** (© **907/225-2133**) is another taxi company in Ketchikan. Taking a cab to the airport terminal is costly because of time that runs up on the meter waiting for and riding the ferry to Gravina Island. Unless you have a lot of luggage, take the cab just to the airport ferry dock and walk on. If you are burdened by luggage, your cab can take you to the terminal, or use the water taxi from downtown (see below).

BY WATER TAXI   Only in Ketchikan could you take a boat from the airport to your hotel. **Tongass Water Taxi** (© **907/225-8294**) also happens to be reasonably priced and quick. The six-passenger boat runs back and forth from near the airport ferry dock to downtown all day. The first person is $18 and each additional person $7. It also crosses the same route as the airport ferry (without going on to downtown) for $7. Several hotels are right on the water, so the water taxi can take you almost to your door. The operator holds up a sign in the baggage claim area to meet arriving flights or you can call to arrange a pick-up.

BY BUS   The least costly way to the airport or ferry dock is the **Ketchikan Gateway Borough bus** (© **907/225-8726**). To get downtown or points south from the airport costs $1. Buses come every half-hour. Your luggage must fit under the seat.

BY RENTAL CAR   **Budget** has locations at the airport or in town (© **800/527-0700** reservations, 907/225-6004 at the airport, 907/225-8383 in town; www.budget.com). **Alaska Car Rental** (© **800/662-0007** or 907/225-5000; www.akcarrental.com) also has offices at the airport and in town.

VISITOR INFORMATION

The **Southeast Alaska Discovery Center,** 50 Main St., Ketchikan, AK 99901 (© **907/228-6220** or 907/288-6237 TDD; fax 907/228-6234; www.fs.fed.us/r10/tongass), is much more than a visitor center. Housed in a large, attractive building of big timbers and cedar, and located a block from the cruise-ship dock, the center is the best museum in the region when it comes to illustrating the interaction of the region's ecology and human society, including both traditional Native and contemporary uses. An auditorium shows a high-tech slide show. Admission to these facilities in summer costs $5, free for children ages 15 and under, with a $15 family maximum; in winter it's free. Without paying, you can get guidance about planning your time and activities in the outdoors. An information kiosk is located near the entrance, and downstairs you'll find a luxurious bookstore decorated like an explorer's private den with room to relax. The center is open May through September daily from 8am to 5pm, October through April Tuesday through Friday noon to 4pm and Saturday 10:30am to 4:30pm.

The **Ketchikan Visitors Bureau,** 131 Front St., Ketchikan, AK 99901 (© **800/770-3300** or 907/225-6166; fax 907/225-4250; www.visit-ketchikan.com), stands right on the cruise-ship dock, offering town information and booths where tourism businesses sell their wares, including tickets for tours. The bureau is open daily in the summer from 8am to 5pm and when cruise ships are in town; weekdays only in winter.

SPECIAL EVENTS

There's a detailed events calendar at www.visit-ketchikan.com.

The **Festival of the North** brings art to Ketchikan audiences for the entire month of February, including theater, ballet, live music, poetry readings, and a wearable art show the first weekend of the month that is a highlight of the winter. The festival is sponsored by Ketchikan Area Arts and Humanities Council, 716 Totem Way (© **907/225-2211;** www.ketchikanarts.org).

King Salmon Derby, a 60-year-old tradition, takes place at the end of May and the beginning of June.

The Fourth of July celebration is huge, with a long parade on Front Street attended by mobs of locals and visitors. After the parade, there's a **Timber Carnival** with an all-afternoon loggers' competition at the baseball field near City Park on Park Avenue; admission is free. Don't miss the legendary **pie sale** at St. John's Church at 423 Mission St., where a slice, ice cream, and beverage is $5. Fireworks are at 11pm on Gravina Island, best viewed from the cruise-ship dock.

Twice weekly through July, the **First City Players** (© **907/225-4792**) perform the melodrama *Fish Pirates Daughter,* as they have for more than 40 years, and serve a crab feed at the Civic Center.

The crowd-pleasing ***Great Alaskan Lumberjack Show*** goes on all summer behind the Alaska Discovery Center (© **888/320-9049** or 907/225-9050; www.lumberjack sports.com). Canadian and U.S. professional teams of lumberjacks—highly skilled and cute, too, according to my friend Charlotte—compete three or more times daily, mostly to an audience of cruise-ship passengers. The show is charming and intentionally a little goofy. The setting is attractive and comfortable. Tickets are $36 for adults, half price for children ages 5 to 12 (including tax)—expensive for a show that lasts 1 hour, but the great majority of clients leave happy.

The Blueberry Arts Festival, held the first weekend of August, has booths, music, and food, and is put on by the Ketchikan Area Arts and Humanities Council, mentioned just above as the sponsor of the Festival of the North. Check with the council for the **Monthly Grind** coffeehouse variety show, as well, which happens in the Saxman Tribal House every third Saturday from September to May.

FAST FACTS: Ketchikan

Banks A bank with an ATM is at 306 Main St.; grocery stores and the visitor center also have ATMs.

Hospital **Ketchikan General Hospital** is at 3100 Tongass Ave. (© **907/225-5171**).

Internet Access **SeaPort Cyberstations** (© **907/247-4615**, www.seaportel.com) is at the ship dock on the second floor at 5 Salmon Landing.

Police Call © **907/225-6631** for nonemergencies.

Post Office 3609 Tongass Ave.; a more convenient downtown substation is 2 blocks from the cruise-ship dock at 422 Mission St.

Taxes **Sales tax** is 6%. **Room taxes** total 13%.

EXPLORING KETCHIKAN

Pick up a copy of the **Official Historic Ketchikan Walking Tour Map,** available all over town, which has three routes through town to follow and loads of information about sites of both great and modest interest on the way.

Many motorized tours of the town vie for customers, getting the majority of their clients from the cruise ships but welcoming independent travelers when space is available. Tickets are for sale at the visitor center on the dock. Besides riding a tour bus through town, you can go into the woods in a Hummer or on a motorcycle or even drive from the streets into the harbor in an amphibious vehicle. That one, called **The Duck** (© **866/341-DUCK** or 907/225-9899), is a favorite of kids. It costs $36 for adults and $22 for children, and lasts 90 minutes.

One of the longest-established tour guides caters only to five visitors at a time—not ships full of clients. Schoolteacher Lois Munch, of **Classic Tours** (© **907/225-3091;** www.classictours.com), has a fun personality and neat concept: She wears a poodle skirt to drive visitors around in her '55 Chevy. A 2-hour tour to the Saxman totem poles is $84; a 3-hour tour adds a natural history stop and costs $99. Rates are per person and include the admission to Saxman.

TLINGIT, HAIDA & TSIMSHIAN CULTURAL HERITAGE

The Ketchikan area has two totem pole parks and a totem pole museum, as well as a wealth of contemporary Native art displayed all over town. Notable pieces stand at Whale Park at Mission and Bawden streets and at the Cape Fox Lodge. Most of what you see in Southeast Alaska is Tlingit—the Haida and Tsimshians generally live to the south and east in British Columbia—but Ketchikan is near the boundary between the three peoples' areas, so their similar cultures mix here.

Totem Bight State Historical Park ★★★   The park presents poles and a clan house carved beginning in 1938 by Natives working with traditional tools to copy fragments of historic poles that had mostly rotted away. The project, funded by the New Deal's Civilian Conservation Corps, helped save a Tlingit and Haida culture that had been essentially outlawed until that time. The setting, purportedly the site of a traditional fishing camp, is a peaceful spot on the edge of Tongass Narrows, at the end of a short walk through the woods, so the experience is both aesthetic and educational. The park also stands out for its excellent interpretive signs, a printed guide, and an interpretive website. There's a small park bookstore.

10 miles out of town on N. Tongass Hwy. Ketchikan Area State Park Office, 9883 N. Tongass Hwy. ✆ 907/247-8574. www.alaskastateparks.org (click on "Individual Parks"). Free admission. Daily 24 hours.

Totem Heritage Center ★★   Located near City Park, the center contains the largest collection of original 19th-century totem poles in existence. The poles, up to 160 years old, are displayed indoors, mostly unpainted, many with the grass and moss still attached from when they were rescued from the elements in villages. Totem poles were never meant to be maintained or repainted—they generally disintegrate after about 70 years, and were constantly replaced—but these were preserved to help keep the culture alive. A high ceiling and muted lighting highlight the spirituality of the art. Well-trained guides are on hand to explain what you're looking at, and there are good interpretive signs. The gift shop, open during the summer, carries authentic Native crafts.

601 Deermount St. ✆ 907/225-5900. Admission $5 in summer; free in winter. Summer daily 8am–5pm; winter Mon–Fri 1–5pm.

Saxman Native Village Totem Pole Park ★   Saxman's park has artifacts similar to those at Totem Bight park, but with an added attraction: You can see carvers at work in the building to the right of the park. It's possible to see the studio and the poles without joining a tour, using a pamphlet that costs $1.50, but Totem Bight is better for that kind of visit—it has a more inspiring location and better interpretive materials. Cape Fox Corp., which operates the tours, caters mainly to cruise-ship passengers with its 2-hour tour, which includes entry to the clan house and a demonstration of traditional dance and song by the Cape Fox Dancers. The tour schedule is different each day, depending on the ships. Buy tour tickets in the gift store on the right as you enter the park.

In Saxman, 2½ miles south of Ketchikan on the S. Tongass Hwy. ✆ 907/225-4846 for tour times and tickets. www.cape-foxtours.com. Tour $35 adult, $18 children 12 and under; unguided visits free. Daily 24 hours. No tours Oct–Apr.

DOWNTOWN ATTRACTIONS

Ketchikan's best downtown attractions are all within walking distance of one another. See Creek Street, then walk up Park Avenue past the Ketchikan Creek fish ladder and

---

Tips Avoiding the Crowds

Ketchikan is overrun with as many as 10,000 cruise-ship passengers every day May through September, far more than the small visitor attractions or even the streets can comfortably handle. Independent travelers can avoid the crush by planning to visit popular spots in the afternoon. Spend the morning on an outdoors activity instead. Ships usually leave the town in early evening.

---

up to lovely **City Park,** site of the Totem Heritage Center, described above. The park is among my favorite places in Ketchikan. The creek splits into a maze of ornamental pools and streams once used as a hatchery, with footbridges, a fountain, and large trees with creeping roots.

The Creek Street boardwalk starts at the Stedman Street bridge, running over the tidal creek. It was Ketchikan's red-light district until not that long ago; now it's a quaint tourist mall. Prostitution was semilegal in Alaska until 1952, recent enough to survive in local memories but distant enough to have made Creek Street historic and to transform the women who worked there from outcasts to icons. Dolly Arthur, who started in business for herself on the creek in 1919 and died in 1975, lived through both eras, and her home became a commercial museum not long after her death. **Dolly's House** (© 907/225-6329) is amusing, mildly racy, and a little sad. Admission is $5; it's open from 8am to 4pm during the summer and when cruise ships are in town.

Creek Street has some interesting shops, described below, but it's also fun just to walk on the creekside boardwalk, into the forest above, and over the "Married Men's Trail"—once a discreet way for married men to reach the red-light district. **The Cape Fox Hill–Creek Street Funicular** (known as "the tram"), a sort of diagonal elevator, runs 211 feet from the boardwalk up to the Cape Fox Lodge on top of the hill. Take it up and then enjoy the walk down through the woods. The summertime fare is $2, but if no one is around, just press the "up" button and go.

Deer Mountain Tribal Hatchery and Eagle Center 🐾🐾   This remarkable nonprofit center combines one of Alaska's best hatchery tours and a great place to see a bald eagle close up. The wooden buildings stand over Ketchikan Creek. You can see fish climbing against the current up into pools where they are sorted before being cut open to complete their biological purpose (salmon die when they spawn anyway). The hatchery tours are special for letting you get so close, right in the action, where you can feed the growing salmon fry yourself. The hatchery produces king and silver salmon and steelhead trout. Visitors can also walk right through the eagle enclosure. Remarkably, the resident pair of injured, flightless bald eagles have mated for life and built a nest where they lay eggs each year. They hunt salmon swimming naturally through their enclosure. No glass stands between you and this activity, only a few feet away.

1158 Salmon Rd. © **800/252-5158** or 907/228-5530. Admission $9, ages 12 and under free. May–Sept daily 8am–4:30pm; winter by arrangement.

Tongass Historical Museum   This one-room museum is where Ketchikan talks back to itself, with well-executed revolving exhibits that have always held my interest. A small permanent area shows Native artifacts. In the same building, the attractive Ketchikan Public Library is a great place to recharge, especially in the children's section downstairs, where big windows look out on Ketchikan Creek's falls.

629 Dock St. ℂ **907/225-5600.** Admission $2 summer; free winter. Summer daily 8am–5pm; winter Wed–Fri 1–5pm, Sat 10am–4pm, Sun 1–4pm.

SHOPPING

The Ketchikan art scene is one of Alaska's liveliest, thanks in part to the Ketchikan Arts and Humanities Council, whose helpful staff operates the **Main Stay Gallery,** near Creek Street at 716 Totem Way (www.ketchikanarts.org). Shows change monthly.

Ray Troll is Alaska's leading fish-obsessed artist. His small gallery, **Soho Coho,** at 5 Creek St., is worth a visit even if you aren't a shopper. It shows Troll's own work and that of other Ketchikan artists from the same school of surreal rainforest humor. In Troll's art, subtle ironies and silly puns coexist in a solidly decorated interior world. T-shirts are his most popular canvas; "Spawn Till You Die" is a classic. Troll's incredible work-of-art website delves far into his strange mind (and sells shirts), at www.trollart.com. The gallery is open summer daily from 9am to 6pm; winter Wednesday through Saturday from noon to 5:30pm; or you can place an order by calling ℂ **800/888-4070.**

Adjacent to Soho Coho, **Alaska Eagle Arts** is a serious gallery featuring the bold yet traditional work of Native artist Marvin Oliver. Upstairs, **Parnassus Books** is a pleasing little cubbyhole with Alaskana, art, cooking, and popular fiction. Down the boardwalk at 18 Creek St., craftspeople carve and interact with visitors at **Hide-A-Way Gifts.** At 123 Stedman St., across the creek, **Blue Heron Gallery and Gifts** carries Alaska arts and crafts that appeal to locals as well as visitors: jewelry, stained glass, clothing, jam, prints, and so on.

Near the Steadman Street Bridge, **Chinook and Company,** at 207 Steadman, is the place to stop for gourmet foods that fit or go beyond the region's specialties, including wonderful smoked salmon, tapenades, marinated veges, dips, flavored oils, and the like, plus clothing made by small, socially responsibly Northwest companies. Back toward the town's center, at 633 Mission St., **Exploration Gallery** is owned by local artist Diane Naab and framer Anna Annicelli and shows original work from all over the region.

Stop for kettle-corn popcorn on your shopping trip at **Orca Corn,** at 602 Dock St., an addictive local favorite that you can get in the usual movie-theater style, or with such flavors as blueberry or maple. Next door is a terrific coffee shop, **Refiners Roast,** open long hours every day and serving killer brownies and other baked goods along with the great coffee.

Moving back toward the waterfront, **Eagle Spirit Gallery of Ketchikan,** at 310 Mission St. shows some very impressive Alaska Native art, including large carved pieces from this region.

At the waterfront, the building that stands right over the dock is Salmon Landing Market Place, at 5 Salmon Landing. Of particular interest here is the **Dockside Gallery,** which shows work of several local artists. Next to Dockside Gallery, hobbyists should check out **The Bead and Yarn Shoppe,** which has an astonishingly diverse selection, and handcrafted jewelry.

Note: Ketchikan is a shopping and art destination, but if you want something authentically Alaskan you have to be careful. For some important tips, see "Native Art: Finding the Real Thing," in chapter 2.

GETTING OUTSIDE

There's a lot to do outdoors around Ketchikan, but most of it will require a boat or plane; drive-by attractions are limited. In any event, your first stop should be the trip-planning room at the Southeast Alaska Discovery Center (see "Visitor Information," in section 2), for details on trails, fishing, and dozens of U.S. Forest Service cabins.

BEAR VIEWING Salmon returning to a fish hatchery on a creek south of town have long attracted black bears. A local business, **Alaska Rainforest Sanctuary,** (© 907/225-5503), takes advantage of the viewing opportunity by hosting visitors on well-made trails with guides. It's an excellent program, however, the firm is solely focused on cruise-ship passengers and hasn't even disclosed a price for individuals to join the tours. As a passenger, you can book onboard. Otherwise, call, but I cannot speak to schedule, availability, or price. On the other hand, you can watch the same bears from public property for free, without a guide. Drive about 10 miles south of town, beyond Saxman on the South Tongass Highway, to the Herring Cove Bridge. From here you have a viewpoint of the same estuary owned by the sanctuary and just as good a chance of seeing black bears. Bears may be present June through September and sightings are most likely in July and August.

For more of a wilderness experience, Ketchikan is a good place to get on a float-plane, soar over water and wooded islands, and land where bears are gathering at streams where the salmon are running. Depending on where the bears are, it costs $250 to $400 per person. **Promech Air** (© 800/860-3845 or 907/225-3845; www. promechair.com) and **Island Wings Air Service** (© 888/854-2444 or 907/225-2444; www.islandwings.com) offer this service; both are described in "Majestic Misty Fjords," p. 118.

CABIN TRIPS The U.S. Forest Service maintains more than 50 **cabins** around Ketchikan; all are remote and primitive, but at $25 to $45 a night, you can't beat the price or the settings. This is a chance to be utterly alone in the wilderness; many of the lake cabins come with a boat for fishing and exploring. For details and descriptions of all the cabins, contact the **Southeast Alaska Discovery Center** (© 907/228-6220; www.fs.fed.us/r10/tongass). The reservations system to use when you're actually ready to book a cabin is described in "Getting Outside in the Tongass National Forest" on p. 102.

If you stay in a cabin, you'll need all your camping gear except a tent, including sleeping bags, a camp stove, your own cooking outfit and food, a lantern, and so on. The easy way to handle this is to contact **Alaska Wilderness Outfitting and Camping Rentals,** 3857 Fairview St. (© 907/225-7335; www.latitude56.com/camping/index.html), which has been supplying cabin trips for more than 15 years. They rent almost everything you need, including small outboards and life jackets for the skiffs, and deliver directly to the air taxi or water taxi.

The cabins are remote. You can hike or take a boat to some of them, but most are accessible only by floatplane (and unless you have loads of stuff, flying is probably the cheapest way to go). Expect to pay around $1,000 round-trip for three passengers. Obviously, it makes sense only if you will stay for a while—we never go for less than 3 nights. For recommended carriers, see "Majestic Misty Fjords," p. 118.

FISHING The **Alaska Department of Fish & Game** produces a 24-page fishing guide to Ketchikan with details on where to find fish in both fresh- and saltwater, including a list of 17 fishing spots accessible from the roads. Get it from the local office of the **Alaska Department of Fish & Game,** at 2030 Sea Level Dr., Suite 205, Ketchikan, AK 99901(© 907/225-2859; www.alaska.gov/adfg, click "Sport Fisheries" then on the Southeast region on the map). More fishing ideas are under "Hiking," below and "Cabin Trips," above. As is generally true in Southeast Alaska, most fishing takes place from boats in saltwater, for which you need a guided charter. **Ketchikan Charter Boats** (© **800/272-7291** or 907/225-7291; www.ketchikancharterboats. com) has a lot of experience in these waters. You can also get a referral from the visitor center. The going rate for a daylong charter for salmon or halibut is around $300 per person, for a half-day about $160.

HIKING   Eight miles out the North Tongass Highway, the **Ward Lake Recreation Area** covers a lovely patch of rainforest, lake, and stream habitat and has a picnic area, several trails, and campgrounds. Ward Creek has steelhead and cutthroat trout, Dolly Varden char, and silver salmon; check current regulations before fishing. The wide, gravel **Ward Lake Nature Trail** circles the placid lake for 1.3 miles among old-growth Sitka spruce large enough to put you in your place. For a more challenging hike, **Perseverance Lake Trail** climbs through forest with steps and boardwalks from the Three Cs Campground, across the road from Ward Lake, to a lake 2.3 miles away that can be reached no other way. There's a good bit of climbing to get there, but the trail is extraordinarily well maintained, without mud even in wet weather. To reach the recreation area, turn right off the highway on Revilla Road and follow the signs.

   Deer Mountain Trail, right behind downtown, is a steep but rewarding climb through big, mossy trees up to great views. You can walk from City Park to the trail head, half a mile and 500 feet higher on steep Fair Street and Ketchikan Lakes Road, but if you take a cab you will save energy for the trail. The first mile rises 1,000 feet to a great ocean view south of Tongass Narrows, and the next mile and 1,000 feet to another great view, this time of Ketchikan. The alpine summit, at 3,000 feet, comes near the 3-mile mark. A public shelter (first-come, first-served) is a bit farther, and the trail continues to another trail head 10 miles away. Pick up a trail guide sheet from the Forest Service at the Southeast Alaska Discovery Center (p. 107).

SEA KAYAKING   The islands, coves, and channels around Ketchikan create protected waters rich with life and welcoming for exploration by kayak. **Southeast Sea Kayaks** (© **800/287-1607** or 907/225-1258; www.kayakketchikan.com), rents kayaks and guides day trips and overnights. They specialize in taking small groups of independent travelers, not big mobs from the cruise ships, and have half-day trips that start with a boat ride to real wilderness with only six paddlers along. Those are $149 for adults, $119 for children, including food and drink. A 2½-hour paddle is $89 for adults, $59 for children as young as 6. The shop is a mile from the cruise-ship dock at 1621 Tongass Ave. They have multi-day Misty Fjords expeditions, too.

WHERE TO STAY

In addition to the hotels and B&Bs listed below, the **Ketchikan Reservation Service,** 412 D-1 Loop Rd., Ketchikan, AK 99901 (© **800/987-5337** or phone/fax 907/247-5337; www.ketchikan-lodging.com), books many bed-and-breakfasts and outfitted apartments, and has online availability and reservations. **Alaska Travelers Accommodations LLC** (© **800/928-3308** or 907/247-7117; www.alaskatravelers.com) is a Ketchikan-based service of long-standing that handles lodgings here, in Juneau, and scattered in other southeast communities.

EXPENSIVE

Best Western Landing ★★   This hotel already boasted newly furnished rooms, done in bright colors and with granite bathroom counters, when 45 brand-new rooms opened in 2006. They're terrific: built with 9-foot ceilings and big opening windows, and equipped with high-quality beds, cherry-wood furniture, flat-screen TVs, and, in nine premium view rooms, fireplaces and covered decks. Every room is loaded with amenities, including both Wi-Fi and wired broadband. Service is professional. The hotel's competition wins only in the category of charm, as an excellent corporate-feeling hotel may not be what you want in Ketchikan. The location, right across from the ferry dock, is distant from the downtown sights, so you'll need to rent a car or use the courtesy van that the hotel offers.

The **Landing Restaurant,** a fountain and grill with lots of chrome, is a local favorite and very kid-friendly. Try the fresh halibut sandwich or Salisbury steak with real mashed potatoes. Lunch and dinner range from $7.25 to $25. You can order from that same steak and seafood menu upstairs, at **Jeremiah's** bar, which also serves sandwiches, pizza, and good pasta in a sumptuous room; the nonsmoking area is glassed off and not smoky.

3434 Tongass Ave., Ketchikan, AK 99901. © 800/428-8304 or 907/225-5166. Fax 907/225-6900. www.landing hotel.com. 107 units. High season $190–$200 double, $210 suite; low season $137–$147 double, $175 suite. AE, DC, DISC, MC, V. **Amenities:** 2 restaurants; bar; exercise room; courtesy van; limited room service; laundry service; dry cleaning; covered parking. *In room:* TV, fridge, coffeemaker, hair dryer, iron, microwave, high-speed Internet, Wi-Fi.

Cape Fox Lodge 🌟🌟

This is Alaska's most beautiful hotel. It stands on a wooded pinnacle above downtown, reached from Creek Street by a funicular. The sheer drop-off and tall rainforest trees create the lofty feeling of a treehouse in the rooms and restaurant. Perfectly proportioned buildings are executed in extraordinarily good taste. Warm wood frames complement the stunning views out of the double-hung windows. The Cape Fox Native corporation built the hotel, and the lobby and parking area are a museum of Tlingit art masterpieces, adding to the peace and rainforest spirit. Rooms are large and airy, appointed in rich-toned wood, and all but a dozen share a view of Ketchikan and the sea and islands beyond (rooms on the opposite side are $10 less). Each room has an attractively tiled bathroom. In the last 2 years we've found rooms ready for renewal, but the housekeeping was good on our latest visit. There's a good coffee shop off the lobby.

The **Heen Kahidi** restaurant has one of Alaska's most attractive dining rooms, a tall, narrow rectangle of windows with a fireplace. Attractive new upholstery in 2007 is another asset. Unfortunately, we've been repeatedly disappointed by the service. Lunch ranges from $7 to $20; dinner main courses range from $17 to $37, with most around $25. The dining room is open from 7am to 9pm daily.

800 Venetia Way, Ketchikan, AK 99901. © 800/325-4000 or 907/225-8001. Fax 907/225-8286. www.westcoast hotels.com. 72 units. High season $190–$200 double; low season $100–$110 double; year-round $250 suite. AE, DC, DISC, MC, V. **Amenities:** Restaurant; bar; limited room service; dry cleaning. *In room:* TV w/pay movies and Nintendo rental, dataport, coffeemaker, hair dryer, iron, Wi-Fi (with fee).

Salmon Falls Resort 🌟🌟

If fishing is your goal, a stay at this huge on-island lodge has several advantages. First, there's the incredible setting, on island-dotted Clover Pass next to a waterfall where 10,000 pink salmon spawn. Next is the cost savings of a road-accessible lodge, since you don't have to fly there. Finally, you're not trapped in the middle of nowhere if one of you doesn't want to fish—the attractions of Ketchikan are a 17-mile drive down the road. The facilities are quite good: large, up-to-date white-walled motel rooms with phones, TVs, and small bathrooms. Those in the upper building are slightly preferable and cost the same. Some 40 lodge-operated boats tie at the dock. Inclusive fishing packages start at $1,210 per person, double occupancy, for a 3-day stay with 2 days on the water, self-guided. With a guide, the price is $1,705 per person. Without fishing, room and board is $743.

The **restaurant** and bar are in a massive log octagon held up in the center by a section of the Alaska pipeline, with great views and a menu of steak and seafood ranging from $18 to $40. It's worth a drive out the road for dinner, even if you aren't staying here (the restaurant doesn't open until May 26).

16707 N. Tongass Hwy. (P.O. Box 5700), Ketchikan, AK 99901. (© 800/247-9059 (reservations) or 907/225-2752. Fax 907/225-2710. www.salmonfallsresort.com. 52 units. $1,705 per person, double occupancy 3-day stay with 2 days on the water with guide; $1,210 per person without guide; $743 per person room and board only. AE, MC, V. Closed Sept 15–May 15. **Amenities:** Restaurant; bar; inclusive guided fishing.

MODERATE

Black Bear Inn ★★ *Finds*   This is a new luxury inn on a large waterfront lot with extensive gardens and a trail to a private beach. The building shows the owners' attention to detail and exquisite taste—wood floors, exceptional tile, fireplaces, the best fabrics, leather furniture, Alaskan art originals, satellite TV (flat screen) and radio, and so on. Each of the five units has its own covered porch and there is a large outdoor hot tub. The hosts, Nicole and Jim Church, offer unusual services, as well: They'll lend a crab pot or teach a guest to smoke fish. Breakfasts are self-served from a shared guest kitchen; a suite has its own kitchen. The location is near the ferry terminal and airport, 4 miles north of downtown.

5528 N. Tongass Hwy., Ketchikan, AK 99901. (© 907/225-4343. www.stayinalaska.com. 5 units. Year-round $150 double, $200 suite. Extra person $50. Rates include self-serve breakfast from stocked kitchen. MC, V. Children by arrangement only. **Amenities:** Hot tub; laundry service; fish cleaning and freezing facilities. *In room:* TV/DVD, fridge, coffeemaker, Wi-Fi, gas fireplace.

The Narrows Inn ★   The motel buildings sit above the water, where fishing charters and floatplanes collect guests for outings. The rooms, done in an outdoors theme, are fresh and nicely decorated, with wallpaper borders. My only complaint is that they are too small—the TV is mounted on the wall. The bathrooms are large. Rooms with balconies rent for $10 more. The location is 4 miles from downtown; they have a shuttle that takes guests to the airport, ferry terminal, and sites within city limits. For flexibility, however, you may want to rent a car if staying here.

The **Narrows Inn Restaurant** ((© **907/247-5900**) is a quiet, comfortable place to eat, with a water view. The food is consistently good enough to bring locals out for dates, celebrations, or brunch with family. For lunch try a half order of one of the rich pasta dishes. Best choices for dinner include the crispy chicken cordon bleu or flavorful Tequila pork.

4871 N. Tongass Hwy. (P.O. Box 8296), Ketchikan, AK 99901. (© 888/686-2600 or 907/247-2600. Fax 907/247-2602. www.narrowsinn.com. 46 units. High season $135–$150 double, $220–$235 suite; low season $99–$115 double, $160–$185 suite. Extra person $10. AE, DC, DISC, MC, V. **Amenities:** Restaurant; bar; courtesy shuttle; marina. *In room:* TV, fridge, coffeemaker, hair dryer, microwave, Wi-Fi.

INEXPENSIVE

Captain's Quarters Bed & Breakfast ★★ *Value*   The rooms here rival the best in Ketchikan, but cost half as much. They are large, quiet, and immaculate, with sweeping views of the city and ocean, and share a self-contained, self-service breakfast room. Little things are done right, such as each room having a private phone with its own outside line and number. A light nautical theme carries through the building. One room has a full kitchen. The setup allows as much privacy as you want—socialize with hostess Toni Bass, a gregarious school secretary, or come and go without seeing anyone. The house is perched in a mountainside neighborhood just north of the tunnel, where half the streets are stairs or wooden ramps. It's a significant but doable walk from downtown. There's no smoking in the house.

325 Lund St., Ketchikan, AK 99901. (© 907/225-4912. www.ptialaska.net/~captbnb. 3 units. High season $100–$110 double; low season $75 double. Extra person $15. Rates include continental breakfast. MC, V. *In room:* TV, hair dryer.

Eagle Heights Bed & Breakfast ⚐ *Finds*   A house with treetop views of the water-front shows exceptional craftsmanship and taste in large, airy guest rooms and a comfortable common room. Two of the units are large suites and all three are equipped with many amenities, including refrigerators stuffed with food and goodies. Hostess Cherry Ferry keeps the place as immaculate as the day it was built and brings the generous continental breakfast to the room. She even washes guests' laundry. Every room has a private entrance, there's plenty of parking, and the downtown sites are about 20 minutes away on foot. Reserve well ahead, as it books up.

1626 Water St., Ketchikan, AK 99901. ⓒ 800/928-3308 or 907/225-1760. www.eagleheightsbb.com. 3 units. $95–$125 double. Extra adult $25. MC, V. **Amenities:** Laundry service. *In room:* TV/VCR, stocked fridge, coffeemaker, hair dryer, iron, microwave.

New York Hotel/The Inn at Creek Street ⚐⚐ *Value*   The same family operates two sets of lodgings in the center of the most historic area. The original portion is the hotel, a funny little 1924 building with a tiny lobby and charming, antique-furnished rooms. It is on the National Register of Historic Places, and the owners have done a good job of adding modern comfort while keeping the essentially funky feel. Four rooms look out on a small boat harbor while five, with less street noise, face the garden. They're not large, but all are a great value—more attractive than other hotel rooms in town that cost much more. To create the new part of the business, the inn, the owners bought apartments above the shops on the Creek Street boardwalk and renovated them into spacious, modern suites. These units are downright luxurious, with kitchens, excellent amenities, and great privacy, and they sit on pilings over the flowing creek. The hotel offers a courtesy van to the airport, ferries, and hiking trails. Note that those who have trouble with stairs shouldn't consider either of these properties.

207 Stedman St., Ketchikan, AK 99901. ⓒ **866/225-0246** or 907/225-0246. Fax 907/225-1803. www.thenewyork hotel.com. 12 units. High season $109–$119 double, $159–$179 suite; low season $79–$89 double, $109 suite. DISC, MC, V. **Amenities:** Restaurant; courtesy van. *In room:* TV, high speed Internet.

A HOSTEL & CAMPING

Three Forest Service campgrounds with a total of 47 sites are located at **Ward Lake** (see p. 113). A salmon stream runs through the middle of the lakeside Signal Creek Campground, which, along with the Last Chance Campground, can be reserved through the national system described in "Getting Outside in the Tongass National Forest," on p. 102. The camping fee at either place is $10.

Eighteen miles out North Tongass Highway, the **Settler's Cove State Park** includes a sandy beach (a good place to watch whales, beachcomb, or even swim); a disabilities-accessible path to a spectacular waterfall; and a short coastal trail. There are 14 campsites, half of which will take rigs of up to 30 feet, without hookups. Camping costs $10 a night. For information, contact the **Alaska Division of Parks** (ⓒ **907/ 247-8574**), 9883 N. Tongass Hwy.

If you need hookups for an RV, try **Clover Pass Resort,** about 15 miles north of the ferry terminal on North Point Higgins Road (ⓒ **800/410-2234** or 907/247-2234; www.cloverpassresort.com). They charge $30 to $32 a night.

Ketchikan Youth Hostel   This downtown hostel in the First United Methodist Church offers utilitarian male and female dorms and guests have use of the church kitchen, although the hostel is independent of the church. Bring a sleeping bag. It is open only June through August; office hours are from 7 to 9am and 6 to 11pm.

400 Main St. (P.O. Box 8515), Ketchikan, AK 99901. (© 907/225-3319. ktnyh@eagle.ptialaska.net. 19 units (beds). $15 per person. Closed Sept–May.

WHERE TO DINE

Besides these restaurants, see the Best Western Landing, Narrows Inn, Salmon Falls Resort, and Cape Fox Lodge, all above, for other choices. A promising Japanese restaurant also serving Chinese food was new in 2007, **Dai Sho Gun,** at 1287 Tongass Ave. (© **907/225-2202**), serving terrific sushi and well-prepared grilled selections; no American food is on the menu and on our visit the staff could speak little English.

There are several good stops for light meals or snacks. The Smith family's **Alaskan Surf Fish and Chips** booth comes back to the dock every summer to the delight of locals and cruise-ship crew members who line up at lunchtime. The fish is halibut with beer batter, and they also serve shrimp and great clam chowder. Picnic tables are handy for seating on a sunny day. **Halibut Hole,** at 7 Creek St., on the deck of the Eagles Club (© **907/225-5162**) serves some of the best fried fish in town, including halibut, salmon, clams, and shrimp in crispy batter, with fries and hush puppies. It's open daily 11am to 4pm in the summer and accepts cash only. **The Alaska Fish House,** at the end of Main Street on the waterfront (© **907/225-4055** ext. 122; www.alaskafish house.com) service high-end seafood takeout from a stylish building that looks like a cannery; you can eat outdoors or take your meal to the nearby Fat Stan's wine bar.

Bar Harbor Restaurant 😤😤 SEAFOOD/ECLECTIC   The wonderful food and attentive service here are the result of a family's commitment to bringing a new class of dining to Ketchikan. They know they're in a small town, so you still find fish and chips and other basics on the menu, but the best of the seafood selections are as good as you find anywhere in Alaska. I was especially impressed by the crab cakes and the clam appetizer. The crab and corn chowder is spicy and satisfying. The halibut tacos are a local obsession (fish, cabbage, cilantro, tomato, onion, lemony sauce). They also do many specials, both to allow the chef-owner to stretch and to educate their audience. Prices are reasonable—usually around $18 for a seafood special. Be ready to settle in, as a meal here can take time. The restaurant operates in an old house over the water a drive from the downtown tourist area, and the dining room consists of a series of partly connected small rooms, all decorated in a cozy fashion with bric-a-brac and white Christmas lights. The name derives from the boat basin that the restaurant overlooks. Given the few seats, reservations are essential.

2813 Tongass Ave. (© **907/225-2813**. www.barharborketchikan.com. Reservations recommended. Dinner main courses $13–$30. DC, DISC, MC, V. Tues–Sat 4:30–9pm.

Burger Queen *Finds* BURGERS   Restaurants with the word "burger" in the name don't often get full write-ups in travel guidebooks, and this place looks unlikely for special treatment as well, but Debbie and Shawn Rahr have turned their four-table restaurant into a Ketchikan institution by doing simple food right. You certainly won't go wrong ordering a burger and milkshake here, but also consider the grilled chicken (teriyaki or barbecue), the cornmeal-breaded halibut, or the oriental grilled chicken salad—teriyaki grilled chicken, loads of veggies, crispy noodles, and homemade tangy soy-sauce flavored dressing. The portions are so large most adults will get plenty to eat ordering from the children's section of the menu. Since the dining room is so small, having your meal delivered for no extra charge makes sense, or get takeout and eat in the park across the street.

Majestic Misty Fjords

In Punchbowl Cove, south of Ketchikan in Misty Fjords National Monument, sheer cliffs rise 3,150 feet straight up from calm water, as high and smooth as those in the Yosemite Valley. Misty is well over twice Yosemite's size, but there isn't a single car here; there isn't so much as a mile of road; in fact, there are hardly any trails. It's something like a great national park before the people arrived.

Visits to the monument are by tour boat, floatplane, or, for the hardy, sea kayak. It isn't a cheap place to go, and you don't see much wildlife. By boat, you don't see glaciers, although glaciated mountains are a spectacular feature of the flights. Unlike Glacier Bay, Tracy Arm, Kenai Fjords, or Resurrection Bay—all places with more wildlife and more glaciers at sea level—the experience at Misty is pure geology. You go for the scenery.

Two companies currently offer boat tours to Misty's Punchbowl Cove, Rudyerd Bay, and back, and both offer meals in the price. Sitka-based **Allen Marine** (© 877/686-8100 or 907/225-8100; www.allenmarinetours.com) has some distinct advantages. The fast, quiet boat makes the round-trip in 4½ hours. All seats face forward. A knowledgeable naturalist interprets the scenery. Adult passengers can peruse regional books, while children work with craft boxes and activities. Tickets are $147 for adults, $91 for children. Sailings every day in the summer coordinate with the cruise-ships' dockings. A Misty Fjords tour operated by **Alaska Travel Adventures,** doing business as Alaska Cruises (© 800/323-5757 or 907/789-0052; www.bestofalaskatravel.com), offers the opportunity see the fjords from above by floatplane and return to Ketchikan by water for $269 for adults, $229 for children; taking the boat both ways is $139 for adults and $89 for children.

I prefer seeing the fjords on an extended floatplane flight (and I certainly recommend it for those susceptible to seasickness). Flying over the scenery is amazing, but it's the floatplane landing that really blows your mind,

518 Water St. © **907/225-6060.** Lunch and dinner $4–$13. MC, V. High season Mon–Sat 11am–7pm; low season Wed–Sat 11am–6pm.

Diaz Cafe ⊀ (Finds FILIPINO   Many Alaskan towns have strong, cohesive Filipino communities, created over decades by large, close families drawn across the ocean one by one for cannery work. In Ketchikan, the heartbeat of the Filipino community has beat in this bright little diner since the early 1950s as ownership passes generation to generation in the same family. The place is so well loved among all ethnicities in Ketchikan that its current owner is unable to change the slightest detail—she even faced an insurrection when she tried to change the color of the menus—so everything remains today as it was half a century ago: the Formica, worn from wiping, the yellow and red walls, and the nondescript street front (which could scare you off, although the restaurant inside is immaculate). If you haven't had Filipino food, this is the place to try it. The spicy chicken adobo, a huge, delicious half chicken bathed in gravy with rice, is $12. The sweet and sour halibut is memorable, too. Regulars order the "Large

— I don't speak sign language.

A hotel can close for all kinds of reasons.
Our Guarantee ensures that if your hotel's undergoing construction, we'll let you know in advance. In fact, we cover your entire travel experience. See www.travelocity.com/guarantee for details.

travelocity·
You'll never roam alone.

because then you get a sudden sense of the scale of everything you've seen from the air. The cliffs are magnified while you shrink to a speck. Go in the late afternoon when the light is pretty and the swarms of planes carrying cruise-ship passengers are gone. Several air-taxi operators in Ketchikan take flightseeing day trips to Misty Fjords or drop clients at remote cabins. **Promech Air** (② **800/860-3845** or 907/225-3845; www.promechair.com) is a large one, charging about $200 for a 75-minute flight including about 10 minutes on the ground.

But I like best a smaller company, **Island Wings Air Service** (② **888/854-2444** or 907/225-2444; www.islandwings.com). The owner and pilot is Michelle Madsen, and my flight with her was among the most memorable of the many I've taken around Alaska. She flew the plane with her long blond hair flowing and her little white dog Perro at her side (although she offered to leave him behind), offering a choice of music on the iPod as background to her impromptu commentary about the fjords. We soared with Van Morrison while Michelle told us about her favorite places down below. The landing was as long as anyone needed to soak in the awesome surroundings. It felt like an outing with old friends. Madsen charges about $200 for a seat on a six-passenger DeHavilland Beaver for a 2-hour flight that includes 45 minutes on the ground at the fjords. She also flies guests to Forest Service cabins (many of them in Misty), places she knows intimately, and she will take the time to help you choose one that suits your interests and budget. Take a look at her informative website for a good start.

Visiting the fjords by kayak is a real expedition, advisable only for those who already know they enjoy this mode of travel, but I can think of few more spectacular places to paddle. **Southeast Exposure** (② 907/225-8829; www.southeastexposure.com) does guided paddles there, and has for 20 years, earning a good reputation. Their 6-day trip is $950 per person.

guy," a bowl of sweet and sour rice mixed with meat, which arrives instantly and costs $5.25. You can also get sandwiches, burgers (also served with rice), and Chinese food.
335 Stedman St. ② **907/225-2257.** Lunch and dinner $5.25–$14. No credit cards. Tues–Sat 11:30am–2pm and 4–8pm; Sun noon–7:30pm.

Good Fortune Chinese Restaurant CHINESE   This restaurant stands on pilings in Creek Street, with small upstairs and downstairs dining rooms. The food is consistently good year after year, with a long and varied menu that allows you to choose by style of cuisine—Cantonese, Szechuan, and so on. Try the broccoli beef.
4 Creek St. ② **907/225-1818.** Lunch $6.25; dinner $12–$19. DISC, MC, V. Mon–Sat 11am–9pm; Sun noon–9pm. Winter closed Mon.

Ocean View Restaurante ⭐ (Finds) MEXICAN/ITALIAN   Everyone in Ketchikan already knows how good the food is at this family restaurant, which is why the place is so lively and festive even on an off-season weeknight—in fact, the dining room can be deafening. Few tourists know about it or make the drive a mile from downtown. The menu is long and reasonably priced, with separate columns of Mexican and Italian cuisine (and an occasional Greek item slipped into the Italian column), a page of seafood and sautéed entrees, plus chicken, veal, steak, pasta, and pizza. Variety is a common technique used by small-town restaurants to make it through the winter; the difference here is remarkably good cooking. They serve beer and wine. The pizza, delivered free, is the best in town. The restaurant's popularity may require dining early on weekends to get a table; call ahead.

1831 Tongass Ave. ⓒ 907/225-7566. Reservations recommended. Lunch $7–$9; dinner $6–$16. MC, V. Daily 11am–11pm.

3 Wrangell

Wrangell, valued for its position near the mouth of the Stikine River, began as a Tlingit stronghold and trading post and became the site of a Russian fort built in 1834. The British leased the area from the Russians in 1840, and their flag flew until the U.S. purchase of Alaska in 1867. Over the balance of the 19th century, Wrangell experienced three gold rushes and the construction of a cannery and sawmill.

Then time pretty much stopped.

While the world outside changed, Wrangell stayed the same from the mid–20th century on. It even moved backward. Elsewhere, Wal-Mart and shopping malls were invented and small-town main streets deflated. Then people noticed what they had lost and tried to bring back their communities. Not out here, beyond the road system. With little incentive for anyone to visit, Wrangell stayed as it was after a 1952 fire burned the downtown: a burly, blue-collar American logging town, simple and conservative. Wrangell cut trees, processed them, and shipped them. The bars stayed busy, and no one thought of opening a health food restaurant. As long as there were trees to saw into lumber, the future was safe in the past.

Or so it seemed until environmental and economic issues closed the mill in 1994. Some feared the town would die, too. Sawing lumber had sustained the local economy for more than 100 years and a third of the paychecks in town came from that one plant. But it hasn't been so simple. The logging industry survived, off and on, and on a much smaller scale. The town grew quieter. Some trailer houses disappeared and stores closed, but the lights didn't go out, although the population declined.

But Wrangell is working to improve on its positive qualities. Residents show an endearing eagerness to please. A new museum was completed by 2005, and eco-tourism operators offer kayaking, hiking, biking, and the like. Tour boats take guests up the wild Stikine River, out on the water for Southeast's great salmon fishing, and over to the mainland to see hordes of black bears at the Anan Wildlife Observatory. The U.S. Forest Service maintains gravel roads that lead to some spectacular places. The community even built a golf course to attract visitors, and **Muskeg Meadow** (ⓒ 907/874-4653; www.wrangellalaskagolf.com) is truly spectacular. The townspeople are so proud of it you'll find it difficult to turn down a round ($20–$40 per day; clubs are for rent).

The town has a nonthreatening, small-scale feel that allows a family to wander comfortably and make friends. We were invited home to dinner by another family we had just met. With so little crime there is no fear of strangers. We picnicked in a totem pole park, hiked in the rainforest, and looked at ancient art strewn across Petroglyph Beach. We were sorry to have to leave. On the ferry back to Juneau, a class of Wrangell

ACCOMMODATIONS ■
Harding's Old Sourdough Lodge **9**
Rooney's Roost B&B **2**
Stikine Inn **1**
Wrangell Hostel **3**
Zimovia B&B **7**

DINING ◆
Diamond C Café **5**
Zak's Café **4**

ATTRACTIONS ●
Grave of Chief Shakes **8**
Nolan Center Museum &
  Visitor Center **6**

sixth graders sat next to us. They talked with excited innocence of all the new things they hoped to experience in the state capital, the most electrifying of which seemed to be the prospect of eating for the first time at McDonald's. Wrangell, I thought, still has a long way to go to catch up with the rest of the world, and that is a condition much to be envied.

ESSENTIALS

GETTING THERE   **Alaska Airlines** (© 800/252-7522; www.alaskaair.com) serves Wrangell once daily with a jet flying 28 minutes north from Ketchikan and another 19 minutes south from Petersburg, a flight that skims treetops the entire way.

Wrangell is on the main line of the **Alaska Marine Highway System** (© 800/642-0066; www.ferryalaska.com). The voyage through the narrow, winding **Wrangell Narrows** north to Petersburg is one of the most beautiful and fascinating in Southeast Alaska. It's quite a navigational feat to watch as the 400-foot ships squeeze through a passage so slender and shallow the vessel's own displacement changes the water level onshore as it passes. The route, not taken by cruise ships, which approach through larger waterways, is also a source of delays, as the narrows are deep enough for passage only at high tide. The walk-on fare is $36 from Ketchikan, $32 from Petersburg. The terminal is downtown (© 907/874-3711) a block from the Stikine Inn.

VISITOR INFORMATION   The city's **Wrangell Visitor Center** is in the new Nolan Center, along with the Wrangell Museum, on the water in the heart of town at 296 Outer Dr. (© **800/367-9745;** www.wrangell.com). Staff from both the Nolan Center and the U.S. Forest Service are on hand to answer questions.

The Forest Service's **Wrangell Ranger District Office** is at 525 Bennett St. (P.O. Box 51), Wrangell, AK 99929 (© **907/874-2323;** www.fs.fed.us/r10/tongass), located on the hill behind town. Forest Service personnel here or at the visitor center have local knowledge of the logging roads and fishing holes, offer printed information on each Forest Service cabin and path, and, for $9, sell a detailed Wrangell Island Road Guide topographic map, which is printed on waterproof material. The district office is open Monday through Friday from 8am to 4:30pm.

ORIENTATION   The main part of town is laid out north to south along the water-front on the northern point of Wrangell Island. **Front Street** is the main business street, leading from the small-boat harbor and **Chief Shakes Island** at the south to the city dock and the ferry dock at the north. Most of the rest of the town is along **Church Street,** which runs parallel to Front Street a block higher up the hill. **Evergreen Avenue** and **Bennett Street** form a loop to the north that goes to the airport. The only road to the rest of the island, the **Zimovia Highway,** heads out of town to the south, paved for about 12 miles, then connects to over 100 miles of gravel logging roads built and maintained by the Forest Service, most of which are usable by two-wheel-drive vehicles in the summer.

GETTING AROUND   You can do the town on foot, but you will need wheels for the airport or Zimovia Highway. **Practical Rent A Car** is located at the Wrangell airport (© **907/874-3975**). **Northern Lights Taxi** is at © **907/874-4646.** Rent **bikes, canoes,** or **kayaks** from Rainwalker Expeditions (© **907/874-2549;** www.rainwalker expeditions.com) at the city dock, described under "Gearing Up," below.

FAST FACTS: Wrangell

Bank **Wells Fargo** is at 115 Front St., with an ATM. There's also an ATM across from the Stikine Inn.

Hospital **Wrangell Medical Center** is at 310 Bennett St. (© **907/874-7000**).

Internet Access At the **Nolan Center,** 296 Campbell Drive (© **907/874-3770**), $5 for the first 20 minutes. Free at the public library on Church Street (© **907/ 874-3535**).

Police For nonemergency calls, dial © **907/874-3304.**

Post Office At 105 Federal Way, across from the Stikine Inn.

Taxes **Sales tax** is 7%. Rooms are taxed at 13%.

SPECIAL EVENTS   The **Garnet Festival,** held the third week of April, marks the arrival of the sea lions, hooligans, shorebirds, and a great concentration of bald eagles on the Stikine River Delta, a spring tornado of wildlife in the region's largest coastal marshes. Community activities take place in town while jet boat tours traverse the delta. **The Wrangell King Salmon Derby,** held during the last half of May and first half of June, started in 1953. Contact the Wrangell Chamber of Commerce for details (© **907/874-3901;** www.wrangellchamber.org). Wrangell also puts on a classic small-town **Independence Day** celebration.

EXPLORING WRANGELL & ENVIRONS

Before white settlers arrived, the Tlingits had already warred for centuries over this strategic trading location near the mouth of the Stikine River. The first Chief Shakes was a successful conqueror who enslaved his enemies, then handed down power through the female line, in the Tlingit tradition, for seven generations. Charlie Jones was recognized as Chief Shakes VII, the last of the line, at a potlatch in 1940, but the position had long since lost most of its status. The decline began after the Alaska purchase, in 1867. Word came of the Emancipation Proclamation, which theoretically freed a third of the residents of the coast's Tlingit villages. Chief Shakes VI sent his slaves in canoes to dry halibut; they kept paddling home to Puget Sound, never looking back. (An excellent pamphlet, *Authentic History of Shakes Island and Clan,* by E. L. Keithhahn, sells for $4 at the Nolan Center Museum, described below.)

Chief Shakes Island, a tiny islet in the middle of the small-boat harbor, is the site of a Tlingit clan house and collection of totem poles constructed by Native workers, using traditional tools, in the Civilian Conservation Corps (CCC) during the 1930s. Unlike some CCC clan house replicas in the region, which mix Tlingit styles, this house is an exact, scaled-down copy of the house in which Chief Shakes VI lay in state in 1916. The inside of the clan house is fascinating, both in the sense it gives of the people's ways, and for some extraordinary artifacts. Unfortunately, it takes some effort to get inside, as it is open mostly only when the cruise ships are in town, a few times a week in the summer. These times are posted around town or at the clan house. Only then can you get in for the single admission of $3. Otherwise, you can pay a $25 minimum to have someone come down and show you around. Call Nora Rinehart at © **907/874-2023** (e-mail norarinehart@yahoo.com), or, if you can't reach Nora, Margret Sturdevant at © **907/874-3747.** Nora can give you the cruise-ship schedule before you come, too. Even if you can't manage that, visit the island to see the totem poles and the charming setting (and, with extra time, visit the overgrown grave of Chief Shakes V, on Case Ave. just across the harbor). You can often see an otter near the island's footbridge.

The carved house posts in the clan house are replicas of the mid-18th-century originals protected by the local museum. These are probably the oldest and certainly the best-preserved Tlingit house posts in existence, still bearing the original fish egg and mineral paints, and a gash where, during a potlatch, a chief hacked off an image that a visitor admired and gave it to him—a gesture that demonstrated the extent of his wealth then, and still does.

The **Nolan Center Museum,** at 296 Campbell Dr. (© **907/874-3770**), opened in 2004. It's an impressive building, with galleries devoted to natural history, logging and fishing, and Native culture. The museum owns many important early Alaska Native pieces, and a lot of just plain old stuff telling the story of Wrangell, one of Alaska's most historic towns. Admission is $5 for adults, $3 for seniors, $2 for children ages 6 to 12; family admission is $12. The museum is open May 1 to September 30 Monday through Saturday 10am to 5pm, the rest of the year Tuesday through Saturday 1 to 5pm, or by appointment. Don't miss the shop, which has an extraordinary collection of books on Alaska and authentic Native crafts for bargain prices.

The museum helped preserve an impressive set of petroglyphs that lie on the beach a mile north of town. The 50 carvings at **Wrangell Petroglyph Beach State Historic Park** probably represent the work of forgotten indigenous people predating the Tlingits and were made over a long period of time. The images, chipped into rocks, are of animals and geometric forms. Their purpose is lost to time. Walk north on Evergreen Avenue and follow the signs down to the beach (don't go within an hour of high tide). Replicas of the petroglyphs were carved so that visitors who want to take rubbings will not destroy the originals; also try not to step on them. The great pleasure here is simply to search for the carvings—they're just lying out there, and it takes some looking— and to wonder at their meaning and age.

GETTING OUTSIDE

ON THE ISLAND   Wrangell Island's network of gravel roads, maintained by the Forest Service, leads to places of awesome beauty rarely visited by non-Alaskans. There are a few day-hike trails, some lovely campsites, and paths to remote shelters and fishing lakes you can have to yourself. There are also a couple of calm and scenic places to start a kayak paddle.

There's only one way out of town: south on the **Zimovia Highway** along narrow Zimovia Strait. The Forest Service map (see "Visitor Information," above) is helpful for anything you might want to do along this route. The first potential stop is **City Park,** just south of town. Besides having a picnic area on the shore among big trees, it's a fine **tide pooling** spot. Go a couple of hours before a good low tide.

Five miles out Zimovia Highway you reach the **Shoemaker Bay Recreation Area,** with a small-boat harbor, campground, and picnic sites (see "A Hostel & Camping," later in this chapter). Continuing south, **Eight Mile Beach** is a good stop for a ramble, and don't miss **Nemo Point,** a high, oceanside overlook from which you can see more than 13 miles along Zimovia Strait all the way back to town. There are eight gorgeous campsites, and a plank walk trail (see "Hiking," below) along the road leads down to the beach.

All the way across the island, about 45 minutes from town, **Earl West Cove** gives access to the protected wilderness waters on the Eastern Passage. There's a campsite there, too.

OFF THE ISLAND   Wrangell provides a stepping-off point for vast, rich wild lands and remote fishing, rafting, sea kayaking, or wildlife-watching. I've described two of the main off-island destinations below—the Stikine River and the Anan Wildlife Observatory—but there are many more, too many to mention. The guides I've listed can give ideas, or look into the Forest Service cabins for rent to the public, many of which provide exclusive access to exceptional fishing. To get beyond the island, you need a boat or floatplane. You can go independently, hiring a water taxi for $200 to $260 an hour; it costs over $500, one-way, to get to a remote Forest Service cabin by boat. That service is offered by various operators (see "Gearing Up," below). If you prefer to go by air, **Sunrise Aviation** (✆ **800/874-2311** or 907/874-2319) is a Wrangell-based operator.

GEARING UP   For a lift over the water, a guide, or rental equipment, there are several long-established businesses. **Alaska Waters,** with a desk in the Stikine Inn, 107 Stikine Ave. (✆ **800/347-4462** or 907/874-2378; www.alaskawaters.com) rents equipment and offers various marine services, including fishing and tours. Check the impressive website for monthly specials and other useful information. **Alaska Vistas,** at the city dock where the cruise ships land, (✆ **866/874-3006** or 907/874-3006;

www.alaskavistas.com) started as a sea-kayaking business, but now offers water taxis, guided hiking, and other services. You can stop in at their office on the dock for advice, books and maps, gear, and espresso. Both companies are listed below under the appropriate headings.

Marie Oboczky's **Rainwalker Expeditions** (© **888/276-2549** or 907/874-2549; www.rainwalkerexpeditions.com) rents bikes ($20 a day) and sea kayaks ($40–$60). She also leads guided activities and offers accommodations on a houseboat in Wrangell or afield (all covered below). Among her choices, Oboczky takes clients for a full day of guided hiking, biking, and sea kayaking for $99 per person, a bargain. Her van tour of the island is $75, including lunch. She also has teamed up with other outdoor businesses in town to offer joint booking and trip planning. Check her website for advice or stop in at the office near the city dock (the sign says TOUR RESERVATIONS & INFORMATION), next-door to the Stikine Inn. Oboczky also organizes unique escorted tours—"Alaskan Lifestyle Programs"—that see the Southeast as locals do.

OUTDOOR ACTIVITIES NEAR WRANGELL

BIKING   A paved 6-mile bike trail along the water next to the Zimovia Highway leads all the way from town to the Shoemaker Bay Loop Road. There's nothing to block the ocean views and a good destination at the end, the Shoemaker Bay Recreation Area, is a well-developed picnic site and the starting point of a hiking trail to a waterfall (see "Hiking," below). There are many more miles of appealing mountain-bike routes on Forest Service roads all over the island. See "Gearing Up," above, for rental information.

FISHING   Anglers can dip a line in various streams and lakes on Wrangell Island reachable by car or a drive and short hike. The Forest Service provides a list, and the **Alaska Department of Fish & Game** (© **907/874-3822**; www.adfg.state.ak.us, click on "Sport Fisheries" then the Southeast region) publishes an extensive *Petersburg/Wrangell Sport Fishing Guide.* May and June are the prime months for king salmon fishing, silvers start in July, and halibut are available all summer.

The well-run **Alaska Waters** (see "Gearing Up," above) offers a long day of saltwater fishing for $250 per person; they're professional and knowledgeable. They also rent skiffs with outboard motors for self-guided fishing. Many other charter boats are available at the harbor; ask at the visitor center. You can often arrange to use part of the day on the boat for sightseeing and wildlife-watching, too.

HIKING   Across the road from the Shoemaker Bay Recreation Area, the **Rainbow Falls Trail** climbs steeply for just under a mile (and 500 ft. in elevation gain) on a boardwalk with steps, up a ridge between two creeks, forested with big, mossy Sitka spruce and western hemlock. The falls seem to tumble down between the branches. From that point, you can continue another 2.7 miles and another 1,100 feet higher into open alpine terrain on the **Institute Creek Trail** to the Shoemaker Overlook, where there are great views, a picnic area, and a shelter. An additional section of the trail continues from there another 8 miles across the island. **Rainwalker Expeditions** (see "Gearing Up," above) leads nature walks on the lower part of the trail, and longer hikes all over the island. The advantage of going with guide Marie Oboczky is that she is a skilled naturalist and teacher and knows all the best places to go.

The Rainbow Falls Trail is sometimes visited by groups from cruise ships. If you want to be sure you won't see anyone, take one of the less-developed walks you can reach along the logging roads—the Forest Service can point the way. The new **Nemo Saltwater Access Trail** is a well-built .5-mile plank walk leading to the beach near

Turn Island, near a wonderful stand of red cedar and the Turn Island Campsite, with two wooden platforms, picnic tables, and dry firewood. Another good choice is the **Salamander Ridge Trail,** which leads a mile to subalpine terrain, where you can go off-trail hiking. The trail begins 27 miles from Wrangell on Salamander Road, also known as Forest Road 50050. The **Long Lake Trail** leads over a half-mile boardwalk to a public shelter and rowboat on the lake, on Forest Road 6271 (you'll need a map).

SEA KAYAKING   Alaska Vistas (see "Gearing Up," above) offers kayaking day-trip paddles starting from the boat harbor, longer day tours to lovely Earl West Cove on the east side of the island, or guided trips of many days. A 5-day trip starts with a jet-boat trip on the Stikine River to Shakes Lake, and then paddles back to Wrangell with stops at the natural hot springs and other sites along the way.

THE STIKINE RIVER

The Stikine's gray, glacial waters rush all the way from the dry Interior of British Columbia to a broad, shallow delta in the rainforest a few miles from Wrangell. It's among the fastest free-flowing navigable rivers in North America, and in early gold-rush years was a route through the Coastal Range. Tours that sometimes go as far as Telegraph Creek, B.C., speed against the current with the roar of high-powered engines that send a jet of water out from under their shallow, metal bottoms. On still water, the jet boats can go as fast as a car on the highway.

The shallow delta is an exceptionally rich wildlife-viewing area, a habitat of grass-lands, braided channels, and marshes populated by sea lions, eagles, and many other species of birds. In late April and early May, when the hooligans run, more than 1,500 bald eagles congregate, and some two million other birds rest on their West Coast migration. Later in the year, when summer's salmon are running, you can see them thrashing in their spawning pools. Farther upriver, tours encounter Sitka black-tailed deer, moose, brown and black bears, mountain goats, river otters, and beavers.

Traveling upriver, tours usually stop at the **Shakes Glacier** and **Shakes Lake,** where there are 3,000-foot cliffs and some 50 waterfalls. Bring a swimsuit for a dip in the Forest Service–owned **Chief Shakes Hot Springs,** where there's an indoor and an outdoor tub for public bathing. The temperature is adjustable up to 120°F (49°C). Alaska Waters and Alaska Vistas offer these tours (see "Gearing Up," above). Alaska Waters goes all the way to Telegraph, B.C., 160 miles upriver, bringing travelers to a remote homestead lodge. Commentary on all their trips includes natural history and Tlingit cultural traditions and legends. A 3-day, 2-night package is $1,399. The going rate for a 6-hour jet boat tour from Wrangell to the glacier, delta, and hot springs is $150 to $180.

Rafting the Stikine offers fast water, expansive scenery, and the potential for a remote, many-day journey. Alaska Vistas offers these guided trips, lasting about 10 days to 2 weeks, for an inclusive price of around $2,500 per person. Alaska Vistas also rents rafts and other gear for floating the Stikine. A raft rents for about $100 a day (see "Gearing Up," above).

ANAN WILDLIFE OBSERVATORY

When the pink salmon are running in July and August (peak is mid-July to Aug 20), a population of more than 40 **black bears** and a few brown bears gather near a water-fall on Anan Creek, on the mainland southeast of Wrangell Island, often walking close to a platform where visitors stand watching. Don't visit outside the time of this salmon run, however, unless you have it on good authority that bears are actively using the creek. Forest Service interpreters are on duty during the bear months; visitors must also follow safe bear behavior (they'll brief you when you arrive; also see "Outdoor Health & Safety," in chapter 2). Most visitors will enjoy a guided day trip from Wrangell more than going on their own. Both **Alaska Waters** and **Alaska Vistas** go by boat (see "Gearing Up," above). Expect to pay $200 to $250 per person for the hour-long run from Wrangell and a few hours with the bears. It's also possible to go without a guide, but you will need a pass issued by the Forest Service **Wrangell Ranger District Office,** at 525 Bennett St. (P.O. Box 51), Wrangell, AK 99929 (© **907/874-2323;** fax 907/874-7595; www.fs.fed.us/r10/tongass/districts/wrangell). Check the website for an explanation of the system, a calendar showing the number of permits available each day, and application forms. A total of 60 passes are allocated for each day of the period from July 5 through August 25, with 12 held back until 3 days before the visit. Passes are given out first-come, first-served by mail, fax, e-mail, or in person and cost $10. There's a Forest Service cabin for rent, too, in very high demand during the bear viewing season. The walk to the observatory is a half mile from the shore where you land, on a good trail. **Sunrise Aviation** (© **800/874-2311** or 907/874-2319) offers charters to Anan for prices competitive with going by boat.

WHERE TO STAY

Besides the places listed below, you will find cozy rooms with private entrances at John and Judy Baker's **Grand View Bed and Breakfast,** Mile 2, Zimovia Hwy. (P.O. Box 927), Wrangell, AK 99929 (©/fax **907/874-3225;** www.grandviewbnb.com). They charge $85 to $100 double and have an outdoor hot tub.

Harding's Old Sourdough Lodge 𝒢   Former mayor Bruce Harding runs this hotel in the style of a fishing lodge, renting the rooms alone or as packages with trips to the Anan Bear Observatory, Stikine River tours, fishing, kayaking, rafting, and other outdoor activities. The attractive building with a wraparound porch is immaculately kept. It stands in a waterfront area about a mile from the ferry dock, but Harding will drive you there or wherever else you want to go. The lodge is decorated in an outdoors theme. Most rooms are small and they generally have only shower stalls, not tubs. Some lack TVs, but all have high-speed Internet access. The suite is huge and has a Jacuzzi tub. Fresh seafood dinners are served nightly, family style (you eat what they cook). Dinner prices are $19 to $24 per person; nonguests by reservation only.

1104 Peninsula (P.O. Box 1062), Wrangell, AK 99929. (C) 800/874-3613 or 907/874-3613. Fax 907/874-3455. www.akgetaway.com. 16 units. $104 double; $149 triple or quad; $179 suite. Rates include continental breakfast. AE, DC, DISC, MC, V. **Amenities:** Sauna; bike rental; tour desk; courtesy car; coin-op laundry; fish freezing.

Rooney's Roost Bed & Breakfast

A warm family has offered this old downtown house with dormer windows to guests for many years. Antiques rest on the hardwood floors in the common areas and the four rooms, while small, are decorated according to cute themes. All have private bathrooms, four-poster beds with thick mattresses, comforters, and oversize pillows. In the summer, elaborate breakfasts with local ingredients, such as seafood or berries, are served in a sunny dining room at the guests' convenience. We ran into some rough spots on our last visit, but I offer this recommendation based on a long record of hospitality.

206 McKinnon (P.O. Box 552), Wrangell, AK 99929. (C) 907/874-2026. Fax 907/874-4404. www.rooneysroost.com. 4 units. $100 double. Extra person $25. Rates include full breakfast. MC, V. **Amenities:** Courtesy car; laundry service.

Stikine Inn

The town's main hotel offers good budget rooms in the most convenient location possible, close to the ferry dock and right on the water's edge. Rooms sharing superb water views carry an $11 to $12 premium. You can watch the sunset on the ocean and hear water lapping the shore. The hotel has been a center of community activity for decades and, despite the building's age, attentive owners are keeping it in good shape. In 2007 rooms received new paint and window treatments and the beds were of good quality and had new linens. Housekeeping was flawless. Although our room had a problem with heat regulation, the rest of the hotel seemed fine.

The **Stikine Inn Restaurant,** after a series of changes in name and ownership, now has begun developing a reputation for pleasant casual dining on a small-town scale. The dining room is noticeably clean and bright and has a terrific view. We found the cuisine a bit inconsistent; best choices are the seafood chowder and the shrimp salad and other salads. The restaurant is open 7am to 9pm in the summer and dinner prices range from $7 to $22.

107 Stikine Ave. (P.O. Box 662), Wrangell, AK 99929. (C) 888/874-3388 or 907/874-3388. Fax 907/874-3923. www.stikineinn.com. 35 units. Year-round $114–$131 double/quad, $131–$143 suite. AE, DC, DISC, MC, V. **Amenities:** Restaurant. *In room:* TV, Wi-Fi ($7 a day).

Zimovia Bed & Breakfast (Finds)

The cedar-shingled house 2 blocks above Front Street contains a pair of extraordinary handcrafted rooms—one with a boat's door on the closet, garnets in the tiles, and a cedar-walled sauna; the other decorated with hand-fused glass tiles and a glass sink atop a display of coral, sand, and glass fish. Both rooms are encased in 10-inch-thick soundproofed walls and have heated floors. Each has a private entrance from a riotously blooming garden outside. The hospitality of hostess Barb Rugo—with her wonderful baking—matches the attention to excellence that has been poured into creating the place. And staying here is the best bargain in town, too. Each room has a single double bed and no room for a third person.

319 Weber St. (P.O. Box 1424), Wrangell, AK 99929. (C) 866/946-6842 or 907/874-2626. www.zimoviabnb.com. 2 units. Year-round $85 double. MC, V. Rate includes continental breakfast. **Amenities:** Courtesy car; laundry service ($6). *In room:* TV/VCR, kitchenette, stocked fridge, coffeemaker.

A HOSTEL & CAMPING

Wrangell Hostel is at the First Presbyterian Church, 220 Church St. (P.O. Box 439), Wrangell, AK 99929 (C) **907/874-3534**). They're open Memorial Day through Labor Day, and the rate is $18 a night.

Rent a Houseboat

Marie Oboczky, the naturalist who owns Rainwalker Expeditions (℃ 907/874-2549; www.rainwalkerexpeditions.com), offers a cute and cozy old wooden houseboat as a summer accommodation. Early in summer it sits in Shoemaker Harbor, then July through September Oboczky keeps it tied up in remote Bradford Canal, 35 miles from town. This is a chance to stay in relative comfort in the wilderness, and for a bargain price. At the dock, the boat rents for $85 a night, including bikes for getting around. In its remote setting, she offers 3- and 5-day packages, including transportation and canoes, starting at $650. The boat isn't large, but a couple or family of three who enjoy the outdoors could be very content here, kayaking and enjoying the outdoors, while still able to cook and use the shower and bathroom onboard. You can put the stay together with an outfitter for guided activities, too.

There are several attractive campgrounds in Wrangell. I've never seen another campground in a spot like the mountaintop **Nemo Point Forest Service Campground** (see "Getting Outside," earlier in this section), but it's more than a dozen miles out of town. Five miles south of town, the **Shoemaker Bay Recreation Area** has sites by the road overlooking the boat harbor, right across from the Rainbow Falls Trail. There are free tent sites and RV sites with electric hookups for $25 a night, $15 without electric; the camping fee includes use of the town pool and its showers. Contact the **Wrangell Recreation and Parks Department** (℃ 907/874-2444) for information. They also manage **City Park,** right at the edge of town on Zimovia Highway, where camping is permitted with a 1-night limit.

For a full hookup RV site, try **Alaska Waters'** small park, at 241 Berger St. (℃ 800/347-4462). They charge $25 a night for rigs up to 35 feet, $30 for rigs over that length.

WHERE TO DINE

Dining has long been a weakness for Wrangell. The situation has improved somewhat, but there continues to be a lack of really good restaurants other than Zak's, described below. The two hotels offer dining. **Harding's Old Sourdough Lodge** (see "Where to Stay," above) serves meals to guests, and to others by reservation. It's a family-style dinner without a menu. The **Stikine Inn Restaurant** is also described above.

You do have a few other choices for deli sandwiches or a simple meal. **Diamond C Cafe,** 215 Front St. (℃ 907/874-3677), is a clean, reliable diner offering speedy, friendly service and well-done food from the grill. It is open Monday through Saturday 6am to 3pm, Sunday 6am to 2pm. The deli at **Bob's IGA,** 223 Brueger St. (℃ 907/874-2341) produces terrific sandwiches and baked goods, and also sells ice cream. It is open Monday through Saturday 9am to 6pm. You can also get a good sandwich at **J&W's Fast Foods** at 120 Front St., open midday only, closed Tuesday.

Zak's Café 🎔🎔 STEAK/SEAFOOD   It's a surprising treat to find food like this in Wrangell, but there's a good explanation: The owners got tired of the lack of good dining options and decided to do something about it. For lunch they serve salads, wraps, burgers, and sandwiches, and for dinner a short but diverse menu of steak, seafood, pasta, and chicken. The stir-fry was seasoned just right, and the steak béarnaise melted in the mouth. Portions tend to be large: The seafood Alfredo was enough for four people. The dining room is small, light, and spare; it doesn't live up to the food. Take the time to talk with the fascinating owners, James and Katherine, who staff the kitchen and dining room respectively.

Front St. ℂ **907/874-3355.** Reservations recommended for dinner. Lunch $6.25–$10; dinner $13–$25. MC, V. Mon–Sat 11am–8pm.

4 Petersburg: Unvarnished Threshold to the Outdoors

Petersburg is the perfect small town, the sort of prosperous, picturesque, quirky place that used to be mythologized in Disney films. Except that Petersburg would never let Disney in the door. People here are too smart for that, and too protective of a place they know would be spoiled by too much attention. For the same reason, Petersburg's residents are just as glad the big cruise ships can't enter their narrow harbor. The town is unspoiled by the ships' throngs of tourists and seasonal gift shops. Instead, locals spend the money that keeps Nordic Drive, the main street, thriving with family-owned grocery and hardware stores, a fish market, and other businesses. Wooden streets over Hammer Slough still serve utilitarian purposes, making them far more appealing than if they were prettied up as tourist areas. As you walk along Sing Lee Alley and check out the stylish little bookstore, you rarely see others like yourselves—instead, you see Norwegian fishermen in pickup trucks and blond-haired kids on bikes.

Because Petersburg is insular and authentic the sublime outdoor opportunities nearby remain little used. There are wonderful trails, mountain-biking routes, and secret places. On the water, the humpback whale-watching is as reliable as anywhere in Alaska and largely undiscovered. There's a glacier to visit, terrific fishing, and limitless sea-kayaking waters. The in-town attractions are few—a day is plenty for simple sightseeing—and little attempt has been made to accommodate lazy gawkers. But Alaska's best is waiting for those willing to spend the effort to look.

Petersburg is named for its founder, Peter Buschmann, who killed himself after living here for only 4 years. But that shouldn't be a reflection on the town, which is in an ideal location and has flourished since that inauspicious beginning. In 1898, or thereabouts (historians differ), Buschmann founded a cannery on Mitkof Island facing the slender, peaceful Wrangell Narrows in what was to become Petersburg. The stunning abundance of salmon and halibut and a nearby source of ice—the LeConte Glacier—made the site a natural. Buschmann had emigrated from Norway in 1891 and, as a proud old Son of Norway told me, he always hired Norwegians. Any Norwegian who came to him, he hired. In a few years, the cannery failed. Perhaps an excessive payroll? My suggestion was met with an icy glance and a change of subject. Teasing aside, Buschmann's mistake was merging his cannery with a firm trying to challenge a monopolistic canning operation, and they went down together.

Buschmann's suicide followed his financial reverses, but the promise of Petersburg remained. The Norwegians stayed and slowly built a charming town of white clapboard houses with steeply pitched roofs, hugging the water. Their living came from the sea, as it still does. Appropriately, the downtown area doesn't stop at water's edge. Roads, boardwalks, and buildings continue over the smooth waters of Wrangell Narrows, out to the cannery buildings that survive on long wooden piers, and into the boat harbors, which branch out in a network far more extensive than the city's streets.

Today the town's economy is based on fishing and government work. The Stikine Ranger District of the Tongass National Forest is headquartered here. That makes for a wealthy, sophisticated, and stable population.

Petersburg

ACCOMMODATIONS ■
Alaska Island Hotel **11**
Bumbershoot B&B **12**
Scandia House **6**
Tides Inn Motel **8**
Water's Edge B&B **12**

DINING ◆
Helse **3**
Java Hus **6**
Joan Mei Restaurant **1**
Papa Bear's Pizza **7**
Rooney's Northern Lights **2**

ATTRACTIONS ●
Clausen Memorial Museum **10**
Eagle's Roost Park **9**
Fishermen's Memorial Park **4**
Sons of Norway Hall **5**

ESSENTIALS

GETTING THERE   Petersburg has the most welcoming **ferry terminal** in the system (*©* **907/772-3855**), with a grassy lawn and a pier from which to watch the boats and marine animals. It's about a mile to the town center. The **Alaska Marine Highway** (*©* **800/642-0066;** www.ferryalaska.com) connects to Juneau directly (an 8-hr. run), or by way of Sitka, far to the west (10 hr. to Sitka from Juneau, then 9 more from Sitka to Petersburg). The fare is $36 from Wrangell (3 hr.), $45 from Sitka, and $66 from Juneau.

Petersburg is served by **Alaska Airlines** jets (*©* **800/252-7522;** www.alaskaair. com) once north and once south each day, with the nearest stops on the puddle jumper being Juneau and Wrangell.

From the airport, call **Metro Cab** (*©* **907/772-2700**) or **Midnight Rides** (*©* **907/ 772-2222**) for a taxi into town.

VISITOR INFORMATION   The Petersburg Chamber of Commerce **Visitor Information Center,** at the corner of 1st and Fram streets (P.O. Box 649), Petersburg, AK 99833 (*©* **866/484-4700** or 907/772-4636; www.petersburg.org), offers guidance on outdoor opportunities, boats, and lodgings, and distributes trail guides and natural history publications. The center is open in summer Monday through Saturday from 9am to 5pm, Sunday from noon to 4pm; winter Monday through Friday from 10am to 2pm.

The full-service **Viking Travel** agency, corner of Nordic Drive and Sing Lee Alley (© **800/327-2571** or 907/772-3818; www.alaskaferry.com), also specializes in booking local guides for tours, kayaks, whale-watching, flights, fishing charters, and other activities. Owners Dave and Nancy Berg are knowledgeable and helpful.

ORIENTATION   Petersburg is on Mitkof Island, divided from the much larger Kupreanof Island by the long, slender channel of the Wrangell Narrows. There are three small-boat harbors and so many docks, boardwalks, and wooden streets that the town seems to sit on the ocean. **Nordic Drive** is the main street, running from the ferry dock through town, then becoming **Sandy Beach Road** as it rounds Hungry Point to the north. At Sandy Beach, you can circle back, past the airport, which stands above the town, to **Haugen Drive,** which meets Nordic again near **Hammer Slough,** right in town. To the south, Nordic becomes the **Mitkof Highway,** which runs to the undeveloped balance of the island.

GETTING AROUND   You can walk downtown Petersburg, but you'll need wheels or a boat to get to most outdoor activities. The **Tides Inn Motel** and **Scandia House** (see "Where to Stay," later) both rent cars, but not many are available in town, so book well in advance for summer.

A boat opens more of the area than any other mode of transportation, allowing exploration of Wrangell Narrows, the trails on the far side, and the opportunity for inexpensive self-guided fishing. **Doyle's Boat Rentals,** in North Harbor (© **877/442-4010** or 907/772-4439; www.doylesboatrentals.com), offers 16-footers with quality outboards and trolling motors for $99 a day, and rents fishing gear and shrimp and crab pots. The Scandia House also rents small boats.

FAST FACTS: Petersburg

Banks There are two banks, both with ATMs, at the intersection of Nordic Drive and Fram Street.

Hospital **Petersburg Medical Center** is at 2nd and Fram streets (© **907/772-4291**).

Internet Access Free at the public library, at Nordic and Haugen drives (© **907/772-3349**).

Police Find them on Nordic Drive near Haugen; nonemergencies © **907/772-3838.**

Post Office Near the airport on Haugen Street. **Trading Union Grocery Store,** 401 N. Nordic (© **907/772-3881**), sells stamps and has a postal drop box.

Taxes **Sales tax** is 6%. The tax on accommodations totals 10%.

SPECIAL EVENTS   **The Little Norway Festival,** which celebrates the May 17, 1814, declaration of independence of Norway from Sweden, is an occasion for Petersburg to go wild. The 4-day schedule of events includes a street fair, food and craft booths, a luncheon and bunad style show (a bunad is a traditional embroidered Norwegian costume), street music and dancing, and a salmon bake on the beach. The celebration is held on the third full weekend of May. **The King Salmon Derby** offers $30,000 in prizes over Memorial Day weekend. **July 4th** is a very big deal in Petersburg and lasts 2 days. **The Canned Salmon Classic** lasts from July 1 to August 15, with a first prize of up to $4,000 going to the person who guesses how many cans of salmon will be packed in Petersburg during the season. The **Festival of Lights** begins the day after Thanksgiving with an evening candlelight parade, the lighting of the Community Christmas Tree, and caroling. **Julebukking,** a Norwegian tradition, happens on Christmas Eve, when merchants offer food and drink to their customers and the streets fill with people under twinkling white lights.

For information on any of the above events, contact the **Petersburg Chamber of Commerce** (© 866/484-4700 or 907/772-4636; www.petersburg.org).

EXPLORING PETERSBURG

A walk around Petersburg should include the boardwalk streets of **Hammer Slough,** the tidal mouth of a creek that feeds into the waterfront. **Sing Lee Alley** leads from North Nordic Drive at the charming center of town, passing by several interesting little shops, including **Sing Lee Alley Books,** at no. 11 (© 907/772-4440), where there's a good collection on natural history and local culture. Petersburg has so many thriving little shops because of its isolation and healthy economy—so far, it's been too small to attract the predation of Wal-Mart and other chains.

Sing Lee Alley turns from solid ground to wooden dock before you reach the **Sons of Norway Hall,** a town center where a large model Viking ship used in the Little Norway Festival is often parked. Next door, also on pilings, is the **Fishermen's Memorial Park.** Plaques memorialize Petersburg mariners lost at sea under a bronze statue of Bojer Wikan, a fisherman and lifelong resident. Across the street, on the outboard side, **Tonka Seafoods** (© 888/560-3662 or 907/772-3662; www.tonkaseafoods.com) is a specialty fish processor with a shop and mail-order operation; they will process your sport-caught fish, too. They offer 1-hour tours for $15 during the summer at 1 and 3pm Monday through Saturday. Continue on to Nordic Drive and turn left, crossing back over the slough to **Birch Street,** which follows the slough's bank on pilings upstream past old, weathered houses that hang over the placid channel. Many have one door for the road and another for the water. It's a charming, authentic place. Step out of the way of cars on the one-lane dock/street.

Back down at the waterfront, stroll the harbor floats to see the frenetic activity of the huge commercial fishing fleet in the summer, then continue north on Nordic Drive to **Eagle's Roost Park,** where there is a grassy area to sit and a stairway that leads down to the water. At low tide an interesting but rugged beach walk starts here. You're almost guaranteed to see eagles, which congregate for the fish waste from the nearby cannery. Look in the tops of the trees. (In fact, you can see eagles almost anytime and anywhere along the water in Petersburg.) Another nice walk leads you on a boardwalk a third of a mile over muskeg swamp from the uphill side of the elementary school, at 4th Street.

The **Clausen Memorial Museum,** at 2nd and Fram streets (© 907/772-3598; www.clausenmuseum.net), interprets Petersburg and its history for the people who live here. It has a living, community feel. On one visit a portfolio of old photographs was on display with notes for visitors to write down the names of anyone they could identify and other memories. No doubt the local fishermen are fascinated by the obsolete fishing gear, rugged old nautical equipment, and a model fish trap, outlawed in 1959 when Alaska became a state. It's like being invited into the town's collective memory. The museum is open in summer Monday through Saturday from 10am to 5pm; call for hours in the winter. Admission is $3 for adults, free for children 12 and under.

GETTING OUTSIDE

I have listed only a few highlights from Petersburg's wealth of outdoor opportunities. For other choices, many of them just as good as those I've written about here, or for the detailed trail and backcountry information you'll need, contact the U.S. Forest Service at the **Petersburg Ranger District** offices at 12 N. Nordic Dr. (P.O. Box 1328), Petersburg, AK 99833 (© **907/772-3871;** www.fs.fed.us/r10/tongass/districts/petersburg).

Some of the best places to go around Petersburg require a boat. **Viking Travel** (see "Visitor Information," above) books most of the dozen or so small charter boats that operate from the harbor at any one time, allowing them to consolidate small groups into 6- to 15-person boatloads for whale-watching, sightseeing, glacier viewing, or fishing. See p. 132 for the option of renting your own boat.

A few operators have made a specialty of natural history and environmentally responsible tours. Barry Bracken, a marine biologist, offers these kinds of trips on his 28-foot vessel. Contact **Kaleidoscope Cruises** (© **800/TO-THE-SEA** or 907/772-3736; www.petersburglodgingandtours.com). To get to remote cabins by air, or for flightseeing, contact **Pacific Wing Air Charters** (© **907/772-4258;** www.pacificwing.com).

SPECIAL PLACES

SANDY BEACH   The beach at City Park is an easy bike ride or a longish walk 1½ miles up Nordic Drive, around Hungry Point at the northern tip of the island, then along Sandy Beach Road to the beach and picnic area. Return by way of the airport, coming back into town on Haugen Drive. The beach itself is coarse sand and fine gravel, and you can't swim in the frigid water, but it's a lovely spot, facing Frederick Sound on the east side of Mitkof Island.

If you go at high tide, you can beachcomb and bird-watch—a great blue heron was hanging around on one visit—but a better plan is to time your visit at low tide (free tide books are widely available, or ask at the visitor center). At tides of 1 foot or lower, you can see the outlines of ancient fish traps built on the beach beginning 2,000 years ago. They look like V-shaped rows of rocks, and at times you can see stakes. The indigenous people who built them knew how to create channels that would corral salmon at high tide, leaving them stranded to be gathered up when the water receded. These ancient people presumably also created the petroglyphs on rocks near the traps, which may depict the traps or could have something to do with the sun. Finding the traps and petroglyphs isn't easy—it's best if you can get someone to lead you, perhaps by joining the occasional Forest Service walks that you can ask about at the Ranger District office. But, if you have the time and inclination to explore, walk out to the left from the picnic area, to the edge of the lagoon near the house with the greenhouse. A major petroglyph is on a black bedrock face, visible when you are looking back toward the picnic area, and the traps are just offshore from there. Please be sensitive to the delicate artifacts so they can last another 2,000 years.

RAVEN TRAIL & RAVEN'S ROOST CABIN   About 4 miles up the steep but spectacular Raven Trail, which begins behind the airport off Haugen Drive roughly a mile from town, the Raven's Roost Forest Service cabin sits atop a mountain with a sweeping view of the town and surrounding waters and islands. It's the sort of place that inspires artists and poets. Allow 3 to 4 hours for the climb along a boardwalk, then up a steep muddy slope, then along a ridge, with an elevation gain of over 1,000 feet. It's possible to continue hiking over the steep, subalpine terrain of the Twin Ridge Ski Trail another 5 miles to the Twin Creek Road, and then get a ride 11 miles back to town. Ask your lodging host about options, or arrange for a pick-up by taxi cab. Check with the visitor center for trail conditions. To stay at the cabin you'll need sleeping bags, cooking gear, lights, and food. Reserve the cabin through the national system described in section 1 of this chapter, "Getting Outside in the Tongass

Finds   Takeout Lunch & Take-Home Fish

Stop in at **Coastal Cold Storage,** at Excel Street and Nordic Drive (© **907/772-4177**), where they sell seafood from freezers and live from tanks. They'll freeze and ship seafood home for you. It's also a good stop for seafood sandwiches, crab specials, chowder, breakfast sandwiches, and espresso at the counter.

National Forest," and check there for information sources on the other 19 cabins in the area, most of which are reached by plane or boat.

MITKOF ISLAND   The Mitkof Highway, leading south from Petersburg, opens access to most of Mitkof Island, with its king salmon fishing; views of swans, fish, and glaciers; salmon hatchery; hiking trails; lakes; and many miles of remote roads for mountain-biking. The town's swimming hole and ice-skating pond are out the highway, too. Anyone can enjoy a day's sightseeing drive over the island, and if you like hiking and the outdoors, you'll find days of fun. Pick up the $9 *Forest Service Mitkof Island Road Guide* map at the visitor center or ranger office; it shows what you'll find along the way.

The **Three Lakes Loop Road** intersects with the highway twice, once 10 miles from Petersburg and again 20 miles from town. From the north intersection, the one closest to town, it's 15 more miles to the level, 4.5-mile boardwalk and dirt **Three Lakes Trail,** which circles four small lakes, each of which contains trout, and three of which have Forest Service rowboats for public use. Besides the fish, it's a place of abundant wildflowers and berries, where you may see deer, beavers, bear, and many birds, including seasonal sandhill cranes.

Fourteen miles down Mitkof Highway from Petersburg, a quarter-mile wheelchair accessible boardwalk leads across the damp, hummocky ground of the rainforest muskeg to **Blind River Rapids,** a peaceful spot with a three-sided shelter where you can watch and fish for king salmon in June and silvers in September, and sometimes see eagles and bears feeding on the fish. A half-mile-long loop leads farther into the forest and muskeg.

At 17 miles, somewhat hidden in the trees on the right, a bird-watching blind looks out on **Blind Slough,** where trumpeter swans winter. Swans normally will be gone by mid-March.

At 18 miles, at the end of the pavement, you'll reach the **Blind Slough Recreation Area,** where locals go to swim in amber water in the summer. Water warms in the narrow slough, more than 5 miles from Wrangell Narrows. In the winter much of the town congregates here for ice-skating and bonfires.

At 20½ miles from Petersburg, the popular **Man Made Hole** picnic area and swimming pond has foot bridges and a pathway; it is accessible to people with disabilities.

At 22 miles you reach the **Ohmer Creek campground,** with a 1-mile trail, a floating bridge over a beaver pond, and trout and some salmon in late summer. The road continues from here along the south shore of Mitkof Island, with great ocean views, to its end at mile 32.

PETERSBURG CREEK   The lovely, grassy Petersburg Creek area could offer either an afternoon frolic among the meadows of wildflowers that meet the water, or could be the start to a challenging 21-mile, multiday hike into the **Petersburg Creek–Duncan Salt Chuck Wilderness.** The fishing is exceptional: The creek contains four species of salmon and two of trout. You'll need a skiff or sea kayak, or get a charter to drop you off, as the creek is on Kupreanof Island, across Wrangell Narrows from town;

the state maintains a dock there. Sea kayaking up the creek makes a wonderful day trip, which you can do on your own or with a guide (see "Sea Kayaking," below). A trail reaches two Forest Service cabins, at Petersburg Lake and East Salt Chuck, each with a boat for public use (reservations are required). The trail to the lake is not difficult, but continuing on to East Salt Chuck is tougher going, including wading some beaver ponds. At the lake you can fish for trout and odds are good of seeing ducks, geese, loons, trumpeter swans, bald eagles, or black bears. The Kupreanof dock also provides access to the 3-mile, 3,000-foot trail that climbs Petersburg Mountain, a challenging hike that has spectacular views from the top.

ACTIVITIES

FISHING   There are various fishing streams and lakes that you can reach on the roads—several are mentioned above, under "Mitkof Island"—and many more accessible by boat or plane. Check at the visitor center, or contact the **Alaska Department of Fish & Game** (© 907/772-5231, www.alaska.gov/adfg). They produce an informative *Petersburg/Wrangell Sport Fishing Guide,* available on paper or on the website (click on "Sport Fisheries," then the Southeast region). The boat harbor has a couple dozen licensed charter fishing boats, mostly six-passenger vessels. As elsewhere, halibut and salmon are usually the target. You can get a list of operators at the visitor center, or book through **Viking Travel** (see "Visitor Information," earlier). Half-day salmon charters cost around $175 per person, while halibut charters or longer salmon charters are $225 to $280 per day. You can rent your own boat and gear for much less. See "Getting Around," p. 132.

SEA KAYAKING   The waters of Wrangell Narrows are protected and interesting, with plenty to see. On longer trips of 3 days to a week, you can get out among the glaciers, Stikine River Delta, and even the whales—there's as much variety here, among these rainforest islands, as anywhere in the region. It's possible to set up a kayak trip linking some of the Forest Service cabins, too, or to use one as a base camp for a few days of exploration. (Get a copy of the free handout *Paddling the Petersburg Ranger District* from the district office.) **Tongass Kayak Adventures** (© 907/772-4600;** www.tongasskayak.com) offers guided and unguided versions of each of these adventures (they rent equipment, too). Their 4-hour paddle crosses Wrangell Narrows from the harbor and penetrates Petersburg Creek, where they stop for a snack and often see bear and deer. No experience is required. They charge $70; reserve through Viking Travel, listed under "Visitor Information," earlier. A 3-night base camp tour costs $930 per person and an 8-night version begins at $1,980; reserve those trips directly with Tongass Kayak.

WHALE-WATCHING   Most summers, Petersburg's **Frederick Sound** is one of the best places in the state to see humpbacks feeding. Whale-watching charters can go any day from May 15 to September 15, but the height is midsummer. You may see stunning bubble-net feeding, when the whales confine a school of fish in a circle of bubbles, then lunge upward to scoop them up, bursting through the surface in a great swoosh. Whales have even been known to spy hop, poking their heads as high above the surface as possible in order to look down into the boats that are watching them. In summer 1995, a humpback jumped right into one of these boats, presumably accidentally. (No one was injured, but a few people fell into the water.) Several charter operators offer trips in small, six-passenger boats. Some, including Kaleidoscope Cruises (p. 134), have hydrophones on board, so you may be able to hear the whales' vocalizations while waiting for them to surface, if their feeding behavior and the water conditions are right. Book trips through Viking Travel or directly with one of the operators. Trips usually leave around 8am and stay out 6 to 10 hours, with several hours among the whales. Prices are $150 to $210 per person. Viking Travel's conference room (at the corner of Nordic Dr. and Sing Lee Alley) houses the Petersburg Marine Mammal Center, where you can use a computer to learn more about whales (www.psgmmc.org).

WHERE TO STAY

Bumbershoot Bed & Breakfast ★ *Finds*   The industrious Gloria Ohmer, who also owns the Tides Inn Motel (see "Tides Inn Motel," below), has opened her extraordinary waterfront home on Frederick Sound to guests as well. The rooms are large, decorated with quilts she made, and Gloria also will happily show off beadwork, woodwork, sewing, stained glass, stone cutting and engraving, a music room, fish-cleaning room, and deck barbecue. The place is brimming with the hosts' enthusiasm for life. Some rooms have water views, and the water is only barely beyond your reach. For $165 a night, you can rent the entire downstairs apartment, with two bedrooms, a kitchen, and a large living room with a fireplace. Bumbershoot also lends bicycles, offers free use of the laundry machines, and arranges transportation from the ferry dock or airport.

901 Sandy Beach Rd. (P.O. Box 372), Petersburg, AK 99833. ✆ **907/772-4683.** Fax 907/772-4627. glohmer@pobox. aptalaska.net. 4 units, 2 with shared bathroom. $80–$90 double. Rates include continental breakfast. No credit cards. **Amenities:** Free bicycle loan; courtesy car; free laundry machines. *In room:* TV/VCR, hair dryer, iron.

Scandia House ★★   Rebuilt in the town's distinctive Norwegian style, this building's solid simplicity puts it in a class by itself. White rooms with blonde-wood trim are blessed with natural light. You have a choice: front rooms with king-size beds, rooms with kitchenettes, twin-bedded rooms, or a magnificent fourth-floor suite with towering ceilings. Most rooms have only one bed and a few have shower stalls, not tubs. The hotel has an elevator and is barrier free. The rooms are some of the cleanest I've ever seen, over various visits, and in 2007 they received new carpet as well. A continental breakfast is offered from 6 to 9:30am, including fresh homemade muffins. Book well in advance for the busy summer season. The owners offer skiff rentals and car rentals.

110 Nordic Dr. (P.O. Box 689), Petersburg, AK 99833. ✆ **800/722-5006** or 907/772-4281. Fax 907/772-4301. www.scandiahousehotel.com. 33 units. $100–$120 double; $140 double with kitchenette; $185–$195 suite. Extra person over age 12 $10. Rates include continental breakfast. AE, DC, DISC, MC, V. **Amenities:** Boat rental; car rental; courtesy van. *In room:* TV.

Tides Inn Motel ★ *Value*   Few hotels in Alaska have such good rooms at such affordable prices. The kitchenette rooms are an incredible bargain. The biggest difference among the rooms is the views, as all are well maintained. Those in the older part of the motel face the other building, while nonsmoking units in the front of the new section get a sweeping view. I watched bald eagles doing aerobatics less than 50 feet from my front window. The management is efficient and committed to quality, and they keep the motel in clean, attractive condition. The hotel has an Avis car-rental franchise and serves a continental breakfast in the lobby, where you'll also find a computer with free Internet access.

307 N. 1st St. (P.O. Box 1048), Petersburg, AK 99833. ✆ **800/665-8433** or 907/772-4288. Fax 907/772-4286. tidesinn@alaska.net. High season $90–$100 double; low season $65–$85 double. Extra person $10. Rates include continental breakfast. AE, DC, DISC, MC, V. **Amenities:** Car rental; courtesy van; Internet access. *In room:* TV, Wi-Fi.

Waterfront Bed & Breakfast   The attraction here is the location, on pilings over the Wrangell Narrows near the ferry dock and steps from Emily's Bakery. Rooms have Mission-style oak beds with excellent mattresses and down comforters, but are otherwise spare and lacking in decoration. Each unit has individual heat control. Bathrooms have shower stalls, not tubs. Four of the rooms have one bed—two with a queen and two with a double—and one has two double beds. The communal living room is cozy and has a great view.

1004 S. Nordic Dr. (P.O. Box 1613), Petersburg, AK 99833. (C) **866/772-9301** or 907/772-9300. Fax 907/772-9308. www. waterfrontbedandbreakfast.com. 5 units. $100–$120 double. Extra person $10. Rates include full breakfast. MC, V. **Amenities:** Covered outdoor Jacuzzi; free laundry machines.

Water's Edge Bed & Breakfast ★★ *Finds*   Barry and Kathy Bracken's house sits right on the beach on Frederick Sound, about 2 miles from town center, with a creek running next to one room. Two units branch off a large common room, each tastefully decorated, well furnished, and outfitted with thoughtful extras such as robes, duvets, and regularly replaced linens. The common room itself is the most memorable, however, a place to sit and watch waterfowl, boats, and icebergs go by through big windows. You can have the whole place for $185 a night. Probably the best thing to do here is to book a package combining a stay at the B&B and an excursion on Barry's 28-foot boat. A marine biologist, he leads natural history glacier- and whale-watching excursions. His knowledge of the area is deep and his enthusiasm infectious. Book well ahead, as it's a rare and popular opportunity. No smoking is permitted.

705 Sandy Beach Rd. (P.O. Box 1201), Petersburg, AK 99833. (C) **800/TO-THE-SEA** (800/868-4373) or phone/fax 907/ 772-3736. www.petersburglodgingandtours.com. 2 units. High season $110 double; low season $70 double. Extra person $10. 2-night minimum stay. Rates include continental breakfast. No credit cards. No children under 12. **Amenities:** Free bike loan; courtesy car; free laundry machines; kitchenette. *In room:* Hair dryer.

A HOSTEL & CAMPING

Friendly little **Alaska Island Hostel,** at 805 Gjoa St. (C) **907/772-3632** or 907/723-5340; www.alaskaislandhostel.com), has male and female dorm rooms with four beds in each and a family room with four beds. The $25 nightly rate includes room tax and Internet access. They're open regularly from April 15 to September 15; call for the winter schedule. Check in and office hours are 5 to 7pm or by arrangement.

The closest natural camping is found 22 miles out the Mitkof Highway at **Ohmer Creek** (see "Mitkof Island," above). **Twin Creek RV Park** is 7½ miles out the highway (C) **907/772-3244**), charging $25 for full hookups, $15 for tent camping.

WHERE TO DINE

For terrific takeout pizza or calzone, burgers, fried fish or other casual choices, try **Papa Bear's Pizza** (C) **907/772-3727;** www.papabearspizza.com), above Coastal Cold Storage at Excel Street and Nordic Drive, open in summer Monday through Saturday 10am to 9pm, Saturday and Sunday 3 to 8pm (in winter Mon–Sat 10am–8pm, closed Sun). It is one of the better bets in town.

Helse, at 13 Sing Lee Alley (C) **907/772-3444**) is a popular lunch spot and health good grocery; the food is much better than the grungy, nine-table dining room would suggest. It is open summer Monday through Friday 8am to 5pm, Saturday 10am to 3pm; winter Monday through Saturday 11:30am to 3:30pm.

Get coffee and bakery items at **Java Hus,** by Scandia House at 110 N. Nordic Dr. (C) **907/772-2626**), a bright, comfortable spot, open Monday through Saturday 6am to 5pm, Sunday 7am to 4pm. The food is from **Emily's Bakery,** at 1000 Nordic

(© **907/772-4555**), which produces truly memorable whole grain pastries, cookies, bars, and cakes, as well as quiche (but the bakery itself has no seating).

Joan Mei Restaurant ⭑ CHINESE   This is an excellent choice for dinner. The whole family works together in a large, bright dining room, serving flaky egg rolls and entrees with vegetables that remain crisp and flavorful rather than being smothered or overcooked. The American food is better than elsewhere in town, too. Locals come here for a nice dinner out, and we saw many happy faces.

1103 S. Nordic, across from the ferry dock. © **907/772-4222**. Lunch $6.25–$13; dinner $10–$25. MC, V. Mon–Tues and Thurs–Sat 11am–2pm and 4–9pm; Sun 8am–2pm and 4–9pm. Closed mid-Jan to mid-Feb.

Rooney's Northern Lights ⭑ SEAFOOD/DINER   You couldn't find a much better site for a restaurant than this one, sitting on pilings in Hammer Slough, overlooking a boat harbor. Call ahead to reserve one of the tables at the window or on the deck, where you can see Kupreanof Island, the fishermen working in the harbor, a cannery, and often waterfowl or seals or a sea lion. The evening menu includes steaks and several ways of having halibut or shrimp, or you can order from inexpensive Mexican selections or burgers, sandwiches, and salads. There are healthy choices as well as heavy selections and a good children's menu. Breakfast is done well, with big skillets, eggs benedict, and the like packing in the locals. The morning crowd rolls dice to see who pays for coffee.

203 Sing Lee Alley. © **907/772-2900**. Lunch $7–$12; dinner $7–$30. MC, V. Mon–Sun 6am–10pm.

5 Sitka: Rich Prize of Russian Conquest

If I could visit only one Alaska town, it would probably be Sitka.

Sitka preserves the Russian legacy of Alaska's initial European invasion and, more deeply, the story of the cultural conflict between Alaska Natives and the newcomers, and the Natives' resistance and ultimate accommodation to the new ways. Here, 18th-century Russian conquerors who had successfully enslaved Aleuts to the west met their match in battle against the rich, powerful, and sophisticated Tlingit. A visit to Sitka reveals the story of that war, and also the cultural blending that occurred in the uneasy peace that followed under the influence of the Russian Orthodox Church—an influence that remained even after the Russians sold Alaska to the U.S. in 1867 (that exchange also happened here), and continues today.

Sitka's history is Alaska's richest, and there's more of real interest in this town than any other you might visit. The fact is, most Alaska towns haven't been on the map long enough to have accumulated much history. Those that have been around for a while often have been wiped out a time or two, leaving little to remind you of the distant past. There's usually a small museum and a few gold-rush sites that can be seen in half a day. Not so in Sitka. Historic photographs bear a surprising resemblance to today's city. The National Park Service protects buildings and grounds of major historic significance—places where the pioneers spoke Russian, with ways much more European than those of the rest of the American West. Even a superficial exploration of the attractions takes a day, and that's without time for the out-of-the way points of interest or the outdoors.

In 1799, the Russians chose these protected waters on Sitka Sound, on the ocean side of Baranof Island, for a new fort as part of a strategy of pushing their sea otter hunting operations and territorial claims east and south along the west coast of North America. The Tlingits understandably considered this to be an invasion and in 1802 they attacked the Russian's redoubt and killed almost everyone inside. The Russians

> **Fun Fact** **Thank You. No, Thank *You.***
>
> In 1867, Russia's Czar Alexander feared that he couldn't hold the unprofitable colony of Alaska and saw a political advantage in doing his American allies the favor of selling it to them. Ironically, the Americans thought they were doing Russia a favor by buying it. Congress balked at paying the $7.2 million price that Secretary of State William Seward had negotiated for this worthless waste, relenting more than a year later partly out of fear of offending the czar. Americans didn't change their dim view of "Seward's Folly" until gold discoveries decades later.

counterattacked in 1804 with the cannons of the ship *Neva* and a swarm of Aleut warriors, eventually forcing the Tlingit battle leader, Katlian, to withdraw. But the Russians never rested easy in their new capital, named New Archangel, and the hostility of the proud and dangerous Tlingit long remained. Some Russian laborers intermarried and essentially adopted Tlingit culture, but the bureaucrats and naval officers sent to run the colony for the czar tended to view Alaska as purgatory and left as soon as they could. Under their ineffective and uninterested control the Russians made surprisingly little impression on the great mass of Alaska. They failed to explore the Interior and held only tenuous control of the vast coastline.

The departing Russians rushed home, leaving only three significant towns—Unalaska, Kodiak, and Sitka—of which only Sitka retains more than a single Russian building. During their century of rule the Russians had nearly wiped out the sea otter and the culture of the Aleuts, but both would eventually bounce back. The Russian Orthodox Church stood as Russia's only lasting cultural gift to Alaska. Thanks to the efforts of one extraordinary cleric, Bishop Innocent Veniaminov, Alaska Natives were able to worship in their own languages, winning for the Russian Orthodox Church many villages' continuing loyalty over less tolerant Protestant churches that came under American rule.

Besides its historic significance, Sitka also is fun to visit. Somehow it has retained a friendly, authentic feel, despite the crush of thousands of visitors. Perhaps because cruise-ship travelers must ride shuttle boats to shore, or because Sitka is a slightly inconvenient, out-of-the-way stop on the Alaska Marine Highway's main-line ferry routes, the city's streets haven't been choked by solid rows of seasonal gift shops, as has occurred in Ketchikan, Skagway, and a large part of Juneau. Sitka remains picturesque, facing Sitka Sound, which is dotted with islands and populated by feeding eagles. Tourism is important here, but Sitka's own residents remain the center of the business and cultural world. The process of being "spoiled" hasn't begun and they seem alert to its hazards. The town recently voted down a proposal to build a new cruise-ship dock.

Even beyond the town and its rich history, Sitka is a gateway to a large, remote portion of Southeast Alaska, in the western coastal islands. This area contains some of Tongass National Forest's least-used outdoor opportunities. The ocean halibut and salmon fishing are excellent and not overexploited, and the bird- and wildlife-watching is exceptional.

Sitka

ACCOMMODATIONS ■
Alaska Ocean View B&B **1**
Alaska Swan Lake B&B **2**
Finn Alley Inn **19**
Shee Atika Totem Square Inn **4**
Sitka Hotel **9**
Super 8 Sitka **12**
Westmark Sitka **14**

DINING ◆
Backdoor Café **10**
Bayview Restaurant **15**
Galley Deli **7**
Highliner Coffee **13**
Ludvig's Bistro **3**
Pizza Express **24**

ATTRACTIONS ●
Alaska Raptor Center **23**
Castle Hill **8**
Harrigan Centennial Hall
    Visitor Center **16**
The Russian Bishop's House **17**
Russian Blockhouse **5**
Sheldon Jackson Museum **21**
Sheldon Jackson College
    Aquarium **20**
Sitka National Historical
    Park **22**
Sitka Tribe of Alaska's
    Community House **6**
St. Michael's Cathedral **11**
St. Peter's by-the-Sea
    Episcopal Church **18**

ESSENTIALS

GETTING THERE   Sitka sits on the west side of Baranof Island, a detour from the Inside Passage for the **Alaska Marine Highway System** (© 800/642-0066; www.ferry alaska.com). Three kinds of ferries come here: the big, main-line ferries; the fast ferry *Fairweather;* and most often the little *LeConte,* which is like a local bus, stopping at all the tiny outlying villages, and giving visitors an insight into their island lifestyle. The *Fairweather* cuts a 9-hour journey from Juneau to less than 5 hours. On any of the ships, the ride through narrow Peril Straits into Sitka is definitely worth the trip. The shore seems close enough to touch, and if you look closely you can sometimes see deer. The fare from either Juneau or Petersburg (10 hr. away by conventional ferry) is $45. The ferry dock (© 907/747-3300) is 7 miles out of town.

 Alaska Airlines (© 800/252-7522; www.alaskaair.com) links Sitka daily to Juneau and Ketchikan with flights that then continue nonstop to Seattle and Anchorage.

 To get to town from the airport or ferry dock, the **Sitka Tours** bus charges $6 one-way, $8 round-trip. No reservations are needed, just climb aboard and pay the driver. **Sitka Cab,** at © 907/747-5001, is among five taxi companies in town; the ride from the ferry dock is around $18. See Hank's Cab on p. 144.

VISITOR INFORMATION   A kiosk in the city-operated **Harrigan Centennial Hall,** 330 Harbor Dr., next to the Crescent Boat Harbor (© 907/747-3225), is the only walk-in information stop. It is staffed by volunteers only when cruise ships are in town, although you may be able to ask questions of hall staff other times. The hall is open Monday through Friday from 8am to 10pm, Saturday 8am to 5pm, and some-times Sunday. The town's professional visitor organization is the **Sitka Convention and Visitors Bureau,** at P.O. Box 1226, Sitka, AK 99835 (© 907/747-5940; fax 907/ 747-3739). They maintain a very useful website at **www.sitka.org**.

 The **Sitka National Historical Park Visitor Center,** 106 Metlakatla St., Sitka, AK 99835 (© 907/747-0110; www.nps.gov/sitk), run by the National Park Service, which maintains key historic sites in Sitka, is an essential stop to gather information and learn about what happened here. The center is open daily from 8am to 5pm in summer, Monday through Saturday from 8am to 5pm in winter. Also see "Exploring Sitka," below, for more on the park.

ORIENTATION   Sitka, on the west side of Baranof Island, has only a few miles of road. The **ferry terminal** is located at its north end, 7 miles out, on **Halibut Point Road;** the site of an abandoned pulp mill is at the south end, roughly the same dis-tance out **Sawmill Creek Road.** The town faces Sitka Sound. Across Sitka Channel is **Japonski Island,** with the **airport** (don't worry, it only looks as if your plane is going to land in the water). **Lincoln Street** contains most of the tourist attractions.

GETTING AROUND   The airport has branches of **Avis** (© 800/230-4898 or 907/ 966-2404; www.avis.com) and **North Star Rent-a-Car** (© 800/722-6927 or 907/966-2552; www.northstarrentacar.com).

 The Visitor Transit Bus operated by the **Sitka Tribe** (see "Exploring Sitka," below) makes a continuous circuit of the sites from May to September when large cruise ships are in town. The fare is $5 round-trip or $10 all day.

 Bike rental makes a good deal of sense in Sitka. **Yellow Jersey Cycle Shop,** at 329 Harbor Dr., right across from the Centennial Hall downtown, (© 907/747-6317; www.yellowjerseycycles.com), rents quality bikes for $25 a day.

FAST FACTS: Sitka

Banks Three banks are at the center of downtown, around 300 Lincoln St., with ATMs, which are also found at local grocery stores.

Hospital **Sitka Community** (📞 907/747-3241) is at 209 Moller Dr.

Internet Access Try **Highliner Coffee**, on Lake Street near Seward Street, or the downtown post office.

Police Call 📞 907/747-3245 for nonemergency business.

Post Office At 338 Lincoln St.; it is open Saturday.

Taxes **Sales tax** is 5% October through March, 6% April through September. The tax on rooms totals 11% and 12% respectively.

SPECIAL EVENTS   The **Starring Ceremony,** January 7, marks Russian Orthodox Christmas with a procession through the streets and song and prayer at the doors of the faithful. Call St. Michael's Cathedral for information (📞 **907/747-8120** or 907/747-3560 voice message).

The **Sitka Salmon Derby** occurs at the end of May and beginning of June, when the kings are running; contact the Sitka Sportsman's Association (📞 **907/966-2281**) for information.

The **Sitka Summer Music Festival,** a chamber-music series that began in 1972, is one of Alaska's most important cultural events, drawing musicians from all over the world in for 3 weeks in June. Performances take place Tuesdays and Fridays, and other events all week. Contact the festival office for information (📞 **907/277-4852;** www.sitkamusicfestival.org).

Alaska Day, October 18, commemorating the Alaska purchase, is a big deal in this former Russian capital city; the **Alaska Day Festival** lasts 4 days leading up to the big event. The Convention and Visitors Bureau has information. The **Sitka Grind,** a music and arts celebration at varying sites around town, takes place the third Saturday of each month from October to March.

The **Sitka WhaleFest** (📞 **907/747-7964;** www.sitkawhalefest.org) takes place over a weekend in early November, during the fall and early winter period when humpback whales congregate in Sitka Sound. Experts come from around the world to present a 3-day symposium, and there are whale-watching tours, concerts, an art show, a run, and community events. Consider combining it with the Alaska Bald Eagle Festival in Haines, coordinated to follow (see section 9 of this chapter).

EXPLORING SITKA

The **Sitka Tribe of Alaska's** Community House is a good starting point, where you can watch dance performances (see "Sitka Tribe Dance Performances," below), join walking or bus tours, or sign up for kayaking or other outdoor activities, including trail hikes. A 2-hour walking tour includes the town, national historic park, and a marine science facility at Sheldon Jackson College. The house is at 200 Katlian St. (📞 **888/270-8687** or 907/747-7290; www.sitkatours.com). **Sitka Tours** (📞 **907/747-8443**) also offers tours, taking more of the Russian perspective. Prices for each choice of tour range from about $15 for a brief downtown tour to $57 for a longer

---

Moments **The Singing Cabbie**

Hank, of Hank's Cab ((C) **907/747-8888**), can drive you around, like any taxi driver, but, if you ask, he offers something more. For $20 to $30 per person he offers a tour of Sitka's Russian and natural history, including a stop at an ocean-side waterfall where he pulls out his guitar and performs. Hank's a good blues/folk musician and can really sing.

---

town tour that includes most of the attractions and dancing; the type of dancing—Native or Russian—depends on which firm you go with. See "Sitka Tribe Dance Performances," below, for a description of the Alaska Native choice. Russian folk dance is performed by the women of the **New Archangel Dancers** ((C) **907/747-5516**) in the Harrigan Centennial Hall at 330 Harbor Dr., next to the Crescent Boat Harbor. Performances are scheduled when cruise ships are in town and most of the audience comes from Sitka Tours. Admission is $8 at the door.

SITKA'S TLINGIT & RUSSIAN HERITAGE

Sitka National Historical Park ★★★   In 1799, the Russian-American Company, led by Alexander Baranof, landed from their base in Kodiak, established Redoubt St. Michael (today the **Old Sitka State Historic Site,** 7½ miles north of town—just a grassy picnic area with interpretive signs), and claimed the Pacific Northwest of America for Russia. The Tlingits, sophisticated traders and who had already acquired flint-locks, attacked with knives, spears, and guns, and destroyed the redoubt in mid-June 1802, killing almost all of the Russians. The Natives immediately began building fortifications on the site now within the national historical park, anticipating a Russian counterattack, which came in 1804. Baranof returned with an attacking force of a Russian gunship and a swarm of Aleut kayaks, which towed the becalmed vessel into position to begin the bombardment. The Tlingits withstood the siege for 6 days, then vacated their fort at night after a canoe delivering gunpowder exploded, leaving them short of ammunition. The Russians founded and heavily fortified the town of New Archangel, and in 1808 it became their administrative capital. But the Tlingit name is the one that stuck: Shee Atika, since contracted to Sitka.

The historic significance of the battle site was recognized early. Pres. Benjamin Harrison, a friend of Alaska missionary Sheldon Jackson, set the land aside as a public park in 1890. In 1902 and 1905, a collection of totem poles from around the Southeast was brought here, and in 1910 the site was designated a national monument. The park visitor center and grounds emphasize the Native perspective. There is no better place to learn about Tlingit art and history. A naturally lit hall with a 30-foot ceiling displays the original poles (reproductions stand outside) in startlingly good condition despite their age. The artistic power of these poles is overwhelming, and their age and value for the Tlingit and Haida cultures only adds to the impact. Moreover, the art still lives. Extraordinary poles by current Native artists stand outside, and within the building artisans of the Southeast Alaska Indian Cultural Center work in a series of windowed workshops creating traditional crafts of metal, wood, beads, textiles, and woven grass. Visitors are invited to enter the workshops and ask questions. A free 12-minute video provides a good historical overview.

The outdoor totem loop trail and the site of the battle and of the fort also must not be missed. The totems stand tall and forbidding along a pathway through massive spruce and hemlock, where misty rain often wanders down from an unseen sky somewhere above the trees. The shoreside battle site and the nearby fort site—only a grassy area now—are along the trail. While plenty of imagination is needed to place a desperate fight in this peaceful setting, it is easy to feel deep down what the Tlingits were fighting for when you stand among the trees and totems and hear the lapping sea and raven's call.

Though they lost the battle for this ground, the Tlingits won the war—they're still here. In 1996, a gathering of clans erected a major new pole in front of the center to explain their story back to mankind's arrival in North America. It took quite a bit of debate to settle the story the pole would tell. For example, the crests of the eagle and raven tribal moieties are traditionally never shown on the same pole, but they had to be to tell the whole history of the Tlingits. In 1999, another new pole rose at the site of the battle to commemorate that story. At the bottom of the pole is a carving of the raven helmet worn by Katlian, the Tlingit leader in the battle of Sitka. You can see the helmet itself in the Sheldon Jackson Museum (see "Sheldon Jackson Museum," below). Contrary to the popular phrase "low man on the totem pole," the position shows the strength with which Katlian led and supported his people.

106 Metlakatla St. Ⓒ 907/747-0110. Admission $4. Visitor center: summer daily 8am–5pm; winter Mon–Sat 8am–5pm. Park: summer daily 6am–10pm; winter daily 7am–8pm.

The Russian Bishop's House ★★★
Bishop Innocent Veniaminov, born in 1797, translated scriptures into Tlingit and other Native languages and trained deacons to carry Russian Orthodoxy back to their Native villages. Unlike most of the later Protestant missionaries led by Sitka's other historic religious figure, Sheldon Jackson, Veniaminov and his followers allowed parishioners to use their own language, a key element to saving Native cultures. When the United States bought Alaska in 1867, few Russians stayed behind, but thanks to Veniaminov's work, the Russian Orthodox faith remains strong in Native Alaska; today there are 89 parishes, primarily in tiny Native villages. In 1977, Veniaminov was canonized as Saint Innocent in the Orthodox faith.

In 1842–43, the Russian-American Company constructed this extraordinary house for Veniaminov as a residence, school, and chapel. It may have survived many years of neglect in part because its huge beams fit together like a ship's. In 1972, the National Park Service bought and began restoring the building, which is the best of only three surviving from all of Russian America (the others are in Kodiak and at 206 Lincoln St. in Sitka, today occupied by Log Cache Gifts). The Bishop's House is Alaska's most interesting historic site. Downstairs is a self-guided museum; upstairs, rangers lead tours of the bishop's quarters, which are furnished with original and period pieces. It's an extraordinary window into an alternate stream of American history, from a time before the founding of Seattle or San Francisco, when Sitka was the most important city on North America's Pacific Coast. The tour concludes with a visit to a beautiful little chapel with many of the original icons Innocent imported from Russia.

Lincoln and Monastery sts. No phone; call Sitka National Historical Park Visitor Center (Ⓒ 907/747-0110). Admission $4 per person or $15 per family (family admission covers both facilities). Summer daily 9am–5pm; winter by appointment.

Sheldon Jackson Museum ★★
Sheldon Jackson, a Presbyterian missionary with powerful friends in Washington, was Alaska's first general agent for education, a paternal guardian of the welfare, schooling, and spiritual lives of Alaska's Natives. His benevolent aim was to defend Natives from exploitation and abuse and bring them into American civilization as equals. Tragically, his strategy to accomplish this goal was to erase indigenous cultures and replace them with Protestantism, causing incalculable,

lasting harm to peoples over a broad swath of Alaska. As a side hobby during his travels from 1888 to 1898, Jackson gathered an omnivorous 5,000-piece collection of Native art, cultural, and everyday objects. That collection, the best in Alaska, has been displayed for more than a century in a concrete building on the college campus that bears Jackson's name. It's a jewel box; the overwhelming wealth is displayed by Alaska State Museum curators in ingenious ways that avoids a feeling of clutter. Many drawers open to reveal more displays. Despite the age of many of the pieces, they appear new, as if just made. Don't miss Katlian's helmet, worn by the Kiksadi clan's war leader in the Battle of Sitka in 1804; raven-shaped, it is that rare piece of great history that's also great art. Native artists demonstrate their skill on summer days, and the gift shop contains almost exclusively authentic Native arts and crafts. Authentic Native art pieces cost more than tourist trinkets: Plan to spend over $100 except for small, simple items. (If you're already here, take time for the college aquarium, mentioned under "Walking Downtown," below.)

104 College Dr. ✆ **907/747-8981**. www.museums.state.ak.us. Admission $4 adults, free for ages 18 and under. Mid-May to mid-Sept daily 9am–5pm; mid-Sept to mid-May Tues–Sat 10am–4pm.

St. Michael's Cathedral ✦

The first Orthodox cathedral in the New World stands grandly in the middle of Sitka's principal street, where it was completed in 1848. Bishop Veniaminov (see "The Russian Bishop's House," above) designed it and oversaw construction. The cathedral contains several miraculous icons, some dating from the 17th century. The St. Michael, the farthest right of six on the front screen, was bound for Sitka aboard the *Neva* in 1813 when the ship went down some 30 miles from Sitka. Thirty days later the icon, in its crate, washed ashore undamaged and was recovered by Sitka's townspeople. The original building burned down in a 1966 fire that started elsewhere and took much of Sitka's downtown, but almost all the contents were saved by a human chain in the 30 minutes before the building was destroyed. One man lifted down the huge central chandelier, which later took six men to carry. Orthodox Christians all over the United States raised the money to rebuild the cathedral exactly as it had been, using a Russian architect who could interpret Veniaminov's original plans. It was completed in 1976. A knowledgeable guide is on hand to answer questions or give talks when large groups congregate. Sunday services are sung in English, Church Slavonic, Tlingit, Aleut, and Yupik. Right across Lincoln Street stop in at the cathedral's well-stocked Archangel Michael Icons, Books and Gift Shop for souvenirs, music CDs, books, and even children's books.

Lincoln and Cathedral sts. ✆ **907/747-8120**. $2 donation requested. Summer Mon–Fri 9am–4pm, but call ahead because hours change and are extended when cruise ships call; winter call for hours.

Sitka Tribe Dance Performances ✦

The Sheet'ka Kwaán Naá Kahidi, Sitka's community house, standing on the north side of the downtown parade ground, is a modern version of a Tlingit clan house, with an air handling system that pulls smoke from the central fire pit straight up to the chimney. The magnificent house screen, a carved wall at the front of the hall, installed in 2000, is the largest in the Pacific Northwest. Performances last 30 minutes, including dances and a story. It's entirely traditional and put on by members of the tribe. You can also sign up for tours and activities in the lobby.

200 Katlian St. ✆ **888/270-8687** or 907/747-7290. www.sitkatours.com. Admission $8 adults, $5 children. Call for times.

OTHER ATTRACTIONS IN TOWN
Alaska Raptor Center ✦✦

This nonprofit center takes in injured birds of prey (mainly bald eagles, but also owls, hawks, and other species) for veterinary treatment and release or, if too badly injured, for placement in a zoo or as part of the collection of 25 that live on-site. Visitors get to see the impressive birds up close in a lecture setting, through the glass wall of the veterinary clinic, and in outdoor enclosures, but the highlight is an extraordinary flight-training center, built in 2003 at a cost of $3 million. This enormous aviary is where recuperating birds learn to fly again, and visitors can walk its length behind one-way glass, watching them preen, feed, and take to the air in a peaceful setting simulating their natural habitat. Watching these giant birds fly from so close is awesome. The center's grounds also include a pleasant nature trail (accessible for travelers with disabilities) that leads down to a river with four species of salmon, where healthy eagles sometimes can be seen feeding.

1000 Raptor Way (off Sawmill Creek Blvd.) Ⓒ **800/643-9425** or 907/747-8662. www.alaskaraptor.org. Admission $12 adults, $6 ages 12 and under. Summer daily 8am–4pm; winter call for hours.

WALKING DOWNTOWN   The grassy park at Lincoln and Katlian was the site of the Russians' barracks and parade ground. Just north on Marine Street is a replica of a **Russian Blockhouse;** across Lincoln Street to the south and up the stairs is **Castle Hill,** a site of historic significance for the ancient Tlingits, for the Russians, and for contemporary Alaskans. The first American flag raised in Alaska was hoisted here in 1867. There are historic markers and cannons. As you walk east past the cathedral and Crescent Harbor, several quaint historic buildings are on the left. My favorite is **St. Peter's by-the-Sea Episcopal Church,** a lovely stone-and-timber chapel with a pipe organ, consecrated in 1899.

At the east end of the harbor is a **public playground** and the **Sheldon Jackson College Aquarium,** in the Sage Building on the ocean side of Lincoln Street. All the tanks contain local marine life (a king crab had just been dismembered by an octopus on our visit), and it's eye opening to realize what's down below. Best of all are the large touch tanks where visitors can handle animals from three different seafloor habitats. The aquarium is open to the public with free admission, however, hours are not published.

SHOPPING

There are some good shops and galleries in Sitka, mostly on Lincoln and Harbor streets. Several are across the street from St. Michael's Cathedral. **Artist Cove Gallery,** at 241 Lincoln St., shows art and contains a small but interesting section of used and out-of-print books about Alaska. **Fishermen's Eye Fine Art Gallery and Graphic,** at 239 Lincoln St., is owned by an artist who shows only work by Alaskans, most of it created in Sitka. **Fairweather Prints,** at 209 Lincoln St., has a fun, youthful feel; it is large and has a diverse selection, including wearable art (including T-shirts), watercolors, prints, ceramics, and cute, inexpensive crafts. Continue west on Lincoln to **Baranov's Russian and American Store** on the right, and, on the left, **Log Cache Gifts,** a typical gift store housed in an 1835 Russian cabin. **Old Harbor Books,** at 201 Lincoln St., is a good browsing store with an excellent selection of Alaska books. Back in the other direction, near the Crescent Harbor dock, the **Sitka Rose Gallery** occupies a Victorian house at 419 Lincoln St., featuring higher-end work, mostly local: sculpture, original paintings, engraving, and jewelry. The **Sheldon Jackson Museum Gift Shop,** 104 College Dr., is an excellent place to buy Alaska Native arts and crafts with assurance of their authenticity.

GETTING OUTSIDE: ON THE WATER

The little islands and rocks that dot Sitka Sound are an invitation to the sea otter in all of us; you must get out on the water.

SIGHTSEEING & WILDLIFE TOURS

When conditions allow, tour boats visit **St. Lazaria Island,** a bird rookery where you can expect to see tufted puffins, murres, rhinoceros auklets, and other pelagic birds. Storm petrels show up by the hundreds of thousands at dawn and dusk for those who charter a boat to stay overnight at the rookery. The volcanic rock drops straight down into deep water, so even big boats can come close, but in rough weather even they won't go to the exposed location of the island. Even then, there's plenty to see in protected waters. Humpback whales show up in large groups in the fall and are often seen by the half dozen in the summer. There are so many bald eagles that you're pretty well guaranteed to see them even from shore. But the lowly sea otter is the most common and, in my experience, most amusing and endearing of marine mammals, and you'll certainly see them from a tour boat. The public tubs at **Goddard Hot Springs,** 17 miles south of town, are another possible stop for charters.

The **Sitka Wildlife Quest,** operated by Allen Marine Tours (© **888/747-8101** or 907/747-8100; www.allenmarinetours.com), runs a popular marine tour with well-trained naturalists to explain the wildlife. You have a good chance of encountering humpback whales and sea otters. Tours visit St. Lazaria Island when sea conditions permit. A 2-hour cruise Tuesday and Thursday at 6pm costs $59 for adults, $39 for children. A 3-hour cruise Saturday and Sunday at 9am costs $79 for adults, $49 for children. The boat leaves from the Crescent Harbor Visitors Dock late May through early September. Buy tickets onboard. These are different excursions from the ones offered cruise-ship passengers. Allen Marine, which also builds vessels, has a long-standing reputation for the quality of its offerings.

For $100 per person, you can charter a six-passenger boat for a 3-hour tour to St. Lazaria Island, for whale-watching, and to learn about the sound with a married couple who are both former wildlife biologists, Kent Hall and Beverly Minn, at **Sitka's Secrets** (© **907/747-5089;** www.sitkasecret.com). They do fishing charters, too. **Ester G Sea Taxi** (see "Forest Service Cabins," below) offers small-boat marine tours as well.

Sea Life Discovery Tours (© **877/966-2301** or 907/966-2301; www.sealife discoverytours.com) offers a chance to see the rich underwater life of Sitka Sound from an extraordinary boat with big windows 4 feet below the waterline; it's really cool. They charge $86 for a 2-hour tour; call for times.

SALTWATER FISHING

Many charter boats are available for salmon or halibut fishing. The Sitka Convention and Visitors Bureau (see "Visitor Information," earlier in this section) keeps a detailed charter boat list online. Using the grid view (www.sitka.org/grid.html), you can compare boats, rates, and services, and link to the vessel's own home page. Or book through **Alaska Adventures Unlimited** (© **907/747-5576**), which has set up charters in Sitka since 1982. If you can handle your own boat, skiffs rent for $95 for a half-day and up from **Sitka Ocean Adventures** (© **907/747-6375;** www.ssocean adventures.com). Make contact at the blue bus in the parking lot of the Harrigan Centennial Hall.

SEA KAYAKING

Sitka's protected waters and intricate shorelines are perfect for sea kayaking. You're almost sure to see sea otters, seals, sea lions, and eagles, and could see whales. **Sitka Ocean Adventures,** mentioned in the previous paragraph, offers tours for beginners every day in the summer when they have at least two customers to go along. Guides don't follow regular routes, seeking wildlife wherever animals have recently been seen. A 2-hour paddle (plus a half-hour for instruction and gearing up) takes kayakers into the islands around Sitka and costs $65. A half-day paddle could also go to a historic World War II fort, where you can walk through the abandoned bunkers. That's $95. The firm offers all-day paddles and rents kayaks, too.

GETTING OUTSIDE: ONSHORE
FRESHWATER FISHING

Anglers should pick up the *Sitka Area Sport Fishing Guide,* which has lots of tips on streams, lakes, and fishing methods in the area. You can download the guide from the **Alaska Department of Fish & Game** at www.alaska.gov/adfg (click "Sport Fisheries," and then the "Southeast region"). The site also has weekly fishing updates. The local fish and game office is at 304 Lake St., Room 103, Sitka, AK 99835 (© **907/747-5355**).

FOREST SERVICE CABINS

The **Sitka Ranger District,** 204 Siginaka Way, Sitka, AK 99835 (© **907/747-6671;** www.fs.fed.us/r10/tongass/districts/sitka), maintains two dozen wilderness cabins on Baranof, Chichagof, and Kruzof islands, in sea-kayaking coves and on remote fishing lakes, where rowing skiffs generally are provided. The cabins and their facilities are described in a Forest Service handout or on their website.

You will need camping gear and a boat or floatplane to get there, a much greater cost than the nightly rental of $35 to $45. For cabins on saltwater near Sitka, the most affordable way is a water taxi, such as **Esther G Sea Taxi** (© **907/747-6481** or 907/ 738-6481 cellular; www.puffinsandwhales.com). Operator Davey Lubin also offers marine wildlife tours and kayak drop-offs to remote shores. **Harris Aircraft Services,** 400 Airport Rd. (© **877/966-3050** Alaska only, or 907/966-3050; www.harris aircraft.com) offers floatplane charters to cabins or anywhere else. Either way, allow time in your schedule in case bad weather prevents backcountry travel. Information on researching and reserving a cabin is under "Getting Outside in the Tongass National Forest," in section 1 of this chapter. Another remote cabin option is the Camp Coogan Bay Hideaway, listed below, under "Rent a Floathouse."

HIKING

Sitka is a great hiking area, with trails threading all over the mountains behind the town. There are a dozen U.S. Forest Service hiking trails accessible from the roads around Sitka and another 20 rough trails you can get to by plane or boat. A beautifully made little book, *Sitka Trails* (Alaska Natural History Association, $8), covers each trail with a detailed description and fine-scale color topographic map. If you need further advice, contact the ranger district office (see "Forest Service Cabins," above).

From downtown, the 4-mile (one-way) **Indian River Trail** is a relaxing rainforest walk rising gradually up the river valley to a small waterfall. Take Indian River Road off Sawmill Creek Road just east of the downtown. For a steeper mountain-climbing trail to alpine terrain and great views, the **Gavan Hill–Harbor Mountain Trail** is near the end of Baranof Street, which starts near the Russian Bishop's House. It gains 2,500 feet over 3 miles to the peak of Gavan Hill, then continues another 3 miles along a ridge to meet Harbor Mountain Road. The **Sitka Cross Trail** connects these trails and neighborhood streets, allowing you to start almost anywhere.

At the north end of Halibut Point Road, 7½ miles from downtown, several wonderful trails loop through the **Starrigavan Recreation Area.** On the right, the **Estuary**

Life Trail and **Forest Muskeg Trail,** totaling about a mile, are exquisitely developed and accessible to anyone, circling a grassy estuary rich with birds and fish. The well-built **Mosquito Cove Trail,** starting from the far end of the bayside loop camping area on the left, circles 1.25 miles along the shore to the secluded gravel beach of the cove, returning over boardwalk steps through the old-growth forest. Camping here is covered under "A Hostel & Camping," below.

TIDE POOLING & SHORE WALKS

Halibut Point State Recreation Area, 4½ miles north of town on Halibut Point Road, is a great place for a picnic, shore ramble, and tide pooling. The Mosquito Cove Trail (see above) is also promising. To find the best low tides, check a tide book, available all over town. It's best to go at the lowest tide possible, arriving on the shore an hour before the low. To identify the little creatures you'll see, pick up a plastic-covered field guide at a bookstore.

WHALE-WATCHING

Humpback whales stop to feed in Sitka Sound on their way south in the winter migration. During October, November, December, and March, you can watch from shore—the local government has even built a special park for the purpose. At **Whale Park,** just south of town on Sawmill Creek Road, spotting scopes are mounted on platforms along a boardwalk and at the end of staircases that descend the dramatic, wooded cliffs. Excellent interpretive signs, located near surfacing concrete whales in the parking lot, explain the whales. The Sitka WhaleFest, in November (see "Special Events," earlier), is the best time for whale enthusiasts, as then you can watch whales in the company of cetacean scientists. For summertime whale-watching, take a boat: Choices are above under "Sightseeing and Wildlife Tours."

WHERE TO STAY

In addition to the places below, you'll find super-clean rooms with many amenities in a quiet building downtown at the **Super 8 Sitka,** 404 Sawmill Creek Blvd. (✆ **800/ 800-8000** for reservations, or 907/747-8804; www.super8.com).

To save money, choose a B&B. The **Sitka Convention and Visitors Bureau** (✆ **907/747-5940;** www.sitka.org) has links to many B&Bs on its website, and can send you a printed list as well. Here are two good options: **Sitka Woodside Lodging,** 411 Wortman Loop (✆ **907/747-8287;** www.woodsidelodging.com), with comfortable rooms for $85 to $100 double in a quiet subdivision a half-hour walk from town; or **Alaska Swan Lake Bed & Breakfast,** 206½ Lakeview Dr. (✆ **907/747-3917;** www.sitka.org/swanlake/index.htm), with rooms with private bathrooms for only $95 a night in a big, white house above the lake just a mile from the downtown area.

Alaska Ocean View Bed & Breakfast 🖈🖈🖈   Ebullient Carole Denkinger and her husband, Bill, have a passion for making their bed-and-breakfast one you'll remember. They've thought of everything—the covered outdoor Jacuzzi where you can watch the eagles, toys and games for the kids, a laptop to borrow, thick robes and slippers, an open snack counter, a big and delicious full breakfast, and even wildflower seeds to take home. Rooms are soft and plush and guests are pampered with unique extras such as DVD players and a media library and HEPA air cleaners in each room for people with allergies. The hospitality is exceptional, too. For example, Carole has stocked her kitchen with vegan and Atkins-approved food for dieters and cooks special meals for those sensitive to gluten or lactose. Moreover, she doesn't charge extra for any of her exceptional amenities. The B&B is on a residential street with a view of the water about a mile from the historic district. No smoking is permitted.

1101 Edgecumbe Dr., Sitka, AK 99835. ℂ **907/747-8310.** Fax 907/747-3440. www.sitka-alaska-lodging.com. 3 units. High season $129–$229 double; low season $89–$169 double. Extra person free–$30 depending on circumstances. Rates include full breakfast. AE, DC, DISC, MC, V. **Amenities:** Outdoor Jacuzzi; business center. *In room:* TV/VCR/DVD, fridge, coffeemaker, hair dryer, iron, microwave, Wi-Fi, CD player, free media library.

Cascade Inn 🟊   Two and a half miles from downtown, this family-operated waterfront hotel puts you in a trim standard room with a balcony over Sitka Sound and a spectacular view. The red building is fronted by gas pumps and a liquor store, but don't let that fool you. The rooms, although small, are an oasis of ocean light where you can fall asleep to the sound of the sea. Each has one or two queen-size beds, and some include handy kitchenette units, which cost $15 more. The sauna has a glass front to take advantage of the view. *Note:* Stay elsewhere if you have trouble with stairs, and plan on having wheels to get around.

2035 Halibut Point Rd., Sitka, AK 99835. ℂ **800/532-0908** or 907/747-6804. www.cascadeinnsitka.com. 10 units. High season $115–$140 double; low season $85–$105 double. Extra person $20. MC, V. **Amenities:** Sauna; coin-op laundry. *In room:* TV, coffeemaker, hair dryer, iron.

Shee Atika Totem Square Inn 🟊   This hotel across the street from the community house is owned by the local Native corporation and makes full use of their Tlingit motifs and colors in its decoration—red, black, white, and earth—and employs many Natives on its staff. The smallish rooms are decorated with Native art and had just received new carpet and bathrooms before our visit in 2007. The common areas are airy and welcoming. The rates include a continental breakfast, served in a nondescript conference room; upgrading to a full breakfast is only $3. The downtown location allows walking to some of the attractions, although the national historic site is a long walk.

201 Katlian St., Sitka, AK 99835. ℂ **866/300-1353** or 907/747-3693. Fax 907/747-2839. www.totemsquareinn.com. 67 units. High season $139–$169 double; low season $49–$119 double. Extra person $10. AE, DC, DISC, MC, V. **Amenities:** Exercise room; airport courtesy van; business center; coin-op laundry; Internet access. *In room:* TV, coffeemaker, hair dryer, iron, Wi-Fi, wired broadband, fan.

Sitka Hotel *(Value)*   After a major fire hit this family-owned budget hotel early in 2006, it blossomed from the ashes (thanks to an insurance settlement) with 15 brand-new rooms and complete redecorating, upgrading what had always been a good deal in a fairly rickety wooden building into a very good deal in a relatively modern building. While the smaller rooms will never be luxurious, the hotel owners have always kept them clean and comfortable. Fourteen of the rooms have shared bathrooms (but there are a good number of them to share). The location is prime, right across from the Russian parade grounds. The brand-new rooms, in the back of the building, have private bathrooms and added amenities, such as coffeemakers.

Victoria's Restaurant, with about a dozen tables in the storefront downstairs, tries for a high Victorian feel, but in actuality it's more of a friendly small-town diner, with hearty breakfasts and lunches in winter and an inexpensive fine-dining dinner menu added in the summer. The hotel has a small bar, too.

118 Lincoln St., Sitka, AK 99835. ℂ **907/747-3288.** Fax 907/747-8499. www.sitkahotel.com. 60 units, 46 with private bathroom. High season $70 double with shared bathroom, $90 double with private bathroom; low season $60 double with shared bathroom, $75 double with private bathroom. Extra person $7. AE, DISC, MC, V. **Amenities:** Restaurant; coin-op laundry. *In room:* TV, iron/ironing board, Wi-Fi.

Finds   **Rent a Floathouse**

Southeast Alaska has a unique kind of dwelling called a floathouse, a house on a barge, permanently anchored in some quiet, forgotten cove. There have even been float-towns, with houses, schools, and other buildings tied together, usually at remote logging sites. **Camp Coogan Bay Hideaway** (*©* **907/747-6375;** www.ssoceanadventures.com) is a floathouse you can rent for $180 a day. It floats in a narrow, placid bay out of a wilderness fantasy, 20 minutes from Sitka by boat (it's also the best place in the area to see bears). A charming, peeling old bunkhouse from town was stuck on a 1940s barge and anchored here, with a rainwater system, a woodstove for heat, propane appliances, and a diesel generator if you want light. A wood-fired sauna and a gas barbecue are out on deck. Don't expect the Hilton: It's primitive and a little grubby. You'll want to rent a boat or sea kayaks for mobility; owners John and Barbara DeLong offer those services too.

Westmark Sitka 🔶   This upscale hotel, above Crescent Harbor in the heart of the historic district, contains many comfortable rooms with sweeping views of Sikta Sound. The lobby suggests the building style of Northwest Native Americans, but the more anonymous rooms will be familiar to any business traveler, with furniture of warm wood and all the expected amenities. There's nowhere to stay that is more convenient to the sites or more comfortable for a broad range of travelers.

The **Raven Dining Room** restaurant shares the hotel's view and is one of the best places in town for an evening meal, with a quiet dining room that, while far from formal, is a bit more refined than the other choices in town. Service was careful and respectful at my last meal. There's a long menu of seafood and beef in the evening and even the more challenging entrees are expertly prepared. For a lighter meal, the bar menu offers excellent choices.

330 Seward St., Sitka, AK 99835-7523. *©* **800/544-0970** for reservations, or 907/747-6241. Fax 907/747-5486. www.westmarkhotels.com. 101 units. High season $149–$159 double; low season $139–$149 double. Extra person over age 13 $15. AE, DC, DISC, MC, V. **Amenities:** Restaurant; bar. *In room:* TV, coffeemaker, hair dryer, iron, high-speed Internet.

A HOSTEL & CAMPING

Hostelling International—Sitka is, as of this writing, a hostel without a home. It remains active as an organization and can be reached at *©* **907/747-8661,** but has moved out of a Methodist church without a place to move into. By the time you're traveling, perhaps this will be resolved. Call ahead.

The Forest Service's **Starrigavan Recreation Area** contains excellent campgrounds at the north end of Halibut Point Road, 7½ miles from town and ¾ mile from the ferry dock. There are three loops. The Backpackers' Loop has six hike-in sites. The Estuary Loop (which joins the Estuary Life Trail), on the right, has 26 sites for RVs or tents, which are widely separated under huge trees. The Bayside Loop, at the water's edge, is the last left on the highway. Three of its sites are situated on the edge of Starrigavan Bay, creating the feeling that you're way out in the wilderness. Fees are $12 to $30 a night. Fourteen sites are available on a first-come, first-served basis, but all the rest must be reserved on the national system (see "Reserving a Cabin or Campsite," p. 103). The recreation area is open all year, but vehicle access is restricted in the winter. May through mid-September, access gates are locked from 10pm to 7am.

There are two RV parks, each with water and electric hookups only and each charging under $22: City-run **Sealing Cove RV Park** (© 907/747-3439) is near the airport and a free dump station, and **Sitka Sportsman's Association RV Park** (© 907/747-6033) is near the ferry dock.

WHERE TO DINE

See other restaurant choices at the Westmark Sitka and Sitka Hotel above, under "Where to Stay." A Subway sandwich shop is at Seward and Lake streets, behind the Westmark.

Bayview Restaurant ✦ BURGERS/PASTA/SEAFOOD   The view of the boat harbor and good food make this small second-story restaurant popular year-round, although it's sometimes noisy and slightly cramped. Everything I've tried from the extensive menu has been well prepared and quickly served by friendly staff. I was quite satisfied with a lunch of a tasty Cajun halibut taco, which came with a salad and the always wonderful clam chowder for $9.75. Dinner prices also are competitive with other places in Sitka, and even then you have the option of simple fare or fancier seafood selections. It's a great spot for breakfast, too.

407 Lincoln St. © 907/747-5440. Main courses $9–$30. DISC, MC, V. High season Mon–Sat 5am–9pm, Sun 5am–3pm; winter Mon–Sat 7am–8pm, Sun 7am–3pm.

Ludvig's Bistro ✦✦ MEDITERRANEAN/OYSTER BAR   This tiny dining room and its young proprietors offer Sitka's only first-rate cuisine, and it's a very pleasant place for a meal. They've taken a formerly grungy concrete space and filled it with charm and warmth, with Mediterranean colors, wine bottles, and whimsical art. They can't serve

---

⎛Tips Hip Eats & Coffee in Sitka

A cool couple owns **The Backdoor Café,** in the back half of Old Harbor Books at 104 Barracks St. (© **907/747-8856**), the kind of place that develops a following among the local poets, musicians, and the like. Besides coffee and the owners' own homemade bagels, the cafe serves fresh pastries for breakfast and a single special for lunch (which can run out). It's open Monday through Saturday from 6:30am to 5pm, Sunday 9am to 2pm. Credit cards are not accepted. **The Galley Deli,** near the big fuel tanks on the waterfront at the end of Lincoln Street (© **907/747-9997**), produces huge sandwiches of homemade bread, delicious wraps and salads, and rich chowder of local clams. The kitchen and dining room are tiny (plan on taking your meal away), and people socialize while waiting for their orders. Summer hours are Monday through Saturday 10am to 5pm, winter closing at 3pm. Only cash is accepted for payment. **Highliner Coffee,** on Lake Street just above Seward Street (© **907/747-4924**), is a fancier place, with free Wi-Fi (or use their computer for $2 for the first 15 min.). A "highliner" is a top commercial fisherman; the name here is a bit of a boast for its fisherpeople owners, who hope to educate customers about their way of life as well as roasting Sitka's coffee. It's open Monday through Saturday from 5:30am to 5pm, Sunday from 8am to 4pm.

many meals a night here, so each one is carefully crafted, coming from a changing menu intended to stretch the chef and introduce the small-town clientele to new tastes. A recent menu included grilled marinated lamb chops, a wild mushroom ragu, and calamari. Or snack in the afternoon on tapas or local oysters in the $13 to $17 price range. Best of all, they're not pretentious—the owners, Colette and Lisa, create a sense of friendship with diners; at times the whole place feels like a big dinner party.

256 Katlian St. ✆ **907/966-3663.** Reservations recommended. Lunch $5–$15; dinner main courses $17–$27. MC, V. Tues–Sat 2–9pm.

Pizza Express (Value) MEXICAN/PIZZA   Come here when you want a filling, inexpensive meal or to order in for a good pizza. The dining room is in a strip mall a little outside the downtown, near the Raptor Center and across from the historical park. The owners are Mexican and produce yummy homemade tortilla chips among other national cuisine.

1321 Sawmill Creek Rd. ✆ **907/966-2428.** Main courses $7–$13. MC, V. Summer Mon–Sat 11am–10pm and Sun noon–10pm; winter Mon–Sat 11am–10pm and Sun noon–9pm.

6 Juneau: Forest Capital

Juneau (*June*-oh) hustles and bustles like no other city in Alaska. The steep downtown streets echo with the mad shopping sprees of cruise-ship passengers in the summer tourist season and the whispered intrigues of politicians during the winter legislative session. Miners, loggers, and eco-tourism operators come to lobby for their share of Southeast's forest. Lunch hour arrives, and well-to-do state and federal bureaucrats burst from the office buildings to try the latest restaurant or brown-bag on one of the waterfront wharves, the sparkling water before them and gift store malls behind. The center of town becomes an ad hoc pedestrian mall as the crush of people forces cars to creep.

My Juneau is close at hand, but very different. As a child, at a magical age, I lived here with my family in a house on the side of the mountains above downtown. My Juneau is up the 99 steps that lead from the cemetery to the bottom of Pine Street—the way I walked home from school—and then to the top of residential Evergreen Avenue, where the pavement gives way to a forest trail among fiddlehead ferns and massive rainforest spruces. That trail leads to the flume (a wooden aqueduct that used to bring water down from the mountains), upon which we would walk into the land of bears and salmon, the rumbling water at our feet. It's still a short walk from the rackety downtown streets to a misty forest quiet, where you can listen for the voices of trees.

Juneau is Alaska's third-largest city (Anchorage and Fairbanks are larger), with a population of 30,000, but it feels like a small town that's just been stuffed with people. Splattered on the sides of Mount Juneau and Mount Roberts along Gastineau Channel, where there isn't room for much of a town, its setting is picturesque but impractical. Further development up the mountains is hemmed in by avalanche danger; beyond is the 1,500-square-mile **Juneau Icefield,** an impenetrable barrier. Gold-mine tailings dumped into the Gastineau created the flat land near the water where much of the downtown area now stands. The Native village that originally stood on the waterfront is today a little pocket several blocks from the shore. There's no road to the outside world, and the terrain discourages building one. Jets are the main way in and out, threading down through the mountains to the airport.

Gold was responsible for the location; it was found here in 1880 by Joe Juneau and Richard Harris, assisted by the Tlingit chief Kowee, who told them where to look. All three men are buried in the Evergreen Cemetery. Their find started Alaska's development. The territory's first significant roads and bridges and its first electrical plant were built in the mountains here, which were carved with miles of hard rock tunnels well before the Klondike Gold Rush began. In a few years these mines removed more gold than the United States paid for all of Alaska, as attested to by a photograph in the Alaska State Museum showing comparative piles. There's plenty of gold left, but mining died out with World War II; efforts to start again have repeatedly faltered in the face of environmental controls and economics. There are several interesting gold mining sites to visit.

In 1900, Congress moved the territorial capital here from Sitka, which had fallen behind in the flurry of gold-rush development. Alaskans have been fighting over whether or not to keep it here for many decades since, but Juneau's economy is heavily dependent on government jobs, and it has successfully fought off a series of challenges to its capital status. In 2002, voters turned down a petition initiative to move the legislature by a two-to-one margin. In 2005, Juneau attempted to cement its place as the capital city by launching a drive to build a new capitol building, but the ploy backfired when the public panned the futuristic design city leaders selected. As a result, the legislature and governor started talking about moving again. The closest the issue came was in the 1970s, when voters approved moving the capital, but then balked at the cost of building a whole new city to house it—a necessity since neither Anchorage nor Fairbanks, which have their own rivalry, would support the move if it meant the other city got to have the capital nearby.

There's plenty to see in Juneau, and it's a good town to visit because the population of government workers supports restaurants and amenities of a quality not found elsewhere in Southeast. Alaska's most accessible glacier, the Mendenhall, is in Juneau, and many businesses have set up tours, including visits to the fish hatchery, the brewery, and an abandoned mine. Juneau is also a starting point and travel hub for outdoor activities all over the northern Panhandle: you'll likely pass through on your way to Glacier Bay or virtually anywhere else in the region. The outdoors is always close at hand in Juneau. You can start from the capitol building for a hike to the top of Mount Juneau or Mount Roberts, or up the Perseverance Trail that leads in between. Sea-kayaking and whale-watching excursions are nearby, as well as some of Alaska's most scenic tide pooling and beach walking.

Downtown, the crush of visitors can be overwhelming when many cruise ships are in port at once. The streets around the docks have been entirely taken over by shops and other touristy businesses. Many of these are owned by people from outside Alaska who come to the state for the summer to sell gifts made outside Alaska. But only a few blocks away are quiet mountainside neighborhoods of houses with mossy roofs, and only a few blocks farther are the woods and the mountains, populated by bear, eagles, and salmon.

ESSENTIALS
GETTING THERE
BY AIR   Jet service is available only from **Alaska Airlines** (✆ **800/252-7522;** www.alaskaair.com), with several daily nonstop flights from Seattle and Anchorage and from the smaller Southeast Alaska towns. Many of the region's commuter and air-taxi operators also maintain desks at the airport and have flights out of Juneau. Among the best is **Wings of Alaska** (✆ **907/789-0790;** www.ichoosewings.com).

BY FERRY   All the main-line ferries of Southeast's **Alaska Marine Highway System** (✆ **800/642-0066;** www.ferryalaska.com) stop at the terminal in Auke Bay

---

> **Tips** **Flying to Juneau**
>
> Juneau's mist-shrouded airport, wedged between ocean and mountain, has a special verb: *to overhead*. That means that when you try to fly to Juneau on a foggy day, you could end up somewhere else instead (although this now happens less frequently thanks to new navigational technology). Planes overhead other Southeast towns, too, but more frequently in Juneau, since it is the region's travel hub, with many flights a day. The airline will put you on the next flight back to Juneau when the weather clears, but they won't pay for hotel rooms or give you a refund. Your only protection is travel insurance and a loose itinerary. This situation is such an ingrained part of Juneau's way of life that a channel on the cable TV system broadcasts the view toward the airport 24 hours a day, showing the weather over the Gastineau Channel (it's called the Channel Channel, 23 on the dial). Residents know the view so well they can tell from the silent image if they'll get out that day.

(© **907/789-7453** or 907/465-3940 recording), 14 miles from downtown, and the fast ferry, *Fairweather*, is based here, too. It cuts off half the 5 hours to Haines or Skagway, with four and five sailings there a week, respectively. The passenger fare is $37 to Haines, $50 to Skagway.

GETTING INTO TOWN FROM THE AIRPORT & FERRY TERMINAL   An airport shuttle may be operating when you visit. Ask at the visitor desk in the baggage claim area.

An express **Capital Transit city bus** (© **907/789-6901**) comes to the airport at 11 minutes past the hour on weekdays from 7:11am to 5:11pm and costs $1.50; your luggage has to fit under your seat or at your feet. Ask the driver for the stop closest to your hotel. Generally, you can walk from there.

Shuttles sometimes operate from the ferry dock downtown in the summer, but the arrangements are changeable. Ask when you arrive, or call ahead to the visitor center (see "Visitor Information," below). A cab downtown from the airport will cost you $22, from the ferry dock $33. One taxi company is **Capital Cab** (© **907/586-2772**), which also offers tours for $55 an hour.

ORIENTATION
Juneau has three main parts: downtown, the Mendenhall Valley, and Douglas. Downtown Juneau is a numbered grid of streets overlying the uneven topography like a patched quilt over a pile of pillows. As you look at Juneau from the water, Mount Juneau is on the left and Mount Roberts on the right; Mount Roberts is a few hundred feet taller, at 3,819 feet. **Franklin Street** extends south of town 5½ miles to good hiking trails and the hamlet of Thane. When the city outgrew its original site downtown, housing spread to the suburban **Mendenhall Valley,** about a dozen miles north out the Egan Expressway or the parallel, two-lane Glacier Highway. The glacial valley also contains the Juneau International Airport, University of Alaska Southeast, and the **Auke Bay** area, where the ferry terminal is located. The road continues 40 miles to a place known as **"The End of the Road."** Across a bridge over the Gastineau Channel from downtown Juneau is Douglas Island. Turn left for the town of **Douglas,**

mostly a bedroom community for Juneau, and turn right for the North Douglas Highway, which leads to the ski area and some beautiful rocky beaches.

GETTING AROUND

BY RENTAL CAR   A car is a hindrance in compact downtown Juneau, but if you're going to the Mendenhall Glacier or to any of the attractions out of downtown or to Douglas Island, renting a car for a day or two is a good idea. Hertz, Avis, Budget, Alamo, and National are based at the airport.

BY BIKE   If you can handle hills, bikes make good sense in Juneau, where separated paths parallel many of the main roads and downtown traffic is slow. The 24-mile round-trip to Mendenhall Glacier keeps you on a bike path almost all the way. Bikes are for rent at the **Driftwood Lodge,** 435 Willoughby Ave. (© **800/544-2239** or 907/586-2280; www.driftwoodalaska.com) for $25 a day, $15 for a half-day.

VISITOR INFORMATION

The **Visitor Information Center** is in the Centennial Hall at 101 Egan Dr., near the Alaska State Museum (© **888/581-2201** or 907/586-2201; fax 907/586-6304; www.traveljuneau.com). Operated by the Juneau Convention and Visitors Bureau, the center distributes a *Juneau Guide & Travel Planner,* online and on paper, that contains exhaustive listings of hotels and B&Bs, charter boats, tours, and other services. The center is open in summer Monday through Friday from 8:30am to 5pm, and Saturday and Sunday from 9am to 5pm; in winter Monday through Friday from 9am to 4pm. The bureau also operates **information desks** at the airport, near the door in the baggage-claim area, and at the Auke Bay ferry terminal. During the summer, centers are staffed at the cruise-ship terminal and at Marine Park.

The office of the **Tongass National Forest Juneau Ranger District** is at 8510 Mendenhall Loop Rd., Juneau, AK 99801 (© **907/586-8800,** 907/790-7444 TDD; fax 907/586-8808; www.fs.fed.us/r10/tongass).

FAST FACTS: Juneau

Banks **Wells Fargo,** at 123 Seward St. (© **907/586-3324**), is one of the many banks and stores that have ATMs.

Hospital **Bartlett Regional,** at 3260 Hospital Dr. (© **907/796-8900**), is 3 miles out the Glacier Highway from downtown.

Internet Access Computers are easy to find downtown at coffeehouses and businesses such as **Copy Express,** at 230 Seward St. (© **907/586-2174**). In the Mendenhall Valley, try **Electronic Adventures,** 9109 Mendenhall Mall Rd. (© **907/790-3658**).

Police The police station is at 6255 Alaway Ave. (© **907/586-0600** for non-emergencies).

Post Office Downtown in the federal building, 709 W. 9th St.; and in the Mendenhall Valley at 9491 Vintage Blvd., near Carr's supermarket. A postal contract station handier to the cruise-ship dock is at 225 Front St., Suite 103, in the mall across the street from the movie theater.

Taxes **Sales tax** is 5%. You pay 12% tax on rooms.

> **Tips The Cruise-Ship Dock: Where Do You Get Off?**
>
> Cruise-ship passengers disembark in Juneau's attractive **Marine Park** waterfront area, where a kiosk dispenses information and tour operators sell their services. Downtown shops and attractions are close by. Among the most popular sights is one right at the dock, the statue of a small dog facing the ships as they come in. This is *Patsy Ann,* a bull terrier that in the 1930s always seemed to know when a steamer was arriving and faithfully stationed herself on the dock to meet the disembarking passengers. There's also a spotting scope in the park for watching mountain goats on Mount Juneau. For a quiet break, visit the beautiful library at the top of the parking garage at the south end of the dock.

SPECIAL EVENTS

An event calendar is posted on the visitors' bureau website at www.traveljuneau.com/discover.

The **Alaska Folk Festival** (© **907/463-3316;** www.alaskafolkfestival.org) is the state's biggest annual coming together of musicians, at Centennial Hall. Musicians take over the town and can be found jamming in every bar and coffeehouse, or wherever a crowd gathers. The 34th annual festival is April 7 to April 13, 2008.

The **Juneau Jazz & Classics Festival** (© **907/463-3378;** www.jazzand classics.org), May 16 to May 24, 2008, presents concerts and workshops in many styles of music—blues, jazz, classical, rock—at various venues, even on a boat, and at many prices—free to $60 a ticket. Most evening performances are around $22.

The simply named **Celebration,** sponsored by the Sealaska Heritage Institute (© **907/463-4844**) is among Alaska's largest cultural gatherings. Alaska Natives gather from every corner of the state to share dance and art, sell crafts, meet and, well, celebrate. Book well ahead if you will be in Juneau at this time, as rooms will be in short supply. It happens only every other year with the next meeting due June 5 to June 7, 2008.

The **Golden North Salmon Derby** (© **907/783-2399;** www.goldennorth salmonderby.org), held annually since 1947, targets kings and silvers, normally the first weekend in August. Unlike some other such fishing contests around the state, this isn't just a tourist thing—it brings out as many as 3,000 local fishermen and is even covered live on the radio.

EXPLORING DOWNTOWN

Alaska-Gastineau Mill and Gold Mine Tour ⭐   A half-day tour visits the ruins of a hard-rock gold operation that operated from 1915 to 1921, then goes 360 feet into one tunnel for a mining demonstration. Guests also get to pan for gold from the mine's tailings. Although Princess Tours provides the buses and sells the tickets, the tour is the work of people who came to Juneau to reopen the A.J. mine (of which this was a part), and stayed to turn it into a tourist attraction when that project failed; their fascination is infectious. The mine site is south of town, but buses pick up visitors at the state museum downtown and at the Mount Roberts Tram. The tour is quite in-depth; those without interest in mining history or mechanical matters may get bored. Dress warmly.

Book through Princess Tours, 151 Mill St. © **907/463-3900.** Admission $59 adults, $39 children. Daily departures during summer; call ahead to reserve.

Alaska State Museum ★★★ The museum contains a large collection of art and historical artifacts, but it doesn't seem like a storehouse at all because the objects' presentation is based on their meaning, not their value. Come here to put the rest of your visit in context. A clan house in the Alaska Native Gallery contains authentic art in the functional places where it would have been used in a memorial potlatch. The Lincoln Totem Pole is here, carved by an artist who used a picture of the president as his model to represent his clan's first encounter with whites. Superb artifacts from Native cultures from around the state are presented to illustrate the lifestyle of those who made them. The ramp to the second floor wraps around the natural history display, with an eagle nesting tree, and at the top a state history gallery uses significant pieces to tell Alaska's story. The children's area is exceptionally fun, with a ship that the kids can play in. Allow at least 2 hours for the museum; half a day would not be out of line. The shop off the lobby is also well worth a look. Although small, it carries lots of quality Alaska Native art, books, and no junk at all (there's a branch at 124 Seward St.)

395 Whittier St. ℂ 907/465-2901. www.museums.state.ak.us. Admission mid-May to mid-Sept $5 adults, free for ages 18 and under; mid-Sept to mid-May $3 adults, free for ages 18 and under. Mid-May to mid-Sept daily 8:30am–5:30pm; mid-Sept to mid-May Tues–Sat 10am–4pm.

The Juneau-Douglas City Museum ★ This fun little museum displays artifacts and photographs from the city's pioneer and mining history and Tlingit culture with special exhibits that change annually. It's quite well done and holds real interest. There are gorgeous stained-glass windows, a large topographical model of the Juneau area, and a 600-year-old fish trap found near a local river. A 26-minute video on Juneau's gold-mining history shows each half-hour. The tiny bookshop is stocked with handy information for your visit to Juneau, including a historic hike guide booklet, free historic walking-tour map, and maps of the Evergreen Cemetery and the old Treadwell Mine. In the summer, the museum leads historic walking tours Tuesday through Thursday at 3pm. The cost is $10 for adults, $7 for children ages 18 and under. The plaza in front is where the 49-star U.S. flag was first raised in 1959—they didn't make many of those, as Hawaii was admitted as the 50th state within a year, but you'll still find one flying here.

At the corner of 4th and Main sts. ℂ 907/586-3572. www.juneau.org/parksrec/museum. Admission $4 adults (free in winter), free for ages 18 and under. Summer Mon–Fri 9am–5pm, Sat–Sun 10am–5pm; winter Tues–Sat 10am–4pm.

The Last Chance Mining Museum and Historic Park ★ *Finds* On the site on forested Gold Creek where gold was first discovered in Juneau, the museum preserves old mining buildings and some of their original equipment, including an immense 1912 air compressor and a layered glass map of the tunnels. This was once a nerve center for one of the world's biggest hard-rock mines. The highlight is its energetic and learned guide, Renee Hughes, who lives above the compressor with her husband Gary Gillette. Both are leaders of the Gastineau Channel Historical Society. Ask Renee about the cave-in of the Treadwell Mine to hear her riveting storytelling. The entrance to the site—which contains relics and buildings spread over several acres—is a bridge across the creek, which leads to a steep trail up to the buildings.

1001 Basin Rd. ℂ 907/586-5338. Admission $4. Daily 9:30am–12:30pm and 3:30–6:30pm. Closed Oct to mid-May. From downtown, take Gold St. up the hill to its end, then join Basin Rd., continuing 1 mile up the valley to the end of the road.

Mount Roberts Tramway ★ The tram takes only 6 minutes to whisk passengers from tourist-clogged Franklin Street to the clear air and overwhelming views at the tree line (at 1,760 ft.), a destination that used to require a day of huffing and puffing to witness. The tram can be crowded; it's once you're up there that the beauty hits you. The Alaska Native owners seem to understand that, and they have done a good job of building a network of paths that take advantage of the views as you pass through a fascinating alpine ecosystem; the owners have even carved clan crests into the living trunks of some of the trees. If you're energetic, you can start a 6-mile round-trip hike to Mount Roberts's summit (at 3,819 ft.), or you can hike the 2.5 miles back to downtown. There's an auditorium at the top tram station showing a film on Tlingit culture, a shop where Native artisans are often at work, and a bald eagle enclosure. The bar and grill serves lunch and dinner. I would choose something else to do on a day when fog or low overcast obscures the view, especially considering the price; however, I am told it is sometimes sunny up top while rainy down on Franklin Street—it can't hurt to ask.

490 S. Franklin St., at the waterfront near the cruise-ship dock. ✆ **888/461-8726** or 907/463-3412. www.goldbelt tours.com. Full-day pass $24 adults, $14 children ages 6–12, free children ages 5 and under; tax included. May–Sept daily 9am–9pm. Closed Oct–Apr.

A JUNEAU WALKING TOUR

Start & Finish:	Alaska State Capitol, 4th and Seward streets.
Time:	1 to 1½ hours for standard tour; 2½ hours for the extended tour, with minimal stops.

❶ The Alaska State Capitol

This structure fills the block between 4th and 5th and Main and Seward streets. Except for the marble portico on the 4th Street side, it is a nondescript brick box, probably the least impressive state capitol in the most beautiful setting in the nation. Legislators hanker for a larger, grander building, but since they can barely agree on the time of day that's unlikely to happen anytime soon. The federal government built the structure in 1931, when Alaska was still a territory. Inside, some of the old-fashioned woodwork and decorative details are interesting, and the public is free to walk through. During the summer, free tours are offered Monday through Friday from 8:30am to 5:30pm, Saturday and Sunday 10am to 5:30pm. Call ✆ **907/465-3800** for information. The legislature is in session from February to mid-May.

Across 4th is the:

❷ State Courthouse

The statue of a bear in front defines official Alaskan taste in art: It replaced a hated abstract steel sculpture called *Nimbus* that was removed by an act of the legislature and that finally came to rest in front of the state museum a few blocks away.

On the opposite, northwest corner is the:

❸ Juneau-Douglas City Museum

Stop in here now to buy the Evergreen Cemetery map if you plan to include that in your walk, or get the *Historic Downtown Juneau Guide* to learn more on the whole walk.

On the southwest corner of Main and 4th is the:

❹ State Office Building

This building is built into the edge of a cliff that forms a major barrier through the downtown area; if you're headed for the lower land, where the Alaska State Museum and Centennial Hall are located, you can avoid eight flights of steps in between by taking the building's elevator down. In any event, visit the towering atrium, with its great views and a 1928 movie theater pipe organ that's played on Fridays at noon. The state library historical collections off the lobby contain historic photographs and artifacts, some of which are often on exhibit. On sunny days, the patio off the atrium is a warm place for a picnic, with a fabulous view.

Leaving again through the door that you entered, turn left and follow Calhoun Street around the curve. An outdoor staircase here leads down to the flat area of town below (but you know about taking the elevator). Those lowlands originally were mostly underwater and this embankment stood just above the shoreline, which continued along Front and South Franklin streets. The land you see below you is made of mine tailings that were dumped in the channel. Continue on Calhoun; the governor uses the pedestrian overpass (which we walk under) to cross Calhoun to get to the capitol from the white, neoclassical:

❺ Governor's Mansion
Located on the left, the mansion was built by the federal government in 1912 for $40,000. It isn't normally open for public tours. Its current occupant is Sarah Palin, a young (for a governor) former beauty queen from Wasilla. Palin walloped Republican governor Frank Murkowski in the primary election and then easily dispatched Murkowski's Democratic predecessor, Tony Knowles, to win the general election in 2006. After taking office her reformist platform looked progressively better as four Republican legislators were indicted by the U.S. attorney for taking bribes and Alaska's most powerful oil executive pleaded guilty; as of this writing, that drama continues to unfold. Meanwhile, Palin's popularity has reached a level never before seen, with an approval rating as high as 90%. She has young children whose play equipment you may see on the lawn of the mansion.

Shortcut: If you don't mind missing the next stop (Gold Creek), you can save yourself some hill climbing by continuing on Calhoun, turning right on Goldbelt Street, climbing past some beautiful houses to 7th, then picking up the tour at the Wickersham House.

Continuing down Calhoun, you'll come to:
❻ Gold Creek
Juneau's founders made their gold strike in this stream in 1880. Trace it upstream

through peaceful **Cope Park,** past the playground and tennis courts to the unique ball field, which is bounded by the stream's forested canyon walls. (To continue this walk to Evergreen Cemetery and up to the top of the town and through the woods on the flume—a long, strenuous hike—return to Calhoun Street and continue in the direction you were going. That route is covered below under "The Extended Walk.")

Go all the way to the right side (that's left field, on your right) of the baseball diamond to find a lovely path and public stairway through the woods steeply up to 7th Street. Seventh runs along a narrow ridge between downtown Juneau and the creek. Across the street from the top of the stairway is:

❼ The Wickersham House State Historic Site
This white, 1898 frame house, at 213 7th St. (© **907/586-9001;** www.alaskatate parks.org, click on "Individual Parks"), was the retirement home of Judge James Wickersham, who was revered by Alaskans for bringing law to the gold rush in Eagle, Nome, and Fairbanks; for exploring the Denali area and helping to make it a national park; for convincing the federal government to build the Alaska railroad and found the state university; and for winning Alaska's right to make its own laws when he represented the territory in Congress. The house was in the family from 1928 until the state bought it in 1984, so it still contains many of Wickersham's belongings, including an Edison cylinder gramophone he took to Fairbanks, and his written assignment to go to Alaska, which is signed by Theodore Roosevelt. The house badly needed repair when a renovation project funded in part by the National Park Service began several years ago. The project was delayed, but I've been assured the house will be open for the 2008 season. During normal operations, the house was open from mid-May to the end of September from 10am to noon

and 1 to 5pm, winter by appointment, and requested a $2 donation. All that may change when it reopens.

Continue on 7th to Gold Street, turn right and follow it downhill to 5th, site of the:

❽ St. Nicholas Orthodox Church

This small structure is a significant architectural and historic landmark. The octagonal building was built in 1893-94 by Serbian miners and Tlingits. Many Tlingits chose the Russian Orthodox faith in the late 19th century when government-sponsored Protestant missionaries arrived with authority to force Christianity on Alaska Natives. The Protestants' civilizing program entailed wiping out Native languages and culture, but the Orthodox allowed people to worship in Tlingit and to continue more of their own customs. Bishop Innocent Veniaminov had translated sacred texts into Tlingit 50 years earlier when the Russians were still in Sitka (learn more under "The Russian Bishop's House," p. 145). Today, Alaska Natives make up the bulk of Russian Orthodox congregations in Alaska, and St. Nicholas still has an active Tlingit parish. Lengthy services are sung in English, Tlingit, and Church Slavonic for Saturday vespers at 6pm and on Sunday morning at 9am; the congregation stands throughout the service. Visitors are welcome for service, or come during the tourist season Monday through Friday from 9am to 5pm, Saturday 10am to 4pm, and Sunday 1 to 5pm. Admission is $2. There is a small gift shop and museum.

Walk 1 block down and 2 blocks to the right to the start/finish point.

THE EXTENDED WALK

This walk of roughly 3 miles includes some steep stairways and streets. Follow the walking tour until you reach Gold Creek (see number 6, above).

Cross the creek and stay on the same road (which goes under various names), bearing right as it becomes Martin Street. On the left is:

❾ The Evergreen Cemetery

The cemetery slopes toward the ocean, opening a wonderful vista over the clear green lawn. One reason the view is so broad and open is that the markers are flush with the ground. The old Alaska Native graves are in the wooded portion on the far side. Joe Juneau and Richard Harris, the city's founders, are buried near the cross at the top end of the cemetery, near where you arrive on the walk.

Across the road from the cross, Hermit Street reaches a little way into the mountainside. Follow the steep public stairs next to house no. 430 up to the bottom of Pine Street. This is the walk I described in the introduction to this section. The views get better and better as you rise to the top of Pine Street then go right on Evergreen Street, following the road to where it dissipates into a trail among shadowy spruce and western hemlock.

Continue on the peaceful forest trail among ferns and evergreens up the valley, coming to the:

❿ Abandoned Wooden Flume

Once the town's aqueduct, the flume now is maintained as a boardwalk into the forest. Since it carried water, it's nearly level, but watch your step in wet weather, as it crosses some high trestles over gullies.

At the end of the flume, cross over the valley to Basin Road and continue upstream. Stop to see:

⓫ The Last Chance Mining Museum

The museum is described on p. 159.

To the left is the Perseverance Trail, which continues up between the mountains; the Perseverance also leads to the trail head for a challenging hike up Mount Juneau (see "Hiking" under "Getting Outside: Onshore," below).

To get back to town, follow Basin Road 1 mile back down the valley. Taking the first right will put you at the top of Gold Street. Descend a block to 7th and pick up the walking tour at stop 7 (the Wickersham House is a block down 7th) or continue down Gold to St. Nicholas Orthodox Church, stop 8 on the tour.

Avoiding Cruise-Ship Crowds

On the busiest days of the summer cruise ships bring more than 10,000 passengers and another 4,000 crew members to the docks on Juneau's Franklin Street. That's simply too many for these narrow old streets; downtown becomes a solid crush of people and attractions are packed, spoiling the experience for everyone. The crush worsens every year and is largely unavoidable, with a minimum of three ships tying up on the light days. Of recent years, those lighter days have been Fridays and Sundays. If you can plan your Juneau sightseeing then, you may find somewhat less crowding; also, the farther you go from the dock, the less crowding you encounter.

SHOPPING

The shops near the dock cater primarily to cruise-ship passengers. After around 500 summer port calls, many close their doors. The year-round community and more local shops tend to be farther up the hill. If you're looking for authentic Alaska Native arts and crafts, be warned that counterfeiting is widespread. For buying tips, read "Native Art: Finding the Real Thing," in chapter 2.

The Raven's Journey, 435 S. Franklin (ⓒ **907/463-4686**), shows Tlingit and other Northwest coast Indian carvings and masks, totemic silver jewelry, and whalebone, ivory, basketry, and fossil ivory carvings and jewelry from the Yup'ik and Iñupiat of western and northern Alaska. Works are displayed with biographical placards of the artists.

Juneau Artists Gallery, in the Senate Building at 175 S. Franklin (ⓒ **907/586-9891;** www.juneauartistsgallery.com), is staffed by a co-op of local artists and shows only the members' work: paintings, etchings, photography, jewelry, fabrics, ceramics, and other media. Much of it is good and inexpensive, and the way it is displayed creates a panorama of artistic visions.

Juneau's Rie Muñoz is one of Alaskans' favorite artists for her simple, graphic, generally cheerful watercolors of coastal Alaskan communities and Native people. Her prints and tapestries are shown downtown at the **Decker Gallery,** 233 S. Franklin (ⓒ **907/463-5536**), and in the Mendenhall Valley at the **Rie Muñoz Gallery,** at 2101 Jordan Ave. (ⓒ **800/247-3151** or 907/789-7449; www.riemunoz.com).

For gifts, try **Annie Kaill's** fine arts and crafts gallery at 244 Front St. It's a little out of the cruise-ship shopping area and gets business from locals. The shop has a rich, homey feeling, with local work at various price levels. The long-established **Ad Lib,** at 231 S. Franklin St., also is a fun little shop.

Hearthside Books (www.hearthsidebooks.com) is a cubbyhole of a bookstore at the corner of Franklin and Front streets, but has a good selection for its size, especially of Alaskan books and maps. (A larger branch, with a good toy department, is in the Mendenhall Valley's Nugget Mall, at 8745 Glacier Hwy., a 5-min. walk from the airport.) Also downtown, **Rainy Day Books** has more than 10,000 new, used, and rare books at 113 Seward St.

The most remarkable shop in Juneau is **The Observatory,** at 299 N. Franklin St. (ⓒ **907/586-9676;** www.observatorybooks.com). This browser's paradise specializes in rare maps and books about Alaska. The collection of antique etchings is mind-blowing in its comprehensiveness. Among the items I've seen here were huge charts drawn by the first 18th-century explorers to trace Alaska's coastline. To get the full effect you must strike up a conversation with the shop's owner, Dee Longenbaugh. She is a fellow of the Royal Geographical Society and the only Alaskan member of the Antiquarian Booksellers Association. One question will start a fascinating tour of Alaska history.

Bill Spear sells his own brightly colored enamel pins and zipper pulls from his studio, hidden upstairs at 174 S. Franklin (© **907/586-2209;** www.wmspear.com). Alaskans collect the vividly executed fish, birds, airplanes, dinosaurs, vegetables, and many other witty, provocative, or beautiful pins, which cost from $4 to $20 each.

Taku Store, at 550 S. Franklin, across the parking lot from the tram station (© **800/ 582-5122** or 907/463-3474; www.takustore.com), is worth a stop if you're nearby, even if you're not in the market for the pricey seafood in the case: It's interesting to watch workers fillet, smoke, and pack salmon through large windows, and to read the explanatory signs about what they're doing. They'll ship fish anywhere in the U.S.

ATTRACTIONS BEYOND WALKING DISTANCE

Mendenhall Glacier Transport (© 907/789-5460; www.mightygreattrips.com) does a 2½-hour town and Mendenhall Glacier tour for $25, or you can ride their "Blue Bus Express" to the glacier for $12. Generally, it runs every half-hour both directions, from the waterfront visitor center to the glacier and back, daily 9am to 6pm in summer. Otherwise, take a rented car or, for vigorous people, bike 24 miles out to the Mendenhall Glacier and back. I've listed these sites by distance from downtown with directions starting from there.

Alaskan Brewing Company   Beer lovers and aspiring capitalists will enjoy the tour of Alaska's most popular craft brewery. Now too big to be called "micro," the brewery started small in 1986 when Geoff and Marcy Larson had the idea of bringing a local gold–rush-era brew back to life. It worked, and now Alaskan Amber and several other brews are everywhere in Alaska and many places down the West Coast, and the brewery has won a long list of national and international awards for its brews. The short, free tour, which starts every half-hour, is fairly interesting, with views of the brewing equipment behind glass and an amazing worldwide beer bottle collection, but it's the tasting that makes it fun. They serve free samples of half a dozen beers, often creating an impromptu party in the lobby. Identification is required.

5429 Shaune Dr. © **907/780-5866.** www.alaskanbeer.com. May–Sept daily 11am–5pm; winter Thurs–Sun 11am–5pm; last tour starts at 4:30pm winter and summer. Turn right from Egan Dr. onto Vanderbilt Hill Rd., which becomes Glacier Hwy., then right on Anka St., and right again on Shaune Dr.

Glacier Gardens   This is the place to see the rainforest if you have mobility problems. The heart of the hour-long tour is a ride in vehicles similar to golf carts up a steep mountainside, past a stream and pools, to a platform with a view of the Mendenhall Valley. Glacier Gardens caters to the cruise ships, but the staff will take groups of just a few visitors for a ride, explaining the forest flora in as much detail as you wish. Gardeners will especially enjoy the extraordinary hanging baskets and other bright and ingenious plantings in the lower area—weddings of cruise-ship passengers are held here almost every day in the summer. The gardens' trademark is upside-down trees whose roots, way up in the air, are planted with trailing flowers. An eagle nest on the grounds has been active in recent years. All good, but as much as I like the place, I have to point out it is priced as a guided tour, not a botanical garden. The garden has a hiking trail for those who don't want to ride on the vehicles, but hikers have plenty of rainforest trails to choose from without fees.

ACCOMMODATIONS ■
Alaska's Capital Inn **15**
Baranof Hotel **24**
Breakwater Hotel **1**
The Driftwood Lodge **7**
The Historic Silverbow Inn **19**
Goldbelt Hotel Juneau **26**
Juneau International Hostel **10**
Prospector Hotel **9**

DINING ◆
The Hangar **27**
Heritage Coffee Co. & Café **25**
Kenny's Wok & Teriyaki Sushi Bar **22**
Pizzeria Roma **27**
Rainbow Foods **13**
Sandpiper Café **6**
Silverbow Bakery **19**
Twisted Fish Co. Alaskan Grill **30**
Valentine's Coffee House & Pizzeria **23**
Wild Spice **21**
Zephyr Restaurant **20**

ATTRACTIONS ●
Abandoned wooden flume **3**
Alaska State Capitol **14**
Alaska State Museum **8**
Evergreen Cemetery **2**
Gold Creek **4**
Governor's Mansion **5**
Juneau-Douglas City Museum **16**
Last Chance Mining Museum **31**
Mount Roberts Tramway **29**
Patsy Ann statue **28**
St. Nicholas Orthodox Church **12**
State Courthouse **18**
State Office Building **17**
The Wickersham House S.H.S. **11**

7600 Glacier Hwy. ℂ 907/790-3377. www.glaciergardens.com. Admission $22 adults, $16 children ages 6–12, free children 5 and under. Summer daily 9am–6pm. Closed Oct–Apr. Near the Fred Meyer store about 1 mile from the airport.

Macaulay Salmon Hatchery ⚓ The hatchery, known by locals as DIPAC (Douglas Island Pink and Chum, Inc.), was ingeniously designed to allow visitors to watch the whole process of harvesting and fertilizing eggs from outdoor decks. From mid-June to October, salmon swim up a 450-foot fish ladder, visible through a window, into a sorting mechanism, then are "unzipped" by workers who remove the eggs. Guides and exhibits explain what's happening. During that period you can often see seals and other wildlife feeding on the returning salmon just offshore from the hatchery. Inside, large and realistic saltwater aquariums show off the area's marine life as it looks in the natural environment. The tour is less impressive in May and June, before the fish are running. At that time visitors see the immature salmon before their release and sometimes get to feed them. The tours don't take long; allow 45 minutes for your entire visit.

2697 Channel Dr. ℂ 877/463-2486 or 907/463-4810. www.dipac.net. Admission $3.25 adults, $1.75 children ages 12 and under. Summer Mon–Fri 10am–6pm, Sat–Sun 10am–5pm; winter call ahead. 3 miles from downtown, turn left at the first group of buildings on Egan Dr.

Mendenhall Glacier ⚓⚓ At the head of Mendenhall Valley, the Mendenhall Glacier glows bluish white, looming above the suburbs like an ice-age monster that missed the general extinction. Besides being a truly impressive sight, Mendenhall is the most easily accessible glacier in Alaska and the state's third-most visited attraction. The parking and an adjacent shelter have a great view across the lake to the glacier's face, and a wheelchair-accessible trail leads close to the water's edge. The land near the parking lot shows signs of the glacier's recent passage, with little topsoil, stunted vegetation, and, in many places, bare rock that shows the scratch marks of the glacier's movement. Atop a bedrock hill, reached by stairs, a ramp, or an elevator, the Forest Service visitor center contains a glacier museum with excellent explanatory models, computerized displays, spotting scopes, and ranger talks. Admission is $3 for adults, free for children under 16. In late summer, you can watch red and silver salmon spawning in **Steep Creek,** just short of the visitor center on the road.

There are several trails at the glacier, ranging from a half-mile nature trail loop to two fairly steep, 3.5-mile hikes approaching each side of the glacier. At the visitor center and a booth near the parking lot the Forest Service distributes a brochure which includes a trail map. The **East Glacier Loop Trail** is a beautiful day hike leading through the forest to a view of a waterfall near the glacier's face and to parts of an abandoned rail tram and an abandoned dam on Nugget Creek; the trail has steep parts but is doable for school-age children. You can park at the visitor center and start from there. The **West Glacier Trail** is more challenging, leaving from 300 yards beyond the Skater's Cabin and following the edge of the lake and glacier, providing access to the ice itself for experienced climbers with the right equipment. You will need wheels to get to the trail head. Take the Mendenhall Loop Road to Montana Creek Road, turn right, and then turn right again on Skater's Cabin Road.

The Skater's Cabin is also the starting point for a groomed cross-country-ski loop on Mendenhall Lake in front of the glacier. Don't go beyond the orange safety markers near the glacier's face. Other trails weave through the pothole lakes across from the glacier.

At the head of Glacier Spur Rd. (right from Egan Dr. on Mendenhall Loop to Glacier Spur). Visitor center ℂ 907/789-0097. Visitor center admission $3 adults, free children under 16. Summer daily 8am–7:30pm; winter Thurs–Sun 10am–4pm.

WHAT TO SEE & DO "OUT THE ROAD"

On sunny summer weekends, Juneau families get in the car and drive "out the road" (northwest along the Glacier Hwy., as it's officially known). The views of island-stippled water from the paved two-lane highway are worth the trip, and there are also several good places to stop. To use this road guide, set your trip odometer to zero at the ferry dock (which is 14 miles from downtown Juneau).

The **Auke Village Recreation Area** is a mile beyond the ferry dock and is a good place for picnics and beach walks. Less than a mile farther is a Forest Service campground.

The Shrine of St. Thérèse ✿ (© **907/780-6112;** www.shrineofsainttherese.org), 9 miles beyond the ferry dock (23 miles from downtown), rests on a tiny island reached by a foot-trail causeway. The wonderfully simple chapel of rounded beach stones, circled by markers of the 15 stations of the cross, stands peaceful and mysterious amid trees, rock, water, and the cries of the raven and eagle. It is the most spiritual place I know. The vaguely Gothic structure was built in the late 1930s of stone picked up from these shores and dedicated by Alaska's first Catholic bishop to St. Thérèse of Lisieux, who died in 1897 at the age of 24. Sunday liturgy services are held from June to September at 1:30pm. The shrine is part of a large retreat maintained by the Juneau Catholic Diocese, which includes a log lodge on the shore facing the island as well as several cabins for rent as lodgings. The shrine's island is a good vantage from which to look upon **Lynn Canal** for marine mammals or, at low tide, to go tide pooling among the rocks. The website covers the shrine's history and gives information on the facilities, gardens, and trails.

Eagle Beach, 14 miles beyond the ferry dock, makes a good picnic area in nice weather, when you can walk among the tall beach grass or out on the sandy tidal flats, watch the eagles, or go north along the beach to look for fossils in the rock outcroppings.

The road turns to gravel, then comes to **Point Bridget State Park,** 24 miles beyond the ferry dock (© **907/465-4563;** www.alaskastateparks.org, click on "Individual Parks"). A flat 3.5-mile path leads through forest, meadow, and marsh to the shore, where you may see sea lions and possibly humpback whales. Three public-use cabins rent for $35 or $45 a night, depending on the season. See "State Parks Cabin Reservations," p. 265. The road ends 26 miles from the ferry dock at pretty **Echo Cove.**

GETTING OUTSIDE: ONSHORE

BIRD-WATCHING   Bald eagles are as common as pigeons in Juneau. Years ago, one of them made off with a tourist's Chihuahua, starting a statewide debate about whether it was funny or horrible. Eagles are most common on the shoreline, especially where fish are plentiful, such as at the hatchery. For more variety, visit the **Mendenhall Wetlands State Game Refuge,** which encompasses 3,800 acres of tidal estuaries in the Gastineau Channel near the airport. More than 100 species of birds use the refuge, mainly during the April and May migrations. Access points are on either side of the channel, including a viewing platform on the downtown-bound side of Egan Drive, at mile six.

FRESHWATER AND SHORELINE FISHING   Juneau isn't known particularly for its stream fishing (boat-charter fishing is covered below under "Getting Outside: On the Water"). But there are a few places on the road system where you can find good fishing in freshwater or even in the ocean. The advice you need is in the free printed **Juneau Sportfishing Guide** available from the Alaska Department of Fish & Game, 1255 W. 8th St. (P.O. Box 25526), Juneau, AK 99802-5526 (© 907/465-4180;

Tips **Gearing Up for Juneau's Outdoors**

You can rent the gear you need for outings on the water or to equip Forest Service cabin visits from **Alaska Boat and Kayak,** at the Auke Bay Harbor (© **907/ 789-6886;** www.juneaukayak.com). They rent sea kayaks ($50 a day for a single, $70 double, with multiday discounts), camping gear, and skiffs with outboard motors ($130-$300 a day) that you can use for fishing or exploring, and they offer guidance in planning where and how to go. They will deliver a sea kayak anywhere on Juneau's road system, to outlying areas, or to Admiralty Island. See "Getting Around," earlier in this section, for bike rentals.

---

www.alaska.gov/adfg, click "Sport Fisheries," then on the Southeast region on the map). For a remote fly-in experience with fly or spinning gear, contact **Alaska Fly 'N' Fish Charters,** 9604 Kelly Court (© **907/790-2120;** www.alaskabyair.com). A guided 5-hour trip is $495 per person, with a two-person minimum. The same reputable guy (Butch Laughlin) also does flightseeing and bear-viewing flights.

HIKING I've mentioned several good hikes at Mendenhall Glacier and out the road, above. More than two dozen are described in a nicely made book with detailed topographic maps of each, *Juneau Trails* (Alaska Natural History Association, $8), which you can find at visitor centers. *In the Miner's Footsteps,* a guide to the history behind 14 Juneau trails, is available for a nominal price from the Juneau-Douglas City Museum. The Juneau city **Department of Parks and Recreation** (© **907/586-5226;** www.juneau.org/parksrec) leads hikes (and other activities) through the year; check the website or call the 24-hour hike line at © **907/586-0428.**

The **Perseverance Trail** climbs up the valley behind Juneau and into the mining history of the area it accesses. It can be busy in summer. The trail head is about 1½ miles from town on Basin Road. The trail is 4 miles of easy walking on the mountainside above Gold Creek to the Perseverance Mine, at the Silverbow Basin, a mining community from 1885 to 1921. Use caution on icy patches, as there are steep drop-offs. A well-documented historic pamphlet is for sale at the Juneau-Douglas City Museum.

Two trails start from points along the Perseverance Trail. The challenging **Mount Juneau Trail** rises more than 3,500 feet over about 2 miles from a point 1 mile along from the Perseverance trail head. Go only in dry weather to avoid disastrous falls. The **Granite Creek Trail,** starting 2 miles in on the Perseverance Trail, climbs 1,200 feet over 1.5 miles to an alpine basin. Both are quieter than the Perseverance Trail.

Another hike right from downtown climbs **Mount Roberts**—just follow the stairway from the top of 6th Street in a neighborhood called Star Hill. The summit is 4.5 miles and 3,819 vertical feet away, but you don't have to go all the way to the top for incredible views and alpine terrain. At the 1,760-foot level, you come to the restaurant at the top of the Mount Roberts tram, mentioned on p. 159. Of course, it's easier to take the tram up and hike down. A third choice: Start from the tram and hike to the summit.

The **Treadwell Mine Historic Trail,** on Douglas Island, is a fascinating hour's stroll through the ruins of a massive hard-rock mine complex that once employed and housed 2,000 men. Since its abandonment in 1922 big trees have grown up through the foundations, intertwining their roots through rails and machinery and adding to the site's exceptional power over the imagination. A well-written guide to numbered posts on the trail is available from the Juneau-Douglas City Museum. This is a great hike for kids. To find the trail head, take 3rd Street in Douglas, bearing left at the Y onto Savikko Street, which leads to Savikko Park, also known as Sandy Beach Park. The trail starts at the far end of the park.

Another great family outing is to the **Outer Point Trail,** 1.33 miles on a forest boardwalk to a beach with good tide pooling, lots of eagles, and possible whale sightings. Many different kinds of loveliness present themselves over the short walk: the mossy rainforest, the stunted muskeg swamp, a glassy little creek, and the pebbled beach and bedrock ocean pools. From there, on the western point of Douglas Island—the opposite side from Juneau—you can see Auke Bay to the east, Admiralty Island to the west, and the tiny islands of Stephens Passage before you. The trail's only drawback is crowding, especially when tour groups tromp through; avoid them by going early or late. To get there, drive over the bridge to Douglas, then right on North Douglas Highway 12 miles to the trail head.

SKIING   For **downhill skiing,** the city-owned **Eaglecrest Ski Area** (© **907/790-2000;** www.skijuneau.com) is the large, steep home hill of Olympic silver medalist Hillary Lindh, Juneau's favorite daughter (her father helped choose the site in the 1970s). A chair goes almost to the top of Douglas Island, with expansive views and 640 acres of skiing terrain. The three lifts serve 31 runs with a total vertical drop of 1,400 feet, rated 40% expert, 40% intermediate, and 20% novice. There's also a hill for innertubing. It's only 12 miles from downtown on North Douglas Highway. An all-day lift ticket is $29 for adults. Even among Alaskans, Eaglecrest is little known, despite being second in size and ski lift development only to Alyeska Resort, near Anchorage.

Finds **Remote Cabins on Foot**

Five U.S. Forest Service cabins and three Alaska State Parks cabins are accessible by hikes of less than a day on trails connected to Juneau's road system. That means that you can get to these cabins without an expensive plane or boat charter, and that's a rarity. The three Alaska State Parks cabins are at Point Bridget State Park (see "What to See & Do 'Out the Road,'" above). The Forest Service cabins include: **Peterson Lake,** with lake and stream fishing for Dolly Varden char and cutthroat trout; **John Muir,** on a 1,500-foot ridge top above Auke Bay, up the Auk Nu Trail; **Dan Moller,** on Douglas Island right across from town; **Eagle Glacier,** overlooking the glacier upriver from Eagle Beach and reached by the Amalga Trail; and beautiful **Windfall Lake,** with fishing. Each cabin rents for $35 a night, and generally there's a 2-night maximum stay. All are popular and must be reserved well in advance (it's wise to book as soon as your dates become available 6 months earlier). If you can afford a charter, or if you are an expert sea kayaker, there are many more choices farther afield, especially on Admiralty Island (see "Getting Outside: On Admiralty Island," below). You'll need camping gear to stay at these primitive cabins (see "Gearing Up for Juneau's Outdoors," p. 168). Get information on cabins from the ranger district (see "Visitor Information," p. 157), then reserve through the national system described in "Getting Outside in the Tongass National Forest" on p. 102.

Eaglecrest has 8 kilometers of **cross-country-skiing** trail, offering the most reliable track skiing in town. Generally, Juneau's warm, damp winters don't provide enough snow for good cross-country skiing at lower elevations. Many of the hiking trails into the mountains become winter backcountry routes, however, and snow does stick up there. Before going out, always check with the Forest Service (see "Visitor Information," earlier) for advice on your route and on avalanche conditions. Several of the Forest Service cabins also serve as winter warm-up houses during the day, and make good skiing destinations. If conditions permit, a network of trails is set around the Mendenhall Glacier (see "Hiking," above).

ZIP-LINE TOURS   A zip line is a cable strung between two high points from which a passenger hangs on a wheeled runner, zipping from one end to the other. Once thought the province of Special Forces training and the like, riding a zip line (with a safety harness) is now considered a cruise activity and is billed as a way of seeing the rainforest. I'm aware of four tours, in Ketchikan, Juneau, and at the Icy Strait cruise-ship stop, but only one, on Juneau's Douglas Island, caters to independent travelers: **Alaska Zipline Adventures** (© **907/790-2547;** www.alaskazip.com) with a tour of seven rides near the Eaglecrest Ski Area. The 3½-hour tour costs $115 for adults, $95 for children 12 and under, including a snack and transfer to the site. Clients must be fit, not pregnant, and between 70 and 250 pounds.

GETTING OUTSIDE: ON THE WATER

SALTWATER FISHING & WHALE-WATCHING   The closest I ever came to a humpback whale—I almost touched it—was on the way back from king salmon fishing out of Juneau on a friend's boat. More than two dozen companies offer charters from Juneau and Auke Bay; you can go to watch whales or fish, or both. Juneau is well protected behind layers of islands, so the water generally is calm.

A lot of companies offer trips. The Juneau Convention and Visitors Bureau maintains a list of businesses and their website has links to each.

Juneau Sportfishing and Sightseeing, 2 Marine Way, Suite 230 (© **907/586-1887;** www.juneausportfishing.com), is one of the largest operators. They charge $269 per person for a full day fishing for salmon, $325 for halibut and salmon; or $169 for 4 hours fishing salmon. They charge $115 for a 2½-hour whale-watching trip.

SEA KAYAKING   The protected waters around Juneau appeal to sea kayakers, and the city is a popular hub for trips on the water farther afield. Besides the sublime scenery, you'll likely see eagles and sea birds and may encounter porpoises, seals, and possibly humpback whales. **Alaska Travel Adventures** (© **800/791-2673** outside Alaska or 800/478-0052 in Alaska; www.bestofalaskatravel.com), offers 3½-hour kayak trips (half that time on the water) in Auke Bay for $85 for adults, $57 for children 6 to 12. The tour includes orientation for beginners, a snack, and transportation from downtown. For a more adventurous option, see "Getting Outside: On Admiralty Island," below. A business that rents and delivers kayaks is listed under "Gearing Up for Juneau's Outdoors" (p. 168).

GETTING OUTSIDE: ON THE ICE

More than 36 major glaciers around Juneau flow from a single ocean of ice behind the mountains, the 1,500-square-mile **Juneau Icefield.** You can land on it in a helicopter just to touch the ice or to take a nature hike or dog sled ride. It's expensive, but there are few other places to see, let alone explore, the kind of ice sheet that carved North America in the last ice age. From the air, glaciers look unreal, like creations by a

A Day Trip to Tracy Arm

The fjords of the Tracy Arm–Fords Terror Wilderness (part of Tongass National Forest) are relatively unknown outside the area, but the scenery and wildlife viewing easily rival those of Glacier Bay National Park. And for those not riding a cruise ship, Tracy Arm has a significant advantage over Glacier Bay: It costs less than half as much and is easier to get to. A Tracy Arm tour takes about 8 hours; going to Glacier Bay from Juneau is an exhausting day trip—it's wiser to overnight there, though that adds more to the cost.

The Tracy Arm fjord is a long, narrow, twisting passageway into the coastal mountains, with peaks up to a mile high that jut straight out of the water, waterfalls tumbling down thousands of feet down their sides. At its head, Sawyer Glacier and South Sawyer Glacier calve ice into the water with a rumble and a splash. Whales and other wildlife usually show up along the way. And, as at Glacier Bay, John Muir paid a visit. No second best here!

Adventure Bound Alaska, at 215 Ferry Way, Juneau (© 800/228-3875 or 907/463-2509; www.adventureboundalaska.com), is a family business operating a 56-foot single-hull boat with deck space all the way around. They charge $130 for adults, $90 for children ages 4 to 17; children must be at least 4 to go.

Another way to visit Tracy Arm is to charter your own boat. Although it may cost twice as much or more per person, you can decide when and where to linger with the animals or ice. Check with the visitor center for a referral, or with **Juneau Sportfishing and Sightseeing** (© 907/586-1887), listed in this section under "Saltwater Fishing & Whale-Watching."

graphic artist, their sinuous lines of blue and white ice striped with darker gray gravel debris. Only standing on the ice, which on closer inspection resembles the crusty compressed snow of springtime snow berms, do you get a clear sense of this entirely unfamiliar kind of terrain.

It's worth noting that these tours have had some major mishaps. While the accidents represent a tiny fraction of all the safe flights, they're a reminder that flying a helicopter to a glacier is not like flying an airliner.

Era Helicopters (© 800/843-1947 or 907/586-2030; www.erahelicopters.com) is a respected operator. Their 1-hour flight over four glaciers with a 15-minute landing on Norris Glacier costs $254 per person. They also offer a program of **dog-sled rides** on the ice, a chance to try a winter sport in the summer. That excursion includes the four-glacier overflight and adds about an hour at a sled-dog camp on a glacier with a ride behind the dogs. It costs $445 per person. One caveat: Poor or even overcast weather makes it difficult to see the ice clearly, but if you wait for a sunny morning all seats will likely be booked. They have a 48-hour cancellation policy, so you have to gamble to some extent on good viewing conditions. Of course, they don't fly in unsafe conditions.

NorthStar Trekking (© 907/790-4530; www.northstartrekking.com), another company with its own helicopters, specializes in hiking and teaching about glaciers. Their small groups (a maximum of 12, with two guides) go on ice-hiking excursions of up to a few miles, with the speed determined by the group. The 4-hour trip, which includes 2 hours on the ice and half an hour in the air (the balance is getting to the helicopter and gearing up), costs $359 per person. They offer longer, more expensive options, overnights, and less expensive options, too.

Wings Airways (© 907/586-6275; www.wingsairways.com) offers glacier over-flights by floatplane and flightseeing tours to the remote Taku Lodge, where they land for salmon for brunch, lunch, or dinner.

GETTING OUTSIDE: ON ADMIRALTY ISLAND

Beyond Douglas Island from Juneau, near the entrance to Gastineau Channel, is 1-mil-lion-acre Admiralty Island, one of the largest virgin blocks of old-growth forest in the country. The vast majority of the island is the protected **Kootznoowoo Wilderness.** Kootznoowoo, Tlingit for "fortress of bears," is said to have the highest concentration of brown bears on Earth. Despite the town of Angoon on the western side of the island, there are more bears than people on Admiralty. The island's **Pack Creek Bear Viewing Area** is the most famous and surefire place to see bears in the Southeast. The area has been managed for bear viewing since the 1930s, when hunting was outlawed. There's a platform for watching the bears up close as they feed on salmon spawning in the creek in July and August. Peak viewing occurs in the middle of that period. The bears gener-ally pay no attention to the people watching them from a safe viewing platform. There's good bird-watching here, too, with an extraordinary abundance of bald eagles.

Only 25 miles from Juneau, Pack Creek is so popular that the Forest Service uses a per-mit system to keep it from being overrun during the day (no humans are allowed 9pm–9am). The great majority of people go for only a few hours. There are no facilities in this wilderness area and you can't even camp without some kind of watercraft to get to a designated area. The easiest way to go is with a tour operator who has permits. The For-est Service District Ranger Office can give you a list of guides. **Alaska Discovery** (© 800/586-1911; www.alaskadiscovery.com), has many permits for Pack Creek sea-kayak trips. Their 1-day excursion flies out and then paddles to the creek; no experience is necessary, but you must be physically capable of hiking and paddling. It costs $595 per person. A 2-night campout and sea kayak near the creek offers more time to see the bears and appre-ciate the scenery. It costs $1,095 per person. **Alaska Fly 'N' Fish Charters** (© 907/790-2120; www.alaskabyair.com), also has permits for its naturalist-guided 5½-hour fly-in Pack Creek visits, which cost $550 per person, with everything you need included.

Twelve permits per day go to the commercial operators and 12 to people who go without any guide; 8 of those 12 private permits can be booked in advance with the Forest Service, and the other 4 are available 3 days before the date on which they're good, or the previous Friday for Tuesday and Wednesday, at 9am at the Juneau Ranger District Office. In the peak season, July 5 to August 25, permits cost $50 for adults, $25 for those ages 16 or under or 62 and over. Lower prices and easier availability pre-vail outside the peak, but then you might not see any bears. After you have the per-mit, you'll still need a way to get there, plus your own gear (including rubber boots and binoculars). The Forest Service lists air taxi operators on its website (www.fs.fed.us/r10/tongass/districts/admiralty).

Protected **Seymour Canal,** on the east side of the island, is good for canoeing and kayaking, and has two other sites besides Pack Creek where bears often show up: Swan Cove and Windfall Harbor. For information on the island, its 15 Forest Service cab-ins, and an excellent $4 map, contact the **Admiralty Island National Monument,** 8510 Mendenhall Loop Rd., Juneau (© 907/586-8800; www.fs.fed.us/r10/tongass/districts/admiralty).

WHERE TO STAY

Hotel rooms can be tight in the summer, so book ahead. Bed-and-breakfasts are a good way to get a better deal and have more fun. The Juneau Convention and Visitors Bureau's free brochure *Juneau Guide & Travel Planner* and the bureau's website contain listings of the hotels and B&Bs with links (℃ **888/581-2201;** www.travel juneau.com).

Besides those places listed below in detail, here are two more good choices: **Prospector Hotel,** 375 Whittier St., Juneau, AK 99801-1781 (℃ **800/331-2711** outside Alaska, 800/478-5866 inside Alaska, or 907/586-3737; www.prospector hotel.com) offers good standard American hotel rooms just across the road from the water and is near the Alaska State Museum and other attractions. **Alaska Wolf House Bed & Breakfast,** 1900 Wickersham Dr., Juneau, AK 99801 (℃ **888/425-9653** or 907/586-2422; www.alaskawolfhouse.com) overlooks Gastineau Channel just off the Glacier Highway a half mile beyond the edge of Juneau's core area. A lot of dark woodwork contributes to a masculine wilderness lodge atmosphere—there's even a wolf pelt draped over the couch.

VERY EXPENSIVE

Pearson's Pond Luxury Inn and Adventure Spa ★★★   Diane Pearson found a vocation when she opened her bed-and-breakfast years ago in a suburban house near the Mendenhall Glacier, and she pursued it with a zeal that's still startling to encounter after all the years I have known her. The result is an extraordinary, sensual retreat of superbly appointed rooms, packed with every conceivable amenity, in a building and on grounds that create the illusion of being in a fairyland somewhere in the Alaska wilderness—there's even a private pond with a rowboat. Diane herself remains the wizard behind the curtain, putting out her husband's freshly baked bread with the wine that greets new guests. On overhearing visitors wish they could have fish for dinner she has been known to grab her rod, ride her bike down to the Mendenhall River, catch a salmon, and light the barbecue in time for the evening meal. As the place has grown, she has added well-trained staff, so you can get a massage or join daily yoga classes, and of course the palaces (I mean rooms) are always immaculate. She hosts business travelers—there's a well-stocked snack room and all units have Ethernet ports and access to a wireless LAN (and she'll lend you a laptop, too)—but it's really a place for couples. Diane plans weddings and even officiates on-site or on the glacier itself; some rooms have wonderful bathing facilities, and all are heavily soundproofed for nights of passion. She also plans custom tour packages, if you want her to set up your whole vacation (see the sample itineraries on the website), and has more conventional condolike lodgings downtown.

4541 Sawa Circle, Juneau, AK 99801. ℃ **888/658-6328** or 907/789-3772. Fax 907/789-6722. www.pearsons pond.com. 5 units. High season $229–$349 double; low season $119–$299 double. Extra person $50. AE, DC, DISC, MC, V. **Amenities:** Health club; 2 outdoor Jacuzzis; concierge; business center; massage; free laundry service; free loan of rowboat, paddleboat, fishing gear, bike, or laptop computer. *In room:* TV/VCR/DVD, kitchenette, coffeemaker, hair dryer, iron, high-speed Internet port, Wi-Fi, CD player.

EXPENSIVE

Alaska's Capital Inn ★★★   This scrupulously restored 1906 mansion offers constant surprises in its fascinating detail: the shining potbellied stove and 1879 pump organ in the parlor, the Alaskan artwork and Persian rugs, the original (electrified) gas lamps, period wallpaper, and even those old-fashioned push-button light switches. It took owners Linda Wendeborn and Mark Thorson 3 years to bring the house back to

this former glory, and they never would have done it without a driving vision, for they poured effort and expense into making details authentic that no one will ever notice. Fortunately, the house was worth it, with many large rooms with high ceilings, good views, fireplaces, claw-foot tubs, and real elegance. The best asset of all, however, may be the warmth and fun of the inn. The common rooms are conducive to socializing and the hosts love to connect with guests and strive to accommodate their needs. For this reason, and the location just steps from the state Capitol Building, the inn fills with affluent lobbyists in the winter; likewise, and because of the lovely garden out back, the place is popular for weddings in the summer. There are some lower-priced rooms, allowing those on midrange budgets to enjoy the ambience, but the real showplaces carry luxury rates. A Scottie dog named Brodie patrols the place. An elaborate breakfast is served at 8am. Smoking is not allowed, and they don't take children under 11.

113 W. 5th St., Juneau, AK 99801. © **888/588-6507** or 907/586-6507. Fax 907/586-6508. www.alaskacapital inn.com. 7 units. High season $159–$299 double; low season $109–$235 double. Extra person $20. Rates include full breakfast. AE, DC, DISC, MC, V. Children under 11 are not permitted. **Amenities:** Jacuzzi; shared computer with Internet access; off-street parking. *In room:* TV/VCR, Wi-Fi.

Goldbelt Hotel Juneau ✪✪   This is a solidly built business hotel on the waterfront downtown. Alone in Juneau, it has an entry where guests can be dropped off out of the rain and enter a full lobby, here filled with superb Tlingit art presented by the Goldbelt Native Corporation, which owns the hotel. The clean, geometrical lines of the building are carried throughout, including large rooms with high ceilings and bold fabrics. There's a special feeling of privacy here, perhaps because even those units facing the busy street on the water side are noticeably quiet. All smell and look immaculate. Rooms with the water view cost $10 more. The best in the house are on the corners, with even more space and light.

The restaurant off the lobby, **Zen,** is among the best in town. The dining room is beautifully decorated in a fully realized Asian theme in shades of green. Tables are widely separated. The Asian fusion cuisine includes items such as ginger halibut and lemongrass salmon, both for $22, as well as steaks and other American dishes.

51 W. Egan Dr., Juneau, AK 99801 © **888/478-6909** or 907/586-6900. Fax 907/463-3567. www.goldbelttours.com. Summer $169–$179 double; winter $139–$149 double. Extra person $15. AE, MC, V. **Amenities:** Restaurant; lounge; airport shuttle. *In room:* TV, coffeemaker, iron, Wi-Fi.

MODERATE

Baranof Hotel ✪✪   The Baranof is the only lodging in Alaska with the pedigree and style to pull off the role of the old-fashioned grand hotel. Built of concrete in 1939, it served for decades as an informal branch of the state capitol. In 2007, the hotel's history gained a chapter when a group of legislators, current and former, were indicted for taking bribes from oil industry executives in suite 604, which happened to be under FBI surveillance. The structure feels historic, in part, because the concrete construction limits modernization—bathrooms and many bedrooms will always be small. In places, past efforts at renovation have made the most of the classic features, retaining glass doorknobs and pressed-tin hallway ceilings. Most bathrooms were remodeled with period tile, porcelain pedestal sinks, and tubs. The upper-floor rooms have great views on the water side. There's a discount on the second floor, which lacks a view, and the rates generally are quite reasonable for this market.

The Baranof's Art Deco **Gold Room** ✪✪ restaurant is Juneau's most traditional fine-dining establishment, and among its best. The dining room combines intimacy

Alaska

Fairbanks o

Anchorage o Cordova **Juneau**
o o Sitka o
Kenai o
Ketchikan

To Mendenhall Lake
and Mendenhall
Glacier ❹

**MENDENHALL
VALLEY**

To Ferry,
Shrine of
St. Thérèse,
and Auke Village
Recreation
Area

Auke
Lake

Auke
Bay

Mendenhall Peninsula

Glacier

Mendenhall R.

Riverside Dr.

Mendenhall Loop Rd.

Egan Dr.

T o n g a s s

N a t i o n a l

F o r e s t

Juneau
International
Airport

❺

❻

**LEMON
CREEK**

Fritz Cove

Douglas Hwy.

0   1 Mi
0   1 Km

Salmon Creek

❼

Douglas Hwy.

Egan Dr.

❽

To Downtown
Juneau ↘

See Downtown
Juneau map

ACCOMMODATIONS ■
Alaska Wolf House Bed &
Breakfast **8**
Pearson's Pond Luxury Inn
and Adventure Spa **3**

DINING ◆
Chan's Thai Kitchen **1**
Hot Bite **2**

ATTRACTIONS ●
Glacier Gardens **5**
Macaulay Salmon Hatchery **7**
Mendenhall Glacier
Visitor Center **4**
Mendenhall Wetlands
State Game Refuge **6**

and grandeur in a showplace of shining brass, frosted glass, and rich wood. The current chef has gained a following. Most entrees are $25 to $35.

127 N. Franklin St., Juneau, AK 99801. ☏ **800/544-0970** or 907/586-2660. Fax 907/586-8315. www.westmark hotels.com. 196 units. High season $139–$169 double; low season $129–$139 double. Extra person over age 12 $15. AE, DC, DISC, MC, V. **Amenities:** 2 restaurants; bar; fitness room; tour desk; salon; limited room service; laundry service; dry cleaning. *In room:* TV, dataport, kitchenettes in some rooms, coffeemaker, hair dryer, iron, high-speed Internet in some rooms.

The Historic Silverbow Inn ✦ There is an oddly pleasing style to this quirky little downtown hotel. The 1914 building, with wood floors, bare brick, and stained glass, is decorated with family pictures and weird postcards, mismatched furniture and varied fabrics. Among the original and considerate touches that show up repeatedly, the cozy little rooms come with extras such as lollipops and popcorn, a shelf of supplies you may have forgotten, an answering machine on the direct-line phone, and a sack breakfast if you have to leave too early for the free full breakfast in the bakery. The proprietors and staff and the scene they have created with their popular Silverbow Bakery give the whole place a communal feel. The building has the feeling of a European pension rather than an American hotel—including five new rooms and a rooftop garden that weren't quite done being built when I inspected. The restaurant, Silverbow Bakery, is described below.

120 2nd St., Juneau, AK 99801. ℂ 800/586-4146 or 907/586-4146. Fax 907/586-4242. www.silverbowinn.com. 11 units. High season $128–$188 double; low season $88–$148 double. Extra person $20. $20 surcharge for 1-night stays in high season. Rates include full breakfast. AE, DISC, MC, V. **Amenities:** Restaurant. *In room:* TV, hair dryer, Wi-Fi.

INEXPENSIVE

Breakwater Hotel   New owners are taking a rectangular building overlooking the boat harbor and bringing it back with friendly service and gradual improvements in the rooms. The units I checked were a bit dated and worn in spots, but perfectly acceptable, with lots of amenities, and a bargain for the rates. The views on the water side are terrific, but you hear traffic from Egan Expressway. The hotel's location is at the edge of downtown at the base of Evergreen Cemetery, a pleasant spot but a long walk to the sites. Upstairs, with the best view, the hotel has a nice, old-fashioned seafood restaurant, with ropes and nets for decoration, and main courses around $20.

1711 Glacier Ave., Juneau, AK 99801. ℂ 800/544-2250 or 907/586-6303. Fax 907/463-4820. www.breakwater inn.com. 55 units. High season $120 double; low season $70 double. Extra adult $10. AE, DC, DISC, MC, V. **Amenities:** Restaurant; lounge; airport shuttle; business center. *In room:* TV, fridge, coffeemaker, Wi-Fi.

The Driftwood Lodge *(Value)*   This downtown motel, next door to the Alaska State Museum, is popular with families, and houses legislators and aides in the winter in its apartment-like kitchenette suites. Although the building can't hide its cinderblock construction and old-fashioned motel exterior, small bathrooms, or lack of elevators, the rooms are comfortable and well kept. The management has held prices low while making improvements, so for a rate that won't get you in the door at other Juneau hotels ($119) you can put four people in a two-bedroom suite with a full kitchen. Don't expect luxury, just a basic, clean motel room for a good price. The round-the-clock courtesy van saves big money to the airport or ferry and the rental bikes will cover your transportation needs downtown.

435 Willoughby Ave., Juneau, AK 99801. ℂ 800/544-2239 or 907/586-2280. Fax 907/586-1034. www.driftwood-alaska.com. 63 units. High season $94 double, $102–$125 suite; low season $66 double, $89 suite. Extra person $10. AE, DC, DISC, MC, V. **Amenities:** Bike rental; courtesy van; coin-op laundry. *In room:* TV, coffeemaker.

A HOSTEL

Juneau International Hostel *(Finds)*   The historic yellow house among the downtown sights is a showplace of custom cabinetry and big, light common rooms. It's a volunteer-operated nonprofit with the mission of uniting people, and it seems to be working. Everyone has to pitch in with a chore, and the shared kitchen was squeaky-clean when I visited. Men and women sleep in a number of small separate dorm rooms, and there is one private room for families with children, which is in high demand. Office hours are from 7 to 9am and 5pm to midnight in the summer, 8 to 9am and 5 to 10:30pm in the winter, with lockout during the day. There's a coin-op laundry, free Internet access and Wi-Fi, lockers, and free local calls. Reservations must be prepaid by mail or phone for a 5-night maximum stay; if there is space available, you can stay up to 7 days. Alcohol, drugs, and pets are not allowed and shoes must be removed at the door.

614 Harris St., Juneau, AK 99801. ℃ 907/586-9559. www.juneauhostel.org. 47 units (46 dorm beds and one private room). $10 per adult; $5 per child ages 6–17 with parent; free children 5 and under. $2 premium for credit card payment. MC, V. **Amenities:** Coin-op laundry; free Internet access. Closed intermittently Nov–March; check website.

CAMPING

Juneau has two exceptional Forest Service campgrounds open from mid-May to mid-September. For information, contact the Juneau Ranger District (℃ **907/586-8800;** www.fs.fed.us/r10/tongass). **The Mendenhall Glacier Campground,** overlooking the lake and glacier and next to the Mendenhall River, is the best built public campground in the state, with granite block construction. The bathrooms have showers and flush toilets and there is a half-mile nature trail for those with disabilities. The 69 sites are huge and broadly separated; nine have full RV hookups and another nine have electricity and water. Tents and RVs are segregated. To get there, turn north on Montana Creek Road from Mendenhall Loop Road. Tent sites are $10, RV sites $26 and $28. The 11-site **Auke Village Campground,** 1¾ miles north of the ferry dock, is in an extraordinary place, with sites among large trees along an ocean beach, looking out on the islands of Auke Bay. The campground, reconstructed in 2006, has vault toilets and running water. Sites are $10 per night.

Spruce Meadow RV Park, at 10200 Mendenhall Loop Rd. (℃ **907/789-1990;** www.juneaurv.com), has full hookups in a natural setting with cable and free Wi-Fi. Full hookups are $30. Reserve ahead.

WHERE TO DINE

After a spell when good food was lacking, Juneau is having a renaissance of dining, with a number of excellent restaurants opening. Besides those detailed below, see the Gold Room, in the Baranof Hotel, on p. 174 and Zen, in the Goldbelt Hotel Juneau, p. 174. For breakfast or lunch, try the **Sandpiper Cafe,** near the Alaska State Museum at 429 Willoughby Ave. (℃ **907/586-3150;** www.thesandpipercafe.com), with an immaculate dining room recalling a sun-faded beachfront eatery. The short menu includes tasty comfort foods, sandwiches, and breakfast all day. A hamburger is $10. It's open daily 6am to 2pm.

Pizzeria Roma, on the waterfront across the hall from the Hanger restaurant at 2 Marine Way (℃ **907/463-5020**) produces some of the best pizza and calzone in the region in a small dining room. Hours are daily 11am to 10pm summer, closing half an hour earlier in winter. **Kenny's Wok & Teriyaki Sushi Bar,** at 126 Front St. (℃ **907/ 586-3575**) offers a seemingly endless menu with reasonable prices with selections ranging from familiar pot stickers or teriyaki chicken to exotic choices such as seaweed salad or sashimi. It's open from around midday to 9:30pm every day.

Chan's Thai Kitchen ★★ *Finds* THAI   The small, overlit dining room in a half basement sees few tourists, but I've heard locals brag about how long they were willing to stand in the small entrance area to get a table. When I went I became a believer, too—the authentic Thai food is that good and the atmosphere, if lacking in polish, is conducive to a good time. You will need a car, as the location is 20 minutes from town across from the Auke Bay boat harbor. Reservations are not accepted and they do not have a liquor license.

11820 Glacier Hwy. ℃ **907/789-9777.** Reservations not accepted. Main courses $10–$14. MC, V. Tues–Fri 11:30am–2pm and 4:30–8:30pm; Sat 4:30–8:30pm.

The Hangar ✿ STEAK/SEAFOOD/PASTA   Situated in a converted airplane hangar on a wooden pier with large windows, this bar and grill has great views and a fun atmosphere; even off-season, it's packed. It's a fine place to drink beer (with 24 brews on tap), listen to live music, or play at one of the three pool tables. What's surprising is that the food is good, too. The seared ahi sashimi appetizer, raw inside, had a pleasant texture and taste, and the jambalaya, a huge portion for $13, was spicy but balanced. Although the menu's steaks and such range up to $30, plenty of choices are under $15.

2 Marine Way. ✆ **907/586-5018.** Reservations recommended. Main courses $13–$30. AE, MC, V. Daily 11am–10pm.

Island Pub ✿ PIZZA/SALADS/SANDWICHES   Across the bridge from Juneau, this is where local people go for a fun night out. The food is good and far from boring—I had a steak salad, which consisted of rare, well-seasoned slices of grilled steak on a bed of lettuce with a load of bleu cheese dressing and onion rings. The specialty is pizza with creative ingredients. The smell of smoke from the wood-fired grill hangs in the air. The dining room, dating from the 1930s, is historic by Alaskan standards and comes by its pub ambience honestly. It's big and open and looks out on the Gastineau Channel through picture windows. At times customers watch killer whales from the bar (they have the photos to prove it). The pub is easy to find. Drive across the bridge to Douglas, turn left, and after entering the town turn left on E Street.

1102 2nd St., Douglas. ✆ **907/364-1595.** www.theislandpub.com. Main courses $8–$11. Pizza $12–$17. MC, V. Daily 11:30am–10pm.

Twisted Fish Co. Alaskan Grill ✿ SEAFOOD/PIZZA/BURGERS   Overlooking the water at the cruise ship dock, in the same building as Taku Smokeries, the dining room is magnificent, with high ceilings and an entire wall of windows on the Gastineau Channel, a fireplace of beach rock, lots of hardwood, and, to keep it from being too grand, cartoon-like fish hanging down. The quality and range of the food brings locals to a tourist zone they would otherwise avoid: items like salmon on a cedar plank or in pastry, halibut or salmon tacos, and also little pizzas, burgers, and terrific desserts. The service is fast and attentive, but the dining room makes you want to stay long after you are done eating.

550 S. Franklin St. ✆ **907/463-5033.** Reservations recommended. Lunch $7–$15, dinner main courses $18–$30. AE, DISC, MC, V. Summer daily 11am–10pm. Closed Oct–Apr.

Wild Spice ✿✿ MONGOLIAN/ECLECTIC   Right in the middle of the downtown, this storefront is a remarkably enjoyable place for lunch or dinner, with interesting food, excellent service, and a fashionable yet relaxed dining room. Guests can use the Mongolian barbecue—picking out ingredients to be cooked on the round grill—or order from an extensive menu of fascinating international dishes in a broad range of prices. The food is quite reasonably priced for the level of quality and it's possible to eat quite inexpensively. I had the Jamaican jerk chicken sandwich, a whole breast with rich but balanced seasonings on a delicious roll with roasted peppers and feta—plus a pasta salad buried in fresh parmesan—for $9. The only downside was the sandwich's structural integrity, as it fell apart under the stress of so many ingredients. Dessert was terrific, as well: two huge, rich brownies with homemade gelato. I was barely walking when I left.

140 Seward St. ✆ **907/523-0344.** www.thewildspice.com. Lunch $8–$14; dinner $11–$28. AE, DISC, MC, V. Summer Sun–Thurs 11am–9pm, Fri–Sat 11am–10pm; winter Mon–Thurs 11am–9pm, Fri 11am–10pm, Sat 2–10pm.

> *Finds* **Quick Bites in Juneau**
>
> The **Silverbow Bakery,** at 120 2nd St. (© **907/586-4146;** www.silverbow
> inn.com), is a happening spot for bagels or hearty sandwiches. It's open daily
> 6am to 8pm. The **Rainbow Food** health-food grocery, an organic hang-out in
> a former church at the corner of Franklin and 4th streets (© **907/586-6476**),
> is the best picnic-packing place downtown, making sandwiches and salads at
> the deli and with a buffet and salad bar. It's also a good place to network
> with a socially conscious crowd. **Hot Bite,** at the Auke Bay boat harbor, is a
> local secret, serving charcoal-broiled hamburgers and halibut burgers and
> mind-blowing milkshakes. Takeout or sit at one of six indoor tables. Down-
> town Juneau's young, professional population supports several good coffee-
> houses. **Valentine's Coffee House and Pizzeria,** 111 Seward St. (© **907/463-
> 5144**), serves light hot meals in an authentic old-fashioned storefront. **Her-
> itage Coffee Co. and Café,** at 174 S. Franklin St. (© **907/586-1087;** www.
> heritagecoffee.com) and 216 2nd St. (© **907/586-1752**) has two trendy, com-
> fortable coffeehouses good for watching people or using the Internet,
> either wireless or on their terminals. They also roast famous coffee.

Zyphyr Restaurant ✦✦✦ MEDITERRANEAN   The dining room, once an old-
fashioned grocery store, was remodeled with restraint and a magnificent sense of style,
using its wooden floors, very high ceilings, and huge storefront windows to create the
illusion of elegance passed down for generations rather than only since late 2006.
Tables robed in linen of dark rust are set so far apart that diners feel they are alone,
and on the winter evening I first ate here the darkness outside contributed to the vel-
vety intimacy. The food and the service—courteous but world-weary—lived up to the
setting. Dishes are from the traditional fine dining palette of colors: calamari, pasta
puttanesca, and veal scallopini, for example. I started with rich, spicy clams and
enjoyed a perfectly textured grilled lamb kabob with asparagus as a main course.
Desserts are excellent, too. Save this place for a romantic meal or a special treat at the
end of the day.

200 Seward St. © **907/780-2221.** Reservations recommended. Main courses $13–$29. MC, V. Tues–Sat 5–10pm.

NIGHTLIFE

Alaska Travel Adventures has offered its **Gold Creek Salmon Bake** (© **907/789-
0052**) for more than 30 years. It's touristy, yes, but fun, with marshmallow roasting,
music, and other entertainment—great for families (I'd avoid it in the rain, however.)
The cost is $34 for adults, $23 for children.

For more substantial performances, try to catch a show by Juneau's **Perseverance
Theatre,** Alaska's largest professional theater. The winter season, starting in September
and lasting until early June, includes Alaska's best cutting-edge drama, including serious homegrown work. Paula Vogel was here when she wrote *How I Learned to Drive,*
which later won the Pulitzer Prize. Summer offerings are limited to youth theater and
workshops. To find out what's playing, contact the theater's office at 914 3rd St., Douglas (© **907/364-2421**), or check the website at www.perseverancetheatre.org.

A political scandal or two put a damper on some of the infamous legislative party-ing that once occurred in Juneau, far away from home districts, but good places to go out drinking and dancing still exist. The **Red Dog Saloon,** at 278 S. Franklin St., is the town's most famous bar, with a sawdust-strewn floor, a slightly contrived but nonetheless infectious frontier atmosphere, and walls covered with Alaska memora-bilia. Locals hang across the street, at **The Alaskan Bar,** 167 S. Franklin St., which occupies an authentic gold-rush hotel with a two-story Victorian bar room. Boister-ous parties and music go on there all year. **The Hangar,** listed above under "Where to Dine," is the place for beer drinkers. They have a big-screen TV and live music Friday and Saturday nights, as well as pool and darts.

7 Glacier Bay National Park

Glacier Bay is a work in progress; the boat ride to its head is a chance to see creation unfolding. The bay John Muir discovered in a canoe in 1879 didn't exist a century ear-lier. Eighteenth-century explorers had found instead a wall of ice a mile thick where the entrance to the branching, 65-mile-long fjord now opens to the sea. Receding faster than any other glacier on Earth, the ice melted into the ocean and opened a spectacular and still-unfinished land. The land itself is rising 1½ inches a year as it rebounds from the weight of now-melted glaciers. As your vessel retraces Muir's path—and then probes northward in deep water where ice stood in his day—the story of this new world unravels in reverse. The trees on the shore get smaller, then disap-pear, then all vegetation disappears, and finally, at the head of the bay, the ice stands at the water's edge surrounded by barren rock, rounded and scored by the passage of the ice but not yet marked by the waterfalls cascading from the clouds above. And there, still doing their landscape-shaping work, are the great, blue glaciers, the largest among them the awesome Grand Pacific Glacier.

Glacier Bay, first set aside as a national monument by Calvin Coolidge in 1925, is managed by the National Park Service, which has the difficult job of protecting the wilderness, the whales, and the other wildlife while serving the huge public visiting the park. This rugged land the size of Connecticut cannot be seen by car, only by boat or plane, and the presence of too many boats threatens the wilderness experience and may disturb the wildlife. The whales appear to be sensitive to the noise of vessels and, since the 1970s, when in some years hardly any whales returned, the Park Service has used a permit system to limit the number of ships that can enter the bay. Any boat sees several other ships on a day's journey up the bay, but how much the vessels bother the whales and other wildlife is difficult to measure precisely, and political pressure always pushes for more huge ships. In response to legislation passed by Alaska's pro-development congressional delegation, the Park Service increased the number of cruise ships entering the bay, but in 2001 environmentalists won a court ruling that briefly reduced the number and held off a further increase pending study. In 2003, the Park Service completed an environmental impact statement on the issue. It allows an increase from 139 cruise ships per year to 184 per year, but only if recommended by a science advisory board. Increases proposed under that program have been more than environmentalists support but fewer than the cruise industry wants. To read more about the park's vessel management plan, go to www.nps.gov/glba.

On my longest visit, I saw humpback whales breaching (leaping all the way out of the water) every day. I saw orcas, too. One day, while fishing for halibut from a small boat in foggy Icy Strait, just outside the park, I heard a sound like thunder not far off.

Glacier Bay National Park

Like thunder, the sound repeated, growing closer, but its source remained hidden behind the white circle of fog that surrounded us. Then the smooth water suddenly bulged and a huge, barnacled creature shot upward and crashed down with a sharp clap and a splash that rocked the boat. And then it happened again. The whale went on performing for most of an hour. A day later, I encountered the same spectacle while sea kayaking in the park's Bartlett Cove.

Leaping whales and falling glaciers are hard to beat. But the park also has major drawbacks to consider. Sightings aren't guaranteed, so there's a risk that you'll spend a lot of money and not see any whales. And even though this is a huge wilderness, the ways to see it are limited, so most people never get away from crowds. The lone concessionaire-operated tour boat into the bay costs $160 per person and is usually full of people. The large cruise ships that bring most visitors to the park view the scenery without getting up close to the shore or wildlife and miss the shore-based attractions. Smaller ships see more, with smaller groups and more chances to get outdoors. Independent travelers can spend a few days in some of Alaska's most attractive remote accommodations, in Gustavus, with great fishing, hiking, sea kayaking, and tour-boat rides into the park. But the only way to see the heart of the park in true solitude is on a boat you charter for yourself (out of range of most budgets) or on a rugged overnight sea-kayaking adventure.

As an alternative, consider the other places to see Alaska's glaciers and whales that are easier and less expensive to visit. If you're in Juneau, consider a day trip to Tracy Arm instead. In Southcentral Alaska, plan a day trip from Whittier to see the glaciers of western Prince William Sound or from Seward to see Kenai Fjords National Park. There are other places in Southeast rich with marine wildlife, as well. Still, Glacier Bay beats them all—and just about anyplace on Earth—for the combination of lots of whales and lots of big glaciers.

ESSENTIALS
GETTING THERE
Most visitors who get to the park enter on cruise ships that pass through the bay without landing, so those readers can skip the material below (although you may be interested in the introduction, above). Others begin their visit to the park at the headquarters area at Bartlett Cove. But once at Bartlett Cove, you're only at the edge of a park with no roads. To go onward into the park, you need some kind of boat. That's covered below under "Activities at the Park."

BY AIR   Gustavus, covered in the next section of this chapter, is the gateway to Glacier Bay National Park, lying 10 miles by road from the Bartlett Cove headquarters. The only practical way to Gustavus is by air. That information is covered in the next section. Getting from the Gustavus airstrip to Bartlett Cove is easy. Vans meet planes, charging $13 for adults, $6.25 for children 8 and under, and carry passengers to Bartlett Cove. It's free if you are traveling with a package tour; also, most of the inns and lodges in Gustavus offer free transfers to the park.

BY WATER   A summer passenger ferry, the fast catamaran *Fairweather Express II*, is operated by the park concessionaire, Glacier Bay Lodge and Tours (© **888-BAY-TOUR;** www.visitglacierbay.com), connecting Juneau's Auke Bay harbor directly to Bartlett Cove. The boat starts from Bartlett Cove Wednesday, Friday, and Sunday at 4:30pm, leaves from Auke Bay at 8pm, and arrives again at Bartlett Cove at 11pm. The fare is $70 one-way for adults, $40 for children 2 to 12 years old. The service was new in 2007 and changes are possible; call ahead for the latest.

VISITOR INFORMATION
Contact the **Glacier Bay National Park and Preserve** at P.O. Box 140, Gustavus, AK 99826 (© **907/697-2230;** www.nps.gov/glba). The Park Service interprets the park mainly by placing well-prepared rangers onboard most cruise and tour vessels entering the bay. The park also maintains a modest visitor center with displays on the park on the second floor of the lodge at wooded Bartlett Cove. Pick up the park map and handy guide, *The Fairweather.* Nearby are the park's offices, a free campground, a backcountry office, a few short hiking trails, a dock, sea kayak rental, and other park facilities. Rangers lead a daily nature walk and present an evening program.

ACTIVITIES AT THE PARK
HIKING AT BARTLETT COVE   There are three short hiking trails through the rainforest of Sitka spruce and western hemlock at Bartlett Cove. Each weaves through the cool, damp quiet created by these huge trees and the moss on the forest floor. Wet spots are often crossed by boardwalks with railings. A map is included in the *Fairweather* visitor guide.

The **Forest Loop** is an easy trail about 1 mile long, beginning at the lodge and passing through the woods and past some park buildings to the cove's pebble beach. The

Now hear this!

Bartlett River Trail is a 4-mile round-trip leading to the Bartlett River Estuary, a good bird-watching spot, especially during migrations. The **Bartlett Lake Trail** branches off the Bartlett River Trail after about .25 mile for a 3.75-mile one-way forest hike to the lake.

BOAT TOURS   Bartlett Cove is nowhere near the park's highlights. Most independent travelers take a day boat to see the vast majority of Glacier Bay. The boat is operated by a park concessionaire called **Glacier Bay Lodge and Tours,** a joint venture of ARAMARK and Huna Totem, with offices at 241 W. Ship Creek Ave., Anchorage, AK 99501 (© **888/229-8687** or 907/264-4600; fax 907/258-3668; www.visitglacier bay.com), or, locally, in the summer only, at P.O. Box 179, Gustavus, AK 99826 (© **907/697-4000;** fax 907/697-4001). The boat leaves from the dock in Bartlett Cove and sails to the fjords' very head and the Grand Pacific Glacier. The 8-hour voyage is too long for many children. There's a snack bar, and a simple lunch is provided. Bring binoculars, good rain gear, and layers of warm clothing. A Park Service employee does the commentary, so you can count on accuracy and a didactic approach missing from most commercial tours. The fare is $160 for adults, half price for children 2 to 12. The company also offers an overnight package that includes the boat ride, meals, and lodging for $334, double occupancy, plus airfare.

CHARTERING A BOAT   Local family operators based in Gustavus take visitors up the bay in comfort, with the spontaneity and intimacy of boating with friends. If you have a group, you can have a boat and guide to yourself. Mike Nigro, a former backcountry ranger and longtime resident, takes groups of four to six for $1,800 per day on a 42-foot yacht, the Kahsteen. His **Gustavus Marine Charters** can be reached at © **907/697-2233** or www.gustavusmarinecharters.com.

KAYAKING IN THE PARK   You won't forget seeing a breaching humpback whale from a sea kayak, sitting just inches off the water. It happens around here. When we breathlessly told our innkeepers about the experience, they smiled politely. They hear the same descriptions all the time.

Inexperienced paddlers should choose a guided trip. **Glacier Bay Sea Kayaks,** based in Gustavus (© **907/697-2257;** www.glacierbayseakayaks.com), offers half-day and all-day paddles in Bartlett Cove good for beginners. Although the trips go nowhere near the glaciers, the paddlers stand a good chance of seeing whales, sometimes quite close up. Any fit person can enjoy it. A half-day costs $85, full-day $135, including a lunch. The same folks rent kayaks for day trips in the cove. These self-guided outings begin with a briefing and novices are welcome. The cost is $30 half-day, $40 full-day. Experienced kayakers ready for an overnight in the wilderness up the bay can rent equipment, too, and get dropped near the glaciers for $214 round-trip. Do your planning and decide what to bring before you leave for the park, as you may not be able to buy or rent what you need once there. Check the gear list and other advice on the Glacier Bay Sea Kayaks website. Before starting off on an overnight you also will have to attend a Park Service briefing and get a backcountry permit from the headquarters. The company operates May 1 to September 30.

Alaska Discovery (© **800/586-1911;** www.alaskadiscovery.com) offers 5-day guided expeditions in Glacier Bay. Although I wouldn't recommend this to someone who hasn't tried kayaking before (what if you hate it?), those who do will find this the most intimate and authentic way to experience this wilderness. A 5-day trip, with 4 days of kayaking, 3 days camping, and 1 day at an inn, costs around $2,000 from Gustavus.

FLIGHTSEEING   One spectacular way to get into the park is by flightseeing. Gustavus-based **Air Excursions** (© 907/697-2375) offers air tours in float or wheeled planes. Other operators fly from various nearby towns, including Haines and Skagway (covered later in this chapter).

You'll see the incredible rivers of ice that flow down into the bay, and you may even see wildlife. What you give up is the sense of scale from ground level.

WHERE TO STAY, CAMP & DINE

Glacier Bay Lodge ★   This is the only place to stay in the park (although Gustavus, 10 miles down the road, has some of the most attractive accommodations in Alaska; see section 8, below). A new concessionaire upgraded the rooms starting in 2005; they have new curtains, phones, and hair dryers. The wood-paneled rooms have a bit of rustic charm, but they're mainly just comfortable lodgings in a pleasant setting. The buildings are set amid the soothing quiet of large rainforest trees and are reached from the main lodge by boardwalks and steps. Laundry facilities and rental of bikes and fishing gear are available. The company offers all-inclusive packages starting at $334 per person, which include lodging, meals, activities, and transfers from the airport.

The **restaurant** has huge windows looking onto Bartlett Cove. The menu includes a wide variety of dishes, including fresh fish. Many visitors enjoy dining—or just having nachos and beer—on the deck, where an international social event lasts all summer among campers and lodge guests watching for whales. A patio menu is served there 11am to 10pm daily. The indoor restaurant serves breakfast as early as 6:30 to 8am, lunch 11am to 2pm, and dinner 5:30 to 10pm.

The lodge also provides public showers and a convenience store for the free Park Service **campground,** about ¼ mile away. The campground lacks running water but has a warming hut, firewood, and bear-resistant food caches. You have to cook in a fire ring in the intertidal zone and observe other bear avoidance rules the rangers will explain. Get a camping permit at the ranger station when you arrive; the campground is almost never full.

Bartlett Cove (P.O. Box 179), Gustavus, AK 99826. © 888/229-8687 or 907/697-4000. Fax 907/258-3668 or 907/697-4001. www.visitglacierbay.com. 53 units. $150–$170 double. Extra person $20. AE, DC, DISC, MC, V. Closed mid-Sept to mid-May. **Amenities:** Restaurant; bike rental; coin-op laundry.

8 Gustavus: Country Inns & Quiet

Gustavus (gus-*tave*-us) remains an undiscovered treasure—or at least it succeeds in making itself feel that way. Although wonderfully remote and easily accessible only by air, the town has a selection of comfortable and even luxurious inns and lodges, plus several days' worth of outdoor activities, excellent salmon and halibut fishing, nearly surefire whale-watching, close access to sea kayaking and other activities at Glacier Bay National Park, and places for casual hiking and bicycle outings. Large cruise ships cannot land here, leaving the roads free of their throngs of shoppers. Miraculously, the 450 townspeople have been smart enough to value what they've got and build on it. Even the gas station is a work of art. Walking, biking, or driving down the quiet roads, everyone you pass—every single person—waves to you.

The buildings, mostly clapboard houses and log cabins, are scattered widely across an oceanfront alluvial plain. Several of the founding homesteads were farms, and the broad clearings of sandy soil wave with hay and wildflowers. The setting is unique in Alaska, and when I had a choice to go anywhere in the state for a 4-day trip with

> ### (*Tips*) Town without a Downtown
>
> This town looks like the country: houses, cabins, and a few businesses spread far apart along gravel roads. Services are limited. On Dock Road the Bear Track Mercantile sells necessities. Bring your own booze and whatever else you will want with you, and reserve all accommodations in advance. The local government, founded in 2004, imposes a 2% sales tax and an added 4% tax on accommodations.

extended family, this is the place I chose. Each of us took something lasting from the trip. My older son, then 8, learned what it was like to be able to bike anywhere at will, making discoveries in the woods and friends on the quiet lanes without his parents reining him in. My parents, in their 60s, glowed when they returned from kayaking among the breaching humpback whales in the park's Bartlett Cove. I often reminisce about a day at the beach when I built dams and sand castles with the children, looking up to see a family of orcas romping just offshore. My cousin won't forget the huge platters of Dungeness crab that came for dinner one night at the inn.

The problem with Gustavus is the expense (and the dampness, but you get used to that). The best outdoor activities involve charters or rentals, which can add more than $200 a day per person to the cost of your trip. Most accommodations have all-inclusive plans, which include great meals but come with price tags of $175 per person per night or more. Less expensive B&Bs exist, but the choice of restaurants for dinner is limited.

ESSENTIALS

GETTING THERE   It's currently possible to take a passenger ferry called *Fairweather Express II* a few evenings a week in summer from Juneau's Auke Bay to Bartlett Cove, 10 miles by road from Gustavus (p. 98). However, the primary mode of transportation to Gustavus is by airplane. During the summer, **Alaska Airlines** (© 800/252-7522; www.alaskaair.com) flies a jet once a day from Juneau to Gustavus and back in the early evening. An advance fare is $150 to $190, round-trip.

For more frequent service by prop from Juneau to Gustavus, at roughly the same fare as Alaska Airlines, use Gustavus-based **Air Excursions** (© 907/697-2375), which flies many times a day on demand, or **Wings of Alaska** (© 907/789-0790 reservations, or 907/697-2201 in Gustavus; www.ichoosewings.com).

VISITOR INFORMATION   The traditional way to plan a trip to Gustavus is to contact a lodge and, once you're comfortable with them, allow them to advise you and book your activities. The **Gustavus Visitors Association** (www.gustavusak.com) is a cooperative website of local businesses, with links and community information; there is no staffed center. Messages sent through the site and calls to an answering machine (© 907/697-2454) are distributed to members for response. Reach them by mail at P.O. Box 167, Gustavus, AK 99826. A local travel agency, **Alaska's Glacier Bay Travel** (© 907/697-2475; www.glacierbaytravel.com), run by the same folks as the TLC Taxi (see "Getting Around," below), also can help with choices and reservations. Be certain to reserve a place to stay before showing up in Gustavus.

GETTING AROUND   There are just a few roads. The main one starts at the airport and runs about 10 miles to **Bartlett Cove,** the Glacier Bay National Park base of operations. **Dock Road** branches off to the left, at the gas station, and leads to the ocean dock and a sandy beach. There's a map and list of businesses posted near the gas station and most businesses will give you one to take along for exploration by bicycle. Many inns and B&Bs have courtesy vans and free bicycles; ask about transportation when you reserve. **TLC Taxi** (© **907/697-2239**) offers transportation between the airport, Bartlett Cove, and points in between, with flat fees depending on the destination. Reserve ahead. A van can accommodate groups, gear, and kayaks. **Bud's Rent a Car** is at © **907/697-2403.**

EXPLORING GUSTAVUS

Everything to do in Gustavus involves the outdoors. I've listed the activities here in priority order.

WHALE-WATCHING & FISHING   Whales keep their own schedule, but you're almost certain to see them on a whale-watching excursion here, where the swirling current of Icy Strait creates such a rich feeding ground that humpbacks come back every summer without fail. The big tour boat in the national park (see "Boat Tours" in section 7) frequently sees whales, but Icy Strait, outside the park, is even more prolific. Currently there are two options. Since arrangements change annually, it's wise to call ahead or get advice from your lodge or B&B host.

    Cross Sound Express (© **888/698-2726** or 907/766-3000; www.taz.gustavus.com) takes two viewing trips a day with up to 23 passengers aboard the *TAZ*, which is also used for kayak drop-offs and other marine transportation. The cost is $95 per person (no discount for children). The park concessionaire, **Glacier Bay Lodge and Tours** (© **888/229-8687** or 907/264-4600; www.visitglacierbay.com), offers a whale-watching dinner cruise on Thursday and Saturday at 5:30pm. The cost is $125 for adults, $63 for children ages 2 to 12. Meal selections include halibut, salmon, or chicken with soft drinks.

    Gustavus has superb charter boat fishing for halibut and salmon (if salmon are running). The waters are protected and seasickness generally is not a concern. Your inn host in Gustavus can make the arrangements. A boat typically charters for $250 to $325 per person for a full day, plus the cost of having your fish professionally packed and shipped home to you. Half-days are rarely available because the boats are fully booked. If you do a fishing charter, and the others onboard agree, you can take some of the time for whale-watching.

SEA KAYAKING   Gustavus-based **Spirit Walker Expeditions** (© **800/KAYAKER** or 907/697-2266; www.seakayakalaska.com) has a good reputation locally. They lead guided day trips to the whale-watching grounds, and overnight expeditions as long as a week. **Alaska Discovery** (© **800/586-1911;** www.alaskadiscovery.com) offers an easy 3-day, 2-night kayaking expedition among the whales for $950 per person. They take a boat to a base camp, then kayak among the whales from there. The outing is suitable for fit beginners and older children.

HIKING & BICYCLING   There are few cars in Gustavus, but most inns provide bikes. The roads are fun to explore, and the sandy beaches, accessed from the town dock, are great for a walk and a picnic, to watch eagles and other birds and wildlife. You can go many miles, if you are of a mind, for a run or long walk, but we saw little reason to go far before stopping to play and picnic on a broad sand beach undisturbed by any other human footprint.

GOLF   If you bring your clubs to Southeast Alaska (a questionable decision), you'll find a unique and spectacular course in Gustavus on the shore of Icy Strait. The 9-hole, par 36 **Mt. Fairweather Golf Course** (✆ **907/697-3080**) was built and is mowed and groomed by Morgan DeBoer on his family's land for his own use. Payment to play is voluntary, but $15 is customary. Reservations are unnecessary as you may have the course to yourself.

WHERE TO STAY

Gustavus contains some of Alaska's best remote accommodations, more than I have room to describe here. Most accommodations are "Gustavus style," which means they charge a daily per-person price for rooms, breakfast and dinner served family style, brown-bag lunches, bicycles and some other outdoor equipment, and transfers, and they book and charge for fishing, sea kayaking, hiking, and Glacier Bay tours. It's expensive, but it's a carefree way to visit. Another set of accommodations charges less, but leaves you on your own for lunch and dinner. Before choosing that less costly, a la carte approach, consider your dining options, which are covered below. Except as noted, rooms in Gustavus don't have phones. Some of the inns do not have licenses to serve alcohol; if that's a consideration, be sure to ask before you book your stay and consider bringing alcohol with you.

Blue Heron Bed and Breakfast at Glacier Bay ✮   Stay here if your budget doesn't allow a pricey all-inclusive package, and you'll still get many of the same comforts in fresh, attractive rooms with features such as VCRs, comforters, and superior linens. The hosts, longtime residents, are enthusiastic about their guests and serve large, gourmet breakfasts. If you rent one of the cottages, you can cook your own evening meal; the rooms have access to microwaves and refrigerators in the sunroom dining area, and a country store and deli are a few minutes' walk away. The location is among the wildflowers and marshland near the Gustavus waterfront.

Off Dock Rd. (P.O. Box 77), Gustavus, AK 99826. ✆ **907-697-2337.** Fax 907/697-2293. www.blueheronbnb.net. 4 units, including 2 cottages. $150 double; $190 double cottage; Extra adult $80; discounts for children. Rates include full breakfast. No credit cards. **Amenities:** Free bike loan; courtesy van; laundry machines ($6 per load). *In room:* TV/DVD, free movie loan.

Glacier Bay Country Inn ✮✮✮   This inn has more of the feel of a wilderness lodge. It sits on 160 acres of unspoiled forest looking out on its own airstrip where a plane waits to take guests out to fish in even more remote spots (the inn has its own charter fishing boat, too). The buildings are quirky and charming, with log beams, strange angles, and an authentically rough-hewn look. Guests make no sacrifices in comfort, however; each of the five rooms and five cabins has its own bathroom, and there is ample room to relax and while away the day if you stay home from the day's activities. Meals are ample, with two main courses offered at the evening, family-style service. As at other Gustavus inns, bicycles and rides in the van are free, but most activities off the property are paid for separately.

35 Tong Rd. (P.O. Box 5), Gustavus, AK 99826. ✆ **800/628-0912** or 907/697-2288. Fax 907/697-2289. www.glacierbay alaska.com. 10 units, including 5 cabins. $185 per person, double; $215 per person, double cabin. Extra adult $100; extra child ages 3–11 $50. Rates include all meals. DISC, MC, V. Closed mid-Sept to mid-May. **Amenities:** Free bike loans; activity desk; courtesy van; laundry; fish cleaning/freezing; Internet access in common room. *In room:* Coffeemaker, hair dryer.

Glacier Bay's Bear Track Inn ✮✮✮   Six miles from Gustavus, this extraordinary log building faces its own field of wildflowers, which, if you walk half a mile across it, leads to the shore. You look out on this scene from a lobby with a huge fireplace, a ceiling 28 feet high, and a wall of windows. The immense logs of the walls and the isolation give the place the feeling of a wilderness lodge, but the rooms are as good as those of any upscale hotel, and have the advantage of large dormer windows with sweeping views. Objectively, it's the best place in Gustavus, and one of the best remote lodges in Alaska, but which place you prefer depends on your taste: what the Bear Track gains from perfection it loses in the funky, quaint atmosphere I like about the area. Another difference compared to other lodges and inns: Meals here are cooked to order from a menu. Those not staying here can buy dinner, too. The inn serves beer and wine.

255 Rink Rd., Gustavus, AK 99826. © 888/697-2284 or 907/697-3017. Fax 907/697-2284. www.beartrackinn.com. 14 units. $495 per person, double occupancy; discounts for additional nights. Rates include round-trip air from Juneau, transfers, and all meals. DISC, MC, V. Closed Oct–Apr. **Amenities:** Restaurant; free bike loan; concierge; tour desk; courtesy van; business center; limited room service; massage; babysitting; laundry service. *In room:* Hair dryer.

Gustavus Inn at Glacier Bay ★★★   This is the original and still my favorite of the Gustavus full-service inns. By objective standards of modern luxury, imitators have surpassed the old homestead farmhouse, but no one could duplicate the extraordinary hospitality of the Lesh family, honed over 40 years of running the inn. Dave and JoAnn know how to make guests feel immediately a part of the place. The site is unsurpassed, too, standing at the center of the community amid blowing grass and with a huge vegetable garden that provides much of the dining room's wonderful food. Dave, the chef, has published a cookbook and his ginger sablefish is now widely copied. The seasonings he uses on seafood are a revelation. He serves big, inexhaustible platters in the dining room, where there's also a beer and wine bar and sushi appetizers. Before going, talk over what you want to do with JoAnn, Dave, or Dave's father, Jack, and let them book everything.

1 Gustavus Rd. (P.O. Box 60), Gustavus, AK 99826. © 800/649-5220 or 907/697-2254. Fax 907/697-2255. www. gustavusinn.com. 13 units. $175 per person per night based on double or triple occupancy. Half price for children under 12. Rates include all meals. AE, MC, V. Closed Sept 16–May 15. **Amenities:** Restaurant; bike loan; courtesy car; laundry service; Wi-Fi; fishing rods (bring your own tackle).

WHERE TO DINE

Even if you do not stay at one of the full-service inns, I recommend taking at least some of your meals there. Some of the best chefs in Alaska cook at these places (I still try to copy some of the flavors prepared by Dave Lesh of the Gustavus Inn at Glacier Bay). Make reservations; you can't just show up and eat. The other choice for fine dining is The Glacier Bay Lodge, which serves three meals a day—but it's 10 miles away at the park's Bartlett Cove headquarters. Otherwise, the dining choices in Gustavus are few and fairly basic.

One free-standing restaurant that's been going strong for years is **A Bear's Nest Cafe,** less than half a mile from the main intersection on Wilson Road (© **907/697-2440;** www.gustavus.com/bearsnest), where the often braided Lynne Morrow serves organic dishes, homemade bread, local seafood, soup, sandwiches, and dessert in a homey dining room with baskets hanging from the open beam ceiling. The cafe is open in summer daily noon to 8pm and accepts Amex, Discover, MasterCard, and Visa. Lynne has a room and a couple of cabins for rent, too.

The other choice is **Homeshore Cafe,** at Gustavus's central intersection on Wilson Road (© **907/697-2822**), where a young family serves meals all year in a dining room with about 40 seats next door to an art gallery. The menu includes pizza, calzones, sandwiches, salad, and the like; a large pizza is $20 to $25, sandwiches $10. Summer hours are Monday through Saturday 11:30am to 2pm and 5 to 8:30pm; winter Tuesday through Friday 11:30am to 1:30pm and 4:30 to 6:30pm, staying open Friday until 7:30pm. The cafe accepts Visa and MasterCard.

9 Haines: Eagles & the Unexpected

For years we always just passed through Haines on the way from the ferry up the highway. I didn't know what I was missing until I stopped and took a couple of days to really investigate. Now Haines is one of my favorite Alaska towns.

Haines is casual, happy, and slightly odd. It waits for you to find it, but, once found, it unveils wonderful charms. If you're looking for the mythical town of Cicely from television's *Northern Exposure,* you'll get closer in Haines than anyplace else I know (in fact, the producers scouted here before choosing to shoot in Roslyn, Washington). As I walked down a sidewalk, I saw a sign in a storefront that said to look in the big tree across the street. I looked, and there was an eagle peering back at me. At the Alaska Indian Arts Native cultural center, seeking an office or a ticket window or someone in charge, I wandered into a totem pole studio where a carver was completing a major commission. He gladly stopped to talk. It turned out there wasn't anyone in charge. Issues that are a big deal in some other towns just aren't in Haines.

Haines's dominant feature, the 1904 **Fort William H. Seward,** gives the town a pastoral atmosphere. The fort is a collection of grand white-clapboard buildings arranged around a 9-acre parade ground, in the middle of which stands a Tlingit clan house—out of place, yes, but wonderfully symbolic of Haines. The town is a friendly, accessible center of Tlingit culture as well as a retired outpost of seemingly pointless military activity.

And Haines has **bald eagles**—always plenty of bald eagles, and in the fall, a ridiculous number of bald eagles. More, in fact, than anywhere else on Earth. The chance to see the birds draws people into the outdoors here. There are well-established guides for any activity you might want to pursue, all cooperating and located together. There are some excellent hiking trails right from town, as well as protected sea-kayaking waters. Also, it's worth noting that because of its location in the flow of weather, adjacent to the drier Interior, Haines is not quite as rainy as towns farther south.

The big controversy of local politics concerns how firmly Haines should embrace tourism. Some want Haines to remain friendly, funky, and forgotten, while others hope new recognition the town has recently received for its attraction to visitors will help start an economic boom. In 2004, two national magazines listed Haines as one of the best places to go. Having written for travel magazines, I can assure you most of those "best of" lists are entirely bogus, made up off the top of the head over doughnuts in the conference room—but in this case they got it right, either letting the cat out of the bag or exposing a suppressed truth, depending on your point of view. Even as tourism growth divides residents, however, another laurel has united them, one that really makes Haines people beam with pride: In 2005 *Library Journal* and the Bill and Melinda Gates Foundation cited Haines' library as the best small library in America. Maybe it's just me, but I think a town that's proudest of its library must have a good heart.

ESSENTIALS

GETTING THERE   The **Alaska Marine Highway System** (© **800/642-0066,** or 907/766-2111 locally; www.ferryalaska.com), is how most people get to Haines, and the cruise on the Lynn Canal fjord from Juneau or Skagway is among the most beautiful in the Inside Passage. The conventional ferry takes almost 5 hours from Juneau, the fast ferry about half that. The Juneau-Haines fare is $37. The trip to Skagway takes an hour and the fare is $31. The dock is 5 miles north of town.

There is currently only one van service meeting the ferry, **Haines Shuttle and Tours** (© **907/766-3138**), which charges a pricey $20 for the short ride.

If you're just going to or from Skagway without a car, a good alternative is the Haines-Skagway Fast Ferry, operated by **Chilkat Cruises and Tours** (© **888/766-2103** or 907/766-2100; www.chilkatcruises.com). The company's 150-passenger catamaran makes at least three daily 35-minute round-trips Monday through Friday and two a day Saturday through Sunday. The boat leaves from the Port Chilkoot dock, below Fort William Seward. Adult round-trips are $54, one-way $30; children 12 and under pay half price.

If you're driving, the **Haines Highway** leads 155 miles to Haines Junction, Yukon Territory, an intersection with the Alaska Highway (you must pass through Canadian Customs—see section 5, "The Alaska Highway," in chapter 9 for rules). The road runs along the Chilkat River and the bald eagle preserve, then climbs into spectacular alpine terrain. Anchorage is 760 driving miles from Haines and Fairbanks is 644.

Several air services offer scheduled prop service, air taxis, and flightseeing tours to surrounding communities from Haines. **Wings of Alaska** (© **907/789-0790** reservations, or 907/766-2030 in Haines; www.ichoosewings.com) has plenty of flights, charging $186 round-trip from Juneau.

VISITOR INFORMATION   The small but well-staffed and -stocked **Haines Convention and Visitors Bureau Visitor Information Center,** 2nd Avenue near Willard (P.O. Box 530), Haines, AK 99827 (© **800/458-3579** or 907/766-2234; www.haines. ak.us), is operated by the local government, which also sends out a vacation-planning packet. It's open summer Monday through Friday from 8am to 7pm, Saturday and Sunday from 9am to 6pm; in winter, hours are Monday through Friday from 8am to 5pm.

ORIENTATION   Haines sits on the narrow Chilkat Peninsula near the north end of the Southeast Alaska Panhandle. Highways run north and east on either side of the peninsula; the one on the east side goes to the ferry dock, 5 miles out, and ends after 11 miles at **Chilkoot Lake.** The other is the **Haines Highway,** which leads to the Canadian border, the Alaska Highway, and the rest of the world. The town has two parts: the sparsely built downtown grid and, a short walk to the west down Front Street or 2nd Avenue, the Fort William Seward area.

GETTING AROUND   Bikes are available from **Sockeye Cycle,** just uphill from the Port Chilkoot Dock on Portage Street in the Fort William Seward area (© **907/766-2869;** www.cyclealaska.com), for $14 for 2 hours or $35 for 8 hours. **Haines Shuttle and Tours** is a taxi and shuttle service. It can be reached at © **907/766-3138.**

Rent cars at the Captain's Choice Motel or Hotel Hälsingland (see "Where to Stay," below).

FAST FACTS: **Haines**

Bank **First National Bank of Alaska,** which has an ATM, is at Main Street and 2nd Avenue.

Hospital The **Haines Medical Clinic** (© **907/766-2521**) is on 1st Avenue, near the visitor center.

Haines

ACCOMMODATIONS ■
Alaska Guardhouse **11**
Captain's Choice Motel **3**
Fort Seward B&B **14**
Hotel Hälsingland **15**
The Riverhouse **16**
The Summer Inn B&B **2**

DINING ◆
The Bamboo Room **4**
Commander's Room **15**
Fireweed Restaurant **10**
The Lighthouse **6**
Mountain Market & Café **8**

ATTRACTIONS ●
Alaska Indian Arts
    Cultural Center **13**
American Bald Eagle Foundation
    Natural History Museum **9**
Fort William H. Seward
    National Historic Site **12**
Hammer Museum **5**
Sheldon Museum &
    Cultural Center **7**
Tsirku Canning Co. **1**

Internet Access The gorgeous **Haines Borough Library,** 111 3rd Ave. S. (© **907/ 766-2545,** www.haineslibrary.org) has eight public terminals.

Police Reach city police in nonemergencies at © **907/766-2121.** Outside city limits, call the **Alaska State Troopers** at © **907/766-2552.**

Post Office At 55 Haines Hwy., just west of Fort Seward.

Taxes The local **sales tax** is 5.5%. Tax on accommodations totals 9.5%.

SPECIAL EVENTS   The 160-mile **Kluane to Chilkat International Bike Relay** (© **867/633-2579;** www.kcibr.org) is held the third Saturday in June, heading steeply down the Haines Highway from Haines Junction, with more than 1,000 entrants riding in teams of two, four, or eight.

The **Southeast Alaska State Fair** (© **907/766-2476;** www.seakfair.org) is the biggest event of the summer, held for 4 days in late July; it's a regional small-town get-together, with livestock, cooking, a logging show, a parade, music, and other entertainment. Buildings constructed for the filming of the movie *White Fang* in 1990 were donated to the fair, and form the nucleus of a retail area. One stop of interest here, at any time, is the local microbrewery, Haines Brewing Co. (© **907/766-3823**), which offers samples and informal tours.

The **Alaska Bald Eagle Festival** (© **907/766-3094;** www.baldeaglefestival.org) offers seminars and special events to mark the annual eagle congregation. Held over 5 days in mid-November.

EXPLORING HAINES

Haines has cemented its position as Alaska's center of odd or unusual museums. In the spirit of this distinction, I've described these attractions in the order of their creation, beginning with the Tlingit art center in an old military hospital and ending with the newest addition, a collection of more than 1,800 hammers.

You can't miss **Fort William H. Seward National Historic Site,** the collection of large, white, wood-frame buildings around sloping parade grounds overlooking the magnificent Lynn Canal fjord. (Get the informative *History Walking Tour* brochure of the national historic site from the Haines Convention and Visitors Bureau to learn about each building.)

The fort led a peaceful life, for a military installation. By the time the U.S. Army built it, in 1904, the Klondike gold rush was over, and there's no evidence it ever deterred any attack on this little peninsula at the north end of the Inside Passage. It was deactivated at the end of World War II, when it was used for training.

In 1947 a group of five veterans from the Lower 48 bought the fort as surplus with the notion of forming a planned community. That idea didn't quite work out, but one of the new white families helped spark a Chilkat Tlingit cultural renaissance in the 1950s. The Heinmillers, who still own a majority of the shares in the fort, formed a youth group that evolved into the Chilkat Dancers. A pair of elders led the group in construction of a Tlingit tribal house on the parade grounds. The **Alaska Indian Arts Cultural Center** (© **907/766-2160**) grew from the same movement. Lee Heinmiller, a member of the family's second generation, still manages the arts center, where you can see totem carving and silversmithing practiced. It is open from 9am to 5pm Monday through Friday. The center occupies the old fort hospital on the south side of the parade grounds.

In the downtown area, the **Sheldon Museum and Cultural Center,** 11 Main St. (© **907/766-2366;** www.sheldonmuseum.org), contains an upstairs gallery of well-presented Tlingit art and cultural artifacts; downstairs is a collection on the pioneer history of the town. There's a uniquely personal feel to the Tlingit objects, some of which are displayed with pictures of the artisans who made them and the history of their relationship with the Sheldons, for whom the museum is named. It's open in summer Monday through Friday 10am to 5pm, Saturday and Sunday 1 to 4pm; in winter, it's open Monday through Friday from 1 to 4pm. Admission is $3 for adults, free for children under 12.

The entirely unique **American Bald Eagle Foundation Natural History Museum,** at 2nd Avenue and Haines Highway (© **907/766-3094;** www.baldeagles. org), is essentially a huge, hair-raising diorama of more than 180 eagles and other mounts of Alaska wildlife. Dave Olerud often sits in a wheelchair behind the desk and will talk your ear off about the museum if you want him to—he worked on it for many years and was paralyzed in a fall during construction. Admission is $3 for adults, $1 for children ages 8 to 12; children need to be with an adult. It's open summer Monday through Friday from 10am to 6pm, Saturday and Sunday from 1 to 5pm; closed during the winter.

The **Tsirku Canning Co.,** at 5th Avenue and Main Street (© **907/766-3474;** www.cannerytour.com), is a museum of Alaska salmon canning, full of 80-year-old machinery salvaged from abandoned canneries around the state, including a 120-foot line that goes through the process of canning imaginary fish, including making the can. The fishing industry remains among the state's largest employers, and was long its largest industry by any measure. In 1929, 157 canneries stood all along the coast, teeming with summer workers and served by frequent steamer service, many in places where nothing remains today but broken dock pilings. Haines had nine. The hour-long museum tour costs $10 for adults, free for children ages 12 and under. Call for a recorded message of the time of the next tour, which is changeable.

The newest addition to Haines' line-up of the unusual is the **Hammer Museum,** at 108 Main St., across from the bank (© **907/766-2374**). Longshoreman Dave Pahl created his collection of hammers over a couple of decades of building a homestead. He found the prize of his collection, an 800-year-old Tlingit war hammer, while digging up the foundation of the museum itself. More than 1,800 hammers from all over the world, old and new, exotic and ordinary, fill a tiny space. The fun part is guessing what each is for. It is open summer Monday through Friday 10am to 5pm, closed off season. Admission is $3 for adults, free for children 12 and under.

GETTING OUTSIDE

EAGLE VIEWING   Haines is probably the best place on Earth to see bald eagles. The **Chilkat Bald Eagle Preserve** protects 48,000 acres of river bottom along the Chilkat River. From October to mid-December, peaking around Thanksgiving, up to 3,000 eagles gather in the cottonwood trees (also known as western poplar) on a small section of the river, a phenomenon known as the Fall Congregation. (A healthy 200–400 are residents the rest of the year.) The eagles come for easy winter food: A very late salmon run spawns here into December in a 5-mile stretch of open water known as the Council Grounds. During the congregation, dozens of eagles stand in each of the gnarled, leafless cottonwoods on the riverbanks, occasionally diving for a fish. The best places to see them are pull-outs, paths, and viewing areas along the Haines Highway from miles 18 to 21. Don't walk on the flats, as that disturbs the eagles. The preserve is managed by **Alaska State Parks** (www.alaskastateparks.org, click on "Individual Parks"). Contact the local ranger at © **907/766-2292;** the headquarters is at 400 Willoughby, 3rd Floor, Juneau, AK 99801.

Cruise passengers often see the river on noisy, high-powered jet boats, which environmentalists maintain are damaging the preserve; if you want a more sensitive way of visiting the eagles, many options are available. Local guides offer trips by raft, bicycle, or bus. Most tours happen in the summer, when the eagles are fewer but visitors more numerous. **Chilkat Guides,** based at 1 Mile Haines Hwy. along Sawmill Road (© **888/282-7789** or 907/766-2491; www.raftalaska.com), does a rafting trip several times a day during the summer down the Chilkat to watch the eagles. The water is gentle—if it's too low, there's a chance you'll be asked to get out and push—and you'll see lots of eagles, mostly at a distance. The company is run by young people who create a sense of fellowship with their clients. The 3½-hour trip, with a snack, costs $79 for adults, $62 for children ages 7 to 12. Serious bird-watchers and others who want an in-depth tour should join **Alaska Nature Tours** (© **907/766-2876;** www.alaska naturetours.net), which leads 3-hour wildlife-viewing tours by bus for $65 year-round. The company also offers longer tours, such as all-day guided hikes, for $110, and cross-country skiing in and around the preserve. **Sockeye Cycle,** directly below, visits the eagle preserve on tours, too.

BIKING   **Sockeye Cycle,** at 24 Portage St., near the dock (© **907/766-2869;** www.cyclealaska.com), leads a variety of guided trips—a couple of hours, half- or full day, or even a 9-day trek along gold-rush routes. A 3-hour ride costs $85, and could include various sites around town. Or you can rent your own bicycle for $35 a day. The area is quite conducive to biking.

FISHING   There are several charter operators in Haines for halibut and salmon fishing, and guided freshwater fishing for silver or sockeye salmon, Dolly Varden, and cutthroat trout. The **Haines Convention and Visitors Bureau,** 2nd Street near Willard (P.O. Box 530), Haines, AK 99827 (© **800/458-3579** or 907/766-2234; www.haines.ak.us) can help you find a guide or fishing lodge through the links on their website or the list of operators they keep at the office. For self-guided fishing advice and weekly updates of what's running, contact the local office of the Alaska Department of Fish & Game (© **907/766-2625;** www.alaska.gov/adfg, click on "Sport Fisheries," then the Southeast region on the state map).

See "Sea Kayaking," below, for self-guided boat rental.

FLIGHTSEEING   This is one of Alaska's best places to go flightseeing. The Inside Passage is beautiful, and one mountain away is Glacier Bay National Park; the icefield and the glaciers spilling through to the sea are a sight you won't forget. It's possible to land on an immense glacial icefield and see the sun slicing between the craggy peaks. **Alaska Mountain Flying and Travel,** 132 2nd Ave. (© **800/954-8747** or 907/766-3007; www.flyglacierbay.com), offers these flights—or, as owner Paul Swanstrom says, adventures. He is known for his glacier and beach landings and offers commentary to make flights fully guided experiences. Prices range from $149 to $499 per person, and reservations are recommended. Other flight services offer these tours, too; ask at the visitor center.

HIKING   There are several good trails near Haines, ranging from an easy beach walk to a 10-mile, 3,650-foot climb of **Mount Ripinsky,** north of town (it starts at the top of Young Street). Get the *Haines Is for Hikers* trail guide from the visitors' bureau. The easiest for families is the 2-mile **Battery Point Trail,** which goes along a beach decorated with wild iris. The trail starts at the end of Beach Road, which leads southeast from the Port Chilkoot cruise-ship dock. **Mount Riley** is south of town, with three trail routes to a 1,760-foot summit that features great views and feels much higher than it is; get the trail guide or ask directions to one of the trail heads. **Seduction Point Trail** is 7 miles long, starting at Chilkat State Park at the end of Mud Bay Road south of town and leading to the end of the Chilkat Peninsula. It's a beach walk, so check the tides; they'll give you a tide table at the visitors bureau.

SEA KAYAKING   **Alaska Mountian Guides and International Leadership School** (© **800/766-3396** or 907/766-2100; www.alaskamountainguides.com), offers instruction, short guided trips, longer expeditions, and rentals ($50 a day for a single). A half-day guided paddle is $85, including a snack; a full day, including lunch, is $125.

WHERE TO STAY

Lodging prices are reasonable in Haines and choices include many friendly little places with lots of charm. Besides the larger establishments described below, here are two more excellent places to stay with just a handful of units between them: **Alaska**

Guardhouse (© **866/290-7445** or 907/766-2566; http://alaskaguardhouse.com), a centrally located B&B overlooking the parade grounds with lifelong Alaskan hosts (a lesbian couple) and a homey atmosphere; and **The Riverhouse** (© **907/766-2641; www.riverhousehaines.com**), a house rental in a spectacular spot at the mouth of the Chilkat, a mile from town, which can be rented in whole or, economically, by individual units.

Captain's Choice Motel ⓡ

Many towns have a lot of chainlike hotels and only one or two unique places with character. In Haines, the situation is reversed, and these trim, red-roofed buildings are the one exception to the general eccentricity. The standard rooms contain all the anticipated amenities, yet the motel still has a certain amount of charm. The room decor is on the dark side, with paneling, and is somewhat out-of-date, but it's quite clean, and many of the rooms have good views on a large sun deck.

108 2nd St. N. at Dalton St. (P.O. Box 392), Haines, AK 99827. © **800/478-2345** or 907/766-3111. Fax 907/766-3332. www.capchoice.com. 39 units. High season $117 double; low season $86 double. Year-round $128–$168 suite. Extra person $5. Rates include continental breakfast. AE, DC, DISC, MC, V. **Amenities:** Tour desk; car rental; courtesy van; limited room service; coin-op laundry. *In room:* TV, fridge, coffeemaker, hair dryer, microwave, Wi-Fi.

Fort Seward Bed and Breakfast ⓡ *Finds*

The fort surgeon's quarters overlook the parade grounds and the Lynn Canal with a big wraparound porch. The inn has an unspoiled historic feel. Norm Smith has lived in this house most of his life and in 1981 started the B&B with his wife, Suzanne, a gifted hostess who instantly makes you feel like an old friend. The rooms have high ceilings, fireplaces, wonderful cabinetry—all kinds of authentic charm. It's a social place, with a barbecue on the porch, and guests are welcome to use the kitchen, where Norm produces a fine full breakfast of sourdough pancakes. Smoking is not allowed.

1 Fort Seward Dr. (P.O. Box 5), Haines, AK 99827. © **800/615-NORM (6676)** or phone/fax 907/766-2856. www.fort sewardalaska.com. 7 units, 4 with private bathroom. High season $99–$135 double; low season $79–$105 double. Extra person $25. Rates include full breakfast. DISC, MC, V. Closed Oct 15–Easter. **Amenities:** Bike loan; kayak rental; courtesy car. *In room:* TV/VCR/DVD.

Hotel Hälsingland ⓡ

This grandly rambling hotel fell on hard times after more than 50 years in the same family until new owners, Jeff and Shannon Butcher, took over in 2002 and started putting in a lot of work, as well as new carpeting, furniture, drapes, paint, and beds. The hotel has always been the most interesting place in town to stay. The group of buildings, designated a National Historic Landmark, served as the commanding officer's quarters for Fort William Seward during both World Wars. You can almost hear well-shined boots on the wood floors, echoing off high ceilings and old-fashioned woodwork. Rooms vary widely, so it's a good idea to take a look before checking in. Some share bathrooms and some of those with private bathrooms have only shower stalls while others have claw-foot tubs. The hotel also books tours and has an RV park out back.

The remodeled **Commander's Room** restaurant, open for dinner only, offers a short menu of well-prepared dishes, with prices for main courses in the $19 to $30 range. The small bar has craft brews on tap. This is a friendly, low-key place in the evening.

Fort William Seward parade grounds (P.O. Box 1649), Haines, AK 99827. © **800/542-6363** or 907/766-2000. Fax 907/766-2060. www.hotelhalsingland.com. 50 units, 45 with private bathroom. $69 double without bathroom, $89–$119 double with private bathroom. AE, DC, DISC, MC, V. Closed mid-Nov to mid-Mar. **Amenities:** Restaurant; bar; tour desk; car rental; courtesy van; coin-op laundry. *In room:* TV, Wi-Fi.

The Summer Inn Bed & Breakfast *Value* This lovely old clapboard house downtown has a big porch and a living room decorated in whites and pale, lacy fabrics, like Grandma's house. The five rooms are cozy but small, and share three bathrooms among them (bathrooms were immaculate when we visited). The house was built by a reputed former member of Soapy Smith's gang in 1912 (see section 10, below for more on Soapy) and the great big claw-foot tub is said to be the first in the history of Haines upstairs bathtubs. No smoking or drinking allowed.

117 2nd Ave. (P.O. Box 1198), Haines, AK 99827. ℂ/fax **907/766-2970.** www.summerinnbnb.com. 5 units, none with private bathroom. High season $90 double, $105 suite; low season $80 double, $95 suite. Extra adult $20, extra child $15. Rates include full breakfast. MC, V.

WHERE TO DINE

Haines has a few consistently good restaurants—which is a few more than most other Alaska towns this size—and you can also eat well during the summer at the Hotel Hälsingland (see "Where to Stay," above). There are lots of places for a casual meal, as well. Among the best lunch places is the **Mountain Market & Café** ⊛, a natural food and grocery store at 3rd Avenue and the Haines Highway (ℂ **907/766-3340**). A primary town hangout and the best espresso stop, it serves hearty and reasonably priced sandwiches, tortilla wraps, and soups, and many fresh baked goods. Pick up a picnic, or stop by for coffee, roasted in-house, or breakfast. The liquor store carries organic wine.

The Bamboo Room ⊛ DINER/SEAFOOD The building started as a French restaurant during the gold-rush era and then became a brothel and speakeasy before the Tengs family got it in 1953. The history is on the back of the menu. In the current generation the food has taken center stage from the bar. The two parts are divided by attractive etched glass but both are smoke-free. The diner serves burgers, salads, pasta, and lots of seafood. Many light and healthful items are on the menu along with the solid fried foods. Get the halibut and chips.

2nd Ave. near Main St. ℂ **907/766-2474.** www.bamboopioneer.net. Lunch $7–$13; dinner $8–$25. AE, DC, DISC, MC, V. Summer daily 6am–11pm; winter daily 6am–8pm.

Fireweed Restaurant ⊛ PIZZA/SANDWICHES A historic building in Fort Seward was remodeled into the most attractive dining room in Haines using salvaged wood from other old buildings: natural tones, handcrafted wood and local art, and photography create a softly aesthetic setting. With only seven tables the place can get a bit crowded and noisy, but the popularity attests to the quality of the casual food. The menu includes pizza starting at $20 for a large pie with diner's choice of many exotic ingredients, and it's consistently great, as are the calzones. Otherwise, there are a few sandwiches and salads (also good), soup, burgers, and the like.

⸢Tips⸣ A Quick Side Trip to Juneau from Haines or Skagway

Without changing your lodgings, you can travel from Skagway or Haines for a tour of Juneau's highlights and a sightseeing day cruise of the Lynn Canal. **Alaska Fjordlines'** high-speed catamaran (ℂ **800-320-0146** or 907/766-3395; www.alaskafjordlines.com) carries passengers for half a day in Juneau, with wildlife sightings on the way. The fare is $159, including a narrated bus tour of Juneau and Mendenhall Glacier. The whole excursion is about 12 hours.

Historic building #37, Blacksmith Rd. ⓒ **907/766-3838.** Lunch $7–$14; dinner $12–$20. MC, V. Summer daily 11am–11pm; Apr and Sept daily 4:30–9pm. Closed Oct–Mar.

The Lighthouse ⭑⭑ SEAFOOD/HAWAIIAN   Chef Song Nash, who grew up in Haines, was avoiding returning to his job cooking at a private resort in Hawaii when he made a suggestion to the owner of a local supermarket buying this threadbare waterfront restaurant. Nash convinced the new owner to turn the restaurant over to him to see what he could do with it. The result is a style of dining Haines has never seen before. Nash remodeled completely, updating the interior by 50 years to make it light and stylish and putting in new windows to take good advantage of the spectacular water view (don't let the saloon exterior scare you away). Drawing on his experience as a chef with flavors from the South Pacific, and his experience as a hand on his family's commercial fishing boat, Nash created a style of cuisine fusing the two. Main courses include ginger Alaskan sable fish with coconut wasabi sauce, which was terrific, and blackened Lynn Canal sockeye salmon with Hawaiian relish; there are also many conventional seafood restaurant staples, steaks, and such. The lunch menu is extensive, too. Service is quick and professional.

Main and Front sts ⓒ **907/766-2442.** Lunch $9–$12; dinner $10–$26. AE, DC, DISC, MC, V. High season daily 8am–10pm; low season daily 11:30am–9pm.

10 Skagway: After the Gold Rush

It's only been 110 years since white civilization came to Alaska. There were a few scattered towns in the Southeast before that—Juneau, Sitka, and Wrangell, for example—but until the Klondike gold rush, the great mass of Alaska was populated only by Natives who had never seen a white face. Then, in a single year, 1898, the population exploded. That year still stands as the greatest in Alaska's short but eventful history, for the influx of those people set the patterns of development ever since.

In the gold-rush years of 1897 and 1898, Skagway and its ghost-town twin city of Dyea were the logical places to get off the boat to head off on the trek to the gold fields near the new city of Dawson City, Yukon Territories. (See "Dawson City & Eagle: Detour into History," p. 418.) Skagway instantly grew from a single homestead to a population of between 15,000 and 25,000. No one knows exactly how many, partly because the people were flowing through too quickly to count and partly because there was no civil authority to count them. This was a wide-open boomtown, a true Wild West outpost that in its biggest years was completely without law other than the survival of the meanest.

Then, almost as quickly as it started, the rush ended and the town deflated.

But Skagway survived by showing off where it all happened. In 1896 there was a single log cabin in Skagway, in 1897 the word of the Klondike strike made it to the outside world, and in 1898 Skagway was a huge gold-rush boomtown. In 1899 the gold rush was ending, and in 1903, 300 tourists arrived in a single day to see where the gold rush happened. By 1908, local businessmen had started developing tourist attractions, moving picturesque gold-rush buildings to Broadway, the main street, to create a more unified image when visitors arrived on the steamers. By 1920, tourism had become an important part of the economy. By 1933, historic preservation efforts had started. Today, more money and more than 20 times as many visitors come through in a year as made the trip to the Klondike during the gold rush.

With 862 residents and more than 900,000 visitors annually, the "real" town has all but disappeared, and most of the people you'll meet are either fellow visitors or summer workers brought north to serve them. Most of the tourists are from cruise ships—it's not unusual for several ships to hit town in a single morning, unleashing as many as 9,000 people at once up the wharf and into the one historic street. There are plenty of highway and ferry travelers, too, and outdoor enthusiasts come to do the Chilkoot Trail, just as the stampeders did.

Is it worth all those visits? Skagway, spared from fire and recognized so long ago for its history, may be the best-preserved gold-rush town in the United States. What happened here in a 2-year period was certainly extraordinary, even if the phenomenon the town celebrates is one of mass insanity based on greed, inhumanity, thuggery, prostitution, waste, and, for most, abject failure. While Canada was well policed by the Mounties, Skagway was truly lawless—a hell on Earth, as one Mountie described it. Soapy Smith ruled this scam-pire with a team of con artists and toughs who milked the suckers for every dollar available. Half of the stories about Soapy are probably lies, but here's one too good not to repeat: He set up a telegraph office for suckers to wire their money home, but with no telegraph line. Such was his influence and high repute in the newspapers he controlled that the governor offered to put Smith officially in charge as a territorial marshal and rode with him in the 1898 Independence Day parade. Four days later, Smith was shot dead in a gunfight with Frank Reid, who led a vigilante committee upset over one of Smith's thefts. Reid died of wounds sustained in the shootout, too, but Soapy Smith's gang was broken. Of course, the gold rush was about to end anyway.

In 1976 the National Park Service began buying many of Skagway's best old buildings for the **Klondike Gold Rush National Historic District,** and now it owns about 15, having completed restoration in 1999. Broadway is a prosperous, freshly painted 6-block strip of gold-rush-era buildings. A few that look like real businesses turn out to be displays showing how it was back then. Other buildings restored by the Park Service are under lease to gift shops and such. Sadly, those historic businesses not preserved by the Park Service have been lost to the onslaught of cruise-ship oriented shopping: A curio shop operating since the gold rush was converted a few years ago, and in 2002 the longest-operating hotel in Alaska, which dated from the earliest days, became a T-shirt shop.

ESSENTIALS

GETTING THERE The **Alaska Marine Highway System** (© **800/642-0066,** or 907/983-2941 locally; www.ferryalaska.com) connects Skagway daily with Haines and Juneau. The fare is $31 from Haines, $50 from Juneau. If you're headed to Haines without a vehicle, consider the private passenger ferry listed under "Getting There," in section 9 earlier in this chapter. Haines is 15 miles away by boat but more than 350 miles by road.

Since 1978, **Klondike Highway 2** has traced the route of the stampeders through the White Pass into Canada, a parallel route to the Chilkoot Trail. The road runs 99 miles, then meets the Alaska Highway a dozen miles southeast of the Yukon capital of Whitehorse. The border is at the top of the pass, 14 miles from Skagway. (See p. 417 in chapter 9 for information on customs.) This is one of the most spectacular drives anywhere in Alaska, with views basically equivalent to those from the White Pass and Yukon Route railway (but a lot cheaper). The road is a well-maintained two-lane high-

Skagway

ATTRACTIONS ●
Corrington Museum of
Alaska History **6**
Mascot Saloon **8**
Mollie Walsh Park **11**
Moore House **10**
National Park Service
Visitor Center **13**
Skagway Museum &
Archives **12**
The White Pass &
Yukon Route Depot **14**

ACCOMMODATIONS ■
At the White House **2**
Mile Zero B&B **1**
Sgt. Preston's Lodge **4**
Skagway Home Hostel **3**

DINING ◆
Glacial Smoothies &
Espresso **5**
Starfire **9**
The Stowaway Café **15**
Sweet Tooth Café **7**

way with wide shoulders. Do it in clear weather, if possible, as in cloudy weather all you'll see is whiteout.

Car rentals in Skagway are available from **Avis,** in the Westmark Hotel at 3rd and Spring streets (© **800/230-4898** or 907/983-2247; www.avis.com).

Riding the ferry to Skagway and then heading inland in a rented RV is an attractive option. Expect to pay around $230 a day, plus many required extras (it's not a cheap option). **Alaska Motorhome Rentals** (© **800/254-9929;** www.bestofalaska travel.com) rents RVs one-way to Anchorage with a drop-off fee of $695 to $895, plus the cost of the rental, mileage, and gas. The same company, under a different name, also offers structured RV tours from Skagway as add-ons to cruise vacations; that's covered in chapter 2 under "Getting There & Getting Around."

Traveling by bus between Skagway and Anchorage or Fairbanks is not a practical option for most travelers. It's a marginal business to be in and operators change annually. At best, the journey takes a couple of days. If taking the bus is your goal, contact the Skagway Convention and Visitors Bureau (see "Visitor Information," below) for the latest advice.

The Gold Rush in Context

The 1898 Klondike gold rush was the single biggest event in Alaska history. You'll be hearing a lot about it. Here's some of the context for the barrage of anecdotes you can expect.

Prospectors sought gold in small numbers even before Russia sold Alaska to the United States in 1867, but the Russians' main interest in Alaska was sea otter pelts, and they made few forays beyond the coast, leaving the great mass of the north and Interior unexplored. When the United States took over, Alaska had virtually no white population, and what it had was concentrated in the Southeast—in Sitka, the Russian capital; in a few other Russian settlements; and at the trading post of Wrangell, which miners used as a jumping-off point for gold fields up the Stikine River in British Columbia.

After the American flag went up over Sitka, prospectors slowly worked their way into Alaska's vastness, often led by or in partnership with Natives who knew the country. Called **sourdoughs** for the live yeast-and-flour mixture they carried to make their bread, these were tough wilderness men living way beyond the law and communication with the outside world. A few of them struck it rich. In 1880, a major find on the Gastineau Channel started the city of Juneau and decades of industrial, hard-rock mining there. Finds followed on the Fortymile River in 1886 (on the Taylor Hwy.), near Circle in 1893 (on the Steese Hwy.), and near Hope on the Kenai Peninsula in 1895 (on the Seward Hwy.). Gold slowly brought more people to Alaska, but not enough to catch the nation's attention.

In 1896, white prospector George Carmack and his Native partners, Tagish Charlie and Skookum Jim, found gold on the Klondike River, a tributary to the Yukon in Canada. Word traveled downriver to the gold fields in the Fortymile Country, and within 48 hours that area was empty and claims on the Klondike were being staked. The miners dug gravel from the creek that winter, and when they washed it in the spring, it yielded big hunks of solid gold, a massive discovery. They were instant millionaires in a time when a million dollars meant something.

It's hard to grasp today the impact of the news on the outside world. The U.S. economy was deeply in depression. The dollar was on a gold standard and the scarcity of gold had caused a deflationary vise that in 1893 brought a banking collapse and national unemployment of 18%. Suddenly, in 1897, a steamer arrived in Seattle bearing men from a place called the Klondike with trunks and gunny sacks full of gold. The supply of money suddenly grew and economic confidence returned. The national economy turned around on the news, and some 100,000 people set off for Alaska to get rich, too, plunging off into a trackless wilderness for which most were completely unprepared.

Contemporary Alaska marks the Klondike gold rush as the start of its history. Before the gold rush, Alaska largely remained as it had been for thousands of years, ruled and inhabited by its indigenous people. As late as the

1880 census, the territory had fewer than 500 white residents, and only 4,000 by 1890—it was virtually empty from the point of view of those who discounted the Alaska Natives. In 1898, the stampede began, bringing an instant population. Even the mayor of Seattle left for Alaska. Within a few years, Alaska had cities, telegraph lines, riverboats, and sled-dog mail routes. About 30,000 made it all the way to Dawson City. Few of that number struck it rich, but those who built the towns and businesses to serve them did—there were suddenly saloons and brothels, dress shops, and photo studios. Promoters sold a credulous public newly laid-out towns on supposed routes to the gold fields, including routes that were essentially impassable.

The White Pass above Skagway and the Chilkoot Pass above Dyea carried the most stampeders. Gold seekers arrived in the crazily lawless settlements by steamer from Seattle, got robbed and cheated, and then ferried their goods over the passes to Lake Bennett. (Upon completion of the railroad through the White Pass in 1901, Dyea and the Chilkoot Pass were abandoned, but Skagway lives on.) The Canadian authorities wisely required each stampeder to bring a ton of supplies, a rule that undoubtedly prevented famine but made the single-file journey over the passes a miserable ordeal. Prospectors sometimes had to make dozens of trips up the trail to get their supplies over the pass. At Lake Bennett, the stampeders built boats, crossed the lake, and floated down the Yukon River, through the dangerous Five Finger Rapids, to Dawson City, a 500-mile journey from the sea.

Imagine their disappointment when they found, on their arrival, that the gold claims had all been staked and big companies were taking over. Prospectors looking to strike it rich had humbling choices. The smart ones started businesses to make money off the other stampeders, and some of them did quite well. Others worked for wages or went home. But many continued in pursuit of the next find. Their wild chase for gold drew the modern map of Alaska, founding dozens of towns. Many of these towns disappeared as soon as the frenzy cooled and now are entirely forgotten or live on only as place names, but some became real cities. Nome came in 1899; Fairbanks in 1902; Kantishna, now within Denali National Park, in 1905; Iditarod in 1908; and many others, until the rush finally ended with the start of World War I in 1914.

Even without a rush, there's still gold to be dug. Ever larger and more sophisticated machinery worked the Klondike claims and washed the gravel until the 1960s, and gold mining remains an important part of that area's economy to this day. Small-time prospectors are still looking all over Alaska and working their claims, and sometimes someone does make a significant new strike. A find still being explored in Alaska's Bristol Bay region is said to contain at least $300 billion in gold and other minerals, making it one of the largest deposits in the world.

Several air taxi operators serve Skagway. A round-trip from Juneau costs $200 on **Wings of Alaska** (© **907/789-0790** reservations, or 907/983-2442 in Skagway; www.ichoosewings.com).

VISITOR INFORMATION   Located in the restored railroad depot, the **National Park Service Visitor Center,** 2nd Avenue and Broadway (P.O. Box 517), Skagway, AK 99840 (© **907/983-9223;** www.nps.gov/klgo), is the focal point for activities in Skagway. Rangers answer questions, give lectures, and show films, and five times a day lead an excellent guided walking tour. The building houses a small museum that lays the groundwork for the rest of what you'll see. The Park Service's programs are free. The visitor center is open early May through late September daily from 8am to 6pm, the rest of the year the museum is open Monday through Friday from 8am to 5pm.

The **Skagway Convention and Visitors Bureau Center,** 245 Broadway (P.O. Box 1029), Skagway, AK 99840 (© **907/983-2854,** fax 907/983-3854; www.skagway.com), occupies the historic Arctic Brotherhood Hall, the building with the driftwood facade. The website contains links to lodgings and activities, or you can request the same information on paper (order by calling © 888/762-1898). Stop in especially for the handy and informative *Skagway Walking Tour Map* of historic sites. The center is open summer daily from 8am to 6pm; winter Monday through Friday from 8am to 5pm.

GETTING AROUND   Skagway is laid out on a simple grid, with streets branching off from Broadway. The main sights can be reached on foot. For places you can't walk, try the **Dyea Dave Shuttle** (© **907/209-5031**), which operates like a taxi. Skagway also has a bus, called **SMART** (© **907/983-2743**), which runs a circuit around town for $1.50 a ride, or out of town to sites such as the Klondike Gold Dredge for $5, leaving on the hour from City Hall and 7th Avenue and Spring Street. A bike is fun and practical transportation in Skagway. **Sockeye Cycle,** on 5th Avenue off Broadway (© **907/983-2851;** www.cyclealaska.com), rents good mountain bikes for $14 for 2 hours and leads guided day trips (see "Getting Outside," below).

FAST FACTS: Skagway

Bank **Wells Fargo,** at Broadway and 6th Avenue, has an ATM.

Hospital The **Dahl Medical Clinic,** staffed by a physician's assistant, can be reached at © **907/983-2255** during business hours.

Internet Access **Alaska Cruiseship Services,** charging $6 an hour, at 2nd Avenue and State Street (© **907/983-3398**).

Police For nonemergency business, call © **907/983-2232.** The station is located at State Street, just south of 1st Avenue.

Post Office On Broadway between 6th and 7th avenues.

Taxes **Sales tax** is 4%. The bed tax totals 8%.

SPECIAL EVENTS   The springtime **Buckwheat Ski Classic,** in the deep snow of the White Pass, is as much for fun as it is for Nordic skiing competition. Various events for adults and kids range from 5 to 50 kilometers. Racers often wear costumes and carry libations, and spectators carve villages from the snow to drink beer and soak up the warm spring sun. A dinner and dance follow. It happens March 22, 2008.

Skagway's July 4th Parade and Celebration, organized by the chamber of commerce and featuring lots of small-town events, has been a big deal since Soapy Smith led the parade in 1898. **The Klondike Road Relay,** a 110-mile overnight footrace over the pass, brings hundreds of runners in teams of 10 from all over the state September 12, 2008. Call the visitor center for information on any of these events.

EXPLORING SKAGWAY

You can see most of Skagway on foot, and everything by bike. Many companies also offer car, van, or bus tours, too. No one goes to greater lengths to give visitors a unique experience than the **Skagway Street Car Company,** 270 2nd Ave. (© **907/983-2908;** www.skagwaystreetcar.com), which uses antique touring vehicles and costumed guides performing "theater without walls." The amusing 2-hour streetcar tour, based on a tour originally given to President Harding in 1923, is $40 for adults and $20 for children 12 and under. The company operates out of a big gift shop with an espresso counter and a theater, where the tour finishes. Book the tour at least 2 weeks in advance, as they're always sold out.

TOURING THE HISTORIC PARK

The main thing to do in Skagway is to see the old buildings and historic gold-rush places. Do it with the *Skagway Walking Tour Map* or join a fascinating National Park Service guided walking tour (see "Visitor Information," above).

Start with a visit to the **museum** at the National Park Service Visitor Center and in the building next door. It helps put everything else in context. Of greatest interest is a collection of food and gear similar to the ton of supplies each prospector was required to carry over the pass in order to gain entry into Canada, a requirement that prevented famine among the stampeders, but made the job of getting to Dawson City an epic struggle.

While they prepared to go over the pass, gold-rush greenhorns spent their time in Skagway drinking and getting fleeced in the many gambling dens and brothels. Nothing was against the law in the town's heyday because there was no civil authority. It's hard to picture at times, because everything looks so orderly now, but the Park Service has tried. For example, the **Mascot Saloon,** at Broadway and 3rd Avenue, has statues bellying up to the bar. It's open daily from 8am to 6pm; admission is free.

The Park Service walking tour ends at the 1897 **Moore House,** near 5th Avenue and Spring Street, open from 10am to 5pm during the summer. Ten years before the gold rush happened, Capt. William Moore brilliantly predicted it and homesteaded the land that would become Skagway, knowing that this would be a key staging area. He built a cabin in 1887, which stands nearby and is open for inspection. But when the rush hit, the stampeders simply ignored his property claims and built the city on his land without offering compensation. Years later, he won in court.

A block east, on 6th Avenue, is **Mollie Walsh Park,** with a good children's play area, public restrooms, and phones. A sign tells the sad story of one of Skagway's first respectable women, a lady who chose to marry the wrong man among two suitors and was killed by him in a drunken rage. The other suitor—who'd previously killed another rival for her affections—commissioned the bust of Walsh that stands in the park.

The **Gold Rush Cemetery** is 1½ miles from town, up State Street. Used until 1908, it's small and overgrown with spruce trees, but some of the charm and mystery of the place is lost because of the number of visitors and the shiny new paint and maintenance of the wooden markers. The graves of Soapy Smith and Frank Reid are the big attractions, but don't miss the short walk up to Reid Falls. The closely spaced dates on many of the markers attest to the epidemics that swept through mobs of stampeders living in squalid conditions. Remember, there was little sanitation for the tens of thousands who passed this way in 1898.

About 9 miles northwest of Skagway is the ghost town of **Dyea,** where stampeders started climbing the Chilkoot Trail. It's a lovely coastal drive or bike ride: From Skagway, go 2 miles up Klondike Highway 2 and then turn left, continuing 8 miles on gravel road. Dyea is a lot more ghost than town. All that remains are a few boards, broken dock pilings, and miscellaneous iron trash. On a sunny day, however, the protected historical site is a perfect place for a picnic, among beach grasses, fields of wild iris, and the occasional reminder that a city once stood here. The National Park Service leads an interesting guided history and nature walk here daily in summer at 2pm; check at the visitor center. (See "Getting Outside," below, for more on going to Dyea.)

The little-visited **Slide Cemetery,** in the woods near Dyea, is the last resting place of many of the 60 to 70 who died in an avalanche on the Chilkoot Trail on Palm Sunday, April 3, 1898. No one knows how many are here, or exactly who died, or how accurate the wooden markers are. In 1960, when the state reopened the Chilkoot Trail, the cemetery had been completely overgrown and the markers were replaced. But somehow the mystery and forgetting make it an even more ghostly place, and the sense of anonymous, hopeless hardship and death it conveys is as authentic a gold-rush souvenir as anything in Skagway.

MUSEUMS & ATTRACTIONS

The White Pass and Yukon Route ⟨★★⟩   A narrow-gauge railroad line that originally ran to Whitehorse, the White Pass was completed after only 2 years in 1900. It's an engineering marvel and a fun way to see spectacular, historic scenery from a train inching up steep tracks that were chipped out of the side of the mountains. Some of the cars are historic, as well—originals more than 100 years old. The railroad "recommends" you don't get out of your seat, but it's a long ride on a slow train, and most people get up and socialize; however, you cannot move from car to car while the train is moving. The trick is to go in clear weather. When the pass is socked in all you see is white clouds. Tickets are expensive, however, and you have to reserve ahead. Take the gamble: Cancellation carries only a 10% penalty and you can change dates for no charge. Also, try to go on a weekend, when fewer cruise-ship passengers are in town taking up all the seats; weekend trains can be booked as little as a week ahead, while midweek excursions can book up months ahead. The summit excursion—which travels 20 miles with an elevation gain of 2,865 feet, then turns back—takes about 3 hours and costs $98 for adults. All fares are half price for children ages 3 to 12 (except for Chilkoot Pass hiker's fares; see "Backpacking," below).

For a longer journey, trains travel to Carcross, Yukon, with a stop for a hot meal at Lake Bennett. That costs $150. But the biggest treat for a train lover is a steam-powered trip. Saturday and Sunday afternoons steam trains go over the pass to Frasier Meadows, 6 miles beyond the pass, and return. The fare is $125. In either case, bring your passport, as the train goes into Canada.

These days, the line operates only as a tourist attraction, May through September. 2nd Ave. depot (P.O. Box 435), Skagway, AK 99840. © **800/343-7373** or 907/983-2217. www.wpyr.com. For the entire schedule and fares, see the website.

Skagway Museum and Archives ★   The museum contains a fine collection of gold-rush artifacts and other items reflecting Skagway's colorful history. The building is the town's most impressive, and one of the state's most dignified architectural land-marks, with crisp granite walls and a high-pitched roof standing among tall shade trees on the edge of town. It began life as a short-lived gold-rush-era college and later became a federal courthouse and jail. The city hall and museum have occupied the building since 1961 except for a brief hiatus for renovations.

7th and Spring sts. ⓒ **907/983-2420.** Admission $2 adults, $1 students, free for children 12 and under. Summer Mon–Fri 9am–5pm, Sat 10am–5pm, Sun 10am–4pm; winter hours vary, call ahead.

Corrington Museum of Alaska History   The eclectic exhibit that leads into the gift shop is well worth a brief stop. Alaska's history is told in 32 tusks of walrus scrimshaw. Besides owning some rare and interesting items, they've done a good job of putting it all together in an understandable way.

Fifth Ave. and Broadway, in Corrington's Alaska Ivory Co. ⓒ **907/983-2580.** Free admission. Daily Mid-May to mid-Sept 9am–7pm; winter closed.

Klondike Gold Dredge Tours   Gold mining never happened in Skagway; it was only a transit point. But more gold-rush tourists come here than anywhere else, so promoters brought a dredge to where the people are. The 1937 rig, weighing 350 tons, dug up and sorted gravel to remove gold first in Idaho, then near Dawson City, and finally near the border on the Top of the World Highway. A 2-hour visit includes a 10-minute video, costumed guides who spice up the tour with humor, and gold pan-ning in heated water. If you visit Dawson City or Fairbanks, you can see larger dredges in authentic historic settings for less money, but if not, this stop can satisfy your mechanical curiosity and fever to pan for gold.

Mile 1.7 Klondike Hwy. ⓒ **907/983-3175.** www.klondikegolddredge.com. $39 adults, $25 children under age 12. Summer Sun–Fri 8:30am–4:30pm (closed in winter); full tours 9:30am and 1:30pm.

GETTING OUTSIDE

The **Mountain Shop,** 355 4th Ave. (ⓒ **907/983-2544;** www.packerexpeditions.com), rents and sells the equipment you need for backpacking or other outdoor activities in Skagway. The owner, who is also the mayor, leads guided day hikes, backpacking trips, and float trips under the name Packer Expeditions, at the same address.

BACKPACKING   The National Park Service and Parks Canada jointly manage the famous **Chilkoot Pass Trail,** publishing a trail guide and offering information at their offices in Skagway and Whitehorse. Some 20,000 stampeders used the trail to get from Dyea—9 miles from Skagway—to Lake Bennett, 33 miles away, where they could build and launch boats bound for Dawson City. Today about 3,000 people a year make the challenging hike, taking 3 to 5 days. The Chilkoot is not so much a wilderness trail as an outdoor museum, but don't underestimate its difficulty, as so many did during the gold rush.

To control the numbers, **Parks Canada,** 205-300 Main St., Whitehorse, Yukon Y1A 2B5 Canada (ⓒ **800/661-0486** or 867/667-3910; fax 867/393-6701; www.pc. gc.ca/chilkoot), allows only 50 hikers with permits per day to cross the summit. To buy the permits, call with a Visa, American Express, or MasterCard, the date you plan to start, and the campsites you will use each night. Permits are C$53 for adults, C$27 for children ages 16 and under, plus a C$12 per person reservation fee. You pick up the permit at the Trail Centre in Skagway; that's also where 8 of the 50 daily permits are held for walk-ins, to be distributed along with any no-shows. The reservation fee is nonrefundable, and the permit fee is refundable only until a month before the hike.

Once over the pass, you're on Lake Bennett, on the rail line 8 miles short of the road. You can walk to the road, or get back to Skagway on the White Pass and Yukon Route railway (p. 204) at 2pm Friday, Saturday, and Sunday. The one-way fare to Frasier, B.C., is $50 and the scenic 3-hour ride to Skagway is $90. Be sure to make your reservations well in advance, including for a meal at Lake Bennett, if you choose to eat there; you will also need a passport to get back into the United States.

There are two **U.S. Forest Service cabins** near Skagway, and official access to both is by the White Pass and Yukon Route railway. Both are on trails described in the *Skagway Trail Map,* mentioned below. The **Denver Caboose** is an old, red White Pass caboose parked next to the tracks 6 miles up the line at the trail head for the 4.5-mile **Denver Glacier Trail.** The **Laughton Glacier Cabin** is 1½ miles up the Laughton Glacier Trail, whose trail head is at the glacier whistlestop, 14 miles up the tracks. For either, you need a $35 cabin permit (see "Getting Outside in the Tongass National Forest," p. 102, for reservations information) and a train ticket from the railroad. For details, contact the National Park Service visitor center (see "Visitor Information," above), or the **Juneau Ranger District,** 8510 Mendenhall Loop Rd., Juneau, AK 99801 (© **907/586-8800;** www.fs.fed.us/r10/tongass).

BIKING   Sockeye Cycle, on 5th Avenue off Broadway (© **907/983-2851;** www. cyclealaska.com), leads bike tours, including one that takes clients to the top of the White Pass in a van and lets them coast down on bikes; the 2½-hour trip is $75. Going up on White Pass and Yukon Route railroad and riding back down brings the price to $175. Riders must be at least 12 years old. The company also leads a 3-hour tour of the quiet ghost town site of Dyea for $75, going over in a van. I rode to Dyea from Skagway on my own over the hilly, 10-mile coastal road, one of the most pleasant, scenic rides I can remember.

FLIGHTSEEING   Skagway, like Haines, is a good place to choose for a flightseeing trip, as Glacier Bay National Park is just to the west. The flightseeing operators listed in the Haines section offer flights from Skagway, too (p. 189). **Temsco Helicopters** (© **866/683-2900** or 907/983-2900; www.temscoair.com) takes 80-minute tours near Skagway with half that time spent on a glacier (not in Glacier Bay); those flights cost $249. A helicopter and dog-sled tour on Denver Glacier is $449.

HIKING   A *Skagway Trail Map* is available from the visitor center, listing 10 hikes around Skagway. An easy evening walk starts at the footbridge at the west end of the airport parking lot, crossing the Skagway River to **Yakutania Point Park,** where pine trees grow from cracks in the rounded granite of the shoreline. Across the park is a shortcut taking a couple of miles off the trip to Dyea and to the **Skyline Trail and A.B. Mountain,** a strenuous climb to a 5,000-foot summit with great views. On the southeast side of town, across the railroad tracks, a network of trails heads up from Spring Street between 3rd and 4th avenues to a series of mountain lakes, the closest of which is **Lower Dewey Lake,** less than a mile up the trail.

WHERE TO STAY

The accommodations in Skagway are within close walking distance of the historic district, except as noted.

At The White House 🏰 The Tronrud family essentially rebuilt a burned 1902 gable-roofed inn, which has dormer and bow windows and two porticos with small Doric columns. They made the rooms comfortable and modern while retaining the authentic gold-rush style of the original owner, Lee Guthrie, a successful gambler and saloon owner of the early years. The inn has hardwood floors and fine woodwork. Bedrooms vary in size, but all have quilts and other nice touches, including ceiling fans.

Corner of 8th and Main sts. (P.O. Box 41), Skagway, AK 99840-0041. ℂ 907/983-9000. Fax 907/983-9010. www.atthewhitehouse.com. 10 units. High season $125 double; low season $85 double. Extra person $10. Rates include continental breakfast. AE, DISC, MC, V. *In room:* TV, fridge, Wi-Fi.

Chilkoot Trail Outpost 🏰 These beautifully crafted log cabins built in 2002 by longtime residents contain comfortable, modern lodgings with carpeted floors and log interior walls, some in the form of two-room suites, with many amenities, including Wi-Fi, but no phones. The hiker's suite consists of two rooms in a duplex with bunk beds that rent for $135 double, including breakfast. The location, in Dyea near the Chilkoot Trail and Taiya River, puts you in quiet, natural surroundings away from the carnival atmosphere created by the crush of tourists in Skagway proper. In good weather, the hosts have a nightly campfire and provide supplies for s'mores. You can also cook your own food at a barbecue and sink in a screened gazebo. Breakfast, served in a remarkable log building with a vaulted ceiling, consists of a buffet with various choices, including one hot selection, such as eggs or pancakes. Computers are available for guests' use.

7 Mile Dyea Rd. (P.O. Box 286), Skagway, AK 99840. ℂ 907/983-3799. Fax 907/983-3599. www.chilkoottrailoutpost.com. 10 units. $135 double duplex; $165 double cabin. Extra adult $25, extra child 2–11 years $13. MC, V. Rates include full breakfast. Closed off season. **Amenities:** Bike loan. *In room:* TV/VCR, fridge, coffeemaker, hair dryer, microwave, Wi-Fi, no phone.

Mile Zero Bed & Breakfast 🏰 This building was designed to be a B&B and it shows in the details such as the soundproofing and the back doors to every room—guests can access the common rooms through one door or go outside through French doors leading to the porch. The idea is to offer the privacy and convenience of a motel and the warmth and character of a B&B, and it works. The site is a few blocks from the historic area. Smoking is not allowed. There are barbecue facilities on-site and wireless Internet throughout.

9th Ave. and Main St. (P.O. Box 165), Skagway, AK 99840. ℂ 907/983-3045. Fax 907/983-3046. www.mile-zero.com. 6 units. High season $125 double; low season $75 double. Extra person $25. Rates include continental breakfast. MC, V. **Amenities:** Wi-Fi.

Sgt. Preston's Lodge Three buildings sit on a landscaped lawn just steps off Broadway, Skagway's main historic street, at 6th Avenue and State Street. U.S., Canada, and Alaska flags fly out front, underlining the theme, along with the trim tan, red, and green paint scheme, of the tidy image of the Royal Canadian Mounted Police. Once inside, however, you will find typical, modern motel rooms, familiar accommodations for those who simply want a comfortable place to sleep. Ten rooms have only shower stalls—no tubs. All are clean and received new bathrooms and other improvements since 2004, but the lobby has been unkempt on our season visits.

370 6th Ave. (P.O. Box 538), Skagway, AK 99840. ℂ 866/983-2521 or 907/983-2521. Fax 907/983-3500. www.sgtprestonslodge.com. 40 units. High season $85–$110 double; low season $80 double. Extra person age 12 and over $10. AE, DISC, MC, V. **Amenities:** Courtesy car; Wi-Fi. *In room:* TV/DVD; fridge; microwave.

A HOSTEL & CAMPING

A primitive **National Park Service Dyea Campground** has 22 well-separated sites near the water at the ghost town site 9 miles from Skagway. The campground has pit toilets and no water. RVs over 27 feet are not allowed. The fee is $6 (possibly going to $10). The **Pullen Creek RV Park** (© **800/936-3731** or 907/983-2768) is near the small-boat harbor, with coin-operated showers. RV sites with power, water, and dump-station use are $30, car camping sites are $22, tenting with no vehicle $16.

Skagway Home Hostel Frank Wasmer and Nancy Schave open up their historic home to hostellers, sharing their meals, refrigerator, bathrooms, laundry machines, bicycles, and hospitality side by side with guests. The atmosphere is like off-campus shared housing at college, except the house is nicer and better kept. Bunks are in separate male and female dorm rooms except for a single private room. To reserve, use the website, as they don't return long-distance calls. In winter, reservations are required, as Frank and Nancy might otherwise not be there. Summer registration hours are from 5:30 to 10:30pm. No pets, alcohol, or smoking.

3rd Ave. near Main St. (P.O. Box 231), Skagway, AK 99840. © **907/983-2131**. www.skagwayhostel.com. 1 private room, 3 dorms. $15 bunk, $50 double private room. MC, V. **Amenities:** Bike loan; laundry machines ($3).

WHERE TO DINE

Restaurants go out of business and open up faster in Skagway's entirely seasonal economy than anywhere else I know. It's not unusual for a third of the restaurants to be new each year. Asking around for a current recommendation may pay off. Restaurants that stay open year-round tend to be better for two reasons: They can keep their staff, and they have to be good or they wouldn't make it through the winter in a town with fewer than 1,000 residents. The **Sweet Tooth Café**, at 315 Broadway (© **907/983-2405**), is a good, year-round diner, open for breakfast and lunch. **Glacial Smoothies and Espresso,** 336 3rd Ave., off State Street (© **907/983-3223**), has built a year-round clientele serving good coffee, bagels, and wraps. It's a fun little place for a light meal where the kids can play Monopoly or Hungry Hippo while you sip.

Starfire ★ THAI Other menu selections are available, but the specialty here is spicy Thai cuisine—stir fries, curries, soups, and salads. The Pad Thai came in a large portion with a cabbage salad and was cooked and seasoned just right. But the small, 10-table dining room is the restaurant's most memorable aspect, with dark hues and art that create an intimate and relatively upscale experience despite the paper napkins and tight quarters. Service is helpful and speedy and the menu is clearly presented to help those not used to the food to order intelligently.

4th Ave. between Spring St. and Broadway. © **907/983-3663**. Reservations recommended. Lunch and dinner $14–$19. MC, V. Summer Mon–Fri 11am–10pm, Sat–Sun 4–10pm; winter closed.

The Stowaway Cafe ★★ SEAFOOD/CAJUN Housed in a small, gray clapboard house overlooking the boat harbor, a 5-minute walk from the historic sites, this little restaurant has for several years turned out many of Skagway's best meals. Grilled and blackened salmon and halibut anchor the menu; there's also beef, pasta, Thai and French cuisine, and all the usual waterfront restaurant items. Part of the attraction is the restaurant's handmade charm. It was founded and operated by a local couple who put their heart into the place, and the tiny dining room is decorated on a mermaid theme that will keep your attention almost as well as the harbor view. They have a beer and wine license.

End of Congress Way near the small boat harbor. (© **907/983-3463**. Reservations recommended. Dinner $13–$29. V. Summer daily 4–10pm; winter closed.

NIGHTLIFE

Incredibly, the ***Days of '98 Show*** has been playing since 1927 in the Fraternal Order of Eagles Hall No. 25, at 6th Avenue and Broadway ((© **907/983-2545**). Jim Richards carries on the tradition each summer with actors imported from all over the United States, doing four shows a day (10:30am, 12:30pm, 2:30pm, and 8pm) during the summer, fewer in the spring and fall. The evening shows begin with an hour of mock gambling at a casino run by the actors. The actual performance, which lasts an hour, includes singing, cancan dancing, a Robert Service reading, and the story of the shooting of Soapy Smith. All shows are $16. Children 15 and under are half price.

The **Red Onion Saloon,** at 2nd Avenue and Broadway, plays up its gold-rush history, with costumed waitresses wearing corsets. It was a brothel originally—what wasn't in this town?—and mock madams offer $5 tours of a "brothel museum" upstairs. The saloon often has live acoustic music. It closes in winter. **Moe's Frontier Bar,** at 5th Avenue and Broadway, is more of a gritty local hangout, open year-round.

6

Anchorage & Environs

As teenagers living in Anchorage, my cousin and I got a job from a family friend painting his lake cabin. He flew us out on his floatplane and left us there, with paint, food, and a little beer. A creek that ran past the lake was so full of salmon that we caught one on every cast until we got bored and started thinking of ways to make it more difficult. We cooked the salmon over a fire and then floated in a boat on the lake under the endless sunshine of a summer night, talking and diving naked into the clear, green water. We met some guys building another cabin one day, but otherwise we saw no other human beings. When the week was over, the cabin was painted—it didn't take long—and the floatplane came back to get us. As we lifted off and cleared the trees, Anchorage opened in front of us, barely 10 minutes away.

The state's largest city, Anchorage—where 40% of Alaska's population resides—is accused crushingly of being just like a city "Outside," not really part of Alaska at all. It's true that the closer you get to Anchorage, the more the human development reminds you of the outskirts of Anytown, USA, with fast-food franchises, occasional traffic jams, and the ugly big-box retail development inflicted everywhere by relentless corporate logic. You often hear the joke, "Anchorage isn't Alaska, but you can see it from there," and writers piously warn visitors to land in

Anchorage but move on as soon as possible, as if it's catching.

When I hear that advice, I think of the many great experiences I've had here—like painting that cabin, years ago. Anyone in Anchorage with a few hundred dollars for a floatplane can be on a lake or river with the bears and salmon in a matter of minutes, in wilderness deeper than any you could find in the Lower 48. **Chugach State Park** is largely within the city limits, but it's the size of Rocky Mountain National Park and has similar alpine terrain, with the critical difference that most of it is virtually never visited. Yet you can be climbing those mountains after a half-hour drive from your downtown hotel. **Chugach National Forest,** the nation's second largest, is less than an hour down the road. In downtown's **Ship Creek,** people catch 40-pound salmon from under a freeway bridge. Within the city's urban neighborhoods you can bike dozens of miles along the coast or through wooded greenbelts, or ski one of the nation's best Nordic skiing parks.

Anchorage is indeed a big American city, with big-city problems of crime and pollution, but it's also entirely unique for being surrounded by pristine and spectacular wild lands. Anywhere else, Anchorage would be known not for its shortcomings, but as one of America's greatest cities for outdoor enthusiasts.

ANCHORAGE YESTERDAY & TODAY

Anchorage isn't old enough to have a sharp identity as a city. The first mayor to be born here was elected only in 2003 (and he was barely 40). The city started as a tent camp for workers mobilized to build the Alaska Railroad in 1915. A few houses and businesses went up to serve the federal employees who were building and later running the railroad, as Steve McCutcheon's father was. McCutcheon, who died in 1998, remembered a remote, sleepy railroad town enlivened by a couple of large World War II military bases, but was never more than strictly functional. As one visitor who came in the early 1940s wrote, the entire town looked like it was built on the wrong side of the tracks.

McCutcheon looked out the picture window from his living room on a placid lake surrounded by huge, million-dollar houses, each with a floatplane pulled up on the green front lawn, and he recalled the year people started to take Anchorage seriously. It was the year, he said, when they started thinking it would be a permanent city, not just an encampment where you went for a few years to make money before moving on—the year they started building Anchorage to last. That year was 1957. Oil was discovered on the Kenai Peninsula's Swanson River, south of here. It was around that time that McCutcheon built his own house all by itself on a lake, far out in the country. At that time, you could homestead in the Anchorage bowl. Those who had the opportunity but chose not to—my wife's family, for example—gave it a pass only because it seemed too improbable that the flat, wet acreage way out of town would ever be worth anything.

Oil fueled Anchorage's growth like nitrogen fertilizer poured on a shooting weed. Those homesteads that went begging in the 1950s and early 1960s now have shopping malls and high-rise office buildings on them. Fortunes came fast, development was haphazard, and a lot was built that we'd all soon regret. I had the bizarre experience of coming home from college to the town I'd grown up in and getting completely lost in a large area of the city that had been nothing but moose browsing the last time I'd seen it. Visitors found a city full of life but empty of charm.

In the last 20 years, that has started to change. Anchorage is slowly outgrowing its gawky adolescence. It's still young, prosperous, and vibrant—and exhausting when the summer sun refuses to set—but now it also has some excellent restaurants, a good museum, a large Native cultural center, a nice little zoo, and culture in the evening besides the tourist melodramas you'll find in every Alaska town. People still complain that Anchorage isn't really Alaska—in Fairbanks, they call it "Los Anchorage" (and in Anchorage, Fairbanks is known as "Squarebanks")—yet the great wilderness around the city remains intertwined with its streets. Along with a quarter million people, Anchorage is full of moose—so many, they're considered pests and wintertime hazards, inspiring debate about hunting them within the city limits. Bears and bald eagles also show up regularly on the system of greenbelts and bike trails that brings the woods into almost every neighborhood.

Anchorage stands on broad, flat sediment between the Chugach Mountains and the silt-laden waters of upper Cook Inlet. At water's edge, mud flats not yet made into land stretch far offshore when the tide is at its low point, as much as 38 vertical feet below high water. There's a **downtown area** of about 8 by 20 blocks, near Ship Creek where it all started, but most of the city lies on long commercial strips. Like many urban centers built since the arrival of the automobile, the layout is not particularly conducive to any other form of transportation. But the roads go only so far. Just beyond, wilds beckon in the Chugach, along the trails of Turnagain Arm, at Alyeska Ski Resort in Girdwood, in

Prince William Sound and in the Matanuska and Susitna valleys. You'll find ways to that wilderness, and the urban pleasures by its side, throughout this chapter.

1 Essentials

GETTING THERE

BY PLANE   You'll probably get to Anchorage at the start of your trip by air, as the city receives by far the most flights linking Alaska to the rest of the world, on many airlines. The **Ted Stevens Anchorage International Airport** is a major hub. Seattle has the most frequent flights connecting to Anchorage, with numerous domestic carriers flying nonstop all day. (See "Getting There & Getting Around," in chapter 2 for more details.) Within Alaska, most flights route through here, even for communities that are much closer to each other than they are to Anchorage. **Alaska Airlines** (© 800/252-7522; www.alaskaair.com) is the dominant carrier for Alaska destinations, and the only jet operator to most Alaska cities. Various commuter carriers link Anchorage to rural destinations not served by jet. **Era Aviation** (© 800/866-8394 or 907/266-8394; www.flyera.com) is one of the largest for Southcentral Alaska destinations and is a convenient, time-saving alternative to driving to communities like Homer and Kenai. Tickets can be booked directly or through Alaska Airlines.

Unless your hotel has a courtesy van or you rent a car, a taxi is probably the best way to get downtown from the airport. A **taxi ride** downtown from the airport runs $18 to $20. Try **Alaska Yellow Cab** (© 907/222-2222). Shuttle vans serve the airport, with arrangements changing frequently. Ask at the visitor information desk in the baggage claim area.

The People Mover city bus connects the airport and the downtown transit center hourly. Take Spenard Route 7A (every other Route 7 bus on weekdays). For finding schedules and other details on using the People Mover see "Getting Around," below.

BY CAR   There's only one road to the rest of the world: the Glenn Highway. It leads through the Mat-Su Valley area and Glennallen to Tok, where it meets the Alaska Highway, 330 miles from Anchorage. Thirty miles out of Anchorage the Glenn meets the Parks Highway, which leads to Denali National Park and Fairbanks. The only other road out of town, the Seward Highway, leads south to the Kenai Peninsula. See "Alaska's Highways a la Carte" (p. 382) in chapter 9 for a review of all the roads. For more on driving to Alaska, see chapter 2.

BY BUS   **Alaska/Yukon Trails** (© 800/770-7275; www.alaskashuttle.com), a van and minibus service, runs between Anchorage and Fairbanks, with stops in Talkeetna and Denali National Park. From Fairbanks, they run to Dawson City and Whitehorse and offer rural highway tours. In Anchorage they stop at various points, including the airport and the downtown Egan Civic and Convention Center. A one-way ticket to Talkeetna is $45, Denali $65, and Fairbanks $91. Various other van and bus services offer transportation to and from Seward, Homer, Talkeetna, Denali National Park, and other points; options are listed in the sections on each of those places.

BY RV   A recreational vehicle is a popular way to explore the region. Renting an RV in Anchorage for a tour is covered below under "Getting Around." Driving an RV to Alaska is covered in chapter 2. It's also possible to come to Alaska with your own RV without making the time-consuming return trip by shipping your RV back from Anchorage to Tacoma, Washington, and flying to meet it (since southbound ships are relatively empty you get a special rate). Contact **Totem Ocean Trailer Express**

Anchorage

ACCOMMODATIONS ■
Courtyard by Marriott **7**
Dimond Center Hotel **26**
Elderberry B&B **25**
Holiday Inn Express **10**
Lake Hood Inn **9**
Lakeshore Motor Inn **11**
Millennium Alaskan Hotel
  Anchorage **8**
Residence Inn by Marriott **22**
Spenard Hostel International **12**

DINING ◆
Arctic Roadrunner **16, 24**
Bear Tooth Theatrepub &
  Grill **15**
Cafe del Mundo **20**
Campobello Bistro **19**
City Diner **13**
The Greek Corner **17**
Jens' Restaurant **18**
Kaladi Brothers **14**
The Lucky Wishbone **3**
The Moose's Tooth Pub & Pizzeria **21**
New Sagaya's City Market **4**

ATTRACTIONS ●
Alaska Aviation Heritage
  Museum **6**
Alaska Botanical Garden **23**
Alaska Museum of Natural
  History **2**
Alaska Native Heritage Center **1**
The Alaska Zoo **27**
Earthquake Park **5**

(© **800/234-8683** in Anchorage, **800/426-0074** in the Lower 48; www.totemocean. com; e-mail rvshipper@totemocean.com).

In addition, several firms offer one-way rentals between Anchorage and Skagway (the ferry terminus) or cities around the U.S. **Alaska Motorhome Rentals** (© **800/ 254-9929;** www.bestofalaskatravel.com) offers Skagway one-way rentals to Anchorage with a drop-off fee of $695 to $895, Anchorage to Seattle for $895 to $1,095, plus the cost of the rental, $209 to $239 a day in the high season, plus mileage (or pay $30 a day for unlimited mileage), gas (budget generously), and tax. Check the website for discounts. The same company has another operation, **Alaska Highway Cruises** (© **800/323-5757**), that provides packages to cruise one-way, tour Alaska in an RV, and fly home. For more on that option and on one-way rentals from the balance of the Lower 48, see chapter 2.

BY RAIL   The **Alaska Railroad** (© **800/544-0552,** 907/265-2494, or 907/265-2620 TDD; www.alaskarailroad.com) connects Anchorage with Seward and Whittier to the south and Fairbanks and Denali National Park to the north. It's a fun way to travel, with expert commentary in the summer, good food, and clean, comfortable cars. However, the train is priced as a tourism excursion and costs more than ordinary transportation. Most trains run only in the summer, but a snowy 12-hour odyssey to Fairbanks runs once a week all winter. The summer fare to Fairbanks is $189 one-way; the winter fare is $137 one-way, $107 for Alaska residents. See "Getting There" in chapter 8 for fares and service details for Denali National Park.

ORIENTATION

Many visitors never make it beyond the **downtown** area, the old-fashioned grid of streets at the northwest corner of town where the large hotels and gift shops are located. Street numbers and letters work on a simple pattern and navigation is easy. Beyond downtown, most of Anchorage is oriented to commercial strips, and you'll need a map to find your way. The map on p. 213 will suffice for major thoroughfares, but to find anything on smaller streets, pick up a detailed map at the visitor centers, at a grocery store, or on the Internet. Some parts of greater Anchorage are in distinct communities outside the bowl formed by the Chugach Mountains, including **Eagle River** and **Eklutna,** within half an hour on the Glenn Highway to the northeast, and **Girdwood** and **Portage,** on the Seward Highway, 45 minutes to the south. The suburban **Matanuska and Susitna valleys** (known as Mat-Su) lie an hour north of the city on the Glenn and Parks highways.

GETTING AROUND

BY RENTAL CAR   Driving is the most practical way for most independent travelers to tour the main part of Alaska, and the location of Anchorage at the hub of transportation networks makes it the handiest place to start. A car improves a visit to Anchorage, too, as the city is spread out and public transportation and taxi service are poor. Most major car-rental companies operate in Anchorage, largely from desks at the airport in a tunnel off the domestic baggage-claim area. A compact car for $50 a day, with unlimited mileage, is a fair deal. The airport adds a 10% concession fee plus a $4-a-day facility fee, which you can avoid by renting off-site from **Avis,** at 5th Avenue and B Street (© **800/230-4898** or 907/277-4567; www.avis.com) or several other firms. The city charges an 8% rental car tax and the state adds an additional 10% tax. Including the airport fees, taxes total well over a third of the rental price. Sorry about that! Cars can sell out in summer, so reserve ahead. Note, rental contracts generally do not allow vehicles on gravel roads, such as the Denali Highway or McCarthy Road; however, an agency that offers this service in Fairbanks is listed on p. 395.

BY RENTAL RV   Several large RV rental agencies operate in Anchorage (see "Getting There," above). High-season rates are around $1,500 to $1,800 a week, plus the large amount of fuel RVs use and taxes. **ABC Motorhome Rentals,** 3875 Old International Airport Rd. (© **800/421-7456** or 907/279-2000; www.abcmotorhome.com), charges no mileage fee. See chapter 2's "Getting There & Getting Around," for more on this option.

BY BUS   It takes patience to go a long way on the **People Mover** buses (© **907/343-6543;** www.peoplemover.org), especially if you have to transfer, but if you have the time, the system is inexpensive, safe, and covers most of the city. Bus fares all over town are $1.75 for adults; $1 for ages 5 to 18; 50¢ for those over age 60, with disabilities, or with a valid Medicare card; free for ages 4 and under. The transit center bus depot is at 6th Avenue and G Street. Buses generally come every half-hour, hourly on weekends, but to use the system conveniently go online and figure out your route and schedule in advance.

BY BIKE   The network of bike trails is a great way to see the best side of Anchorage, but not a practical means of point-to-point transportation for most people. The **Tony Knowles Coastal Trail** starts right downtown (see "Getting Outside," later in this chapter). Good street bikes are usually for rent near Elderberry Park downtown, at the start of the Coastal Trail, from **Pablo's Bike Rental,** a booth at the corner of 5th and L (© **907/250-2871**). Rates are $20 for 4 hours, $40 for a day. An established bike rental shop with a wide choice of equipment is in the 4th Avenue Market Place at 4th and C: **Downtown Bicycle Rental** (© **907/279-5293;** www.alaska-bike-rentals.com). Rates start at $16 for 3 hours, $4 for each additional hour, $32 max per day. The shop also carries tandems, kids' bikes, and trailers, and clip in shoes and pedals for advanced cyclists. The shop also offers a hikers' shuttle to the Glen Alps parking lot, the trailhead for Flattop Mountain (p. 243).

VISITOR INFORMATION

The **Anchorage Convention and Visitor Bureau,** 524 W. 4th Ave., Anchorage, AK 99501-2212 (© **907/276-4118;** fax 907/278-5559; www.anchorage.net), offers information on the city and the entire state at its centers and extensive website (the site even has a feature to allow visitors to ask questions of volunteers by e-mail). The main location is the **Log Cabin Visitor Information Center,** downtown at 4th Avenue and F Street (© **907/274-3531;** open daily June–Aug 7:30am–7pm, May and Sept 8am–6pm, Oct–Apr 9am–4pm). If it's crowded, go to the storefront office right behind it. You'll also find visitor information desks at the airport: one in the baggage-claim area in the C concourse and in the international terminal.

The **Alaska Public Lands Information Center,** located at 605 W. 4th Ave. (across the intersection from the log cabin at 4th and F), Suite 105, Anchorage, AK 99501 (© **866/869-6887** or 907/271-2737; www.nps.gov/aplic; open daily 9am–5pm in summer, Mon–Fri 10am–5pm in winter), can help anyone planning to spend time outdoors anywhere in Alaska. Exhibits in the grand room with high ceilings—the building was a 1930s post office and federal courthouse—orient visitors to Alaska's geography and outdoor activities and make an excellent starting point for your trip. When you're ready for details, you will find all the land agencies represented by rangers whose advice is based on personal experience. Be sure to pick up the free booklets they distribute on the highways and parks you will be visiting and pick from an excellent selection of trail and field guides at the bookstore. Even if you have no need for information, stop in for free films, presentations, and children's programs. You'll have to pass through a federal security checkpoint at the entrance, but the center is well worth the trouble.

SPECIAL EVENTS

For more events, and online calendars, see "The Performing Arts," later. The **Anchorage Folk Festival** (© 907/566-2334; www.anchoragefolkfestival.org), the last two weekends of January, imports musicians and shows off local talent in free concerts, workshops, and jam sessions, as well as four guest musician dances that raise money for the festival. They have other events through the year, including an August fiddle camp and a Novemberfest; check the website for times and venues.

The **Fur Rendezvous Winter Festival** (© 907/274-1177; www.furrondy.net), February 22 through March 2, 2007, is a winter celebration of many decades longevity, featuring community events, a parade, fireworks, a carnival, craft fairs, snowshoe softball, dog-sled rides, and other fun. Of late, the festival has suffered shaky finances, so check ahead if you're planning it as part of your trip. The Rondy's traditional centerpiece is the **World Champion Sled Dog Race,** a 3-day sprint event of about 25 miles per heat. In addition, the last weekend of the festival coincides with the start of the **Iditarod Trail Sled Dog Race** (© 907/376-5155; www.iditarod.com). The Iditarod, long Alaska's biggest winter event, has recently grown dramatically as a tourist attraction, bringing in a flood of visitors who combine seeing the race with winter sports and festivals in Anchorage and Fairbanks. On the weekend of the start, the streets of Anchorage fill with foreign languages, as European visitors come in disproportionate numbers. The Iditarod begins from Anchorage the first Saturday in March (in 2008, March 2) and then proceeds in trucks to the restart the next day in the Mat-Su Valley for the 1,000-mile run to Nome (see section 6 in chapter 10 for more details).

The **Native Youth Olympics** (© 907/793-3267), held by the Cook Inlet Tribal Council in April at the Sullivan Arena (a children's event is in January), is a tough competition in traditional Alaska Native games such as the seal hop (done on the knuckles) and the spectacular high kick, in which young men kick a ball suspended as high as 9 feet off the floor. Admission and parking are free.

The **Anchorage Market & Festival** is a big street fair and farmer's market held every weekend from mid-May through mid-September at 3rd Avenue and E Street (© 907/272-5634; www.anchoragemarkets.com).

The stocked salmon runs in Ship Creek, which runs right through downtown Anchorage, produce one of the town's most popular summer activities (see "Roadside Fishing," p. 244). The **Slam'n Salm'n Derbies** (© 907/646-4846; www.shipcreek salmonderby.com) add the possibility of winning money and prizes for fishing. The derby for kings is in early June and another for silvers is in early August. One-day tickets are $10 and benefit the Downtown Soup Kitchen; they are available at the derby headquarters in the Alaska Railroad plaza near the creek.

The **Blues on the Green** music festival, the first weekend in June, takes place under the sky in the natural amphitheater at Kincaid Park. It is an all-day, all-evening blues concert. Headliners in the past have included Taj Mahal, Bo Diddley, and Buddy Guy.

The **Alaska State Fair** (© 907/745-4827; www.alaskastatefair.org), which culminates a 12-day run on Labor Day each year, is the biggest event in the area. It takes place in Palmer, 40 miles north of Anchorage on the Glenn Highway. In most ways, it's a typical state fair, with rides, booths, exhibits, contests, fireworks, and live music.

Not typical are the vegetables. The good soil and long days in the Matanuska Valley around Palmer boost their growth to massive size, the stuff of childhood nightmares. Cabbages are the size of beanbag chairs. A mere beach-ball-size cabbage would be laughed off the stage. And it's not just the 100-pound cabbages. Imagine a 19-pound carrot, 35-pound broccoli, 43-pound beet, 63-pound celery, or 76-pound rutabaga (all world records from the fair, among others you can check out on the website). The flower gardens are amazing too, although not in the same way. Note that on the weekends the fair ties up traffic between Palmer and Anchorage, so it's wise to go midweek if possible.

The **Carrs/Safeway Great Alaska Shootout basketball tournament** (© 907/ 786-1250; www.goseawolves.com), hosted by the University of Alaska Anchorage, brings top-ranked college men's and women's teams to the Sullivan Arena over Thanksgiving weekend and the preceding week.

FAST FACTS: Anchorage

Banks A bank is rarely far away, and all grocery stores and gas stations also have **ATMs.** Downtown, **Wells Fargo** (© 907/263-2016) has a branch in the 5th Avenue Mall (5th Ave. and D St.), with a foreign exchange desk and wire transfer services.

Hospitals **Alaska Regional Hospital** is at 2801 DeBarr Rd. (© **907/276-1131;** www.alaskaregional.com), and **Providence Alaska Medical Center** is at 3200 Providence Dr. (© **907/562-2211,** www.providence.org).

Internet Access and Business Services Downtown, the **UPS Store,** at 645 G St., next to City Hall (© **907/276-7888**), has computers with high-speed connections for $1 per 5 minutes, or $10 an hour, as well as other services.

Police The **Anchorage Police Department** has main offices at 4501 S. Bragaw Rd., south of Tudor Road; for a nonemergency call © **907/786-8500.** For non-emergency police business outside the city, call the **Alaska State Troopers,** 5700 E. Tudor Rd. (© **907/269-5511**).

Post Office Downtown, it's downstairs in the brown building at 4th Avenue and D Street.

Taxes There's no **sales tax** in Anchorage. The **bed tax** is 12%. **Car rental taxes** amount to over a third of the price between the state, local, and airport taxes and fees.

---

2 Where to Stay

Hotel rooms are overpriced in Anchorage, so this is a good place to choose a B&B or small inn. I've searched for such places, choosing those with character and reasonable prices. There are hundreds more, many of them just as good. Dozens of B&Bs are listed on a website maintained by the cooperative **Anchorage Alaska Bed and Breakfast Association** (www.anchorage-bnb.com). You can search by area of town or preferred amenities, or browse alphabetically. Links go directly to the B&Bs' own sites. Many have online availability calendars. If you don't have access to a computer, call the association's hot line (© **888/584-5147** or 907/272-5909), which is answered by hosts at member properties, for referrals to places that meet your requirements.

DOWNTOWN

VERY EXPENSIVE

Besides the Hotel Captain Cook, described in full below, three other high-rise hotels downtown offer a similar level of service without as much character or quite as many amenities. **Hilton Anchorage,** 500 W. 3rd Ave. (© **800/HILTONS** or 907/272-7411; www.hilton.com), is a large conference hotel right at the center of downtown activities. The **Sheraton Anchorage,** 401 E. 6th Ave. (© **800/478-8700** or 907/276-8700; www.sheratonanchoragehotel.com), is comparable to the Hilton, but in a slightly less attractive area a few blocks away. The newer **Anchorage Downtown Marriott,** 820 W. 7th Ave. (© **800/228-9290** or 907/279-8000; www.marriotthotels.com), has a nice pool and fabulous views from rooms with wall-size picture windows.

Hotel Captain Cook ★★★   This is Alaska's great, grand hotel, where royalty and rock stars stay. Former governor Wally Hickel built the first of the three towers after the 1964 earthquake, and now the hotel fills a city block and anchors the downtown skyline. Inside, the earth tones and dark wood decor contribute to a fully realized (maybe a little excessive) nautical theme, with art memorializing Cook's voyages and enough teak to build a square-rigger. The regularly renewed rooms are decorated in a rich, sumptuous style using exquisite fabrics, unique pieces of custom-built furniture, and lots of varnished trim. The hotel never abandoned the deep colors that are now returning to fashion—not a scrap of pale wood or generic beige ever came in. Rooms are comfortable in size, but not as large as those in modern upscale chains, and all have a choice only of a king or two twin beds. Lots of custom tile and mirrors make up for the relatively small size of the bathrooms. There are great views from all sides and you don't pay more to be on a higher floor. The pool, spa, and fitness facilities in the below-ground lower lobby are among the best in town.

Sophisticated food and elaborately formal service justify the high prices at **The Crow's Nest** ★★★, the city's most traditional fine-dining restaurant, on the hotel's top floor. Most tables have stupendous views, and high-backed booths lend intimacy for a romantic dinner. No other restaurant in Anchorage makes its patrons feel as special and important. The cuisine draws on many influences without being trendy and all our food looked wonderful on the plate. Everything was prepared perfectly as well. Main courses range from $26 to $50. The wine list is huge, with few bottles under $40. **Fletcher's,** off the lobby, is an English pub serving good Italian-style pizza, pasta, and sandwiches. **The Pantry** is an above-average hotel cafe, with good service and interesting entrees in moderate serving sizes. The **Whale's Tail** serves light meals, coffee, and cocktails amid overstuffed chairs and big TVs. It's a good place for a drink without feeling like you're in a bar.

4th Ave. and K St. (P.O. Box 102280), Anchorage, AK 99510-2280. © **800/843-1950** or 907/276-6000. Fax 907/343-2298. www.captaincook.com. 547 units. High season $245–$255 double; $260–$1,500 suite. Low season $145–$155 double; $160–$1,500 suite. Extra person $20. AE, DISC, MC, V. **Amenities:** 4 restaurants; 3 bars; indoor pool; separate men's and women's health clubs; Jacuzzi; steam room and sauna; concierge; car-rental desk; business center; shopping arcade; salon; 24-hr. room service; massage; dry cleaning; concierge-level rooms; racquetball courts. *In room:* TV w/pay movies, hair dryer, iron, Wi-Fi.

EXPENSIVE

Here are a few chain-hotel options downtown for those who prefer national brands: the **Days Inn,** 321 E. 5th Ave. (© **800/DAYS INN** or 907/276-7226; www.daysinn alaska.com), which has a courtesy van to the airport and rail depot; the **Clarion Suites,** 325 W. 8th Ave. (© **877/424-6423** or 907/274-1000; www.clarionsuites.com), an

Downtown Anchorage

ACCOMMODATIONS ■

Anchorage Downtown Marriott **11**
Anchorage Grand Hotel **24**
Anchorage International Hostel–Downtown **12**
Caribou Inn **7**
Clarion Suites **28**
Copper Whale Inn **5**
Days Inn **32**
G Street House **18**
Hawthorn Suites **6**
Hilton Anchorage **25**
Hotel Captain Cook **10**
The Oscar Gill House B&B **1**
Sheraton Anchorage **33**
Susitna Place **2**
The Voyager Hotel **9**

DINING ◆

The Bridge **30**
Café Savannah **23**
Club Paris **27**
The Crow's Nest **10**
Dianne's Restaurant **21**
Downtown Deli & Café **22**
Fletcher's **10**
Glacier Brewhouse **14**
Kaladi Brothers **20**
Kumagoro **26**
The Marx Brothers Café **19**
The Muffin Man **13**
Orso **14**
The Pantry **10**
Sacks Café **16**
Side Street Espresso **17**
Simon & Seafort's
  Saloon & Grill **4**
Snow City Café **8**
Whale's Tail **10**

ATTRACTIONS ●

Alaska State Troopers Museum **29**
Anchorage Museum at Rasmuson Center **31**
The Imaginarium **15**
The Oscar Anderson House Museum **3**

219

all-suite building across from the Federal Building, with a small pool; and the **Hawthorn Suites**, 1110 W. 8th Ave. (© **800/527-1133** or 907/222-5005; www.hawthorn.com), with similar facilities as the Clarion Suites, plus a Benihana restaurant on-site.

Anchorage Grand Hotel 👍👍

This all-suite hotel has a rare combination of advantages: a superb, central location; solid, quiet rooms; fully equipped kitchens in every unit full of housewares and with dishwashers and automatic ice makers; generous amenities such as free high-speed Internet in the bedroom and living room; and rates competitive for this area of town. The hotel lacks much of a lobby, as the main entrance and handicap entrance lead directly into a stairway or hallway; that's because it is a reincarnation of an old, concrete apartment building. But the rooms and tiled bathrooms are immaculate and quite large, decorated in a trim, subdued style with fine cabinetry. Despite the full kitchens, I've never noticed odors in the many rooms I've checked on several occasions. Also despite the kitchen, they serve a free continental breakfast in the morning (and deliver the newspaper). Every unit has a bedroom and a queen-size sofa sleeper in the living room.

505 W. 2nd Ave., Anchorage, AK 99501. © **888/800-0640** or 907/929-8888. Fax 907/929-8899. www.anchorage grand.com. 31 units. Summer $199 double; winter $99 double. Extra person over age 13 $20. Rates include continental breakfast. AE, DISC, MC, V. **Amenities:** Business center; guest laundry. *In room:* TV, kitchen, hair dryer, iron, high-speed Internet, voice mail.

Copper Whale Inn 👍👍

A pair of clapboard houses overlook the water and Elderberry Park right on the Coastal Trail downtown, with attractive rooms of various shapes and sizes. New ownership in 2006 took the historic main building, which was growing worn, and redecorated in fashionable tans and browns with comfortable new beds, huge nature photographs, and even granite countertops in the bathrooms and common areas. The small upstairs rooms still have wonderful views and funny angles, and now have a style that requires no excuses for the high rates. Two of those rooms share a bathroom. Lower-level rooms open on a patio but lack the view. The rooms in the lower, newer building, have cherry wood furniture, high ceilings on the upper level, and are larger, although none are very large. The common area, where the staff serves a large continental breakfast, is a comfortable place to gather or check e-mail. Rooms also have free Wi-Fi and telephones, but the rooms have TVs only by request.

440 L St., Anchorage, AK 99501. © **866/258-7999** or 907/258-7999. Fax 907/258-6213. www.copperwhale.com. 14 units, 12 with private bathroom. High season $165 double with shared bathroom, $195 double with private bathroom. Low season $75 double with shared bathroom, $105 double with private bathroom. Extra person $20. Rates include continental breakfast. AE, DISC, MC, V. **Amenities:** Access to health club; bike rental; concierge; guest computer. *In room:* Hair dryer, iron, Wi-Fi.

The Voyager Hotel 👍👍

Thanks to its exacting proprietor, Stan Williams, The Voyager is just right, down to the high quality of the linen and memory foam mattresses. The size is small, the location central, the rooms large and light, all with well-designed kitchenettes, and the housekeeping is exceptional. The whole place has a feel of crisp professionalism. Remodeling projects have been moving through the building for several years, most recently updating the facade and adding big, opening windows that bring in light and air (the hotel also has central air-conditioning). The hotel is best for business travelers. The desks have speakerphones, free high-speed Internet ports (Wi-Fi is available in the lobby), and extra electrical outlets. The pick of the rooms are those on the northwest corner, which have an added meeting or sitting room but cost the same as the units that have only the bedroom. There's nothing ostentatious or outwardly remarkable about the hotel, yet experienced travelers return again and again.

501 K St., Anchorage, AK 99501. © **800/247-9070** or 907/277-9501. Fax 907/274-0333. www.voyagerhotel.com. 40 units. High season $189 (up to 3 people per room); low season $89 (up to 3 people per room). Extra person $10. AE, DC, DISC, MC, V. Nonsmoking hotel. **Amenities:** Restaurant; access to nearby health club with $10 day pass; dry cleaning; coin-op laundry. *In room:* A/C, TV, broadband dataport, kitchenette, coffeemaker, hair dryer.

INEXPENSIVE

Caribou Inn *Value*   A big old wood frame house stands among office buildings, parking lots, and high-rise hotels on a corner in the very best part of downtown Anchorage. Instead of the luxurious rooms you would expect on such valuable property, budget accommodations are inside—rooms decorated with as much country style as could be managed with older furniture and limited funds (for example, a flowered bedspread covering an old couch). It's clean, and the management makes an effort to cater to visitors who simply want good value for their money, rather than people who can't afford to go anywhere else. The best room in the house, a large unit with dormers and a kitchenette, costs what you normally pay for a depressing little compartment on the edge of downtown. Add the hot breakfast served from 6 to 9am, airport transportation, and a free parking pass, and you are getting an amazing deal. If you don't need polish, you can save $50 a night here.

501 L St., Anchorage, AK 99501. © **800/272-5878** or 907/272-0444. Fax 907/274-4828. www.cariboubnb.com. 14 units, 9 with private bathroom. Summer $99 double with shared bathroom, $119 double with private bathroom; winter $49 double with shared bathroom, $59 double with private bathroom; Extra person $25. Rates include full breakfast during summer. AE, DISC, MC, V. **Amenities:** Courtesy van. *In room:* TV w/digital cable, fridge.

G Street House Bed & Breakfast ★ *Value*   This elegant home lies within easy walking distance of the downtown sights, in one of the city's oldest intact residential neighborhoods. The classy rooms have private bathrooms and are priced reasonably. It's a home B&B where you get to socialize with the hosts, the Tesches, who happen to be knowledgeable and charming. Pam is an expert on local history, a gourmet cook and energetic community volunteer. Allan has served for nearly a decade on the Municipal Assembly. The garden out back features a cigar court. You can book through the website.

1032 G St., Anchorage, AK 99501. © 907/276-3284. Fax 907/279-8253. www.gstreethouse.com. 3 units. $115 double. Rates include full breakfast. AE, MC, V. **Amenities:** Internet access. *In room:* Wi-Fi.

The Oscar Gill House Bed & Breakfast ★★   On the Delaney Park strip, just a few blocks from downtown, this is truly the oldest house in Anchorage—it was built in 1913, in Knik, before Anchorage was founded, and moved here on a barge a few years later. Oscar Gill was an early civic leader. The house was to be torn down in 1982 but was moved to storage by a historic preservation group; Mark and Susan Lutz saved it in 1993, transferring it to its present location and, with their own labor, restoring it authentically as a cozy bed-and-breakfast. Now it's on the National Historic Register. Appropriate antiques sit on plank floors in rooms sized in those more modest times. With the period decoration, it's like visiting your grandmother's house when it was brand new. The outgoing Lutzes create a warm, social setting. Book early, as rooms fill quickly; you can check availability and even select a room on their website.

1344 W. 10th Ave., Anchorage, AK 99501. ©/fax **907/279-1344**. www.oscargill.com. 3 units, 1 with private bathroom. High season $105 double with shared bathroom, $135 double with private bathroom; low season $75 double with shared bathroom, $85 double with private bathroom. Extra person $20 (except infants). Rates include full breakfast. AE, MC, V. **Amenities:** Bike loan; babysitting by arrangement. *In room:* TV, hair dryer, iron, Wi-Fi.

Susitna Place ★★ *Value*   Just a few blocks from the downtown core, where a narrow residential street reaches a quiet end, a nondescript door under a carport leads into a rambling house of rooms ranging from comfortable and inexpensive to grand. It turns out the street side is really the back of the house, which sits at the top of a high bluff facing an unobstructed view of Cook Inlet and Mount Susitna beyond, a view so unlike most urban vistas it is easy to forget you are right in town. A large, gracious common room and breakfast area and an adjoining balcony command this extraordinary view, and its enough to make you stop right there and just spend time looking. Remodeling completed in 2007 filled the house with new furniture. The suite is quite luxurious, but the four rooms that share two bathrooms are the rarer find: cozy and very clean, sharing this prime location, they allow travelers to save money without compromise. A good, simple room with two double beds and its own bathroom rents for $125 double. The hosts, successful journalists, are hospitable Alaskans.

727 N St., Anchorage, AK 99501. (℃ **907/274-3344.** Fax 907/272-4141. www.susitnaplace.com. 9 units, 5 with private bathroom. High season $100–$105 double with shared bathroom, $125–$135 with private bathroom, $155–$180 suite; low season $60–$65 with shared bathroom, $75–$80 with private bathroom, $90–$110 suite. Extra person $15. Rates include continental breakfast. AE, DISC, MC, V. **Amenities:** Free covered parking. *In room:* TV w/HBO.

A HOSTEL

Anchorage International Hostel—Downtown, 700 H St. ((℃ **907/276-3635;** www. anchorageinternationalhostel.org), has 95 beds and an urban feel. A coin-op laundry, kitchen, and storage are available, and they have Internet access and a courtesy phone in the lobby. Dorm rooms are small, with just a few bunks each. A bunk is $20, a private room $55. Dorms close between 10am and 5pm daily. The curfew is 1am and checkout is 10am. A homier hostel outside the downtown area is detailed below.

BEYOND DOWNTOWN

These lodging choices are spread across Anchorage, with its long, wide commercial strips. Like most residents, you need a car to stay here. On the other hand, by leaving downtown you can sometimes find larger, newer rooms for less cost, and you avoid downtown parking problems.

VERY EXPENSIVE

Residence Inn by Marriott ⚐   Families who can afford it should stay here, and many business travelers would find it convenient, too. All units are suites with cooking facilities and most have full kitchens. They're big enough to provide family members with privacy and sanity breaks, and you will save money over renting adjoining rooms in an ordinary hotel and dining out for all meals. Room decoration is light and hotel typical; common areas have an Alaska Native motif reflecting the Native corporation management of the hotel. The clapboard building has a gabled roof and stone accents, standing in a parklike enclave in the midtown commercial area, next to a high-rise office building and across the road from a large Fred Meyer grocery and department store. On-site, there's a pool and fitness area, an outdoor basketball and mini–tennis court, and a restaurant serving breakfast daily and light evening meals with beer and wine 4 days a week, included in the room rate. Get driving directions, as it's a little tricky.

1025 35th Ave., Anchorage, AK 99508. (℃ **877/729-0197** or 907/729-0197. Fax 907/563-9636. www.residence inn.com. 148 units. Summer $265–$375 suite; winter $145–$175 suite; rates for any number of guests in unit. AE, DC, DISC, MC, V. Rates include full breakfast. **Amenities:** Pool; basketball and mini-tennis court; fitness room; spa; courtesy shuttle; business center; coin-op laundry; valet service; complimentary newspaper; Wi-Fi. *In room:* TV w/pay movies, kitchenette or full kitchen, iron/ironing board, wired broadband.

EXPENSIVE

Dimond Center Hotel 🐾🐾 *Finds*   This hotel is unique in several ways. Owned by the Seldovia Native Association, its primary clientele consists of rural Alaska residents coming to the big city for shopping and entertainment. That explains the location, on the south side of town, far from downtown sites or midtown office buildings, in the parking lot between a Wal-Mart store and a large shopping mall (where the large health club and pool are accessible to hotel guests). Strange as it sounds, however, the location makes sense for many visitors: Chugach State Park, the zoo, and the Seward Highway and its many attractions are closer than anywhere else you could stay. Since the owners built the hotel for themselves, the attention to comfort and detail are impressive. The common areas are stylish and decorated with Native art, and the rooms are grand: high ceilings, granite counters, attractive modern furniture, 36-inch TVs, and pillow-top beds with comforters. The bathrooms are elaborate, with large shower areas and separate soaking tubs that can connect to the bedroom by opening wooden shutters. Amenities are exhaustive: wired broadband and Wi-Fi, snacks, slippers and bathrobes, a breakfast of Belgian waffles, and so on. Note that a car is essential at this location, and you'll have to drive when you want to eat. You should also avoid the smoking rooms.

700 E. Dimond Blvd., Anchorage, AK 99515. ⓒ **866/770-5002** or 907/770-5000. Fax 907/770-5001. www.dimond centerhotel.com. 109 units. Summer $229–$269; winter $119–$149; rates for up to four guests in a room. AE, DC, DISC, MC, V. Rates include continental breakfast. **Amenities:** Bar; breakfast room; fitness area; access to health club; free airport shuttle; coin-op laundry. *In room:* TV, fridge, coffeemaker, microwave, Wi-Fi, wired broadband.

MODERATE

Lake Hood Inn 🐾🐾 *Finds*   Pilot Bill Floyd built this place right next to his floatplane slip (he flies a C-180) and filled it with fascinating aviation stuff: photographs, propellers, and even rows of seats from a Russian airliner. The guestbook is an aircraft log book. On the comfortable balconies that look over the lake, headphones are available to listen to radio traffic between the tower and the aircraft that you can see taxiing on the lake in front of you. Floyd invested in commercial-quality construction and the rooms have the feel of a solid, upscale hotel room, not a family B&B; they are decorated in cool, muted shades with Berber carpet and light flooding in through big windows. The bathrooms have large shower stalls. Beds can be configured as two twins or as one king. Two front rooms have their own balconies and cost $20 more; the two back rooms have access to a shared balcony and are smaller. All four rooms are up a flight of stairs.

4702 Lake Spenard Dr., Anchorage, AK 99509. ⓒ **866/663-932** or 907/258-9321. www.lakehoodinn.com. 4 units. $149–$169 double. Extra person over age 16 $20. Rates include continental breakfast. AE, MC, V. **Amenities:** Coin-op laundry; guest kitchen; fish freezing. *In room:* TV/VCR, fridge, coffeemaker, hair dryer, safe, high-speed Internet.

INEXPENSIVE

Elderberry Bed & Breakfast *Finds*   If you want to make new friends, stay at this bed-and-breakfast, where visitors mingle in the residents' living quarters like houseguests. Linda and Norm Seitz, brimming with old-time Alaskan hospitality, enjoy talking about their experiences as longtime residents. The house is a typical middle-class subdivision home, surrounded by flowers and, inside, immaculate and full of memorabilia. Located near the airport, it makes a good first stop on a trip—the Seitz's take pride in orienting their guests and letting them in on local secrets. The three rooms are cute but small. Two have bathrooms attached and one has a private bathroom across the hall.

8340 Elderberry St., Anchorage, AK 99502. ⓒ **907/243-6968**. www.elderberrybb.com. 3 units. Summer $85–$95 double; winter $75 double. Extra person $15. Rates include full breakfast in summer, continental breakfast winter. MC, V. **Amenities:** Internet access. *In room:* TV.

Tips Rooms near the Airport

Good, inexpensive standard motel rooms near the airport are rare to the vanishing point, although upscale rooms and B&Bs are readily available. The prize winner in my search for reasonably priced hotel rooms with consistently high quality is the **Lakeshore Motor Inn** (© 800/770-3000 or 907/248-3485; www.lakeshoremotorinn.com). The rate of $149 a night double, at peak season, includes a continental breakfast, Wi-Fi, and use of a 24-hour courtesy van. The hospitality is warm and the rooms are inviting, despite the older concrete building. Two good chain hotels stand near the airport, with higher rates: **Courtyard by Marriott** (© 800/314-0782 reservations or 907/245-0322; www.marriott.com/anccy), with many amenities and a pool, at $209 double in summer; and the **Holiday Inn Express** (© 800/HOLIDAY or 907/248-8848; www.hiexpress.com), at $229 double in the summer. The **Millennium Alaskan Hotel Anchorage** (© 800/544-0553 or 907/243-2300; www.millenniumhotels.com/anchorage) is a large, full-service hotel that stands lakeside near the airport. It might look like a huge fishing and hunting lodge judging by the large lobby, with its warm colors and fly rods and animal mounts on display, but the rooms, on long corridors in a wooden building, are loaded with comfort and amenities. The hotel has two restaurants and offers many services. High season rates are $239 to $285 double. I also recommend Lake Hood Inn (p. 223) and Elderberry Bed & Breakfast (p. 223), both of which are handy to the airport.

A HOSTEL

Spenard Hostel International, 2845 W. 42nd Ave. (© **907/248-5036;** www.alaskahostel.org), is a friendly place near the airport, with free phones, inexpensive bike rental, storage, Internet access, and laundry machines. It feels more like communal housing than an impersonal hostel. There are three lounges for different activities and three kitchens. The owner has installed heat exchangers in the bedrooms to keep the air fresh. You can come and go 24 hours a day. The office is open daily from 9am to 1pm and from 7 to 11pm in summer, 7 to 11pm winter. Beds are $21 by cash or check, a dollar more if you use a credit card (Visa, MasterCard, Amex, or Discover).

CAMPING

Anchorage is a big city, but you can find natural camping right on the urban outskirts. The municipally owned **Centennial Park** is on Boundary Road at the Muldoon Road exit from the Glenn Highway (© **907/343-6986,** or 907/343-6992 off season; www.muni.org/parks/camping.cfm), just as you enter town from the north. Although it is near Muldoon's run-down commercial strip, many of the 88 sites are nicely wooded. The campground has hot showers and is suitable for tents and RVs. Sites are $20. Use of the dump station is $8 for nonguests.

The two closest state park campgrounds to Anchorage are at Bird Creek, to the south of town, and Eagle River, just to the north. The **Bird Creek Campground** is one of my favorites. It sits next to Turnagain Arm and the salmon-filled creek. A paved pathway passes by under the large spruce trees. There are 28 sites and the fee is $15 per night. From Anchorage drive 25 miles south on the Seward Highway to milepost 101.

The 57-site **Eagle River Campground** sits in a thickly wooded riverside spot, and it's well developed with paved roads and large sites with lots of privacy. It costs $15 a night and sites can be reserved in advance. Book up to a year ahead at © **800/952-8624** or 907/694-7982 (www.lifetimeadventures.net). The hosts also book rafting on the Eagle River. Take the Glenn Highway 12 miles north from Anchorage and exit at Hiland Road.

If you seek a place to hook up your RV in town, Anchorage Ship Creek Landings RV Park (© **888/778-7700;** www.bestofalaskatravel.com) is nearest to downtown. The site is in an industrial area a short drive but a little too far to walk to the attractions. Water, sewer, and power sites are $39 to $45 in the summer.

3 Where to Dine

DOWNTOWN
EXPENSIVE

The Bridge ✦✦ SEAFOOD/ECLECTIC   The restaurant was built upon a former roadway bridge over the water of Ship Creek, a short but steep downhill walk from downtown, and some tables have pleasant water views. Many others are in a soothing dining room with warm colors and historic photographs. The menu is difficult to categorize, but includes plenty of Alaska seafood with Pacific influences—for example, as appetizers, a crab and mango summer roll or beer tempura halibut. After several meals here, I've been drawn back by the memory of interesting flavors, truly exceptional service, and the pleasant ambience (although we never seem to get one of those waterside tables). But at each visit we've also had some dishes that went wrong, including, at worst, an alarmingly undercooked chicken that went back to the kitchen. With greater consistency, the place would have my unqualified recommendation.

221 W. Ship Creek Rd. © **907/677-6771.** www.thebridgealaska.com. Reservations recommended. Lunch $7.50–$14, dinner main courses $18–$30. AE, DISC, MC, V. Summer daily 11am–10pm; Winter Mon–Fri 11am–9pm, Sat 11am–10pm, Sun 11am–3pm (brunch). Winter limited menu 2:30–5pm.

Club Paris ✦✦ STEAK/SEAFOOD   Coming from a bright spring afternoon into midnight darkness, under a neon Eiffel Tower and past the bar, I sat down at a secretive booth for two and felt as if I should lean across the table and plot a shady 1950s oil deal with my companion. And I would probably not have been the first. In contrast to Sullivan's Steakhouse, across the street, which contrives a masculine, retro feel, Club Paris is the real thing, decorated with mounted swordfish and other cocktail-era decor. The club is the essence of old Anchorage boomtown years, when the streets were dusty and an oil man needed a classy joint in which to do business. Steak, of course, is the thing to order, and rare really means rare. It's consistently voted the best in town. Ask for the blue cheese stuffing; the stuffed filet is worth the years it probably takes off your coronary arteries. They have a full bar.

417 W. 5th Ave. © **907/277-6332.** www.clubparisrestaurant.com. Reservations recommended. Lunch $5.75–$15; dinner $14–$44. AE, DC, DISC, MC, V. Mon–Thurs 11:30am–2:30pm and 5–10pm; Fri–Sat 11:30am–2:30pm and 5–11pm; Sun 5–10pm.

The Marx Brothers Cafe ✦✦✦ ECLECTIC/REGIONAL   A restaurant started by three friends back when gourmet food was an exotic hobby in Anchorage long ago became the standard of excellence in the state. Treatments of Alaska seafood that began here as cutting-edge creative cuisine now turn up in many of the best restaurants, yet Chef Jack Amon's signature macadamia nut encrusted halibut is nowhere done better. He still presides in the kitchen of the cottage downtown, one of the city's first houses, while maitre d' Van Hale manages the front, preparing his famous Caesar salad at tableside, a ritual that allows him to schmooze with anyone he chooses in the tiny dining

> ### *Finds* The Best Takeout in Town
>
> Anchorage has great takeout food (as my family's continued survival attests). Downtown, **The Muffin Man,** at 817 W. 6th Ave. (© **907/279-6836**) produces some of the best meals eaten at desks in Anchorage, including the memorably delicious smoked red salmon and cream cheese sandwich. You can eat in the sunny, tiled dining room, too. The best, most original burgers are at **Arctic Road-runner,** with locations on Arctic Boulevard at Fireweed Lane and on Old Seward Highway at International Airport Road. Try the Kodiak Islander, which has peppers, ham, onion rings, and God knows what else on top. We get carry-out Chinese from **New Sagaya's City Market** (© **907/274-6173;** www.newsagaya.com) at the corner of 13th and I streets. It's also a wonderful gourmet grocery and community meeting place, and has a good deli and Italian-style brick-oven pizza. Pack a picnic here, or eat in the enclosed or sidewalk dining areas.

rooms. His attitude mirrors the casual elegance of the entire evening, where those wearing ties are in the minority. The cuisine is eclectic, ranging from Asian to Italian, and always turned out flawlessly. The changing menu is not long, but the wine list is the size of a dictionary. With plenty of bottles over $1,000, it has won many awards, but the novice may find it intimidating. A meal is an experience that takes much of the evening and most entrees are over $30. Save room for the exceptional desserts.

627 W. 3rd Ave. © 907/278-2133. www.marxcafe.com. Reservations required. Main courses $18–$36. AE, DC, MC, V. Summer Tues–Sat 5:30–10pm, winter Tues–Thurs 6–9:30pm, Fri–Sat 5:30–10pm.

Orso ✸✸ ITALIAN/MEDITERRANEAN   This restaurant is unique in Anchorage for serving interesting food even though it is large and oriented to the downtown tourist trade. The warm colors of the ornate dining room are lightened with big modern paintings. The cuisine is amped up with bold flavors and the menu is long and full of surprises. The mushroom ravioli, with a generous dose of smoked salmon, was rich and strongly flavored. The rice that came with my nicely seared scallops had to be passed around and started a conversation—I'm still not sure exactly what made it taste so good. Service is professional but not stuffy, and the food comes fast enough not to use up the entire evening. Generally, the prices are reasonable for this kind of food. We also enjoy the bar later in the evening for a drink and dessert at the end of an evening out (it's open an hour later than the dining room). Dining in the bar lets you in on the festive, sophisticated atmosphere for less money.

737 W. 5th Ave. © 907/222-3232. www.orsoalaska.com. Reservations recommended. Lunch $10–$15; dinner pasta or main course $12–$33. AE, MC, V. Summer Mon–Tues 11:30am–4pm and 5–10pm, Wed–Fri 11:30am–4pm and 5–11pm, Sat 5–11pm, Sun 5–10pm. Winter Mon–Tues 11:30am–2:30pm and 5–9:30pm, Wed–Thurs 11:30am–2:30pm and 5–10pm; Fri 11:30am–2:30pm and 5–11pm; Sat. 5–11pm, Sun 5–9:30pm.

Sacks Cafe ✸✸✸ CREATIVE/ECLECTIC   This is the most fashionable restaurant in town, and also one of the best. The storefront dining room, in warm Southwest colors and sharp angles, resembles a showcase for the food and diners, who can sit at tables or at a tapas bar. The cuisine defies categorization, but is consistently interesting and creative, frequently with Thai influences. The menu changes, but one consistent offering is chicken with scallops, shiitake mushrooms, snow peas, udon noodles, ginger cream sauce, and black bean salsa. Vegetarians do as well as meat eaters. For lunch, the sandwiches are unforgettable, with choices such as shrimp and avocado with herb cream cheese on sourdough. Do not fail to try the tomato soup with Gorgonzola. The beer and wine list is extensive and reasonably priced. They serve brunch Saturday and Sunday 10am to 2:30pm.

328 G St. © **907/274-4022.** www.sackscafe.com. Reservations recommended. Lunch $5–$15; dinner main courses $18–$34. AE, MC, V. Mon–Thurs 11am–2:30pm and 5–9:30pm; Fri 11am–2:30pm and 5–10:30pm; Sat 10:30am–2:30pm and 5–10:30pm; Sun 10:30am–2:30pm and 5–9:30pm.

Simon and Seafort's Saloon and Grill ⋆⋆ STEAK/SEAFOOD   Simon's, as it's known, is a jolly beef and seafood grill where voices boom off the high ceilings. On sunny summer evenings, the rooms, fitted with brass turn-of-the-20th-century saloon decor, fill with light off Cook Inlet, down below the bluff; the views are magnificent. The food is consistently good. Besides a nightly list of specials the restaurant boasts of its macadamia nut stuffed halibut, but most of the cuisine is simpler—prime rib, for example. Service is warm and professional, and quick enough to allow time for other evening activities. Children are treated well. To enjoy the place on a budget, order a sandwich and soup for lunch in the well-stocked bar; it's open until 11pm every night. Getting a table in the restaurant at a reasonable hour requires advance planning in peak season or on off-season weekends; call a couple of days ahead.

420 L St. © **907/274-3502.** Reservations recommended. Lunch $7.50–$18; dinner main courses $16–$42. AE, DISC, MC, V. Summer Mon–Fri 11am–2:30pm and 4:30–10pm, Sat–Sun 4:30–10pm; winter Mon–Thurs 11:00am–2:30pm and 5–9:30pm, Fri 5–10pm, Sat 4:30–10pm, Sun 4:30–9pm.

MODERATE

Cafe Savannah ⋆⋆ SPANISH   Right across from the town square, this storefront restaurant is stylish, relaxing, and serves interesting and delightful food. The specialty is tapas, made for ordering many plates and then sharing them. Selections under $7 include items such as *hongo relleno con chorizo* (stuffed portobello mushroom caps with Spanish chorizo and manchego cheese) or cold *gambas embueltas con jamon* (shrimp with cilantro sauce wrapped with prosciutto). I learned a lot eating here! For a simpler lunch, the grilled sandwiches and soups are spicy and satisfying. The dining room has tables and a bar decorated with colored stones and bent flatware under a hard, clear surface. Monthly art shows hang on the walls. Don't choose to dine here if you're in a rush, or if you're looking for warm Alaskan hospitality; although I enjoyed the waiter's classy attitude, we didn't become buddies.

508 W. 6th Ave. © **907/646-9121.** All items $4–$29. MC, V. Mon–Thurs 11am–3pm and 5–10pm; Fri–Sat 11am–3pm and 5–11pm.

Glacier Brewhouse ⋆ GRILL/SEAFOOD/PIZZA   An eclectic and changing menu is served in a large dining room with lodge decor, where the pleasant scent of the wood-fired grill hangs in the air. It's a lively place to see others and be seen. There are lots of agreeable if trendy touches: the glass wall showing off the brewing equipment, which produces eight or more hearty beers, and also turns out spent grain for bread that's then set out on the tables with olive oil. An advantage for travelers is the wide price range—a pizza with feta cheese, sun-dried tomatoes, pesto, and garlic is $10; crab legs are $37. The food is usually quite good. Choose this place for a boisterous meal with quick, casual service that will get you out in time to do something else with the evening. Do reserve ahead, however, as waits can be long.

737 W. 5th Ave. © **907/274-BREW.** www.glacierbrewhouse.com. Reservations recommended. Lunch $8–$15; dinner $9–$34. AE, DC, DISC, MC, V. High season daily 11am–11pm; low season Mon 11am–9:30pm, Tues–Thurs 11am–10pm, Fri–Sat 11am–11pm, Sun 4–9:30pm.

Kumagoro ✦ JAPANESE   Anchorage has several good, authentic Japanese restaurants, but this one, right on the main tourist street downtown, has the most convenient location. Among my favorite lunches anywhere is their lunch box ($15), a large sampler of many dishes, including sushi, sashimi, and other tasty things, always a little different, that I can't always identify. The dining room is pleasantly low-key, with tables in rows, so you may have the opportunity to meet those seated next to you. The restaurant has a beer and wine license.

533 W. 4th Ave. © **907/272-9905.** Lunch $8–$15; dinner main courses $14–$42. AE, DC, DISC, MC, V. Summer daily 11am–10:45pm; winter Mon–Sat 11am–9:45pm, Sun 1–9:45pm.

INEXPENSIVE

Dianne's Restaurant _Value_ SOUP/SANDWICH   This is my first choice for a quick, healthful, inexpensive lunch downtown. Located off the lobby of a tall, glass office building, Dianne's cafeteria line fills with well-dressed folk seeking the hearty freshly baked bread, soups, sandwiches, and specials turned out for the lunch hour. The atmosphere is bright and casual and you don't waste your day eating. The restaurant does not have a liquor license.

550 W. 7th Ave., Suite 110. © **907/279-7243.** Main courses $4.25–$9. AE, DISC, MC, V. Mon–Fri 7am–4pm.

Downtown Deli and Cafe DELI   When this restaurant was started by a pair of young politicians in the 1970s, the idea of a kosher deli in Anchorage that sold the Sunday _New York Times_ was just this side of bizarre. As their careers rose—one became governor and the other helped create Alaska's Permanent Fund—the restaurant became a local institution and political hot spot. In 1994, President Clinton came for dinner. The restaurant that exists today, however, is less interesting than its history. The look is outdated and the food similar to what you would find in a hotel cafe. The restaurant is convenient for tourists, who are the primary clientele: a handy location, reasonable prices (especially at dinnertime, when downtown is short on inexpensive sit-down places), and kids are treated well. They serve beer and wine.

525 W. 4th Ave. © **907/276-7116.** All items $6.25–$15. AE, DC, DISC, MC, V. Summer daily 6am–10pm; winter Mon–Sat 7am–3pm, Sun 9am–3pm.

Snow City Cafe ✦ VEGETARIAN/HOME STYLE   This is _the_ happening spot downtown for breakfast or lunch. What started as a smaller, granola-crowd place grew on the basis of hearty, tasty food and a friendly young wait staff into a large, busy restaurant with lots of life and energy and a diverse clientele. It's especially popular in the morning, when you'll rarely do better than the salmon cakes and eggs or omeletes. Breakfast is served all day. Lunch, starting at 11, includes comfort food such as mac and cheese or meat loaf, but also unusual sandwiches, such as roast beef and blue cheese or the delicious portabello burger. The dining room is light and colorful, with a clean feel, and with tables out in the open amid lots of movement. Bring your laptop, as the restaurant offers free Wi-Fi. The only demerits I can give are that on occasion I've had food take too long, and there's often a wait at busy hours. They're open Wednesday nights for an Irish music jam. Small monthly art shows begin with artist receptions every first Friday, a pattern shared with all the downtown galleries. They serve beer and wine.

Coffeehouses

There are coffeehouses all over the city to get a cup of java and a pastry, and to meet people and engage in conversation. My favorite is **Side Street Espresso,** on G Street between 4th and 5th, a gathering place for artists, activists, and anyone who wants to trade ideas, sometimes with live acoustic music in the evening. **Cafe del Mundo,** at Northern Lights and Denali midtown, gets an older crowd of businesspeople, yuppies, stay-at-home parents, and those looking for a comfortable meeting spot. **Kaladi Brothers** has several locations with Internet access, including in a classy space in the back corner of the Alaska Center for the Performing Arts downtown, at 6th Avenue and G Street. Their location in the shopping center on Northern Lights Boulevard between Arctic and Minnesota is extremely popular, sharing space with the huge Title Wave used bookstore and just down from the essential REI sporting goods store.

1034 W. 4th Ave. ✆ **907/272-CITY.** www.snowcitycafe.com. Breakfast and lunch $8–$12. AE, DISC, MC, V. Daily 7am–4pm (espresso counter only after 3 on weekdays).

BEYOND DOWNTOWN

EXPENSIVE

Jens' Restaurant ✸✸✸ INTERNATIONAL   Chef Jens Hansen is truly gifted. His restaurant is for the kind of diner who loves exciting food, surprises, and beautiful plates of new tastes and textures; the meals are about the food, sharing bites, and saying "Wow," and "How did he do that?" The cuisine is highly eclectic, but I won't call it experimental, despite the raw kangaroo I tried on one visit, because these dishes work far more often than any experimentalist has a right to expect. There's often only one item on the changing menu that isn't unusual or challenging: the superb pepper steak. Like everything, even that dish has a sauce, and it is complex and memorable. The wine list is exceptional but manageable and reasonably priced, and you can sip your selection while dining inexpensively on appetizers in a pleasant bar area; try the incredible spinach ravioli with Gorgonzola, for example. Desserts are sublime. The dining room is light and clean, decorated with modern art. Service is highly professional, with each formally attired waiter assigned to just a few tables, and they earn their keep as well by helping diners learn about food and wine they have probably never tried.

701 W. 36th Ave. ✆ **907/561-5367.** www.jensrestaurant.com. Reservations recommended. Lunch $9–$29; dinner main courses $18–$37. AE, DC, DISC, MC, V. Mon 11:30am–2pm; Tues–Fri 11:30am–2pm and 6–10pm; Sat 6–10pm; wine bar serves appetizers starting at 4pm. Closed Jan.

MODERATE

Bear Tooth Grill ✸ *Value* SOUTHWESTERN   You can't find food of this quality for prices this low anywhere else in Anchorage. Dishes such as the soy grilled halibut are sophisticated and nicely done, but take up only a small part of a menu that goes on and on with Mexican choices, sandwiches, and other selections inexpensive enough to make the restaurant fit for a late-afternoon impulse—most main courses are under $11. The partners who own the restaurant started in business by making beer and then opened a pizzeria to sell the beer (see the Moose's Tooth, below); next they opened a theater-pub (see "Anchorage Nightlife," later in this chapter); the grill, in the same building, was the final addition. Eat tacos, wraps, or pizza while watching a movie or at tables in the movie theater lobby—a loud, free-flowing setting perfect for kids. The grill is in a separate, calmer, and more confined dining room, best for couples and parties of four or less. The food comes out slowly, as befits the atmosphere. Tables are more comfortable than booths, but at peak times you have to take what you can get, often with a wait, so try to dine here early or late. Besides the beer, they have a full bar serving many margaritas and 20 wines by the glass.

1230 W. 27th Ave. ℂ **907/276-4200.** Reservations not accepted. All items $6–$20. AE, DC, DISC, MC, V. Summer Sun–Thurs 4–11:30pm, Fri–Sat 4pm–midnight; winter Sun–Thurs 4–11pm, Fri–Sat 4–11:30pm.

Campobello Bistro 👁👁 NORTHERN ITALIAN/BISTRO   This quiet little midtown restaurant is amazingly like stepping into northern Italy, except for the Alaska seafood. Even the service has the quality of jocular professionalism I remember from Italy. The same priceless pair of waiters has developed a following for almost a decade. Unlike most of Anchorage's best restaurants, the bistro doesn't try to reinvent the cookbook. Most of the menu consists of recognizable dishes, such as veal Marsala or Italian sausage and polenta. Meals are bold, highly flavored, and entirely satisfying. The seafood crepe is fantastic. Those seeking the bland tomatoes and cheese of a typical Italian family restaurant should go elsewhere (Sorrento's and Romano's, both on Fireweed Lane, each do that tried-and-true formula well). The wine and food are reasonably priced.

601 W. 36th, Suite 10. ℂ **907/563-2040.** Lunch $10–$13; dinner main courses $15–$25. DC, MC, V. Mon–Fri 11am–2:30pm and 5–9pm; Sat 5–9pm.

City Diner 👁 DINER   In 2007, a pair of well-known local chefs opened this chrome and neon diner that looks right out of a Hollywood movie set, and immediately had a hit on their hands. Standing at the corner of busy Benson Boulevard and Minnesota Drive (on the route downtown for the airport), the building is unmistakable and nearly irresistible, with its big clocks labeled "Time to Eat" and shiny metal siding. The counter, booths, and finishes inside carry the theme to its conclusion. It's all bigger, cleaner, and more contrived than any "real" diner, but fun anyway, and the food is better than you would expect. The grilled Reuben was probably the best I've had—and that's saying something. The menu includes many classic sandwiches, including an open-faced meatloaf, for nonclassic prices (the meatloaf is $13). Entrees, including seafood and steak, are reasonably priced under $20. Six beers are on tap, including craft brews. Service was good on my visit. The diner doesn't take reservations and lines form at popular hours.

3000 Minnesota Dr. ℂ **907/277-CITY.** All main courses $7–$19. AE, DISC, MC, V. Mon–Tues 10am–10pm; Wed–Sun 7am–10pm.

The Greek Corner 👁 GREEK/ITALIAN   When we need a relaxed place for a three-generation family meal, this place always seems to come to the top of the list. The exterior is not promising and the small, well-lit dining room is decorated with travel posters and has a homemade look, but somehow that just makes the restaurant feel more real and the warm hospitality of the service even more sincere. Sometimes it's as if you've been adopted by the waitstaff, and the food comes fast. I usually order the lamb chops, which are tender and seasoned and cooked just right, and come with perfectly prepared asparagus and baby potatoes. A dozen authentic traditional Greek dishes are on the menu, mostly priced around $15, or you can order from a list of old Italian favorites such as spaghetti or lasagna. They serve pizza, too, and reasonably priced lunches—a gyro with soup or a salad is $9.

302 W. Fireweed Lane ✆ 907/276-2820. Lunch $5.50–$10; dinner main courses $10–$20. MC, V. Mon–Fri 11am–10pm; Sat noon–10pm; Sun 4–10pm.

INEXPENSIVE

The Lucky Wishbone ✪ *(Finds* DINER   This Anchorage institution of half a century (in high school we called it "The Bone") is where the real pioneer Alaska meets families out for a delicious, not-too-greasy fried chicken dinner, famous milkshakes (try the hot fudge), and other delights from the fountain. It is our children's favorite. One section of the counter is reserved for discussion of aviation and golf. When the beloved owners outlawed smoking years ago, it made the front page of the newspaper. You'll see few other tourists, as the location, among the car dealerships at the extreme east end of downtown, is too far to walk to from the hotels. On the other hand, I once ran into Alaska's powerful senior U.S. senator, Ted Stevens. They have a drive-in.

1033 E. 5th Ave. ✆ 907/272-3454. All items $3.50–$11. MC, V. Summer Mon–Sat 10am–11pm; winter Mon–Thurs 10am–10pm, Fri–Sat 10am–11pm.

The Moose's Tooth Pub and Pizzeria ✪✪ *(Kids* PIZZA   The best pizza and beer in Anchorage undoubtedly come from this fun and friendly place. The microbrewery came first, but the pizza really is the greater accomplishment. It has a soft, light crust like Italian pizza but the oomph of American pizza. They offer many ingenious toppings, but not just to dump on: The combinations really work. The ambience is youthful, casual, and loud; the high energy means kids aren't out of place. The dining room, although handsomely rebuilt, still looks from top to bottom like a college town pizzeria. The only drawback is the restaurant's popularity, which can make for long waits at peak times.

3300 Old Seward Hwy. ✆ 907/258-2537. www.moosestooth.net. Large pizza $13–$25. AE, DC, DISC, MC, V. Summer Sun noon–midnight, Mon–Thurs 11am–midnight, Fri–Sat 11am–1am; winter Sun noon–11pm, Mon 11am–11pm, Tues–Thurs 11am–midnight, Fri–Sat 11am–1am.

4 What to See & Do

I've arranged this section starting with a self-guided walking tour through downtown Anchorage, followed by details on the downtown museums and then attractions that are farther afield. If you'd prefer to tour by bus, **Gray Line of Alaska's** Anchorage Highlights Tour (✆ 800/544-2206; www.graylineofalaska.com) takes 3 hours to visit downtown and the Ship Creek area, the Anchorage Museum, and the Alaska Native Heritage Center. It spends an hour at the center, not as long as I like to stay. The tour costs $47 for adults, half price for children 12 and under, including admission to the center.

Tips **Helper Bees**

The people you see downtown on bikes and on foot in bright yellow-and-black outfits are the Downtown Ambassadors, employees of a downtown business improvement district, sometimes known as the "bumblebees" for their color scheme. Stop one to ask a question or report a problem, or call ✆ 907/277-**SAFE** (7233; www.anchoragedowntown.org).

WALKING TOUR   DOWNTOWN ANCHORAGE

Start & Finish: 4th Avenue and F Street.
Time: 2 hours (use the shortcuts noted for a briefer tour).

Start at the **Log Cabin Visitor Information Center** at 4th Avenue and F Street. Outside is a sign that shows the distance to various cities and a 5,114-pound jade boulder put on display by Stewart's Photo Shop, an Anchorage institution that is just across the street.

Walk east, toward the mountains, to:

❶ Old City Hall (1936)
This building is on the right of 4th Avenue as you approach E Street. The lobby contains a fun and illuminating free display on city history, including dioramas of the early streetscape, old photographs, and the fire bell and fire pole that once were used in this building.

Crossing E Street, notice on the left side of 4th Avenue that all the buildings are modern—everything on that side from E Street east for several blocks collapsed in the 1964 earthquake. The street split in half lengthwise, with the left side ending up a dozen feet lower than the right. That land was later reinforced with a gravel buttress by the U.S. Army Corps of Engineers and the slope below forever set aside as open space because of the earthquake risk. This stretch of 4th Avenue is where the **Iditarod Trail Sled Dog Race** and the **Anchorage Fur Rendezvous World Championship Sled Dog Race** start each year in March and February, respectively.

Continue walking east. At 4th Avenue and D Street is the:

❷ Wendler Building (1915)
The old Club 25 is among the oldest buildings in Anchorage. The bronze statue of the dog commemorates the sled-dog races that start here. Across D Street is a mural that depicts a map of coastal Alaska and B.C., with the Iditarod Trail faintly marked.

Cross 4th Avenue to the north side to see:

❸ 4th Avenue Market Place
The blue building on the north side of 4th is a "village mall," collecting together Alaska Native artists and businesses in the heart of downtown. One shop represents the Alaska Native Heritage Center (p. 230) and another, the Two Spirits Gallery, is owned by the Cook Inlet Tribal Council, which presents carvers and artists working on-site every day. Alaska Natives demonstrate their work in the common area, and you can sometimes catch free performances here as well. On the eastern end of the building, take in large, interesting graphics about the 1964 earthquake and other historic topics. The Rusty Harpoon (p. 247) is a good craft and gift shop in the yellow building next door.

Cross back to the south side of 4th and walk a block south on D Street to see:

❹ The Culture of D Street
This one-block street contains two of the city's most interesting cultural outlets. First on the left, at 4th and D, is **Cyrano's Off-Center Playhouse** (© 907/274-2599; www.cyranos.org), home of its own theater company. They really are good; the tiny theater can cause quite a stir in town and has won many awards. They also have poetry readings and the like, and you can stop in the cozy little cafe for a glass of wine or beer on performance days. Tickets are sold through **CenterTix** (© 907/263-ARTS or www.centertix.net). A little farther on the left, the **International Gallery of Contemporary Art** (www.igcaalaska.org) is the community's nonprofit forum for art that's happening right now. Typically, the gallery is given over to a single artist or theme. Hours are on p. 249.

Downtown Anchorage Walking Tour

1 Old City Hall
2 Wendler Building
3 4th Avenue Market Place
4 The culture of D Street
5 The 5th Avenue Mall
6 Town Square
7 Alaska Center for the
   Performing Arts

🐧 Humpy's
8 City Hall
9 Offbeat businesses
10 Holy Family Cathedral
11 Elderberry Park
12 Resolution Park
13 The Last Blue Whale
14 Courthouse Plaza

15 Totem poles
16 Historic houses
17 Ship Creek overlook
18 Anchorage Market &
   Festival
19 Old Federal Building
20 4th Avenue Theater

Cross 5th Avenue at the end of D Street and enter:

❺ The 5th Avenue Mall

This grand, four-story shopping center is Alaska's fanciest mall, with Nordstrom and JCPenney as its anchor stores. A large, airy food court is on the top floor. Take a look, or walk straight through to the doors on the opposite side. (Just a block east, you'll find the Anchorage Museum at Rasmuson Center and the Alaska State Troopers Museum, described below.)

Cross the mall to the doors opposite, exiting onto 6th Avenue, turn right and walk a block and cross E Street to the:

❻ Town Square

The community raised money for improvements to the square by collecting

donations of $40 each for the granite bricks, with an inscription of the contributor's choosing. There are 13,344 (bet you can't find mine). On the east side of the square, behind you, the huge whale mural was painted freehand by Wyland in 1994. He painted similar whale murals in cities all along the West Coast. Changes are in the offing to redo the square, improve E Street for pedestrians, and do other work in the area, so it may be torn up when you visit. The building on the northeast corner of the square is one of the city's oldest and was saved from demolition when the park was created; it contains a charming gift and candy shop owned by the mayor's wife.

Dominating the west side of the square is the massive, highly decorated:

⑦ Alaska Center for the Performing Arts

The center was completed in 1988 amid controversy about its design, among other things—it's either clever and bold or garish and busy. Take a look and decide for yourself. The lobby is usually open, and whatever your opinion of the decor, a peek inside will spark a discussion. Alaskans have grown used to it, and now we think of the building mostly as a focal point of our cultural life. Tours are held Wednesday at 1pm; a $1 donation is requested (reach the center's administrative offices at ℰ 907/263-2900; www.alaskapac.org). Thespians believe the building is haunted by the ghost of painter Sydney Laurence, who makes lighting mysteriously vary and elevators go up and down with no one in them. An auditorium demolished to make room for the center was named for Laurence. Check the box office for current performances in the three theaters and rehearsal hall, Alaska's premier performance venues (and see "The Performing Arts," later in this chapter).

Take a Break
From the performing arts center, cross 6th Avenue at the F Street light and turn right (west) to **Humpy's,** a popular tavern on the south side of 6th with a huge selection of microbrews, live music, and good casual meals, including halibut tacos.

The square green office building next door to Humpy's is:

⑧ City Hall

Turn left through the pedestrian walkway between Humpy's and City Hall. A large mural showing a timeline of the history of Anchorage faces the parking lot. An artistically superior mural, by Duke Russell, is on the wall in Humpy's outdoor seating area on the near side of the parking lot.

Walk west through the city hall parking lot to G Street, turn right, and proceed north to 5th Avenue. G Street between 4th and 5th avenues contains some of the downtown's best:

⑨ Offbeat Businesses

First comes **Aurora Fine Arts,** an attractively cluttered arts and craft shop with plenty to see. Next up are: **Darwin's Theory,** a friendly, old-fashioned bar with character that shows up in an Indigo Girls song ("Cut It Out" from the album *Shaming of the Sun*); **Suzi's Woollies** (www.suziswoollies.com), a Celtic shop carrying imported sweaters, jewelry, and CDs, and with live Irish music Saturday afternoons and the first Friday of the month; **Tracy Anna Bader Design Studio,** a studio and shop of bright, graphic, wearable art; and **Side Street Espresso,** where you can get into a lively discussion on art or politics and make contact with thinking people. On the opposite side of the street, at 423 G Street, the light-filled storefront of the **Alaska Glass Gallery Downtown** (www.alaskaglassgallery.com) exhibits fanciful and dramatic glass sculptures by glassblower and gallery director Cynthia England and by other artists from all over the United States and Canada.

Shortcut: You can cut an hour off the tour here by continuing north on G Street to 4th, then turning right and walking 1 block to the starting point at F Street.

Backtrack to 5th and G, and then proceed west (away from the mountains) on 5th. The Imaginarium, described under "Downtown Museums," below, is on the right. Continuing west on 5th Avenue and crossing H Street, you'll see the:

⑩ Holy Family Cathedral

This concrete Art Deco church is the seat of the Roman Catholic archbishop. The interior is unremarkable.

Keep going toward the water, crossing L Street and going down the hill to:

⑪ Elderberry Park

The yellow-and-brown house in the park is **The Oscar Anderson House Museum,** described under "Downtown Museums," below. Besides the good playground equipment, the park offers the easiest access point to the **Tony Knowles Coastal Trail** (see "Walking & Biking," later). The trail tunnels under the Alaska Railroad tracks from the bottom of the park.

Now hike back up the hill to L Street and turn left. At 3rd Avenue is:

⑫ Resolution Park

The bronze **Captain Cook Monument** stands on a large wooden deck, but he's gazing out to sea—the opposite of the way he was facing when he explored Cook Inlet in 1778 aboard HMS *Resolution*. Cook didn't personally come as far as Anchorage, instead sending a boat with his ship's master, William Bligh (later the Captain Bligh who inspired mutiny aboard the HMS *Bounty*). Failing to find the Northwest Passage here, Cook considered his 2 weeks in Cook Inlet a waste of time, grousing in his journal, "Nothing but a trifling point in geography has been determined." The park's informative signs, powerful mounted binoculars, and commanding vantage point make this a rewarding stop for gazing out at the water and the mountains beyond. The waters you see are ferocious and wild, with whirlpool currents and a tidal range of almost 40 vertical feet. The shore across the inlet, about 2 miles away, is virtually uninhabited.

Follow 3rd Avenue east (back toward the mountains) 1 block and turn right on K Street. On the right is:

⑬ The Last Blue Whale

Joseph Princiotti's huge 1973 bronze of combat between a whale and whalers in small boats shows the whale's point of view.

Cross K Street to walk through the

⑭ Courthouse Plaza

The plaza frames the **Nesbett State Courthouse;** the sinuous shapes of the plaza's concrete walkways are supposed to suggest both the flow of people through the court system and a braided glacial river. The metal *Grizzly Bear and Cub,* by Homer sculptor Mike Sirl, was installed in 2004; local and state law require projects to construct public buildings to set aside 1% of their budget for art, and this work is one result.

Cross the plaza to 4th Avenue, cross I Street, and take a look at the two:

⑮ Totem Poles

Carved of red cedar by Lee Wallace, of Ketchikan, and erected in 1997, they represent the eagle and raven moieties of the Tlingit people, intended to symbolize the balance of justice. A Tlingit creation story tells of how raven stole the moon and stars and brought them to mankind; here, the moon and stars are the features of the Alaska flag.

Walk around past the courthouse on 4th Avenue and turn left onto H Street. Follow H as it crosses 3rd Avenue and becomes Christensen Drive. Descend the hill on Christensen and turn right on 2nd Avenue, toward the mountains. Look around at the:

⑯ Historic Houses

The old wooden houses along 2nd are mostly attorneys' offices now, but once this was one of the better residential areas in town. Several houses are marked and a kiosk at 2nd and F relates some town history. If you imagine houses like this over much of downtown, you'll know what Anchorage looked like before oil.

Continue east on 2nd Avenue to E Street, where you will find:

⑰ A Ship Creek Overlook with a Monument to President Eisenhower

The bust commemorates Alaska's 1959 admission to the Union (in fact, Eisenhower was a major barrier to statehood).

More interesting is the overlook. You can see the Alaska Railroad yards from here, and part of the port of Anchorage and the neighborhood of Government Hill across the Ship Creek river bottom. This is where the tent city of Knik Anchorage, later shortened to Anchorage, was set up in 1914. An informative set of signs on the overlook explains the history. The Alaska Railroad, which helped build Anchorage, still has its headquarters in a modern brick building that stands by the creek. The nearer concrete building is the railroad's stately depot. The restored steam engine on the pedestal in front was used on construction of the Panama Canal, then worked in the yard here as a switch engine. The creek itself is full of salmon in June and August (see "Fishing," later in this chapter), and a walkway that crosses a dam just upstream from here is a good place to watch the fish and to feed ducks. Keep in mind that the walk down the stairs to the river bottom and back is strenuous.

Walk up the hill on E Street to 3rd Avenue. The extensively landscaped parking lot on the left becomes the:

⑱ Anchorage Market & Festival

This street fair, held every weekend from mid-May to mid-September, draws hundreds of vendors and thousands of shoppers. You can buy everything from local vegetables to handmade crafts to tourist junk. There are food booths and music, too.

Turn right on 3rd Avenue, and then left on F Street. F Street Station, on the left, is a fun bar with an after-work crowd. Proceed to 4th Avenue, and you're back at the Log Cabin Visitor Information Center, but don't stop. Turn right on 4th Avenue. On the right side is the:

⑲ Old Federal Building

This grand, white, Depression-era structure now contains the Alaska Public Lands Information Center, with interesting displays and lots of information about the outdoors (p. 215). Don't let the security checkpoint deter you—go in and look around.

Across the street is Anchorage's most attractive historic building, the:

⑳ 4th Avenue Theater (1947)

The theater was built by Cap Lathrop, Alaska's first business magnate, who created it as a monument to the territory and the permanence of its new society. An old-fashioned movie palace, it features bas-relief murals and a blinking Big Dipper on the ceiling. It flourished for decades, but began losing money when one-screen, downtown movie theaters became obsolete in the 1980s. It was saved from destruction in 1991 and made a tourist attraction by a local businessman with a sentimental attachment to the building. However, the theater again closed its doors in 2006 and faced doom. A lively political battle ensued over a city bail-out. As of this writing, it seems unlikely the theater will be torn down, but it is unclear whether it will be open for viewing.

DOWNTOWN MUSEUMS

Alaska State Troopers Museum   This charming little museum has more than one way into the heart. For law enforcement people, the appeal is obvious (the official name is the Fraternal Order of Alaska State Troopers Law Enforcement Museum). Others may enjoy perusing a trove of law enforcement insignia, equipment, a 1952 Hudson Hornet patrol car, and old Alaska memorabilia—even a grinning mug shot of Steve McQueen, who was picked up in 1973 spinning doughnuts in city streets in an Olds Toronado. The whole place conveys the positive spirit of pioneer Alaska.

245 W. 5th Ave. ✆ **800/770-5050** or 907/279-5050. www.alaskatroopermuseum.com. Free admission. Mon–Fri 10am–4pm; Sat noon–4pm.

Anchorage Museum at Rasmuson Center ★★★   The state's largest museum doesn't have its largest collection, but it has the room and staff to teach and to serve as a center of contemporary culture for this part of the world. Most visitors tour the large Alaska Gallery, an informative and enjoyable walk through the history and some of the anthropology of the state. In the art galleries, you can see what's happening in art in Alaska today; Alaskan art isn't all scenery and walrus ivory, but the grandeur of the state does influence almost every work. The Anchorage museum also gets the best touring and temporary exhibits. Depending on your interest, you could spend most of a day there. The restaurant, operated by the excellent Marx Brothers Cafe (p. 225), serves some of the best lunches to be had downtown. Call or check the website for information on films, lectures, openings, and jazz happenings staged many summer evenings, a great opportunity to meet like-minded locals. The shop is an excellent place to buy authentic Alaska Native art. A $100 million expansion project is under-way, but will not be completed until 2010.

121 W. 7th Ave. ☎ **907/343-4326.** www.anchoragemuseum.org. Admission $8 adults, $7 seniors 65 and older, free for children 17 and under. May 15–Sept 15 Fri–Wed 9am–6pm, Thurs 9am–9pm; Sept 16–May 14 Wed–Sat 10am–6pm, Sun noon–5pm.

The Imaginarium *(Kids)*   Located in the mall with the Orso Restaurant and Glacier Brewhouse, mostly in the basement, this small museum is a favorite of Anchorage children under age 10, with room to play and interesting things to look at. The highlights are the excellent marine touch tanks, which are like indoor tide pools, and the display of live reptiles and amphibians. Other exhibits cover astronomy, insects, flight, and miscellaneous science topics. For families, it's a worthwhile stop; less so, if you're used to larger science museums in major cities.

737 W. 5th Ave., Suite G. ☎ **907/276-3179.** www.imaginarium.org. Admission $5.50 ages 13–64, $5 ages 2–12 and 65 and older. Mon–Sat 10am–6pm; Sun noon–5pm.

The Oscar Anderson House Museum   This house museum, moved to a beauti-ful site in Elderberry Park over the water, shows how an early Swedish immigrant lived. Although far from grand, the house is quaint, surrounded by a lovely little gar-den, and dates from the city's founding in 1915. The 45-minute guided tour provides a good explanation of Anchorage's short history. In those small-town days, Anderson found success in the meat, coal, and aviation businesses. He died in 1974, and the house contains many of the family's original belongings, including a working 1909 player piano around which the structure was built. If you come at Christmas, don't miss the Swedish Christmas tours, the first two weekends in December.

420 M St. ☎ **907/274-2336.** Admission $3 adults, $1 children 5–12. Summer Mon–Fri noon–5pm. Closed in winter.

SIGHTS BEYOND DOWNTOWN

Alaska Aviation Heritage Museum ★★   Alaska's late development meant it skipped a technological step: Travel and mail went straight from dog sleds and riverboats to air-planes, without the intervening development of a significant road or rail network. One day towns were separated from the outside world by perilous journeys that could last a month; the next day, people could come and go in hours. However, the peril still remained. In the early days, Alaska aviators crossed vast wilderness without proper maps, landmarks, weather reports, or even formal airstrips. This museum on the shore of the Lake Hood floatplane base contains many of their planes, most of them beautifully restored (you can sometimes watch restoration work in progress), as well as artifacts from

Alaska's eventful military history, films, and a flight simulator. Aviation enthusiasts shouldn't miss it. Others can get a strong feel for that pioneering time with a little effort: More interpretive information would be helpful, as the context of the planes and artifacts sometimes requires prior knowledge. There's an aviation-themed gift store, of course.

4721 Aircraft Dr. ⓒ 907/248-5325. www.alaskaairmuseum.org. Admission $10 adults, $8 seniors, $6 children ages 5–12. Summer daily 9am–5pm; winter Wed–Sun 9am–5pm. The museum is near the international airport; driving toward the airport on International Airport Dr., turn right toward Postmark Dr., then right again on Heliport Dr., and right again on Aircraft Dr.

Alaska Botanical Garden *Finds*   The garden is a pleasant place to walk and learn about native flora and some of the garden flowers and herbs that grow in this region. The plantings are in a few small clearings connected by gravel paths on thickly wooded grounds at the edge of a large wildland park. The quiet, shady setting of the boreal forest sets a muted tone. Gardeners will be interested in the two perennial gardens, the small rock garden and a formal herb garden. The placards on the wildflower trail will help you identify plants you see on Alaskan hikes. The Lowenfels Family Nature Trail is a 1-mile loop with a guide brochure that is pitched at an unusually thoughtful level. Along the walk is a chance to see salmon in Campbell Creek. Those without strong interest in gardening or native plants may find other attractions more deserving of limited time, however—especially considering the drive from downtown, which is 20 minutes without traffic, and possibly twice that at rush hour. The garden is open during daylight hours year-round, but the gardens are best viewed mid-May to mid-September.

Campbell Airstrip Rd. (off Tudor Rd.). ⓒ 907/770-3692. www.alaskabg.org. Suggested donation $5 per person, $10 per family. Summer daily 9am–9pm. Guided tours June–Aug Wed and Sat at 1pm. From downtown, drive out New Seward Hwy. (Gambell St.) to Tudor Rd., exit to the east (left), turn right off Tudor onto Campbell Airstrip Rd., and park at the Benny Benson School.

Alaska Museum of Natural History   This young museum 3 miles east of downtown focuses on paleontology with a permanent exhibit of Alaskan fossils belonging to the Bureau of Land Management with interactive features that children especially enjoy. Alaska's Arctic once was warm and humid, and now is a hotspot for dinosaur bone hunters. Temporary annual exhibits have been good, too.

201 North Bragaw St. ⓒ 907/274-2400. www.alaskamuseum.org. Admission $5 adult, $3 ages 5–12. Summer Mon–Sat 10am–5pm; winter Tues–Sat 10am–5pm.

Alaska Native Heritage Center *★★★*   Alaska Natives built this extraordinary center to bring their cultures to visitors. It's Alaska's best Native cultural attraction. What makes it so is not the graceful building or the professional and informative displays, but the Native people themselves, who often create a personal connection with visitors and rarely come across as practiced or distant. The three main parts of the center take half a day to absorb. First, there's a hall where storytellers, dancers, and Native athletes perform, with three 30-minute programs rotating through the day. Next, there is a gallery of educational displays with a theater showing short films and a series of workshops, where artisans practice and show off traditional crafts and often teach crafts to visitors. Finally, there's a pond surrounded by six traditional Native dwellings representing each cultural group, each hosted by a member of that group. There's a snack bar and grill that serves soup, sandwiches, and other meals, and a gift shop carries inexpensive items and real Native art and crafts for sale by the center or on consignment from artisans. Getting to the center requires wheels. The center offers a free shuttle from various points around town. Call for details on where and when to catch it.

From the Glenn Hwy. take the North Muldoon exit. (✆) **800/315-6608** or 907/330-8000. www.alaskanative.net. Admission $24 adults, $21 seniors and military, $16 children 7–16; Alaska residents $10 adult, $7 children. Discounts in winter for families and for joint admission to Anchorage Museum at Rasmuson Center. Summer daily 9am–5pm; call for winter hours.

The Alaska Zoo ★★ (Kids)

Don't expect the variety of a big-city zoo, but what the Alaska Zoo lacks in size it makes up with a charm all its own. Anchorage residents have developed personal relationships with the animals, naming many of them. That affection has made the national controversy over Maggie the African elephant an especially hot topic—animal welfare groups don't think she belongs in Alaska, and everyone from children's magazines to Jay Leno and David Letterman have weighed in. The zoo is trying to keep Maggie happy with improved indoor facilities, including a one-of-a-kind elephant exercise treadmill (which, like most human treadmills, has gone unused). The zoo's best attractions, however, are the Alaskan animals. I enjoy watching Ahpun the polar bear play and swim underwater (you can check that out on a webcam, too). Gravel paths meander through the woods past large enclosures with natural flora for bears, seals and otters, musk oxen, Dall sheep, moose, caribou, waterfowl—all the animals you were supposed to see in Alaska but may have missed. (Don't get the Amur tigers, yaks, snow leopards, or Bactrian camels in your snapshots—they'll blow your story.) You can easily spend half a day here. If you don't have a car, consider using the free summer-only shuttle from downtown. It is timed to meet up with 2-hour naturalist tours that take place every day at noon and include some backstage stops. The tours are $25 for adults, half price for children 12 and under. A snack bar serves basic meals and there is a gift shop.

4731 O'Malley Rd. (✆) **907/346-3242**. www.alaskazoo.org. Admission $10 adults, $8 seniors and military, $6 ages 3–17, free under 3. MC, V. May–Aug daily 9am–6pm, till 9pm Tues and Fri Memorial Day to Labor Day, summer educational programs most Tues at 7pm, live music most Fri at 7pm; off-season daily 10am–closing (time varies depending on the time of sunset). Drive out the New Seward Hwy. to O'Malley Rd., then turn left and go 2 miles; it's 20 min. from downtown, without traffic.

Earthquake Park

The 1964 Good Friday earthquake was the biggest ever in North America, registering at 9.2 on the Richter scale, killing 131 people, and flattening much of the region. Downtown Anchorage and the Turnagain residential area, near the park, suffered enormous slides that turned neighborhoods into chaotic ruins. A sculpture and excellent interpretive signs commemorate and explain the event, but you can't see much through the trees that have grown up since the quake. If you are up to a walk in the woods, however, descend into the park on the paved coastal trail, and then explore the dirt paths that branch from it. Those quiet pathways climb over the strange topography of hummocks and small ponds created when the ground went liquid. This also is a good access point to the Coastal Trail and a likely place to see birds and moose. Early in the summer the mosquitoes are horrendous. Continue west on the Coastal Trail or Northern Lights Boulevard to outlooks at Airport Park and Point Woronzof, within 2 miles of Earthquake Park, where Mount McKinley is visible in clear weather.

West end of Northern Lights Blvd. Free admission. Daily 24 hrs. From downtown, take L St. (it becomes Minnesota Dr.) to Northern Lights Blvd. and turn right. The park is on your right after you cross Lakeshore Dr.

Eklutna Historical Park ★

The Native village of Eklutna has a fascinating old cemetery, still in use, in which each grave is enclosed by a highly decorated spirit house the size of a large dollhouse. These little shelters excite the imagination in a way no ordinary marker would. The unique practice evolved from the melding of Athabascan and Russian Orthodox beliefs. There are two small Russian Orthodox churches on the site, including the **St. Nicholas Orthodox Church.** Built north of here of logs sometime before 1870, it is among the oldest churches on Alaska's mainland, and among the oldest buildings in the state. Tour guides offer an orientation talk before leading visitors through the site and both churches. Arrangements recently changed, however; given the half-hour drive from Anchorage, it would make sense to call ahead. If you go, wear mosquito repellent and also take the time to see Thunderbird Falls, described below under "Hiking & Mountain Biking."

About 26 miles out the Glenn Hwy. ℭ **907/688-6026.** Admission $5 adult, $3 ages 10–18, free under 10. Summer Mon–Fri 10am–4pm, Sat–Sun noon–4pm. Closed winter. Take the Glenn Hwy. 26 miles to the Eklutna exit, and then go left over the overpass.

SPECTATOR SPORTS

Most big events in Anchorage happen at the **Sullivan Arena,** at 16th Avenue and Gambell Street (sometimes known as the Sully, it is named after a still-living former mayor). Tickets can be purchased through Ticketmaster (ℭ **907/562-4800,** www.ticketmaster. com), which also sells through local Fred Meyer grocery stores. Ticketmaster also handles events at the downtown Egan Civic and Convention Center.

BASEBALL   Anchorage has two semipro baseball teams—the **Anchorage Glacier Pilots** (ℭ **907/274-3627;** www.glacierpilots.com) and the **Anchorage Bucs** (ℭ **907/ 561-2827;** www.anchoragebucs.com)—with college athletes playing in a six-team Alaska league during June and July. Cool summer nights under the natural light at Mulcahy Stadium are among our family's favorite outings. You hear, smell, and feel the rhythm of the game when you sit so close in the tiny park. The quality may be uneven, but exceptional players grow up here and many make the majors: Among famed alumni are Mark McGwire, Rick Aguilera, Tom Seaver, Dave Winfield, Barry Bonds, Wally Joyner, and Randy Johnson. Check the *Anchorage Daily News* or the websites above for game times. Mulcahy is at 16th Avenue and A Street, a long walk or a short drive from downtown. Tickets are around $5. Dress warmly for evening games; a blanket is rarely out of order. A weekend day game is warmer, but then you won't get to see baseball played at night without lights.

BASKETBALL   The University of Alaska Anchorage hosts an NCAA Division I preseason basketball tournament, the **Carrs/Safeway Great Alaska Shootout** (ℭ **907/ 786-1250;** www.goseawolves.com) in late November. The noted men's tournament takes place at the Sullivan Arena over Thanksgiving weekend. The women's tournament is held on the 2 days prior to Thanksgiving. The Seawolves, themselves in Division II, play the regular season at the Wells Fargo Sports Complex, on campus on Providence Drive.

HOCKEY   Anchorage is a hockey town. The biggest headline I've ever seen in the local newspaper is when the minor league hockey team won the national ECHL championship in the spring of 2006. The team, the **Alaska Aces** (ℭ **907/258-2237;** www.alaskaaces.com) competes at the Sullivan Arena. The western division that Alaska faces regularly includes cities such as Las Vegas and Phoenix. The season lasts from October to May.

Most years, the **University of Alaska Anchorage Seawolves** (ℭ **907/786-1250;** www.goseawolves.com) get plenty of attention all winter. They play NCAA Division I hockey at the Sullivan, a notoriously noisy and raucous venue for opposing teams.

5 Getting Outside

Anchorage is unique in Alaska (and anywhere else I know) for the number of places right in and near town to hike, bike, ski, and otherwise get into the wild. I've broken the options down by activities below. In town, the city's bike trails connect through greenbelts that span the noisy, asphalt urban core with soothing creekside woods. Kincaid Park and Far North Bicentennial Park are both on the trail system within the city, and encompass thousands of acres and scores of miles of trails for Nordic skiing, mountain biking, and horseback riding. The Chugach Mountains, which form the backdrop to the town, offer tundra hiking, backpacking, mountain biking, and climbs that range from easy to technical. More trails and streams, only slightly farther afield, are covered in the "Out from Anchorage" sections later in this chapter. Many cruises, tours, fishing charters, and sea-kayaking trips leave from nearby **Whittier,** easily managed as a day trip; see section 4 of chapter 7 for details.

INFORMATION   The **Alaska Public Lands Information Center** (p. 215; $\textcircled{C}$ **907/ 271-2737;** www.nps.gov/aplic) offers guidance for all these recreation areas and more throughout Alaska.

For information on the bike trails, parks, swimming, and other city recreation, contact **Anchorage Parks & Recreation** at $\textcircled{C}$ **907/343-4355** (www.muni.org/parks). Cross-country skiers can get information from the **Nordic Ski Association of Anchorage** ($\textcircled{C}$ **907/276-7609;** www.anchoragenordicski.com). For current trail conditions, check www.crosscountryalaska.org/trails.

Get information specific to **Chugach State Park** from the public lands center, or directly from the park at $\textcircled{C}$ **907/345-5014** (www.alaskastateparks.org; click on "Individual Parks"). Their *Ridgelines* newspaper is packed with useful information about the park, including a map adequate for most day hikers.

Chugach National Forest can be reached at $\textcircled{C}$ **907/743-9500** or www.fs.fed.us/ r10/chugach.

The best trail guide to the entire region is John Wolfe, Jr., and Helen D. Nienhueser's *55 Ways to the Wilderness in Southcentral Alaska,* fifth edition (The Mountaineers Books, $17) available in any bookstore in the area. Two excellent trail maps are widely available: "Chugach State Park" by Imus Geographics, covers the entire park, while "Anchorage & Vicinity" by Alaska Road & Recreation Maps, covers the park's southern portion as well as the entire Anchorage bowl and is at a finer scale than the Imus map. You can find either at sporting-goods stores or information centers.

EQUIPMENT   You can rent most anything you need for outdoor activities. For bike rentals, see "Getting Around," p. 214. Get advice, buy gear, and rent cross-country skis, snowshoes, bear-proof containers, and mountaineering equipment at **Alaska Mountaineering and Hiking,** at 2633 Spenard Rd. ($\textcircled{C}$ **907/272-1811;** http://alaska mountaineering.com). It's a small shop where the staff takes the time to help you plan a trip. A block away, at 1200 W. Northern Lights Blvd., **REI** has a larger store ($\textcircled{C}$ **907/272-4565;** www.rei.com) that rents a wide range of gear, including lightweight canoes and touring kayaks with car-top carriers, camping gear, packs, tents, sleeping bags, and cross-country skis (but not bikes or ice climbing gear). It is the best stocked place in town to buy outdoor athletic clothing as well. (For Arctic cold weather gear and where to buy it, see "What to Wear" on p. 19.)

WALKING & BIKING

Anchorage has an award-winning network of paved **bike trails** spanning the city along wooded greenbelts. You rarely see a building and almost always cross roads and rail lines through tunnels and over bridges, so you're never in traffic. Here are two of the best.

TONY KNOWLES COASTAL TRAIL 🍀🍀🍀   Leading 10 miles from the western end of 2nd Avenue along the shore to **Kincaid Park,** the coastal trail is among the best things about Anchorage. It's a unique pathway to the natural environment from the heart of downtown. I've ridden parallel to beluga whales swimming along the trail at high tide and encountered as many as six moose on a single ride. (Don't approach moose or bear or try to slip by; wait at a safe distance for them to go their own way.) The most popular entrance is at **Elderberry Park,** at the western end of 5th Avenue. **Westchester Lagoon** (a pond) is 10 blocks south of Elderberry Park. From downtown, the lagoon is a good destination for a lovely stroll and a fine place to picnic and feed the ducks, which nest on small islands.

LANIE FLEISCHER CHESTER CREEK TRAIL 🍀   Starting at an intersection with the Coastal Trail at Westchester Lagoon, this trail runs about 4 miles east along the greenbelt to **Goose Lake,** where you can swim or paddle a rented boat in a cool woodland pond at the end of a hot bike ride and buy ice cream or other snacks from a little cafe—still, improbably enough, in the middle of the city. South from the lake, a wooded trail leads partway through the university campus. The paved bike trails, including the Fleischer, stay well back in the trees, so you rarely see a building, and tunnels and bridges span all road and railroad crossings, so you're never in traffic.

HIKING & MOUNTAIN BIKING

Besides these hikes and bikes in Anchorage proper, more excellent, nearby options are along Turnagain Arm and in Girdwood, covered in sections 8 and 9 of this chapter.

KINCAID PARK 🍀🍀   Covered in more detail below, Kincaid Park is an idyllic summer setting for mountain biking and day hikes. Moose sightings are a common daily occurrence on wide dirt trails that snake for about 40 miles through the birch and white spruce of the park's hilly 1,500 acres of boreal forest, often with views of the sea and mountains beyond, including McKinley. Trails open to bikes around June 1, or as soon as they dry, and a mountain bike race series runs through the summer. On the busiest summer day, however, there is plenty of room for relaxed, solitary rambling or cycling. Within the park, wooded Little Campbell Lake is a picturesque spot for family canoeing and fishing for stocked trout; there is no lifeguard. There's also an 18-hole Frisbee golf course. Note that the park gates are locked at 10pm, so get your car out before then or park in one of the lots outside the gates.

FAR NORTH BICENTENNIAL PARK/CAMPBELL TRACT 🍀   A rectangle totaling 4,730 acres of city park and Bureau of Land Management (BLM) land brings wilderness into the city on the east side of town, a habitat for bears, moose, and spawning salmon. People use it for dog mushing and skiing in winter, and for exceptional mountain biking and day hiking in summer. The Alaska Botanical Garden, listed earlier, and the Hilltop Ski Area, described later, are both within the park's boundaries. A good place to start a hike or ride through the woods is the **Campbell Creek Science Center** (© 907/267-1247; www.blm.gov/ak/st/en/prog/science center.html), an educational facility operated by the BLM. Staff are often on hand to answer questions and you can consult books and maps and look at an aquarium of native fish. To get to the science center from downtown, take Gambell Street (it becomes New Seward Hwy.) south to Dowling Road, go east (toward the mountains), turn right on Lake Otis Road, turn left on 68th Avenue, and follow 68th to its end, then left at the BLM Campbell Tract entrance sign.

FLATTOP MOUNTAIN & THE GLEN ALPS TRAILHEAD ★★★ There are many ways to reach the alpine tundra, intoxicating fresh air, and cinematic views in the Chugach Mountains behind Anchorage, but the easiest and best developed portal is the Chugach State Park Glen Alps Trailhead. Even those who aren't up to hiking should go for the drive and a walk on a short, paved loop with incredible views and interpretive signs. If you are ready for a hike, you can start at the trailhead for trips of up to several days, following the network of trails or taking off across dry, alpine tundra by yourself, but usually within cellphone range. Camping is permitted anywhere off the trails.

Flattop Mountain is the most popular hike from Glen Alps and a great family climb, if a bit crowded on weekends. It's a steep afternoon hike, easy for fit adults and doable by school-age children. There's a bit of a scramble at the top, easiest if you stick to the painted markers on the rocks. Dress warmly and don't go in the rain, when slick rocks at the top could cause a fall.

For a longer or less steep hike or a mountain-biking trip, follow the broad gravel trail that leads up the valley from the Glen Alps Trailhead to several other great routes. Trails lead all the way over the mountains to Indian or Bird Creek, on Turnagain Arm, up some of the mountains along the way or to round alpine lakes in high, rocky valleys. You're always above the tree line, so you don't need to follow a trail if you have a good map. This is wonderful backpacking country.

To get to the trail head, take New Seward Highway to O'Malley Road, head east toward the mountains, then turn right on Hillside Drive and left onto Upper Huffman Road. Finally, turn right on the narrow, twisting Toilsome Hill Drive. Don't forget to bring cash or a check for the self-service day-use fee of $5 (not required if you are going only to the overlook and park in the designated spaces).

A hikers' shuttle runs summer afternoons daily from Downtown Bicycle Rental at the 4th Avenue Market Place downtown (p. 247) when enough passengers sign up. The fare is $22 for adults, $15 for children ages 6–12, $5 for children 5 and under. Call ⓒ 907/279-3334 to sign up.

EAGLE RIVER VALLEY ★★ The **Eagle River Nature Center,** at the end of Eagle River Road, 12 miles up Eagle River Valley from the Glenn Highway exit (ⓒ **907/694-2108;** www.ernc.org), resembles a public wilderness lodge, with hands-on nature displays about the area and daily nature walks in the summer and weekends year-round (2pm weekends, call for other times). Operated by a nonprofit concessionaire for Chugach State Park, it's open June through August Sunday to Thursday from 10am to 5pm, Friday and Saturday from 10am to 7pm; May and September from 10am to 5pm except Monday; October through April Friday to Sunday from 10am to 5pm. There's a $5 parking fee.

The .75-mile **Rodak Nature Trail,** with interpretive signs, leads to viewing platforms over a beaver pond. The **Albert Loop Trail** is a 3-mile route; a geology guide from the center matches with numbered posts on the way. Both trails have good bird- and wildlife-watching. The 25-mile **Crow Pass Trail,** a portion of the historic Iditarod Trail, continues up the valley into the mountains along the river. You can make a day-hike loop of 6 miles or less by returning on the **Dew Mound Trail.** Continuing, the Crow Pass Trail eventually surmounts the Chugach in alpine terrain and passes near Raven Glacier before descending into Girdwood (p. 254). There are campsites with fire rings along the way, and a mile up the trail the center rents out a public-use cabin for $65 a night. A yurt on the Crow Pass Trail and another on the Albert Loop rent for the same price. Reserve well ahead for weekends. Availability is shown on the website.

THUNDERBIRD FALLS & EKLUTNA LAKE 👁👁 The hike to Thunderbird Falls is an easy, 1-mile forest walk with a good reward at the end; you can see the falls without the steep final descent to their foot. Take the Glenn Highway north to the Thunderbird Falls exit, 25 miles from Anchorage. Continuing 10 miles up the Eklutna Lake Road, you come to an appealing state parks campground ($10 a night, $5 day-use fee) and a glacial lake for canoeing, hiking, and exceptional mountain biking. The Lakeside Trail leads 14 miles to Eklutna Glacier; you can camp on the way, stay at the state park's Yuditna Creek Cabin at 3 miles or stay in the communal Serenity Falls hut at 13 miles. Advance reservations are required for the cabin or hut. See "State Parks Cabin Reservations" on p. 265. For the hut, you can reserve in person only. Rental bikes, kayaks, and other equipment, and guided kayak tours are offered by **Lifetime Adventures,** with a booth at the trail head of the Lakeside Trail (📞 **907/ 746-4644;** www.lifetimeadventures.net). For $75 you can kayak 8 miles to the other end of the lake and pick up a bike there to ride back.

BIRD-WATCHING

The Anchorage bowl contains varied bird habitat that is easily accessed and close at hand: lakes, streams, marshes, seashore, woodlands, and mountains. Visiting birders can see species they don't encounter at home (Pacific loons, Hudsonian godwits, boreal chickadees) and familiar birds in breeding plumage unique to these northern latitudes (a red-necked grebe that actually does have a red neck, for example). Local birders have recorded more than 225 species in the city. You will need the help of a rental car or at least a bike. Potter Marsh is a superb freshwater birding area (see section 8, later in this chapter). Salt marshes and mud flats lie along much of the Tony Knowles Coastal Trail (see above). Right downtown, Ship Creek provides a river habitat. You can join field trips and network with local birders through the **Anchorage Audubon Society** (www.anchorageaudubon.org). The site contains an updated log of unusual sightings, which you can also check on a recorded hot line (📞 **907/338-BIRD**).

A terrific booklet, *Anchorage Wildlife Viewing Hot Spots,* published by the Alaska Department of Fish & Game, is sold for $6 at the Alaska Public Land Information Center. It has more places to go than I can include here, detailed directions, and helpful information. Learn more about wildlife viewing around Alaska at www.wildlife viewing.alaska.gov.

FISHING

There are hatchery salmon in several of Anchorage's streams, and stocked trout, salmon, or char in 28 lakes, so you need not leave town to catch a fish. The **Alaska Department of Fish & Game,** 333 Raspberry Rd., Anchorage, AK 99518-1599 (📞 **907/267-2218;** www.alaska.gov/adfg, click on "Sport Fisheries," then navigate by using the maps), publishes informative booklets on the Web and on paper and an online fishing report updated weekly in season. There's also a recorded information line (📞 **907/267-2503**) with what's hot and lots of other advice. See chapter 2 for general guidance and license information, and information for planning a fishing vacation, and see chapter 7 for the famous fishing opportunities on the Kenai Peninsula.

ROADSIDE FISHING Although the setting (under a highway bridge in an industrial area) might not be the wilderness experience you've dreamed about, the 40-pound king salmon you pull from **Ship Creek** may make up for it. From downtown, just walk down the hill to the railroad yard. A couple of shacks sell and rent gear in the summer. Fishing for kings is best in June and for silvers in August and September. You should fish only on the rising tide, when the fish come into the creek. Fishing near the end of the rising tide will mean crossing less mud, but one successful angler I know insists it's the start of the tide that's best. Either way, you'll need rubber boots, preferably neoprene chest waders, for the muddy banks, but don't go too far out, as the mud flats are dangerous and several times every summer the Fire Department has to rescue stuck fishermen.

Campbell Creek, a more natural urban stream, is stocked with silver salmon that make good fishing in August and September, and rainbow trout and Dolly Varden char are in the creek year-round. The creek runs along a greenbelt across the city through residential and industrial neighborhoods; the adjacent bike trail is a good access route. You can join the trail on Dimond Boulevard east of Jewel Lake Road, or where C Street crosses the creek just north of Dimond, among other places; or ask for directions and tips at the Public Land Information Center.

Bird Creek, 25 miles south of Anchorage on the Seward Highway (see "Out from Anchorage: Turnagain Arm & Portage Glacier" later in this chapter), is known for hot silver salmon fishing in the late summer and fall. Pinks run from late June to early August during even-numbered years. Other creeks along the Arm have similar but smaller runs.

FLY-IN FISHING ✯✯✯ Serious anglers will use Anchorage as a base from which to fly to a remote lake or river with more fish and fewer people. Such a flight can be an unforgettable experience for those who are less than enthusiastic about fishing, too. The plane lifts off from Anchorage's Lake Hood floatplane base and within half an hour smoothly lands on a lake or river. You climb out and watch as the plane lifts off and disappears, leaving behind the kind of silence unique to true wilderness. It's on these trips that avid anglers are made—or spoiled. I've heard people complain of how sore their arms got from pulling in too many salmon.

Several companies offer fly-in trips; the best established is **Rust's Flying Service** (© 800/544-2299 or 907/243-1595; www.flyrusts.com). It's a family-owned company with a strong safety ethic. They can take you out guided or on your own, for the day or for a longer stay in a cabin or lodge. If you fly to a lake, they'll provide a boat. They can't make fish appear if none are running, but they will try to take you to the hot spots. You can bring your own gear, or they can provide it. Prices for an unguided day trip start around $230 per person, with a two-person minimum; guided trips start around, $425. Pickup from your hotel is included, but not fishing licenses.

OTHER SUMMER ACTIVITIES

FLIGHTSEEING/BEAR VIEWING Small planes are the blood cells of Alaska's circulatory system, and Anchorage its heart. There are several busy airports in Anchorage, and Lake Hood is the world's busiest floatplane base. If you will travel to Talkeetna, Denali National Park, Juneau, Glacier Bay National Park, or Ketchikan, you may want to save your flightseeing splurge for those extraordinary places, which are close to famous attractions. Likewise, for bear-viewing flights, Katmai National Park, Homer, Kodiak, Juneau, and Wrangell may be closer to the action. (All those places are covered in this guide with the details for flights; see the table of contents or index.) On the other hand, plenty of spectacular territory is near Anchorage, and, if time is short, you can see bears or Denali in an afternoon. I recommend Rust's Flying Service (see "Fly-In Fishing," above), a reliable operator that has designed a menu of choices around visitors' most common interests. They can take you on a floatplane ride for as little as $95. A flight to see Mount McKinley (without landing) is $295 and takes 3 hours. An all-day bear-viewing tour from Anchorage is $550 to $695 per person. The exact destination—Lake Clark or Katmai national parks, or somewhere else—depends on where bears are active when you are traveling.

RAFTING There are several whitewater rivers within a 90-minute drive of Anchorage. **Nova Raft and Adventure Tours** (© **800/746-5753** or 907/745-5753; http:// novalaska.com) has more than 30 years of experience offering trips all over the state, and five different half-day floats in the Anchorage area. Various rafting trips are available, ranging from the relatively easygoing Matanuska and Kings rivers to the Class IV and V whitewater of Six Mile Creek, which begins with a required instructional swim and includes fun optional swims. That wild whitewater is about an hour south of Anchorage on the Seward Highway. Whitewater rafting always entails risk, but Nova's schedule allows you to calibrate how wild you want to get. Call to reserve and let them guide you as to the float that fits you best. The company also offers add-ons for self-paddling, helicopter flightseeing, or glacier hiking. The half-day trips range in price from $70 to $250. Children 5 to 11 can go on the calmer Matanuska River float for $35. Other trips are suitable only for older children and adults. You'll need your own transportation to the river and may need to bring your own lunch. **Chugach Outdoor Center** (© **866/277-RAFT** or 907/277-RAFT; www.chugachoutdoorcenter.com) also offers several rafting options south of Anchorage. The company has two daily choices on Six Mile Creek, floats in Turnagain Pass and in Seward's Resurrection River, and sea-kayaking on Kenai Lake.

If you want to go rafting without traveling to the Matanuska River or Six Mile Creek, you can save time and money by taking a shorter, somewhat less dramatic ride closer to town on the Eagle River, which runs past the Anchorage suburb of the same name. A whitewater ride is as little as $35 with **Lifetime Adventures** (© **907/746-4644;** www.lifetimeadventures.net) and they have longer floats that also include more smooth water. The rides go several times a day every day of the summer.

SEA KAYAKING Except at Eklutna Lake (see above), kayaking day trips from Anchorage go through Whittier, on Prince William Sound (see section 4 of chapter 7 for complete details).

SWIMMING I'm betting that most visitors from warmer climes won't be interested in chilly lake swimming in Anchorage (the best spot is Goose Lake, off Northern Lights Blvd. east of Lake Otis Rd.). If you have children and need to burn off some energy, however, you won't find a better spot than an indoor waterpark called **H2Oasis** (© **888/H2OASIS** or 907/522-4420; www.h2oasiswaterpark.com), near the intersection of O'Malley Road and the New Seward Highway. A big wave pool and a 500-foot "watercoaster" are the top attractions. Adults should bring earplugs, as the noise is unbearable, and a full wallet, as admission is $22 for ages 13 and older, $17 for ages 3 to 12, and free for children under age 3.

WINTER ACTIVITIES
The best downhill skiing and snowmobile tours are covered in the Girdwood section, on p. 254.

ICE SKATING **Westchester Lagoon,** just 10 blocks from downtown (see "Walking & Biking," earlier), is a skating paradise in the winter. When the ice gets thick are coordinated to happen on the first Friday of each month, allowing for an evening of free party hopping and art shopping.

The **International Gallery of Contemporary Art,** 427 D St. (www.igcaalaska.org) is a nonprofit space dedicated to artists. Come here for an in-depth look at just a few artists' work and to meet people who really care about art. Since it is run on contributions by volunteers, hours are short and changeable; currently open Wednesday through Sunday noon to 4pm; Tuesday 5:30 to 8:30pm; closed Monday. They're also open for first Friday, 6 to 8pm.

Artique, at 314 G St., is Anchorage's oldest gallery and has a large selection. Half of the gallery is given over to big oils and other impressive originals; the other half is chock-full of prints, less-expensive ceramics, and some mass-produced and/or corny stuff. At 5th and G, **Aurora Fine Arts** carries pottery, prints, and gifts. Directly across G is a gallery showing only glass sculpture.

7 Anchorage Nightlife

THE PERFORMING ARTS

WHAT'S PLAYING   The primary arts season begins in the fall and ends in the spring, but in the summer you can catch traveling performers, music festivals, and live music at the nightclubs and coffeehouses. To find out what's happening, check Friday's edition of the *Anchorage Daily News,* which has a section called "Play" that includes reviews and listings information in grid format. The website (www.adn.com/play) includes an exhaustive event calendar. The free weekly *Anchorage Press,* given away in racks all over town, also offers extensive event coverage aimed at a younger audience. See "Special Events" earlier in this chapter for some major happenings.

BUYING TICKETS   Ticketmaster (© 907/562-4800; www.ticketmaster.com) handles the Sullivan Arena and Egan Civic and Convention Center, and sells tickets at Fred Meyer grocery stores. The Alaska Center for Performing Arts, at 631 W. 6th Ave. (www.alaskapac.org) operates its own ticket agency, **CenterTix** (© 907/263-ARTS; www.centertix.net). The call center and box office in the center are open Monday through Friday 9am to 5pm, Saturday noon to 5pm, and evenings prior to events.

PRESENTERS   The **Anchorage Concert Association** (© 907/272-1471; www.anchorageconcerts.org) offers a fall-through-spring schedule of classical music, theater, dance, and other performing arts. **Whistling Swan Productions** (www.whistlingswan.net) promotes folk and acoustic alternative performers in intimate venues all year. The **Anchorage Symphony** (© 907/274-8668; www.anchoragesymphony.org) performs during the winter season. Anchorage also has lots of community theater and opera, and limited professional theater, including the experimental **Out North Contemporary Art House** (© 907/279-3800; www.outnorth.org), which produces local shows and imports avant-garde performers. Downtown, **Cyrano's Off Center Playhouse** (© 907/274-2599; www.cyranos.org), at 4th Avenue and D Street, is a tiny theater with its own semiprofessional repertory company.

NIGHTCLUBS & BARS

I've mentioned some fun downtown bars in the walking tour, including Humpy's, Darwin's Theory, and F Street Station. The largest and hippest downtown club is **Bernie's Bungalow Lounge,** 626 D St. (© 907/276-8808) which grew from a little bungalow into a large, artsy playground with a backyard patio enclosed by a hedge.

You can sometimes find foreign films, poetry readings, and similar cultural fare here, and, more often, you can socialize with people interested in such things.

Blues Central/Chef's Inn, 825 W. Northern Lights Blvd. (© **907/272-1341**), is dedicated to showcasing the best blues performers available, virtually every night. Major names come through on a regular basis. Shows start at 9:30pm. They're also known for their beef.

The most famous bar in Anchorage, with the slogan, "We cheat the other guy and pass the savings on to you," is the huge **Chilkoot Charlie's,** at Spenard Road and Fireweed Lane (© **907/272-1010;** www.koots.com). It has two stages, three dance floors, and 10 bars on different themes, including a historic old dive from the Seward Highway called the Bird House that was picked up and moved into the building. The place is huge and full of entertainment, like an adult Disneyland, but I find it claustrophobic when crowded, with its low ceilings and confusing layout. It's open every day of the year from 10:30am until after 2am. If you do go there late, avoid conflict and use caution when leaving, as it can be a wild crowd and rough neighborhood.

THE MOVIES

A movie at the **Bear Tooth TheatrePub,** at 1230 W. 27th Ave. (© **907/276-4200;** www.beartooththeatre.net) is a chance to sit back with a big glass of craft-brewed beer and a plate of nachos or a full dinner—it feels a lot like watching at home except for the big screen and the other people around you in the dark. (Well, our home is usually a bit cleaner, but our cooking isn't as good.) The films tend to be independent or second-run, either campy or deep. The dining choices include gourmet tacos, pizzas, and other hand-held selections. Everything is quite good. They also put on concerts monthly: check the website. And now the fine print. Even bad movies sell out and there's often a crush. You must arrive quite early to find parking, get your ticket and seat, order your food and beer, and finish waiting in various lines before the movie starts. The staff brings the meal to you in the theater. Eating here without taking in a movie is covered under "Bear Tooth Grill" on p. 229. There are several multiplexes in Anchorage playing all the current Hollywood output; check the sources at the beginning of this section for listings and reviews. The closest large theater to the downtown area is the **Century 16,** 301 E. 36th Ave. (© **907/929-3456;** www.cinemark.com).

8 Out from Anchorage: Turnagain Arm & Portage Glacier

One of the world's great drives starts in Anchorage and leads roughly 50 miles south on the Seward Highway to Portage Glacier. It's the trip, not the destination, that makes it worthwhile. The two-lane highway along Turnagain Arm, chipped from the foot of the rocky Chugach Mountains, provides a platform to see a magnificent, ever-changing, mostly untouched landscape full of wildlife. I've listed the sights in the style of a highway log, for there are interesting stops all the way along the road. It will take at least half a day round-trip, and there's plenty to do for an all-day excursion. Use your headlights for safety even in daylight and be patient if you get stuck behind a summertime line of cars—if you pass, you'll just come up behind another line ahead. Mileage markers count down from Anchorage. Continue with this highway log on to the Kenai Peninsula and Seward in chapter 7, starting at p. 265. Car rental is covered in "Getting Around," earlier in this chapter.

Bus tours follow the route and visit Portage Glacier. **Gray Line of Alaska** (© **800/ 544-2206** or 907/277-5581; www.graylineofalaska.com) offers a 7-hour trip that includes a stop in Girdwood and a boat ride on Portage Lake for $69 adults, $35 children 12 and under, twice daily in summer.

You can also see this incredible scenery—and more—from a train, although, of course, without stopping along the way for hikes or wildlife viewing. The **Alaska Railroad** (© **800/544-0552** or 907/265-2494; www.alaskarailroad.com) operates summer trains to Whittier and Seward that trace Turnagain Arm on the way, as well as a day-trip tour to the glaciated interior of the Kenai Peninsula, where no road extends. You can join that tour, called the "Glacier Discovery Train to Grandview" in Anchorage, Girdwood, Whittier, or Portage; if starting from Anchorage, the return from Portage is by bus. The tour is $99 for adults from Anchorage or Girdwood, $79 from Portage or Whittier, and roughly half price for children. It takes all day. They have a whitewater rafting option, too.

POTTER MARSH (Mile 117)   Heading south from Anchorage, the Seward Highway descends a bluff to cross a broad marsh formed by water impounded behind the tracks of the Alaska Railroad. The marsh has a boardwalk from which you can watch a huge variety of birds. Salad-green grasses grow from sparkling, pond-green water.

POTTER SECTION HOUSE (Mile 115)   Located at the south end of Potter Marsh, the section house was an early maintenance station for the Alaska Railroad. Today it contains the offices of Chugach State Park, open during normal business hours, and, outside, a few old train cars and interpretive displays. Just across the road is the trail head for the **Turnagain Arm Trail.** It's a mostly level path running down the arm well above the highway with great views breaking now and then through the trees. Hike as far as you like and then backtrack to your car; or, if you can arrange a one-way walk with a ride back from the other end, continue 4 miles to the McHugh Creek picnic area and trail head, or 9 miles to Windy Corner.

McHUGH CREEK (Mile 111)   Four miles south of Potter is an excellent state park picnic area and a challenging day hike with a 3,000-foot elevation gain to Rabbit Lake, which sits in a tundra mountain bowl, or to the top of 4,301-foot McHugh Peak. You don't have to climb all the way; there are spectacular views within an hour of the road. From this point onward, most of the stops are on the right or ocean side of the road: Plan your stops on the outbound trip, not on the return when you would have to make left turns across traffic.

BELUGA POINT (Mile 110)   The state highway department probably didn't need to put up scenic overlook signs on this pullout, 1½ miles south of McHugh Creek—you would have figured it out on your own. The terrain is simply awesome, as the highway traces the edge of Turnagain Arm, below the towering cliffs of the Chugach Mountains. If the tide and salmon runs are right, you may see beluga whales, which chase the fish toward fresh water. Sometimes they overextend and strand themselves by the dozens in the receding tide, farther along, but they usually aren't harmed. The pullout has spotting scopes to improve the viewing. The further right-hand pullouts over the next few miles have interpretive signs about the 1895 gold rush in this area and other topics.

WINDY POINT (Mile 106)   Be on the lookout on the mountain side of the road for Dall sheep picking their way along the cliffs. It's a unique spot, for the sheep get much closer to people here than is usual in the wild; apparently, they believe they're safe. Windy Point is the prime spot, but you also have a good chance of seeing sheep virtually anywhere along this stretch of road. If cars are stopped, that's probably why;

Tidal Wave

Tides in Turnagain Arm rise and fall over a greater range than anywhere else in the United States, with a difference between an extreme high and low of more than 41 feet. When the tide is rising, the water can grow deeper by as much as 7 feet an hour, or a foot of water every 8½ minutes. If your foot gets stuck in the mud, it takes less than an hour to drown. (Yes, that has really happened.) Amazing as that speed is, the tide here can go even faster. A breathtaking wall of water up to 6 feet tall called a bore tide can roar up Turnagain Arm twice a day. To see the ocean do such a thing is so unfamiliar it looks almost like science fiction, as the wide arc of foam rushes ahead of a noticeably deeper sea. You can (theoretically) predict the bore tide. Get a tide-table book or look up the tide change on the Web (start at http://tidesandcurrents.noaa.gov and pull down "Products"). Note the size of the tidal range for the day you are visiting: The bore tide will be most noticeable during periods of large tides. (The magnitude of tides varies on the lunar cycle.) Find the time of low tide in Anchorage. Now add the following intervals to the time of the Anchorage low for a prediction of when the bore tide will pass each of these spots on the highway:

- Beluga Point (Mile 110): 1 hour 15 minutes
- Bird Point (Mile 96): 2 hours 15 minutes
- Twentymile River (Mile 80): 4 hours

The best viewing is Beluga Point to Bird Point; at the latter wayside, a set of signs explain the tides.

get well off the road and pay attention to traffic, which will still be passing at high speeds.

You may also see windsurfers in the gray, silty waters of the Arm. They're crazy. The water is a mixture of glacial runoff and the near-freezing ocean. Besides, the movement of water that creates the huge tides causes riverlike currents, with standing waves like rapids.

INDIAN VALLEY (Mile 104)   Up the road by the Turnagain House restaurant is the **Indian Valley** trail head, a gold-rush–era trail that ultimately leads 24 miles to the other side of the mountains. The path, while often muddy, rises less steeply than other trails along the Arm.

BIRD RIDGE TRAIL (Mile 102)   This is a lung-busting climb of 3,000 vertical feet in a little over a mile. It starts with an easy, accessible trail, then rises steeply to views that start at impressive and get more amazing as you climb. With the southern exposure, it's dry early in the year.

BIRD CREEK (Mile 101)   The excellent state campground on the right side of the highway, over the water, is described on p. 224, and the productive salmon fishing in the creek is described on p. 245. If you stop, use the lot on the left side of the road before you reach the creek. There is also a short trail, interpretive signs, an overlook, and a platform that makes fishing easier for people with disabilities. Pink salmon run from late June to mid-August, silver salmon mostly in August. A scenic bike trail starts here and runs 10 miles to Girdwood, much of it on an older highway alignment.

BIRD POINT (Mile 96)   The remarkable wayside here is not to be missed. A paved pathway rises up to a bedrock outcropping with a simply wonderful view—all the severity of the Turnagain Arm, but framed by the soft green of a freshwater wetland with a beaver lodge. Take a look at the fascinating interpretive signs on many subjects.

THE FLATS (Miles 96–90)   At Bird Point the highway descends from the mountain-side to the mud flats. Several pullouts on the right side of the highway have interpretive signs. At high tide, water comes right up to the road. At low tide, the whole Arm narrows to a thin, winding channel through the mud. The Arm is not practically navigable and navigational charts are not even available. Few have ever tried to navigate it other than gold prospectors in rowboats a century ago or today's occasional death-defying canoeist or kayaker. The first to try was Capt. James Cook, in 1778, as he was searching for the Northwest Passage on his final, fatal voyage of discovery (he was killed by Hawaiians later that year). He named this branch of Cook Inlet Turnagain Arm because the strength of the currents and shoals forced the boat he sent to keep turning around.

TURNOFF TO GIRDWOOD (Mile 90)   The attractions of Girdwood, covered below, are worth a visit, but the shopping center here at the intersection is not chief among them. Stop for a simple meal or a restroom break (the convenience store has large public restrooms), or to fill your gas tank for the last time for many a mile.

TWENTYMILE RIVER (Mile 80)   Three species of salmon and a small smelt, the eulachon, known locally as the hooligan, spawn in this river. In the spring you can see Native families dip-netting the hooligan. There is good bird-watching here and from turnouts farther on, but venturing out on Turnagain Arm's tidal mud carries the real risk of getting stuck in quicksand-like mud and drowning in the tide. Don't do it.

OLD PORTAGE (Mile 80)   All along the flats at the head of Turnagain Arm are large marshes full of what looks like standing driftwood. These are trees killed by salt-water that flowed in when the 1964 quake lowered the land as much as 10 feet. On the right, 7⁄10 mile past the Twentymile River and across from the rail depot, a few ruins of the abandoned town of Portage are still visible, more than 40 years after the great earthquake.

ALASKA WILDLIFE CONSERVATION CENTER (Mile 79)   Originally conceived as a tourist attraction, the center has become a nonprofit organization giving homes to injured and orphaned deer, moose, owls, elk, bison, musk ox, bear, fox, and caribou (© **907/783-2025;** www.alaskawildlife.org). Visitors drive through the 200-acre compound to see the animals in fenced enclosures as large as 110 acres—you can often get a close look at the animals, but the larger enclosures give them natural vegetation and the ability to get away from view if they want to. There's no need to visit both here and the Alaska Zoo (p. 239). The zoo has more kinds of animals and it's a fun place to stroll, but the cages there are much smaller and often seem constricting. Here the animals' settings are more natural and perhaps more humane, but viewing is car based. A big, log gift shop and outdoor snack bar are at the end of the tour. Admission is $7.50 for adults; $5 for military, seniors, and children 4 to 12, with a maximum of $25 per vehicle. In summer, it's open daily from 8am to 8pm (last vehicle in at 7:30pm); in winter, daily from 10am to 5pm.

Gone but Not Forgotten

The **Begich, Boggs Visitor Center** at Portage Glacier is named for Hale Boggs, who was U.S. House majority leader, and Rep. Nick Begich, then Alaska's lone congressman, who disappeared together in a small plane during Begich's 1972 reelection bid. The most likely theory is that the wings iced up in Portage Pass, causing a crash into Prince William Sound just beyond the mountains. No trace was ever found—as with many other Alaskan planes that have simply flown off into oblivion. Begich was reelected anyway. His opponent, Republican Don Young, later won a special election and continues to serve as Alaska's only congressman. Boggs' wife, Lindy, went on to serve out his term and eight more. Boggs' daughter, Cokie Roberts, is the famous broadcast journalist. Begich's son, Mark, is mayor of Anchorage.

PORTAGE GLACIER (Take the 5½-mile spur road at Mile 78)   The named attraction has largely melted, receding out of sight of the visitor center. (The glacier you *can* see is Burns.) When the center was built in 1985, it was predicted that Portage Glacier would keep floating on its 800-foot-deep lake until 2020. Instead, it withdrew to the far edge of the lake in 1995. Today the exhibits in the lakeside **Begich, Boggs Visitor Center** focus on the Chugach National Forest as a whole, rather than just the glacier, and they're worth an hour or two to become oriented to the area's nature, history, and lifestyles. Children and adults find much to hold their interest here. To see Portage Glacier itself, take the road toward Whittier that branches to the left just before the visitor center and stop at a pullout beyond the first (toll-free) tunnel; or take the boat mentioned below.

Several short trails start near the center. Check at the center for rangers-led nature walks. The Moraine Trail is an easy, paved .25 mile. Another trail leads less than a mile to Byron Glacier, in case you're interested in getting up close to some ice. Always dress warmly, as cold winds are the rule in this funnel-like valley.

A **day boat** operated by **Gray Line of Alaska** (© **800/478-6388,** 907/277-5581 for reservations, or 907/783-2983 at the lake; www.graylineofalaska.com) traverses the lake right up to Portage Glacier on hour-long tours, ice conditions permitting. It costs $29 for adults, $15 for ages 12 and under, and goes five times daily in summer, every 90 minutes starting at 10:30am. If this is your only chance to see a glacier in Alaska, it's a good choice, but if your itinerary includes any of the great glaciers in Prince William Sound, Kenai Fjords National Park, or the like, you won't be as impressed by Portage.

Sandwiches and other simple meals are sold at a cafeteria near the visitor center called the **Portage Glacier Lodge** (© **907/783-3117**).

There are no lodgings in Portage, but two **Forest Service campgrounds** are on the road to the visitor center, with 72 sites between them (more details are in the Chugach National Forest section in chapter 7). At the Williwaw Campground, there's also a place to watch red salmon spawning in mid-August, but no fishing.

9 Out from Anchorage: Girdwood & Mount Alyeska

Girdwood, 37 miles south of Anchorage, is proof that a charming little town can coexist with a major ski resort, as long as the resort goes undiscovered by the world's skiers. Girdwood still has a sleepy, offbeat character. Retired hippies, ski bums, a U.S. senator, and a few old-timers live in the houses and cabins among the big spruce trees in the valley below the Mount Alyeska lifts. They all expected a development explosion to follow the construction of an international resort here a number of years ago, but it hasn't happened. That may not have been good news for the Japanese investors who finally sold the resort late in 2006, but it is for skiers and other visitors who discover this paradise. They find varied, uncrowded skiing through long winters, superb accommodations, and an authentically funky community.

The primary summer attractions are the hiking trails, the tram to the top of Mount Alyeska, and the Crow Creek Mine, described below. In winter, it's skiing. Mount Alyeska doesn't have the size of the famous resorts in the Rockies, but it's more than large and steep enough. Better still, there's plenty of room, half the mountain is above the tree line, and the snow lasts a long time. Olympian Tommy Moe trained here and the Alpine national championships raced down these slopes in 2004 and 2007. Skiers used to tamer, busier slopes rave about the skiing here, with long, challenging downhills, few lift lines, and stunning views of the Chugach Mountains and glistening Turnagain Arm below.

A wealthy skiing enthusiast bought the ski resort in 2006 from owners that had paid it little attention for several years. He pledged to make many welcome improvements on the mountain and at the skiing facilities, but nothing concrete had happened yet when I completed this edition. Be aware changes are likely as you use the information you find here.

ESSENTIALS   A **rental car** is the most practical means for getting to Girdwood. If you will only ski, however, you may be able to take a shuttle; call the resort before you come. The **Girdwood Chamber of Commerce** maintains a website at **www.girdwood alaska.com**. For more guidance, check the Anchorage visitor information listed in section 1 of this chapter.

EXPLORING GIRDWOOD

Crow Creek Mine ⚡   This mine, opened in 1898, is still operated in a small way by the Toohey family, but mostly they use the paths and eight small original buildings as a charming tourist attraction. You get a glimpse of the frontier lifestyle and can watch rabbits and ducks wandering around. A bag of dirt, guaranteed to have some gold in it, is provided for gold panning, and you can dig and pan to get more if you have the patience for it. Crow Creek Road, off the Alyeska Highway, can be quite rough and muddy in the spring. Camping is $5 a night, with portable toilets.

Crow Creek Rd. (off the Alyeska Hwy.), Girdwood, AK 99587. ⚡ **907/278-8060.** Admission $3 adults, free for children; gold panning $10 adults, $4 children 11 and under (includes admission). May 15–Sept 15 daily 9am–6pm.

Mt. Alyeska Tram ⚡   The tram isn't cheap, but I think it's worth it for anyone who otherwise might not make it to high alpine tundra during an Alaska trip. (In winter ride on your lift ticket; in summer ride free with a meal at the Seven Glaciers Restaurant at the top, p. 250.) The tram takes 7 minutes in summer to get to the 2,300-foot level, where it stops at a station containing both the Seven Glaciers Restaurant and an attractive but pricey cafeteria. Whether or not you eat here, the tram presents an opportunity for everyone, no matter how young, old, or infirm, to experience the pure light, limitless views, and crystalline quiet of an Alaskan mountaintop. Take the opportunity to walk around and enjoy it. Dress very warmly.

At the Hotel Alyeska (see below). Admission $16 adults, $15 ages 55 and older, $14 adult Alaska residents, $12 ages 8–17, $7 ages 7 and under. Summer daily 10am–9:30pm; winter when lifts operate (call to check as hours vary).

Tips Ski Conditions

The rainforest of Girdwood and the dry Anchorage bowl often have different weather, despite being within the same municipality. Before heading down the road for a day of skiing, check out the conditions. Call *©* **907/SKI-SNOW** for snow, weather, and visibility conditions, or check that information online at www.alyeskaresort.com. For visibility from below, check out the cam at www.chairfive.com.

ACTIVITIES

Here I have covered activities right in Girdwood. In nearby Whittier (p. 273), you can go ocean fishing, sea kayaking, or take a glacier and wildlife cruise. The Turnagain Arm and Portage area (p. 250) offers sightseeing along Turnagain Arm, hiking, and other summer activities.

SKIING   Mount Alyeska, at 3,939 feet, has 1,000 acres of skiing, beginning from a base elevation of only 250 feet and rising 2,500 feet. The normal season is from early November to April, and it's an exceptional year when there isn't plenty of snow all winter (although the warming climate has brought some poor ski seasons). Skiing on the upper mountain usually lasts through Memorial Day weekend (not for beginners). The average snowfall is 721 inches, or 61 feet. Because Mount Alyeska is near the water, the weather is rarely very cold. Light is more of an issue, with short days in midwinter. There are 27 lighted trails covering 2,000 vertical feet on Friday and Saturday evenings from mid-December to mid-March, but the best Alaska skiing is when the days get longer and warmer in the spring.

Alyeska has 10 lifts, including the tram. Two chairs serve beginners, with a vertical drop of around 300 feet. The other 89% of the mountain is geared to intermediate to expert skiers. The biggest drawback for less-experienced skiers is a lack of runs in the low-intermediate ability range. After graduating from the primary beginners' lift, Chair 3, skiers must jump to significantly more challenging slopes. That explains the long lines in busy periods on Chair 3 (it is the only lift on the mountain with real lines). More confident skiers like the mountain best. Most of it is steep and the expert slopes are extreme. Helicopter skiing goes right from the resort's hotel as well.

Children and nonskiers enjoy the Glacier Tubing Park. Riders go uphill on a lift that is designed to carry passengers and inner tubes, and then slide down a long, bouncy run. Tickets are for 90-minute sessions during the day and cost $15 for adults and $10 for ages 6 to 13. Children must be at least 42 inches tall.

An all-day lift ticket costs $55 for adults ($48 for Alaska residents, $44 for hotel guests), $36 for ages 14 to 17 or 60 to 69, $28 for ages 8 to 13, and $10 for ages 7 and under or over 70. Discounts apply for families. Private and group instruction is available and you can save a lot by buying your lessons, lift ticket, and equipment rental at the same time. The day lodge rents basic gear and the hotel rents high-performance gear. A basic rental package costs $29 a day for adults, $20 for ages 13 and under or over 60; high-performance gear is $34 and $21 respectively. There are groomed **cross-country trails** as well, and gear for rent at the hotel, but the best Nordic skiing is in Anchorage.

A center operated by **Challenge Alaska** (*©* **907/783-2925** or 907/344-7399; www.challengealaska.org) allows skiers with disabilities to use the mountain, skiing down to the lift to start and back to the center at day's end. It's called the Keil Center for Adaptive Sports and Therapeutic Recreation. They also rent the latest adaptive ski equipment.

The resort's new owner has said he will demolish and replace the utilitarian **day lodge,** a large, noisy building with snack and rental counters and located at the front of the mountain. The relatively cozy **Sitzmark Bar,** nearby, has long been a more comfortable place for a meal (burgers are around $8). The Hotel Alyeska (p. 258) is on the other side of the mountain, connected to the front by the tram to the top and beginner-level Chair 7 (you can ski right from the door). It makes a quieter and more genteel starting point for day-trippers as well as guests, as it has its own day lockers and an equipment rental counter with higher-quality equipment (and higher rates) than the day lodge. There are several dining choices here and at the top of the tram (see "Where to Stay," below).

HIKING   There are a couple of great Chugach National Forest trails starting in Girdwood.

Among the best trails in the region for a family hike is the **Winner Creek Trail,** which begins behind the Hotel Alyeska and leads to a roaring gorge where Winner Creek and Glacier Creek meet; a hand-operated tram crosses the water. The trail is essentially level and a good length for an afternoon: the round-trip to the gorge is about 4.5 miles. People with mobility problems may not make it that far, but can still enjoy the first .65 miles of the trail, which are built up with wide boardwalks and gravel nearly to the point of wheelchair accessibility. Beyond that part, the trail has roots and muddy spots, but is still well maintained. A winter ski trail takes a separate route, through a series of meadows, to the same destination.

The **Crow Pass Trail** is more ambitious. The route rises into the mountains and continues all the way over to Eagle River, after a 26-mile hike that can take a couple of days. But with less expenditure of time you can make a strenuous day hike of it going just up to the pass, where you can see the glaciers, wildflower meadows, and old mining equipment. The Forest Service's A-frame Crow Pass public-use cabin makes an excellent destination for an overnight from Girdwood; it lies on a lake at an elevation of 3,500 feet, half a mile from the pass. The trail head is up Crow Creek Road, off the Alyeska Highway. For more information on the national forest and cabin reservations, see section 3 of chapter 7.

SNOWMOBILING   **Glacier City Snowmobile Tours** (© 877/783-5566 or 907/783-5566; www.snowtours.net) operates out of the Great Alaskan Tourist Trap gift shop in the shopping center on the Seward Highway. Guides suit up clients—most of whom have never been on a snowmobile—and drive them to a promising site, determined according to snow conditions. At best, the winter tours make it all the way to Spencer Glacier. Groups are no larger than six and the attitude is casual: After a brief introduction, you are driving your own machine, using your own judgment. The entire outing lasts as long as 6 hours, with 3½ hours riding. The cost is $225 per person. The same outfit offers summertime snowmobiling May through September. For $389 each, a helicopter carries clients to the Eagle Glacier for more than 2 hours of riding on the snowfield.

WHERE TO STAY

Besides the resort hotel, there are plenty of condos and B&Bs in town. **Alyeska Accommodations,** on Olympic Mountain Loop (© 888/783-2001 or 907/783-2000; www.alyeskaaccommodations.com), offers rooms, condos, cabins, and luxurious houses.

Hotel Alyeska ✦✦✦   This hotel is among Alaska's best. The beauty of the building alone separates it from the competition, as does its location in an unspoiled mountain valley among huge spruce trees. Studded with dormers and turrets, it impresses on first sight. Inside, sumptuous cherrywood and rich colors unite the welcoming common rooms and elegant guest rooms. Although not large, rooms have every convenience. The saltwater swimming pool is magnificent, with a cathedral ceiling and windows by the whirlpool overlooking the mountain. The location and activities alone make the hotel worth visiting. A full-service spa was added in 2006, offering all the latest pampering. A few days spent here skiing, swimming, and relaxing make the rest of life seem too drab. Now for the bad news. On weekends and school holidays in the winter the hotel is overrun by partying families from Anchorage who overtax the facilities and destroy the peaceful ambience. Children run wild, the pool becomes impossibly crowded, and service deteriorates to an unacceptable level. Perhaps the new owner can get it under control. In the meantime, avoid these times for a skiing vacation.

Four restaurants vie for attention. The **Seven Glaciers,** 2,300 feet above the lobby by tram on Mount Alyeska, serves trendy and beautifully presented dinners in a sumptuous dining room floating above the clouds. Service is warm and highly professional. Meals are expensive, especially since the small servings make it desirable to order several courses. The restaurant opens only on the weekends in the winter. A mountain-top cafeteria is right next door (great views, limited choices). At the base level, the cuisine at the Teppanyaki Sakura has developed a good reputation. The **Pond Cafe** is good when not jammed on the weekends and has a nice view.

1000 Arlberg Ave. (P.O. Box 249), Girdwood, AK 99587. ☎ **800/880-3880** or 907/754-1111. Fax 907/754-2200. www.alyeskaresort.com. 304 units. Summer and Christmas $275–$360 double, $420–$2,200 suite; winter $145–$240 double, $260–$2,200 suite. Extra adult $25; children stay free in parent's room. AE, DC, MC, V. **Amenities:** 4 restaurants; 2 bars; indoor pool; health club; spa; bike rental; children's programs; concierge; tour desk; business center; shopping arcade; limited room service; massage; babysitting. *In room:* TV w/pay movies, fridge, coffeemaker, hair dryer, iron, safe, Wi-Fi floors 2 & 3.

WHERE TO DINE

Also see directly above for restaurant options at the Hotel Alyeska.

Chair 5 Restaurant ✦ *(Kids* SEAFOOD/BURGERS/PIZZA   This is where Girdwood locals meet their friends and take their families for dinner, and it's also one of our favorites after skiing or on a drive to the Kenai Peninsula. One afternoon, Bob Dylan music accompanied a friendly game of pool while men with ponytails and beards sipped microbrews. Another evening, a guy in the entryway entertained the children with magic tricks and the waitress asked them to draw pictures to enter into a contest. The menu offers choices pleasing to each family member, including pizza, burgers, fresh fish, and steaks, and the food is consistently good.

5 Lindblad Ave., in the New Girdwood Town Square. ☎ 907/783-2500. www.chairfive.com. Lunch $9–$15; dinner $18–$24; large pizza $18–$21. AE, DC, DISC, MC, V. Daily 11am–11pm (bar open till 2am).

Double Musky Inn ✦✦✦ CAJUN   The ski-bum-casual atmosphere and rambling, cluttered dining room among the trees match the wonderful Cajun and New Orleans food in a way that couldn't have been contrived—it's at once too improbable and too authentic. Service is relaxed to a fault, and food takes a long time to arrive, but when it does every dish is flawless. I love the jambalaya and the steaks are famous (by which I mean, really famous—Food Network chose this as one of the 10 best restaurants in America). On my most recent visit, with two couples, each item on our plates from appetizers through dessert was remarkable; since I love talking about the food over dinner, I love this place. The Double Musky isn't to everyone's taste, however; your senses can feel raw after the extreme noise, highly spiced food, and crowds, and parking can be difficult. Loud groups will enjoy it more than couples, and families don't really fit. Since the restaurant doesn't take reservations, here's an important tip: Grab seats in the bar and dive into your meal there with appetizers and drinks rather than simply waiting.

Mile 3, Crow Creek Rd., Girdwood. ✆ 907/783-2822. No reservations. www.doublemuskyinn.com. Main courses $18–$37. AE, DC, DISC, MC, V. Tues–Thurs 5–10pm; Fri–Sun 4:30–10pm. Closed Nov.

10 Out from Anchorage: The Matanuska & Susitna Valleys

On a longer visit to Anchorage, you may want to spend a day or two in the suburbs to the north, known as the Mat-Su Valley. Reached by the Glenn Highway about 40 miles from Anchorage, the area is both a bedroom community for the city and a former frontier farming region with its own quirky identity. If you are driving anywhere north from the city you will pass through this area and there are some interesting places to stop if you have the time. In this summary I've covered a few highlights in the central area (the whole thing is the size of West Virginia). Some of the best attractions are covered in other parts of the book. **The Alaska State Fair,** held before Labor Day, is covered under "Special Events," earlier in this chapter. **The Musk Ox Farm** is under "Shopping," also earlier in this chapter. Funky Talkeetna, a gateway to Denali National Park, is in chapter 8. The Matanuska Glacier area (on the Glenn Hwy.), with its great canyon views and late-season cross-country skiing and snowmobiling, is in chapter 9.

You can learn more about visitor attractions, lodging, and the area's greatest strength, its hiking, fishing, and skiing, from the **Mat-Su Visitors Center,** 7744 E. Visitors View Court, Palmer, AK 99645 (✆ **907/746-5000;** www.alaskavisit.com). The center is open mid-May to mid-September, 8:30am to 6:30pm. To find it, take the Trunk Road exit from the Parks Highway near the intersection with the Glenn Highway.

THROUGH HATCHER PASS

If you're headed north to Denali National Park or Fairbanks, the winding road through Hatcher Pass to Willow makes a glorious alpine detour around the least attractive part of your drive. Note, however, that past the mine and skiing area the road is unpaved, open only in summer, and not suitable for large RVs. From the Parks Highway, just after it branches from the Glenn Highway, exit to the right on the Trunk Road and keep going north when you reach Palmer-Fishhook Road, which becomes Hatcher Pass Road. From the Glenn Highway near Palmer, take Palmer-Fishhook just north of town.

Even if you're not headed north, a trip to Hatcher Pass combines one of the area's most beautiful drives, access to great hiking and Nordic skiing, and a look at interesting old buildings. The **Independence Mine State Historical Park** ✮✮ (✆ **907/745-2827** or 907/745-3975; www.alaskastateparks.org, click on "Individual Parks," then "Matanuska and Susitna Valleys") takes in the remains of a hard-rock gold-mine operation that closed down in 1951. Some buildings have been restored, including an assay office that's a museum and the manager's house that's a welcoming visitor center, while a big old mill, towering on the hillside, sags and leans as a picturesque ruin. A visit is interesting even if you don't go inside, using the interpretive panels and map on a self-guided tour. The paved trails are easily navigable by anyone. The setting, in a bowl of rock and alpine tundra, is spectacular. The day-use fee is $5 per vehicle. A guided tour is an additional $5 per person and leaves at 1:30pm and 3:30pm weekdays, plus 4:30pm weekends. Tours depend on staffing and may be increased or decreased from these hours. The visitor center is open from 10am to 7pm daily in the summer, closed off season.

Leave some time for a summer ramble in the heather if you visit the mine. In the winter, the Nordic or telemark skiing is exceptional, with a few kilometers of groomed trail and miles of open country to explore. (See the Hatcher Pass Lodge, below, for more details.) There are four hiking trails and two mountain-biking routes in the area—ask at the visitor center. The **Gold Cord Lake Trail** is less than a mile. The **Reed Lakes Trail** is spectacular for its mountain scenery and waterfalls; starting from the Archangel Road, it gains 3,000 feet over 4.5 miles to Upper Reed Lake. Another challenging hike is the 8-mile **Gold Mint Trail,** which starts across the road from the Motherlode Lodge on Hatcher Pass Road and ends at the Mint Glacier, where you have to turn around to hike back.

ON THE PARKS HIGHWAY

The Museum of Alaska Transportation and Industry ⋇, off the Parks Highway at mile 47 on Museum Drive, west of Wasilla (© 907/376-1211; www.museumofalaska. org), is a paradise for gearheads and tinkerers. The volunteers have gathered every conceivable machine and conveyance—14 airplanes, 13 fire trucks, 7 locomotives, and 2 steam cranes, for example—and fixed up to running order as many as they can. An indoor museum displays their finished masterpieces, while the 20 acres outside are crammed with deteriorated treasures—trains, tractors, fishing boats, and mining equipment—all grist for memories and imagination. It's open May 1 to September 30 daily 10am to 5pm, winter by appointment. Admission is $8 for adults, $5 for students and seniors, $18 for families.

WHERE TO STAY & DINE

Three good places to eat in the valley are at the three accommodations described below. In addition, there are unlimited fast-food spots and roadhouse burger places. One place of note is **Vagabond Blues,** in Palmer at 642 S. Alaska St. (© **907/745-2233**), a coffeehouse and cafe offering sandwiches, wraps, baked goods, homemade bread and soup, and music. The food is great, and the music is exceptional: A steady stream of national folk and alternative acoustic acts that come to Anchorage also make a pilgrimage to this small town venue; many are booked by Whistling Swan Productions, whose website lists dates (p. 249). The coffeehouse is open Monday through Saturday 7am to 9pm, Sunday 7am to 6pm.

HATCHER PASS

Hatcher Pass Lodge ⋇ *(Finds*   A charming family presides at this tiny mountain lodge in the treeless alpine bowl that also contains the Independence Mine State Historic Park, 3,000 feet above the sea, which glistens in the grand vista down below. Out on the open snowfield in winter, or the heather in summer, the nine cabins and A-frame lodge seem far more remote than they really are, just 90 minutes from Anchorage. There is a phone in the main lodge for emergencies but no TV. Our family went for a glorious Nordic skiing vacation there, and the 12 of us, ages 2 through 75, all had a great time. A place with nothing to divert you but snow, a warm cabin, and good meals brings a family closer. The cabins are clean and nicely set up, with no rustic edge except chemical toilets and a lack of running water. The rates reflect the off-grid remoteness, not exceptional luxury. Guests go to the main lodge for showers, meals, and drinks; the family produces surprisingly professional meals there. Stay in summer for a taste of the real Alaska with doorstep access to wonderful alpine hiking.

P.O. Box 763, Palmer, AK 99645. (907/745-5897. www.hatcherpasslodge.com. 12 units (3 lodge rooms, 9 cabins). $95 lodge room double; $157 cabin for 2. Extra person $15. AE, DC, DISC, MC, V. **Amenities:** Restaurant; bar; sauna.

WASILLA

Best Western Lake Lucille Inn ⊛ This well-run, attractive lakeside hotel in Wasilla has the best standard rooms in the valley. They're large and well appointed, and those facing the lake have balconies and a grand, peaceful view. The hotel helps with activities and offers discounts on some. Flightseeing trips take off from the dock below the lawn. The **restaurant** is one of the best in the area, with a light, quiet dining room looking out on the water. It's open for three meals a day. The dinner menu of beef and seafood ranges from $16 to $40. The property is nonsmoking except the lounge.

1300 W. Lake Lucille Dr., Wasilla, AK 99654. (800/528-1234 or 907/373-1776. Fax 907/376-6199. www.bestwestern lakelucilleinn.com. 54 units. High season $179 double, $239 suite; low season $109 double, $185 suite. Rates includes $6 breakfast voucher. Extra person $10. AE, DC, DISC, MC, V. **Amenities:** Restaurant; exercise room; Jacuzzi; sauna; coinop laundry. *In room:* TV, coffeemaker, hair dryer, iron, free high-speed Internet, Wi-Fi.

PALMER

Colony Inn ⊛ *(Finds* This classic country inn occupies a restored teacher's dormitory from the New Deal Colony Project, right in the middle of Palmer. The rooms are attractively old-fashioned, although a little worn in spots, with rockers and comforters but also Jacuzzi bathtubs in most rooms, and big TVs with VCRs. A large sitting room and a dining room downstairs are decorated with historic photographs that help tell the building's story. Meals are served here during the summer at the **Inn Cafe** ((**907/746-6118**): lunch Monday through Friday and a popular Sunday brunch. Guests check in at the comparatively downscale Valley Hotel, at 606 S. Alaska St., and there often is no innkeeper on-site to let you in or help with problems.

325 E. Elmwood, Palmer, AK 99645. (907/745-3330. Fax 907/746-3330. 12 units. $110 double; $196 suite. AE, DISC, MC, V. **Amenities:** Restaurant; laundry machines. *In room:* TV/VCR, dataport, fridge.

The Kenai Peninsula & Prince William Sound

The Gulf of Alaska arcs at its northern edge, forming the rounded northern shore of the Pacific Ocean, a zone of great collisions. This is where the earth's tectonic plates collide, spewing forth froths of hot lava from dozens of volcanoes and fracturing and folding the earth with titanic earthquakes. Here, the ocean's wildest weather hits mountains jutting miles high from the sea, growing immense prehistoric ice sheets and glaciers that carve the rock into long, deep, intricate fjords. The sea proffers prodigious biological wealth on these shores, including the salmon it unleashes into the rivers in furious swarms of life that climb over the mountains and into the Interior to spawn. Nature seems giant and superabundant along this magnificent arc of land and water.

Geography endowed this one stretch of coast with several of the world's great natural places. On the east, near Cordova, the **Copper River**'s immense, entirely unspoiled delta is the largest contiguous wetlands in the Western Hemisphere. On a day trip, you're immediately alone with flocks of rare, graceful waterfowl that congregate on shallow ponds surrounded by miles of waving grass. **Prince William Sound** is a vast protected sea of wooded mountains and mammoth glaciers. This is our family's favorite place on Earth, where we go each summer to camp among the otters and eagles on tiny islands out of contact with the rest of mankind. **Kenai**

Fjords National Park takes in bays off the open ocean where the mountains soar a mile straight up from the water. Boats travel here among humpback, gray, and orca whales; spot otters, seals, and sea lions; and visit swarming colonies of puffins and other seabirds. The **Kenai River** harbors the world's biggest salmon, on the western side of the Kenai Peninsula; and on its southern tip, **Kachemak Bay** is like a miniature Prince William Sound, but with people. The bay's shores are dotted by tiny towns with lodges, art galleries on pilings, and some of Alaska's best restaurants.

The whole region is exceptionally accessible, by Alaska standards. The Kenai (*keen*-eye) Peninsula, in particular, is easy to get to without the expense and exhausting travel that can make much of the state difficult. Most of what you're looking for in Alaska lies along a few hundred miles of blacktop, within reach of a rental car and perhaps a tour boat ticket: glaciers, whales, legendary sport fishing, spectacular hiking trails, interesting little fishing towns, bears, moose, and high mountains.

People from Anchorage go to the peninsula for the weekend to fish, hike, dig clams, paddle kayaks, and so on, and certain places can get crowded. There's a special phrase for what happens when the red salmon are running in July on the Kenai and Russian rivers: *combat fishing*. At hot times in certain places, anglers stand elbow to elbow on the bank, each casting into his or her own yard-wide slice of river, and still catch plenty of hefty salmon. The peninsula also exerts a powerful magnetic force on RVs, those road-whales that you find at the head of lines of cars on the two-lane highways. During the summer, the fishing rivers, creeks, and beaches on the west side of the peninsula and the end of the Homer Spit can become sheet-metal cities of hundreds of Winnebagos and Airstreams parked side by side. Often some local entrepreneur will be selling doughnuts or newspapers door-to-door.

Yet the decision is yours as to whether you spend time in the company of tourists. If the roadside fishing is hairy, hiking a little farther down the bank usually means you can be by yourself. In this chapter, I'll describe some towns of unspoiled charm, where you can kayak virtually from your room. Being alone is easy. You can paddle among otters in Resurrection Bay; tramp over the heather in Turnagain Pass; hike, bike, or ski one of the many maintained trails in Chugach National Forest. And, when you're ready to come back to the comforts of civilization, you'll find that some of the state's best restaurants and most interesting lodgings are here, too.

1 Exploring the Kenai Peninsula & Prince William Sound

THE TOWNS

Kenai, on Cook Inlet on the west side of the Kenai Peninsula, is the largest town in the region. Ten miles up the Kenai River, **Soldotna** is Kenai's twin, and together they form a unit with about a fourth of the Kenai Peninsula's population of 50,000. They're also the least interesting of the peninsula's communities. **Homer,** at the southern end of the peninsula, has wonderful art and character and lots of ways to get out on the water. **Seward,** on the east side, is smaller and quieter, a charming gateway to Kenai Fjords National Park.

There are three towns on Prince William Sound. **Valdez** is an oil town at the southern terminus of the trans-Alaska pipeline where tankers are loaded. **Cordova** is more attractive, a historic community on the eastern side of the sound, with outdoor activities close at hand. **Whittier** is a grim former military outpost, but a convenient gateway to the protected fjords and glaciers of the western sound.

GETTING THERE & GETTING AROUND

BY CAR   Highways connect all the region's large towns, except Cordova, which is reached only by air or water. Like all of Alaska's main highways, these are paved two-lane roads. The Seward Highway runs south from Anchorage to the Kenai Peninsula. That route is described in the following section. A road built in a railway tunnel connects Whittier, on Prince William Sound, to the Seward Highway. The Glenn and Richardson highways reach from Anchorage to Valdez through Alaska's Interior. Stops along that route are described in chapter 9, and all of Alaska's highways are summarized on p. 382.

BY FERRY   The ferry system connects Whittier with Valdez and Cordova via the fast ferry *Chenega,* launched in 2005. Driving from Anchorage to Whittier, taking the ferry to Valdez, and then driving back to Anchorage (or north to Fairbanks) makes a great loop (see chapter 3). The Chugach National Forest usually has rangers onboard offering programs and interpretation. The ferry *Tustumena* (the *"Tusty"*) connects Homer to Kodiak Island and the Aleutian Archipelago (see chapter 10), and also runs from Homer to Seldovia. The schedule is not convenient for Seldovia, however; for that trip, it's easier to take one of the private passenger ferries that serve the towns and remote sites around Kachemak Bay from Homer. A U.S. Fish & Wildlife Service ranger offers programs on the *Tusty*. For more on the ferry system, see section 1 of chapter 5, call © **800/642-0066,** or visit www.ferryalaska.com.

BY AIR   Commuter aircraft connect Anchorage to Kenai, Homer, Valdez, and Cordova. You can also fly between Anchorage and Cordova on an Alaska Airlines jet once a day in each direction (the northbound originates in Seattle). Scheduled and air-taxi services use these smaller towns as bases for the villages, carrying passengers, mail, and cargo, and flying to remote lodges and cabins for fishing or other outdoor activities. Valdez, Cordova, and Anchorage operators serve the Prince William Sound region. Kenai and Anchorage companies cover Cook Inlet and remote public lands such as Lake Clark National Park. Homer is the base for villages around Kachemak Bay and lower Cook Inlet bear-viewing sites.

BY TRAIN   The **Alaska Railroad** (© **800/544-0552** or 907/265-2494; www. alaskarailroad.com) runs from Anchorage south to Seward or Whittier and back daily in the summer.

VISITOR INFORMATION

For information on the peninsula as a whole, contact the **Kenai Peninsula Tourism Marketing Council,** 35477 Kenai Spur Hwy., Suite 205, Soldotna, AK 99669 (© **800/535-3524** or 907/262-5229; www.kenaipeninsula.org), which distributes a vacation planner with information on businesses and trip planning in the area (order through their website). The staff will answer inquiries during normal business hours.

GETTING OUTSIDE

The towns of the region are like beads strung along the laces of the highways; everything else is wilderness. You can find all the activities and isolation you seek here, yet the presence of the towns means that comfort is closer at hand than in other parts of Alaska.

   Chugach National Forest takes in all of Prince William Sound and most of the eastern Kenai Peninsula. At 5.3 million acres, it's more than double the size of Yellowstone National Park. Anywhere else but Alaska it would be a national park, and one of the largest and most spectacular, with some of the best sea kayaking, hiking, backpacking, wildlife-watching, and scenery anywhere. General information, camping, and ideas on remote areas in the Chugach are covered in section 3, while details about National Forest areas near towns are in the appropriate town sections.

   Kenai Fjords National Park (see section 6) protects the outer edge and ice cap of the Kenai Peninsula's southern side. The park is incomparable in its remoteness, stark beauty, and abundance of marine wildlife. Access is though Seward (see section 5).

   On the peninsula's western side, **Kenai National Wildlife Refuge** (see section 9) has Alaska's most accessible wilderness lake and river canoeing as well as extraordinary fishing, with access from roads near Soldotna (see section 8).

   Kachemak Bay State Park offers good sea-kayaking waters and wilderness hiking not connected to any road. The **Alaska Maritime National Wildlife Refuge** protects the wildlife habitat of remote islands and seashores around the state. Both are covered in section 10 of this chapter, on Homer.

VISITOR INFORMATION   The region's best and most central place to get outdoor information is the **Alaska Public Lands Information Center,** 605 W. 4th Ave., Suite 105, Anchorage, AK 99501 (© **866/869-6887** or 907/271-2737; www.nps.gov/aplic).

Tips State Parks Cabin Reservations

Alaska's state parks rent remote public cabins like the famous Forest Service cabins (see section 3), but they're usually newer, larger, and easier to get to. Most are in Southcentral Alaska—in this chapter, they're mentioned near Homer, Seward, and Valdez. Like the Forest Service cabins, it takes a hike, boat ride, or air taxi to get to the cabins, and you need cabin equipment, such as a cookstove and sleeping bags, but once there you can experience the real Alaska all by yourself.

Some of these cabins book up the minute they become available and, since Alaska residents get a jump on the reservation system, visitors are unlikely to be able to use the most popular cabins at peak periods. But if you can be flexible about where you go, or if you can travel out of the peak season, you can probably find a cabin. Alaska residents can reserve 7 months ahead, nonresidents 6 months ahead; however, reservations do not initially open on weekends or holidays, only at 10am Alaska time on the following business day. Once a date opens on the system, it stays open 24 hours a day until someone takes it.

The easiest way to reserve is by using the online system with a MasterCard or Visa, but you can also reserve in person, by mail, or by fax (you can ask questions by phone, but not apply). The staff is friendly and will guide you around the system, and help you find a cabin where you can get a permit, even if it's not your first choice. The main information and reservations desk is the **Department of Natural Resources Public Information Center—Anchorage,** 550 W. 7th Ave., Suite 1260, Anchorage, AK 99501-3557 (*�C* **907/269-8400,** or 907/269-8411 TDD; fax 907/269-8901; www.alaskastateparks.org). The website is the best source of information about the cabins, with a picture and description of each and a real-time availability calendar. The center is open Monday through Friday 10am to 5pm. Cabins rent for $25 to $75 a night, with fees highest for popular cabins at peak periods.

You'll be able to receive guidance from residents who have spent time in the places you'll be visiting, and there are exhibits on the wildlife and outdoor opportunities in the region—even maps showing where to find various species of fish. Land agencies present information on the whole state and the bookstore is well stocked with maps, field guides, and such. Summer hours are daily from 9am to 5pm, winter Monday through Friday from 10am to 5pm. Visitor centers for particular areas are covered in the appropriate sections.

2 The Seward Highway: A Road Guide

The Kenai Peninsula's lifeline is the road down from Anchorage, a 127-mile drive to Seward on a good two-lane highway, most of it through public land without development or services. Highway 1, commonly known as the Seward Highway, is more than scenic—it's really a wonderful attraction in itself, designated a National Scenic Byway and an All-American Road. A detailed booklet about the highway with maps and mile-by-mile descriptions, *The Seward Highway: Alaska's All-American Road,* is distributed by the public land information center in Anchorage (p. 215).

There are excellent campgrounds and hiking trails all along the way in the Chugach National Forest, which I've covered in section 3 of this chapter.

The mileposts start in Seward. Here we count backward, since you'll likely start from Anchorage.

MILES 127–79   The highway begins at the south end of Anchorage, the only way out of town in that direction, and runs along Turnagain Arm 48 miles to the Portage Glacier. I've written about that spectacular portion of the drive in chapter 6 under section 8, "Out from Anchorage: Turnagain Arm & Portage Glacier."

MILES 79–75   Beyond the Portage Glacier turnoff, the road traverses the salt marshes to the south side of the Arm. These wetlands are good bird-watching grounds. The dead trees on the flats are left over from before the 1964 earthquake. The area was inundated in the quake, when the entire region shifted—including the Kenai Peninsula and Prince William Sound—lowering this area 12 feet and raising areas to the east as much as 30 feet. Everything moved laterally, too. Besides being the second strongest earthquake ever recorded, the '64 quake moved more land than any other. People who were here tell of their surprise when the tide came far higher than they had ever seen it before in the days after the earthquake, until finally they realized that the land itself had sunk. Large parts of Homer, Hope, and Seldovia disappeared under the waves at high tide. Seward, Whittier, Valdez, and Kodiak were swept by destructive tsunami waves.

MILES 75–68   The highway steeply climbs through the spruce forest to the fresh, towering alpine terrain of the 1,000-foot-elevation **Turnagain Pass.** The vistas here are stupendous year-round.

Why All the Dead Trees?

There are whole mountainsides on the Kenai Peninsula and in Anchorage that lack large trees or have huge groups of dead, weathered, or downed trees. The spruce bark beetle is to blame. Although a natural part of the forest system, the beetles' population exploded in the last 2 decades and swept across Southcentral Alaska, wiping out 4 million acres of white and Sitka spruce, the biggest single insect kill of trees ever in North America up to that time. The beetles bore under the outer bark layer to eat the trees' phloem, the soft inner bark that carries food manufactured in the needles down to the roots. The beetles reproduce in the tree, sending the next generation in flight in May and June in search of more victims. The blight stopped spreading only when susceptible trees were dead.

Scientists believe global climate change allowed short, spotty beetle outbreaks to become a long, widespread plague. Cool, damp springs can stop beetles in a year or two, but since 1987 the state has had a solid string of exceptionally warm, dry seasons. Ecologists also have noticed shrinking ponds, a rising tree line, and many other indicators of a changing climate on the Kenai Peninsula. In places, the ecological makeup in the forest appears to be transformed, but it will be decades before we learn if natural succession leads back to a new spruce forest, or if large tracts become grassy parklike areas. In the meantime, be careful with fire. (You can learn more on my website at www.wohlforth.net/SpruceBarkBeetles.htm.)

MILE 68   If you find the meadow and tundra hard to resist for a walk, go ahead. Park at the pullout with the toilets on the right side at the pass summit and follow the path, or just amble off into the wildflowers (assuming the ground is dry when you're there). In the winter and spring, this is a backcountry skiing and snowmobiling paradise. Skiers go on the left (east) side of the road and snowmobilers on the right. Always check with the Chugach National Forest (see section 3, below) for avalanche conditions first. An avalanche near here killed five riders in spring 1999.

MILE 68–57   The pass forms a divide; crossing it, Granite Creek flows down toward the south. The road follows, falling back below the tree line of stunted spruce and then popping back up into sweeping views. Arcing to the northwest after the Granite Creek Campground, the highway follows another north-flowing river, Six Mile Creek.

MILE 57 & HOPE HIGHWAY   The Hope Highway divides off to the north and west along Six Mile Creek while the Seward Highway continues south. Rafting companies based in Anchorage use this wild stretch of water for some of their most challenging rides (see "Rafting" in chapter 6 on p. 246).

A Side Trip to Hope   If you want a break, you'll find **Hope** at the end of the 17-mile Hope Highway. It's a charming gold-rush–era village and the starting point for some great hikes (see the information on Resurrection Pass Trail, p. 270, and Porcupine campground, p. 272). A few white-frame buildings remain from the days when Hope was a gold-mining boomtown after a strike in 1894. Before the 1964 earthquake, the rest of the town used to stand where the creek gives way to a tidal meadow. Wandering the gravel roads, you'll find more quaint spots. Today, Hope's year-round population is about 150. For information, contact the **Hope-Sunrise Community Library** (© 907/782-3121), which is open daily in summer from 11am to 4pm, when volunteer manpower allows. You can also find Hope information online at www.advenalaska.com/hope. The **Hope and Sunrise Historical and Mining Museum** (© 907/782-3740) is a one-room log cabin displaying historic objects and photographs, a barn, blacksmith's shop, miner's bunkhouse, and old-time school. Volunteers keep the museum open Memorial Day to Labor Day daily noon to 4pm. Hope has several places to eat, all with very small-town flavor. Locals have been gathering at one cafe since 1896 (it shows). Another local restaurant was rebuilt by volunteer labor after it burned down. Likely Hope's best place for a meal—or even to overnight in a cozy cabin—is **Bowman's Bear Creek Lodge** (© 907/782-3141; www.bowmansbearcreeklodge.com). Cabins are $125 double in summer, $100 in winter. The restaurant is open in summer Tuesday through Sunday 2 to 10pm, in winter Thursday through Sunday the same hours.

MILE 57–46   The Seward Highway climbs steeply from the Hope Highway intersection, up the canyon of Canyon Creek, before leveling out above the tree line at an elevation of about1,400 feet. Next come a series of alpine lakes in a narrow mountain valley.

MILE 46   Upper Summit Lake lies smooth and reflective in a steep alpine valley. On the far side is the Tenderfoot Creek Campground, a calming spot warmed by sun off the water (p. 272). On the near side is a traditional highway stopping place without neighbors for miles in any direction, the **Summit Lake Lodge**, at Mile 45.5 (© 907/244-2031). The main building is a traditional log roadhouse that's been updated to house a modern restaurant. Meals can take some time, so eat here only if you've not in a rush. Even if you don't want dinner, however, the location can't be beat for a driving break. You can enjoy an ice-cream from the counter in the log gift shop while you stroll near the lake. The lodge rents six motel rooms with private bathrooms, but without TVs or phones.

MILE 46–37   The highway continues through similar mountain terrain before descending into the trees again and branching at **Tern Lake.** This is a stirringly beautiful spot year-round, and a good place to get out and taste the fresh mountain air and watch for moose, waterfowl, and other birds. There's a picnic area. To the right at the intersection, the Sterling Highway leads to Cooper Landing, Soldotna, Kenai, and Homer.

MILE 36   Look on the right to turn for the luxurious **Inn at Tern Lake** (© 907/ 288-3667; www.ternlakeinn.com), a family-operated lodge surrounded by mountains and hiking opportunities with four airy, well-made rooms overlooking a pond. The inn has many amenities—even a tennis court. It's a place to enjoy a few days of quiet, as you'd be too sorry to leave if you stop only overnight. Summer rates are $145 to $175 double, winter $90.

MILE 32   Moose Creek has a viewing platform to watch thousands of spawning salmon, in season; half a mile on, the Trail Lake Fish Hatchery sits on the edge of Upper Trail Lake. This is the first of a string of sparkling mountain lakes that the road will follow for the next 15 miles.

MILE 30   The community of Moose Pass, with a population of about 200, sits on the shore of Upper Trail Lake.

MILE 18–0   Down among the big spruces of the coastal forest, the highway comes to Seward.

3 Chugach National Forest: Do-It-Yourself Wilderness

I've lived near the Chugach National Forest all my life, but it wasn't until well into adulthood that I had seen all its parts and appreciated its vastness and variety. Still, I doubt I'll ever really know this seemingly infinite land. **Prince William Sound,** just one of the national forest's three parts, has 3,500 miles of shoreline among its folded islands and deeply penetrating fjords and passages. It would take a lifetime to completely know all those cove beaches, climb all the island mountains, and explore to the head every narrow bay under big rainforest trees. The **Copper River Delta** is another world entirely. Unlike the musty secrets of the sound's obscure passages, the delta opens to the sky like a heavenly plain of wind and light, its waving green colors splashed by the airiest brushstrokes. It's another huge area: Just driving across the delta and back from Cordova takes most of a day. Finally, there's the western part of the national forest, on the **Kenai Peninsula.** This is largely an alpine realm. The mountains are steep, their timber quickly giving way to rock, tundra, and wildflowers up above. It's got remote, unclimbed peaks, but also many miles of family hiking trails, accessible fishing streams, and superb campgrounds. This is where you go in Alaska for multiday trail hikes.

The Chugach is managed primarily for recreation and conservation. Logging in Prince William Sound essentially stopped after the 1989 *Exxon Valdez* oil spill, when conservationists recognized the need to prevent further environmental damage to support recovery from the disaster. Exxon was forced to pay $1 billion to a recovery fund and government trustees spent much of the money to buy back timber rights in the sound and beyond to protect the trees. They bought 1,419 miles of coastline and almost as much land as is in all of Yosemite National Park. Still, that was only a sixth of the area the Chugach already encompassed.

ESSENTIALS

GETTING THERE & GETTING AROUND There are many ways to the Chugach National Forest. For Prince William Sound, use Whittier, Valdez, or Cordova as gateways; for the Copper River Delta, go through Cordova. Trails and campgrounds on the Kenai Peninsula generally meet the Seward or Sterling highways, or spur roads from the highways. The individual town listings later in this chapter provide details on how to get there and into that part of the national forest. Section 2, above, describes the Seward Highway.

VISITOR INFORMATION The most central place for information on the national forest is the Alaska Public Lands Information Center in Anchorage (p. 215). For general forest inquiries, you can also contact the **forest headquarters,** 3301 C St., Suite 300, Anchorage, AK 99503 (© **907/743-9500;** www.fs.fed.us/r10/chugach). The national forest also has three ranger district offices, where you can get up-to-date local information and personal advice: **Glacier Ranger District,** on Monarch Mine Road, near the Seward Highway off Alyeska Road, in Girdwood (© **907/783-3242**); **Seward Ranger District,** 4th Avenue and Jefferson Street, in Seward (© **907/224-3374**); and **Cordova Ranger District,** 2nd and Browning streets, in Cordova (© **907/424-7661**). You can't reserve campground sites and remote cabins through these local offices—for that you must use the national system listed below under "Where to Stay"—but you can call them with questions.

GETTING OUTSIDE
HIKING, MOUNTAIN BIKING & BACKPACKING

Alaska's best long trails lead through the mountain passes of Chugach National Forest, including historic gold-rush trails and portions of the original Iditarod Trail (the race doesn't use these southern portions). The Forest Service maintains **public cabins** on many of these trails, and in other remote spots reachable only with a boat or small plane. If the nights you need are available, you can use the cabins instead of a tent on a backpacking trip. Or make a cabin your destination and spend a few days there hiking or fishing. I've covered trails near Cordova in section 12 of this chapter, and some shorter hikes are mentioned below with the campgrounds under "Where to Stay." In addition, the superb Winner Creek Trail and Crow Pass Trail, from Gridwood, are described on p. 257. Two excellent trail guides cover the peninsula. *55 Ways to the Wilderness in Southcentral Alaska,* fifth edition by Helen D. Nienhueser and John Wolfe, Jr., (The Mountaineers Books, $17), is the most complete, with detailed coverage in readable prose. The newer *Kenai Trails* (Alaska Natural History Association, $8), includes an extremely detailed topographic map along with each trail description. **Trails Illustrated** publishes excellent plastic maps of the region (© **800/962-1643;** http://maps.nationalgeographic.com).

CARTER LAKE TRAIL An excellent day hike starts from mile 33 of the Seward Highway, a few miles east of Tern Lake (p. 268), rising about 1,000 feet over 2 miles to alpine views and Carter Lake, which is stocked with rainbow trout. Continuing another 1.3 miles brings you to the east end of Crescent Lake.

RESURRECTION PASS TRAIL This gold-rush trail begins 4 miles above the town of Hope (see section 2) and runs over the top of the Kenai Peninsula to Cooper Landing (see section 7). It's a beautiful, remote, yet well-used trail for hiking, mountain biking, Nordic skiing, or snowshoeing; it rises through forest, crosses the alpine pass, and then descends again to a highway trail head where you'll need to have transportation waiting. The 39-mile trail has eight public-use cabins, available for $35 to $45 a night. (See "Where to Stay," below, for reservation information.) The cabins are well spaced to cover the trail in an easy 5 days, and those on lakes have boats for fishing. Cabins book up well ahead winter and summer, but there are lots of good camping spots, too. The **Devil's Pass and Summit Lake trails** cut off from the Resurrection to the Seward Highway south of Summit Lake, shortening the route. The difficulty of doing the whole trail, by any of the entrances, is that you either need two cars or someone willing to drive you back to your starting point.

RUSSIAN LAKES TRAIL This trail begins in Cooper Landing (see section 7 of this chapter), near the end of the Resurrection Pass Trail, and leads to three remote cabins and a series of lakes. There's excellent fishing and wildlife viewing (bears are common). It's less than 3 miles with little elevation gain to Lower Russian Lake and the cabin there, or you can make a backpacking trip over the entire 21 miles.

JOHNSON PASS TRAIL The 23-mile trail climbs to a pair of lakes above the tree line at the 1,450-foot Johnson Creek Summit, tracing impressively narrow mountain valleys. The route, part of the Iditarod National Historic Trail, leads from near the Trail Lake Fish Hatchery, at mile 32 of the Seward Highway, to near the Granite Creek Campground, on the highway at mile 63. Plan to do the trail as an overnight and have transportation ready at each end.

LOST LAKE TRAIL & PRIMROSE TRAIL With their fields of alpine wildflowers and small lakes, these connected trails offer one of the most beautiful hikes in the area. Snow lasts until late in the season up at the top. The upper, northern trail head is at the 10-site Primrose Campground, on vast Kenai Lake, 17 miles from Seward off the Seward Highway on Primrose Road. The trail rises through hemlock past a waterfall about 2 miles up (look for the spur to the right when you hear water), past an old mining cabin, and then through ever smaller trees and above the tree line. A Forest Service cabin is on a 2-mile spur about 11 miles along the 16-mile route. Strong hikers can do the whole trail in a long day, but it makes more sense to hike in and out on the upper end, or to spend the night along the way. The lower, Lost Lake trail head is in a subdivision near Seward; ask for directions at one of the visitor centers to find it.

FISHING

The national forest contains some of the most famous, and crowded, fishing banks in Alaska, including the **Russian River,** near Cooper Landing, with its incredible run of red salmon in July and good fishing lasting into September. Easiest access is at the Russian River Campground, just west of the village. There are plenty of other roadside salmon streams and remote fishing rivers and lakes in the national forest where you can lose sight of other anglers. Some remote lakes have Forest Service cabins for rent on their shores, with rowboats. The Forest Service publishes information on these opportunities. See chapter 2 for other information sources.

SEA KAYAKING & BOATING

A variety of Prince William Sound tour boats are listed in the Whittier, Valdez, and Cordova sections of this chapter. Whittier offers the greatest number of boats and the most impressive scenery, with big glaciers that come right to the water. It's also possible to rent your own boat there.

All three communities also have operators offering sea-kayak rentals and guided outings of various lengths. The best sea kayaking is near Cordova or east of Whittier. The long fjords reached from Whittier feature calving glaciers, narrow passages, and Forest Service cabins, but to get out there you need a boat ride first—the waters right around Whittier aren't as interesting—and that is expensive. The local sea-kayaking operators can help you arrange drop-off service. Cordova has more interesting waters right near town, so you can paddle from the boat harbor. Those who haven't done much sea kayaking should consider only a guided trip; if it's your first time, start with a guided day trip rather than an overnight.

WHERE TO STAY

CABIN AND CAMPSITE RESERVATIONS

Some campsites in the Chugach can be reserved in advance and public-use cabins are available only by reservation. **The National Recreation Reservation Service** works well, but it is operated by Ticketmaster in upstate New York, so reservation agents are not the best people to ask for information about which remote cabin or campground is right for you. Instead, use the Chugach National Forest website (www.fs.fed.us/r10/chugach) and follow up with questions with the ranger stations (p. 269). The easiest way to reserve a cabin or campsite is online at **www.recreation.gov**, because the interactive maps and availability calendars allow you to shop for open days at various places. To reserve by phone, call ✆ **877/444-6777** or 518/885-3639 with toll from overseas. The phone lines are open March through October daily 10am to midnight eastern time, November through February 10am to 10pm. The system accepts payment by bank card only: American Express, Discover, MasterCard, or Visa. Campsites can be reserved starting 240 days ahead, cabins 180 days ahead.

REMOTE CABINS

There is no more authentic Alaska accommodation than a pioneer cabin with a woodstove—a place to give you a better feel for the soul of a wild place. Chugach National Forest maintains more than 40 remote recreation cabins for rent to the public. This is simple shelter: Cabins don't have electricity or plumbing; you bring your own sleeping bags, cooking equipment, and other gear; and the cabin is only as clean as the last user left it. But no other room you can rent has a better location or greater privacy. Some cabins are along hiking and skiing trails, others on shores where boats and kayaks can pull up, and others on remote fishing lakes accessible only by floatplane. You can stay up to a week in most, with a summer limit of 3 days in the Resurrection Trail cabins.

The Forest Service prints a free listing of the cabins with short descriptions of each. You will also need a trail guide and detailed map (see "Getting Outside," above). Cabins rent for $35 or $45 a night, with most priced at $45 a night. Typically, the price of the cabin itself is not your major expense: You'll need a way to get there, either by plane, by boat, or by having a vehicle to drive to a trail head and then hiking. If you're flying, contact flight services in the nearest town (listed in the sections later in this chapter) to find out the cost before you book a cabin. Flight time is several hundred dollars an hour. You can rent the camping equipment you'll need at the businesses listed in the Anchorage chapter on p. 269, but you should talk to a ranger first to get details about access and what to take. And start planning early: For summer dates, many cabins book up the second they become available on the reservation system, 6 months prior. This is not an exaggeration. Reservation details are above.

CAMPGROUNDS

Forest Service campgrounds mostly have pit toilets and water from hand pumps, and roads usually are not paved. But some of these places are truly spectacular. I've listed them in order of distance from Anchorage, counting in reverse direction on the Seward Highway mileposts. For information on campgrounds below mile 60, call the Seward Ranger District; for the others, call the Glacier Ranger District, in Girdwood (p. 269 for phone numbers). Sites in a few of the following campgrounds, as noted, take reservations through the national system explained above. RVs and cars can access and park at all of the campgrounds, but Williwaw is the only campground intended primarily for RVs.

Williwaw & Black Bear   These two campgrounds are next to each other near Portage Glacier, along a creek where you can watch spawning red salmon in mid-August (no fishing is allowed). Williwaw is one of the better-developed campgrounds in the national forest, with paved roads and pumped water, and is intended primarily for RVs.

Mile 4, Portage Glacier Rd. (turn at mile 78.9 Seward Hwy.). Williwaw: 60 sites. Reservations accepted with additional fee. $10 per night. Black Bear: 12 sites. $9 per night.

Bertha Creek   This one's in the high country.

Mile 65.5, Seward Hwy. 12 sites. $10 per night.

Granite Creek   Near the Johnson Pass trail head.

Mile 63, Seward Hwy. 19 sites. $10 per night.

Porcupine   This campground near the gold-rush village of Hope is among the most beautiful in the Chugach National Forest. The sites are on a mountainside over-looking Turnagain Arm, five with sweeping ocean views. The thick trees make for privacy, but also mosquitoes. Bring repellent. Two good day hikes leave from the campground: The level 5-mile trail to **Gull Rock** makes a good family ramble, and with some effort you can scramble down to remote beaches along the way, where we've enjoyed a picnic. The **Hope Point Trail** is a stiff climb that rises 3,600 feet to expansive views.

At the end of the Hope Hwy. 24 sites. $10 per night.

Tenderfoot Creek   This pleasant campground lies across Summit Lake from the Seward Highway as it passes through a narrow mountain valley above the tree line. Campsites look out on the water from a peaceful, sunny hillside. The nearby Summit Lake Lodge, described on p. 267, offers meals and is the only business on the Seward Highway for many a mile.

Mile 46, Seward Hwy. 27 sites. $10 per night.

Ptarmigan Creek & Trail River   Near the tiny towns of Moose Pass and Crown Point, the Ptarmigan Creek campground is at the trail head for the trail to Ptarmigan Lake, 4 miles away with only 500 feet in elevation gain—a good place for a picnic or fishing for Dolly Varden char and rainbow trout. Trail River campground is a mile away and on the other side of the highway.

Mile 23, Seward Hwy. 16 and 63 sites, respectively. $10 per night. Reservations accepted, with additional fee.

Primrose   Another favorite, this lovely campground lies on the edge of Kenai Lake and at the base of the Primrose Trail to Lost Lake, one of the area's most beautiful (see "Getting Outside," above). This campground is the closest to Seward that has a sense of natural isolation.

Mile 17, Seward Hwy. 10 sites. $10 per night.

Russian River   This large, well-developed campground mainly serves fishermen pursuing red salmon on the river. When the fishing is good, the campground overflows and can be noisy. Overnight parking is $6. Reserve ahead.

Mile 52, Sterling Hwy., just west of Cooper Landing. 84 sites. $13 per night. 3-day limit. Reservations accepted, with additional fee. Flush toilets.

Cooper Creek   The campground has two halves bisected by the highway right in Cooper Landing. Ten sites are on the Kenai River and the balance is across the road and somewhat better screened and separated.

Mile 50.7, Sterling Hwy. 26 sites. $10 per night. Reservations accepted.

Quartz Creek   Thickly wooded sites stand well separated a bit off the highway, many right on Kenai Lake and others with good mountain views. There is a boat ramp in the campground and a lodge nearby.

Quartz Creek Rd., at mile 45 Sterling Hwy. 45 sites. $13 per night. Reservations accepted. Flush toilets, boat launch.

Crescent Creek   This campground is quieter and more secluded than others near Cooper Landing, at the Crescent Lake trail head. The 6.5-mile trail leads to the Crescent Lake Forest Service Cabin, where renters have a boat for grayling fishing.

Mile 3 Quartz Creek Rd., at mile 45 Sterling Hwy. 9 sites. $10 per night.

4 Whittier: Dock on the Sound

Whittier is Anchorage's portal to Prince William Sound. Although Anchorage itself is on Upper Cook Inlet, that muddy, fast-moving water is little used for recreational boating. Whittier, on the other hand, stands on the edge of a long fjord in the northwest corner of the sound, whose clear waters are full of salmon, orcas, and otters, and bounded by rocky shores, rainforests, and glaciers. In the past, getting to Whittier meant riding through a mountain by train. Now the railway tunnel is paved, creating North America's longest highway tunnel and, in theory, putting Whittier only an hour away from the city. But only in theory, because the tunnel is also among the most inconvenient to use in North America. It has only one lane, and that lane must be shared by traffic and trains in both directions, and in between trips the tunnel often must be aired out. You usually have to wait.

Whittier certainly has major advantages for visitors seeking to get out on the water. The water is calmer here than on excursions to Kenai Fjords National Park, so seasickness is rare, and the glaciers are even more numerous. One company's selling point is a "26-glacier cruise," all done in a day trip from Anchorage by rail and large tour boat (see "Phillips' Cruises and Tours," below). Prince William Sound boats also see otters and sometimes whales; Kenai Fjords tours, on the other hand, more often see whales

---

Tips **Be Prepared**

Whittier lacks a bank, large stores, or downtown businesses. Bring what you need.

---

and see more birds. Sea kayakers also have great places to go from Whittier. Almost all of Prince William Sound is in Chugach National Forest, with its public-use cabins in lovely, remote spots on the shores (see "Campgrounds," above).

There's little other reason to go to Whittier, unless you're on a quest to find the oddest towns in America. Most of the roughly 180 townspeople live in a single 14-story concrete building with dark, narrow hallways. The grocery store is on the first floor and the medical clinic on the third. The rest of the people live in one other building. **The Begich Towers,** as the dominant structure is called, was built during the 1940s, when Whittier's strategic location on the Alaska Railroad and at the head of a deep Prince William Sound fjord made it a key port in the defense of Alaska. Today, with its barren gravel ground and ramshackle warehouses and boat sheds, the town maintains a stark military-industrial character. The pass above the town is a funnel for frequent whipping winds, it always seems to rain, and the glaciers above the town keep it cool even in summer. As one young town ambassador told me once when I was on a visit, "You're thinking, 'Thank God I don't live here,' right?" The official boosters look more on the bright side: Having everyone live in one building saves on snow removal in a place that gets an average of 20 feet per winter. Kids don't even have to go outside to get to school—a tunnel leads from the tower to the school.

ESSENTIALS

GETTING THERE   By Car   Take the Seward Highway to the Portage Glacier Road, at mile 78.9 (48 miles from Anchorage). The road through the 2¾-mile-long World War II rail tunnel to Whittier is only one lane and also accommodates trains, so you'll have to wait your turn. Get the schedule through the tunnel's website (www.tunnel.alaska.gov), through its phone recording (© **877/611-2586** or 907/566-2244), or by tuning to 1610AM in Portage or 530AM in Whittier. Checking the schedule helps you avoid a wait of an hour or more if you miss the opening, but you can also wait if you arrive just on time at peak hours, when there may be too many vehicles in line to get through during one open period. Typically, the crowding comes in the summer around 6 to 7pm Friday through Sunday. The tunnel closes altogether at night. In summer the first opening from Whittier is at 5:30am and the last to Whittier is at 11:15pm. Winter hours are shorter and changeable, so check ahead. The toll is $12 for cars; $20 for RVs, cars with trailers, and large vans. It is charged only going toward Whittier. Special permits are required for really huge vehicles (over 14 ft. high or 10 ft. wide). Parking in Whittier is $10 a day. As I mentioned in the introduction, Whittier really isn't worth the trouble unless you are going out on the water.

By Train   If you plan to take a day trip on the sound from a base in Anchorage (or Girdwood)—the way most people use Whittier—you can leave the car behind and take the train. The large tour operators will book it for you when you buy your boat ticket. The **Alaska Railroad** (© **800/544-0552** or 907/265-2494; www.alaska railroad.com) runs a daily train timed to match the schedules of Prince William Sound tour boats. Unless you have planned an activity or tour on the water, however, you'll find the 6-hour stay in Whittier is too long to just hang around. The round-trip fare is $72, one-way $58, half price ages 2 to 11. The train ride is scenic and fun, but a rental car will take about half as long and save money if there is more than one of you along.

By Bus   Boat tour operators have buses that can save time and money over the train. Reserve when you buy your boat cruise ticket.

By Ferry   Ferries of the **Alaska Marine Highway System** (© **800/642-0066,** or 800/764-3779 TDD; www.ferryalaska.com) connect Whittier, Valdez, and Cordova. The new fast ferry *Chenega* has dramatically cut travel times and increased sailings in the summer. The fare from Whittier to either Valdez or Cordova is $89 for adults, half price for ages 6 through 11, free for children under 6. A 15-foot car costs $105 to take along. The Whittier-Valdez run creates the opportunity for a wonderful loop tour of a couple days or more: Drive Anchorage to Whittier, take the ferry to Valdez, then return to Anchorage via the Glenn Highway or continue up the Richardson Highway to Fairbanks and drive back to Anchorage on the Parks Highway. See chapter 3 for a complete loop itinerary.

Whittier is the system's main port connecting Southeast and Southcentral Alaska via the oceangoing ferry *Kennicott.* The ship's route spans the state, from Prince Rupert, B.C., to Juneau, across the Gulf of Alaska to Whittier, around the Kenai Peninsula to Homer and out to Kodiak. The entire loop takes 2 weeks. The fare for the 2-day voyage between Whittier and Juneau is $221 for adults, $508 for a 15-foot vehicle, and roughly $200 to $350 for a cabin. See section 1 in chapter 5 for information about the system. A Chugach National Forest ranger interprets the scenery for passengers on the Prince William Sound ferry.

VISITOR INFORMATION   There is no visitor center, but you can contact the City of Whittier (© **907/472-2327;** www.ci.whittier.ak.us). **The Whittier Chamber of Commerce** (© **907/472-2493;** www.whittieralaskachamber.org) includes a business directory with links on its website. The people at the harbormaster's office are helpful and maintain public toilets and showers; it's the two-story building at the harbor (© **907/472-2327** extension 110 or 115).

GETTING OUT ON THE SOUND

Whittier is the entrance to western Prince William Sound, at the end of one of many long, deep fjords where marine mammals and eagles are common. Glaciers at the heads of many of the fjords dump ice in the water for the tour boats that cruise from Whittier.

LARGE TOUR BOATS

Several companies with offices in Anchorage compete for your business for day-trip tours to the sound's western glaciers. Besides having incredible scenery, the water is calm, making seasickness unlikely—for the queasy, this is a much better choice than Kenai Fjords National Park. Each operator times departures to coordinate with the daily Alaska Railroad train from Anchorage, described above, which means they have up to 6 hours for the trip. Some try to see as much as possible, while others take it slower to savor the scenery and wildlife sightings. Between the train and boat fare, expect to spend $190 per person for this day's outing, leaving Anchorage at 10am and returning at 9:30pm. You can save $10 to $15 a person and up to 3 hours by taking a bus the tour boat arranges instead of the train. If you have two or more people, you can save by renting a car and driving. You will be able to buy meals onboard or one will be provided.

Phillips' Cruises and Tours The 26-glacier cruise travels the sound on a fast three-deck catamaran, covering many miles of scenery and counting the glaciers as they go. The boat ride is 4½ hours, so if you use their bus you cut the total time from Anchorage to under 8½ hours. The boat has a snack bar and bar, and a hot lunch is provided with the fare.

519 W. 4th Ave., Anchorage, AK 99501. ✆ **800/544-0529** or 907/276-8023. www.26glaciers.com. 4½-hour cruise $139 adults, $89 children under 12.

Major Marine Tours This company operates a smaller, 149-passenger vessel at a slower pace than Phillips—they hit a mere 10 glaciers, but spend more time waiting for them to calve. Another important feature: The tour is narrated by a Chugach National Forest ranger, not the company. The route goes up Blackstone Bay. The boat is comfortable, with reserved table seating. They put emphasis on their food, which costs extra; the salmon and prime rib buffet is $15 for adults, $7 for children. It's quite good. Time on the water is 5 hours.

411 W. 4th Ave., Anchorage, AK 99501. ✆ **800/764-7300** or 907/274-7300. www.majormarine.com. $99 adults, $49 children ages 11 and under.

SMALL BOAT TOURS

Instead of getting on a giant tour boat with a crowd of people, you can go on a small boat with a local who will show off favorite places and beaches where you can picnic and walk. If you see a whale or other point of interest, you stay as long or as short a time as you like. What you give up is the comfort of a large, tour-bus-like vessel, you pay more, and most small boats have a four-person minimum.

Sound Eco Adventures Beloved Gerry Sanger is a retired wildlife biologist who spent years researching the waterfowl and ecology of Prince William Sound. Now he carries up to six passengers at a time on whale, wildlife, and glacier tours from his speedy 30-foot aluminum boat, which has a landing-craft-like ramp perfect for pulling up on gravel beaches and suitable for wheelchairs. Gerry's success rate at finding whales is better than 90% since 1999, and he has gone years without missing once. His shorter, 5-hour tours usually do not encounter whales. Fares include snacks, but bring your own lunch. Gerry is considering retiring again, so this may be the last year to take his tour.

P.O. Box 707, Whittier, AK 99693. ✆ **888/471-2312** or 907/472-2312. www.soundecoadventure.com. 10-hr. whale and wildlife cruise $210–$235 per person; 8-hr. tour $180 per person; 5-hr. sightseeing cruise $160 per person; charter the whole boat $125–$150 per hr.

Honey Charters A family runs three sturdy aluminum boats built for these waters, specializing in personal tours, water transportation, and kayaker drop-offs. They operate with a minimum of four passengers; by paying the four-person minimum, you can have a boat to yourself. For larger groups, their *Qayaq Spirit* carries up to 30 passengers for kayaking or sightseeing cruises. Bring your own food.

On the Whittier waterfront (P.O. Box 708), Whittier, AK 99693. ✆ **888/477-2493** or 907/472-2493. www.honeycharters. com. 3-hr. cruise $99 per person; 6 hr. cruise $149 per person.

FISHING

About 30 charter fishing boats operate out of Whittier, the closest saltwater fishing to Anchorage, mostly targeting halibut but also getting salmon at certain times. The **Whittier Harbormaster** can give you a list of operators (✆ **907/472-2327,** extension 110 or 115). **Bread-n-Butter Charters** (✆ **888/472-2396** or 907/472-2396;

Finds **The Sound by Yacht**

I came across the *Discovery* one evening in a secret little cove in the remote southwestern corner of Prince William Sound's Knight Island. Briefly pulled from my rough camping existence, I suddenly found myself sitting on a soft couch in a sumptuous mahogany lounge, eating a delicious chocolate dessert, and sipping wine. The *Discovery* is a classic old wooden vessel, and accommodations are nautical and yachtlike, not as fancy even as a small cruise ship. But it's comfortable, groups are only about a dozen per trip, and the owner and skipper know the sound well, taking passengers to its most intimate and beautiful spots—places like that cove that hardly anyone knows about. It's like a first-class wilderness lodge afloat. Seven-day voyages are around $3,650 per person, double occupancy. Contact **Discovery Voyages** at ✆ **800/324-7602;** www.discoveryvoyages.com.

---

www.breadnbuttercharters.com) has been around for many years. They charge $245 per person for a day of halibut fishing and have an office on the waterfront. Honey Charters, listed above under "Small Boat Tours," has a similar service.

You can also rent your own boat for fishing, camping, or even sleeping onboard, from **Whittier Boat & Tackle Rentals** (✆ **866/667-2628** or 907/632-1188; www.whittierboatrentals.com). The company carries quality equipment, including boats suitable for an extended trip. Full-day rentals range from $300 to $725.

SEA KAYAKING

Whittier is a popular starting point for kayak trips to beautiful and protected western Prince William Sound. Day trips for beginners paddle along the shore near Whittier, often visiting a bird rookery, or take a boat 5 miles from the harbor to Shotgun Cove and paddle back. Longer multiday trips go by boat to even more interesting waters where you can visit glaciated fjords and paddle narrow passages. Several businesses compete in Whittier. **Alaska Sea-Kayakers** (✆ **877/472-2534** or 907/472-2534; www.alaskaseakayakers.com) offers 3- and 5-hour day trips, for $79 to $175; paddles at Blackstone Glacier that begin and end with a charter boat ride, for $300; and extended trips. Guides are well trained and they occasionally offer weekend instructional clinics (check the website for times). Offices are at each end of Whittier Harbor. They rent to experienced paddlers, too. **Prince William Sound Kayak Center** (✆ **877/472-2452** or 907/472-2452; www.pwskayakcenter.com) offers guided half-day trips starting at $75 as well as full days and other options, and rents kayaks. They've been in business since 1981.

Most self-guided kayakers charter a boat to drop them off among the islands beyond the long, deep fjord in which Whittier is located. Honey Charters, listed above under "Small Boat Tours," offers a drop-off service. There are six Forest Service cabins in this idyllic area, which must be reserved 6 months ahead. Flat sites suitable for a tent are not plentiful on these rocky shores, which dropped in the 1964 earthquake, so do some research with the Forest Service or Alaska Public Lands Information Center in Anchorage before you go (the tent platforms at Surprise Cove State Marine Park make an excellent remote base camp). For information and cabin reservations, see section 3, "Chugach National Forest: Do-It-Yourself Wilderness."

WHERE TO STAY & DINE

Most meals served in Whittier are for people grabbing a sandwich or fish and chips while waiting for a boat or otherwise passing through. Several such restaurants are in the triangle at the east end of the harbor where you can conveniently check them all out before making a choice. For something a bit fancier, try the inn, below. Most visitors to Whittier don't need overnight accommodations, but there are places to stay.

Inn at Whittier ★★   This is an exquisite Arts and Crafts style building with authentic post-and-beam construction using enormous cedar timbers and natural rock, yet it stands at the harbor mouth, amid gravel, marine junk, and plywood shacks. When this improbable venture ran into financial trouble in 2006, it didn't come as a great surprise. The inn is back in business, and visitors who need to spend the night in Whittier and have a generous travel budget will find luxurious rooms. The restaurant is good, and the dining room is gorgeous, with superb woodwork and sweeping ocean views.

Harbor Loop Rd. (P.O. Box 609), Whittier, AK 99693. ℂ 866-472-5757 or 907/472-7000. www.innatwhittier.com. 25 units. High season $219–$299 double, $399–$599 suite; low season $99–$169 double, $249–$399 suite; $10 each additional person. AE, MC, V. **Amenities:** Restaurant. *In room:* satellite TV, coffeemaker, Wi-Fi.

June's Whittier Bed and Breakfast Condo Suites ★   Nine of these condo units are in the top two floors of the Begich Towers, the concrete building that dominates Whittier, allowing guests to live as Whittier people do, with narrow corridors and a small elevator leading to rooms with breathtaking views and hummingbirds feeding at the high-rise windows (one unit is on the first floor). Rather than a traditional B&B, you are essentially renting an equipped apartment for the night. All units have full kitchens, and some have stereos and big living rooms that are the equivalent of a nice family home. Housekeeping is first-rate. The friendly hostess, June Miller, and her husband, Ken, also have a fishing charter and sightseeing business, Bread-n-Butter Charters, listed above; you check in at their harborside office.

P.O. Box 715, Whittier, AK 99693. ℂ 888/472-2396 or 907/472-2396. Fax 907/472-2503. www.breadnbutter charters.com. 10 units. $125–$450 double. Extra adult $15. AE, MC, V. **Amenities:** Harbor shuttle; coin-op laundry. *In room:* TV/DVD, kitchen, Internet.

5 Seward: Gateway to Resurrection Bay & Kenai Fjords

Located by the broad fjord of Resurrection Bay, Seward's main reason to exist has always been its ocean dock. The agreeable little town started life as a place to fish and to get off boats arriving in Alaska, then continued as a place for Alaskans and visitors to get *on* boats and see the bay and Kenai Fjords National Park (see section 6 of this chapter). With the growth of the cruise industry, Seward again is a place to get off the boat. Many cruises that cross the Gulf of Alaska start or end here, with their passengers taking a bus to or from the airport in Anchorage. The minority of those cruise passengers who spend any time in town find a mountainside grid of streets lined with old wood-frame houses, the sort of place where pedestrians casually wander across the road, hardly glancing for cars, for there likely won't be any, or, if there are, they'll be ready to stop. Increasing tourism has brought more traffic and development, but the growth mostly has been of a quality that hasn't damaged the town's character. Seward isn't spoiled yet.

Seward's history is among the oldest in Alaska. The great Russian governor Alexander Baranof stopped here in 1793, named Resurrection Bay, and built a ship, which later sank, probably because Baranof's workers didn't have proper materials. Gold

The following labels appear on the map:

to Exit Glacier
Port Ave.
Alaska R.R.
0 ... 1/2 mi
0 ... 1/2 km
Fresh Water Lagoon
Seward Hwy.
4th Ave.
Harbor
Cruise Ship & State Ferry Dock
Resurrection Bay
D St.
C St.
B St.
A St.
Monroe St.
Madison St.
P.O.
Jefferson St.
Adams St.
Washington St.
Railway Ave.
Mt. Marathon Trail
1st Ave.
2nd Ave.
3rd Ave.
4th Ave.
5th Ave.
6th Ave.
Ballaine Blvd.
Anchorage
Seward
Juneau

ACCOMMODATIONS ■
Ballaine House B&B **6**
The Breeze Inn **2**
Harborview Inn **5**
Holiday Inn Express Seward **1**
Hotel Edgewater **13**
Moby Dick Hostel **7**
Murphy's Motel **4**
Van Gilder Hotel **9**

DINING ◆
Apollo Restaurant **11**
Christo's Palace **15**
Ray's Waterfront **3**
Ranting Raven **12**

ATTRACTIONS ●
Alaska SeaLife Center **16**
Iditarod Trailhead **14**
Seward Museum **8**
St. Peter's Episcopal Church **10**

prospectors blazed trails from here to finds on Turnagain Arm starting in 1891, and in 1907 the army linked those trails with others all the way to Nome, finishing the Iditarod Trail. Today that route is discontinuous south of Anchorage, but you can follow it through Seward and hike a portion of it on the Johnson Pass Trail north of town (p. 270). More relevant for current visitors and the local economy, the federal government took over a failed railroad-building effort in 1915, finishing the line to Fairbanks in 1923. Until the age of jet travel, most people coming to the main part of Alaska arrived by steamer in Seward and then traveled north by rail. The train ride to Anchorage, daily during the summer, is still supremely beautiful.

Seward's in-town highlight is the Alaska SeaLife Center, a research aquarium that's open to the public. Combined with Seward's excellent ocean fishing, the national park, the wonderful hiking trails, and the unique and attractive town itself, the center helps make Seward well worth a 2-day visit.

ESSENTIALS

GETTING THERE **By Car** See section 2 of this chapter, on the Seward Highway, for how to make the spectacular 127-mile drive down from Anchorage. All major car-rental agencies are represented in Anchorage.

By Bus   The **Seward Bus Line** (© 907/224-3608 in Seward or 907/563-0800 in Anchorage) makes a round-trip from Seward to Anchorage and back daily, year-round (except Sun Oct–Apr); the fare is $45 one-way, $85 round-trip. They'll pick up and drop off passengers anywhere en route and, for an extra $5, take you to the airport. **The Park Connection Motorcoach Service** (© 800/266-8625 or 907/245-0200; www.alaskatravel.com/bus-lines) connects Seward with Anchorage and Denali National Park twice daily in summer in each direction with big, comfortable coaches. The fare is $56 between Seward or Whittier and Anchorage, $135 between Seward or Whittier and Denali, half off for children under age 12. Passengers going to Anchorage get a free pass to the Anchorage Museum at Rasmuson Center.

By Train   The train ride between Anchorage and Seward is one of miraculous beauty. The **Alaska Railroad** (© 800/544-0552 or 907/265-2494; www.alaskarailroad.com) offers passenger service from Anchorage and back daily in summer. The route is even prettier than the highway, passing close by glaciers and following a ledge halfway up the narrow, vertical Placer River gorge, where it ducks into tunnels and pops out at bends in the river. The landscape looks just as it did when the first person beheld it. The railroad's young guides are well trained. The fare is $65 one-way, $109 round-trip; children ages 2 to 11 half price. A rental car will almost always be cheaper, but the train ride is unforgettable. The railroad also offers packages with lodging and activities in Seward. Don't try to do it in 1 day from Anchorage—the 16-hour marathon is too much.

GETTING AROUND   You can easily cover downtown Seward on foot, although a little help is handy to get back and forth from the boat harbor. If it's not raining, a bike may be the best way. **Seward Bike Shop** (© 907/224-2448), in a railcar near the depot at the harbor, rents high-performance mountain bikes and models good for just getting around town, plus accessory equipment. A cruiser is $12 for a half-day, $19 for a full day; a mountain bike is $18 and $30. **PJ's Taxi** (© 907/224-5555) is one of the cab companies in Seward.

VISITOR INFORMATION   The **Seward Chamber of Commerce,** P.O. Box 749, Seward, AK 99664 (© 907/224-8051; www.sewardak.org), has two visitor centers. The one on the right side of the Seward Highway as you enter town is open year-round (summer daily 8am–6pm; winter Mon–Fri 9am–5pm). A summer-only information kiosk is on the cruise-ship dock. The chamber can provide business information and last-minute help in finding a room. In addition to these town information sources, the **Kenai Fjords National Park Visitor Center** is covered in section 6, later in this chapter. For contacts for the Chugach National Forest, see section 3.

SPECIAL EVENTS   The **Fourth of July** is the biggest day of the year in Seward, when the whole town explodes with visitors, primarily from Anchorage. Besides the parade and many small-town festivities, the main attraction is the 3¼-mile **Mount Marathon Race,** run every year since it started as a bar bet in 1915. The racers go from the middle of town straight up rocky Mount Marathon to its 3,022-foot peak, then tumble down again, arriving muddy and bloody at the finish line in town. Strong binoculars allow you to see the whole thing from town, including the pratfalls of the runners on their way down.

The **Silver Salmon Derby** starts the second Saturday of August, although the peak of silver season comes later. The chamber of commerce visitor centers can provide tickets and rules.

FAST FACTS: Seward

Bank **Wells Fargo** is at 908 3rd Ave., with an ATM.

Hospital **Providence Seward Medical Center** is at 417 1st Ave. (© **907/224-5205**).

Internet Access Free at the **Seward Public Library,** 5th and Adams.

Police For nonemergency situations, call the **Seward Police Department** (© **907/ 224-3338**) or, outside the city limits, the **Alaska State Troopers** (© **907/224-3346**).

Post Office At 5th Avenue and Madison Street.

Taxes Sales tax is 6%. The room tax totals 10%.

GETTING OUTSIDE

Here I've described things to do out of Seward other than visiting the national park, which includes the fjords and Exit Glacier. See section 6, "Kenai Fjords National Park," later in this chapter, for that information.

SEA KAYAKING & WATER TAXI

Sunny Cove Sea Kayaking (© **800/770-9119** for reservations, or 907/224-4426; www.sunnycove.com) has earned a good reputation for guided kayaking in Resurrection Bay and beyond. Their day trips suitable for beginners are offered as part of the Kenai Fjords Tours trips to its Fox Island lodge. For a more ambitious day trip, and for multiday trips, they venture into the fjords themselves (see "Kenai Fjords National Park" later in this chapter). On a budget, you can take one of Sunny Cove's tours right from Seward. They launch from Lowell Point, following the shore toward Caines Head State Recreation Area, where you can see sea otters, seabirds, intertidal creatures, and the salmon in Tonsina Creek. Three-hour paddles are $59; 8-hour trips are $125. A trip to Fox Island is more expensive but comes with a fjords boat tour and salmon bake, so the cost of the kayaking comes out roughly the same.

Another highly regarded sea kayaking firm in Seward, **Kayak Adventures Worldwide** (© **907/224-3960;** www.kayakak.com) offers a wide selection of day trips and expeditions, and offers packages involving other activities, such as glacier hiking. The company also rents kayaks and gear to experienced paddlers ($60 a day single, $75 double) and arranges water taxi drop-off for clients.

Miller's Landing, at Lowell Point, 3 miles south of town (© **866-541-5739** or 907/224-5739; www.millerslandingak.com) is the primary water-taxi operator in Seward, charging flat rates to take travelers to remote beaches and public cabins around the bay or to the national park—great for sea kayakers or those who just want to get off on their own ($45 per person round trip to Caines Head, $275 to the park service cabin in Aialik Bay). The company rents skiffs, too ($80 for 4 hr.) and offers many other services.

FISHING

Seward is renowned for its saltwater silver salmon fishing. The silvers start showing up in the bay in mid-July and last through September. You can catch the fish from shore, from Lowell Point south of town, or even near the boat harbor, but your chances of success are far greater from a boat. I prefer small, six-passenger boats because you can get to know the skipper better and can learn more about fishing. If your party has the whole boat, you can control where it goes, perhaps adding whale-watching or sightseeing to the day. Larger boats add more comfort and stability in the waves. The going rate for a guided charter, with everything provided, is around $175 per person, or $245 to go for salmon and halibut on the same day. Andrew Mezirow, a marine biologist and maritime instructor, operates two boats, including a 12-passenger vessel and a six-passenger boat custom-built for fishing salmon in Resurrection Bay year-round. Besides day fishing, he takes guests on multiday fishing expeditions to extremely remote and beautiful places. His business is **Crackerjack Sportfishing Charters** (© **800/566-3192** or 907/224-2606; www.crackerjackcharters.com). The office is on the boardwalk at the top of the harbor ramps. There are many other fishing charter companies, mostly booked through central charter agencies, which make life simpler for visitors. **The Fish House** is the largest charter fishing agency in Seward, located at the Small Boat Harbor. The store also sells and rents ocean-fishing and spin-casting gear, and carries some fly-fishing supplies. For charters, reserve ahead at P.O. Box 1209, Seward, AK 99664 (© **800/257-7760** or 907/224-3674; www.thefishhouse.net). If you want a small boat, ask to be put on a "six pack," as vessels licensed for six or fewer passengers are known.

HIKING

There are several excellent hiking trails near Seward. You can get a complete list and directions at the Kenai Fjords National Park Visitor Center (p. 289).

The **Mount Marathon Trail** is a tough hike right to the top of a 3,022-foot mountain in less than 4 miles. The route of the famous Mount Marathon footrace is the most strenuous choice, basically going straight up from the end of Jefferson Street; the hikers' route starts at the corner of 1st Avenue and Monroe Street. Either trail rises steeply to the top of the rocky pinnacle and the incredible views there. Allow all day, unless you're a racer; in that case, expect to do it in under 45 minutes.

The **Caines Head State Recreation Area** (www.alaskastateparks.org, click on "Individual Parks") has a 7-mile coastal trail south of town. Parts of the trail are accessible only at low tide, so it's best done either as an overnight or with someone picking you up or dropping you off in a boat beyond the beach portion—the Miller's Landing water taxi (p. 281) offers this service for $35 per person one-way, $45 round-trip. The trail has some gorgeous views, rocky shores, and a fascinating destination at the end, a towering promontory with the concrete remains of Fort McGilvray, a World War II defensive emplacement. Take flashlights and you can poke around in the spooky, pitch dark underground corridors and rooms and imagine what each was used for (going in without lights would be foolhardy). We've rarely enjoyed a hike more. Three campsites are at Tonsina Point, about 2 miles in, and a state park public-use cabin is 2 miles farther (see "Where to Stay," below; and "State Parks Cabin Reservations," p. 265). At North Beach, 4½ miles from the trail head, are two camping shelters, a ranger station, and the trails to the fort and South Beach. For an easy 2-mile hike to Fort McGilvray, start with a boat ride to North Beach. The main trail head is south of town on Lowell Point Road; pull off in the lot right after the sewage plant, then cross the road through the gate and follow the dirt road a bit until it becomes the actual trail. Stop at the Kenai Fjords National Park Visitor Center for tide conditions and advice.

DOG MUSHING

When Mitch Seavey won the Iditarod Trail Sled Dog Race in 2004, many agreed it couldn't have happened to a nicer guy. He had made a lot of friends over the years from offering rides with his dogs. It's a family business, including the four boys (one is a Junior Iditarod champ), making use of their kennel on Old Exit Glacier Road off Herman Leirer Road. They offer summer rides in Seward and in winter in Sterling (near Soldotna). The summer ride uses a wheeled sled and a full, 12-dog team—not the real thing (no snow), but you'll get a feeling for the dogs' power and intelligence. The 90-minute tour costs $59 for adults, $29 for children 11 and under. Husky puppies are available for cuddling, too. They call their company **IdidaRide** (© **800/ 478-3139** or 907/224-8607; www.ididaride.com).

Those willing to spend much more should consider mushing on snow at the height of summer by joining a helicopter tour to Godwin Glacier from the Seward Airport with **Godwin Glacier Dog Sled Tours** (© **888/989-8239** or 907-224-8239; www. alaskadogsled.com). A chopper lands at a camp of 100 dogs, where guests take a ride in a dog sled (the company also offers glacier hikes and overnight camping on the ice). They charge $430 for adults, $390 for children 12 and under.

EXPLORING THE TOWN

Besides the Alaska SeaLife Center (see below), most of Seward's in-town attractions are of the modest, small-town variety. The **Iditarod trail head,** on the water just east of the SeaLife Center, is where pioneers entered Alaska. The broken concrete and twisted metal you see on the beach walking north are the last ruins of the Seward waterfront, which was destroyed by a tsunami wave in the 1964 earthquake. Sometimes you can see sea otters swimming just offshore. During silver salmon season, in August and September, it's possible to catch them by casting from shore here, although your chances are far better from a boat (see "Fishing," above).

The **Seward Museum,** at 3rd and Jefferson (© **907/224-3902**), is a charming grandma's attic of a place, with clippings, memorabilia, and curiosities recalling the history of the town and of the Iditarod Trail, painter Rockwell Kent, and the ways of the past. Admission is $3 for adults, 50¢ for children under age 18. It's open during the summer daily from 9am to 5pm, in winter usually weekends noon to 4pm (call ahead). Evening slide programs take place during the summer months.

The steep-roofed **St. Peter's Episcopal Church** (© **907/224-3975;** www.stpeters-seward.org) is a sweet little chapel under the mountains at 1st Avenue and Adams Street finished in 1906, within a few years of the town's founding. Behind the altar is a mural painted in 1925 by Dutch artist Jan Van Emple showing the Resurrection as if it had happened at Resurrection Bay. The apostles are depicted as real Alaska Natives and pioneers who were living in town at the time, in their contemporary dress. To get into the church attend a Sunday morning service or ask for the key at the Seward Museum.

Alaska SeaLife Center ★★★   The center's role as an important research institution makes it an especially vibrant and fascinating aquarium to see creatures from nearby Alaska waters. There's always something happening. You may have seen puffins diving into the water from a tour boat; here you can see what they look like flying *under* the water. Seabirds, harbor seals, octopus, and sea lions reside in three spectacular exhibits viewed from above or below—you can get within a few feet of the birds without glass. There are smaller tanks with fish, crab, and other creatures, a touch tank where you can handle starfish and other tide-pool animals, and exhibits on current ocean changes and hot research issues. An exhibit built in 2007 traces the life cycle of salmon; the staff hatches salmon eggs on a schedule so fish at each stage of development will always be present in their realistic habitats. I don't want to oversell the place, however: The center is not as large as a big-city aquarium, and you'll likely spend no more than a couple of hours unless you sign up for one of the lectures or special behind-the-scenes programs for adults and children that happen all day. To make the most of the admission price call ahead so you can catch a program that interests you.

301 Railway Ave. (P.O. Box 1329), Seward, AK 99664. © 888/378-2525 or 907/224-6300. www.alaskasealife.org. $15 adults, $12 children 7–12, free for children 6 and under. Apr 15–Sept 15 daily 8am–7pm; Sept 16–Apr 14 daily 10am–5pm.

WHERE TO STAY

Alaska's Point of View Reservation Service (© 907/224-2323; www.alaskasview. com) is a Seward lodging and tour booking agency. The website has a handy search function for B&Bs, cabins, hotel rooms, and all other lodgings. You can get a list of B&Bs from the chamber of commerce visitor center (p. 280).

Seward has several hotels beyond those I can list here; in fact, I'm not aware of a bad hotel in Seward. The **Holiday Inn Express Seward Harbor** (© 800/HOLIDAY or 907-224-2550; www.hieseward.com) stands right on the small boat harbor wall, with its ramp down to the floats, and is only steps from the railroad depot. The hotel has a shopping arcade, charter booking office, Wi-Fi, and a tiny pool. The well-equipped rooms have red carpets, but otherwise are typical of a national chain. Summer rates are $189 to $299 double, with the lower-priced units facing the parking lot instead of the harbor. Breakfast is included in the price.

Equally attractive to the Holiday Inn, and with better rates, is the downtown **Hotel Edgewater,** 200 5th Ave. (© 888/793-6800; www.hoteledgewater.com). The unique building looks across the street to the bay on two sides near the Alaska SeaLife Center. Rooms vary in shape and size and are decorated in bold colors. Lower-priced units have lesser views or have only frosted windows on the lobby atrium. Summer rates are $155 to $235 double.

Save over either of those choices at **Murphy's Motel** (© 800/686-8191 or 907/ 224-8090; www.murphysmotel.com), near the boat harbor, which has attractive rooms with views in a new building and good budget rooms in an older building.

Ballaine House Bed and Breakfast *Finds* This 1905 house near downtown is a classic B&B, with wooden floors, a large living room, and tall, double-hung windows. It's on the National Register of Historic Places and the town walking tour, decorated with antiques and handmade quilts. It's a social place with service that is accommodating and fun, and the hostess offers raincoats, binoculars, and other gear for outings, cooks breakfast to order, and even does laundry. The B&B can also book your activities and boats in Seward and some other towns, giving you the booking commission, which can save as much as 20%. The rooms are not large, suitable for only one or two people, and all bathrooms are shared. The B&B does not take children under 8.

437 3rd Ave. (P.O. Box 2051), Seward, AK 99664-2051. © 907/224-2362. www.superpage.com/ballaine. 5 units, none with private bathroom. $95 double. Rates include full breakfast cooked to order. No credit cards. No children under 8. **Amenities:** Tour booking; laundry service; shared Internet access. *In room:* TV/VCR.

The Breeze Inn ★ Located right at the busy boat harbor, this large, three-story, motel-style building is constantly renewed and, when I visited in 2007, was in the midst of a major expansion. The location is the most convenient in town for a fishing or Kenai Fjords boat trip, which means the building is in the strip of asphalt and activity between the highway and the harbor. The original wing is a bargain: old-fashioned motel rooms, but clean and well maintained. An annex building has good upscale rooms, some overlooking the harbor. The newest wing wasn't done yet.

1306 Seward Hwy. (P.O. Box 2147), Seward, AK 99664-2147. © **888/224-5237** or 907/224-5237. Fax 907/224-7024. www.breezeinn.com. 100 units. Summer $139–$199 double; winter $49 double. Extra person $10. AE, DC, DISC, MC, V. **Amenities:** Restaurant; bar; courtesy van; guest laundry. *In room:* A/C, TV, dataports, fridge, coffeemaker, hair dryer, iron, Wi-Fi.

Harborview Inn ★★ The inn grew from Jerry and Jolene King's bed-and-breakfast operation and still shows the taste and attention to detail that made it such a success. The rooms are among the most attractive in town, with lots of light, Mission-style furniture, and Tlingit art based on Jolene's tribal crest. The rates are not out of line by Seward's high standards, and the location, midway between the Small Boat Harbor and downtown, puts both within long walking distance. Families and large groups especially should consider a stay. The inn has a four-bedroom family suite with the features and size of a house—it's 2,500 square feet—renting for $199 double plus $10 for each additional person. Two two-bedroom apartments on the beach along Ballaine Avenue are perfect for families as well and rent for $189 a night for four. There are other suites, too.

804 3rd Ave. (P.O. Box 1305), Seward, AK 99664. © **888/324-3217** or 907/224-3217. Fax 907/224-3218. www.sewardhotel.com. 39 units, including 4 apts. High season $144 double, $159–$259 apt. Low season $59 double, $69–$219 apt. Extra person $10. AE, DISC, MC, V. *In room:* TV, coffeemaker, hair dryer, Wi-Fi.

Seward Windsong Lodge ★★ This hotel is the only one at Kenai Fjords National Park with a national park atmosphere. The big lobby could be at Yellowstone with its high ceiling, huge wood beams, fireplace, and cedar shingles. Moreover, the posh, solidly finished quality of the place puts it in first place among Seward's hotels. The location is out of town, among spruce trees on the broad valley of the Resurrection River, and the collection of buildings goes on and on. Rooms are in separate lodges with entry from exterior porches. They have a crisp feel, all with two queen beds and rustic-style furniture and good amenities. Family suites are available with TVs and video games in the kids' room.

The hotel restaurant, the **Resurrection Roadhouse** has lots of natural light, pale wood and an exhaustive selection of Alaska craft brews on tap. The menu includes fish, venison, and ribs smoked in-house as well as hand-thrown gourmet pizzas. Main courses for dinner range from $9 to $24. The view of the mountains is great and the feeling relaxed, a low-key alternative to a noisy waterfront restaurant. Do call ahead, as they fill at dinnertime. The restaurant closes mid-September to mid-May.

½ mile, Exit Glacier Rd., also known as Herman Leirer Rd. (Mailing address: 2525 C St., Suite 405, Anchorage, AK 99503). © **888/959-9590** or 907/265-4501 in Anchorage, or 907/224-7116 in Seward. www.sewardwindsong.com. 144 units. High season $215–$259 double; low season $129–$179 double. Extra person over age 11 $15. AE, DISC, MC, V. Closed Oct–Apr. **Amenities:** Restaurant; tour desk; courtesy van, Wi-Fi, and Internet station in lobby. *In room:* TV/VCR, coffeemaker.

Van Gilder Hotel ★ This historic building was restored and decorated with the wallpaper of a century ago, Victorian reproductions, and other authentic period details. Even the tiny bathrooms, mostly with shower stalls, not tubs, are tiled in the appropriate style and immaculately clean. Three rooms share bathrooms. The rooms tend to be small and oddly shaped, as you would expect, but all have queen-sized beds and some also have a fold-down Murphy bed for a third person. In Seward's high-priced lodging market, these rooms are a great value for a party of three. Perhaps best is the warm, professional management: They thought of including a community kitchen on the main floor where guests can stop for a free hot drink at any time, or even cook their own meals. The location, right downtown, is prime.

308 Adams St. (P.O. Box 609), Seward, AK 99664. © **800/204-6835** or 907/224-3079. Fax 907/224-3689. www.vangilderhotel.com. 23 units. High season $109 double shared bath, $155–$175 double private bath, $195 suite; low season $59 double shared bath, $69–$79 private bath, $129 suite. $10 each additional person. AE, DC, DISC, MC, V. *In room:* TV.

A HOSTEL, CAMPING & CABINS

A friendly family runs the **Moby Dick Hostel,** at 432 3rd Ave. (© **907/224-7072;** www.mobydickhostel.com). They charge $19 for a bunk, $50 for private hostel rooms, and $65 to $70 for kitchenette rooms.

The best campgrounds near Seward are those in Chugach National Forest, described earlier in section 3, especially Primrose Campground on Kenai Lake (p. 273). The only campground in Kenai Fjords National Park is near Seward, the **Exit Glacier Campground** at mile 8.5 of Herman Leirer Rd. (aka Exit Glacier Road). The campground is on willow-covered, gravel ground that plants haven't yet reclaimed from the retreating ice. Sites are far apart and almost completely private, but lack any amenities—no picnic tables, fire grates, or anything. Use the food lockers and central cooking to keep bears away. Snow lingers into early June; later in the summer, the campground often fills by early evening. There is no fee for the 12 sites, and reservations are not taken. It's open for tents only and has pit toilets and hand-pump water.

In the town of Seward itself, the seaside **Waterfront Park** on Ballaine Boulevard is good for RV camping—units stand side by side like townhouses facing the ocean—but the tent sites are too noisy and exposed for my liking. Seward has tried to crack down on drinking and rowdiness in its campgrounds with partial success. The fee is $8 for tents, $12 for RVs plus $25 for a site with utilities, and showers are $2. It's operated by the city Parks and Recreation Department (© **907/224-4055;** www.cityofseward. net/parksRec). A quieter town campground is **Forest Acres Park,** among the spruce trees at Hemlock and Sealion Boulevard, just off Seward Highway near the Army Recreation Center. Fees are the same. Neither campground accepts reservations. RVs are welcome, but there are no hookups.

The Alaska Division of Parks maintains two cabins for rent in the **Caines Head State Recreation Area,** south of town, and two in **Thumb Cove State Marine Park,** across the bay from Caines Head (see "State Parks Cabin Reservations," earlier in this chapter). These cabins are in high demand and difficult to reserve, but there are good areas for camping in both parks. It's possible to hike to the Caines Head cabins (see "Hiking," above), but to get to Thumb Cove you need a boat. Water-taxi service is offered by Miller's Landing (p. 281). The Thumb Cove cabins lie in an impossibly steep bowl of mountains, a grand and lovely setting that, along with the excellent salmon fishing nearby, explains their popularity. Camping is permitted along the same beach without a permit, with plenty of space and an outhouse for campers' use. Cabins in Chugach National Forest and Kenai Fjords National Park are mentioned in those sections.

WHERE TO DINE

Besides the dining options described here, see the restaurant at the Seward Windsong Lodge, described above. There are various places at the harbor to grab a sandwich or other quick meal on the way out to sea; they change too frequently for me to include here. Downtown, the **Ranting Raven,** at 228 4th Ave. (© **907/224-2228**), is a great little gift and coffee shop serving pastries, sandwiches, and soup, open April through Christmas.

Apollo Restaurant ✦ (Kids) MEDITERRANEAN/SEAFOOD   This is a surprisingly good small-town restaurant. Seward families come back for a menu that includes anything they might want: Greek and southern Italian cuisine, steaks, seafood, pizza, and much more. They'll even cook your own day's catch. But the food is much better than you expect in such a place, especially the seafood dishes, and the service is fast, skilled, and flexible, great for families with children. The dining room, with many booths, takes the Greek theme as far as it will go—I especially enjoyed the miniature Doric columns. They serve beer and wine.

229 4th Ave. (© **907/224-3092.** www.apollorestaurantak.com. Main courses $10–$24. AE, MC, V. Daily 11am–11pm.

Christo's Palace ✦ SEAFOOD/ITALIAN/MEXICAN   I was skeptical of a restaurant with faux 1890s decor and Formica tables serving a family-friendly menu of pizza, pasta, tacos, burgers, subs, fried fish, steaks, and much finer dining, including rack of lamb and stuffed halibut. Who could do so many things well? But I'm now a believer. First, the service was too friendly and efficient for me to keep up my guard. Next, the children's menu met their needs exactly and my teen said the pizza was first rate. Finally, the seafood sauté was richly endowed with king crab and other delicacies, and the chicken and artichoke penne pasta was rich and cooked perfectly. Everything was served so quickly the children didn't have time to squirm. Christo's has found the way to please everyone.

133 4th Ave. (© **907/224-5255.** Lunch and dinner main courses $8–$36. AE, DC, DISC, MC, V. Summer daily 11am–11pm; winter Mon–Fri 11am–10pm, Sat–Sun noon–10pm.

Ray's Waterfront ✦ STEAK/SEAFOOD   The lively, noisy dining room looks out from big windows across the small-boat harbor, with tables on terraces so everyone can see. The atmosphere is fun and the consistently good food is just right after a day on the water. While not perfect, it's more nuanced than the typical harborside place; the seafood chowder is great. Most important, they don't overcook the fresh local fish—and that's really all you can ask. Consider the popularity of the restaurant, however, when choosing where to dine on a busy summer weekend; although the owner disagrees, I've found the place can get overwhelmed. They have a full bar.

At the small-boat harbor. (© **907/224-5606.** Dinner reservations recommended. Lunch $8–$15; dinner main courses $15–$30; 18% gratuity added for parties of 6 or more. AE, DISC, MC, V. Daily 11am–11pm. Closed Oct to mid-Mar.

6 Kenai Fjords National Park

Kenai Fjords is all about remote rocks, mountains, and ice that meet the ocean, and the animals that live there. The park comprises 670,000 acres of the south coast and interior landmass of the Kenai Peninsula. The shore here is exposed to the Gulf of Alaska, whose wild, recurrent storms beat against the mountainous shore unbuffered by any landmass from the vast expanse of the Pacific to the south. Wildlife thrives, but humans have never made a mark.

The geological events that formed this landscape are vast and ongoing. The steep, coastal mountains amount to a dent in the earth's crust where the northward-moving Pacific tectonic plate is colliding and adding land to the southern edge of Alaska. As the Pacific plate pushes under Alaska, it slams islands onto the Alaska coast, then pulls them under into the molten layer down below. These mountains are shrinking measurably as the earth swallows them up. The 1964 earthquake dropped them by 6 to 8 feet. As your boat passes the park's small, sharp, bedrock islands, now populated by seabirds and marine mammals, you are seeing the tips of ancient peaks that once stood far above the shore like today's coastal mountains.

The park's history has barely started. The fjords became a park only in 1980. In 1976, when the National Park Service explored more than 650 miles of coastline, including the park area, they didn't find a single human being. The same was true when geologists came in 1909. British explorer Capt. James Cook made the first maps of the fjords area in 1778, but the coast was too rugged and rocky for him to land. We don't know much about Native Americans who lived in the fjords. Scientists have found some areas where people lived, or at least had camps, but no one knows exactly who they were or what they were doing here. The earth, through earthquakes or glacial action, has erased most remains. Anthropologists call these people *Unegkurmiut,* and believe they were Alutiiq, Eskimos who lived on the Pacific coast, closely related to the people of Prince William Sound and Kodiak Island. Those groups are still around; scientists are studying the Unegkurmiut and what happened to them from the little evidence they can find on the fjord's beaches.

The Natives probably never ventured inland over the impossibly rugged interior of the Kenai Peninsula, leaving its heart to be discovered in 1968, when the first mountain climbers crossed the Harding Ice Field, which covers most of the national park. **Exit Glacier** and all the glaciers of Kenai Fjords flow from this ice age leftover, which may be a mile thick. The ice field lies in a high bowl of mountains that jut straight out of the ocean to heights of 3,000 to 5,000 feet. When moisture-laden ocean clouds hit those mountains, they drop lots of rain and snow—up on the ice field 40 to 80 feet of snow fall each winter, with a water equivalent of 17 feet. Summer weather isn't warm enough to melt the snow at that elevation, so it packs down ever deeper until it turns into the hard, heavy ice of glaciers and flows downward to the sea.

The area's history finally got an ugly start in 1989, when the tanker *Exxon Valdez* crashed into a rock about 150 miles northeast of the park in Prince William Sound and spilled about 11 million gallons of oil. Exxon did a poor job of catching the oil before it spread, and by the end of the summer the sticky, brownish-black muck had soiled beaches in the western sound, across the fjords, and all the way to Kodiak Island and the Alaska Peninsula. More than 1,000 miles of shoreline were oiled to some degree, 30 miles in the park. Hundreds of sea otters and hundreds of thousands of seabirds were killed in the sound and on the islands near the fjords. Nature scrubbed the oil off the rocks again, and you will see no evidence of it in the park today; but government scientists say some of the affected species of birds and animals still haven't come back completely. Nonetheless, there are few places you can see more wildlife than on a boat ride here.

Most of the park is remote and difficult to reach. A large vessel, such as a tour boat operating out of Seward, is the only practical way for most people to see the marine portion of the park. That's not cheap or quick, and there are better destinations for people subject to seasickness. The inland portion is accessible only at Exit Glacier, near Seward.

ESSENTIALS

GETTING THERE   Seward is the threshold to the park. Exit Glacier is 13 miles from the town by road; the Kenai Fjords National Park Visitor Center is at the Seward Small Boat Harbor; and the tour boats that visit the park leave from Seward.

Some visitors try to see the park in a day, coming from Anchorage by train or road, touring the park by boat, and then returning that evening. I do not recommend this.

To really get to the park, you need to be on an all-day boat trip—most half-day trips barely leave Resurrection Bay and hardly see the park proper. More important, a lot of visitors riding the train back to Anchorage after a 16-hour marathon to Kenai Fjords are so tired they can't keep their eyes open for the extraordinary scenery passing by. A better plan is to spend at least 1 night in Seward and take in the full Kenai Fjords boat trip and Exit Glacier.

VISITOR INFORMATION   At the **Kenai Fjords National Park Information Center,** Seward Small Boat Harbor (P.O. Box 1727), Seward, AK 99664 (© **907/ 224-7500;** www.nps.gov/kefj), you will find rangers to answer questions about the park and provide information on the all-important tour boats, and a small but handy bookstore. Call or drop by here for advice on public-use cabins for rent in the fjords, guidance on a sea-kayaking expedition there, or information on hikes and trail conditions. They're open late May through early September daily 8:30am to 7pm, the balance of May and September 9am to 5pm. The center is closed October through April.

ACCOMMODATIONS & CAMPING   There are no hotels in the park; it's best to base yourself in Seward (see my recommendations earlier in this chapter). The **Exit Glacier Campground,** the only campground in the park, also is listed on p. 286. In the heart of the park you can camp anywhere if you observe correct backcountry precautions. A free park service map shows the location of food lockers and hanging cables to keep your stuff away from bears in the kayaking waters of Aialik Bay and Northwestern Fjord. The Park Service gives voluntary permits to record your itinerary and an emergency contact phone number in case you don't return. The park will send a packet of information, which you can request through the website. They also rent out three **public-use cabins** in the fjords, reachable only by boat or floatplane. Contact the Alaska Public Lands Information Center in Anchorage (p. 215) for a $50-a-day cabin permit, open for reservations starting January 2 each year.

SEEING THE PARK
SIGHTSEEING & WILDLIFE CRUISES

Kenai Fjords is essentially a marine park. On a boat tour, you'll see its mountains, glaciers, and wildlife. On any of the tours you're sure to see sea otters and sea lions, and you have a good chance, depending on the season, conditions, and luck, of seeing humpback whales, orcas, mountain goats, and black bears. I saw all those on one trip to Aialik Bay. Gray whales come in the early spring and huge fin whales show sometimes, too, but are hard to see. Bird-watchers may see bald eagles, puffins (both tufted and horned), murrelets (marbled, ancient, and Kittlitz's), cormorants (red faced, pelagic, and double-crested), murres (common and thick billed), auklets (rhinoceros and parakeet), and various other sea ducks, alcids, and gulls.

The farther you go into the park, the more you'll see. If you really want to see Kenai Fjords National Park and glaciers that drop ice into the water, the boat has to go at least into Aialik Bay to Holgate Glacier or Aialik Glacier. Northwestern Glacier is even deeper in the park. Half-day Resurrection Bay cruises offer plenty of impressive scenery but pass only one large glacier, at a distance. They have less chance of seeing whales, and see fewer species of birds. The longest trips into the heart of the park proper encounter the greatest variety and number of birds and animals. If you're lucky with the weather, you can make it to the exposed Chiswell Islands, which have some of the greatest bird rookeries in Alaska, supporting more than 50,000 seabirds of 18 species. I've seen clouds of puffins swarm here. The day-long trips also allow you more

(*Tips* **It's Not Easy Being Green**

A critical factor in choosing your boat tour is your susceptibility to **seasickness.** To reach the heart of the park, vessels must venture into the unprotected waters of the North Pacific. Large, rolling waves are inevitable on the passage from Resurrection Bay to the fjords themselves, although once you're in the fjords the water is calm. On a rough day, most boats will turn back for the comfort of the passengers and change the full-day trip into a Resurrection Bay cruise, refunding the difference in fare. Of course, they'd rather not do that, and the decision often isn't made until the vessel is out there and some people are sick. This has happened to us more than once. On one trip, about 80% of the passengers were already vomiting when the boat turned around. (Even for those who don't lose it, being around that much puke isn't fun.) If you get seasick easily, my advice is to stick to the Resurrection Bay cruise, or take a boat tour in protected Prince William Sound, where the water is always smooth, from Whittier or Valdez (see section 4 or 11 of this chapter). Detailed advice for seasickness is on p. 49.

time to linger and really see the behavior of the wildlife. Whatever your choice, binoculars are a necessity, but if you didn't bring your own you can often rent them onboard.

Prices are around $160 to go to Northwestern Glacier in Northwestern Fjord off Harris Bay, a 10- to 12-hour trip; $130 to $140 to go to Holgate or Aialik Glacier in Aialik Bay, which takes 6 to 8 hours (the most common destinations); and $60 to $80 for a 3- to 5-hour Resurrection Bay tour, which doesn't go to the national park at all. Children's prices are around half off. I have seen vague or misleading publicity material from tour operators, so ask exactly where the boat goes or get a map of the route. They sometimes brag about going to Bear Glacier, but that's a let-down because boats can't get close to it. You have to go at least to Aialik Bay for a noteworthy glacier encounter.

The season begins in April with tours to see the gray whale migration, mostly within Resurrection Bay. That's done by mid-May, when the regular schedule of tours begins, which lasts into September. Fares with each operator differ little, although you can sometimes get early season or Web specials; instead shop for the destination, length of trip, food service, interpretation, and size or intimacy of the boat. Consider the seating arrangement. How many passengers will be onboard? Is lunch provided, and what does it consist of? Another important point of comparison is whether you have a ranger doing the commentary, or the captain—some of these captains don't know when to shut up, and they can give inaccurate information.

Try to schedule loosely so that if the weather is bad on the day you choose for your boat trip you can wait and go the next day. If the weather's bad, you'll be uncomfortable and the animals and birds won't be as evident, or the boat may not go out of Resurrection Bay. If you pay up front to hold a reservation on a boat—probably a good idea in the busy season—find out the company's refund and rescheduling policy.

Most operators offer packages with the Alaska Railroad and the SeaLife Center, or even with a local hotel, which may save money, but make sure you have enough time to do everything you want to do in Seward. All have offices at the Seward Small Boat Harbor. Here are two of the best.

Kenai Fjords Tours   This is the dominant tour operator, with the most daily sailings and choices of destination. The main part of the operation uses 90- to 150-passenger vessels, many of which have forward-facing seats, like an airplane's. They're professionally staffed. The whole operation runs remarkably smoothly and we found the crew extremely attentive. When the ships are crowded, however, the experience becomes more impersonal. Onboard, the captain or an employee provides the commentary. The same company also owns **Mariah Tours,** which operates more intimate 16-passenger vessels. Their trips are more spontaneous and go farther; the downside is that the smaller boats move more in the waves.

Most of the large Kenai Fjords vessels call on a lodge the company owns on Fox Island, in Resurrection Bay, for lunch and park service ranger talks. The lodge sits on a long cobble beach near Sunny Cove, where painter Rockwell Kent lived in seclusion with his son in 1918 and 1919 and produced the art that made him famous. It is an inspiring spot. The lodge itself stands on a narrow strip of land between the beach and a pond, which visitors overlook from large wooden decks. Lunch is grilled salmon. Big, touristy salmon bakes tend to overcook the food, and we found no exception here, but it was a pleasant meal nonetheless. Some passengers spend the night at the lodge on all-inclusive packages, and half-day sea-kayaking paddles from the island are offered for day-trippers or overnight guests: $79 to $89 per person as an add-on for overnighters; or $149 to $169, including a Resurrection Bay tour boat ride, for day-trippers.

At the Seward Small Boat Harbor. © **800/478-8068,** 907/224-8068 in Seward, or 907/276-6249 in Anchorage. www.kenaifjords.com.

Major Marine Tours   This company pioneered first-class onboard dining and commentary by park rangers, who go on every trip—a decisive advantage in my judgment. Their boats are slower than some of the competitors', so they don't make the long trip to Northwest Glacier; they either go to Aialik Glacier or tour Resurrection Bay around Seward. Instead of bringing sandwiches or stopping for a meal, they serve a buffet of salmon and prime rib onboard for $15 per person, $7 for children. The food is surprisingly good. I also like their table-seating arrangement with forward-facing seats. Your seat is assigned, so there's no need to rush aboard or try to stake out your spot.

411 W. 4th Ave., Anchorage. © **800/764-7300,** 907/274-7300, or 907/224-8030 in Seward. www.majormarine.com.

SEA KAYAKING

The fjords are calm yet rugged, intricate, and full of wildlife and soaring vistas. It's hard to imagine a better place for a sea-kayaking expedition. They also are extremely remote and very rainy, however, so a trip there is a poor choice for your very first outing. Experienced cold-water paddlers can rent kayaks and explore on their own, using the park service cabins for shelter (see "Accommodations & Camping," above). I've listed an agency that rents kayaks and offers water taxis under "Sea Kayaking & Water Taxi" in the Seward section on p. 281. **Sunny Cove Sea Kayaking** offers a kayaking day trip to Aialik Bay. They take guests out on a small charter boat for a wildlife tour, and then you launch and paddle in front of the glacier while the boat stands by. The price for the day trip is $375; expensive, but it is the best of the best. For a visit with time to get more of a feel for the place, spend a couple of days. Sunny Cove's 2-day, 3-night glacier trip costs $899.

EXIT GLACIER

When I visited Italy years ago, I got to the point where I thought I'd scream if I saw another painting of the Madonna. If your trip to Alaska is long, you may start to feel the same way about glaciers. Nevertheless, though relatively small, Exit Glacier really is unique, and my family still enjoys visits there even as jaded lifelong Alaskans. (And I've probably seen even more glaciers than Madonnas.)

You can walk close to Exit Glacier, see its brittle texture, and feel the cold, dense spires of looming ice. Cold air breathes down on you like air from an open freezer door. Approaching the glacier, you can see the pattern of vegetation reclaiming the land that the melting ice has uncovered, a process well explained by interpretive signs and a nature trail. The National Park Service opened a nature center here in 2004, adding to the comfort and educational content of a visit (the building is also interesting technically, as it is powered by a hydrogen fuel cell). You can easily spend a couple of hours on a casual, pleasant visit to the glacier (longer if you do a hike). *A safety note:* Big chunks fall off the glacier ever more frequently as Alaska's climate warms. Stay behind the signs or you stand a good chance of being crushed.

The easiest way to get to the glacier is to drive. The clearly marked 9-mile road splits from the Seward Highway 3⅔ miles north of town. In winter, the road is closed to vehicles. If you don't have a car, a shuttle may be available; check with the park visitor center (p. 289) to see who is currently offering service. Entrance to the park is currently free.

Following the road along the broad bed of the wandering Resurrection River, you'll see in reverse order the succession of vegetation, from mature Sitka spruce and cottonwood trees down to smaller alders and shrubs. It takes time for nature to replace the soil on sterile ground left behind by a receding glacier. As you get closer, watch for signs with dates starting a couple of centuries in the past; they mark the retreat of the glacier through time.

The Exit Glacier Nature Center is open Memorial Day weekend through Labor Day daily 9am to 8pm. Ranger-led nature walks start daily at 10am, 2pm, and 4pm on the short trail to the glacier. It's easy to find your way to the glacier and back on a variety of short trails.

One of the glacier's striking features is a high berm of gravel that fits around its leading edge like a necklace. This is a moraine, the glacier's refuse pile. The glacier gouges out the mountains with its immense, moving weight as new ice flows down from the ice field above and melts here. It carries along the rock and gravel torn from the mountain like a conveyor belt. This moraine is where the conveyor belt ends and the melting ice leaves the debris behind in a big pile. Probably without knowing it, you've seen hundreds of moraines all over North America, where the glaciers of the last ice age piled debris into hills, but this is the most obvious moraine I've ever seen, and it helps you understand how they work.

An all-day hike, 8 miles round-trip, climbs along the right side of the glacier to the Harding Ice Field—the glacier gets its name for being an exit from that massive sheet. It's a challenging walk with a 3,000-foot elevation gain, but it's the easiest access I'm aware of to visit an ice field on foot. The upper trail isn't free of snow until late June or early July. The ice field itself is cold and dangerous, and there's an emergency shelter maintained by the park service. Don't trek out on the ice unless you have glacier climbing experience. The park service leads hikes up the trail Saturdays in July and August, leaving at 9am from the nature center.

The Resurrection River Trail, in Chugach National Forest, begins from the road just short of the last bridge into the Exit Glacier area. It's a pleasant day hike, with lots of wildflowers in the fall, or the start of a long hike deep into the mountains.

7 Cooper Landing: Road Meets River

The little roadside community of Cooper Landing, in a wooded mountain valley along Kenai Lake and the Kenai River, begins about 8 miles west of Tern Lake, where the Sterling Highway splits from the Seward Highway, and continues sporadically along the highway for about 7 miles. (The Sterling runs generally west until Soldotna, where it heads south again.) The frothing upper **Kenai River** is the community's life-line, each summer bringing the salmon that in turn draw visitors, who fill hotels, restaurants, and the date books of fishing guides. The **Russian River** meets the Kenai at the western edge of the community, where a mad fishing frenzy for the July red salmon season occurs. A ferry takes anglers across the river from the highway. For information on how to fish the Kenai, see "Fishing" in section 8 of this chapter on Kenai/Soldotna; there's additional information in chapter 2.

If you're not an angler, there's not much here—a couple of operators do rafting trips and some trails start here. Cooper Landing is the starting or ending point for back-packing trips in the Chugach National Forest, described in section 3 of this chapter. Look there also for descriptions of several campgrounds for tents or RVs (there are also RV hookups at the Kenai Princess Lodge, reviewed below).

Cooper Landing has a post office, service stations, and small stores selling fishing gear and essentials, but it's not a real center of commerce. For banking or anything else not directly related to catching a salmon, you'll have to drive to Sterling, 30 miles away to the west, or Soldotna, 14 miles beyond that.

VISITOR INFORMATON   The **Cooper Landing Chamber of Commerce Visitor Center** is at Mile 47.5 of the Sterling Highway, right before the Kenai River Bridge, next to Wildman's Convenience Store (© **907/595-8888;** www.cooperlanding chamber.com). There's a plan to put in a picnic area and free Wi-Fi.

FISHING LODGES

The four lodges below can take care of everything, so you can set up your fishing and other activities with a single phone call. If what you need is a simple room that is clean, comfortable, and inexpensive, try **The Hutch Bed and Breakfast,** Mile 48.5, Sterling Highway (© **907/595-1270;** www.arctic.net/~hutch). In nice weather, you can sit at the fire pit and watch the bunny rabbits hop by. The B&B has Wi-Fi.

Gwin's Lodge   This is the town's old original log roadhouse, dating from the 1940s. Standing just a mile east of the Resurrection trail head and the Russian River Camp-ground, Gwin's is convenient and has loads of character. The owner, a dynamic for-mer F-15 fighter pilot, keeps it open 24 hours a day all summer long as the nerve center for the 24-hour fishing on the Russian River. It includes a liquor store and a large store selling tackle, snacks, and clothing and freezing anglers' fish. You can also book fishing, rafting, flightseeing, and many other activities. The lodgings range from old-fashioned cabins to modern trailer-size units called "chalets" with kitchenettes, mock log exteriors, and sleeping lofts with tiny dormers. All have shower stalls, not tubs. The least expensive cabins are old log structures and not as plush. All are quite clean, with a woodsy, cabin smell.

For over 55 years, the **restaurant** has welcomed many a tired angler or backpacker for a hearty meal; after a long day outdoors it's hard to be objective about food, but the chowder has won awards. Choices range broadly: burgers, quiche, steak, pies, and seafood. Meals are hearty and good, well above the greasy spoon tradition of such places. Sit in the small original dining room or the recently added pavilion. Both the restaurant, bar, and espresso stand are open around the clock in summer, and the "gourmet to go" shop sells the restaurant's fare for takeout. You can also get pizza or ice cream at the complex.

14865 (Mile 52) Sterling Hwy., Cooper Landing, AK 99572. © 907/595-1266. www.gwinslodge.com. 14 units (all cabins). High season $115–$194 double; low season $79–$99 double; $15 each additional person age 3 or older. DISC, MC, V. Amenities: Restaurant; bar; fishing rentals; activity desk. In room: Coffeemaker, Wi-Fi.

Kenai Princess Lodge ⭐⭐⭐ This is one of the best in the region. Each room in the red-roofed buildings feels like a remote cabin, with balconies overlooking the wooded valley, woodstoves stocked with firewood, and many unique details; yet they're luxurious hotel rooms at a resort with a fine restaurant. There are three classes of rooms with a $30 price difference between each. The middle, premium class, is halfway up the hill, with rooms separated by a divider into two parts, like a real cabin. At the top level the deluxe rooms, highest on the hill, have more of a clean, elegant feel. Bathrooms are surprisingly small in all the rooms. Currently closed off-season, most rooms fill in the summer with Princess cruise-ship passengers. The cycle of the ships determines if there are rooms open for independent travelers. The lodge books guided fishing, horseback riding, tours, and other activities, and there are hiking trails nearby. An attractive 35-space RV park with full hookups is on-site, with access to the facilities.

The Eagle's Crest restaurant has a varied and sophisticated menu, with good use of Alaskan seafood, professional service, and a light dining room that follows the hotel's generally rustic theme. Dinner main courses are $20 to $30; the lunch menu has the expected items, plus choices such as calamari and some unusual salads, generally under $10. Even if you have no reason to stay in Cooper Landing, consider planning your drive to include a meal here that will be several steps up from highway fare and enjoy the relaxing ambience of the lodge. The service is relatively quick considering the level of quality.

Up Bean Creek Rd. above Cooper Landing (P.O. Box 676, Cooper Landing, AK 99572). © 800/426-0500 or 907/595-1425. Fax 907/595-1424. www.princesslodges.com. 86 units. High season $239–$299 double; low season $159–$189 double; RV sites $35. AE, DC, DISC, MC, V. Amenities: Restaurant; bar; exercise room; Jacuzzi; tour desk; coin-op laundry. In room: TV, dataport, coffeemaker. Closed Oct–Apr.

Kenai River Sportfishing Lodge/Kenai Riverside Lodge ⭐⭐ The compound lies between the highway and the river, but down among the trees it feels like a remote lodge. I'd call the cabins faux rustic—I've never seen real Bush cabins with smooth walls, wainscoting, bright rag rugs, and private bathrooms, but these trim places still feel like the outdoorsy real thing, with no TVs or phones. The location is the real advantage: Kenai River fishing frontage. Whitewater rafting rides and fishing floats leave right from the riverfront. The lodge also possesses much-coveted guide permits for the hot fishing river section that runs through the Kenai National Wildlife Refuge.

Everything is covered by one price: transportation from Anchorage, meals in a central lodge building, guided salmon fishing or fly-fishing for rainbow trout in drift or power boats, and, on longer visits, halibut fishing (done from boats in saltwater). You provide your own booze and fishing license and pay the tip. The company customizes fishing trips of 2 to 7 days, including nonfishing activities such as Kenai Fjords sight-seeing or Alaska Railroad tours. Or come as part of a "safari" package that includes outdoor activities and sites, such as the Alaska Wildland Adventures safari that's described in chapter 2 on page 38.

Floating the Kenai River

The Kenai is more famous for fishing than rafting, but the area is beautiful and the Kenai Canyon, below Cooper Landing and above Skilak Lake, has frothy water between vertical canyon walls. Alaska Wildland Adventures, at the Kenai Riverside Lodge (© **800/478-4100** or 907/783-2928), is the most established operator and has a great reputation. They offer a 7-hour float through the canyon for $139 for adults, $99 for children; and a placid 2-hour float down the upper Kenai for $49 for adults, $29 for children. Their guided fishing is $250 for a full day, including lunch and gear. Alaska Rivers Co., Mile 50, Cooper Landing (© **907/595-1226;** www.alaskariverscompany.com), has more than 25 years of experience. They offer scenic rafting three times daily ($49 for adults, half price for children) and daily canyon floats ($122), as well as guided fishing ($99 half-day, $185 all day). They rent cabins, too.

Alaska Wildland Adventures, Mile 50.1 Sterling Hwy. (P.O. Box 389, Girdwood, AK 99587-0389). © **800/478-4100** or 907/783-2928. www.alaskasportfish.com. 16 units (all cabins). 3-day, 4-night inclusive package $2,050. MC, V. **Amenities:** Restaurant (family style); sauna; river equipment included.

A WILDERNESS LODGE

Kenai Backcountry Lodge ★★   On the far side of Skilak Lake from the Sterling Highway, reached by boat, this lodge is not about fishing—it's about being in a beautiful place, hiking to the tree line, lake kayaking, and enjoying quiet in an environmentally sustainable place. The tent cabins and log cabins are hidden in the woods on the lakeshore, connected by gravel paths, and the feeling is authentically wild and remote, but there are flush toilets and hot showers in the shower house and the food offered in the central lodge is terrific. The owners, Alaska Wildland Adventures, who also have the establishment listed directly above, have established a superb reputation for reliable service and a positive ethic of doing things right. You can stay as part of one of their package trips, or come for the lodge alone. Log cabins are $50 more than tent cabins; a cabin with its own bathroom is $100 more.

Alaska Wildland Adventures, Skilak Lake (P.O. Box 389, Girdwood, AK 99587-0389). © **800/478-4100** or 907/783-2928. Fax 907/783-2130. www.alaskawildland.com. 10 units (all cabins). $1,075–$1,175 adult; $875–$975 child. 2-night stay, double occupancy. Rates include all meals and guiding. DISC, MC, V. Closed Sept–May. **Amenities:** Restaurant (family style); boating; outdoor equipment. *In room:* No phone.

8 Kenai/Soldotna & Sterling: Giant Salmon

These quintessential western U.S. towns, dominated by shopping malls and fast-food franchises facing broad highways, have a single claim to fame, but it's a pretty good claim: The largest sport-caught king salmon in the world, almost 100 pounds, came from the Kenai River. The Kenai's kings run so large there's a different trophy class for the river—everywhere else in the state, the Alaska Department of Fish & Game will certify a 50-pounder as a trophy, but on the Kenai it has to be at least 75 pounds. That's because kings in the 60-pound class—with enough wild muscle to fight ferociously for hours—are just too common here. Anglers prepared to pay for a charter will be in their element on the river when the fish are running hot. Catching a big king is not easy or quick, however, and success rates vary greatly year-to-year and week-to-week.

Those not interested in fishing will find, at most, a day's sightseeing in these towns. Instead, use the towns as a base for the outdoors. Kenai has a strangely beautiful ocean beach and the Kenai River mouth has exceptional bird-watching during migrations. Beyond the towns, you'll find a wealth of outdoor activities, primarily in the lake-dotted **Kenai National Wildlife Refuge,** which has its headquarters in Soldotna. The refuge is covered in the next section.

Kenai came into being with the arrival of the Russians at the mouth of the Kenai River more than 200 years ago, but it came into its own only with the discovery of oil on the peninsula in 1957. Today its economy relies on oil, commercial fishing, and, to a smaller extent, tourism. Soldotna, a smaller, newer, and less attractive town, is the borough seat and the primary destination for anglers. Sterling is just a wide place in the road—incredibly wide, as a matter of fact (no one is quite able to explain why such a small town needs such a big road).

ESSENTIALS

GETTING THERE   From Anchorage, the drive on the Seward and Sterling highways to Soldotna is 147 miles. Allow 3 hours, without stops: In summer, traffic will slow you down; in winter, speeds are limited by ice and the fear of hitting moose. Kenai is 11 miles from Soldotna on the Kenai Spur Highway, the first major right as you enter Soldotna from the north on the Sterling Highway.

The **Homer Stage Line** (© 907/235-2252 or 907/399-1847 on the van, www. homerstageline.com) connects Anchorage, Homer, Seward, and points between with van service. In summer they run to Homer daily from Anchorage and Seward, less frequently in winter. The fare from Anchorage to Soldotna is $50 one-way, $90 round-trip. The pick-up point in Soldotna is the Thompson's Corner gift store at 44224 Sterling Hwy. The Anchorage ticket office is at 2607 Eagle St. (© **907/868-3914**).

Kenai receives very frequent flights from Anchorage from **Era Aviation** (© **800/ 866-8394;** www.flyera.com).

GETTING AROUND   The area is so spread out that walking most places really isn't possible, and there's no public transportation. Everyone drives. Several major car rental companies operate at the Kenai airport: **Hertz, Avis, Budget,** and **Payless.** If you plan only to fish, however, you may not need a car, instead getting rides from your guide, your host, or a taxicab. Ask about transportation options when you reserve your rooms. There are several cab companies; try **Alaska Cab** (© **907/283-6000** in Kenai or **907/262-1555** in Soldotna).

VISITOR INFORMATION   The **Soldotna Visitor Information Center,** 44790 Sterling Hwy., Soldotna, AK 99669 (© **907/262-9814** or 907/262-1337; www.soldotna chamber.com), is located on the south side of town; drive through the commercial strip and turn right after the Kenai River Bridge. It's open daily in summer from 9am to 7pm; in winter, Monday through Friday from 9am to 5pm. Besides the usual brochures and free maps, they offer a computer loaded with comparative information about lodgings, camping, and other services, and will help you find a room or charter. Anglers should stop in to see the world-record 97-pound King salmon and a 20-pound rainbow trout.

In Kenai, the **Kenai Visitors and Cultural Center** at 11471 Kenai Spur Hwy., Kenai, AK 99611 (© **907/283-1991;** www.visitkenai.com) is an attraction in itself. A museum does a good job of using artifacts to explain the cultures that passed through the Kenai: the Natives; Captain James Cook, who explored Cook Inlet in 1778 (a first edition of his journals is on display); the Russians, who settled in 1791;

and the later pioneers and oil workers. Look for the "King of Snags," an immense conglomeration of lost fishing lures, rods, and sticks from the bottom of the river. Temporary art exhibitions are mounted, too (see "Special Events," below). To get there, follow the Spur Highway past Main Street and look for the large, landscaped building on your left. In summer, admission to the museum portion is $3, free for students through high school; off season, admission is free. They are open summer Monday through Friday from 9am to 7pm, Saturday and Sunday from 10am to 6pm; and off season Monday through Friday from 9am to 5pm and Saturday 11am to 4pm.

SPECIAL EVENTS   Kenai Visitors and Cultural Center (see above) hosts invitational art shows each summer. Works usually cross media and include contemporary art and traditional Alaska Native work. Admission is $3 for adults, free for minors.

In Soldotna, the **Tustumena 200 Sled Dog Race** (✆ 907/262-3270), an Iditarod qualifier, is held in late January and helps kick off the mushing season. **Progress Days** (✆ 907/262-9814), in late July, offers a parade, rodeo, car shows, and other festival events commemorating the completion of a gas pipeline in 1960. That's the area in a nutshell—but, if you miss it, you can still catch Kenai's **Industry Appreciation Days** the last Saturday in August.

In Ninilchik, the **Kenai Peninsula State Fair** (✆ 907/567-3670), south at mile 136 on the Sterling Highway, is the third weekend in August (Aug 15–17, 2008), with rodeo, music, crafts, games, agricultural and craft exhibits, and other country attractions, plus a few kids' rides. One-day admission is $8 for adults, $6 for children ages 6 to 12 and seniors.

FAST FACTS: Kenai & Soldotna

Banks   You will find them on the Kenai Spur Highway in the middle of town; and in Soldotna, on the Sterling Highway commercial strip. In addition, ATMs are in grocery stores all over the area.

Hospital   **Central Peninsula General** is in Soldotna at 250 Hospital Place (✆ 907/262-4404); from the Sterling Highway, take Binkley Street to Marydale Avenue.

Internet Access   Connect to the Web for free at the **Kenai Public Library,** 163 Main St. Loop (✆ 907/283-4378), or at the **Soldotna Public Library,** 235 Binkley St. (✆ 907/262-4227).

Police   For nonemergencies in Kenai, call the Kenai Police Department (✆ 907/283-7879); in Soldotna, call the Soldotna Police Department (✆ 907/262-4455); outside city limits, call the Alaska State Troopers (✆ 907/262-4453).

Taxes   There's a 5% **sales tax** in Kenai and Soldotna, and 2% outside city limits.

FISHING

Fishing the Kenai River is the whole point of coming to the area for most visitors. Check at the Soldotna Visitor Information Center (p. 296) for information and regulation booklets. Or contact the **Alaska Department of Fish & Game,** 43961 Kalifornsky Beach Rd., Suite B, Soldotna, AK 99669 (✆ 907/262-9368 or 907/262-2737, for a recorded fishing report; www.adfg.state.ak.us). Serious anglers shouldn't miss the website, which includes daily sonar counts of salmon in the river and information on biology and fishing techniques; click on "Sport Fishing" under Fisheries, and then click on the Southcentral region on the map. Licenses are for sale on the site and in virtually any sporting-goods store. Also, read "A Salmon Primer" and "Fishing" in chapter 2. There are more than two dozen public access points over the 80 miles of the Kenai River. A **guide brochure** with a map is available from the state **Division of Parks,** P.O. Box 1247, Soldotna, AK 99669-1247 (© **907/262-5581;** www.alaskastateparks.org); you also can pick up a copy at one of the visitor centers.

KINGS   King salmon, the monsters of the river, come in two runs. The early run comes from mid-May to the end of June, peaking in mid-June. On average less plentiful and smaller, in the 20- to 40-pound range, the run did also produce the sport caught world's record (97 lb., 4 oz.). The second run comes during the month of July and includes more of the massive fish. Most people fish kings from a boat, fishing certain holes. Boats hold stationary or back slowly down the river; or fishermen drift down river. Your chances from the bank are low; on average, with or without a boat, it takes 29 hours of fishing time to land a king (you'll likely get at least a dozen strikes for every fish that makes it into the boat). With a guide, the average time to land a fish is cut in half, but that still means that if you fish for only 1 day, chances are good that you'll get skunked. A boat of three anglers on a half-day guided charter has roughly a 50% chance of landing a king between them.

A guided charter averages $150 to $170 for a 6½-hour day trip, $250 to $265 for a full day. There are dozens of guides. Contact the visitor center in Kenai or Soldotna (p. 296) to get in touch with a guide; also, many hotels and lodges have their own. It's possible to rent a boat, but this is advisable only if you are experienced in boats and stay out of the hazardous, faster flowing parts of the river. The **Sports Den,** at 44176 Sterling Hwy. in Soldotna (© **907/262-7491;** www.alaskasportsden.com), is one charter operator, with river and ocean trips for salmon or halibut, fly-in fishing and hunting, and they also offer lodging packages with large units. I've found them friendly and helpful over the years.

REDS   The area really goes crazy when the red (or sockeye) salmon join the kings in the river, from mid-July to early August. You can fish reds from the bank or from a boat. Reds are plankton eaters; some say they won't strike a lure, some say they do. In the most popular fishing areas, near the confluence of the Russian River or Moose River with the Kenai, regulations allow only the use of flies. Most people around here cast the flies with spinning gear, weighting the line 18 inches from the fly so it bounces along the bottom. Cast upstream from shore and allow the fly to drift down, keeping near the bank. While waiting for a strike, debate whether the fish really attack the flies, or if they get caught when they instinctively move their mouths in an eating motion, which they do in quick-moving water.

SILVERS   Silvers first arrive in late July, peaking during August, but continuing to be in the river through September and even in October. They're easiest to catch anchored in a boat, but you can also do well from shore. Lures work well, as does bait of salmon eggs.

OTHER SPECIES   Trophy-size rainbow trout and Dolly Varden char also come out of the river. Anglers using light tackle may also enjoy catching pink salmon, which are plentiful in the Kenai during even-numbered years, arriving in late July and lasting until mid-September. Use spinning gear and lures. Most Alaskans turn up their noses at this easy-to-catch 4-pound fish; just smile and keep hauling them in. Fresh, bright pinks taste great over a campfire.

EXPLORING THE TOWNS

Kenai's historic sites, beach walking, and bird-watching can occupy you for much of a day. Start at the visitor and cultural center mentioned above and get a copy of the *Old Town Kenai Walking Map;* follow the numbered markers. Not many of the simple, weathered buildings remain from Kenai's life before oil, but those that do are interesting and lie only a few blocks down Main Street from the center, along the Cook Inlet and Kenai River bluff.

The **Holy Assumption of the Virgin Mary Russian Orthodox Church** is the area's most significant building. The parish was founded in 1845 and the present church was built in 1895. It's a quaint, onion-domed church, brightly kept but with old icons. A donation is requested. Several nearby buildings are interesting for their interlocking log construction and weathered exteriors.

The bluff nearby overlooks the broad, sandy ocean beach. A dirt path runs down from Alaska Avenue between the apartment building and the houses that contain professional offices (please don't park near here, as an excess of tourists' cars has caused a problem for the apartment building). To drive down, return to the Kenai Spur Highway, turn to the northwest (left), and then turn left on South Spruce Street. There's a big parking lot with a $10 fee, which seems strange on the deserted beach unless you arrive during dipnetting season, the last few weeks in July (the only time the fee is actually charged). If you come then, you'll see a fish gold rush. Alaska residents are permitted to fish from this beach by scooping up passing red salmon with long-handled dip nets. It's a time for filling freezers and smokers for the winter. That's also when you can see white beluga whales chasing salmon upriver, sometimes in great numbers. If you just want to watch, the viewpoint from the top of the bluff at Erik Hansen Scout Park, at Cook and Mission avenues, is a prime spot. However, the beach also is a lovely place for a walk. It's easy to imagine the Russians' first arrival. On a calm day the beach sand, the mud flats, and the inlet's gray, glacial water seem to meld together into one vast shimmering plain. The water is far too cold for swimming.

The mouth of the river and the wetlands of its delta make for fine **bird-watching,** especially during spring and fall migrations. One of the best places to get to the tidal Kenai River Flats is along Bridge Access Road, which branches from the Spur Highway, where one sometimes also sees caribou and moose. The state of Alaska has developed viewing areas at each end of the bridge.

A family looking for something to do while one parent is off fishing may enjoy the magnificent **North Peninsula Recreation Area Nikiski Pool** (© **907/776-8472**), 10 miles north of Kenai on the Kenai Spur Road. The facility occupies a large dome and has a 136-foot water slide, mushroom fountains of water, and a raised hot tub from which parents can watch their children play in the pool below. The water slide is open Tuesday through Sunday from 1 to 5pm and from 6 to 9pm in the summer (lap swimming opens those days at 7am); the winter hours are complicated, so call for details. Pool admission is $3, or $6 to use the slide and pool. Weekends can be crowded.

WHERE TO STAY

Rates at many hotels are on seasonal schedules with three, four, or even more levels linked to the salmon runs. I've listed the highest and lowest. One unique lodging choice, worth an exploratory visit even if you don't stay there, is the **Historic Kenai Landing** (© **907/335-2500;** www.kenailanding.com), where a complex of cannery buildings dating from 1912 has been remodeled into simple rooms, a restaurant, and shops. The location is scenic but out of the way, on the opposite side of the river mouth from Kenai: after crossing the bridge, turn right on Kalifornsky Beach Road and right again on Cannery Road.

Aspen Hotel Soldotna 🐾🐾   Try here for accommodations with high-end amenities in an up-to-date corporate style. The building is a rectangle without much personality, visible from the Sterling Highway as your drive through town, but inside it has high ceilings and a solid feeling of quality. Room choices include family suites with bunk beds, privacy between parents and kids, and PlayStation video games. Suites with cooking facilities are available, too, as well as other handy configurations. All rooms are decked out with lots of amenities, including DVD players and speakerphones, and the hotel has a small pool and whirlpool. The hotel is near Arby's on the commercial strip, but offset from traffic and with a view out the back of a settling pond and the river, where a walkway provides access to fishing.

326 Binkley Circle, Soldotna, AK 99669. 📞 888/308-7848 or 907/260-7736. Fax 907/260-7786. www.aspenhotelsak. com. 63 units. High season $169–$179 double, $199 suite. Low season $99 double, $119 suite. $10 each additional person over age 18. Rates include continental breakfast. AE, DC, DISC, MC, V. **Amenities:** Pool; whirlpool; exercise room; business center with computers; coin-op laundry. In room: TV/DVD, fridge, coffeemaker, hair dryer, iron, microwave, Wi-Fi.

Great Alaska Adventure Lodge 🐾🐾   For anglers, it's the location that counts, and for that this lodge is hard to top. It contains a third of a mile of river frontage where the Moose and Kenai rivers converge, a hot fishing spot since time immemorial, as an ancient Native site attests. In the evening, the lodge keeps a guide and campfire on the beach so you can keep casting in the midnight sun. Lodge rooms overlooking the river are spacious and have gas fireplaces and private bathrooms. Unfortunately, the site suffers from vehicle noise from the adjacent Sterling Highway. The lodge offers a wide variety of guided fishing activities, including fly-fishing and halibut outings. For guests interested in seeing wildlife and the glorious wilderness of the Kenai National Wildlife Refuge, the lodge offers trips to cushy backcountry tent camps. They also arrange day trips and overnights to a camp across Cook Inlet to watch resident brown bear engaging in natural behavior. Check the lodge's website for information on the many tours and wilderness safaris that they offer as well as rates, which are too complicated to itemize here.

Moose River, 33881 Sterling Hwy., Sterling, AK 99672 (in winter, P.O. Box 2670, Poulsbo, WA 98370). 📞 800/544-2261 or 907/262-4515. Fax 907/262-8797 in summer, 360/697-7850 in winter. www.greatalaska.com. 25 units. $175–$345 day trip without lodging; $995–$4,995 packages of 2 to 10 days. Rates include all meals, guide service, transfers and travel from Anchorage. AE, MC, V. Closed Oct to mid-May.

Harborside Cottages Bed and Breakfast 🐾   On a grassy compound at the top of the bluff over the mouth of the Kenai River in Old Town, these little white cottages make the most of a perfect site. The view and quiet can keep you in a peaceful reverie all day. Inside, the cottages are as immaculate as if brand-new, each with its own light country decoration. They have either king-size beds or pairs of twin beds. There are no tubs, just shower stalls. The hostess stocks a self-serve breakfast the night before. Outside is a patio with a picnic table and gas barbecue.

13 Riverview Dr. (P.O. Box 942), Kenai, AK 99611. 📞 888/283-6162 or 907/283-6162. www.harborsidecottages.com. 5 units (all cottages). High season $175 double; low season $135 double. Rates include continental breakfast. AE, DISC, MC, V. Closed winter. In room: TV, fridge, coffeemaker, iron, microwave.

Log Cabin Inn 🐾   Ted and Carol Titus built this log house specifically to be a B&B, but with its huge common room—with a fireplace and towering cathedral ceiling—it feels more like a wilderness lodge. Located off Kalifornsky Beach Road a little south of the bridge in Kenai, the house stands over an active beaver pond with a deck and lots of windows to watch the beavers. The upstairs rooms, which cost $10 more, are well worth it—they're large and airy. A room on the main floor has French doors to a deck over the pond. Several other rooms, in the half basement, are cute but smaller, with country decoration. If you like to stay up late or rise early, the strict 10pm to 7am quiet hours in the house could make the cabins an attractive choice. They are large and comfortable, but authentic, with plank floors, rag rugs, and rough-cut wood walls. Carol serves a full breakfast.

49860 Eider Rd. P.O. Box 2886, Kenai, AK 99611. ℂ/fax 907/283-3653. www.acsalaska.net/~ted.titus. 9 units, including 3 cabins. High season $100–$110 double; low season $80–$100 double. Extra adult $25; extra child under 12 $10. Rates include full breakfast. AE, DISC, MC, V. **Amenities:** Jacuzzi.

CAMPING

Soldotna's appealing **Centennial Park Campground** extends along a long section of the Kenai River bluff among thick spruce and birch trees with ramps down to fishing spots on the river. Although natural in its setting, it has a coffee stand and newspaper vending machine and is next door to the visitor center and close to stores. Turn right on Kalifornsky Beach Road just after the bridge on the Sterling Highway. Camping fees are $11 a night and day use is $5, payable at a manned entrance booth. The park is open May 1 to October 1. There's a dump station, usable for a $10 fee. **Swiftwater Park** is a similar city-operated riverside campground near the Fred Meyer grocery store and Taco Bell as you enter town from the north. For a quieter, oceanfront public campground, see Captain Cook State Recreation Area, p. 304.

RV parks are scattered about. The one with the best location is **Beluga Lookout Lodge and RV Park,** 929 Mission Ave. (ℂ **907/283-5999;** belugarv@ptialaska.net). It's in Kenai's Old Town, at bluff's edge over Cook Inlet at the mouth of the Kenai River. Full hookups are $20 to $50 a night. They offer bike rentals and charters for salmon and halibut fishing and bear- or beluga-watching.

WHERE TO DINE

Franchise fast-food and burger-steak-seafood places dominate in Kenai and Soldotna. Among the most popular restaurants without a name brand is **Sal's Klondike Diner,** at 44619 Sterling Hwy. (ℂ **907/262-2220**) a classic Western highway diner, with big portions, fast service, cheap prices, and nothing fancy that doesn't have to be. It's open 24 hours a day all year long.

Charlotte's Bakery, Café, Espresso ⋆ SANDWICHES Rich-textured bread from the bakery anchors the sandwiches, and unique combinations enliven the large, filling salads, but the motherly owner doesn't make a point of that—hers is not a trendy or gimmicky place. Locals fill the big wooden chairs in the bright dining room because the food is wonderfully flavored, the service sweetly attentive, and the prices reasonable. The cafe serves beer and wine

115 S. Willow, Kenai. ℂ 907/283-2777. www.charlottesrestaurant.net. All items $5–$11. MC, V. Mon–Fri 7am–4pm.

Mykel's ⋆⋆⋆ STEAK/SEAFOOD This is a traditional fine-dining restaurant for a date or an especially relaxing evening. Located in the Soldotna Inn, near the intersection of the Sterling and Kenai Spur highways, the dining room, with high-backed booths and Formica-topped tables, is well kept but dated and not up to the style of the food. That's the only demerit I can give. The cuisine is exceptional and the service professional and more than friendly. Nothing else in the area even plays in the same league, and Mykel's is only a half step below Alaska's best. The dinner menu contains many familiar beef and chicken dishes done just right. When they "borrowed" the pepper steak created by Jens Hansen at his restaurant in Anchorage they admitted it on the menu—classy. In addition, the restaurant offers various ways of having local seafood in creative ways. The nightly specials, with wine pairings, run to a full page. Servings are large, even for the exceptional desserts, so don't order extra courses. The lounge has 18 wines by the glass and many microbrews. At lunchtime there are lots of salads to choose from besides the expected sandwiches.

35041 Kenai Spur Hwy., Soldotna. ⓒ 907/262-4305. www.mykels.com. Reservations recommended. Lunch $8–$13, dinner $18–$28. V. High season daily 11am–10pm; low season Tues–Thurs and Sun 11am–9pm, Fri–Sat 11am–10pm, Mon closed.

Paradisos ⓐ GREEK/ITALIAN/MEXICAN   The restaurant is a fine example of an old-fashioned type that was once common: a place that's fancy enough to take Grandma for Sunday dinner, but also has a lengthy menu with choices for each member of the family and a relaxed atmosphere where children fit in. I suppose chains have taken over in this category elsewhere—Olive Garden, Appleby's, and such. In business here since 1971, Paradisos has the formula right: big portions of familiar food, reasonable prices, and speedy, friendly service. The owner's specialty is Greek cuisine, but they also turn out Italian and Mexican food, pizza, and steaks, crab and the like, if you're of a mind.

Main St. and Kenai Spur Hwy. in Kenai. ⓒ 907/283-2222. Lunch $8–$18; dinner $8–$38. AE, DISC, MC, V. Summer daily 11am–11pm; winter 11am–10pm.

Suzie's Cafe ⓐ DOWN-HOME   If you are traveling the Sterling Highway and want a pleasant and filling lunch or dinner, you'll do no better than this local favorite on the east side of the road in the town of Sterling itself. Cheerful, efficient servers bring big plates of comfort food and hearty sandwiches—the jalapeño Swiss burger is great. The dining room, heavily decorated in burly country style, has only seven tables and a small lunch counter, and no room for waiting. Busy winter and summer, it is kept bright and immaculate.

Mile 87.2, Sterling Hwy., Sterling. ⓒ 907/260-5751. All items $7–$25. MC, V. Summer daily 11am–8pm; winter Thurs–Sun 11:30am–9pm.

9 Kenai National Wildlife Refuge

Floating through the Kenai National Wildlife Refuge in a canoe narrows the world into a circle of green water, spruce, and birch. You can paddle and hike for days without encountering more than a few other people, your only expense the cost of your canoe and the vehicle that carried you to the trail head. Out there with my older son, I once noticed that, other than his voice, the only sounds I had heard in 2 days were the gurgling of the water and the wind shushing in the birch leaves. You rely on yourself, but your greatest tests are not overly taxing. Trail a line behind the canoe and when you catch a rainbow trout, land it and make a fire to cook it. Launch your body into the clear, frigid water to rinse off the sweat on a warm day. Float slowly, watching eagles circle the treetops and puffy clouds drift like ships past your little world.

Most of the western half of the Kenai Peninsula lies within the 2 million acres of the refuge—it's almost as large as Yellowstone National Park—and much of that land is impossibly remote and truly dedicated to the wildlife. The Kenai River flows through part of the refuge, but the refuge is just a name to the anglers who pursue its salmon (for information about fishing and rafting the river see sections 7 and 8 earlier in this chapter). Canoeists will be more interested in the lowlands on the west side, west of the Sterling Highway and north of Kenai and Soldotna. The lakes there are as numerous as the speckles on a trout's back, or at least that's how they appear from the air. From the ground, the region is a maze of lakes connected by trails—more than 70 lakes you can reach on canoe routes stretching more than 150 miles. It's the easiest way to real Alaska wilderness I know.

ESSENTIALS

GETTING THERE   The refuge surrounds much of the land from Cooper Landing at the north to Homer at the south and Cook Inlet to the west. The Sterling Highway and roads that branch from it are the main ways to the lakes, trails, and rivers, and there is no practical way there without a vehicle.

VISITOR INFORMATION   Stop in at the **Kenai National Wildlife Refuge Visitor Center,** Ski Hill Road (P.O. Box 2139), Soldotna, AK 99669 (© **907/262-7021;** http://kenai.fws.gov), for guidance before plunging into the wilderness. The U.S. Fish & Wildlife Service, which manages the refuge, exhibits natural history displays here, shows a film each hour in the afternoon in the summer, and maintains a 3-mile nature trail. The staff offers advice and sells books and maps that you'll definitely need for a successful backcountry trip. To find the center, turn left just south of the Kenai River Bridge, taking a right turn in front of the building-supply store uphill on the unpaved road. It's open June through August Monday through Friday from 8am to 5pm, Saturday and Sunday from 9am to 5pm; October through May, Monday through Friday from 8am to 4:30pm, Saturday and Sunday from 10am to 5pm. The website also contains detailed trip-planning information for the canoe routes.

GETTING OUTSIDE
CANOEING

Once known as the Kenai National Moose Range, the refuge's brushy wetlands are paradise for moose, rich in their favorite foods of willow and birch shoots and pond weeds. Moose like to dine while wading. Waterfowl and other birds, beavers, muskrats, and other aquatic animals are common on the lakes. People also must be partly aquatic to explore the lakes, paddling canoes across their surfaces, pushing through lily pad passages between lakes, and frequently hiking in rubber boots between lakes while carrying the canoe and camping gear.

There are two main canoe routes, both reached from Swanson River and Swan Lake roads, north of the Sterling Highway from the town of Sterling. The **Swan Lake Canoe Route** is a 60-mile network of 30 connected lakes. It meets Swan Lake Road twice, allowing a loop of several days, and in between adventurers can penetrate many lakes deep into the wilderness, visiting remote lakes they'll have all to themselves. It's also possible to canoe through to the Moose River and ride its current 17 miles over a long day back to the Sterling Highway.

Getting anywhere requires frequent portages of a quarter mile or so, and more ambitious routes have mile-long portages. You can skip all the portaging, however, by floating 2 days down the **Swanson River** to its mouth, at the Captain Cook State Recreation Area (see "Camping," below), joining the river at a landing at mile 17.5 of Swanson River Road. The water is slow and easy all the way.

The most challenging of the routes is the **Swanson River Canoe Route,** which connects to the river's headwaters through a series of lakes and longer portages. The route covers 80 miles, including 40 lakes and the river float. Both routes have many dozens of remote campsites—just lakeside areas of cleared ground with fire rings—and most of the portages are well marked and maintained with wooden planking over the wet areas.

You can rent canoes and everything else you need for a wilderness trip on the refuge canoe routes near the intersection of Swanson River Road and the Sterling Highway in Sterling, where the Finch family operates **Alaska Canoe & Campground** (© 907/ 262-2331; www.alaskacanoetrips.com). Coleman canoes rent for $40 for 24 hours and lighter, fiberglass canoes for a little more. They offer a shuttle service to carry canoeists from one entrance to another so you don't have to double back on your trip and they can give valuable expert advice. And they rent a lot of other outdoor stuff: kayaks, mountain bikes, rafts, and so forth. Call ahead to check on equipment and to reserve. Their campground is fully equipped, too, a good base where you can return for showers and laundry.

The Finch's business also offers guided trips, but you don't need a guide if you know how to canoe and are prepared for wilderness. If that's your approach, among your most important tools will be the book *The Kenai Canoe Trails,* by Daniel L. Quick (Northlite Publishing, $19). This extraordinary guide contains super-detailed maps and directions, and advice on how to plan your trip and fish and camp on your way. I haven't provided detailed driving instructions because you'll need detailed maps to go at all. **Trails Illustrated** produces a good detailed map of the whole area, printed on plastic (see "Fast Facts: Alaska," in chapter 2 for details). A serviceable free map is distributed by the refuge visitor center.

There's much more to do in the refuge too, including several upland hiking trails. The refuge visitor center provides guidance and maps.

CAMPING

For car camping away in a wild, oceanfront setting, remote from the region's fishing mayhem, try the **Captain Cook State Recreation Area.** The lovely and underused 3,460-acre area faces Cook Inlet 25 miles north of Kenai on the North Kenai Road at the mouth of the Swanson River. There are lots of attractive sites among large birches, trails, beach walking, a canoe landing at the end of the Swanson River Canoe Route, and lake swimming. The state parks camping fee is $10. There are many campgrounds within the refuge, too, some of them lovely, quiet spots on the edge of uninhabited lakes, such as the small **Rainbow Lake** and **Dolly Varden Lake campgrounds,** on Swanson River Road near the start of the canoe routes, and the **Watson Lake** and **Kelly-Peterson Lake campgrounds** on the Sterling Highway between Sterling and Cooper Landing. Get a complete listing from the visitor center. Only two campgrounds have fees: **Hidden Lake** and **Upper Skilak Lake,** which are closer to Cooper Landing, charge $10.

10 Homer & Kachemak Bay: Cosmic Hamlet by the Sea

Homer's leading mystic, the late Brother Asaiah Bates, always maintained that a confluence of metaphysical forces causes a focus of powerful creative energy on this little seaside town. It's hard to argue. Homer is full of creative people: artists, eccentrics, and those who simply contribute to a quirky community in a beautiful place. Indeed, Brother Asaiah may have been the quintessential Homeroid, although perhaps an extreme example, with his gray ponytail, extraordinary openness and generosity, and flowery rhetoric about "the cosmic wheel of life." Homer is full of outspoken, unusual, and even odd individualists—people who make living in the town almost an act of belief. I can say this because I'm a former Homeroid myself.

The geography of Homer—physical as well as metaphysical—has gathered certain people here the way currents gather driftwood on the town's pebble beaches. Homer is at the end of the road; the nation's paved highway system comes to an abrupt conclusion at the tip of the Homer Spit, almost 5 miles out in the middle of Kachemak Bay, and believers of one kind or another have washed up here for decades. There were the "barefooters," a communal group that eschewed shoes, even in the Alaska winter (Brother Asaiah came with them in the early 1950s). There are the Russian Old Believers, who organize their strictly traditional communities around their objection to Russian Orthodox Church reforms made by Peter the Great. There are the former hippies who have become successful commercial fishermen after flocking here in the late 1960s to camp as "spit rats" on the Homer Spit beach. And there are even the current migrants—artists and retired people, fundamentalist preachers and New Age healers, wealthy North Slope oil workers and land-poor settlers with no visible means of support—all people who live here simply because they choose to.

The choice is understandable. Homer lies on the north side of Kachemak Bay, a branch of lower Cook Inlet of extraordinary biological productivity. The halibut fishing, especially, is exceptional. The town has a breathtaking setting on Homer Spit and on a wildflower-covered bench high above the bay. The outdoors, especially on the water and across the bay, contains wonderful opportunities. And the arts community has developed into an attraction of its own. There are several exceptional galleries and the Pratt Museum, which has a national reputation.

You'll be disappointed, however, if you expect a charming little fishing village. Poor community planning has created a town that doesn't live up to its setting—indeed, highway sprawl is in the process of ruining some of it. Homer Spit in summer is a traffic-choked jumble of cheap tourist development and RVs.

Homer began to take its modern form after two events: In the 1950s the Sterling Highway connected it to the rest of the world, and in 1964 the Good Friday earthquake sank the spit, narrowing a much larger piece of land with a small forest into the tendril that now barely stands above the water. If not for constant reinforcement by the federal government, the spit long since would have become an island, and Homer would hardly exist. As long as it survives, however, the town makes the most of that unique finger into the sea. Whether or not it is a cosmic focal point, it certainly is an exceptional launching point to one of the nation's great marine recreation areas.

ESSENTIALS

GETTING THERE   By Car   At about 235 miles, Homer is roughly 4½ hours from Anchorage by car, if you don't stop at any of the interesting or beautiful places along the way. It's a scenic drive. If you take a rental car, drive it both ways, as the drop-off fees from Anchorage to Homer are high.

By Bus   Homer Stage Line (© 907/235-2252 or 907/399-1847 on the van, www. homerstageline.com) runs to Anchorage and Seward and back daily during the summer, less frequently the rest of the year. The Anchorage-Homer fare is $60 one-way, $110 round-trip. Tickets are for sale at 1213 Ocean Dr. in Homer (© **907/235-2252**). In Anchorage, the ticket office is at 2607 Eagle St. (© **907/868-3914**).

By Air   Era Aviation (© **800/866-8394;** www.flyera.com) serves Homer from Anchorage several times a day. Small air-taxi operators use Homer as a hub for outlying villages and the outdoors.

By Ferry   The **Alaska Marine Highway System** (© **800/642-0066;** www.ferry alaska.com) connects Homer to Seldovia, Kodiak, and points west along the Alaska Peninsula and Aleutian Archipelago, with the ferry *Tustumena*. The *Kennicott* also goes to Kodiak, and to the east rounds the Kenai Peninsula to Whittier and thence across the Gulf of Alaska to Southeast Alaska and British Columbia (see "Getting There," in section 4, earlier in this chapter). The run to Kodiak takes 10 hours and costs $74 for an adult walk-on passenger (children 6–11 are half off). It's a long trip, but a memorable one.

VISITOR INFORMATION   The **Homer Chamber of Commerce Visitor Information Center,** 201 Sterling Hwy. (P.O. Box 541), Homer, AK 99603 (© **907/235-7740;**

www.homeralaska.org), is on the right as you enter town. In summer, staff is on hand Monday through Friday from 9am to 7pm, Saturday and Sunday 10am to 6pm. Besides answering questions and handing out brochures on local businesses and public lands, they sell tickets for the halibut derby (p. 308). Winter hours are Monday through Friday from 9am to 5pm.

The **Alaska Islands & Ocean Visitor Center,** 95 Sterling Hwy., Homer, AK 99603 (② **907/235-6961,** www.islandsandocean.org), is more than a visitor center, it's one of Homer's best attractions—a sort of museum of the outdoors for the Alaska Maritime National Wildlife Refuge and the Kachemak Bay Research Reserve, the cosponsoring organizations. Everyone coming to Homer should stop in to see the building, an architectural gem that perfectly reflects the rocky shores that the refuge and reserve take in, and to experience exhibits that use technology and a deft sense of theater to recreate those remote places in thought and feel. A film shows frequently about the research of the brave scientists who work in the fierce wilderness of the refuge's outer reaches, in the Aleutian Islands. The center is also the best place to stop for information if you plan to go outdoors anywhere in the area. An easy nature trail descends to the salt marsh below the center. Admission is free. The center is open daily 9am to 6pm in summer; check the website or call for winter hours.

The refuge itself consists of islands off Alaska from the Arctic to near British Columbia that include some of the world's most prolific bird and marine mammal habitat. The U.S. Fish & Wildlife Service manages these lands for the benefit of the animals and people rarely set foot on their shores, but rangers in Homer offer bird and guided tide pool treks frequently in the summer, and give programs at the center. Call for times and see more on tide pooling below. In addition, birders can call the **Kachemak Bay Bird Alert Information Line** (② **907/235-7337**) to find out about recent sightings and upcoming birder events, and to leave news of your own observations, in season.

The **Kachemak Bay State Park District Office,** Mile 168.5, Sterling Hwy., 4 miles from town (② **907/235-7024;** www.alaskastateparks.org), can help answer questions about planning a trip to the trails and beaches across Kachemak Bay from Homer and give advice on renting remote cabins (although you make the reservation through the Anchorage office—see "State Parks Cabin Reservations," p. 265). Depending on staffing, the office should be open Monday through Friday from 9am to 5pm.

GETTING AROUND The best way to get to and around Homer is by car. If you didn't bring one, you can rent a car at the airport from **Hertz** (② **800/654-3131** or 907/235-0734; www.hertz.com) or one of three local firms. Taxis are available from **CHUX Cab** (② **907/235-CHUX**), among others.

For strong riders, a bike is a good way around town. You do have to dodge traffic in places downtown, but a paved trail parallels the road for the 5 miles of the spit and another runs 5 miles east of town. Some excellent mountain-biking routes are mentioned below. **Homer Saw and Cycle,** 1532 Ocean Dr. (② **907/235-8406;** www.homersaw.com), rents mountain bikes, street bikes, kid's bikes, and trailers. Bike rentals start at $25 a day and come with helmets and locks. The shop keeps track of trail conditions and is a good source of advice. It is open Monday through Friday from 9am to 5:30pm, Saturday from 11am to 5pm. They rent as well from Land's End Resort at the end of the spit, open every day. It's wise to reserve bikes a day or two ahead, especially if an outing depends on getting one.

SPECIAL EVENTS **Homer's Winter Carnival** (② **907/235-7740**), February 9–10, 2008, is a big community event, a small-town celebration with a beer-making contest, a parade, a Mardi Gras celebration, and auto racing on the ice of Beluge Lake, among other highlights.

The **Kachemak Bay Shorebird Festival** (© **907/235-7740;** http://homeralaska. org/shorebird.htm), May 8–11, 2008, includes guided bird-watching hikes and boat excursions, natural history workshops, art shows and performances, and other events. It's organized by Alaska Maritime National Wildlife Refuge and the Homer Chamber of Commerce to mark the return of the annual migration.

The **Kachemak Bay Sea Festival** (© **907/235-7740;** www.kachemakkayakfestival. com), over 10 days in late May, focuses on kayaking, wooden boats, and marine safety. See handmade boats from around the region and join kayak events, instruction, and paddles.

Concert on the Lawn, July 26–27, 2008, by KBBI public radio (© **907/235-7721**), is a 2-day outdoor music, craft, and food festival that brings together the whole town.

The **Jackpot Halibut Derby** (© **907/235-7740;** www.homerhalibutderby.com), lasting May 1 to September 30, has a top prize that has reached over $50,000 for the biggest fish of the season, and smaller monthly prizes and tagged fish prizes. Grand prize fish are usually 300 pounds or more. Of course, you must buy your $10 ticket before you fish.

FAST FACTS: Homer

Bank Three banks with ATMs, including **Wells Fargo** (which has a lovely mural inside), are on the Sterling Highway near Heath Street.

Hospital **South Peninsula Hospital** is at the top of Bartlett Street, off Pioneer Avenue (© **907/235-8101**).

Internet Access **Tech Connect Computer Sales and Services,** 432 E. Pioneer Ave. (© **907/235-5248**) offers broadband access for $5 an hour on their computers or Wi-Fi on yours. Other Wi-Fi hotspots are not hard to find, too.

Police For nonemergencies within the city limits, call the **Homer Police Department** (© **907/235-3150**); outside the city, phone the **Alaska State Troopers** (© **907/235-8239**). The police station is across Pioneer Avenue from the intersection with Heath Street.

Post Office Sterling Highway at Heath Street.

Taxes **Sales tax** in Homer is 6.5%. Outside the city, you pay 2%.

EXPLORING THE TOWN

The best activities are on the beaches, in the hilltop meadows, and on Kachemak Bay, and the best man-made attractions all somehow relate to that setting. The art inspired by Homer's environment shows in more than a dozen galleries and studios in town, not including those across the bay in Halibut Cove (discussed later). New shows open all over town on the first Friday of the month, when restaurants hold special evenings and the entire community comes out for an evening of gallery hopping.

A widely distributed brochure lists most of the galleries in town, with a map. Most are close together on Pioneer Avenue. You'll mostly find photography, prints, pottery, fabric, woodwork, and other crafts, since these are small businesses owned by local people trying to make a living. But there is some expensive fine art, too. Among my favorite galleries are **Ptarmigan Arts,** at 471 E. Pioneer Ave. (© **907/235-5345**), an artists' co-op showing a cross section of what the area offers; the **Fireweed Gallery** (© **907/235-3411,** www.fireweedgallery.com), next door to Ptarmigan, with true fine art in an elegant, airy space; and the large, friendly, and well-stocked **Art Shop Gallery** (© **907/235-7076,** www.artshopgallery.com), in the two-story, octagonal building at 202 W. Pioneer Ave.

There are galleries on Homer Spit, too, among all the ticky-tacky gift shops, food stands, and fishing charters offices. My favorite there is Gary Lyon's **Sea Lion Gallery,** on the Central Charters Boardwalk at 4241 Homer Spit Rd. (© **907/235-3400;** www.sealiongallery.com). Lyon's work captures Alaska wildlife in spectacular detail but also transforms his subjects with a distinctively dreamy vision. His gallery is a tiny jewel box of valuable works.

Bunnell Street Gallery ✷✷ This nonprofit gallery, located in a perfect space in an old hardware store near Bishop's Beach at the lower end of Main Street, is my favorite in Alaska. Unlike most other Alaska galleries, which double as tourist gift shops, Bunnell was made by and for artists, and the experience is noncommercial and often challenging. You may be tempted to become a member of the nonprofit corporation that runs it, for membership comes with a one-of-a-kind plate made by one of the artists. As with all Homer art, the themes of the work tend to be fishy, and the medium and style can be anything. The gallery also mounts invitational or juried art shows from beyond the community and also puts on folk and classical music concerts, poetry readings, and films.

106 W. Bunnell Ave. © **907/235-2662.** www.bunnellstreetgallery.org. Summer daily 10am–6pm; winter, Tues–Sat 10am–6pm.

Norman Lowell Studio & Gallery ✷ *Finds* Lowell built his own huge gallery on his homestead to show his life's work. The immense oils of Alaska landscapes, which are not for sale, hang in a building that counts as one of Alaska's larger art museums. Although Lowell's work is traditionally representational, many of the paintings carry raw emotions capable of reaching the most cynical viewer. Admission is free, and Lowell and his wife, Libby, usually host guests who walk through. Their old-time Alaskan hospitality is a delight. At the end of the exhibit a large gift shop sells nothing but Lowell's work; paintings range from $750 to $30,000 and prints start at $100. They don't take credit cards. Take a moment to wander the grounds, too, as it's an opportunity to see a real wilderness homestead that has survived largely unchanged from the early days.

Norman Lowell Dr. © **907/235-7344.** Free admission. Mon–Sat 9am–7pm; Sun 1–5pm. Closed mid-Sept to May 1. Turn from Sterling Hwy. at mile 160.9 (4½ miles from Anchor Point, about 12 miles from Homer).

Pratt Museum ✷✷ The Homer Society of Natural History's museum is as good as any you'll find in a town of this size. The Pratt displays art and explains local history, too, but it is strongest in natural history. It helped pioneer technology that allows viewing of wildlife through live remote control cameras without disturbing the animals. Visitors at the museum can watch puffins and other birds on Gull Island, and operate the camera's controls. Another remote camera focuses on the brown bears of McNeil River. There is a saltwater aquarium housing local marine life, and if you're curious about all the fishing boats down in the harbor, you can find out about the different types of gear as well as the fish they catch. In the small botanical garden outside you can learn to identify all the local wildflowers, and a forest trail teaches about the area's ecology. There's much more to see, too, including a good gift shop.

Late March Is Perfect

On a spring break trip to Homer, in late March, I enjoyed spectacular cross-country skiing on deep snow on lengthy trails leading to lofty Diamond Ridge, and from there I could see a fleet of hundreds of small boats returning across the bay from salmon fishing. We'd spent time viewing the galleries, eating in fantastic restaurants, and staying in a luxurious waterfront room for an amazing bargain price. A smart visitor touring Alaska could combine skiing and fishing in Homer with other March highlights, including the Iditarod Trail Sled Dog Race in Anchorage and the World Ice Art Championships in Fairbanks (see "Alaska Calendar of Events," p. 21). Homer even has a B&B where you can ski the trails from your room, **Alaska Ridgetop Inn** (𝄐 888/357-4343; www.alaska ridgetopinn.com). The owner is one of the volunteer ski trail groomers.

3779 Bartlett St. (at Pioneer Ave.). 𝄐 **907/235-8635.** www.prattmuseum.org. Admission $6 adults, $5.50 seniors, $3 children ages 6–18, $20 family rate. High season daily 10am–6pm; low season Tues–Sun noon–5pm. Closed Jan.

GETTING OUTSIDE

The best **map of the Kachemak Bay area** is produced by Alaska Road and Recreation Maps and is available all over town.

ON THE HOMER SIDE OF KACHEMAK BAY

TIDE POOLING   Exploring Kachemak Bay's tide pools is the best way to really get to know the sea and meet the strange and wonderful animals that live in it, and it doesn't cost anything but the price of a pair of rubber boots. First, check a tide book, available for free in virtually any local store, or ask a local to check one for you. You'll do best on a low tide of –2 or lower, meaning that low water will be at least 2 feet below the normal low, some 25 feet below the high. Extra-low tides expose more of the lower intertidal zone that contains the most interesting creatures. At a –5 tide, you could find octopus and other oddities. Also, the lower the tide, the more time you'll have to look. Keep track of the time: The tide will come in faster than you can imagine, and you could get stranded and drown in the cold water.

The best place to go tide pooling right in town is reached from Bishop's Beach Park, near the lower end of Main Street. Walk west on the beach toward the opening of the bay to Cook Inlet. It's at least a half-hour brisk walk to the Coal Point area, where the sand and boulders end. This is where you'll find pools of water left behind by the receding tide, many full of life. Explore patiently and gently—look at the animals and touch them, but always put them back as they were and try not to crush them underfoot. Marine invertebrate identification keys and many other field guides are sold at the Alaska Islands & Ocean Visitor Center (see "Visitor Information," above), where rangers happily give advice. They also offer ranger-guided tide pool beach walks. If you want to keep going beyond Coal Point, there's usually a raft of sea otters offshore about 3 miles down the beach. Just continue walking, keeping your eyes on the water. As always when watching wildlife, binoculars will improve the experience.

HIKING AND NATURE WALKS   The **Wynn Nature Center,** operated by the nonprofit **Center for Alaskan Coastal Studies** (𝄐 907-235-6667; www.akcoastal studies.org) offers a chance to learn about the ecology of the area and see its birds and wildflowers on an easy walk or hike while taking in sweeping ocean views. The center encompasses 140 acres of spruce forest and wildflower meadow off Skyline Drive, with an 800-foot boardwalk accessible to people with disabilities. This is a lovely area, and the center has done a fine job of adding an educational component without diminishing it—including a log cabin where you can meet a host and ask questions. The center is open daily from 10am to 6pm mid-June through Labor Day, with guided walks twice a day. You can also hike on your own with a printed guide. Fees are $5 for adults, $4 for seniors, and $3 for children younger than 18. Call about interesting weekly programs as well.

More ambitious hikes explore more of the bench of land above Homer or the mountains across the bay at Kachemak Bay State Park (see below). The 7-mile **Homestead Trail** is an old wagon road used by Homer's early settlers. The largely informal trail is lovely and peaceful, tunneling through alders, crossing fields of wildflowers, and passing old homestead cabins. From a hilltop meadow you can see all the way to the inlet and the volcanoes beyond. The eastern trail head is at the reservoir on Skyline Drive—drive up West Hill Road from the Sterling Highway, turn right, and follow Skyline to the fourth left. The western trail head is on Rogers Loop, which branches from the Sterling Highway just before it crests the last big hill before entering Homer. (That's also the place to join Homer's outstanding cross-country ski trails.) A map and guide produced by the Kachemak Heritage Land Trust is available at the visitor center.

DRIVING OR MOUNTAIN BIKING   Several gravel roads around Homer make for exquisite drives or bike rides. Mountain bikers can use the Homestead Trail, too (see "Hiking and Nature Walks," above). A lovely drive leads out **East End Road,** through seaside pastures, a forest, and the village of Fritz Creek, and then follows the bluff line through meadows toward the head of the bay. When the road gets too rough, explore onward on a mountain bike. **Skyline Drive** has extraordinary views of high canyons and Kachemak Bay; drive up East Hill Road just east of Homer. **Homer Saw and Cycle** (see "Getting Around," above) can give you many more ideas. The great mountain biking across the bay is described below.

HORSEBACK RIDING   Ranchers have worked around Kachemak Bay for decades. Drive east of town on East End Road to see pastures overlooking spectacular marine and mountain views. Go beyond the road, and you're in some of Alaska's most beautiful untamed country. Mark Marette guides trail rides to the head of Kachemak Bay, leading every group himself, as he has since 1986. Guests used to typical, boring tourist horseback riding come back thrilled at how adventurous their ride has been. Marette's business is **Trails End Horse Adventures** (© **907/235-6393**), 11 miles out East End. He charges $25 per hour, or $80 for a 4-hour trip. He takes all ages and raw beginners.

ON & ACROSS KACHEMAK BAY

Along the south side of the Kachemak Bay, glaciers, fjords, and little wooded islands are arranged like a smorgasbord before Homer. A quick boat ride puts you there for sea kayaking, mountain biking on unconnected dirt roads, hiking in the mountains, or eating sushi in a top-tier restaurant on pilings. Or gallery hopping, or resting at a remote lodge, or studying at a nature center, or walking the streets of a forgotten fishing village. The far side of the bay has no road link to import the mundane, mass-produced world, but it does have people, and they make the landscape even richer and more enchanting than it would be alone. And underneath the water, there's a wealth of halibut and salmon.

PLANNING AN OUTING   **Central Charters,** 4241 Homer Spit Rd., Homer, AK 99603, (© **800/478-7847** or 907/235-7847; fax: 907/235-2895; www.centralcharter. com), is a long-established booking agent that represents businesses for many of the most popular activities, including halibut fishing, water taxis, boat tours to Seldovia and Halibut Cove, and even local theater. They have a ticket office on the right side of the spit as you drive out.

TRANSPORTATION ACROSS THE WATER   Many water taxis operate from Homer to wilderness cabins, kayaking waters, hiking trails, and mountain biking roads accessible from the Jakolof Bay Dock, Seldovia, Halibut Cove, Kachemak Bay State Park, and other remote points. Rates vary little; it's around $65 per person to get to Kachemak Bay State Park, plus a $4 park fee, for example. Water taxis can be booked through Central Charters, mentioned above. **Mako's Water Taxi** (© **907/ 235-9055;** www.makoswatertaxi.com) has experience and a good reputation. Mako Haggerty also rents sea kayaks and drops them off; with his advice, you can plan a one-way paddle, with the water taxi providing a lift at each end. Karl Stoltzfus's **Bay Excursions Water Taxi and Tours** (© **907/235-7525;** www.bayexcursions.com) offers transportation across the bay, but also specializes in small-group tours—he takes no more than 12 at a time—for serious bird-watching or, on other days, to encounter sea otters as well as see the bird rookeries. Stoltzfus rents kayaks, too.

KACHEMAK BAY STATE PARK   The park comprises much of the land across the water that makes all those views from Homer so spectacular. For around $65 you can be dropped off there after breakfast, walk the beach, hike in the woods, climb the mountains, and meet your boat in time to be back in Homer for dinner. Enough people are doing it now that some water taxis offer scheduled service to the most popular trail head—perhaps with a stop for espresso at a floating coffee house in Halibut Cove on the way home. If you want to be on your own, there are plenty of lesser-used trails as well. The park's main office is at the ranger station listed on p. 307. Its center is the summer-only **ranger station** in Halibut Cove Lagoon, where there's a dock and mooring buoys for public use, three public rental cabins over the water, a campsite, and excellent king salmon fishing in mid-June.

The park has about 80 miles of trails, many linking at the ranger station; a free trail guide is available there, but you're well advised to get a good map before you leave Homer. The trails generally start at tidewater amid a lush, mossy forest and rise into the craggy mountains—up sharp peaks, or, if you don't want to climb, over the hills to the next secluded beach. The most popular is the **Saddle Trail,** which rises through forest from a staircase at the east side of Halibut Cove over a low ridge to the icy lake in front of Grewink Glacier. It's an easy hike of around 3 miles total. If you want to be away from other hikers, however, discuss that with a ranger or your water-taxi provider, as there are plenty of quieter trails. All hikers should prepare with proper shoes and clothing and bring mosquito repellent. Review bear avoidance skills (see "Outdoor Health & Safety," in chapter 2). Cellphones do work, so bring one along if you have it.

Besides the cabins at Halibut Cove Lagoon you can hike to a public rental cabin on secluded China Poot Lake less than 3 miles from the lagoon's dock. The park's fifth cabin is on Tutka Bay, off the Halibut Cove trail network. You can also use one of these places as a base for self-guided sea kayaking. Cabin permits are $65 a night and usually must be reserved 6 months in advance (see "State Parks Cabin Reservations," p. 265).

SELDOVIA   This historic fishing village is like Homer without all the cars and peo-ple: just a lot of quiet, the lovely ocean waters, and some nice places to stay. It belongs in this outdoor section only because there's nothing at all to do there other than bike, paddle, or fish (you can do nothing there very well, too).

The trip across Kachemak Bay to Seldovia is one of the best parts of going there. For most people, the **Rainbow Tours** (② **907/235-7272;** www.rainbowtours.net) daily round-trip is the practical alternative. They leave Homer Harbor at 9am and

---

A Day Trip to Halibut Cove

The artists' colony of Halibut Cove sits on either side of a narrow, peaceful channel between a small island and the mainland; the water in this channel is the road. Boardwalks connect the buildings, and stairs reach down to the water from houses perched on pilings over the shore. The post office and espresso stand float on docks. Visitors arrive each afternoon to walk the boardwalks, visit the galleries, and eat at the restaurant, the **Saltry.** That's a place to sit back on the deck and sip microbrews and eat fresh-baked bread, mussels, sushi, and locally grown salads, followed by fresh fish grilled over charcoal.

The classic wooden boat *Danny J* (book through Central Charters at ② **800/ 478-7847** or 907/235-7847; www.centralcharter.com) leaves Homer daily in the summer at noon, brings back day-trippers, takes guests to the Saltry Restaurant at 5pm, and brings back the diners later in the evening. The noon trip includes bird-watching at Gull Island. Seating is mostly outdoors, and I would choose something else to do in bad weather. You also take the *Danny J* if you're spend-ing the night in Halibut Cove. The noon trip is $48 for adults, $43 for seniors, $25 for children; the dinner trip is $28 for everyone, regardless of age, but to go you must have a dinner reservation at the Saltry, usually made at least a few days ahead, also with Central Charters. On the noon trip only, they sometimes take more passengers than *Danny J* can carry, putting the overflow aboard the steel *Storm Bird.* Reservations and fares are identical to those of the *Danny J.* Reserve at least a few days ahead for dinner.

On the afternoon trip you can bring lunch or eat at the Saltry, described above, and then explore the **boardwalk** that runs from the restaurant along Ismailof Island past the galleries, boat shops, and houses. There's also a barn-yard, perched on a patch of ground along the boardwalk, where kids, who already will be in heaven, can look at rabbits, pigs, chickens, ponies, and other animals. The summer-only **Halibut Cove's Experience Fine Art Gallery** (② **907/ 296-2215**) is the first building past the farm on the boardwalk, on pilings above the water. The airy room contains works by Halibut Cove artists only.

Farther on, Diana Tillion, who, with her husband, Clem, pioneered the com-munity, opens her **Cove Gallery** (② **907/269-2207**) and studio to guests year-round. Since the 1950s, she has worked in many media, but is best known for her sepia paintings made with octopus ink, which is painstakingly extracted with a hypodermic needle. Trails branch from the boardwalk across the island to broad views of the bay or to the quiet opposite end of the island.

Exceptionally appealing overnight accommodations at Halibut Cove are cov-ered under "Lodgings Across the Bay," p. 320.

return from Seldovia Harbor at 5pm. After subtracting the time on the boat, you have 6 hours free in the village—plenty of time for lunch, a bike ride, a kayak tour, or seeing the town. While visitors are in Seldovia, the boat continues on for whale-watching (see "Whale-Watching," below). Round-trip fares to Seldovia are $35 for adults, $30 for seniors, $25 for children 12 and under; one-way $20 for everyone.

Go sea kayaking in Seldovia with **Kayak'atak** (© **907/234-7425;** www.alaska. net/~kayaks). The couple doing the tours, longtime Seldovia residents, takes pride in showing off the wildlife and beauty of this little-used area. They charge $120 for a 5-hour tour, including lunch, or $80 for a 3-hour tour, without lunch. They also offer kayaks for rent and overnight trips. For a less taxing look at Seldovia Bay, take their evening skiff tour for $35 per person (with two to four passengers).

King salmon are stocked in Seldovia Slough, which passes right through the town. The run peaks in mid-June, and you can fish from shore. Seldovia also has an edge for halibut anglers, because you start out an hour closer to the **halibut** grounds than anglers at Homer, potentially giving you more time to actually fish. Get more information from the **Seldovia Chamber of Commerce** by leaving a message at © **907/ 234-7612,** or check the town's extraordinary website, www.seldovia.com.

JAKOLOF BAY   A state-maintained dock opens an area of gentle shorelines and abandoned roads to visitors who seek the wilderness without paying to stay at a wilderness lodge. West of Kachemak Bay State Park and east of Seldovia, the lands have roads, but the roads aren't connected to anything and are used as much by mountain bikers as by anyone else. You can take a water taxi straight to the Jakolof dock. Lodgings are nearby at Across the Bay Tent and Breakfast (p. 321). There's plenty to do in the area. The waters of Jakolof, Little Jakolof, Kasitsna, and Little Tutka bays, and the tiny Herring Islands are appealing and protected for sea kayaking. Supreme mountain-biking trails lead along the shore and right across the peninsula through forest and meadows for berry picking. The Red Mountain and Rocky River roads are prime routes, different each year depending on washouts and intermittent maintenance—that's part of the adventure. A maintained 10-mile road west leads to the charming village of Seldovia, described above.

GULL ISLAND   The island is a rock across the bay from Homer Spit that serves as a busy bird colony in the summer. It's easy to get to and boats can edge close, as the water is deep all around it. You can often see tufted and horned puffins, black-legged kittiwakes, common murres, red-faced and pelagic cormorants, pigeon guillemots, and glaucous-winged gulls. Tour boats to Halibut Cove or Seldovia may cruise by the island, and if you are taking a water taxi to Halibut Cove Lagoon, ask to take a look on your way.

ACTIVITIES

FISHING   Homer is known for **halibut,** those huge, flat bottom fish, and the harbor is full of charter boats that will take you out for the day for around $225 per person in the high season. Every day, a few people catch fish that are larger than they are, and halibut over 50 pounds are common. Getting out to where the fish are plentiful requires an early start and a long ride to unprotected waters. People who get seasick easily shouldn't go, as the boat wallows on the waves during fishing. (For advice on avoiding seasickness, see p. 49.) Using gear and lines that look strong enough to pick up the boat, you jig the bait (chunks of herring or cod) up and down on the bottom. Halibut aren't wily or acrobatic, and fighting one can be like pulling up a sunken

Tips   Getting Your Fish Home

A typical angler comes back from a halibut charter with around 60 pounds of fish that, when cleaned, will yield 30 pounds of filets. A large serving is less than a pound of halibut. Eat as much fresh as you can, as it will never be better, but be prepared for how you will deal with the rest of your bounty. The typical 30 pounds is worth more than $250 at grocery store prices (it's illegal to sell sport-caught fish). If it is properly and quickly frozen, it will retain much of its quality well into the winter; if not, you waste this superb food. If you're lucky enough to catch that much salmon, the problem is even more immediate, as salmon is more sensitive to proper handling. Most fishing towns have a sport processor who can vacuum-pack and flash-freeze your catch for around $1 a pound. The best way to get it home is as checked baggage; the processor can provide sturdy fish boxes and cold packs. If you aren't leaving right away, processors will hold the fish, and many hotels have freezer facilities. If you have to ship it, use an overnight service (expensive) and make sure someone is there to put it in the freezer on the other end. Above all, keep the fish *hard frozen;* thawing and refreezing diminishes the quality off any fish and can turn salmon into mush (if your fish thaws, call the processor for advice on how to proceed). Consider having some of your salmon smoked, if possible, making it a ready-to-eat delicacy very welcome as a homecoming gift. Halibut can be smoked, too, but because of its low fat content and delicate flavor and texture it doesn't smoke as well as salmon. In Homer, **Coal Point Trading Co.,** 4306 Homer Spit (© **907/235-3877;** www. welovefish.com), will process, pack, and ship your catch as ordered. Ask your charter captain—if you don't want to, you don't ever have touch your fish until you're ready to eat it back home.

Buick. One good, full-day operator is **Silver Fox Charters** (© **800/478-8792** or 907/235-8792; www.silverfoxcharters.com).

Half-day charters have less chance of getting way out to the biggest fish but cost a lot less. **Rainbow Tours** (© **907/235-7272;** www.rainbowtours.net) operates a big boat for the shorter outings, charging $95 for adults, $85 for seniors, and $75 for juniors. This choice makes good sense if you are not a fishing fanatic or are taking kids along, as a full day halibut fishing is exhausting and can be tedious. Other charter boats can be booked through Central Charters (see "Planning an Outing," above).

Salmon use Cook Inlet year-round, not only when they're returning to the streams to spawn, and Homer anglers pursue them with trolling gear even in the dead of winter. The town has a Winter King Salmon Tournament in March (check with the chamber of commerce). Most people, however, fish salmon in summer. Although without as many great road-accessible, streamside fishing spots as found farther north, the bay does have some good salmon fishing. A small inlet called the Nick Dudiak Fishing Lagoon on the Spit is stocked with king and silver salmon by the Alaska Department of Fish & Game. Kings return to the lagoon from late May to the end of June. Silvers arrive in mid- to late July, peaking in early August and finishing by midmonth. These salmon have nowhere to spawn, so all must be caught (some anglers scorn such "fish-in-a-barrel" fishing). At the end of the runs, Fish & Game announces that snagging is permitted, which is something like mugging salmon and can be a lot of fun, if not something you'll brag about later at the Rod and Gun Club. For salmon fishing in a more natural setting, head across the bay to Halibut Cove Lagoon (see "Kachemak Bay State Park," above) or Seldovia, or drive back up the Sterling Highway to the Anchor River, a famous steelhead trout stream (catch-and-release only) also good for salmon, rainbow trout, and Dolly Varden char. Several popular fishing streams cross the Sterling Highway between Homer and Soldotna. The **Alaska Department of Fish & Game** maintains a fishing hot line at ✆ **907/235-6930.** They're located at 3298 Douglas Place (✆ **907/235-8191**).

NATURAL HISTORY TOURS The nonprofit **Center for Alaskan Coastal Studies** (✆ **907/235-6667;** www.akcoastalstudies.org) is dedicated to educating the public about the shore, interpreting Kachemak Bay for visitors on daily explorations of the Peterson Bay and China Poot Bay area, across the water from Homer. At low tide they lead guests on a fascinating guided tide-pool walk. The center also has access to lovely woodlands where nature walks cover forest ecology and geology and visit an archaeological site. Saltwater tanks at the lodge contain creatures from the intertidal zone and microscopes to inspect your finds. It's a relaxed and truly Alaskan outing. You can add on sea kayaking or an overnight stay. Reserve by calling the center at the number above. The all-day tour is $100 for adults, $63 for children 12 and under, and operates daily Memorial Day to Labor Day. Pack your own lunch and bring footwear suitable for hiking and potentially wet beach walks and warm clothing for the boat ride.

SEA KAYAKING Silence fell as the boat pulled away from the beach, leaving us behind with the kayaks and our guide. For the rest of the day my son and I absorbed the water-reflected sunlight and glided past fancifully shaped rocks and resident sea otters around Yukon Island. We explored beaches, picnicked, raced, and discovered tiny bays too small for any other craft. At the end of the day, we had a new friend in our quietly cheerful guide, Alison O'Hara, and discovered that she'd imperceptibly taught us a lot about sea kayaking. O'Hara runs **True North Kayak Adventures** (✆ **907/235-0708;** www.truenorthkayak.com). Her 8-hour beginner day trips cost $139, including lunch and passage across the bay. Most kayaking day trips in Alaska towns barely get out of the small boat harbor. This trip doesn't feel so tame—it's more like a mini-expedition. True North Kayak also offers more challenging overnight and multiday trips to remote waters in the area, and a $235 package that includes the day tour, a night in the attractive Hesketh Island Cabins, and a second day of hiking.

Various others offer Kachemak Bay kayak trips. You can choose through Central Charters (p. 312). The protected waters, tiny islands, and remote settlements are fascinating paddling no matter who you go with, or, for experienced paddlers, if you go on your own. Kayakers can take a water taxi across and explore at will, camping or staying in cabins over much of the bay. Check with Kachemak Bay State Park for guidance. **Mako's Water Taxi** (✆ **907/235-9055;** www.makoswatertaxi.com) offers rides and rents and delivers kayaks. True North Kayak (see above) also rents to experienced paddlers, and rents camping gear. For kayaks expect to pay $65 a day for a double, $45 for a single.

FLIGHTSEEING & BEAR VIEWING One gets used to thinking of the mountains across Kachemak Bay from Homer as the far side of a magnificent stage set, so it's somewhat mind-blowing to fly beyond that first line of mountains and see how they are just the beginning of much more complex topography of peaks, glaciers, chasms, and ice fields. The best person to show you that wild country is Bill de Creeft. His **Kachemak Bay Flying Service** (© **907/235-8924;** www.alaskaseaplanes.com) offers spectacular scenic flights starting at $150 per person. Having flown out of Homer since 1967, de Creeft is experienced enough to qualify as a pioneer aviator, but the real old-timer is his favorite plane, a restored 1929 Travel Air S-6000-B, one of only six remaining examples of the executive aircraft, with mahogany trim and wicker seats, which he has been flying and caring for since 1969. Jim Reardon wrote a book about this relationship of man and plane (see the website). The tours begin with the thrill of a water take-off from Beluga Lake in this unique aircraft.

Homer has several air taxis providing access to the very remote areas of the southern Kenai Peninsula and lower Cook Inlet that you can't easily reach by boat. You can also use their scheduled service to explore, flying to Seldovia or even one of the two Alaska Native villages across the bay. If your main objective is to see bears, however, the best guides are at **Emerald Air Service** (© **907/235-6993;** www.emeraldairservice.com). Ken and Chris Day specialize in all-day bear-viewing flight expeditions. Unlike some air services I've flown with, whose pilots may not know much about bears and land only briefly, the Days make a point of teaching about bears and their habitat in extended visits. They helped the National Wildlife Federation film an IMAX movie called *Bears,* and starred in it along with the title characters. Trips include a flight by floatplanes on fresh or saltwater and then a naturalist-guided hike to see the wildlife. The couple pride themselves on their care for the environment. The trips cost $556 per person.

WHALE-WATCHING   Whales can't be counted on to come into Kachemak Bay, but a long-established tour boat operator, **Rainbow Tours** (© **907/235-7272;** www.rainbowtours.net), takes visitors beyond the bay to where whales turn up more predictably in the waters at the entrance of Cook Inlet and in the Barren Islands. That's a long ride and the waters outside the bay are unprotected—the operators don't go in bad weather, but you should take seasickness preventative measures anyway (see "Health & Safety," in chapter 2). The trip is a good chance to see humpback and orca whales and sometimes minke and fin whales. It takes all day, from 9am to 6pm, and includes lunch onboard a comfortable, 100-passenger vessel, the *Rainbow Connection,* which also serves the town of Seldovia as a passenger ferry. The fare is $125 for adults, $110 for seniors, and $85 for children.

WHERE TO STAY

Homer has many good B&Bs. The Homer Chamber of Commerce (www.homer alaska.org) has links to a prodigious number of them. In addition to the places I've listed in detail, **The Sea Lion Cove,** above the Sea Lion Gallery on Homer Spit (© **907/235-3400** in summer or 907/235-8767 in winter; www.sealiongallery.com/cove), has two spacious units with limited cooking facilities, private phones, and a deck right over the beach where you can hear the waves roll in at night. They rent for $120 and $130 a night.

Up the hill on the other side of town, **A Memorable Experience Bed and Breakfast** (© **800/720-9275** ext. 7374 or 907/235-7374; www.amemorableexperience.com) offers huge rooms and a large cottage with spectacular views and an expansive garden setting. The owners know how to do things right. They also run the Fresh Sourdough Express restaurant and, besides a great breakfast, offer guests a voucher for goodies there.

If you just want good, simple lodgings downtown, you'll find an extraordinary value at the clean and friendly **Pioneer Inn,** 244 W. Pioneer Ave. (© **800/782-9655** or 907/235-5670; www.pioneerinnhomerak.com), which offers big, apartment-style units for $109 in summer ($119 in July) with up to four people in the room. Rooms with two twins or a queen bed are $89 to $99 in summer. They also have a house that sleeps up to nine for $275 a night.

Driftwood Inn *(Value*   The historic building a block from Bishop's Beach and across from the Bunnell Gallery resembles a lodge or B&B with its large fireplace of beach rock, the hot coffeepot and inexpensive self-serve breakfast in the lobby, and friendly attitude. There are two parts to the inn. The old section has a cozy feel that's somehow enhanced by sloping floors and old fixtures. Its rooms are like Pullman compartments in size and configuration, but they are cute and clean and have some real style. They're also quite inexpensive. Nine bedrooms share two bathrooms. The walls are thin, so there's a no-noise policy during evening hours. A newer section has larger rooms, all with king size beds. There's also an appealing 22-site RV park. The inn offers a fish cleaning station and freezing facility and year-round fishing charters.

135 W. Bunnell Ave., Homer, AK 99603. © 800-478-8019 or ph/fax 907/235-8019. www.thedriftwoodinn.com. 27 units, 16 with private bathroom. High season $65–$175 double; low season $45–$99 double. RV sites $29–$35, full hookup. Extra person $10. DISC, MC, V. No smoking. **Amenities:** Coin-op laundry. *In room:* TV.

Land's End Resort *⊀⊀⊀*   Traditionally *the* place to stay in Homer, Land's End would be popular no matter what, due to its location at the tip of Homer Spit, the best spot in Homer and possibly the best spot for a hotel in all of Alaska. It's composed of a line of weathered buildings that fittingly straggle along the beach crest like driftwood logs. Inside, the local owners keep high standards and make constant improvements. Rooms and public areas are decorated with town history and old photographs, nautical memorabilia, and bold colors. Rooms range from cute shiplike compartments with fold-down Murphy beds to big, two-story suites. Two-room suites sleep five comfortably, with a small private balcony in the parents' room. Resort attractions include a spa in a calming space with a professional massage staff, called the Raven's Nest; a tiny moving-water lap pool; an outdoor hot tub; bike rentals; and an activities desk. The hotel is near the boat harbor, and some people fish right from the beach in front. The front desk also rents a series of privately owned townhouse condos next door; for groups or couples on extended visits, these are the best accommodations in the region, with stylish furniture, lots of space and light, and a beachfront location second to none. The condos rent for $300 to $425 a night.

The **Chart Room restaurant** makes good use of its wonderful location, looking out over the beach and bay from big windows. There's a casual, relaxing atmosphere in the long, wood-trimmed dining room. The deck outside has glass wind shields, making it a warm, satisfying place to sit over coffee on a sunny day. You can watch otters, eagles, and fishing boats while you eat. The selection of main courses, priced $16 to $38, is fairly typical of a seaside fine dining restaurant, and the food is good if not memorable. The appetizer menu, however, is much more extensive and interesting, and the appetizer portions are easily large enough to make a full meal.

4786 Homer Spit Rd., Homer, AK 99603. © 800/478-0400 or 907/235-0400. Fax 907/235-0420. www.lands-end-resort.com. 95 units. High season $125–$210 double; low season $69–$99 double. Extra person $10. AE, DC, DISC, MC, V. **Amenities:** Restaurant; bar; indoor lap pool; exercise room; spa; outdoor Jacuzzi; sauna; tour desk. *In room:* TV, coffeemaker, Wi-Fi.

Magic Canyon Ranch Bed and Breakfast ⚛ At the top of a canyon road off East End Road, the Webb family shares its charming home, 74 unspoiled acres, a tree house, and sweeping views with guests, a cat, and a herd of retired llamas. The air is mountain clear and quiet between the high canyon walls—you start to relax as soon as you get out of the car. The Webbs serve sherry in the evening and a full breakfast in the morning. The four rooms, some nestled cozily under the eaves, are decorated in country and Victorian style, with lots of nice details and some family antiques. The house isn't historic by any means, but it feels like it is.

40015 Waterman Rd., Homer, AK 99603. ℭ/fax **907/235-6077**. www.magiccanyonranch.com. 4 units, 2 with private bathroom. High season $100–$115 double; low season $70–$85 double. Extra adult $25; extra child 12 and under $20. Rates include full breakfast. MC, V. Closed in winter.

Ocean Shores Motel ⚛ These buildings on a grassy compound have a commanding view of Kachemak Bay, with a path leading down to Bishop's Beach, yet the location is right off the Sterling Highway as you enter town, within walking distance of downtown Homer. Rooms are fresh and bright, most with private balconies, refrigerators, and microwaves; four have full kitchens (one rents for only $109). The less-expensive rooms lack the views and are older, but are still modern and have cute touches. The place is decorated with photographs and art collected over a family's five generations in Alaska. Smoking is not allowed.

451 Sterling Hwy. no. 1, Homer, AK 99603 ℭ **800/770-7775** or 907/235-7775. Fax 907/235-8639. www.oceanshores alaska.com. 38 units. High season $99–$159 double; low season $59–$75 double. Extra person $5. AE, DISC, MC, V. *In room:* TV, dataport, kitchen in some, fridge, microwave.

Old Town Bed and Breakfast ⚛ *(Finds* These rooms combine the artiness of the excellent Bunnell Street Gallery downstairs (see "Exploring the Town," earlier) and the funky, historic feel of the old trading post/hardware store that the building used to house. The wood floors undulate with age and settling, their imperfections picked out by light from tall, double-hung windows that look out at Bishop's Beach. The antiques, handmade quilts, and wonderful original art fit in as if they have always been there, yet the rooms are comfortable, fresh, and clean. The B&B has no TVs or in-room phones. The rates include a hot breakfast from 8 to 10am in the parlor and afternoon tea. This place is not a good choice for people who have any trouble with stairs.

106–D W. Bunnell, Homer, AK 99603. ℭ **907/235-7558**. Fax 907/235-9427. www.oldtownbedandbreakfast.com. 3 units, 1 with private bathroom. High season $95 double shared bathroom, $115 double private bathroom; low season $56 double shared bathroom, $70 double private bathroom. Extra person $15. Rates include full breakfast and tax. MC, V.

Seaside Farm *(Finds* Mairiis Kilcher's farm, its meadows dotted with cottonwood trees, slopes spectacularly to Kachemak Bay. The land is populated by Morgan horses, cows, chickens, latter-day hippies, and international backpackers, many of whom do chores in exchange for lodging (when chores are needed): 2 hours of work equals a night in the hostel bunks, and 1 hour earns a campsite in the pasture above the bay. Campers have use of an outdoor cooking and washing area, fire pit and barbecue, and autumn raspberry picking. The hostel dorms seemed a bit dark and close to me; I'd choose to camp in a tent or cabin. The cabins are quaint and unpolished, in some cases sitting in lovely, quiet places—two are right on the water. Mairiis, better known as Mossy, is a member of Homer's pioneering and beloved Kilcher family, which spawned the singer Jewel (rarely seen hereabouts any longer). Mairiis runs the place as casually as a cloud scurrying through the sky.

40904 Seaside Farm Rd. (5 miles from downtown off East End Rd.), Homer, AK 99603. © 907/235-7850. www.xyz.net/~seaside. 9 units (4 bedrooms), 4 cabins, 12 hostel beds (co-ed dorms). $55–$75 cabin for 2; $50–$75 private room with shared bathroom; $20 per person hostel bunk; $10 campsite. Extra adult or teen in room or cabin $15, free under age 12. MC, V. Dogs only on prior approval.

CAMPING & HOSTELS

The most popular place to camp in Homer is out on the spit, amid the sand and pebbles. It can be windy and crowded, but waking up on a bright, pebbled beach makes up for much. The city charges $8 for tents, $15 for RVs, payable at the Camp Fee Office (© **907/235-1583,** summer only) in a small log cabin on the spit across the road from the fishing hole (RVers should read the next paragraph for another option on the spit). The city also operates the more protected Hornaday Campground near the hospital: from Pioneer Avenue, take Bartlett Street uphill; turn left on Fairview and right on Campground Road. Both camping areas are managed by **Homer Public Works** (© **907/235-3170;** http://publicworks.ci.homer.ak.us and click on "Parks & Recreation"). If RV hookups are a priority you can still stay on the Homer Spit—for a price. **Heritage RV Park** is on the spit right next to the fishing hole (© **800/ 380-7787** or 907/226-4500; http://alaskaheritagervpark.com) and has all the usual amenities. Sites with full hookups, including telephone with voice mail and satellite TV, are available for $75 a night. There are plenty of places to go off the spit and get RV hookups more affordably, including the Driftwood Inn, above. **Oceanview RV Park,** 455 Sterling Hwy. (© **907/235-3951;** www.oceanview-rv.com), has 100 spaces near the downtown area overlooking the water with a trail to the beach. Rates are $37 a night for full hookups, including cable TV, Wi-Fi, laundry, and showers. Campers also get halibut charter discounts.

Tent campers will find a natural, pastoral setting at Seaside Farm, mentioned above, which also has hostel beds. More conveniently located hostel rooms are at **Homer Hostel,** 304 W. Pioneer Ave. (© **907/235-1463,** www.homerhostel.com), charging $23 a night for beds in gender-separated or co-ed dorms with four to six bunks each, or $63 double for private rooms (tax included). It's open from April to October. It's a nice old house with a shared full kitchen, but common areas are small. They also rent bikes and fishing rods and have a grill on the porch that guests can use.

LODGINGS ACROSS THE BAY

These places to stay all are based across Kachemak Bay from Homer, each in its own remote cove, bay, or village, and each in its own market niche, from family lodgings to luxurious accommodations. It's wise to reserve rooms at any of these places months in advance (the preceding winter isn't too soon). I regret I can't include many more that are also deserving—and there are many—but you can find a score of them listed with links at www.homeralaska.org (click on "Where to Stay," then "Across Kachemak Bay"). Here are some other standouts to consider: The **Otter Cove Resort** (© **800/ 426-6212** or 907/235-7770; www.ottercoveresort.com), with a collection of attractive, affordable cabins and a shower house, where guests can cook their own meals or dine in a well-made restaurant, and access to excellent hiking and sea kayaking (see "Dining across the Bay," below); **A Stillpoint in Halibut Cove,** home of the Center for Creative Renewal (© **907/296-2283;** www.centerforcreativerenewal.com), which offers an all-inclusive individual wilderness lodge experience as well as retreats and art workshops for groups—it's an astonishing work of art itself, full of exquisite stone, dramatic spaces, and even an indoor creek and waterfall—making a good site for a vacation or, as they say, "to provide an optimal nurturing atmosphere to inspire personal discoveries"; and, in Seldovia, **Alaska Dancing Eagles B&B and Cabin Rental** (© **907/234-7627** in summer or 907-360-6363 in winter; www.dancingeagles.com) a picturesque and relaxing house on the town's historic boardwalk overlooking calm water and, usually, a sea otter or two.

Across the Bay Tent and Breakfast ⚹   Tony and Mary Jane Lastufka created this unique place, a spot where you don't have to be rich to stay for a few days in a backwoods paradise, beachcombing by day and feasting on Tony's grilled seafood in the evening. It looks like a summer camp, with large canvas tents on wooden platforms that stand off by themselves on a steep hillside among towering spruce trees. There's a central house for relaxation, evening games, or conversation, an organic garden to produce the food, two outhouses with stained-glass windows, a bathhouse with plumbing, and a forest volleyball court. The beachfront faces placid Kasitsna Bay—that's where water taxis drop off visitors and where guided sea-kayaking excursions depart ($85 half-day, $105 full day per person). Up the stairs to the road, mountain bikes are for rent ($15 half-day, $25 full day) to explore the area's network of abandoned logging roads or to pedal to Seldovia. The tents have beds, but you sleep in your own bag. You can save further by cooking your own meals. Check the website for workshops you may want to join.

On Kasitsna Bay (P.O. Box 81), Seldovia, AK 99663. © **907/235-3633.** (Winter P.O. Box 112054, Anchorage, AK 99511; © 907/345-2571.) www.tentandbreakfastalaska.com. 6 tents. $75 per person with breakfast; $110 per person with all meals; half price for children 6–11; free for children 5 and under. MC, V. Closed mid-Sept to Memorial Day.

Kachemak Bay Wilderness Lodge ⚹⚹⚹   I can think of no more idyllic way to become acquainted with Alaska's marine wilderness than by staying at this intimate lodge, run for more than 25 years by hospitable and generous Mike and Diane McBride. I only wish it were affordable for more people, because it's a place of unforgettable experiences. The site, on China Poot Bay, is uniquely perfect: on an isthmus, arrayed among big trees, beach grass, and interesting topography, a peaceful and lovely setting with excellent tide pooling, kayaking, and good hiking trails nearby. Environmentally conscious guides, who have included noted experts on the science and history of the area, lead just a few guests at a time for sea kayaking, hiking, wildlife-watching, and learning about nature; guests set the agenda, and everything is included. The man-made part of the lodge is extraordinary, too. Instead of trying to pack glossy luxuries into their cabins and main lodge, the McBride's have retained the rough texture of a remote Alaskan camp while subtly enhancing it: One cabin has linoleum floors and well-used furniture, but also fine rugs, a hidden Ethernet connection, and a wine list. Each unit has a history to tell. The McBrides' meals are legendary, and guests can spend the rest of the evening in yoga classes, or the private, 1930-vintage sauna, or the hot tub, or viewing a natural history slide show. With a 3-day add-on a lucky few can visit the remote Loonsong Mountain Camp, where Mike and Diane personally guide and cook for just two couples or one family of four at a time in a lodge on its own mountain lake reached by floatplane.

China Poot Bay (P.O. Box 956), Homer, AK 99603. © **907/235-8910.** Fax 907/235-8911. www.alaskawildernesslodge.com. 5 cabins. $2,100 per person for a 3-night stay; $3,800 per person for a 6-night stay. Rates all-inclusive. Mon–Fri package only. V. Closed Oct 15–May 1. **Amenities:** Hot tub and sauna; boating, kayaking, and all guiding included.

Quiet Place Lodge ⚹⚹⚹   A series of beautifully finished cabins and lodge buildings perch on the edge of the narrow waterway that is the main street of the artists' colony of Halibut Cove (p. 313), putting a few guests in the heart of this fascinating community in complete, relaxed comfort. You can walk down to the floating dock whenever you like and get aboard your own hand-built wooden row boat or sea kayak to explore the village or paddle across the water for a spot of sushi at the Saltry Restaurant or an espresso from a stand on a floating dock. The lodge itself serves all meals, included in the package prices. The required two- or four-day packages also include guided fishing and sea kayaking. A wonderful family created this place and for years has treated guests as friends; their openness and authentic hospitality are among the lodge's best assets.

Halibut Cove (mail: 64362 Bridger Rd, Homer, AK 99603). ℂ 907/235-1800. www.quietplace.com. 3 cabins. $480 per person, per day. Rate includes all meals and limited guiding. 2- or 4-day package only. MC, V. Closed Sept–May. **Amenities:** Sauna; rowboats; sea kayaks; guided fishing.

Tutka Bay Wilderness Lodge ✸✸✸ Jon and Nelda Osgood's personalities are reflected in the amazing place they've built—open and enthusiastic, perfectionist and safety conscious, clean-cut but truly Alaskan. On pilings and on a narrow, grassy isthmus by the green water of the Tutka Bay fjord, they've put together what amounts to an upscale hotel in the wilderness, with cabins connected by long boardwalks, a deck large enough for a helicopter to land on, and a kitchen capable of producing gourmet meals. It's quite a feat—the water system alone is a wonder. There's plenty to do: guided tide-pool and forest walks, bird-watching, hiking, berry picking, rowing, fishing from the dock, and other activities around the lodge; you can pay extra for guided fishing or kayaking, bear-viewing flights, and other outdoor experiences that go farther afield.

P.O. Box 960, Homer, AK 99603. ℂ 800/606-3909 or 907/235-3905. www.tutkabaylodge.com. 6 cabins. $390–$450 per person per night. Rates include all meals. 2-night minimum stay. MC, V. Closed Oct–Apr. **Amenities:** Sauna; hot tub; high-speed Internet access. *In room:* TV/VCR, stocked fridge, coffeemaker, hair dryer.

WHERE TO DINE

Besides those places listed here, don't miss the **Chart Room** at Land's End, described under "Where to Stay," above.

Our current favorite in Homer for a quick, casual meal is **Cosmic Kitchen** (ℂ 907/235-6355; www.cosmickitchenalaska.com), a cheerful place on Pioneer Avenue producing Mexican lunches and breakfasts, especially large burritos stuffed with fresh, high-quality ingredients along with rice and other side items in disposable baskets. An enormous meal comes in at under $8 per person. Limited indoor seating is supplemented by a pleasant deck out front protected from the wind by glass, but during peak hours the place is jammed and ordering takeout would be advisable.

For fresh local halibut and cod, salmon, burgers, chicken, and milkshakes in an attractive beachfront dining room, try **Boardwalk Fish and Chips** (ℂ 907/235-7749), on the boardwalk across from the harbormaster's office on the spit. It's relaxed fast food, but the place is clean and grown-up and serves local beer. **Duncan House Diner** (ℂ 907/235-5344) downtown at 125 E. Pioneer Ave., is a friendly, traditional place, popular with coffee-sipping locals (but smoke free). You can eat at the counter or in a booth. It is open for breakfast and lunch daily. **Panarelli's Cafe & Deli,** next to the Bunnell Gallery at 106 W. Bunnell St. (ℂ 907/235-1555), produces tasty sandwiches to eat in a small dining room, on the porch, to take away, or as sack lunches to take fishing. It is open in summer Monday through Saturday 9am to 6pm, winter 11am to 6pm. The cafe doesn't take credit cards.

Dining across the Bay

In a lovely dining room and bar with vaulted ceilings, wood and tile floors, and extraordinary views of wooded Eldridge Passage, you can order draft beer, a delicious halibut or steak dinner, and simpler meals. But you can't get there without a boat. That turns out to be okay, because the ride to **Otter Cove Resort** (© **800/426-6212** or 907/235-7770; www.ottercoveresort.com) is one of the best parts of dining there. The owner, Homer Ocean Charters, carries passengers across for only $20 in the evening; at lunch time, the price is $60, but the meal is included in the price (and you still get to order from a menu). It's the cheapest way to get out on the water. They offer inexpensive cabins, too (p. 320). For another dining option across the bay, see "A Day Trip to Halibut Cove," p. 313.

Café Cups ✸✸✸ SEAFOOD/SANDWICHES   The facade of the yellow house on Pioneer Avenue is unmistakable with its elaborate bas-relief sculpture. The small dining room is a work of art, too, a masterpiece of wood, light, and space. Jennifer Olsen seats guests, and her husband, David, is the chef. As the owners, they've combined a love for good food with practicality in a small town. The menu comes in two parts. The regular daily menu is mostly mainstream—aimed at local diners looking for something familiar—but they also have an extensive daily menu of orally described specials, usually including many interesting choices based on local seafood. Do not make a choice before considering these, which are the heart of the experience. David has a terrific sense of the texture of food—the lamb chops I had on a recent visit were a sensual delight, crisply seared on the outside, tender and juicy inside, on rich mashed potatoes. Portions are large. They serve beer and wine.

162 W. Pioneer Ave. © **907/235-8330.** Reservations recommended. Lunch $6–$10; dinner main courses $16–$23. MC, V. Mon–Sat 4:30–10pm.

Fat Olives ✸✸ NORTHERN ITALIAN   Built with great style in a former school bus garage on the Sterling Highway near the visitor center, this restaurant is a wonder of warm Mediterranean colors, shiny metal, and primitive art—not the sort of place you expect to find in a small town in Alaska. The cuisine brings further surprises: bold flavors and textures, a little Tuscany, and plenty of Homer, too, including local seafood. The centerpiece is a wood-fired Italian brick oven that produces enormous slices of pizza, grilled sandwiches, and other delights. They serve local beers on tap and 30 wines by the glass. This can be a good place to go with kids, but not if you arrive at peak hours, when it can take a long time to get a table. The area for waiting—shared with the takeout counter—is not very comfortable.

276 Olson Lane. © **907/235-8488.** Reservations not accepted. Lunch $7–$12; dinner main courses $16–$26. MC, V. Daily 11am–10pm.

Fresh Sourdough Express Bakery and Restaurant ✸ (Kids) BAKERY/CAFE   Ebullient Donna and Kevin Maltz's organic eatery is quintessential Homer, starting with its motto: "Food for people and the planet." But there's no New Age dogma here. The Sourdough Express is fun and tasty, even as it grinds its own grain and recycles everything in sight. An inexpensive lunch menu includes many vegetarian choices as well as hearty sandwiches. The evening menu includes many specials; elaborate dishes, including huge portions of local seafood with rich sauces; and, perhaps more remarkably, simple, solid choices, too, for those who don't want to spend a lot. All-you-can-eat crab is served from 3 to 8pm. Families will enjoy the relaxed atmosphere and the big sandbox and an old van out front where kids can play while you wait for your meal. Stop by on the way to a day on the water for a hearty breakfast or to pick up the brown bag lunch you will need for a charter fishing trip. Don't miss dessert from the made-from-scratch bakery.

1316 Ocean Dr. ⓒ 907/235-7571. www.freshsourdoughexpress.com. Breakfast $6–$10; lunch $6.50–$12; dinner main courses $9–$25. MC, V. High season daily 7am–9pm; low season daily 8am–3pm.

The Homestead ★★★ STEAK/SEAFOOD The ambience is that of an old-fashioned Alaska roadhouse, in a large log building decorated with contemporary art and lots of summer light. The food is wonderfully satisfying. The seafood is done simply but right, often just grilled to a turn, which is a good call with this fresh Alaskan fish. The salads and the side dishes let the chef show more sophistication, and we've always been impressed. The seafood portions are generous, and if you want a big piece of rare prime rib, go no farther. After a day outdoors, it's a warm, exuberant place for dinner, but with polished edges: white table linens and intimate but professional service. We chose the restaurant for our 20th anniversary, and we couldn't have been happier. The wine list is well selected and arranged—not intimidating; plenty of bottles are in the $21 to $34 range. They also have a full bar with local beers on tap.

Mile 8.2, East End Rd. ⓒ 907/235-8723. www.homesteadrestaurant.net. Reservations recommended. Main courses $21–$39. AE, MC, V. June–Aug daily 5–10pm; March–May and Sept–Dec Wed–Sat 5–9pm. Closed Jan–Feb.

HOMER NIGHTLIFE

The **Pier One Theatre** (ⓒ 907/235-7333; www.pieronetheatre.org) is a strong community theater group housed in a small, square, red building on the spit, between the fishing hole and the small-boat harbor. Instead of the ubiquitous gold-rush melodrama and Robert Service readings, Pier One often presents serious drama, musicals, and comedy—not just schlock. They also produce dance, classical music, and youth theater events during the summer. There's generally something playing Thursday through Sunday nights in the summer. Check the *Homer News* or the website for current listings. They strongly recommend making reservations by phone; they can be changed or canceled if necessary. Tickets may also be available at the door.

The landmark **Salty Dawg Saloon** is a small log cabin on the spit with a lighthouse on top. It's the place to swap fish stories after a day on the water. Wherever you go to hoist a beer, order a draft from the **Homer Brewing Company** (Red Knot Ale is my favorite).

11 Valdez

Big events have shaped Valdez (val-*deez*). The deepwater port, at the head of a long, dramatic fjord, first developed with the 1898 Klondike gold rush and an ill-fated attempt to establish an alternative route to the gold fields from here. Later, the port and the Richardson Highway, which connected Valdez to the rest of the state, served a key role in supplying materials during World War II. On Good Friday, March 27, 1964, all of that was erased when North America's greatest recorded earthquake occurred under Miners Lake, west of town off a northern fjord of Prince William Sound. It set off an underwater landslide that caused a huge wave to sweep over the waterfront and

Valdez

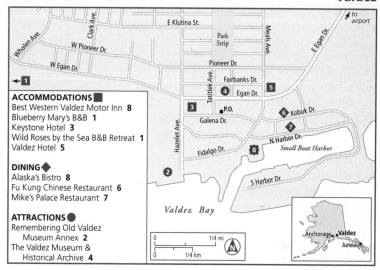

ACCOMMODATIONS ■
Best Western Valdez Motor Inn **8**
Blueberry Mary's B&B **1**
Keystone Hotel **3**
Wild Roses by the Sea B&B Retreat **1**
Valdez Hotel **5**

DINING ◆
Alaska's Bistro **8**
Fu Kung Chinese Restaurant **6**
Mike's Palace Restaurant **7**

ATTRACTIONS ●
Remembering Old Valdez
   Museum Annex **2**
The Valdez Museum &
   Historical Archive **4**

kill 32 people. The U.S. Army Corps of Engineers moved the town, rebuilding a drab replacement in a safer location that slowly filled with nondescript modern buildings.

The construction of the trans-Alaska pipeline, completed in 1977, brought a new economic boom to Valdez and enduring economic prosperity as tankers came to fill with the oil. Then, on March 24, 1989, on Good Friday 25 years after the earthquake, the tanker *Exxon Valdez*, on its way south, hit the clearly marked Bligh Reef, causing the largest and most environmentally costly oil spill ever in North America. The spill cleanup added another economic boom. Nearly 20 years later, most wildlife populations have recovered but some have not, though visible signs of the spill are difficult to find.

Today, Valdez is a regular American town, driven by industry but turning to the vast resources of Prince William Sound for outdoor recreation. In town you can tour two small museums and take a hike or a river float. The town has made major strides in improving its appearance, especially on the waterfront, but it isn't the sort of historic or charming fishing village that justifies a trip all by itself. Instead, come for the setting—the wildlife, fishing, and sightseeing in the sound, and the spectacular drive down the Richardson Highway.

Because Valdez lies at the end of a funnel of steep mountains that catches moisture off the ocean, the weather tends to be overcast and rainy in summer and extremely snowy in winter.

ESSENTIALS

GETTING THERE   By Car   The **Richardson Highway** (see section 7 in chapter 9) dramatically crosses Thompson Pass and descends into the narrow valley where Valdez lies. Try to do the trip in daylight, in clear weather, and stop at the Worthington Glacier. This is the only road to Valdez. The drive from Anchorage is 6 hours without stops.

By Ferry   The **Alaska Marine Highway System** (© **800/642-0066** or 907/835-4436; www.ferryalaska.com) connects Valdez, Whittier, and Cordova by ferry. One time-tested way to see the sound is to put your vehicle on the ferry in Whittier for the run to Valdez and then drive north on the Richardson Highway. The fast ferry *Chenega* cuts travel time from Anchorage to Valdez to less than driving (about 90 min by car from Anchorage to Whittier and 4 hr. by ferry from Whittier to Valdez). The current fare is $89 for an adult, half price for ages 6 through 11, free for children under 6. A 15-foot car costs $105 to take along.

By Air   **Era Aviation** (© **800/866-8394;** www.flyera.com) flies several times a day each way between Anchorage and Valdez.

GETTING AROUND   The main part of the town and boat harbor are compact enough to walk, but you will need wheels for the airport, the attractions on Dayville Road, and most of the hiking trails.

Rental cars are available at the airport from **Valdez-U-Drive** (© **907/835-4402;** www.valdezudrive.com).

Taxis are available from **Valdez Yellow Cab** (© **907/835-2500**).

VISITOR INFORMATION   The Valdez Convention and Visitors Bureau maintains a **Visitor Information Center** at 200 Fairbanks Dr., a block off Egan Drive (P.O. Box 1603), Valdez, AK 99686 (© **907/835-4636;** www.valdezalaska.org). Pick up the free town map and useful *Vacation Planner.* They're open in summer daily 8am to 7pm and winter Monday through Friday 8am to 5pm.

SPECIAL EVENTS   The town has three **summer fishing derbies:** The **Halibut Derby** runs all summer, the **Silver Salmon Derby** runs from late July to early September, and the **Women's Silver Salmon Derby** is the second Saturday in August. Derby tickets are available all over town.

The **Fireweed Bicycle Race Across Alaska** (www.fireweed400.com) covers big mileage on the Glenn and Richardson highways between Sheep Mountain and Valdez, with 50-, 100-, 200-, and 400-mile events the first weekend in July.

The **Last Frontier Theater Conference** (© **907/834-1614;** www.pwscc.edu) brings playwrights, directors, and actors from all over the U.S. for seminars and performances from June 14 to June 21, 2008. Performances are staged every night over the 8-day event and workshops and readings last all day. Those interested in literature and theater will find it worth arranging a trip around the event.

FAST FACTS: Valdez

Banks Two **banks** are on Egan Drive, both with ATMs.

Hospital **Providence Valdez Medical Center** (© **907/835-2249**) is at 911 Meals Ave.

Internet Access You can go online free at **Valdez Consortium Library** (© **907/835-4632**) at 260 Fairbanks St., but you may need to call ahead to reserve a time.

Police For nonemergencies phone the **Valdez Police Department** at © **907/835-4560**, at 212 Chenega Ave.

Post Office Galena Drive and Tatitlek Street, 1 block back from Egan Drive.

Taxes Valdez has no sales tax but does charge a 6% **bed tax.**

GETTING OUTSIDE
SIGHTSEEING & WILDLIFE TOURS

For most visitors, a daylong ride on a tour boat into the sound is likely to be the most memorable part of a visit to Valdez. The main tour boat company in town is **Stan Stephens Glacier and Wildlife Cruises** (© 866/867-1297 or 907/835-4731; www.stanstephenscruises.com). The office is on the dock at the end of the small-boat harbor near the Best Western Valdez Harbor Inn. Stephens has been showing off the sound and defending it from pollution for decades. After passing through the long fjord of Port Valdez, boats enter an ice-choked bay in front of **Columbia Glacier** on a 6-hour tour that often encounters birds, seals, sea otters, and sea lions, and sometimes whales, for $95 for adults. A light lunch is served. Going on to Meares Glacier, farther west, adds 3 hours to the round-trip, but brings you to a glacier you can get a better look at and that may drop ice into the water. That cruise is $130 and includes a hot lunch and a snack. Prices are half for children ages 2 to 11 on either trip.

SEA KAYAKING & SAILING

Raven Charters, Slip C-25, Valdez Boat Harbor (© 907/835-5863; www.alaska.net/~ravenchr), is run by a family who shares its home on a 50-foot boat with clients to sail and explore the sound. The wind tends to be light and changeable, but a sailboat makes a comfortable base for discovering interesting, isolated places. All-inclusive prices for the whole boat start at $850 per night for up to four passengers, or $700 for a day charter, with discounts for longer trips.

Right around Valdez, short sea-kayaking day trips to see wildlife on the Duck Flats may be just what you want for a first try at the sport; but that area is hardly wilderness, as it's also reached by road and is within sight of the oil facilities. Day trips to Shoup or Columbia glaciers get you into more of the beautiful, remote country that makes Prince William Sound so exceptional. **Pangaea Adventures** (© 800/660-9637 or 907/835-8442; www.alaskasummer.com) offers guided sea kayaking from Valdez, or rentals for experienced paddlers, for whom the sound is a paradise. They also offer multiday guided camping trips deeper into the sound, or, for those who prefer a bed and home base, lodge-based tours where clients paddle by day and stay in a lodge at night. Pangaea offers many other services as well: water taxi and kayak drop-off, ice climbing and glacier hiking, river rafting, and even trips that combine these activities in the sound and Wrangell-St. Elias National Park. Check out the website for more details.

FISHING & BOATING

The ocean waters around Valdez are rich in salmon and halibut. It's possible to fish for salmon from shore. Popular spots include Dayville Road west of the fish hatchery, the city dock near the ferry dock in town, or even the harbor floats. Except at the hatchery, you're hoping a fish swims by your lure or bait at the right moment: There isn't a freshwater destination to concentrate the fish. Chances and the fishing experience are improved if you get out on the water. Many small fishing charter boats are available in the boat harbor, or you can rent your own boat and gear; book through **Fish Central** (© 888/835-5002 or 907/835-5002; www.fishcentral.net). They can also take care of processing and freezing your catch for shipment.

HIKING & MOUNTAIN BIKING

Valdez has a broad selection of good day hikes and an overnight. The visitor center can advise you on choices beyond those I list here. In addition, you can join guided hiking and glacier activities, including ice climbing, with Pangaea Adventures (see "Sea Kayaking & Sailing," above).

The easiest hike is a pleasant forest and shore walk to **Dock Point,** starting at the east side of the boat harbor, at the end of North Harbor Drive. It's a peaceful, natural walk close to town, with boardwalks and overlooks and berries along the way in season.

For a longer hike and perhaps an overnight, the **Shoup Glacier Trail** runs 12 miles west from town along the shore of Port Valdez to a lagoon in front of the glacier's face. The going is generally flat and there are many places to get down to the beach, with wild iris and many other flowers. Cool yourself in a waterfall. Camping is unrestricted, but be sure to bring mosquito repellent and review bear avoidance techniques (see "Outdoor Health & Safety," p. 46). If you plan to go all the way, consider reserving one of the three state parks cabins near the glacier (see "State Parks Cabin Reservations," in section 1 of this chapter). Or you can get a lift one way from a water taxi, such as the service offered by Pangaea Adventures. The trail starts at the end of West Egan Drive.

The **Solomon Gulch Trail** starts across from the fish hatchery on Dayville Road (see "Exploring the Town," below) and goes steeply up to Solomon Lake, where locals swim. Be prepared for bears. Trails off **Mineral Creek Road,** above town off Hanagita Street, are great for walking, mountain biking, or berry picking, and in winter there is a fine cross-country skiing trail network. The **Valdez Goat Trail** runs from the spectacular Bridal Veil Falls at mile 13.8 of the Richardson Highway for a distance of 2.5 miles on an abandoned roadbed, past some great views.

RAFTING

Keystone Raft and Kayak Adventures (© **907/835-2606;** www.alaskawhitewater.com) takes five trips a day 4½ miles down the amazing Keystone Canyon, a virtual corridor of rock with a floor of frothing water, past the crashing tumult of the 900-foot Bridal Veil Falls. The whitewater is rated Class III, meaning it is not too wild for most people, but rafting is not without risk—serious mishaps can sometimes occur. Keystone charges $40 per person. The company also has numerous longer trips, ranging from a day to 10 days, on many of the region's rivers.

HELI-SKIING

Valdez is a magnet for backcountry alpine and extreme skiing and snowboarding thanks to its prodigious snow and limitless steep mountains. A bunch of guide companies offer these trips, operating by helicopter from mid-February to mid-May. One established operator is **Valdez Heli-Ski Guides** (© **907/835-4528;** www.valdezheli skiguides.com). Expect to pay around $850 a day, or book a package with lodgings.

EXPLORING THE TOWN

The community college's **Maxine & Jesse Whitney Museum,** at the airport (© **907/834-1614;** www.pwscc.edu), contains a large collection of Alaska Native arts and crafts and animal mounts accumulated by the couple over 50 years. It is open from May to mid-September daily from 9am to 6pm and by appointment in winter; admission is $5.

The Solomon Gulch Hatchery When the pink salmon return from late June to early August, they swarm on the hatchery in a blizzard of fish. The hatchery releases more than 200 million pinks and 2 million silvers (or coho) each year. There is no stream for the salmon to return to, so they try to get back into the hatchery, crowding together in a solid sea of fighting muscle. Seals and birds come in to feed, and you can stand on shore and watch (and smell) the spectacle. Surefire fishing is allowed up the shore on Dayville Road. Popular tours at the hatchery were suspended by construction through 2007, but managers expected to open to the public again in 2008. Call or ask at the visitor center to learn the current status.

On Dayville Rd. on the way to the tanker terminal. ℂ 907/835-1329.

The Valdez Museum and Historical Archive ★★ The museum's primary exhibit is a chronological walk through the area's history from explorers' visits through the oil spill in 1989. Objects and photographs bring back some of those moments and places with emotional force, with humor, or with something like nostalgia—if that's the word to describe longing for a time before one's own birth. Despite its professionalism, the museum has friendly, small-town hospitality and shows items of small-town pride: In the lobby are shiny old fire engines, dating back to 1886, and the annual summer show of local quilting and fiber crafts. An annex, near the ferry dock, is less polished, but shouldn't be missed. It contains the "Remembering Old Valdez" exhibit, a ¹⁄₂₀-scale model of how Valdez looked at its old site, before the 1964 earthquake forced the town to move. Using photographs, records, and old-timers' memories, a dedicated worker brought that lost city back with 400 miniature buildings on tables, like model train dioramas without the trains. A film puts it in context. The annex is at 436 S. Hazelet Ave. Admission covers both buildings.

217 Egan Dr. ℂ 907/835-2764. www.valdezmuseum.org. $5 adults; $4.50 adults over 65; $4 children 14–17, free for children under 14. Memorial Day through Labor Day both buildings daily 9am–6pm; low season main building Mon–Fri 1–5pm, Sat noon–4pm, annex by appointment.

WHERE TO STAY

Best Western Valdez Harbor Inn ★ This up-to-date hotel commands the best location in town, right on the harbor near the tour boats, although few rooms have views. The rooms are well equipped, set up to make snacks or breakfast and with DVD players connected to the big TVs to play movies rented at the front desk. A good restaurant on-site, Alaska Bistro, is described below. Wireless Internet is available throughout; business-class rooms have wired DSL connections and king size beds.

100 N. Harbor Dr. (P.O. Box 468), Valdez, AK 99686. ℂ 888/222-3440 or 907/835-3434. Fax 907/835-2308. www.valdezharborinn.com. 88 units. High season $139–$149 double; low season $69–$79; $15 each additional person age 12 or older. AE, DISC, MC, V. **Amenities:** Restaurant; exercise room; limited room service; coin-op laundry. *In room:* A/C, TV/DVD, fridge, coffeemaker, hair dryer, iron, microwave, Wi-Fi.

Blueberry Mary's Bed and Breakfast ★ (Value) A lucky few get to sleep under Mary Mehlberg's handmade quilts on her feather beds, gaze at the ocean views, bake in the sauna, and breakfast on her blueberry waffles made from wild berries that grow just outside the house. She only takes parties of two or less and sometimes closes for breaks. Those who do stay here get a good deal on immaculate, handcrafted rooms at a prime location.

810 Blueberry Hill Rd., off W. Egan Dr. (P.O. Box 1244), Valdez, AK 99686. ℂ 907/835-5015. http://home. gci.net/~blueberrymary. 2 units. $100–$115 double (including tax). Rates include full breakfast. No credit cards. Closed Sept 15–June 1. **Amenities:** Sauna. *In room:* TV/VCR, fridge, coffeemaker, hair dryer, iron, microwave.

Keystone Hotel (Value) This basic budget hotel, made of modular units, was built by Exxon to serve as its offices for the oil-spill cleanup operation, but it wasn't completed until late summer 1989, so the company occupied it for only about a month.

It stood vacant for 5 years before a new owner remodeled it into a hotel, with small rooms that mostly have two twin beds or one double bed, though some have two doubles. Select a room when you check in, as they vary in decor.

401 W. Egan Dr. (P.O. Box 2148), Valdez, AK 99686. © **888/835-0665** or 907/835-3851. Fax 907/835-5322. www. keystonehotel.com. 98 units. $95 double. Extra person over age 12 $10. Rate includes continental breakfast. AE, MC, V. Closed in winter. **Amenities:** Coin-op laundry. *In room:* TV.

Valdez Hotel 🏠🏠   Stay here for standard rooms at the quality level you would find in a corporate travel hotel. Service is good and common areas spacious and well equipped—there's a small pool and business center, and the lobby is a handy dining room where you can serve your own breakfast of cereal, waffles, fruit, and the like. Rooms are decorated in burgundy, hunter green, and dark wood, with lots of extras, large TVs, and mirrors. Our family of six fit nicely in a family suite, which has a large main bedroom and a separate children's room with bunk beds with its own TV. Ask about discounts you may qualify for.

100 Meals Ave., Valdez, AK 99686. © **800/478-4445** or 907/835-4445. Fax 907/835-2437. 104 units. High season $129–$149 double; low season $99 double. AE, DC, DISC, MC, V. **Amenities:** Indoor pool; exercise room; spa; business center (computer, printer, copier, dataport); coin-op laundry. *In room:* TV/VCR, fridge, coffeemaker, hair dryer, iron, microwave, Wi-Fi.

Wild Roses by the Sea B&B Retreat 🏠🏠   Light pours from bay windows that overlook the water and surrounding woods into large, elegantly appointed rooms with high ceilings, decorated with Asian and contemporary art, and finished in light colors, wood floors, and Berber-style carpets. Best of all is the spacious and private "Ocean View Guesthouse," a downstairs suite with a kitchen and living room. The hostess, Rose Fong, prepares elaborate breakfasts in the summer and feeds guests snacks and beverages all day. The location is half a mile from the Shoup Glacier Trail (see "Hiking & Mountain Biking," above) and less than a mile from a state park beach.

629 Fiddlehead Lane (P.O. Box 3396), Valdez, AK 99686. © **907/835-2930.** Fax 907/835-4966. www.alaskabythe seabnb.com. 3 units. Summer $128–$165 double, including full breakfast; winter $79 double, including continental breakfast. Extra adult $20, child $15. MC, V. *In room:* TV, dataport, hair dryer, iron.

CAMPING

The **Sea Otter RV Park,** P.O. Box 947, Valdez, AK 99686 (© **907/835-2787**), sits on the outside of the boat harbor breakwater, a mosquito-free spot with views and beachfront where you can fish for salmon or watch the harbor otters. The RV park has a laundry and other facilities, and charges $29 for full hookups.

The best campground in the area is the state's **Blueberry Lake Campground,** 24 miles out of town on the Richardson Highway, just below Thompson Pass. The campground is above the tree line, with mountaintop views and access to limitless alpine hiking. It can be windy and cold. The small lake is stocked with trout. Fifteen well-screened sites are $15 on a self-serve system. There are pit toilets. RVs are welcome, but there are no hookups.

WHERE TO DINE

Alaska Bistro 🍴 MEDITERRANEAN/PIZZA   A harborside dining room with big windows creates a proper setting for a restaurant with fine dining aspirations. The food includes lots of local seafood prepared in Northern Italian and similar styles; the chicken, pork, and beef also get more than the typical small-town treatment, although you can also get a simple grilled steak. The pizza is European, too, with toppings such as pesto, sun-dried tomatoes, and feta cheese. There's a downside to trying to do too much, however; on our last visit the wine we ordered had turned and the service was chaotic. They have a full bar.

102 N. Harbor Dr. ℭ **907/835-5688**. Reservations recommended. Lunch $9–$15, dinner main courses $10–$30. AE, MC, V. Daily 6–10:30am, 11:30am–2:30pm, and 5–10pm.

Fu Kung Chinese Restaurant ★ CHINESE   This long-established family restaurant near the harbor serves some of the best meals in town; in Valdez, that's not a huge claim to fame, but this place is good. The interior is clean and pleasant, with a fish tank, warm colors, and plenty of room. The food is plentiful and tasty, especially the gingery bean curd with vegetables, the hot and sour soup, and the kung pao chicken. They feature local seafood in Chinese dishes and serve some Thai and sushi selections, too. Service is fast and attentive. In winter, they often close earlier than the hours listed below.

207 Kobuk Dr. (1 block from the boat harbor). ℭ **907/835-5255**. Lunch $8–$11; dinner main courses $12–$16. AE, DISC, MC, V. Daily 11am–11pm.

Mike's Palace Ristorante PIZZA/STEAK/SEAFOOD   This is a good family pizza restaurant, a place where Valdez residents come for a casual evening out. The calzone is good, the service skilled, and everything consistent. The owners' national Greek cuisine is on the menu as well, and the restaurant serves beer and wine. It's a warm, cheerful place, perfect after a day on the water—the boat harbor is right across the street. Mike's also has a place in history: Capt. Joseph Hazelwood was waiting for a takeout pizza here when he slipped next door to the Club Bar for his last drink before starting the fateful voyage of the *Exxon Valdez* that hit Bligh Reef.

201 N. Harbor Dr. ℭ **907/835-2365**. Lunch $5–$10; dinner main courses $9–$26. AE, DISC, MC, V. Daily 11am–11pm.

12 Cordova: Hidden Treasure

The first time I ever went to Cordova, my companion and I arrived at the Mudhole Smith Airport in a small plane and happened upon an old guy with a pickup truck who offered to let us ride in back with some boards the 10 miles to town. The highway led out onto a broad, wetland plain—the largest contiguous wetland in the Western Hemisphere, as it happens. Our guide's voice, studded with profanity, boomed through the back window as he told us proudly about the diversity of the wildlife to be found out there. Then, absolutely bursting with enthusiasm, he leaned on the horn and bellowed, "Look at them f—ing swans!" We looked; trumpeters paddling in the marsh looked back. He would have invited them along to the bar, too, if he'd known how.

Every time I've been to Cordova since, I've been taken under the wings of new friends. Although they usually don't express themselves the same way that first gentleman did, they are just as enthusiastic to show off the amazing natural riches of their little kingdom. Tourists are still something of a novelty here, for Cordova isn't just off the beaten track—it's not on the track at all. There's no road to the rest of the world, and the town is an afterthought on the ferry system. Boosters call their town "Alaska's Hidden Treasure." For once, they're right.

Our family has had some of our happiest times in Cordova, visiting the Childs Glacier and seeing the swans and geese on the delta; hiking into the mountains behind town; boating on the sound to meet the sea otters, sea lions, eagles, and spawning salmon; hiking and canoeing at a remote lake cabin—and meeting no other people at all. In town, we made new friends whenever we turned around and received hearty greetings from old friends from previous visits. Leaving on the ferry for Valdez, I've watched Cordova shrinking behind us with a wistful hope that it would never change.

So far, I've gotten my wish. You can feel a bit like an anthropologist discovering a tribe lost to time, for Cordova has the qualities small towns are supposed to have but lost long ago in America. Walking down 1st Street, you pass an old-fashioned independent grocery store and drugstore, the fishermen's union hall, and Steen's gift shop, run by the same family since 1909—no chains or franchises. My children thought the street looked like a movie set on our most recent visit. The best part of their week was the novel freedom to roam and shop on their own. It was clearly safe. People leave their keys in the car and their doors unlocked at night. When a friend of mine bought one of the quaint, moss-roofed hillside houses years ago, he didn't receive a key—the simple reason was that the front door didn't have a lock.

Cordova owes much of its uniqueness to a rich history and remote location. Its biggest political controversy—simmering for 70 years—concerns whether to build a road to the outside world. The town's heyday was in 1911, when the Copper River and Northwestern Railroad opened, carrying copper ore down from the mine at Kennecott; it hit a low when the mine closed in 1938. Since then, boosters have been trying to get a road built on the old rail line, north along the Copper River to Chitina (that fascinating area is covered in chapter 9, under "Wrangell–St. Elias National Park & Kennecott"). The road builders have made it only about 50 miles out of town so far. From Cordova, the **Copper River Highway** provides access to the best bird-watching and, in my judgment, the most impressive glacier in Alaska, as well as trails and magnificent vistas and areas to see wildlife. In town, the small-boat harbor is a doorway to Prince William Sound.

ESSENTIALS

GETTING THERE   By Ferry   Cordova is served by ferry from Valdez and Whittier by the **Alaska Marine Highway System** (© **800/642-0066** or 907/424-7333 local dock; www.ferryalaska.com). It's a spectacular ride, with a good chance of seeing wildlife aboard the fast ferry *Chenega*. The passenger fare from Valdez is $50, from Whittier $89; half price for children ages 5 to 11. Taking a vehicle under 15 feet one-way from Valdez to Cordova is $94, from Whittier $105. You can also rent a car in Cordova. See section 1 of chapter 5 for information about the ferry system.

By Air   Alaska Airlines (© **800/426-0333,** www.alaskaair.com) flies daily each direction, from Anchorage to the west and Yakutat, Juneau, and Seattle to the southeast, with more flights from Anchorage operated by **Era Aviation** (© **800/866-8394;** www.flyera.com).

GETTING AROUND   You can easily walk around downtown Cordova, but that's not where the most interesting sights are. To get out on the Copper River Highway,

ACCOMMODATIONS ■
The Northern Lights Inn 8
Orca Adventure Lodge 1
Reluctant Fisherman Hotel 2

DINING ◆
Ambrosia 5
Baja Taco 4
Killer Whale Cafe 6

ATTRACTIONS ●
Cordova Historical Museum 7
Ilanka Cultural Center 3

you'll need a car, bus, or, if you're vigorous, a bike. Cars are for rent from **Chinook Auto Rentals** (*C* 877/424-5279 or 907/424-5279) at Northern Nights Inn (p. 338). Taxis are available from **Cordova Taxi** (*C* 907/424-5151).

Water taxis and rental of bikes, kayaks, skiffs, canoes, and fishing and camping gear are available at **Cordova Coastal Outfitters,** south of the boat harbor near the Alaska Commercial grocery store (*C* 800/357-5145 or 907/424-7424; www.cordovacoastal. com). They also offer drop-off and pick-up service on the Copper River Highway, allowing visitors to go for a canoeing or cabin trip without renting a car. They're described in full later.

To get to remote cabins and fly-in fishing, try **Cordova Air** (*C* 907/424-3289) or **Copper River Air Taxi** (*C* 907/424-5371), both based on Eyak Lake, just north of town.

VISITOR INFORMATION The **Cordova Chamber of Commerce Visitor Center** (*C* 907/424-7260; www.cordovachamber.com) is at 404 1st St., north of Council Avenue (P.O. Box 99, Cordova, AK 99574). They're open Monday through Friday 10am to 4pm, with occasional Saturday hours. Besides the usual information, the center has a 60-minute recorded walking tour that you can listen to as it guides you around town.

The **Cordova Ranger District** of the Chugach National Forest, upstairs in the old white courthouse at 2nd Street and Browning (P.O. Box 280), Cordova, AK 99574 (*C* 907/424-7661; www.fs.fed.us/r10/chugach), has displays and provides maps and guide information that's indispensable for planning outdoor activities. The staff will sit down and help you figure out what you want to do.

SPECIAL EVENTS The **Cordova Ice Worm Festival,** from February 1 through February 3, 2008, is a winter carnival culminating in the appearance of the big ice worm—or, to be precise, ice centipede—in a parade. The town's centennial will be celebrated at a **Cordova Birthday Party** May 3, 2008. **The Copper River Delta Shorebird Festival,** May 8 through May 11, 2008, revolves around the coming of dizzying swarms of millions of shorebirds that use the delta and beaches near the town as a migratory stopover. The whole community gets involved to host bird-watchers and put on a full schedule of educational and outdoor activities that lasts 3 days. **Copper River Wild! Salmon Festival,** July 11 and July 12, 2008, includes a marathon and a music festival. For details on any of these happenings, contact the Cordova Chamber of Commerce or check their website, www.cordovachamber.com.

FAST FACTS: Cordova

Banks There are two banks on 1st Street, with **ATMs**.

Hospital **Cordova Community Medical Center** and **Ilanka Community Health Center** are located together on Chase Street (© **907/424-8000**), off the Copper River Highway near the Odiak Slough.

Internet Access Find it at the **Cordova Public Library** (© **907/424-6667**) and at **Orca Book and Sound** (© **907/424-5305**), both on 1st Street.

Police For nonemergency business, call © **907/424-6100**.

Post Office At Railroad Avenue and Council.

Taxes **Sales tax** is 6%; rooms and car rentals carry an additional 6% tax.

EXPLORING THE TOWN & HIKING NEAR TOWN

ATTRACTIONS   Cordova mostly is for outdoor activities (covered below), but save some time to wander around town, make discoveries, and meet people, possibly with the help of the **historic walking tour booklet** produced by the historical society and available from the chamber of commerce.

The **Cordova Historical Museum,** at 622 1st St. (© **907/424-6665**, www.cordova museum.org), mostly in one room, does a good job of presenting some valuable artifacts reflecting Cordova's eventful past, a collection of classic Alaskan art, and some odd and fascinating stuff. There's a historic lighthouse lens, a Linotype machine, the interior of a fishing boat, a parka made of bear gut, basketry, and photographs of fishing and historic scenes. Our entire family enjoyed it. The museum is open summer Monday through Saturday from 10am to 6pm, Sunday from 2 to 4pm; winter Tuesday through Friday from 10 to 5pm, Saturday from 1 to 5pm. Recommended donation is $1.

Cordova is a center for the Eyak, a small but linguistically and ethnographically distinct people. Make a point of stopping in at the Native Village of Eyak's **Ilanka Cultural Center,** at 110 Nicholoff Way (across from the Fishermen's Memorial at the small-boat harbor; © **907/424-7903**). Although small, the center is new and growing, and we experienced a warm link with the Eyak people we met. The collection includes Eyak, Alutiiq, Tlingit, and Ahtna artifacts, photographs, and oral histories. There is also a fully reconstructed orca whale skeleton. The gallery sells art, books, and other items made in Alaska, especially by Alaska Natives. Artists sometimes offer classes and demonstrations. Hours are summer Tuesday through Saturday 10am to 5pm. Admission is free, but donations are encouraged.

HIKING   Cordova has more good hiking trails per capita than any place I know. The Cordova Ranger Station can provide you with a free trail-guide booklet with lots of ideas and maps. There are three hikes close to town and more on the Copper River Delta, covered below in the section on the Delta, and at Hartney Bay (ask at the ranger station).

The **Tripod Mountain Trail** begins right from town and climbs 1,255 feet over less than a mile up the first mountain back from the shore, a half-day hike with views that present the sound and Cordova like a map below you. The trail begins at the foot of the town ski lift, on 6th Street—take Browning up the hill.

Partway up Tripod Mountain, near the middle drop-off of the ski lift, a 1-mile trail links to the **Crater Lake Trail,** which eventually joins the **Power Creek Trail** on a loop of 12 miles. An easier start for that route is Power Creek Road—drive it along the north side of Eyak Lake to the end, 7 miles from town. The creek has spawning red salmon in July and attracts a lot of bears; watch, but don't get out of your car if you come upon one. The trail follows the creek through dramatic scenery 4.25 miles to the Power Creek Forest Service cabin, with a great view (you can reserve it through the system described on p. 271).

THE COPPER RIVER DELTA

The delta and its star attraction, the **Childs Glacier,** make an unforgettable day trip by car or tour bus from Cordova, but if you have a couple of days, you can do much more. The backwaters, sloughs, and ponds beg to be explored by canoe. Bird-watchers will especially enjoy paddling here and visiting the boardwalks and blinds set up by the Forest Service. You can raft the rivers. There are excellent hiking trails and mountain-biking routes branching from the road, and Forest Service cabins to stay in. And the river itself has many miles of deserted sandy beaches for long walks or sand castles on a sunny day.

The delta seems to go on forever, a vast patchwork of marsh, pond, small hills of trees, and the huge, implacable gray river itself. The glacial silt it carries away—some 2 million tons a day—has built this 700,000-acre wetland. A well-maintained gravel road leads across it, all in Chugach National Forest, and the rangers have done a good job of providing ways and places to enjoy and learn about the area. The road itself is the old bed of the Copper River and Northwestern Railroad. It leads 48 miles to the **Million Dollar Bridge.** Built by Michael Heney, a magician of a 19th-century railroad builder who also constructed the White Pass and Yukon Route in Skagway, the 200-mile Copper River line was an engineering triumph that brought the mind-boggling wealth of the Kennecott Copper Corporation to ships in Cordova (read more about the mining in section 8 of chapter 9). The bridge over the Copper River was built in a race against time between two surging glaciers in 30-foot-deep, fast-flowing glacial water, during winter. It stood for 56 years, until the 1964 earthquake knocked down one end of one of the spans, driving it into the riverbed. In 2004 your highway dollars repaired that span and once again you can drive to the other side, where only an unmaintained road soon peters out into a rough trail.

GETTING THERE

BY CAR   Driving gives you the most freedom. The Copper River Highway is gravel, but it's wide and level. If you've brought a rental car and your contract does not allow driving on gravel, I recommend parking in Cordova and renting a car there for the drive on the Copper River Highway. The Northern Nights Inn (p. 338) offers rentals. Beyond the Million Dollar Bridge, the road becomes a rough four-wheel-drive track at best, and if you get stuck you'll be there for a long time. Check at the Forest Service Cordova Ranger Station for the latest news about the road and pick up their road guide.

BY BIKE   Mountain biking the highway is the adventurous way to travel, camping or staying in a Forest Service cabin on the way. The drawbacks are the distances, the delta's strong winds, and a lot of road dust. Of course, you don't have to ride all the way to see lots of birds and wildlife, and there are good mountain-biking routes on the delta away from the road. The 3-mile **Saddlebag Glacier Trail,** at mile 25 of the Copper River Highway, leads to a vista of a glacial lake surrounded by rocky peaks. Bikes are for rent from Cordova Coastal Outfitters (see "Out on Prince William Sound," below) for $18 a day.

ALONG THE ROAD

Keep your eyes scanning the wetlands and mountains around you as you drive out the road. The **wildlife** you may see along the way includes black and brown bears, wolf, coyote, moose, and mountain goats. The entire world population of dusky Canada geese nests on the delta, and you're likely to see eagles and trumpeter swans without really looking. The ranger station provides a wildlife-viewing guide and several places to stop along the way designed for bird-watching. The first is a platform with interpretive signs as you leave town, an introduction to the delta; this stretch of the road is fine for bird-watching.

Don't skip the **Alaganik Slough Boardwalk.** Take the 3¼-mile spur road to the right 17 miles out the Copper River Highway; it's marked. The sky here is big and certain while the land is ambivalent—it doesn't know if it wants to be waving grass of green and gold or shallow, shimmering ponds and tendrils of water. The road leads to the start of the 1,000-foot boardwalk with a blind and to a riverside path. Water reflects the sun and the colors of the marsh. We were speechless one evening at sunset, even in the complete absence of birds. Often in the summer you can see breeding trumpeter swans, ducks, and grebes, and in the spring and fall migrating waterfowl and shorebirds make appearances. The path is on the left just before you arrive at the boardwalk and picnic area; the 1-mile Fisherman's Trail is a meandering route among water and brush.

You can stop at any of the bridges crossing the Copper River for a romp in the sand. The river beaches of fine sand extend practically forever.

The highway ends with the area's best attraction, the advancing **Childs Glacier.** This is the most amazing glacier I've ever seen and no one seems to know about it outside Cordova. The advancing wall of ice, 300 feet tall, comes right down to the quarter-mile-wide river, battling the flowing water for control of the land here. The glacier tries to divert the river while the river tries to cut the glacier like a knife, eroding the base and bringing down huge ice chunks. As you sit on the opposite bank, the glacier on the opposite side is too large to see—it completely fills your field of vision, creating an eerie and hypnotic sense of scale. On a warm summer day, you can feel the glacier's thunder as the ice shifts, and see pieces fall off. A chunk the size of a car barely registers, but when an office building–size hunk falls, there's a roar and gray breakers radiate out across the river. Falling glacier pieces have made waves large enough to uproot trees here, not to mention hurl a few fish around—at the Forest Service viewing and picnic area across the river, salmon have been found high up in the trees and boulders have been found in odd places. Several years ago, such a wave injured some visitors, and now the Forest Service warns that anyone who can't run fast should stay in the observation tower. A path leads less than a mile to the **Million Dollar Bridge** or drive by on your way out.

ACTIVITIES

CANOEING   The delta's canoe routes are little used, leading to remote places where birds and aquatic animals rule. You can launch on Alaganik Slough at a picnic area at mile 22 on the Copper River Highway, paddling placid waters into stunningly beautiful marsh lands, perhaps headed for the Tiedeman Forest Service Cabin for a few days. Taking the "Wrong Way" route that starts a couple of miles up the road, you can float several miles of challenging water down to McKinley Lake, stay at the Forest Service cabin, and then float downstream again to the slough launch, back at the road. It's ideal overnight, or you could do it in a day, or, as we did, spend an extra day and night at the cabin. The couple who run **Cordova Coastal Outfitters** (see "Out on Prince William Sound," below) rents canoes for $35 a day, offers drop-off, and will help you decide what route to take. You can ride out on one of their bicycles and pick up the canoe already at the launch site. They rent camping gear, too. Make sure to get their advice on current conditions before setting out on the water.

FISHING   Anglers can fish the delta's lakes and streams for all species of Pacific salmon except kings (which you can fish in saltwater), as well as Dolly Varden char and rainbow and cutthroat trout. The Cordova Ranger Station can offer guidance or contact the Cordova office of the **Alaska Department of Fish & Game** (© 907/ 424-3213; www.adfg.state.ak.us, click on "Sport Fisheries," then the Southcentral region, then "Prince William Sound Area"). See "Fishing" in chapter 2 for general guidance.

HIKING   The Forest Service maintains several trails on the delta. The **Alaganik Slough Boardwalk** and **Saddlebag Glacier Trail** are mentioned on p. 336. The Copper River beaches make for sublime off-trail hikes. The **Haystack Trail,** starting on the right just past the 19-mile marker on the highway, climbs through mossy rainforest from the delta's floor onto an odd little hill. The glaciers that once covered the delta spared this bedrock outcropping. The trail is steep in places but only three-quarters of a mile in length, and it leads to an overlook. The **McKinley Lake Trail,** at mile 21.6 on the highway, leads 2.5 miles through rainforest vegetation to a lake bearing trout (though we got no bites) and a little further to the overgrown ruins of a gold mine. You can also get there by canoe (see above). There are two Forest Service cabins on the trail, the small McKinley Trail Cabin, near the highway, and the McKinley Lake Cabin, beautifully situated among big trees above the lake. Each costs $35 a night and can be reserved through the national system described on p. 271. You can also join a guided glacier hike or ice climb with Alaska River Expeditions (see "Rafting," below).

RAFTING   The immense quantity of water draining the Wrangell–St. Elias Mountains through the Copper River Delta, and the Copper River Highway that provides river access, make this a perfect venue for rafting. **Alaska River Expeditions** (© **800/ 776-1864** or 907/424-7238; www.alaskarafters.com) is well regarded by locals. Their diverse territory means they can offer quite a range of trips, from easy floating to whitewater, or even rafting right in front of the Childs Glacier. Trips range in duration from half- to multiday. A 4½-hour trip is $85 for adults, $65 for children ages 6 to 12; all day, with flightseeing, is $275. They guide glacier hikes, ice climbing, and mountain biking, too.

OUT ON PRINCE WILLIAM SOUND

The waters of Prince William Sound around Cordova, although lacking the tidewater glaciers found in the western sound, are protected and rich in marine life. Sea otters don't receive a second glance from locals, congregating in rafts of many dozens or even hundreds. Sea lions can be found predictably, too, and orcas and humpback whales are not out of the ordinary. Bird-watchers can expect harlequin ducks and many other marine birds.

Cordova Coastal Outfitters is a good place to start for any outdoor activities (© **800/357-5145** or 907/424-7424; www.cordovacoastal.com). Andy Craig and Seawan Gehlbach know the equipment, the skills, and the area, and they convey that knowledge with casual enthusiasm. Their office is south of the boat harbor, between the Alaska Commercial grocery store and Baja Taco. They guide sea kayaking, rent kayaks, and offer water taxi drop-off for kayakers. The **guided sea-kayaking trip** for beginners lasts 4 hours and costs $75, concentrating on wildlife sightings; a 7-hour guided trip is $125, including lunch. An advantage of planning your kayaking here is that there is plenty to see near the harbor and not much boat traffic. If your group isn't up to kayaking, consider renting a motorboat. You won't believe the sense of freedom you feel clearing the harbor breakwater to explore Orca Inlet and the bays of Hawkins Island, on the far side. Boats rent for $150 a day, fishing gear extra.

Several vessels are available for fishing charters or day trips to see whales and other wildlife. The chamber of commerce (p. 333) has links to charter operators on its website, or call them for a referral.

WHERE TO STAY

The Northern Nights Inn ★★ (Value) Our family spent a week here, and the visit was supremely relaxing and pleasant, both because of the wonderful hospitality and a big apartment-style room that fit our six perfectly. Cordova is so safe the kids were able to walk out the front door and explore on their own—they couldn't believe it. Each room has been lovingly renovated, with antiques, reproductions, and quilts. They're generally spacious, some have views, and all are loaded with amenities—an almost unreal value. All but one has a full kitchen, and breakfast supplies are provided. The inn is Becky Chapek and Bill Myers's historic 1906 house, a couple of blocks above the town's main street. Becky loves to talk and share her enthusiasm for Cordova, and you couldn't start with a better person for figuring out what you want to do. She also rents older model vehicles that are OK to drive on the Copper River Highway out to Childs Glacier.

500 3rd St. (P.O. Box 1564), Cordova, AK 99547. © **907/424-5356.** Fax 907/424-3291. www.northernnightsinn.com. 5 units. $75–$95 double. Extra adult $10. Children stay free in parent's room. AE, DISC, MC, V. **Amenities:** Free bike loan; car rental; babysitting; free laundry machines. *In room:* TV/VCR and HBO, fridge, coffeemaker, hair dryer, iron, microwave, Wi-Fi.

Orca Adventure Lodge ✱   A picturesque old cannery north of town was renovated into simple guest rooms with private bathrooms (no phones or TVs, however) while retaining the exterior and muscular ambience that made it attractive in the first place. But it's the location and the activities here that make the place special: It's set on a gravel beach with a dock where sea kayaks, fishing boats, and floatplanes pick up guests, and where thousands of pink salmon spawn in a small creek. In the late winter, helicopters land on the grounds to carry guests to ski in the vast and trackless Chugach Mountains. Guests can use the place as a hotel paying the regular nightly rates listed below, or come with a package, which includes all meals and outdoor equipment, such as kayaks, bikes, and fishing poles (guiding is extra), for $145 per person per day.

2500 Orca Rd. (P.O. Box 2105) Cordova, AK 99574. ✆ **866/424-ORCA** or 907-424-7249. www.orcaadventure lodge.com. 34 units. Summer $140 double, $175 suite; winter $95 double, $110 suite. **Amenities:** Restaurant.

Reluctant Fisherman Inn ✱✱   Once among Alaska's best, this hotel fell on hard times and closed—a blow like the loss of a vital organ for the town—but a commercial fishing family with three generations of history in Cordova took over and poured money and effort into reviving the place. The sale of Greg Meyer and Sylvia Lange's fishing assets became a new roof, snow white comforters in all the rooms, a new deck with a teak railing, a renovated kitchen, and even four new furnaces. The location certainly justifies the effort, overlooking the boat harbor at the heart of the town, as does the comfortable yet historic feel of the property. The rooms have the look of an upscale hotel, with great views on the water side. A bar and grill serves casual lunches and dinners every day, and a continental breakfast is provided to guests in the lobby.

407 Railroad Ave. (P.O. Box 150), Cordova, AK 99574. ✆ **877/770-3272** or 907/424-3272. Fax 907/424-7465. www. reluctantfisherman.com. 40 units. High season $100–$150 double, $210 suite; low season $85–$120 double, $160 suite. $10 each additional adult. Children free to age 18. Rates include continent breakfast. AE, MC, V. **Amenities:** Restaurant; bar; airport shuttle ($10); guest coin-operated laundry Internet station; fish cleaning station; fish freezing. *In room:* TV w/HBO, Wi-Fi.

CAMPING

Alaska River Expeditions (✆ **800/776-1864** or 907/424-7238; www.alaskarafters. com) offers a campground with 20 sites, some with hookups, at mile 12.5 of the Copper River Highway. It has pit toilets and an office to check in.

WHERE TO DINE

Some of Cordova's best meals, breakfast, lunch, or dinner, come from **Baja Taco** (✆ **907/424-5599**), near the south end of the boat harbor. The kitchen and espresso machine are in an old bus, with a window for ordering, and there are comfortable indoor and outdoor seating areas for diners, with free Wi-Fi. The salmon tacos are exceptional, and all the meals are tasty and generous. The restaurant serves wine and both Alaskan and Mexican beer. The proprietor, who lives in Baja in the winter, operates here May through September.

Ambrosia, at 410 1st St, (✆ **907/424-7175**) is a solid standby, a well-run family restaurant in a light storefront with an extensive menu, including pizza. It's the kind of place that stays in business in a small town: The food is reliable, the portions large, and the service friendly and helpful. My children became addicted to the gooey fettuccine alfredo with chicken. The restaurant serves beer and wine. Prices range from $10 to $21. Hours are Monday through Saturday 4 to 10pm.

The primary small-town eat-and-meet place is the vegetarian-friendly **Killer Whale Cafe** (© **907/424-7733**), on 1st Street. All-day breakfast includes a selection of omelets, and for lunch there are sandwiches in the $8 to $11 range, including salmon and halibut, burgers, and the like. Besides the expected, the cafe serves salmon cakes and smoothies. Hours are Monday through Saturday 7am to 3pm, Sunday breakfast only 8am to 1pm. They take Visa and MasterCard.

The Denali National Park Region

Denali (Den-*al*-ee) stands alone among the national parks: It gives regular people easy access to real wilderness, with sweeping tundra vistas, abundant wildlife, and North America's tallest mountain. Other wilderness areas in Alaska may have equally inspiring scenery and even more animals, but Denali is unique because of its accessibility to visitors—and because that accessibility hasn't spoiled the natural experience, as it has at so many other parks.

It's a sad truth that even the largest national parks in the Lower 48 are too small to comprise complete ecosystems. The dream of leaving nature undisturbed is essentially lost in those places and only through human intervention do the natural systems within the parks stay as close to their primeval state as they do (this is demonstrated by the efforts of Yellowstone rangers to drive bison back within park boundaries so they won't come to harm outside). Millions of cars driving through the parks further interfere with nature. At Rocky Mountain National Park, there's a crossing guard for bighorn sheep. Yosemite Valley and Grand Canyon Village can be choked with cars in summer, yet attempts to get rid of the cars have so far been thwarted.

On the other end of the spectrum, Alaska has many parks with immense, intact ecosystems that have remained unchanged, still existing as they did before the first white contact. More than two-thirds of America's national park acreage is in Alaska, taking in inconceivably huge swaths of land without roads, buildings, or landing strips. They're natural, all right, but almost no one goes there. Some of these parks receive a few hundred visitors a year—only the indigenous people of the surrounding villages and the hardiest and wealthiest outdoors people. Just chartering a plane to get to some of these places can cost as much as most people spend on their entire vacations. With so many people on the earth, wilderness survives only when it's rationed somehow. In most of Alaska, the rationing system is simply the expense and difficulty of getting to the wilds.

At Denali, on the other hand, you can see the heart of the park for little more than it would cost for you to visit Yellowstone. And when you get there, it's a pristine natural environment where truly wild animals live in a nearly complete ecosystem without much human interference. A single National Park Service decision makes this possible: The only road through the park is closed to the public. This means that to get into the park, you must ride a bus over a dusty gravel road hour after hour, but it also means that the animals are still there to watch and their behavior remains essentially normal. From the window of the bus, you're likely to see grizzly bears doing what they would be doing even if you weren't there. It may be the only $30 safari in the world.

What's even more unique is that you can get off the bus pretty much whenever

---

Tips **Denali Changes**

A massive round of changes to the main Denali National Park visitor area is complete, but work farther inside the park continues. The Eielson Visitor Center, 65 miles within the park, is closed for reconstruction. A larger building is scheduled to open in 2008. During the project, shuttle buses that normally turn around at Eielson have turned around a few miles short of there, at Fish Creek Turnaround, at mile 63. An information center, bookstore, and bus dispatch operate out of tents at Toklat Visitor Contact Center, Mile 53, with all buses stopping for a 30-minute break. Upon completion of the reconstruction, buses will turn around at the new visitor center instead. Big projects can be delayed, however, so visitors will need to check for arrangements.

---

you want to, walk across the tundra, out of sight of the road, and be alone in this wilderness. Unfortunately, many Denali visitors never take the opportunity, which normally would cost a lot of money or require a lot of muscle and outdoor skill. Being alone under God's big sky makes many people nervous. Most people have never been entirely away from other people, much less apart from anything people have made. But that's the essence of Alaska—learning, deep down, how big creation is and how small you are, one more mammal on the tundra under the broad sky. At Denali, you can experience that wonder, and then, when you're ready to return to civilization, you can just walk to the road and catch the next bus—they come every half-hour.

The Denali experience spreads beyond the park. After all, the park boundary is an artificial line—the wildlife and the scenery of the Alaska Range don't observe its significance. To the east, the **Denali Highway** runs through the same extraordinary terrain, with opportunities for hiking over the tundra and canoeing on the lakes managed by the Bureau of Land Management. To the south, **Denali State Park** and the town of **Talkeetna** provide another vantage on Mount McKinley, with the advantage of salmon fishing in the rivers. The construction of comfortable new lodges

and a variety of good outdoor guides have helped make Talkeetna a popular alternative gateway to Denali. Even though it's 150 miles from the park entrance by car, Talkeetna is physically closer to the mountain than is the park headquarters.

Visitors often skip the area's other attractions, however, and focus on **Mount McKinley,** which, at 20,320 feet, is the tallest mountain in North America. It is an impressive peak, but you don't need to go to the park to see it—in fact, most people who do go *don't* see it. Summer weather patterns usually sock in the mountain by midafternoon, at least as seen from the ground in the park.

Unfortunately, Denali has become a thing people feel they must do, and seeing Mount McKinley is a thing they must do when they visit Denali. Many package tours rush through the park so quickly it becomes a blur outside a window rather than an experience. If they miss the mountain, passengers may wonder why they traveled so far to stay at a hotel in the developed area near the park's entrance and ride on a bus over a bumpy road. A friend swears she overheard a tourist ask, as she boarded the train leaving Denali, "Why did they put the park way out here in the boondocks?"

The answer is there for you to find, at the bottom of the steps of the shuttle bus door.

1 Planning a Visit to the Park

ORIENTATION

Denali National Park and Preserve is rock- and ice-robed in tundra and stands of stunted black spruce, a huge slice of the Alaska Range that stands like a pivot in the center of Alaska. It encompasses 6 million acres, a roughly triangular polygon about 20% larger than Massachusetts. The only park entrance is 237 miles north of Anchorage and 120 miles south of Fairbanks on the paved George Parks Highway or the Alaska Railroad. Although **Mount McKinley** is visible from as far away as Anchorage, you can't see it at all from the park entrance (where you will find the railroad depot and all services accessible by private vehicle) because it's on the far side of the park. A mile north of the park entrance on the Parks Highway, along a cliff-sided canyon of the Nenana River, is **Glitter Gulch,** the local term for the seasonal roadside strip that's home to hotels and restaurants (boosters call it the **Nenana Canyon Area**). Other services are at **Carlo Creek,** 13 miles south on the Parks Highway; at another roadside development 7 miles south of the park entrance; and in the year-round town of **Healy,** 12 miles north of the park entrance. From the park entrance, a road accessible only by shuttle bus leads west 89 miles through the park, past a series of campgrounds and a visitor center, and ends at the **Kantishna district,** a patch of park-surrounded private land with wilderness lodges.

WHEN TO GO & HOW FAR AHEAD TO PLAN

Crowding is relative. Once you're out in the park, Denali is never crowded. The bottleneck created by the shuttle and tour bus system, which prevents vehicles from entering the heart of the park, protects it from overuse. What makes the July to mid-August season difficult is getting through that bottleneck from the crowded park entrance into the wilderness. At that time, travelers who just show up at the visitor center without any reservations might have to spend a day or two outside the park before they can get a desirable shuttle bus seat, a campground site, or a backcountry permit.

The flow of visitors varies greatly from year to year. After dropping for 4 years, it has been quite busy for the last few. Some years, you needed to make **reservations** by March for a July visit; other years, a few weeks of advance planning has been enough. To be on the safe side, get your shuttle tickets and campsites as soon as you know the dates of your visit. Lodgings also get tight in July but are not as critical to the success of your visit. Reserve as far ahead as you can, but don't worry about getting stuck in a dive if you don't get your first choice of rooms or cabins, as there are few really bad places near the park.

Summer residents come to the park beginning in early May, when snow remains; they migrate south again in mid- to late September, when winter is closing in. In the off season, fewer than 200 residents stay in the area, and sled-dog-driving rangers patrol the backcountry. The shuttle bus system doesn't begin operation until the last week of May; going any earlier is inadvisable and even early June can be iffy. The visitor season gets into high gear in mid-June and starts to wind down in mid-August. There are several weeks of relative quiet, reduced hotel prices, and easy reservations at the end of the season, a wonderful time to go to Denali. The weather gets nippy at night, and there can be surprise snowfalls, but rain is less likely, and the trees and tundra turn wonderful colors. By early September visitors are few. By mid-September the shuttle buses stop operating and private cars can drive on the park road for a few days—the park service holds a lottery in July to determine who will get that treat.

Another way to avoid the crowds is to book a stay in a **wilderness lodge.** Lodges in Kantishna, listed in section 10 of this chapter, have the right to carry clients to their businesses over the park road in buses and vans, avoiding the bottleneck.

SAMPLE ITINERARIES

The more you're willing to rough it, the closer you can get to the real Denali. There are no hotels inside the park.

THE HOTEL STAY ITINERARY

Drive to the park or arrive by train and choose accommodations near the park—shuttles and courtesy vans can get you around. Visit the exhibits at the Denali Visitor Center, attend a ranger talk, see the *Cabin Nite* dinner-theater show, or go on a short nature walk around the park hotel in the evening. Get to bed early, and the next morning take a shuttle bus before 7am into the park to see the terrain and animals, and possibly to get a view of the mountain. By late morning you'll be at a point with a commanding view of McKinley (in good weather). Now ride partway back toward the entrance before getting off the bus at a place of your choosing for a walk and to eat the bag lunch you've brought along with you (pack out all trash, of course), or take one of the National Park Service guided walks. After enjoying the wilderness for a few hours, head back on the bus, finishing a long day back at the hotel. The next day, try an educational program at the Murie Science and Learning Center or take a rafting ride, a flightseeing trip, or another activity near the park entrance before driving onward or reboarding the train.

THE FAMILY CAMPING ITINERARY

Arrive at the park entrance by car with your camping gear and food for a couple of nights. (You can rent the camping gear and car in Anchorage or Fairbanks.) Camp that evening at the Riley Creek Campground near the visitor center. Enjoy the evening ranger program, see the exhibits at the visitor center, take a nature walk, or go straight to a campsite farther within the park (either way, you'll need to reserve well ahead). The next day, catch a shuttle bus to get deeper into the park for sightseeing and hiking. If you have another day after that within the park, you can do more hikes and have the cushion of a weather day. Add a rafting excursion at the park entrance before driving on, if you like, and possibly a night in a hotel with a soft bed and your very own bathroom.

THE BACKCOUNTRY CAMPING ITINERARY

Arrive by train, bus, or car with your backpack, camping gear, and food for at least several days' hiking. Go immediately to the Backcountry Information Center to orient yourself to the backcountry permit process, buy the information you need for your trek (see section 4 of this chapter), and choose the unit area that looks most promising. Backcountry permits cannot be reserved in advance; you can apply for them in person only at the center 2 days in advance, and they go fast. If you're lucky, permits will be left for the day after you arrive; more likely, you'll need to camp for a night nearby and arrive at the visitor center by the 9am opening (in high season) to get your permit for the following day. Now you've got another day to wait; if you've reserved a shuttle-bus seat, you can get a preview of the park and see some wildlife. The next morning you can start your backcountry hike, taking the camper bus to your unit, and then traveling for up to 2 weeks in a huge area of wilderness reserved almost exclusively for your use.

Denali National Park

ACCOMMODATIONS ■
Camp Denali/North Face Lodge **1**
Cedar Hotel at Denali Grizzly
  Bear Resort **17**
Denali Bluffs Hotel **27**
Denali Cabins **17**
Denali Crow's Nest Log Cabins **25**
Denali Grizzly Bear Cabins
  and Campground **17**
Denali Mountain Morning
  Hostel and Lodge **19**
Denali Princess Lodge **24**
Denali River Cabins **16**
Dome Home B&B **14**
Earthsong Lodge **14**
Kantishna Roadhouse **1**
McKinley Chalet Resort **23**
McKinley Creekside Cabins **20**
McKinley RV and Campground **12**
Motel Nord Haven **13**
The Perch **21**
Riley Creek Campground **28**
Sanctuary River Campground **9**
Savage River Campground **10**
Teklanika River Campground **8**
Touch of Wilderness B&B **14**
Wonder Lake Campground **3**

229 Parks Restaurant and
  Tavern **18**

ATTRACTIONS ●
Eielson Visitor Center **4**
Mt. Healy **22**
Polychrome Pass **6**
Sable Pass **7**
Toklat River **5**
Wonder Lake **3**

DINING ◆
Black Diamond Grill **11**
Bub's Subs **26**
Courtyard Cafe **23**
Denali Salmon Bake **26**
King Salmon Restaurant **24**
Lynx Creek Pizza **26**
Nenana View Bar and Grill **23**
The Overlook Bar and Grill **25**
The Perch/Panorama Pizza Pub **21**

The Denali Highway: The Drivable Denali

From Cantwell, 27 miles south of the Denali National Park entrance, the Denali Highway leads 133 miles east to another tiny village, Paxson, on the Richardson Highway. The little-known road is a lesson in how labels influence people. It runs due east from the Denali National Park border, a natural extension of the park over the Alaska Range, with scenery that's equal to and in some ways more impressive than the park's. Yet without the national park name the terrain along the Denali Highway is comparatively little used.

The Bureau of Land Management (BLM) controls the land along the Denali Highway and it's pretty much open for any recreational activity. Much of the highway passes through high, alpine terrain, with views that extend infinitely and good chances of seeing caribou, moose, and black and grizzly bears. At **Maclaren Pass**, at 4,086 feet, you stand in high Alaska Range terrain of tundra and rock, with views of Maclaren Glacier. The land invites you to walk at least a little way out across it. The **Tangle Lakes** are perfect canoeing waters, where you can see an extraordinary variety of waterfowl, including trumpeter swans, sandhill cranes, and loons. **Tangle River Inn,** at mile 20 (© **907/822-3970**; www.tangleriverinn.com), rents canoes for $5 an hour or $35 for 24 hours.

Simply **driving** the road is an experience. If you're traveling to Denali National Park from Anchorage or Fairbanks, consider making a return trip via the Denali Highway and Richardson Highway. But check out road conditions first. The road is gravel and sometimes in poor condition. Consult the Alaska Department of Transportation's **road condition hot line** (© **511;** http://511.alaska.gov). When the road is good, you can cover its length in less than 4 hours. Two agencies that rent cars and RVs for use on these gravel highways are listed under "Equipped for the Back Roads" on p. 395. Most companies don't allow their vehicles on the Denali. For the adventurous, **biking** the road is one of the best ways to see it. Trails and remote roads from the highway offer some exceptional mountain-biking and hiking routes, especially in the Tangle Lakes National Register Archaeological District.

Lodgings on the highway are limited to a few small roadhouses. At mile 42, the friendly **Maclaren River Lodge** (© **907/822-5444;** www.maclaren lodge.com) makes a welcome break with good basic food from the grill and boat tours on the river. Check the cabins before deciding on a night's stay; although inexpensive and clean, they are definitely no-frills. One reportedly has a ghost. The BLM maintains **campgrounds** at Brushkana Creek and Tangle Lakes, and you can camp anywhere you want outside a campground.

For more details, get the BLM's *Denali Highway Points of Interest* road guide and its *Trail Map and Information Guide to the Tangle Lakes Archaeological District.* They're available at the Alaska Public Lands Information Centers in Fairbanks, Anchorage, or Tok, or directly from the BLM's Glennallen Field Office (p. 423), where rangers can give advice on a Denali Highway trip. The agency also has a website devoted to the highway at www.blm.gov/ak/st/en/fo/gdo/0.html.

THE KANTISHNA WILDERNESS LODGE ITINERARY

For those who can afford it, this may be the best way to see Denali. The lodge will drive you through the park and you'll immediately be away from the crowds in remote territory. The lodges all have activities and guides to get you out into the wilderness.

THE TALKEETNA OPTION

Drive or take the train only as far as Talkeetna, about 110 miles north of Anchorage, and board a flightseeing plane from there to the park, perhaps landing on a glacier on Mount McKinley. You'll stand a better chance of seeing the mountain than anyone else, since the weather tends to be better on the south side and you can fly above most clouds. You'll also save yourself hours of driving to the park and the bus ride into the park, and you'll have the pleasure of staying in a town with some character, unlike the park entrance area. If you want the on-the-ground wildlife-viewing opportunities that can be had only in the park, you can fly from Talkeetna for the day, for a price. (See section 11 of this chapter for more information.)

2 Park Essentials

VISITOR INFORMATION

Getting the information you need to plan your visit is especially important at Denali because of the need for advance reservations.

The most important resource for setting up a trip is the concessionaire: **Doyon/ARAMARK Joint Venture,** 241 W. Ship Creek Ave., Anchorage, AK 99501 (© **800/622-7275** or 907/272-7275; fax 907/258-3668; www.reservedenali.com). The concession is operated by a joint venture of ARAMARK, which manages affairs at many parks around the country, and the Doyon Native Corporation of Interior Alaska. They handle the reservations system for the campgrounds and shuttle buses, as well as several hotels, bus tours, a rafting operation, and a dinner theater. The best place to make in-person contact with the concessionaire is at the reservation and ticketing desks in the **Wilderness Access Center,** on the Denali Park Road, half a mile from the park entrance. The access center is open from mid-May to mid-September daily from 5am to 7pm; it's closed October through April. You can even buy an espresso inside to drink while you stand in line. Since there's no park entrance station, this center is also a good stop for the park map, a copy of the *Alpenglow* park newspaper, and other handouts. A small store offers a limited selection of conveniences and camping supplies, including hiking boots.

The **National Park Service** can be reached at P.O. Box 9, Denali National Park, AK 99755 (© **907/683-2294;** www.nps.gov/dena). Make contact in person at the spectacular **Denali Visitor Center,** near the railroad depot at mile 1.5 of the park road on the right side. It is open summer daily 9am to 6pm. Find more on park service educational facilities under "Learning About the Park," p. 361.

Besides the centers at the park and the website, you can get park information on the way there at the interagency **Alaska Public Lands Information Centers** in Anchorage, Fairbanks, and Tok, listed in chapters 6 and 10. The park's nonprofit publishing arm is the **Alaska Natural History Association,** Denali Branch, P.O. Box 230, Denali National Park, AK 99755 (© **907/683-1272** summer, 907/683-1258 off season; www.alaskanha.org). They operate the shops in the park visitor centers, and you can use their website to order books and maps before coming.

THE RESERVATIONS SYSTEM

Here's the system for reserving shuttle-bus tickets and sites at the developed campgrounds. This section may look long, but paying attention to the details of the reservations system greatly improves your chances of a good visit to the park. (The backcountry permit system is covered in section 4 of this chapter.)

FOR ADVANCE RESERVATIONS

Sixty-five percent of shuttle-bus seats and all campground sites (except Sanctuary and Igloo) are offered for booking by Internet, telephone, fax, or mail; the balance is held back for walk-ins up to 2 days before the trip. Use the Doyon/ARAMARK Joint Venture information above under "Visitor Information."

Reservations by Internet or mail open for the whole summer on December 1 of the preceding year. Reservations by phone open in mid-February. Lines are answered daily from 7am to 5pm Alaska time (remember, that's 4 hours earlier than Eastern Standard Time, where the hours would be 11am to 9pm). By using the Internet (www.reserve denali.com), you can get a big jump on those who call for reservations. The site has been redesigned and is easy to use. You will need a Visa, MasterCard, American Express, or Discover Card. You can also pay by check if you're reserving by phone or mail; payment is due within 10 days. But this option is not available within 30 days of the date you are arriving. It's also possible to reserve by fax, but I'm unable to think of a reason for doing so.

A **confirmation** will be sent out within 2 days of making the reservation. Take it to the "will call" desk at the Wilderness Access Center or to the camping check-in desk at the Riley Creek Merchantile, near the Riley Creek Campground, exchanging the confirmation for a camping permit and bus ticket. The center closes at 7pm and the Merchantile closes at 11pm. If you'll be even later, call © **907/683-9274** to avoid losing your site or shuttle seat.

FOR WALK-INS

Internet, mail, and fax orders are not accepted the day before the visit starts (in fact, they're mostly sold out weeks earlier), but walk-in reservations begin 2 days out, offering 35% of the shuttle-bus seats that are held back and any leftover car-camping sites (usually none), and all sites at Sanctuary and Igloo campgrounds. (Igloo is currently closed, but may reopen.) If it's a busy time of year, desirable shuttle reservations are snapped up early in the day. That means you may not get a good reservation for the day of your arrival or even the day after, only the next day after that. That's why it's so critical to reserve in advance.

On the other hand, don't despair if you arrive without reservations, as the flow of visitors rises and falls unpredictably. It's perfectly possible that you'll walk into the visitor center and get a shuttle seat on the same day.

FEES

Park entrance fees are $20 per vehicle (up to eight passengers) or $10 per person, good for 7 days. There is no entrance station to collect the fee, but it is automatically added to your bill when you make shuttle or campground reservations. If you have one of the national passes for senior citizens, those with disabilities, or frequent park users (now called the "America the Beautiful—National Park and Federal Recreational Lands Pass," p. 51) mention it when you reserve to get your discount. Entrance fees are in place year-round and are collected at the Murie Science and Learning Center during winter months.

Campground fees are $16 to $20 per night for car or RV camping, $12 for walk-in tent camping sites at Riley Creek Campground, and $9 at Sanctuary Campground and Igloo Campground (if open). A reservation fee of $4 is charged for the first night of stays in campgrounds other than Riley Creek and Savage River. (See "Where to Stay," later in the chapter for more particulars.) **Bus fees** are listed in the chart "Denali Park Road Bus Facts," in section 3 of this chapter. A $4 fee is charged for canceling or changing a campsite or bus ticket, except for free children's tickets. You can cancel until 5pm for campground reservations or 2 hours before departure for shuttle tickets. Tundra Wilderness Tour reservations can be canceled only 7 days or more in advance.

GETTING THERE
BY TRAIN
The **Alaska Railroad** (© **800/544-0552** or 907/265-2494; www.alaskarailroad.com) pioneered tourism to the park before the George Parks Highway was built in 1972. In summer, trains leave both Anchorage and Fairbanks daily at 8:15am, arriving at the park from Anchorage at 3:45pm and from Fairbanks at noon, crossing and going on to the opposite city for arrival at 8pm in each. The basic fare from Anchorage to Denali is $135 one-way for adults, from Fairbanks $59, half price for children ages 2 to 11, free under 2. First-class "Gold Star" seats are $59 more per leg. Descriptions of the different classes of service are below under "Train Choices." The train also stops in Wasilla and Talkeetna; see the website for details. The full train runs only from mid-May to mid-September, with somewhat lower fares in the first and last few weeks of the season. During the winter, the Alaska Railroad runs a single passenger car from Anchorage to Fairbanks and back once a week—a truly spectacular, truly Alaskan experience.

BY CAR
Renting a car and driving from Anchorage or Fairbanks is far cheaper and far faster than taking the train. It's easy to average 65 mph on a good two-lane highway, making the drive about 4½ hours from Anchorage and 2½ hours from Fairbanks. (The train averages 40 mph and takes 7½ hr to get from Anchorage to Denali.) Many of the views along the **Parks Highway** are equal to the views on the train, but large stretches, especially in the Matanuska and Susitna valleys, near Anchorage, have been spoiled by ugly roadside development (which you don't see from the train). A long but spectacular detour around the mess leads through **Hatcher Pass** on a mountainous gravel road open only in the summer (see "Through Hatcher Pass," in section 10 of chapter 6). Farther north from Anchorage, the Parks Highway passes through **Denali State Park.** If the weather's clear, you can see Mount McKinley from the pullouts there. The state park also contains several campgrounds, public-use cabins, hiking trails, and a veterans' memorial. Byers Lake is a nice stop with a good campground and with canoe and kayak rental from **Denali Southside River Guides** (© **877/425-7238;** www.denaliriverguides.com)—the company also offers guided river rafting, kayaking, and fly-fishing. The park has a visitor contact station at the memorial, at mile 147. For information before you go, contact the **Mat-Su Area Park Headquarters** (© **907/745-3975;** www.alaskastateparks.org, click on "Individual Parks"). From Fairbanks, the drive is pleasant but rarely spectacular. Allow an hour to stop in the quaint, riverside town of Nenana, where you can see an old railroad depot museum (p. 388).

Tips Train Choices

Alaska Railroad executives know that their fares are high for a simple ride to Denali. As one told me, "We're selling entertainment," and that's how you should judge your choices. So, to review the entertainment: All the cars are luxurious, and some are grand and highly memorable; the rail line follows a historic, unspoiled route through beautiful countryside; there's a good chance of seeing moose and caribou; the commentary by well-trained Alaska high-school students is fresh and engaging; and the food is good. There are disadvantages, too. The train is very expensive. You can rent a small car for a week for the same price as one round-trip on the train. It's slow, adding 3 hours to a trip from Anchorage to the park, and when it's late, it can be very late. And, once you arrive, you have to rely on shuttles and courtesy vans to get around outside the park.

After you decide to ride the train, you have to choose which part of the train. One set of Alaska Railroad locomotives pulls the Alaska Railroad cars and other sets of cars with full glass domes owned by cruise lines, two of which have seats for independent travelers (although 90% or more are filled with their older cruise-ship customers). **Princess Cruises and Tours** (© 800/426-0500; www.princesslodges.com) has tall, all-dome cars with table seating upstairs and dining rooms downstairs; there's plenty of head room and large balconies at the ends of the cars on the lower deck where you can ride outdoors. **Gray Line of Alaska Package Tours,** a part of Holland America (© 800/544-2206 or 907/277-5581; www.graylinealaska.com), has newer cars that are even better than Princess's. They're huge and comfortable, with all seats facing forward upstairs—an advantage over table seating—and dining rooms below that are large enough so only two seatings are needed for each meal. (All meals are served at assigned seatings in the cruise-line cars.)

The **Alaska Railroad** offers two classes of service. The basic service is in traditional railroad cars. They're clean and have big windows and forward-facing seats. Passengers stroll around and dine when and how they please rather than at assigned seatings. Old-fashioned VistaDome cars provide a limited but adequate number of shared dome seats. By paying another $59, you can upgrade to "Gold Star" service, with your own full-dome seat for the entire trip on custom-built double-decker cars like the cruise lines', with a sumptuous white-tablecloth dining room downstairs (eat when you like). These are my favorite cars on the train. They're decorated with original fine art and are very luxurious, but you still know you're on a train, not a cruise ship, and you're not treated as a herd animal. Also, the cars have large outdoor vestibules on the upper deck. The views and open air there are incredible.

All passenger seats are assigned on all the cars. You can't walk from one company's cars to another, but you can walk between cars in your own train section. Fares on all three options are similarly high, but they're more advantageously priced as part of lodging and tour packages, which you can buy from the railroad or the cruise lines.

BY BUS

Several van and bus services inexpensively connect Anchorage and Fairbanks to Denali. Most will carry bikes and other gear for an additional fee. **The Park Connection Motorcoach Service** (© **800/266-8625** or 907/245-0200; www.alaskacoach.com) runs big, comfortable coaches to Denali from Seward and Anchorage, with two buses daily in each direction. The Anchorage fare is $79, Seward $135. Children under 12 ride for half price; those 4 and under need a car seat. **Alaska/Yukon Trails** (© **800/770-7275;** www.alaska shuttle.com) offers daily service from Anchorage and Fairbanks, with stops at any other point on the way. The one-way fare is $65 from Anchorage, $46 from Fairbanks.

BY AIR

Talkeetna Aero Services (© **888/733-2899** or 907/683-2899; www.talkeetna-aero.com) offers the only scheduled air service to Denali from their base in Talkeetna, or from Anchorage, in the summer only. The flights are sold as 1-day packages, including flightseeing on the way, a bus tour at the park, a box lunch, and ground transfers. It's the only way to "do" Denali in a day. The package from Anchorage is $495, from Talkeetna $375.

GETTING AROUND

If you take the train or bus, you'll find that most accommodations have arrangements to get you around, although this becomes less convenient as you get farther from the park entrance. Ask how courtesy transportation works when you book your room. There are cabs available, too, but they have been a poor option because of sky-high rates. If you must rely on cabs, get a firm quote when you call. Try **Denali Transportation** (© **877/683-4765** or 907/683-4765). You can also take the train to Denali, rent a car there, and drop it in Fairbanks or Anchorage. **Teresa's Alaskan Car Rentals** (© **907/683-1377;** www.denalicarrental.com) is in Healy.

If you drive to the park, you'll still need to take the shuttle bus, described below, to get into its heart, except under certain circumstances. You can drive past mile 14 on the park road only if you have a 3-day camping permit at Teklanika Campground, 29 miles in; then your vehicle must remain parked at the campground for the entire 3 days. The rules loosen at the end of the season, when winners of a drawing can drive the road for a few days in late September (check with the park service for lottery details). After the permit driving is over, the road is open to anyone as far as mile 30 until the snow flies; then it's maintained only as far as the headquarters, 3 miles from the entrance.

Bicycles have free access to the park road. For that option, see section 5 of this chapter.

FAST FACTS: Denali National Park

Banks There are no banks near the park entrance. A couple of ATMs are in the Glitter Gulch (Nenana Canyon) area, including one at the Lynx Creek Store and Deli. A couple more are at gas stations in Healy, 12 miles north of the park. Do your banking before leaving Anchorage or Fairbanks.

Emergencies © **911** will work inside the park, but be sure to tell the operator you are within Denali National Park. However, cellphone coverage reaches only along the highway and there are no telephones except at the developed areas. Bus drivers on the park road are equipped with radios.

Gear Rental **Denali Mountain Works** ((C) **907/683-1542**; www.akrivers.com), a clothing and outfitting shop, rents binoculars, sleeping bags, tents, backpacks, and stoves. It is right across from the McKinley Chalet Resort. Bikes are for rent at **Denali Outdoor Center** ((C) **888/303-1925** or **907/683-1925**; www.denali outdoorcenter.com); see p. 364.

Hospital The seasonal **Canyon Health Clinic Urgent Care Center** ((C) **907/683-4433**) is among the big hotels near the park entrance. In Healy, 12 miles north of the park entrance, the year-round **Community Interior Health Center** ((C) **907/683-2211**) is open 24 hours a day for emergencies, or normal office hours for nonemergencies. Neither clinic has a full-fledged doctor.

Police The **Alaska State Troopers** ((C) **907/683-2232** or 907/768-2202) have a post in Healy, 12 miles north of the park, and in Cantwell, 28 miles south.

Post Office The post office is just within the park entrance, right before the Riley Creek Campground.

Stores You should do major shopping before leaving Anchorage or Fairbanks, but there are handy little stores at Denali. **Riley Creek Mercantile** ((C) **907/683-9246**) is at the Riley Creek Campground, near the park entrance. It's open daily from 7am to 11pm in the summer. Besides convenience groceries, they have firewood, some basic camping supplies, RV supplies, a dump station, made-to-order sandwiches, Wi-Fi, fax and copy service, binocular rentals, showers, and laundry. In the Glitter Gulch (Nenana Canyon) area across from the McKinley Chalet Resort, the locally owned **Denali General Store** ((C) **907/683-2920**) carries a variety of goods at better prices than in the hotel gift shops, and packs picnics to take along on the shuttle bus ride.

Taxes The local **bed tax** is 7%. There is no sales tax.

3 Denali by Shuttle Bus

Your visit to Denali will likely revolve around a ride on the shuttle bus into the park to see the wildlife and to stop for a walk in the wilderness. Some planning will make it a more successful trip.

CHOOSING YOUR DESTINATION

You can buy shuttle tickets to the Toklat (*Toe*-klat) River, 53 miles into the park; to Fish Creek Turnaround or Eielson Visitor Center (depending on construction at the center), at around 63 or 66 miles, respectively; Wonder Lake, at 85 miles; or Kantishna, at 89 miles (see "Denali Park Road Bus Facts," below for fares). On any day trip, you have to go both ways, so you're in for a long ride. If you don't get off the bus along the way, the round-trip takes 5 hours to Toklat (with a temporary visitor center), nearly 8 hours to Fish Creek Turnaround or Eielson, 11 hours to Wonder Lake, and 12 hours to Kantishna. You must bring your own water and food.

In choosing your destination, you need to balance your stamina, your desire to save time for a day hike, and your desire to see wildlife. There are no firm rules about where wildlife shows up, but my own observations are that in the early morning, you can often see moose on the first part of the road; in midsummer, brown (grizzly) bears seem to appear most in the higher country, beyond Toklat, which also is the best area for caribou; in the fall berry season, the grizzlies show up all along the drive.

The best views of Mount McKinley show up beginning around Highway Pass at the east side of the causeway at about mile 58, beyond Toklat (where the mountain cannot be seen at all). The mountain is most likely to be visible in the morning, as clouds often pile up during the day. Going all the way to Wonder Lake provides more amazing views, including the land-covered Muldrow Glacier and many classic images of Mount McKinley. There's really no reason to go as far as Kantishna unless you are headed to a lodge there (see section 10, "Denali Wilderness Lodges," later). In general, I think Fish Creek Turnaround (or Eielson Visitor Center, when open) is the best destination for most people, offering them the chance to see the mountain and some wildlife while leaving them time to get out and walk (I've included ideas on where to hike later).

You won't be able to time your trip for good weather, as you need to book ahead. But don't despair if it rains—the sun may be out at the other end of the park. The best weather for wildlife sightings is cool, overcast skies without rain. One trick of the system that allows visitors to wait for sun is to stay at Teklanika Campground. If you drive to a campsite there, agreeing to stay for a minimum of 3 nights, you're eligible to buy a special shuttle ticket for $25 for adults, $13 for children ages 15 to 17, free for children under 15, that's good for rides deeper into the park the entire time you're staying at the campground. Wherever you stay, you can buy a three-trip pass for the price of two.

Denali can be a challenge for families. Young children will go nuts on an 8-hour bus ride and often can't pick out the wildlife—this isn't a zoo, and most animals blend in with their surroundings. Older children also have a hard time keeping their patience on these trips, as do many adults. The only solution is to get off the bus and turn your trip into a romp in the heather. When you've had a chance to revive, catch the next bus. Besides, just because you buy a ticket to Wonder Lake doesn't mean that you have to go that far. Keep in mind, too, that if your child normally needs a car seat, you must bring the seat along on the bus.

The park has alternatives to the shuttle bus, with commentary, more comfortable seats, and other amenities. Doyon/ARAMARK Joint Venture operates two narrated

---

(Tips) Bus Concerns & Complaints

The Denali concessionaire uses only school bus–type vehicles for shuttles on the park road, which are not as comfortable as highway motorcoaches and do not have bathrooms onboard. Safety concerns permit only these tough, lightweight buses to operate on the narrow, gravel park road. Some of the Tundra Wilderness Tour buses—unlike the shuttles and camper buses—are tricked out with higher-backed cloth seats and video monitors that allow the driver to zoom in on wildlife, but the basic bus is essentially the same. (I haven't been on these yet, but I have my doubts about going to the park to watch wildlife on a TV screen.) The road itself can be an issue, too. I've heard from visitors complaining of white knuckles on the ride. The buses act a bit like mountain goats on the heights of Polychrome Pass and near Eielson Visitor Center as the road climbs without guardrails. If you're afraid of heights, it might not be to your liking.

bus tours, booked mostly as part of package tours. The **Denali Natural History Tour** provides just a taste of the park, going 17 miles down the park road, but also includes a cultural component, with a film, a history talk at a cabin, and a presentation by an Alaska Native, which could include singing, storytelling, or information about living off the land. The **Tundra Wilderness Tour** goes to Toklat when the mountain is hidden by clouds, and 8 miles farther, across Highway Pass to Stony Hill, when it is visible. Programmed commentary provides background on what you are seeing. Food is provided, but you can't get off the bus along the way (that's the fatal flaw, in my opinion). Two other narrated tours are offered by privately owned lodges in the Kantishna area, at the far end of the park road. **Kantishna Wilderness Trails** (© **800/230-7275** or 907/683-1475; www.seedenali.com) and **Denali Backcountry Adventure** (© **888/ 560-2489** or 907/683-2643) each cover 190 miles in around 13 hours, with a stop halfway through, at the far end, for a meal and gold panning (with either), or a sled-dog demonstration (with Kantishna), or a hike (with Denali Backcountry). Either way, it's a marathon and you can't get off the bus along the way, but there is no other choice for a 1-day, narrated tour that covers the whole road. The cost is $125 to $135 with no discount for children (nor could any kid I know stay sane on a 13-hour bus ride).

GETTING READY

Reserve your shuttle ticket for as early as you can stand to get up in the morning. This strategy will give you more time for day hikes and enhance your chances of seeing the mountain and wildlife. Many animals are more active in the morning, especially on hot days. During peak season, the first bus leaves the visitor center at 5:30am and then one leaves roughly every 15 to 30 minutes in the morning. A few buses leave in the afternoon, mostly to pick up stragglers on the way back, returning late under the midnight sun.

By taking an early bus, you have more time to get off along the way for a hike, walking back to the road, and getting the next bus that comes along with a spare seat. Time it right, and you could have more than 8 hours for hiking plus a tour of most of the park road before returning on a late bus. (To be on the safe side, don't push it to the very last bus.) The sun won't set until after 11pm May through July and it will be light all night. If you need to get back to the park entrance at a certain time, leave yourself plenty of time because after getting off your westbound bus, you can't reserve seats going back the other way, and you may have to wait an hour for a bus with room to take you.

Before you leave for the Wilderness Access Center to get on your shuttle bus, you'll need a packed lunch and plenty of water. You should wear sturdy walking shoes and layers of warm and lighter clothing with rain gear packed, you should have binoculars or a spotting scope at the ready, and you should have insect repellent. You may also want a copy of Kris Capps' worthwhile booklet *Denali Road Guide,* sold at the Denali Visitor Center bookstore and published by the Alaska Natural History Association (ANHA; see "Visitor Information," earlier in section 2). It provides a milepost commentary you can follow as you ride. ANHA also publishes guides to Denali birds, mammals, geology, and trails. If you'll be doing any extensive day hiking, you may also want to bring a detailed topographic map printed on waterproof plastic (published by Trails Illustrated and sold for $9.95 from the visitor center or by ordering from ANHA) as well as a compass; if you're just going to walk a short distance off the road, you won't need such preparations.

Denali Park Road Bus Facts

Note: WAC is Wilderness Access Center. All prices rounded to nearest dollar.

Bus	Purpose	Route	Frequency	Fare
Hotel Courtesy Shuttle	Links Denali Park Resorts (DPR) hotels to park entrance	Hotels 1 mile north and 7 miles south	Continuous loop	Free, even if not staying within park at a DPR hotel
Riley Creek Loop	Links facilities within park entrance area	Visitor facilities, Riley Creek Campground, rail depot	Continuous loop	Free
Savage River Shuttle	Public transport to hiking near the Savage River, which can also be reached by car into the park	From visitor center to Savage River day-use area, about 14 miles	Peak season every hour 9am–9pm	Free
Camper Shuttle (Green Bus)	Access to campgrounds and backpacking beyond the park entrance	From the WAC to Wonder Lake Campground, 85 miles into the park	Several times a day	$29 adults, half price ages 15–17, free 14 and younger
Shuttle bus (or just "the shuttle"; Green Bus)	General access to the park and wildlife viewing; limited commentary, depending on the driver; no food or water	From the visitor center as far as Kantishna, 91 miles away through the park	Every 30 minutes to Fish Creek/Eielson, everyhour to Wonder Lake, 4 times daily Kantishna	$23 to Toklat, $29 to Fish Creek/Eielson, $39 to Wonder Lake, $43 to Kantishna; half price ages 15–17, free 14 and younger
Tundra Wilderness Tour (Tan Bus)	6- to 8-hour guided bus tour with lunch provided; passengers may not get off en route	From the WAC to the Toklat River or Stony Hill, 53–61 miles into the park	Twice daily	$84 adults, half price ages 14 and younger (includes park entrance fee)
Natural History Tour (Tan Bus)	5-hour guided bus tour at the edge of the park	From the WAC 17 miles into the park	Three times daily	$56 adults, half price ages 14 and younger (includes park entrance fee)

> ### ⌐*Tips* **Shuttle-Bus Etiquette**
>
> It's common courtesy on the shuttle bus to yell out when you see wildlife so others can see it, too. The driver will stop and everyone will rush to your side of the bus. After you've had a look, give someone else a chance to look out your window or get a picture. Be quiet and don't stick yourself, your camera, or anything else out of the bus. You will scare away the animals or, worse, help habituate them to humans.

ON YOUR WAY

There are no reserved seats on the bus, but if you arrive early, you can find a place on the left side, which has the best views on the way out. Bus riders often see grizzly bears, caribou, Dall sheep, moose, and occasionally wolves, but, as one driver said, the animals aren't union workers, and it's possible that you won't see any at all. Of course, you have to stay on the bus when animals are present.

The shuttle-bus drivers often offer commentary about the sights on the road, but they aren't required to do so. Some do a great job and some don't say much. The tour bus drivers do a formal presentation, but you can't get off the bus on the way.

A ROAD LOG

Here are some of the highlights along the road (check the visitor center or the park service information handouts to confirm times of the guided walks):

MILE 9   In clear weather, this is the closest spot to the park entrance with a view of Mount McKinley. This section also is a likely place to see moose, especially in the fall rutting season.

MILE 14   At the end of the paved road at the Savage River Bridge, this is generally as far as private vehicles can go. A park service checkpoint stops anyone who doesn't have a proper permit. From the parking lot by the bridge, a simple climb over dry tundra leads to Primrose Ridge, also known as Mount Wright.

MILE 17   The portable toilets here are as far as the Natural History Tour bus goes.

MILE 29   An hour and 10 minutes into the drive, a large rest stop overlooks the Teklanika River, with flush toilets, the last plumbing on the road. The Teklanika, like many other rivers on Alaska's glacier-carved terrain, is a braided river—a stream wandering in a massive gravel streamed that's much too big for it. The braided riverbeds, sometimes miles wide, were created by water from fast-melting glaciers at the end of the last ice age. Each is kept free of vegetation by its river, which constantly changes course as it spreads the debris of rock and dust from the glaciers. Flat plains in glacial terrain usually are laid down by this mechanism.

MILE 34   Craggy Igloo Mountain is a likely place to see Dall sheep. Without binoculars, they'll just look like white dots. Manageable climbs on Igloo, Cathedral, and Sable mountains take off along the road in the section from Igloo Creek to Sable Pass.

MILES 38–43   Sable Pass, a critical habitat area for bears, is closed to people. A half-eaten sign helps explain why. Bears show up here mostly in the fall. This is the start of the road's broad alpine vistas.

MILE 46   Here you'll find the top of 5-mile-wide Polychrome Pass, the most scenic point on the ride, and a toilet break, 2 hours and 25 minutes into the trip. Caribou look like specks when they pass in the great valley below you, known as the Plain of Murie after Adolph Murie, a biologist who pioneered study here and helped develop the park service's scientific ethic (the name does not always appear on maps, however). Note how the mountains of colored rock on either side of the plain match up—they once were connected before glacial ice carved this valley. Huge rocks on its floor are glacial erratics, plucked from the bedrock by moving ice and left behind when the ice melted.

MILE 53   The Toklat River, another braided river, is a flat plain of gravel with easy walking. The glaciers that feed the river are 10 miles upstream; the river bottom is habitat for bears, caribou, and wolves, and a good place for picnics. During construction at Eielson Visitor Center, this has been the main rest area for westbound buses, with all of them stopping for 30 minutes here. If construction is completed on schedule in 2008, the main stop will move there. During the interim, a large tent has housed a station for the National Park Service and a tiny bookstore operated by the Alaska Natural History Association. Doyon/ARAMARK has had a bus dispatch tent where you can ask about changing buses if you want to go back later or continue onward. There is no food or water, but there are outhouses.

MILE 58   Highway Pass is the highest point on the road. In good weather, dramatic views of Mount McKinley start here. The alpine tundra from here to the Eielson Visitor Center is inviting for walking, but beware: Tundra is soft underfoot and can conceal holes and declivities that can twist an ankle.

MILE 62   Stony Hill Overlook is a mountainous highway point with great views of McKinley, 36 miles away. The Tundra Wildlife Tour turns around here on days with good mountain viewing.

MILE 63   Fish Creek Turnaround is where the 8-hour shuttle-bus trip turns around during Eielson Visitor Center reconstruction. There are no facilities.

MILE 64   Thorofare Pass, where the road becomes narrow and winding, is a good area to look for bears and caribou. Bus drivers know best where the animals are on any particular day, since they talk to fellow drivers.

MILE 66   This is the site of the **Eielson Visitor Center,** closed while under reconstruction. Completion of the project is planned for 2008. The site is a fine vantage point for seeing McKinley. Seismic measurements here show frequent small earthquakes accompanying McKinley's prodigious growth—about an inch every 3 years. This region is a jumble of rocks pushed together by the expanding Pacific tectonic plate; the mountain and the whole Alaska Range are folding upward in that great collision.

MILE 68.5   The incredibly rugged terrain to the north is the earth and vegetation covering Muldrow Glacier. The ice extends to McKinley's peak and was an early and arduous route for climbers; these days, they fly to a base camp at a 7,200-foot elevation on the Kahiltna Glacier, on the south side. McKinley's glaciers, falling 15,000 vertical feet and extending up to 45 miles in length, are among the world's greatest. The Ruth Glacier has carved the Great Gorge on the south side, which is almost 6,000 feet deep above the ice and another 4,000 below—almost twice the depth of the Grand Canyon. The park road comes within a mile of the Muldrow's face, then continues through wet,

The Alaska-Ohio Name Game, Round 30

Mount McKinley is so large that Athabascan people speaking different languages had different names for it. The Koyukon, on the north and west, called it Deenaalee, while the Dena'ina and Ahtna on the far side called it Dengadh. In 1839 the name was recorded on a Russian map as Tenada. It often has been translated as "the great one," but a closer translation is the more generic "the high one." The Athabascans never named mountains after people, nor did the Denali area get much use, since fish and game are relatively sparse and the weather extreme, but they did regard high places as spiritually important.

The name McKinley became associated with the mountain in the haphazard way common of the Alaska gold-rush period. A businessman and Princeton graduate named William Dickey was prospecting in the area in 1896, constantly arguing with his traveling companions about the big political issue of the day, the gold monetary standard supported by the Republicans and opposed by the Democrats. The Democratic presidential candidate, William Jennings Bryan, declared at his nomination convention that year, "You shall not crucify mankind upon a cross of gold." It was the gold standard that caused a deflationary economic disaster in those years, which was relieved only by the 1898 Klondike gold rush, which also led to Alaska's settlement. Anyway, when Dickey came out of the Bush, he published a piece about his travels in the *New York Sun* in which he reported his "discovery" and his name for North America's highest mountain—in honor of William McKinley, the Republican candidate who won the White House and was then assassinated. Dickey later admitted he chose the name only to spite his former traveling companions.

Alaskans have long believed McKinley is an irrelevant name for the mountain, especially since it already had a name. In 1975, the state of Alaska petitioned the U.S. Geographic Names Board to change the name back to Denali. In 1980, Congress changed the name of the national park to Denali, but a single congressman from Ohio has blocked changing the name of the mountain itself. McKinley was an Ohio governor and congressman before running for president. Rep. Ralph Regula, a Republican who has represented McKinley's former seat since 1972, and who even attended William McKinley Law School, found a clever maneuver to keep the name on the mountain. The names board has a policy of taking up no issue that is also being considered by Congress. In each Congress since 1977, Regula has introduced a single sentence as a budget amendment or as a standalone bill that states that McKinley is the mountain's permanent name. Although the bill never gets so much as a committee hearing, its existence is enough to invoke the board's policy and prevent it from considering the change.

Alaskans call the mountain Denali anyway and haven't given up on changing its official name. Their chief hope is persistence. Regula can't stay in Congress forever.

This box is largely based on an article from Alaska Magazine, *July 2005, by Peter Porco.*

rolling terrain past beaver ponds, and finally descends into a small spruce patch near mile 82.

MILE 73   Buses to Wonder Lake may use this rest stop. Four chemical toilets are here temporarily.

MILE 86   Wonder Lake campground is the closest road point to Mount McKinley, 27 miles away. Some buses continue another half-hour to Kantishna. The fact that McKinley looks so massive from this considerable distance, dominating the sky, is testament to its stupendous size. You'll likely never see a larger object on this planet. From its base (your elevation here is only 2,000 ft.) to its top is an elevation gain greater than that of any other mountain on Earth. Other mountains are taller overall, but they stand on higher ground.

4 Denali on Foot: Day Hiking & Backpacking
DAY HIKING IN THE BACKCOUNTRY

One of the unique aspects of Denali is the lack of developed trails—you really can take off in any direction. I've covered some of the best hiking areas above, in "A Road Log," including Primrose Ridge, Teklanika River, Igloo and Sable mountains, and the Toklat River. The park service long resisted building any trails, but finally gave in and recognized some trails visitors had created, including those at the Eielson Visitor Center (currently a construction site) and the 2-mile path that leads from the Wonder Lake Campground to the McKinley River Bar, which extends far to the east and west. You can drive or take a free shuttle to the Savage River Day Use Area, at mile 15, which has a 1-mile loop trail and longer, informal routes for great alpine tundra hiking. Kris Capps' *Denali Walks* (ANHA, $7) is a handy Denali hiking guide covering all the trails in the park. No permit is needed for day hiking.

The broad, hard-gravel flats of the **braided riverbeds,** such as the McKinley, Toklat, Teklanika, and Savage, are among the best routes for hiking in the park. **Stony Creek,** leading up a gorge to the north from the road at mile 60, is an excellent walk into the mountains. You can also hike on the tundra, of which there are two varieties: The **wet tundra** lies on top of permanently frozen ground called permafrost; it's mushy, at best, like hiking on foam rubber laid over bowling balls. At worst, it's swamp. **Dry tundra** clothes the mountainsides and generally makes for firmer footing and easier walking. The brush and stunted forest of the region are virtually impenetrable.

The major risks of hiking here relate to the weather and rivers. It can get cold and wet in midsummer, and if you're not prepared with warm, waterproof clothing, you could suffer the spiraling chill of hypothermia. The rivers are dangerous because of their fast flow and icy-cold water. Experienced backcountry trekkers plan their routes to avoid crossing sizable rivers. See the notes on handling river crossings, managing hypothermia, and getting lost in the "Outdoor Health & Safety" section of chapter 2. Bears, which people worry most about, have never killed a Denali visitor. Tips on avoiding them are in chapter 2 and are widely distributed at the park.

For a first foray beyond the trails, consider joining one of the park service guided hikes. One or two daily **Discovery Hikes** take off from the park road. One follows a route well inside the park toward the Eielson Visitor Center, and the other goes nearer to the entrance end of the park. A ranger takes only 15 hikers, leading them into wilderness while teaching them about the nature of the places they visit. Plan a 5- to 11-hour day, including the shuttle ride; actual hiking time is about 4 hours. The hikes

---

Tips **Ranger Programs in the Park**

Check the park newspaper, the *Alpenglow,* for ranger talks and slide shows that happen as often as several times a day in the front-country area (near the entrance) and at the Riley Creek, Savage River, and Teklanika campgrounds.

---

generally are not too strenuous for families with school-age children, although it is wise to inquire how steep it will be if you have any doubts. They cost no more than the price of your shuttle ticket. You need to wear hiking shoes or boots and bring food, water, and rain gear. Reserve a place in advance, as hikes fill up in July and you'll need to know when and where to catch the special bus. Rangers lead other walks, too, although the lineup can change each year. There often is a walk on the short Savage River Loop, 15 miles into the park, and another along the Toklat River, at mile 53. Check with the visitor center for the current offerings and crucial details about which bus to take.

DAY HIKING IN THE PARK ENTRANCE AREA

There are several trails at the park entrance, weaving through the boreal forest around small lakes. Only one strenuous trail leads from the entrance area, but it is a gem. The steep and spectacular hike to the **Mount Healy overlook** is a 5-mile round-trip. The trail breaks through the tree line to slopes of tundra and rock outcroppings, where you can see just how small the pocket of human infestation at the park entrance area is: The Alaska Range and its foothills extend far into the distance. If you continue on an all-day hike right to the top of Mount Healy, you can see all the way to McKinley on a clear day. Several new interpretive trails offer the chance to learn, stroll, or even get somewhere. A new bike and pedestrian trail connects the entrance area, near the Riley Creek Mercantile, to Glitter Gulch, allowing pedestrians to get back and forth without walking on the road. The McKinley Station, Morino, and Spruce Forest trails teach about nature and history. Get the book *Denali Walks,* mentioned in the previous section, to learn more.

BACKPACKING

Imagine backpacking over your own area of wilderness, without trails, limits, or the chance of seeing other people. There's no need to retrace your route to get back: Anywhere you meet the 91-mile Denali Park Road you can catch a bus back to the world of people. Any experienced backpacker should consider a backcountry trek at Denali.

Yes, it can be challenging. Hiking on the tundra, broken-rock mountainsides, and braided rivers is tiring, and it's easy to fall or turn an ankle. You must be prepared for river crossings and cold weather, know how to find your way with a map and compass, and know how to avoid attracting bears. But if you've done a backpacking trip in a less challenging area, you surely can manage it here, so long as you prepare and don't underestimate the additional time you'll need in trail-less terrain. Nor do you need to trek far—you can camp just a few miles off the road and still be in a place that looks like no one has ever been there before.

You must be flexible about where you're going and be prepared for any kind of terrain because you can't choose the backcountry unit you will explore until you arrive at the Backcountry Information Center, adjacent to the Wilderness Access Center, and find out what's available. This information, and a map of the units, is posted on a board at the center. Groups of four or more may have a hard time finding a place to hike, but there's almost always *somewhere* to go. You can reserve permits only 2 days in advance, and you're unlikely to get one for the day you arrive, but you can reserve permits for continuation of your trip for up to 14 days at the same time. The first night of a trip is the hard one to get—for one thing, you can reserve only units that are contiguous to the park road for the first night—but after that, each night gets progressively easier. A couple of rangers are there to help you through the process.

Buy the *Denali National Park and Preserve* **topographical map,** published by Trails Illustrated, available for $10 from the Alaska Natural History Association (ANHA), listed earlier under "Visitor Information." Printed on plastic, the map includes the boundaries of the 43 backcountry units and much other valuable information. Also, you'll want a copy of the *Backcountry Companion* (ANHA, $9), which describes conditions and routes in each area (a new edition is planned for 2008). You'll find it at the visitor center, or you can glance at a well-thumbed copy kept at the backcountry desk.

The alpine units from the Toklat River to Eielson Visitor Center are the most popular. That's where you get broad views and can walk across heathery dry tundra in any direction. But to travel far, even there, you may have to climb over rugged, rocky terrain, and the tundra can be deceptively difficult to walk on—it's soft and hides ankle-turning holes. The wooded units are the least popular, since bushwhacking through overgrown country is anything but fun. The best routes for making time here (and anywhere in the Alaska Bush) are along the braided river valleys and streambeds. Be ready to walk in water. You'll have to take the **camper bus** to get to your backcountry unit, at a cost of $29 for each adult.

Before venturing into the backcountry, everyone is required to watch an **orientation film** covering safety and environmental issues, including how not to attract bears. I've spoken to competent backpackers who considered abandoning their trip because of the severity of the warnings they received about bears. That's unfortunate because sensible people taking normal precautions don't need to worry. The park service provides bear-resistant food containers in which you are required to carry all your food. Guns are not permitted in the park; carrying a pepper spray, such as CounterAssault, for self-defense from bears is allowed. Bear safety is covered in chapter 2 under "Outdoor Health & Safety."

Before you decide to go backpacking at Denali, however, you may want to broaden your thinking—if you're up to a cross-country hike without a trail, there are tens of millions of acres in Alaska available for backpacking that don't require a permit. Check with the Alaska Public Lands Information Center in Anchorage or Fairbanks for ideas about road-accessible dry tundra and other suitable areas on the Denali Highway (see "The Denali Highway: The Drivable Denali," earlier), and on the Dalton Highway and in Wrangell–St. Elias National Park (see chapter 9). I've listed some great trail hikes in chapter 7, under Chugach National Forest, and in chapter 9, in the sections on Chena Hot Springs Road and the Steese Highway.

5 Activities within the Park

LEARNING ABOUT THE PARK

The Denali experience changed significantly with the completion in 2005 of magnificent new educational facilities in the front country. What once was a rudimentary stepping-off point for journeys into the park became something of a destination in itself, with superb exhibits and opportunities to learn about nature.

The 14,000-square-foot **Denali Visitor Center** introduces the park and its connections to the rest of the world in a building that takes stock of its surroundings. The

First to the Top

It's the biggest. That's why climbers risk their lives on Mount McKinley. You can see the mountain from Anchorage, more than 100 miles away. On a flight across Alaska, McKinley stands out grandly over waves of other mountains. It's more than a mile taller than the tallest peak in the other 49 states. It's a great white triangle, always covered in snow, tall but also massive and strong.

The first group to try to climb Mount McKinley came in 1903, led by Judge James Wickersham, who also helped explore Washington's Olympic Peninsula before it became a national park. His group made it less than halfway up, but on the trip they found gold in the Kantishna Hills, setting off a small gold rush that led to the first permanent human settlement in the park area. Wickersham later became the Alaska Territory's nonvoting delegate to Congress and introduced the bill that created the national park, but the government was never able to get back land in the Kantishna area from the gold miners. Today that land is the site of wilderness lodges, right in the middle of the park.

On September 27, 1906, renowned world-explorer Dr. Frederick Cook announced to the world by telegraph that he had reached the summit of Mount McKinley after a lightning-fast climb, covering more than 85 miles and 19,000 vertical feet in 13 days with one other man, a blacksmith, at his side. On his return to New York, Cook was lionized as a conquering explorer and published a popular book of his summit diary and photographs.

In 1909, Cook again made history, announcing that he had beat Robert Peary to the North Pole. Both returned to civilization from their competing treks at about the same time. Again, Cook was the toast of the town. His story began to fall apart, however, when his Eskimo companions mentioned that he'd never been out of sight of land. After being paid by Peary to come forward, Cook's McKinley companion also recanted. A year later, Cook's famous summit photograph was re-created—on a peak 19 miles away and 15,000 feet lower than the real summit.

In 1910, disgusted with Cook, four prospectors from Fairbanks took a more Alaskan approach to the task. Without fanfare or special supplies—they carried doughnuts and hot chocolate on their incredible final ascent—they marched up the mountain carrying a large wooden flagpole they could

structure is environmentally advanced, using solar power for electricity and clever design to save solar warmth. Inside, life-size models of cranes overhead lead to an enormous mural, 60×28 feet in size, showing the landscape types found at the park. The carpet simulates a flowing river of gray and brown, making a path to an exhibit area with recreations of Denali wildlife, including a full-scale moose stepping through deep snow. You will also find exhibits on the Athabascan people, mining, tourism, and scientific research. On the upper floor, a large topographic model of the park demonstrates the arbitrary nature of its boundaries and another exhibit shows the six-continent routes of migratory birds found at Denali. Drawers open to reveal discoveries: a plant on top to prove they'd made it. But on arriving at the summit, they realized that they'd climbed the slightly shorter north peak. Weather closed in, so they set up the pole there and descended without attempting the south peak. Then, when they got back to Fairbanks, no one could see the pole, and they were accused of trying to pull off another hoax.

In 1913, Episcopal archdeacon Hudson Stuck organized the first successful climb to reach the real summit—and reported he saw the pole on the other peak. Harry Karstens led the climb (he would become the park's first superintendent in 1917), and the first person to stand at the summit was an Alaska Native, Walter Harper.

Although McKinley remains one of the world's most difficult climbs, about 10,000 people have made it to the top since Hudson Stuck's party. Since 1980 the number of climbers has boomed. Garbage and human waste disposal are a major problem. One recent June day, 115 climbers made it to the summit. In 1970, only 124 made the attempt all year; now more than 1,200 try to climb the peak each year, with about half making it to the summit. The cold, fast-changing weather is what usually stops people. From late April into early July, climbers fly from the town of Talkeetna to a base camp at an elevation of 7,200 feet on the Kahiltna Glacier. From there, it takes an average of about 18 days to get to the top, through temperatures as cold as $-40°F$ ($-40°C$).

Climbers lose fingers, toes, and other parts to frostbite, or suffer other, more severe injuries. More than 90 climbers have died on the mountain, not counting plane crashes. During the season, the park service stations rescue rangers and an emergency medical clinic at the 14,200-foot level of the mountain, and keeps a high-altitude helicopter ready to go after climbers in trouble. In 2002, under pressure from Congress, the park service started charging all climbers a $150-a-head fee, defraying a portion of the rescue costs. The park and the military spend about half a million dollars a year rescuing climbers, and sometimes much more. The cost in lives is high as well. Volunteer rangers and rescuers die as well as climbers. Plane crashes, falls, cold, and altitude all take a toll. Monuments to those who never returned are in the cemetery near the airstrip in Talkeetna.

cross section of Earth, or of different kinds of trees. An award-winning orientation film, *Heartbeats of Denali,* lasts 18 minutes. The photography is impressive and the narration says much with few words. Summer hours are daily 8am to 6pm; the center is closed in the winter.

The **Murie Science and Learning Center** (© **866/683-1269** or 907/683-1269; www.murieslc.org), supports research and offers programs about the park. It is located about a mile in along the park road on the right side. The lobby houses changing science exhibits. A variety of organizations participate in programming, with evening lectures, morning walk-in science presentations, youth camps, and natural history field seminars for adults and for families with older or younger children. Three-day courses are around $320 per person. Check topics and register well in advance on the website. The center is open summer 9:30am to 4:30pm, winter daily 10am to 4pm.

MOUNTAIN BIKING

A bicycle provides special freedom in the park. Bicyclists can ride past the checkpoint where cars have to turn back, at mile 14 on the park road. Riding is gritty, however, as buses come frequently and kick up a lot of dust. Bikes are not permitted off-road. Park campgrounds have bike stands and, with enough prior planning, you can set up a trip riding from one to the next. The longest stretch on the park road between campgrounds is 52 miles. With a reservation, you can take a bike on the camper bus so you can ride one-way. The shuttle system lacks much capacity for bikes, however, as only two can fit on each camper bus (I'm not sure why they don't install racks). Given this shortage, it can be hard for cyclists to find room on buses returning to the park entrance; instead, get a reserved spot on an outbound bus and bike back. Groups larger than two must split up onto different buses. Pick up a copy of the bicycle rules from the Backcountry Information Center before you start. **Denali Outdoor Center** (© **888/303-1925** or 907/683-1925; www.denalioutdoorcenter.com) rents front-suspension bikes for $40 for 24 hours, $25 for 6 hours, with discounts for longer rentals. The center has an office in Glitter Gulch and headquarters near Healy, at Otto Lake Road and Parks Highway, Mile 247. On the highway in the Nenana Canyon, you can also rent a bike at the **Denali Parks Resorts Activity Center** (© **907/683-2591**) for $15 for 4 hours, $30 for 8 hours.

SLED-DOG DEMONSTRATIONS

In the winter, rangers patrol the park by dog sled, as they have for decades. In the summer, to keep the dogs active and amuse the tourists, they run a sled on wheels around the kennel, and a ranger gives a talk, normally at 10am, 2pm, and 4pm. Although it's no substitute for seeing dogs run on snow, you can get a sense of their speed and enthusiasm from the show. It was the highlight of my older son's trip to Denali when he was 3 years old. There's no parking at the kennels, near the headquarters at mile 3.4 on the park road, so take a free bus that leaves the Denali Visitor Center 40 minutes before each show. Times are listed in the *Alpenglow* park newspaper. The park service is considering charging a fee for the demonstration starting in 2008; in the past it has always been free.

FISHING

Fishing is poor at Denali. There are grayling in some rivers, but the water is too cold and silty for most fish. Those who don't care if they catch anything, however, do enjoy fishing in this wonderful scenery. You don't need a fishing license within park boundaries, but you do have to throw back everything you catch. Bring your own gear.

For a better chance of catching something—and an opportunity to learn about fly-fishing, too—go to a private lake outside the park with guide Rick McMahan of **Denali Fly Fishing Guides** (© **907/768-1127**). He picks up clients at their hotels and takes them lake or stream fishing, on the bank or wading, mostly for Arctic grayling but also rainbow trout. The per-person cost is $150 for a half-day, $260 for a full day, lunch included.

CLIMBING MOUNT MCKINLEY

Because of its altitude and weather, Mount McKinley is among the world's most challenging climbs. Summer temperatures at the high camp average 20 to 40 degrees below zero. If you're looking here for advice, you're certainly not up to an unguided climb. A guided climb is a challenging and expensive endeavor requiring months of conditioning and most of a month on the mountain. Get names of guides from the park service's **Talkeetna Ranger Station,** P.O. Box 588, Talkeetna, AK 99676 (© **907/733-2231**). The climbing season lasts from late April or early May until the snow gets too soft, in late June or early July. Climbers fly from Talkeetna to a 7,200-foot base camp on Kahiltna Glacier. About 1,200 climbers attempt the mountain annually in about 300 parties; about half typically make it to the top each year, and usually a few die trying.

6 Attractions & Activities outside the Park

FLIGHTSEEING

Getting a good, close look at Mount McKinley itself is best accomplished by air. Frequently you can see McKinley from above the clouds even when you can't see it from the ground. Best of all, some Talkeetna operators that fly mountaineers also land visitors on the mountain, a unique and unforgettable experience (see section 11 of this chapter). Regardless of how close you approach the mountain, a flight shows how incredibly rugged the Alaska Range is.

Small planes and helicopters fly from the park airstrip, from private heliports, and airstrips along the Parks Highway, and from the Healy airstrip. **Denali Air** (© **907/683-2261;** www.denaliair.com) has an office in the Nenana Canyon area and operates flights at mile 229.5 of the Parks Highway. An hour-long flight going within a mile of the mountain costs $295 for adults, $150 for children ages 2 to 12. **Era Helicopters** (© **800/843-1947** or 907/683-2574; www.erahelicopters.com) has 50-minute flights for $299, including van pickup from hotels in the area. Their heli-hikes land for a 4-hour walk on a mountain ridgeline, the difficulty tailored to the customers' ability, for $399. A 2-hour glacial hike costs the same.

RAFTING

Rafting on the Nenana River, bordering the park along the Parks Highway, is fun and popular. Several commercial guides float two stretches of the river: an upper portion, where the water is smoother and the guides explain passing scenery; and the lower portion, where the river roars through the rock-walled Nenana Canyon and rafts take on huge splashes of silty, glacial water through Class III and IV rapids. Guides take children as young as 5 on the slow trip (although I wouldn't let my kid go at that age); the youngest accepted for the fast portion is age 12. Whitewater rafting carries risks you shouldn't discount just because a lot of people do it, as a fatal accident on the supposedly easy tour confirmed in 1999. Each session takes 2 to 2½ hours, including safety briefings, suiting up, and riding to and from the put-in and take-out points. Prices vary from $73 to $98 for adults, with discounted rates for children (from $10 less to half off). **Denali Outdoor Center** (© **888/303-1925** or 907/683-1925; www.denalioutdoorcenter.com) is a professional operation, offering rafting trips and instruction in river techniques. The firm also offers self-paddled inflatable kayaks, popular with those who want to take an active hand in their float. Its riverside office is located 2½ miles north of the park entrance at Otto Lake Road, at Mile 247 of the Parks Highway; the company also has an office right in Glitter Gulch. Whoever you go with, plan a shower afterward—the silt in the river water will stick to your skin and hair.

HORSEBACK RIDING

There is no riding in the park itself, but various companies offer rides in similar terrain outside the park's boundaries. One- to 2-hour rides cost from $79 to $125. Among the operators are **Denali Saddle Safaris** (© **907/683-1200;** www.denalisaddlesafaris. com), which also offers pack trips and extended journeys.

7 Where to Stay

PARK SERVICE CAMPGROUNDS

I've explained how to make camping reservations under "The Reservations System," p. 348. Camping fees are listed here, but reservation fees and entrance fees may be added when you pay. Only Riley Creek Campground is open after September (water is off in winter). The rest reopen when the snow is gone in May, except Wonder Lake, which opens in June. I have noted where RVs are permitted in the description of each campground. There are no RV hookups at any campground in the park.

CAR-ACCESSIBLE CAMPGROUNDS

In addition to these, see **Teklanika River** under "Bus-Accessible Campgrounds," below; you can drive to it as long as your stay is at least 3 nights.

Riley Creek This large campground right across the road from the visitor center is best for those who want to be in the middle of things. It's near the Riley Creek Mercantile, with its showers, laundry, Wi-Fi, and sewage dump station. The free front-country shuttle connects the campground with other facilities. Reservations are relatively easy to get. Sites are wooded with small birch and spruce, and they're adequately separated, but this isn't exactly wilderness camping. Twenty-seven walk-in sites are only for tent users without vehicles.

Near the visitor center. 147 sites; RVs or tents. $20 vehicle sites; $12 walk-in sites. Campfires allowed; flush toilets.

Savage River On the taiga—the thin spruce forest and tundra—this is a wonderful campground with unforgettable views. Campers can wander from their sites on some of the park's best hikes. This is the only campground you can readily drive to that's away from the activity at the park entrance. There is no telephone.

On Denali Park Rd., 13 miles from entrance. 33 sites; RVs and cars or tents. $20 per site. Campfires allowed; flush toilets.

BUS-ACCESSIBLE CAMPGROUNDS

To use these campgrounds, you'll need a camper ticket on the shuttle bus, which costs $29 for adults, half price for children ages 15 to 17, free for ages 14 and under. There are no businesses and no phones beyond the park entrance area; you must bring in everything you need. Wildlife management concerns sometimes close these campgrounds unexpectedly.

⟨*Tips* **Keeping Clean at Denali**

The only showers within the park are at **Riley Creek Mercantile,** the store near the Riley Creek Campground, which also has laundry machines and other services. You pay by the shower, so there's no coin-operated timer to feed. You can also wash your clothes and shower at **McKinley RV and Campground** in Healy, covered below under "Commercial Campgrounds." The larger park campgrounds have the typical cold-water bathrooms found in the national parks, while others have vault toilets.

Sanctuary River & Igloo   These two small, primitive campgrounds offer a back-country experience away from cars. You can't reserve sites in advance; permits are available only in person at the visitor center when you arrive. Igloo has been closed for several years, but the park hopes to reopen it someday.

On Denali Park Rd., Sanctuary River Mile 23, Igloo Mile 34. 7 sites each; tents only. $9 per site. No campfires; stoves permitted; chemical toilets.

Teklanika River   This is the only car campground beyond the checkpoint on the park road. To hold down traffic, the park service requires campers to keep their vehicles in place for 3 nights. Sites are among the small trees of the boreal forest. The big advantage of staying here is that you begin the morning much closer to the heart of the park, cutting the time you have to spend on the bus. You can buy one bus ticket for the regular price and use it for your entire 3-night stay. That makes Teklanika a good base to really explore different areas of the park in varying kinds of weather.

On Denali Park Rd., 29 miles from entrance; access by camper bus, or drive in with a minimum 3-night stay. 53 sites; RVs only, no tents. $20 per site. Campfires allowed; flush toilets.

Wonder Lake   It takes almost 6 hours to get here on the bus, but this campground by placid Wonder Lake, at the foot of Mount McKinley, puts you in the most beautiful and coveted area of the park. Set among a patch of spruce trees on the mountain side of the lake, the sites can be tough to get, especially those with views of McKinley. The secret is to stay more than 1 day. When campers with a coveted site leave in the morning, grab it. A central area with bear-resistant food storage lockers has tables covered by an awning where campers prepare food and meet each other; choose a site away from this area and the noise and foot traffic there. The mosquitoes at Wonder Lake can be horrendous.

On Denali Park Rd., 85 miles from entrance. 28 sites; tents only. $20 per site. No campfires; stoves permitted; flush toilets.

COMMERCIAL CAMPGROUNDS

There are several commercial campgrounds in the general vicinity of the park entrance, although none in walking distance. **Denali Grizzly Bear Cabins and Campground** (© 866/583-2696 or 907/683-2696; www.denaligrizzlybear.com) is about 7 miles south of the park entrance at mile 231.1 of the Parks Highway. Some sites sit on an exposed hillside, while others are among small trees. Small cabins and tent cabins dot the property as well; they range from $59 without a bathroom to $248 for a unit with a full bathroom. There are coin-operated showers. Tent sites are $21 for up to four people, with electrical and water hookups $6 more. (The hotel on the property is described on p. 370.)

A campground with birch trees and attractive sites is 10 miles north of the park, in Healy. **McKinley RV and Campground,** at mile 248.4 on the Parks Highway (© 800/478-2562 or 907/683-2379), has a deli, a gas station, a token-operated laundry, and hot showers. Basic tent sites are $10, full hookups $32. The campground is operated by Denali Park Resorts, which is owned by ARAMARK; the toll-free number is their main reservation line.

HOTELS

Patterns of land ownership and the uncontrolled development around Denali have led to a hodgepodge of roadside hotels, cabins, lodges, campgrounds, and restaurants in pockets arrayed along more than 20 miles of the Parks Highway. There are rooms of good quality in each of the pockets, but the going rates vary widely. The most expensive rooms, and the first booked, are in the immediate vicinity of the park entrance. Better bargains are in pockets south of the park, with prices getting lower the farther you go. Both these areas are entirely seasonal. Good deals are had in **Healy,** too, 12 miles north of the park, where you can find a hotel room for $50 less than a comparable room near the park entrance. A few links to B&Bs are on the **Healy Chamber of Commerce** website (www.denalichamber.com, click on "Directory"). If you don't have a car Healy is not convenient; in that case, stay nearer the park entrance. The other choices are a wilderness lodge in the **Kantishna** area (see section 10 of this chapter); or **Talkeetna,** the back door to the park (see section 11 of this chapter). Despite their high prices, rooms can be hard to find at the peak of the season, and it's wise to book ahead.

NEAR THE PARK

This area, known formally as Nenana Canyon or more commonly as "Glitter Gulch," extends about a mile north of the park entrance on the Parks Highway. Large, luxurious hotels dominate. Owned by the Princess and Holland American cruise lines, each hotel has superb rooms and public areas that were rebuilt in grand style within the last few years. Objectively the best lodgings in the area, I give them brief mention mainly because they serve package-tour passengers nearly to the exclusion of other guests. The giants are the **Denali Princess Lodge,** Mile 238.5, Parks Hwy. (© **800/426-0500** reservations, 907/683-2282 local; www.princesslodges.com), and the **McKinley Chalet Resort,** Mile 239.1, Parks Hwy. (© **800/622-7275** or 907/272-7275; www.reservedenali.com). Rack rates are high at each of these places, but you usually don't have to pay them. You can stay for much less if you arrive on one of the days when the flow of cruise-ship passengers is down, or early or late in the season, or if you book one of their packages. Good deals are to be had there as packages with the Alaska Railroad or out of peak season.

At one time the canyon contained a variety of smaller, locally owned hotels catering to independent travelers, but the extraordinary value of the property and ever-growing flow of cruise-ship passengers has led to consolidation of lodgings, campgrounds, shops, restaurants, and other businesses into the hands of the two main cruise lines (which are, in reality, only two arms of the same corporation, Carnival), and ARAMARK, the park concessionaire, which operates under the name Denali Park Resorts outside park boundaries.

All of the hotels in this area are open only during the tourist season, roughly from May 15 to September 15.

Denali Bluffs Hotel ✦ A series of 12 buildings on a steep mountainside looks down on the Nenana Canyon area from above the highway. The light, tastefully decorated rooms have two double beds and good amenities, and those on the upper floor have vaulted ceilings and balconies with great views. There's little to explain the rates, however, than the overheated Denali market. The courtesy van will take you anywhere in the area. ARAMARK manages the hotel and the 154-room **Grande Denali Lodge,** which perches impossibly high above the Nenana Canyon and charges more for the view. Use caution and observe the mirrors at the switchbacks on the gravel road up from the highway. The information below is for Denali Bluffs, but the toll-free number and website are good for either.

Mile 238.4, Parks Hwy. (Mailing address: 241 W. Ship Creek Ave., Anchorage, AK 99501). ℭ **866/683-8500** or 907/683-8500. Fax 907/258-3668. www.denalialaska.com. 112 units. High season $225 double; low season $189 double. Extra person age 12 and older $20. AE, DISC, MC, V. **Amenities:** 2 restaurants; tour desk; courtesy van; coin-op laundry. *In room:* Satellite TV, coffeemaker.

Denali Crow's Nest Log Cabins ⌖   Perched in five tiers on the side of Sugarloaf Mountain above the canyon area, looking down on Horseshoe Lake and the other, larger hotels, the regularly updated cabins are roomy and comfortable, especially those on the 100 and 200 level. A log cabin and the warmth of the Crofoot family create a truer Alaskan feeling than the modern, standard rooms that have filled the canyon, and the rates are reasonable for the area (believe it or not). You spend a lot of time climbing stairs, however; and the rooms have shower enclosures, not tubs. All rooms are nonsmoking. The restaurant, **The Overlook Bar and Grill,** is recommended separately under "Where to Dine," below.

Mile 238.5, Parks Hwy. (P.O. Box 70), Denali National Park, AK 99755. ℭ **888/917-8130** or 907/683-2723. Fax 907/683-2323. www.denalicrowsnest.com. 39 cabins. High season $189 cabin for 2; low season $139 cabin for 2. Extra person $10. MC, V. **Amenities:** Restaurant; bar; outdoor hot tub; tour desk; courtesy van.

IN HEALY

Healy is 10 miles north of the park entrance, but a world away. It's a year-round community with an economy based partly on a coal mine. It sits in a large, windy valley with a few patches of stunted trees and big, open spaces of tundra. There are hotels and B&Bs with rooms well below the cost of those near the park, and most businesses stay open in the winter when the rest of the region shuts down tight. They say the water tastes better, too. On the downside, you need a car to stay in Healy. Besides the lodgings listed below, **Denali Dome Home** (ℭ **800/683-1239** or 907/683-1239; www.denalidomehome.com) is a neat place, a huge house in a geodesic dome on 5 acres, run year-round by a family for many years. The seven rooms are $148 double in summer and have many amenities.

Denali Touch of Wilderness Bed and Breakfast Inn ⌖   This special inn has won a place in the hearts of residents of this remote region, who congregate for retreats, quilting, wedding rehearsals, and the like. Visitors will find immaculate rooms, all with private bathrooms and phones, in one large building, decorated in a Victorian-tinged country theme. The common areas most memorably create the inn's warm feeling, however—large sitting rooms with expansive views on the nearby Alaska Range, a library of Alaskana and a selection of movies for the TV, and a kitchen guests can use. The inn has Wi-Fi and a free shared guest computer as well, and an outdoor Jacuzzi on an attractive deck. The location is away from the noisy highway, about 3 miles out in the country on the Stampede Road. The hosts serve fabulous breakfasts from 7 to 9am.

Mile 2.9, Stampede Rd. (P.O. Box 397) Healy, AK 99743. ℭ **800/683-2459** or 907/683-2459. www.touchofwilderness bb.com. 9 rooms. High season $180 double; low season $85 double. Extra person $20. AE, DISC, MC, V. Rates include full breakfast. **Amenities:** Outdoor Jacuzzi; laundry service; coin-op laundry. *In room:* fridge, coffeemaker, hair dryer, microwave.

Earthsong Lodge ⌖⌖ 𝒱alue   This place is well off the beaten path, but it's worth the trip to stay in an authentically Alaskan dwelling and meet interesting people, such as year-round residents Jon and Karin Nierenberg. Guests gather in the main lodge building, with its library, living room, and piano. There's a coffeehouse, Henry's, serving

breakfast and dinner and packing sack lunches. The lodge and individual cabins are all solid log construction. The cabins, with one or two bedrooms, have quilts on the beds and other cozy features, as well as private bathrooms (these are operational only in the summer; in the off season, guests use a shower house). Outside is the windy open tundra with sweeping views of the Alaska Range. In the evening a naturalist puts on a slide show in the coffeehouse. In the winter the lodge offers dog sledding, and in the summer kennel tours. The lodge is 17 miles north of Denali National Park, 4 miles down the scenic Stampede Trail Road.

Stampede Trail Road, off the Parks Hwy. at mile 251 (P.O. Box 89), Healy, AK 99743. ⓒ **907/683-2863.** Fax 907/683-2868. www.earthsonglodge.com. 12 units. Summer $145–$185 double cabin; winter $75–$85 double cabin. Extra person 18 and over $10, ages 12–17 $5, 11 and under free. DISC, MC, V. **Amenities:** Restaurant (coffeehouse). *In room:* Coffeemaker, hair dryer, Wi-Fi.

Motel Nord Haven 🐾🐾   This fresh little gray hotel with a red roof has large, immaculate rooms, each with one or two queen-size beds. They're equal to the best standard rooms in the Denali Park area and a lot less expensive. Bill and Patsy Nordmark offer free continental breakfast in the summer, and newspapers, coffee, tea, hot chocolate, free Wi-Fi, and a guest computer in a common area, and a sitting room with a collection of Alaska books. The rooms, decorated with Alaska art and oak trim, all have interior entrances and have been smoke-free since their construction. Up to four people can stay in the rooms with two beds for the price of a double. There are three kitchenette units. The Nordmarks pack sack lunches for $10.

Mile 249.5, Parks Hwy. (P.O. Box 458), Healy, AK 99743. ⓒ **800/683-4501** or 907/683-4500. Fax 907/683-4503. www.motelnordhaven.com. 28 units. Summer $131–$157; spring/fall $94–$104; winter $80–$85. AE, DISC, MC, V. *In room:* TV, Wi-Fi.

SOUTH OF THE PARK

Lodgings south of the park are in widely separated pockets of private land concentrated 7 and 14 miles south of the park. (Anything south of that is covered with Talkeetna, in section 11 of this chapter.) I've listed a few in detail below, but you may also want to try **Denali Cabins,** Mile 229, Parks Hwy. (ⓒ **877/233-6254** or 907/376-1992; www.denali-cabins.com).

Cedar Hotel at Denali Grizzly Bear Resort 🐾   The owner of the adjoining campground (Denali Grizzly Bear, p. 367) opened the hotel in 2006, producing comfortable, modern rooms in three buildings standing right over the Nenana River with the highway mostly out of view. You can hear the water from your bed or emerge on a small deck to enjoy the view (and the company of other guests, who are an arm's length away). Rooms are decorated in the Alaska rustic motif with lots of cedar. They don't have phones.

Mile 231.1 Parks Hwy. (P.O. Box 7) Denali National Park, AK 99755. ⓒ **866/583-2696** or 907/683-2696. www.denaligrizzlybear.com. 54 rooms. High season $179 double; low season $149 double. Extra person $10. DISC, MC, V. **Amenities:** Internet access in common area (fee). *In room:* TV, coffeemaker, hair dryer, no phone.

Denali Mountain Morning Hostel and Lodge *Value*   The hostel offers cozy accommodations in an octagonal log building. A store mainly carries organic food and a $5 shuttle runs to the park entrance four times a day. Accommodations include hostel bunks, private rooms, or separate private cabins, all reasonably priced. All guests use the shared bathhouse and have access to a fully equipped kitchen and Internet access, which carries an additional fee. The hostel is in the Carlo Creek area, where there are a couple of good casual restaurants.

Mile 224.5, Parks Hwy. (P.O. Box 208), Denali National Park, AK 99755. ☎ **907/683-7503.** www.hostelalaska.com. 14 units (2 female dormitories, 2 male dormitories, 1 co-ed dormitory; 9 private cabins). $25 adult bunk; $19 children 12 and under bunk; $75 double private room; $95 double cabin. Extra adult $10; extra child ages 5–12 $5; extra child under 5 free. 2-night minimum in private rooms and cabins. AE, DISC, MC, V. **Amenities:** Shared kitchen; Internet access in common room (fee). *In room:* No phone.

Denali River Cabins/Cedar Lodge ☆☆   The cedar cabins arrayed on a maze of boardwalks above the Nenana River are fresh and well appointed. Unlike some accommodations outside Denali, they have an outdoorsy, national park feel, lent in part by the riverside location. They have shower stalls, not tubs, and lack closets. They do have phones. The cabins on the river, with decks over the water, are $40 more. The sauna has a picture window on the river. The Cedar Lodge, on the same property, offers more of a hotel experience, with 48 rooms with two double beds, TVs, and telephones. Ride the free Denali Park Resorts shuttle to the park entrance and rail depot. Don't confuse this place with Denali Cabins.

Mile 231.1, Parks Hwy. (P.O. Box 210), Denali National Park, AK 99755. (Winter mailing address: 1 Doyon Place, Suite 200, Fairbanks, AK 99701.) ☎ **800/230-7275** or 907/683-8000. Fax 907/683-8095. (Winter ☎ 907/459-2121; fax 907/459-2160.) www.seedenali.com. 102 units (48 rooms, 54 cabins). High season $159–$209 cabin for 2, $194 double in lodge; low season $129–$209 cabin for 2, $164 double in lodge. Extra person 11 and older $20. MC, V. **Amenities:** Restaurant; bar; sauna; tour desk; coin-op laundry. *In room:* TV.

McKinley Creekside Cabins ☆   These cozy cabins are right by the highway and the pleasant cafe of the same name (covered below), but you would never know it thanks to how they are situated in the woods on the banks of Carlo Creek. Cabins are decorated in subdued tones and have decks and nice private bathrooms, and some have refrigerators and microwaves. Family units sleep up to 6, a real money saver. The decoration stresses rustic, northern themes, with log bedposts made by a local craftsman. There are communal spots for visiting around barbecues and fire pits, some at the river's edge. Cabins have Wi-Fi, but no TV or telephone.

Mile 224, Parks Hwy. (P.O. Box 89), Denali National Park, AK 99755. ☎ **888/5DENALI** or 907/683-2277. www. mckinleycabins.com. 38 units (6 rooms, 24 cabins). High season $125–$199 unit for 2–6; low season $79–$179 unit for 2–6. Extra person $5. DISC, MC, V. Closed Oct–Apr. **Amenities:** Restaurant; barbecue. *In room:* Coffeemaker, Wi-Fi, no phone.

The Perch *Value*   In the trees along rushing Carlo Creek, 13 miles south of the park entrance, cabins range from large, modern units with private bathrooms to cozy if spartan A-frames with lofts that share a bathhouse. Two cabins have kitchens. There's a sense of privacy and of being out in the woods along the wooden and gravel walkways. The Perch is a good value, open year-round, which will be most appealing to budget travelers and those who enjoy a few rough edges when they visit an outdoor destination such as Denali. The restaurant and bar, set atop a steep hill, are described below under "Where to Dine"; down on the highway level, their Panorama Pizza Pub is a local gathering place.

Mile 224, Parks Hwy. (P.O. Box 53), Denali National Park, AK 99755. ☎ **888/322-2523** or ☎/fax 907/683-2523. www.denaliperchresort.com. 22 units (cabins, 14 with private bathroom). $85 cabin for 2, shared bathroom. $125 cabin for 2, private bathroom. Extra adult $16. Rates include breakfast. AE, DISC, MC, V. **Amenities:** 2 restaurants; tour desk. *In room:* No phone.

8 Where to Dine

Since Denali is entirely seasonal, it lacks the range of inexpensive family restaurants that develop in year-round communities. While you may find reasonably priced food in Healy, to the north, or Carlo Creek, to the south, near the park most meals are overpriced by 25% to 50% due to the short season and captive audience. Unless otherwise stated, all restaurants listed are open only during the visitor season.

NEAR THE PARK ENTRANCE

You'll have no trouble finding an espresso at Denali. The large hotels in the canyon each have fine dining and casual restaurants; I've described the best in detail below. There are plenty of spots for a low-key meal or takeout. The **Courtyard Cafe** at the McKinley Chalet Resort serves a buffet and has a children's menu. **Lynx Creek Pizza** is something of a tradition but inconsistent from year to year. For takeout sandwiches and a great cheese steak, it's hard to beat **Bub's Subs,** located in the Rainbow Mall, next door to the Lynx Creek Store. You can eat and people watch in the casual seating area.

You can't miss the homemade highway frontage of the hip **Denali Salmon Bake** (© **907/683-2733;** www.thebakerocks.com) in Glitter Gulch. Although extremely casual, the staff is friendly, led by owners who are involved in the community. It's fun and a hot spot for live music as well. Check the website for a calendar of who is playing and the amount of the cover charge. They'll also come to pick you up and drive you back to your hotel. The food is tasty and relatively inexpensive, including Tex-Mex selections, king crab, and grilled reindeer in addition to the grilled salmon.

King Salmon Restaurant ★★ STEAK/SEAFOOD   This is a terrific place for a special night of dining out right near the park. First, there's the waiting area, newly remodeled with a cozy fireplace in 2007. Next, the dining room, perched on the edge of the Nenana Canyon, where you can watch rafters float by during your meal. Then there's the food and service, which are up to Princess Tours' excellent standards—steak and salmon, the usual choices for Alaska tourists—prepared expertly. For something a bit more casual the Basecamp Bistro is in the same building.

In the Denali Princess Lodge, Mile 238.5, Parks Hwy. © **907/683-2282.** Reservations recommended. Dinner main courses $17–$37. AE, DC, DISC, MC, V. Summer daily 5–11am, noon–2pm, and 5–10pm. Basecamp Bistro daily 5–9am and 10am–midnight.

Nenana View Bar & Grill ★ PIZZA/STEAK/SANDWICHES   This attractive restaurant in the McKinley Chalet Resort has a fireplace at one end of the dining room and outdoor seating overlooking the river at the other. They serve delicious pizza and great fire-grilled steaks.

Mile 238.9, Parks Hwy., in McKinley Chalet Resort. © **907/683-8200.** All items $12–$28. AE, DISC, MC, V. May–Sept daily 11am–2:30pm and 5–11pm. Bar until 1am. Closed off season.

The Overlook Bar and Grill ★ BURGERS/STEAK/SEAFOOD   This fun, noisy place has the feel of a classic bar and grill, with a vaulted ceiling of rough-cut lumber and a spectacular view of the Nenana Canyon. There are two dining rooms, one with the bar, and another, behind a glass partition, which is quieter and has tablecloths. A huge variety of craft beers is available, with several on tap. At times I've gotten excellent fare here. Call © 907/683-2723 for courtesy transportation from all area hotels.

Mile 238.5, Parks Hwy., up the hill above the Denali Canyon area. © **907/683-2641.** Lunch main courses $9–$15; dinner main courses $16–$30. MC, V. Daily 11am–11pm. Bar until 1am. Closed mid-Sept to mid-May.

WITHIN DRIVING DISTANCE

These restaurants are as much as 13 miles from the park entrance, so you will need a car.

Black Diamond Grill ✿✿ STEAK/SEAFOOD/ITALIAN   A unique 9-hole golf course lies amid the mountains and rolling taiga north of the park. The associated restaurant produces excellent meals from a menu mostly influenced by Northern Italian cookery. For lunch, sandwich choices include a pesto chicken hoagie for $7.50, and for dinner there is halibut in parchment with fresh rosemary and garlic for $20. Although not as perfect as at the best restaurants in Anchorage, the cuisine is memorable and satisfying. The dining room is light and cheery, with pine furniture and flowers on the table. Children will enjoy the mini–golf course and wagon rides.

Mile 247, Parks Hwy. (take the hwy. north 10 miles, then turn left at Otto Lake Rd.). © **907/683-4653**. Lunch $7.50– $9; dinner main courses $14–$24. AE, DISC, MC, V. Daily 7am–11pm. Closed off season.

McKinley Creekside Cafe ✿ *Kids* STEAK/SEAFOOD/SANDWICHES   This friendly spot in the Carlo Creek area, south of the park, is a favorite of the locals. You can dine on steak or baked salmon with brown sugar, apples, and toasted almonds for around $20, or order a burger for around $9. The food is consistently good, including breakfast, and craft brews and wine are served. There is a playground outside and a kid's menu. They also pack substantial sack lunches for the park shuttle-bus ride.

Mile 224, Parks Hwy. © **888/333-6254** or 907/683-2277. www.mckinleycabins.com. Lunch $6–$10; dinner $8–$21. DISC, MC, V. Summer daily 6am–10pm.

The Perch/Panorama Pizza Pub ✿ STEAK/SEAFOOD/PIZZA/DELI   An odd, knoblike hill gives the Perch its name (the attractive cabins described above sit below the restaurant). It's a friendly, family-run place serving a straightforward steak and Alaskan seafood menu—they don't try anything fancy, just good ingredients done right. The home-baked bread is noteworthy. The dining room is light, with well-spaced tables and big picture windows on three sides. Down on the highway level, the Panorama Pizza Pub is a hot spot for pizza, and also includes a bakery/deli that packs lunches in cloth tote bags for the park bus. You can often hear local musicians playing there in the evening.

Mile 224, Parks Hwy., 13 miles south of the park. © **888/322-2523** or 907/683-2523. www.denaliperchresort.com. The Perch: Dinner main courses $14–$40. AE, DISC, MC, V. Summer daily 6–9am and 5–9pm; winter hours vary. Panorama Pizza Pub: Pizza $15–$25. AE, DISC, MC, V. Summer daily 11am–midnight.

229 Parks Restaurant and Tavern ✿✿ ECLECTIC   The name comes from the milepost, which puts the restaurant in a quiet area about 8 miles south of the park entrance, where it occupies a beautiful post-and-beam building. Year-round residents Laura and Land Cole own the restaurant—Laura is a professionally trained chef and veteran of the Marx Brothers Cafe, one of Alaska's best restaurants, and cooked for 12 years at Camp Denali, the park's most famous lodge, which is also owned by family. Whenever possible, she uses organic ingredients and local produce—eggs are naturally nested by free-range chickens. The menu changes daily and has included main course items such as tenderloin filet, lemon pasta with asparagus, venison chops, and, of course, salmon. A sweet potato soup with king crab meat was fabulous. The appetizer list is long and interesting, including spring rolls second to none. Breakfast is coffeehouse fare, such as quiche, granola, and fruit. Locals keep the place busy even winter weekends, but they close at 1pm on winter Sundays so everyone in the community can go play hockey on Deneki Lakes.

Mile 229, Parks Hwy. © **907/683-2567.** www.229parks.com. Reservations recommended. Dinner $15–$33. MC, V. Summer Tues–Sun 7–11am and 5–10pm; winter Fri–Sat 9am–10pm, Sun 9am–1pm.

9 Denali Nightlife

The main evening event is the concessionaire's **Cabin Nite Dinner Theater,** at the McKinley Chalet Resort (© **800/276-7234** or 907/683-8200), a professionally produced musical revue about a gold-rush-era woman who ran a roadhouse in Kantishna. You can buy the $57 tickets (half price ages 2–12) virtually anywhere in the area. The actors, singing throughout the evening, stay in character to serve big platters of food to diners sitting at long tables, doing a good job of building a rowdy, happy atmosphere for adults and kids. Shows happen nightly at 5:30 and 8:30.

Princess Cruises and Tours puts on its own evening show, **The Music of Denali,** at the Denali Princess Lodge. The musical performance lasts an hour, the entire dinner 2 hours. Tickets are for sale at the hotel's tour desk (© **800/426-0500** or 907/683-2282) for $49 (half price ages 6–12).

10 Denali Wilderness Lodges

Staying in a wilderness lodge makes for a completely different experience of Denali, and that's why I've segregated these choices here. These lodges are self-contained vacations, and if you choose to stay you don't need to worry about the shuttle bus or the other issues of escaping the "frontcountry." The lodges also are expensive and require a significant commitment of time. It doesn't make sense to spend less than 3 days, and some lodges require longer minimum stays.

All lodges within Denali National Park are in the Kantishna district, an inholding of private land where gold miners staked claims before the park was created. The lodge operators who later obtained this land gained something more valuable than gold: the opportunity to bring visitors to the far end of the park from the entrance, as near as a vehicle can get to Mount McKinley, without using the park's shuttle system. Hosts drive visitors to Kantishna in their own buses or vans over the 91-mile park road. These lodges are open only in summer.

Besides the three lodges I have room to describe here in detail, I also recommend **Denali Backcountry Lodge** (© **877/233-6254** or 907/376-1992; www.denalilodge.com).

Camp Denali/North Face Lodge ✸✸✸ At this pioneering eco-tourism establishment, you can wake to the white monolith of Mount McKinley filling your window. The naturalist guides here have the right to use the park road free of the shuttle system for hikes, biking, lake canoeing, bird-watching, photography sessions, and other outdoor learning activities, all included in the substantial price. During some sessions, nationally respected academics and other experts lead the program. All arrivals and departures are on fixed session dates of 3, 4, or 7 days and start with a picnic supper on the park road on the way out to the lodges. Each of the Camp Denali cabins has its own outhouse, and all share a central bathhouse and wonderful lodge common rooms—it has the best views and would be my first choice for anyone who can get by without his or her own flush toilet. North Face Lodge has smallish traditional rooms with private bathrooms. Each lodge has its own dining room for family-style meals. A conservation ethic pervades the operation, from the homegrown vegetables to the proprietors' efforts to preserve the natural values of private land in the park.

Kantishna (P.O. Box 67), Denali National Park, AK 99755. ⓒ **907/683-2290.** Fax 907/683-1568. www.camp denali.com. 32 units (17 cabins), none with private bathroom at Camp Denali; 15 units with bathroom at North Face Lodge. 3-night stay $1,365 per person, $1,024 per child 11 and under; 7-night stay $3,185 per person, $2,389 per child 11 and under. Rates include all meals and guided activities. Minimum stay 3 nights. No credit cards. No smoking in buildings or vehicles. *In room:* No phone.

Kantishna Roadhouse 🌟🌟   This well-kept property of many buildings along Moose Creek in the old Kantishna Mining District trades on both the mining history and outdoor opportunities of the area. Some rooms are large and luxurious, while others are in smaller single cabins with lofts. The log central lodge has an attractive lobby with people coming and going—it's got more of a hotel feel and might be more attractive to an older, less active set or to families than the other lodges in the Kantishna District. It also has a bar. Guided hikes, fishing, interpretive programs, biking, gold panning, a daily sled-dog demonstration, and the bus ride from the park entrance are included in the rate.

Kantishna District, Denali National Park (Mailing address: 1 Doyon Place, Suite 300, Fairbanks, AK 99701). ⓒ **800/ 942-7420** or 907/683-1475. Fax 907/683-1449. (Winter: ⓒ 907/459-2120; fax 907/459-2160.) www.seedenali.com. 32 units. $385 per person double; $300 per child ages 3–11. Extra person $275. Rates include all meals and guided activities. Minimum stay 2 nights. AE, DISC, MC, V. **Amenities:** Bar; sauna; mountain bikes. *In room:* No phone.

Skyline Lodge 🌟 *(Value)*   Run by pilot Greg Lahaie, owner of Kantishna Air Taxi, the lodge offers a unique alternative in Denali's backcountry: a place you don't have to be a millionaire to afford. With room for only eight guests and a self-serve philosophy, it's far simpler and more casual than the full-service lodges in Kantishna, and costs less than a fourth as much. Also, there's no minimum stay, and you can fly there with Greg. It costs $30 a day to join the family-style lunch and dinner (breakfast is already included in the price). Rooms are in cabins, each with a double or queen-size bed and a loft. Large windows overlook Moose Creek. The kitchen, TV, and other amenities are in the central lodge building. The most important amenity, however, is that you are in the heart of Denali's backcountry. Nonsmoking.

Kantishna District (P.O. Box 46), Denali Park, AK 99755. ⓒ **907/683-1223.** Fax: 907/683-1223. www.katair.com. 3 units, none with private bathroom. $185 double. Extra person age 2 and over $50. DISC, MC, V. Rates include continental breakfast. **Amenities:** Sauna; free mountain bikes; courtesy van.

11 Talkeetna: Back Door to Denali

Talkeetna, a historic and funky little town with a sense of humor but not much happening, slept soundly from its decline around World War I until about a decade ago. Now there are paved streets (both of them), a fancy National Park Service building, a larger railroad depot, and two large luxury lodges. It seems that while Talkeetna slumbered in a time capsule, an explosion of visitors was happening at Denali National Park. Now, not entirely voluntarily, Talkeetna has been enveloped in that boom.

As a threshold to the park, Talkeetna has significant pros and cons that you should take into account. On the positive side, it's closer to Anchorage; the development is much more interesting and authentic than that at the park entrance; there's lots to do outdoors; and Mount McKinley is seen more frequently, both because of geography and weather. On the negative side, a big minus: You can't get into the park from here without a long drive or a flight. That may mean you miss the dramatic scenery, easy backcountry access, and unique wildlife viewing on the park road.

The town dates from the gold rush and has many charming log and clapboard buildings. With 15 sites of historic note, the entire downtown area has been listed on the National Register of Historic Places. You can spend several hours looking at two small museums and meeting people in the 2-block main street, then go out on the Talkeetna or Susitna rivers for rafting, a jet-boat ride, or fishing, or take a flightseeing trip to the national park.

ESSENTIALS

GETTING THERE   Talkeetna lies on a 14-mile spur road that branches from the Parks Highway 99 miles north of Anchorage and 138 miles south of the park entrance.

The **Alaska Railroad** (© 800/544-0552 or 907/265-2494; www.alaskarailroad. com) serves Talkeetna daily on its runs to Denali National Park during the summer, and weekly in the winter. (See section 2 of this chapter for additional details.) The summer fare from Anchorage to Talkeetna is $82 one-way for adults, half price for children, for basic service.

The **Talkeetna Shuttle Service** (© 907/733-1725 office or 907/373-8548 cellular; www.denalicentral.com) runs to and from Anchorage. Fares are $65 one-way, $125 round-trip.

It's possible to stay in Talkeetna but do the Denali National Park shuttle bus ride and other park activities by flying there for the day. **Talkeetna Aero Services** (© 888/733-2899 or 907/733-2899; www.talkeetnaaero.com) offers daily round-trips for this purpose during the summer with a flightseeing tour circling Mount McKinley en route. They charge $395 as a package with ground transfers, a bus tour, and a box lunch.

VISITOR INFORMATION   Built to serve people aiming to climb Mount McKinley, the **Denali National Park Talkeetna Ranger Station,** at 1st and B streets (P.O. Box 588), Talkeetna, AK 99676 (© 907/733-2231; www.nps.gov/dena), makes a fascinating stop for anyone curious about mountaineering. Inside the handsome structure a large sitting room contains a river rock fireplace, climbing books, and pictures of the mountain—it's like an old-fashioned explorers' club. Fascinating records open for inspection cover the history of McKinley climbs. Rangers are on hand to answer questions, too. It's open May through Labor Day daily from 8am to 6pm; winter, Monday through Friday from 8am to 4:30pm.

The **Talkeetna/Denali Visitor Center,** located in a tiny cabin at the intersection of the Parks Highway and Talkeetna Spur Road and on Main Street (P.O. Box 688), Talkeetna, AK 99676 (© 800/660-2688 or 907/733-2641; www.talkeetnadenali.com), is a commercial center belonging to a local flight service and providing brochures, information, and advice while earning commissions from bookings. It's the handiest commercial information stop in the region. The center is open daily from 8am to 8pm in summer, and they respond to inquiries year-round with free trip-planning help.

FAST FACTS: Talkeetna

Bank   A local credit union is near the Parks Highway on the Talkeetna Spur Road. There is no bank in the town center, but several businesses have ATMs, including Nagley's General Store and Tanner's Trading Post, both on Main Street.

Hospital   Talkeetna Denali Family Medical Clinic, 125 1st St. (© 907/733-2708).

Internet Access Free for up to 20 minutes at the **Talkeetna Public Library** (© 907/ 733-2359), at mile 13.5 of the Talkeetna Spur Road, just across the tracks.

Police For nonemergencies, call the **Alaska State Troopers** at © 907/733-2256. The station is near the Parks Highway on the Talkeetna Spur Road.

Post Office In the town center, near the intersection of Talkeetna Spur Road and Main Street.

Taxes There is no **sales tax. Bed tax** in the area is 5%.

SPECIAL EVENTS   The **Talkeetna Moose Dropping Festival,** held over the second weekend in July, is the big community event of the year, a fair beginning its fourth decade as a fundraiser for the Talkeetna Historical Society (© **907/733-2487**). The named event doesn't involve dropping moose, as an aggrieved animal lover once complained, but tossing moose droppings. Another event, the mountain mother contest, open only to mothers, is a race of Bush skills, including splitting wood and diapering a baby.

EXPLORING THE TOWN

Talkeetna is famous for its laid-back atmosphere and outdoors, not for "attractions," but there are several places to stop in to get the sense of the place. One is the ranger station mentioned above under "Visitor Information." If you come in May or June, you're sure to meet many international mountain climbers; you'll have no difficulty picking them out (see "Climbing Mount McKinley," in section 5 of this chapter). Along Main Street are shops where artists and craftspeople often can be found at work.

The **Talkeetna Historical Society Museum,** in five buildings on the Village Airstrip a half block south of Main Street (© **907/733-2487,** www.talkeetnahistorical society.org), is well worth a stop. The first building contains artifacts and displays on local mining history, including engaging photographs and biographies of individual characters. The second is an attempt to re-create the old railroad depot. The third holds climbing displays and a huge scale model of Mount McKinley and the nearby mountains (don't miss it if you will fly over the mountain). The fourth is a 1916 trapper's cabin and the fifth a 1924 cabin, both with period artifacts. The museum also is a handy information stop. It is open daily in summer from 10am to 6pm; generally closed in winter, although you may get lucky on a weekend. Admission is $3, free for children 12 and under.

I've found the most affecting site in town to be the **Mount McKinley Climbers' Memorial** at the town cemetery, near the airstrip on the east side of the railroad tracks. Besides a memorial of granite plaques for lost mountaineers, there is a small garden of monuments to many individual climbers, some in Japanese. The bodies of at least 34 climbers who died on the mountain have never been recovered. The propellers in the cemetery mark the graves of Bush pilots.

GETTING OUTSIDE
FLIGHTSEEING

There is no more dramatic or memorable experience available to the typical tourist in Alaska than to fly with one of the glacier pilots who support Mount McKinley climbs. Climbers typically begin with a flight from here to the 7,200-foot level of the Kahiltna

Glacier. These immense mountains grow ever larger as you fly toward them until, like a tiny insect, you fly among their miles-tall folds, watching the climbers toiling on the ice below you. I was simply speechless.

Several operators with long experience offer the flights. The least expensive excursions cost around $180 and approach McKinley's south face. If at all possible—and if the weather is good—buy an extended tour that circles the mountain and flies over its glaciers, for $225 to $275 per person. Best of all, arrange a landing on the mountain itself, just as the climbers do. The Don Sheldon Amphitheater on the Ruth Glacier is a stunning spot high on McKinley; only after you stand there do you realize the incredible scale of what you have seen from above. In the past this was not possible from mid-July through August, as the snow was too soft for the ski planes to land on the glaciers, but air taxis using different equipment and different landing areas have often been able to land all summer in recent years. These landings are usually treated as add-ons to the tours mentioned above, for an additional price of around $75 per person, plus the $10 park entrance fee.

Should you reserve ahead or wait to see the weather? It used to be you could reliably walk in and grab a seat, but the popularity of these flights now makes reservations advisable. That's the best way to get a guaranteed price, too; otherwise, prices sometimes depend on the number of passengers aboard the plane. If you do decide on the walk-in approach, make your appearance early in the morning.

A number of air taxi companies offer these flights, all operating out of the Talkeetna airport, including these three that I can wholeheartedly recommend: **Talkeetna Air Taxi** (© **800/533-2219** or 907/733-2218; www.talkeetnaair.com), **K-2 Aviation** (© **800/764-2291** or 907/733-2291; www.flyk2.com) and **Talkeetna Aero Services** (© **888/733-2899** or 907/733-2899, www.talkeetnaaero.com).

FISHING & JET BOAT TOURS

Talkeetna is at the confluence of the Talkeetna and Big Susitna rivers. **Mahay's Riverboat Service** (© **800/736-2210** or 907/733-2223; www.mahaysriverboat.com) covers these fast moving waters of glacier silt on speedy jet boats. Tours that leave several times a day from a dock near the Talkeetna River public boat launch range from 2 to 5 hours, priced at $55 to $145 per person. Owner Steve Mahay is legendary, the only person ever to shoot Devil's Canyon in a jet boat. He offers fishing charters as well.

RAFTING

Talkeetna River Guides, on Main Street (© **800/353-2677** or 907/733-2677; www.talkeetnariverguides.com), offers a 2-hour wildlife river-rafting tour, without whitewater, over 9 miles of the Talkeetna three times a day for $69 for adults, $49 for children 10 and under. They also offer longer rafting expeditions.

WHERE TO STAY & DINE

There are good restaurants at each of the lodgings listed here. One other place stands out, **Café Michele,** in a quaint little house at the corner of Talkeetna Spur Road and 2nd Street (© **907/733-5300**). It's a classy little bistro, serving sandwiches on homemade focaccia bread for lunch, and dinner entrees ranging from $24 to $34. Save room for dessert, as the baking is exceptional—Michelle even bakes the area's wedding cakes. It's easy to find a burger, pizza, or sandwich on Main Street.

A public campground for tents only is at the end of Main Street and costs $10. A larger campground with more privacy is at the boat launch (cross the railroad tracks to the airport and then turn left) and charges $13 a night.

Mt. McKinley Princess Lodge 🌟🌟   The Princess Cruise Line built the main lodge building to take advantage of a striking view of the mountain, only 42 miles away as the crow flies. The property isn't near any town—100 miles south of the park entrance and about 45 road miles from Talkeetna—but, like a resort, they offer everything you need on-site and a full set of activities, including a short network of trails. If you want a ride to Talkeetna, the lodge provides free shuttle service three times a day. The design and decoration are an inspired modernization of the classic national park style. There are several dining choices, including a steak and seafood place, a cafe, and a bar and grill.

Mile 133.1, Parks Hwy., Denali State Park, AK 99683. ℂ **800/426-0500** or 907/733-2900. Fax 907/733-2922. www.princesslodges.com. 460 units. Summer $189 double, $289 suite; spring/fall $149 double, $249 suite. AE, DC, DISC, MC, V. Closed mid-Sept to mid-May. **Amenities:** 3 restaurants; bar; exercise room; tour desk; courtesy shuttle to Talkeetna, coin-op laundry. *In room:* TV, hair dryer.

Swiss-Alaska Inn *Finds*   This is the essence of Talkeetna: a family business in the same hands for decades where guests are made to feel like old friends among the real old friends often found sipping coffee with the proprietor in the small restaurant. They serve good, familiar American meals, plus a few German dishes. Most of the rooms are decorated in light colors and, although small, are clean, comfortable, and reasonably priced. The larger rooms in the newer building are quite preferable.

F St., near the boat launch (P.O. Box 565), Talkeetna, AK 99676. ℂ **907/733-2424.** Fax 907/733-2425. www.swiss alaska.com. 20 units. $130 double. Extra person $10. AE, DISC, MC, V. **Amenities:** Restaurant; bar; courtesy car (to railroad station). *In room:* TV/DVD (no broadcast reception), hair dryer.

Talkeetna Alaskan Lodge 🌟🌟   The Cook Inlet Region Native corporation spared no expense building this magnificent hotel of big timbers and river rock, but it's not a gaudy showplace. Trim of regionally harvested birch finishes rooms and hallways in understated geometric designs, hung with Native art. Because the hotel sits atop a high river bluff, views from common rooms and many guest rooms take in a broad-canvas masterpiece of the Alaska Range, with McKinley towering in the center. Although just 2 miles from the town, the hotel feels like it's out in the wilderness. Rooms in the main building are preferable. They're somewhat larger and have either one king- or two queen-size beds, and the hallways connect to several sumptuous lobbies with reading areas. As much as I like the hotel, however, the rates are high.

Mile 12.5, Talkeetna Spur Rd. (Mailing address: P.O. Box 727, Talkeetna, AK 99676). ℂ **888/959-9590** or 907/265-4501 reservations; 907/733-9500 at lodge. Fax 907/733-9545. www.talkeetnalodge.com. 212 units. Summer $265–$395 double; off season $149–$219 double. Extra person 12 and over $15. AE, DISC, MC, V. Closed Oct–Apr. **Amenities:** 2 restaurants (dining room; bistro); bar; fitness center; tour desk; courtesy van; business center; Wi-Fi in lobby. *In room:* TV, dataport, coffeemaker, hair dryer, iron.

9

The Alaskan Interior

A warm summer evening in a campground; a slight breeze rustling the leaves of ghostly paper birches, barely keeping the mosquitoes at bay; the sounds of children playing; a perpetual sunset rolling slowly along the northern horizon—this is Interior Alaska. You know it's time to gather up the kids, separate them according to who belongs to whom, and put them to bed; it's 11 o'clock, for heaven's sake. But it's too difficult to feel that matters, or to alter the pace of a sun-baked day that never ends, meandering on like the broad, silty rivers and empty two-lane highways. Down by the boat landing, some college kids are getting ready to start on a float in the morning. An old, white-bearded prospector wanders out of the bar and, offering his flask to the strangers, tries out a joke while swatting the bugs. "There's not a single mosquito in Alaska," he declares. Waits for the loud, jocular objections. Then adds, "They're all married with big, big families." Easy laughter; then they talk about outboard motors, road work, why so many rabbits live along a certain stretch of highway. Eventually, you have to go to bed and leave the world to its pointless turning as the sun rotates back around to the east. You know it'll all be there tomorrow, just the same—the same slow-flowing rivers, the same long highways, the same vast space that can never be filled.

Interior Alaska is so large—it basically includes everything that's not on the coasts or in the Arctic—you can spend a week of hard driving and not explore it all. Or you can spend all summer floating the rivers and still have years of floating left to do before you see all the riverbanks. It's something like what the great mass of America's Midwest once must have been, perhaps a century and a half ago, when the great flatlands had been explored but not completely civilized and Huckleberry Finn could float downriver into a wilderness of adventures. As it happens, I have a friend who grew up on a homestead in the Interior and ran away from home at age 15 in that exact same fashion, floating hundreds of miles on a handmade raft, past the little river villages, cargo barges, and fishermen. During an Interior summer, nature combines its immensity with a rare sense of gentleness, patiently awaiting the next thunderstorm.

Winter is another matter. Without the regulating influence of the ocean—the same reason summers are hot—winter temperatures can often drop to –30°F or –40°F (–34°C or –40°C), and during exceptional cold snaps, even lower. Now the earth is wobbling over in the other direction, away from the sun. The long, black nights sometimes make Fairbanks, the region's dominant city, feel more like an outpost on a barren planet, far off in outer space. That's when the northern lights come, spewing swirls of color across the entire dome of the sky and crackling with electricity. Neighbors get on the phone to wake each other and, rising from bed to put on their warmest parkas and insulated boots, stand in the street, gazing straight up. Visitors lucky enough to come at such times may be watching from a steaming hot-spring tub. During the short days, they can bundle up and watch sled-dog racing or race across the wilderness themselves on snowmobiles.

Fairbanks stands second in Alaska in population, with over 80,000 in the greater area, but the Interior otherwise is without any settlements large enough to be called cities. Instead, it's defined by roads, both paved and gravel, which are strands of civilization through sparsely settled, often swampy land. Before the roads, development occurred only on the rivers, which still serve as thoroughfares for the Athabascan villages of the region. In the summer, villagers travel by boat. In the winter, the frozen rivers become highways for snowmobiles and sled-dog teams. White homesteaders and gold miners live back in the woods, too. Gold-rush history is written on the land in piles of old gravel tailings and abandoned equipment, as well as in the prettier tourist attractions and historic sites. Gold mining goes on today, in small one-man operations and huge industrial works employing hundreds, but today the economy is based more on military and other government spending, the oil industry, and, of course, tourism. You'll find warm rural hospitality along with the great vistas on these highways, and, perhaps, a sense of slow-river laziness Huck Finn would have recognized.

1 Exploring the Interior

More than anywhere else in Alaska, the Interior is the place where having your own car provides you with the freedom to find the out-of-the-way places that give the region its character. Trains and buses run between Fairbanks and Anchorage, but that approach will show you only the larger, tourist-oriented destinations.

If you have the time and money, you may enjoy driving one of the remote gravel highways, or just poking along on the paved highways between the larger towns, ready to stop and investigate the roadhouses and meet the people who live out in the middle of nowhere. You'll find them mostly friendly and often downright odd—*colorful,* to use the polite term. As I drove an abandoned highway a few years ago, I saw a hand-lettered sign advertising coffee. It wasn't your typical espresso stand, just a log cabin dozens of miles from the next nearest building. A squinting high plains drifter stepped out of the cabin, wearing a cowboy hat on his head and a huge revolver on his hip, and asked, "Yeah?" The coffee came from a percolator warming on the woodstove, and the proprietor and I struck up a good conversation in his dark little dwelling. He was living the life of the old-time frontier. Another favorite roadside sign, sighted on the Alaska Highway, in spray paint on plywood: SALE—EEL SKINS—ANVILS—BAIT. I've always wished I'd stopped in to window-shop and meet the person who came up with that business plan.

Of course, not every mile of back road is scenic, nor are all the stops interesting. Driving a car through Alaska takes a long time, including many hours spent in dull, brushy forest, and calls for a high tolerance for greasy hamburgers and a willingness to occasionally relieve yourself in the bushes. Paved highway sections can develop frost heaves in this often-frozen land—backbreaking dips and humps caused by the freeze and thaw of the road base and ground underneath. The gravel roads generate clouds of dust and quickly fatigue drivers, and windshields and headlights often succumb to their flying rocks. For information on renting a vehicle to drive on gravel roads, see "Equipped for the Back Roads," on p. 395.

Alaska's Highways a la Carte

You won't need a detailed highway map of Alaska, because Alaska doesn't have detailed highways. A triangle of paved two-lane highways connects Tok, Fairbanks, and Anchorage. From this triangle, a few routes reach to discrete destinations, and gravel roads penetrate the periphery of the Bush. Beyond a few miles of freeway around Fairbanks and Anchorage, highways all are narrow strips of asphalt or gravel through the wilderness. (See "The Roster of Rural Roads," on p. 406, for a rundown of Alaska's unpaved and minor highways.) Always fill your tank before leaving town, as gas stations are far apart. A centralized report on road conditions and construction is operated by the Alaska Department of Transportation (© 511; http://511.alaska.gov). To help readers figure driving times, I have included my estimate of reasonable average speeds on each road (without stopping). These are based purely on my experience and assume dry, daylight conditions in summer.

Alaska Highway

Route 2 from the border to Delta Junction

Average speed (Alaska section): 55–65 mph

Running nearly 1,400 miles from Dawson Creek, British Columbia, to Delta Junction, Alaska, a couple of hours east of Fairbanks on the Richardson Highway, this World War II road today is paved and generally easy driving. Two tiny towns lie on the Alaska portion of the road, Delta Junction and Tok. The prettiest part is on the Canadian side, in the Kluane Lake area. See section 5, later in this chapter.

Glenn Highway

Route 1 from Anchorage to Tok

Average speed: 55–65 mph, except 45 mph on Matanuska Glacier section

From the Alaska Highway, this is how you get to Southcentral Alaska, including Anchorage, 330 miles southwest of Tok. The northern section, from Tok to Glennallen (sometimes called the "Tok Cut-Off"), borders Wrangell–St. Elias National Park, with broad tundra and taiga broken by high, craggy peaks. Glennallen to Anchorage is even more spectacular, as the road passes through high alpine terrain and then close by the Matanuska Glacier, where it winds through a deep canyon valley carved by the glacier's river. See section 6, later in this chapter.

Parks Highway

Route 3 from near Anchorage to Fairbanks

Average speed: 60–65 mph

The George Parks Highway goes straight from Anchorage to Fairbanks, 360 miles north, providing access on the way to Denali National Park. The best parts are the vistas of Mount McKinley from south of the park and the alpine terrain on either side of Broad Pass, where the road crosses the

Alaska Range and the park entrance. However, the Parks Highway is mostly a transportation route, less scenic than the Richardson or Glenn highways. From the northern (Fairbanks) end, the highway passes Nenana (p. 388), then Denali and Talkeetna (see chapter 8), and finally the towns of the Matanuska and Susitna valleys (see chapter 6). Pick up a free road guide called "The Corridor" from the Alaska Public Lands Information Center in Anchorage or Fairbanks.

Richardson Highway

Route 4 from Valdez to Delta Junction, Route 2 from Delta Junction to Fairbanks

Average speed: 50–60 mph, except 45 mph in Thompson Pass section

The state's first highway, leading 364 miles from tidewater in Valdez to Fairbanks, lost much of its traffic to the Parks Highway, which saves more than 90 miles between Anchorage and Fairbanks, and to the Glenn Highway, which saves about 120 miles from Glennallen to Tok. But it's still the most beautiful paved drive in the Interior. From the south, the road begins with a magnificent climb through Keystone Canyon and steep Thompson Pass, just out of Valdez (see chapter 7), and then passes the huge, distant peaks of southern Wrangell–St. Elias National Park. North of Glennallen, the road climbs into the Alaska Range, snaking along the shores of long alpine lakes. The road descends again to the forested area around Delta Junction and meets the Alaska Highway before arriving in Fairbanks. The highway is covered in section 7.

Seward Highway

Route 1 from Anchorage to Tern Lake, Route 9 from Tern Lake to Seward

Average speed: 45–60 mph, depending on traffic

The highway leaves Anchorage on the 127-mile drive to Seward following the rocky edge of mountain peaks above a surging ocean fjord. Abundant wildlife and unfolding views often slow cars. Later, the road climbs through high mountain passes above the tree line, tracing sparkling alpine lakes. Alaska's best trail hikes are here. The section from Anchorage 50 miles south to Portage Glacier is covered in chapter 6; the remainder, to Seward, in chapter 7.

Sterling Highway

Route 1 from Tern Lake to Homer

Average speed: 50–60 mph, except 45 mph near Cooper Landing

Leading 142 miles from the Seward Highway to the tip of the Kenai Peninsula, the highway has some scenic ocean views on its southern section, but is mostly a way to get to the Kenai River, the Kenai National Wildlife Refuge, Kachemak Bay, and the towns of Cooper Landing, Soldotna, Kenai, and Homer.

Finds Rollin' on the River

Floating any of the thousands of miles of the Interior's rivers opens great swaths of wilderness. Beginners will want to take a guided trip before venturing out on their own. (See the list of operators in chapter 2.) To plan your own trip, start with the **Alaska Public Lands Information Center** in Fairbanks (p. 387), Tok (p. 419), or Anchorage (p. 215). Among the most accessible and historic rivers in the region are the Chena, Chatanika, and Yukon (see sections 2 and 3 as well as the boxes "The Steese Highway: Drive into the Wild" and "Dawson City & Eagle: Detour into History," in this chapter).

2 Fairbanks: Alaska Heartland

If the story of the founding of Fairbanks had happened anywhere else, it wouldn't be told so proudly, for the city's father was a swindler and its undignified birth contained an element of chance not usually admitted in polite society. As the popular story goes (and the historians' version is fairly close), it seems that in 1901, E. T. Barnette decided to get rich by starting a gold-mining boomtown like the others that had sprouted from Dawson City to Nome as the stampeders of 1898 sloshed back and forth across the territory from one gold find to the next. He booked passage on a riverboat going up the Tanana with his supplies to build the town, having made an understanding with the captain that, should the vessel get stuck, he would lighten the load by getting off with the materials on the nearest bank. Unfortunately, the captain got lost. Thinking he was heading up a slough on the Tanana, he got sidetracked into the relatively small Chena River. That was where the boat got stuck and where Barnette got left, and that was where he founded Fairbanks.

Fortunately for Barnette, an Italian prospector named Felix Pedro was looking for gold in the hills around the new trading post and the next summer made a strike in the Tanana Hills, north of the Chena. On that news, Barnette dispatched his Japanese cook, Jujiro Wada, off to Dawson City to spread the word. Wada's story showed up in a newspaper that winter after Christmas, and a stampede of hundreds of miners ensued, heading toward Fairbanks in weather as cold as −50°F (−46°C). Barnette's town was a success, but the cook nearly got lynched when the stampeders found out how far he'd exaggerated the truth. Much more gold was found later, however, and half the population of Dawson City came downriver to Fairbanks. Barnette had made it big.

The town's future was ensured thanks to a political deal. Barnette did a favor for the territory's judge, James Wickersham, by naming the settlement for Wickersham's hero in Congress, Sen. Charles Fairbanks of Indiana, who later became vice president. Wickersham then moved the federal courthouse to Fairbanks from Eagle—he loaded his records on his dog sled and mushed here, establishing the camp as the region's hub. Wickersham's story is interesting, too. He was a notable explorer, Alaska's first real statesman as a nonvoting delegate to Congress, and father of the Alaska Railroad. Houses he lived in are preserved at Pioneer Park in Fairbanks and in Juneau just up the hill from the capitol building. Barnette didn't do as well in history's eyes: He was run out of the town he founded for bank fraud.

Fairbanks is Alaska's second-largest city now, with a population of about 30,000 in the city limits and 85,000 in the greater metropolitan area, but it has never learned to

Fairbanks

put on airs. It sprawls, broad and flat, along big highways and the Chena. It's a friendly, easygoing town, but one where people still take gold and their independence seriously. They're still prospecting and mining around here, fighting off environmental regulation and maintaining a traditional Alaskan attitude that "it's us against the world." Fairbanks is the birthplace of strange political movements, including the secessionist Alaskan Independence Party. It's an adamant, loopy, affable place; it doesn't seem to mind being a little bizarre or residing far from the center of things. And that makes it an intensely Alaskan city, for those are the qualities Alaskans most cherish in their myth of themselves.

Fairbanks can strike a visitor a couple of ways, depending on what you expect and what you like. Fairbanks can come across as a provincial outpost, a touristy cross between Kansas and Siberia. Driving one of the franchise-choked commercial strips, you can wonder why you went out of your way to come here. Or you can relax and take Fairbanks on its own terms, as a fun, unpretentious town that never lost its sense of being on the frontier.

My children love it here. There's plenty for families to do in Fairbanks, much of it at least a little corny and requiring drives to widespread sites at the university, on the Chena River, in the gold mining area north of town, and at Pioneer Park. (You *must* have wheels in Fairbanks.) There are good opportunities for hiking and mountain biking, and great opportunities for canoeing and slow river-float trips.

ESSENTIALS

GETTING THERE   By Car or RV   Fairbanks is a transportation hub. The Richardson Highway heads east 100 miles to Delta Junction, the end point of the Alaska Highway, and then south to Glennallen and Valdez. The Parks Highway heads due south from Fairbanks to Denali National Park, 120 miles away, and Anchorage, 360 miles south.

By Van   Alaska/Yukon Trails (© 800/770-7275; www.alaskashuttle.com) offers daily service in summer (3 days a week in winter) to and from Denali National Park and Anchorage (one-way fares are $46 and $91, respectively). In Fairbanks, the van stops at the visitor center and at Billie's Backpackers Hostel (p. 403), among other places. The shuttle also runs to Dawson City and from there to Whitehorse, Yukon. On most routes they pick up and drop off along the way, but not in Canada.

By Train   The **Alaska Railroad** (© 800/544-0552; www.alaskarailroad.com) links Fairbanks with Denali National Park and Anchorage, with tour commentary provided along the way. The high-season one-way fare is $59 to Denali and $189 to Anchorage (more than twice the cost of flying between the cities).

By Air   Alaska Airlines (© 800/252-7522; www.alaskaair.com) connects Fairbanks to Anchorage. A bargain round-trip fare is under $250. The airport is a hub for various small carriers to Alaska's Interior and Arctic communities. A cab downtown from the airport is $16 to $18 with **Yellow Cab** (© 907/455-5555). **Fairbanks Shuttle** (© 800/770-2267) charges $7 for the ride from the airport.

VISITOR INFORMATION   The **Fairbanks Log Cabin Visitor Information Center** is in a large log building with a sod roof at 550 1st Ave., on the Chena River at the center of town, at Cushman Street, Fairbanks, AK 99701 (© 800/327-5774 or 907/456-5774; fax 907/452-2867; www.explorefairbanks.com). Besides answering questions, the staff and volunteers provide useful maps, driving tour pamphlets, and walking tour audio players, and can help you find a room with their daily vacancy listing.

Several computers are set up for free Internet access. The center is open May to mid-September daily 8am to 8pm, the rest of the year 10am to 5pm. The same organization has information desks at the airport and train depot.

The **Alaska Public Lands Information Center,** down the stairs at 3rd and Cushman streets (© **907/456-0527;** www.nps.gov/aplic), is an indispensable stop for anyone planning to spend time in the outdoors, and an interesting one even if you're not. The staff is remarkably knowledgeable and can tell you about trips and activities based on first-hand experience. Besides providing maps and other details, the center houses a small museum about the state's regions and the gear needed to explore them. Daily free films and naturalist programs show in a small auditorium. Open in summer daily from 9am to 6pm, in winter Tuesday through Saturday from 10am to 5pm.

GETTING AROUND   Fairbanks is designed around the car, and that's the practical way to get around. Without one, sticking downtown, you will leave with a low opinion of the place. The city is too spread out to use taxis much. **Avis, Hertz, Dollar, Budget, Payless, Alamo,** and **National** are located at the airport. **National** rents vehicles for gravel roads; for that, contact them at their local number (see "Equipped for the Back Roads," p. 395).

Fairbanks Shuttle (© **800/770-2267;** www.alaskashuttle.com, click on "Local Shuttles") offers transportation to many attractions in downtown Fairbanks and the greater area for reasonable prices.

The Fairbanks North Star Borough's **MACS bus system** (© **907/459-1011;** www.co.fairbanks.ak.us, click on "Departments," then "Transportation") links the university, downtown, the nearby North Pole community, shopping areas, and some hotels. Service is every 30 minutes, at best, worse Saturday, and nonexistent Sunday. Pick up timetables at the visitor center. All buses connect at the transit park downtown, at 5th Avenue and Cushman Street. The fare is $1.50 for adults; 75¢ for seniors, children, teens, and people with disabilities; free for children under age 5.

Fairbanks's car-oriented layout does not lend itself to using bikes as a primary means of transportation, but there are great mountain-biking opportunities (see "Getting Outside," later in this chapter).

FAST FACTS: Fairbanks

Banks Fairbanks has numerous banks with **ATMs** in the downtown area and along the commercial strips. **Key Bank** is at 100 Cushman.

Business Services **FedEx Kinko's Copy Center** is at 418 3rd St. (© **907/456-7348**).

Hospital **Fairbanks Memorial** is at 1650 Cowles St. (© **907/452-8181**).

Internet Access Free at the **Log Cabin Visitor Information Center** on Cushman Street at the river downtown (see "Visitor Information," above).

Police For nonemergency police business, call the **Alaska State Troopers** (© **907/451-5100**) or, within city limits, the **Fairbanks Police Department** (© **907/459-6500**).

Post Office At 315 Barnette St.

Taxes Fairbanks has no sales tax. North Pole charges 4% with a cap of $8 in tax on any one purchase. **Bed tax** is 8%.

Finds Nenana: Tom Sawyer's Alaska

If you are driving south from Fairbanks toward Denali National Park or Anchorage, plan a short stop in the town of Nenana, about 60 miles along your way. It's a town out of a Mark Twain novel, a sleepy, dusty riverside barge stop left over from the past. Here President Warren Harding drove the golden spike on the Alaska Railroad in 1923; a monument with a depiction of it is on display outside the memory-stirring old depot museum, although the train hasn't stopped regularly in 20 years. On the waterfront, riverboats are still loaded with cargo for villages down the Tanana and Yukon rivers. That's also where you can see the Alfred Starr Nenana Cultural Center, with its own little museum and Native craft shop, including some crafts by locals. The oldest building in town is the picturesque 1905 log cabin church on Front Street. Stop in at the visitor center on the Parks Highway to learn more and to see the big book of guesses from the Nenana Ice Classic (www.nenanaakiceclassic.com). The contest is a drawing to guess the exact minute the ice on the Tanana will go out, with a jackpot around $300,000. Thanks to the game, this is one of the most carefully kept climate measurements in the north; scientists are using it to demonstrate long-term warming of the weather. See "Special Events," above, to learn about ice classic festivities. Learn more about Nenana at the city's website (www.nenanahomepage.com).

SPECIAL EVENTS   A recording of current local happenings can be reached at © 907/456-INFO (4636), maintained by the Fairbanks Convention and Visitors Bureau, which also posts an event calendar at **www.explorefairbanks.com**.

The **Yukon Quest International Sled Dog Race** (© 907/452-7954; www.yukon quest.com) starts the second weekend in February 2008 in Fairbanks and ends more than a week later in Whitehorse (in odd-numbered years, the direction is reversed). Mushers say this rugged 1,000-mile race is even tougher than the Iditarod.

The **Nenana Ice Classic** (© 907/832-5446; www.nenanaakiceclassic.com) is a sweepstakes held annually since 1917 based on who can guess closest to the exact minute when the ice will go out on the Tanana River. The classic starts with Tripod Days, the first weekend in March, when they set up the so-called four-legged tripod; when it moves 100 feet it trips a clock, determining the winner. The Tripod Days celebration includes dance performances, dog mushing, and other activities.

Also in March, the **World Ice Art Championships** (© 907/451-8250; www. icealaska.com) brings carvers from all over the world to sculpt immense, clear chunks cut from a Fairbanks pond. It's worth planning a visit around. Ice sculptures stand in the Ice Park near the corner of Peger and Phillips Field roads. In 2008, professional carving will be February 27 to February 28 (single block) and March 2 to March 7 (multiblock), with the best viewing of completed sculptures March 8 to March 18. Amateur and junior carving will take place March 1 to March 14. The park stays open until the last Sunday in March. Among ice carvers, Fairbanks' ice is famous for its clarity and the great size of the chunks. Some spectacular ice sculptures stand as tall as two-story buildings. Check the website for pictures of past winners.

The **North American Sled Dog Championships** (© 907/457-MUSH [6874]; www.sleddog.org) are the oldest running, taking place over two weekends in mid-March.

Sprint mushers from all over the world compete with teams of as many as 24 dogs, streaking away from the starting line on 2nd Avenue or the Chena River.

Lots of events happen around the **summer solstice,** usually June 21. The **Midnight Sun Run** (© 907/452-6046; www.midnightsunrun.org) is a 10K race and walk, with winners chosen for both their times and their funny costumes. The race is run on or near the solstice. It starts at 10pm on the University of Alaska Fairbanks campus and ends at Pioneer Park.

The **Midnight Sun Baseball Game,** hosted by the semipro Alaska Goldpanners of Fairbanks (© 907/451-0095; www.goldpanners.com), begins at 10:30pm on the solstice. The game, which began with a pair of pick-up teams in 1906, is played with no artificial lights. The 'Panners have hosted since 1960.

Also in June, the free **Fairbanks Summer Folk Fest** (© 907/460-7014 or 455-6528; www.alaskasbest.com/fairbanksfolkfest) fills a Pioneer Park lawn with music, food, and art booths; live music starts at 1pm and lasts late into the night.

The Fairbanks Summer Arts Festival, held the last 2 weeks in July on the University of Alaska Fairbanks campus (© 907/474-8869; www.fsaf.org), brings artists of international reputation for performance and teaching. Classes are for all levels in music, dance, theater, opera, creative writing, visual arts, healing arts, and other subject areas (July 13-27, 2008).

The **Tanana Valley State Fair** (© 907/452-3750; www.tananavalleyfair.org), in early August, shows off the area's agricultural production, arts and crafts, businesses, and entertainment, and includes rides and competitive exhibits.

In late August, Friends of Creamer's Field (© 907/459-7307) hosts an annual **Sandhill Crane Festival,** with nature walks, lectures, and other activities, mostly at Creamer's Field (see "Special Places," later in this chapter).

The **BP Top of the World Classic,** November 20 to November 23, 2008, brings NCAA Division I basketball teams to the University of Alaska Fairbanks for a weekend tournament (© 907/474-5977; www.alaskananooks.com, click on "Tournaments" under "Nanook Links").

EXPLORING THE TOWN
STROLLING AROUND DOWNTOWN

Exploring downtown won't take more than an hour or two, but there are a few interesting spots in addition to the ice museum and community museum covered below. The log cabin visitor center at 1st and Cushman lends audio players with spoken tours (you have to leave a credit card imprint as a deposit). Among the highlights is the **Golden Heart Park,** a waterfront plaza next to the center, with a fountain and a bronze statue of a Native family, where community events often occur. A graceful footbridge spans the river, and on the other side is the town's most interesting building, the Roman Catholic **Church of the Immaculate Conception.** The white clapboard structure, built in 1904, has ornate gold-rush decoration inside, rare for its authenticity, including a pressed-tin ceiling and stained-glass windows—an appealing if incongruous mix of gold-rush and sacred decor. Also on this side of the river, peek into the lobby of the Doyon Native corporation offices to see Native cultural displays from all over Alaska, the traditional Athabascan tool collection, and the colorful modern art hanging from the walls and ceiling.

Back on the visitor center side of the river, at 1st Avenue between Kellum and Bonnifield streets, east from the center, **St. Matthew's Episcopal Church** is a cute old log church with a working rope-pull bell. It was founded by missionary and dog-sled explorer Hudson Stuck in 1904, who organized the first successful climb of Mount McKinley. The original church burned; the present structure dates from 1948.

At 500 2nd Ave., the **Fairbanks Ice Museum** ⊛ (℃ **907/451-8222;** www.ice museum.com) aims to show summer visitors what winter is like, with seven large ice displays and a freezer you can enter to feel –20°F (–29°C). A big-screen, high-tech slide show plays hourly, explaining the annual World Ice Art Championships (see "Special Events," above), and the freezers contain impressive ice tableaux with an ice artist usually at work. Admission is $12 for adults, $11 for seniors and military, $6 for children ages 6 to 12, $2 for ages 5 and under; except noon lunch shows, which include food and cost $18 for everyone. It's open from 10am to 8pm daily from mid-May to mid-September.

The **Fairbanks Community Museum** ⊛, in the old city hall at 410 Cushman St. (℃ **907/457-3669**), is well worth a stop for the charming historical exhibits and the sense of local pride it contains. A series of cramped galleries offers up old photographs, maps, newspapers, and other bric-a-brac, as well as skillfully created explanatory exhibits, mostly focusing on the area's gold-mining history and development. Whimsical photographs show how modern-day Fairbanksans entertain themselves in the winter. You could spend quite some time wandering this maze of small discoveries. The Yukon Quest International Sled Dog Race (see "Special Events," above) shares these quarters, teaching about mushing with displays of equipment and supporting the race with souvenirs sold in the tiny gift shop. The museum is open Tuesday through Saturday from 10am to 6pm. Admission is free. It is closed during April.

Another little downtown museum recently opened: **Historic Hall,** at 825 1st Ave., in the Golden North Rebekah Lodge. Highlights include panoramic pictures of the Fairbanks waterfront throughout the decades, historic local home movies, and Alaska travel maps and brochures from the past. The museum relies on volunteer staff and so is open "most" summer days from 1:30 to 8pm.

PIONEER PARK ⊛⊛

Built for the Alaska purchase centennial in 1967, **Pioneer Park** (formerly **Alaskaland**) is the boiled-down essence of Fairbanks on grounds at the intersection of Airport Way and Peger Road (℃ **907/459-1087;** www.co.fairbanks.ak.us, click on "Parks and Recreation," then "Pioneer Park"). It's called a theme park, but don't expect Disneyland or anything like it. Instead, Pioneer Park is a city park with a theme. It's relaxing and low-key, entrancing for young children and interesting for adults if you can give in to the charm of the place. Admission to the park is free and the tours and activities are generally inexpensive. The park is open year-round, but the attractions operate only Memorial Day weekend to Labor Day, daily from 11am to 9pm. Pick up a map and schedule when you arrive; here I've listed the highlights, but there is more to see. Depending on the pace you like to keep and the age level of your group, you can spend anything from a couple of hours to most of a day here.

The **SS** *Nenana* ⊛⊛ (℃ **907/456-8848**) is the park's centerpiece. Commissioned by the federally owned Alaska Railroad in 1933, the large sternwheeler plied the Yukon and Tanana rivers until 1952. In 1967 the *Nenana* came to what was then Alaskaland but was unmaintained and had nearly collapsed from rot when it was saved by a community restoration effort, completed in 1992. There are two decks of sumptuous mahogany, brass, and white-painted promenades to see, and the wheelhouse, well-preserved engine room, and the like. Self-guided entry to the entire boat is $3 (free for ages 5 and younger), or for $2 you can see the ground-floor cargo deck with

Moments Seeing the Aurora Borealis

One fall evening I left the house of friends in Fairbanks to the sight of a swirling green glow that filled the dark sky. I knocked on the door and brought them out to see, only to have my friends laugh in my face. They informed me, with mock contempt for my Anchorage home, that in Fairbanks they don't even bother to bend their necks back for northern lights as dim as these. It's true—a bright aurora borealis is routine in Fairbanks. Some of the world's top experts on the phenomenon work here, at the University of Alaska's Geophysical Institute (their aurora predictions, in season, and extensive background on the aurora are posted at **www.gi.alaska.edu**). Hours-long displays can be incredibly spectacular and even moving.

Unfortunately, most visitors never see these wild strands of bright colors whipping across the sky, because when most visitors come, the sky is never dark. Alaskans rarely see the stars from late May to early August, and to see the aurora well you need an especially dark night sky. To improve your chances, plan your trip in the fall or winter. An early September trip offers brilliant fall foliage, dark night skies, and the remnants of summer weather. In midwinter, the sky is dark all night and most of the day. Many hotels near Fairbanks cater to travelers coming to see the aurora in winter, as well as visitors who come for such winter sports as dog mushing and snowmobiling; the best for that kind of trip is Chena Hot Springs Resort, covered in the next section.

its engaging set of dioramas showing all the riverside towns and villages where the boat called, modeled as they looked in its heyday.

Much of Fairbanks's history has been moved to Pioneer Park. A village of log cabins contains shops and restaurants, each marked with its original location and place in town history. **Judge Wickersham's house,** built around 1904, is kept as a museum, decorated appropriately according to the period of the town's founding. The house is less than grand—it may remind you of your grandmother's—but it's worth a stop to strike up a conversation with the historical society volunteers who keep it open. **Pres. Warren Harding's railcar,** from which he stepped to drive the golden spike on the Alaska Railroad, sits near the park entrance. The **Pioneer Air Museum (© 907/451-0037)** is housed in a geodesic dome toward the back of the park. Besides the aircraft there are displays and artifacts of the crashes of Alaska's aviation pioneers. Admission is $2 for adults, free for children 12 and under with a parent, $5 for families. Other attractions include dog-sled rides, an illustrated gold-rush show, kayak and bike rentals, a dance hall, an art gallery, and Alaska Native and gold-rush museums.

If you have children, you certainly won't escape Pioneer Park without a ride on the **Crooked Creek and Whiskey Island Railroad** that circles the park twice, with a tour guide pointing out the sights; rides cost $2 for adults, $1 for children and seniors. Kids also will enjoy the large **playground,** with equipment for toddlers and older children, where lots of local families come to play, and the 36-hole miniature golf course. The only carnival ride is a nice old **merry-go-round,** which costs $1.

Tour groups generally come to Pioneer Park in the evening from mid-May to mid-September for the **Alaska Salmon Bake,** at the mining valley area (© **907/452-7274**), and the **Golden Heart Revue,** at the Palace Theatre (© **907/456-5960;** www. akvisit.com for both). The cost for all-you-can-eat prime rib and fish (halibut, cod, or salmon) is $31. Beer and wine are available. The seating area is pleasant, with indoor or outdoor dining. The revue, nightly at 8:15pm from mid-May to mid-September, covers the amusing story of the founding of Fairbanks with comedy and song in a nightclub setting; admission is $18 for adults.

UNIVERSITY OF ALASKA FAIRBANKS

The state university's main campus contains several interesting attractions and makes a point of serving tourists. The campus is on the west side of town; the main entrance is at the intersection of University Avenue and College Road. A widely distributed brochure lists tours, hours, and fees. A free 2-hour **walking tour,** led by students, meets at the museum Monday through Friday at 10am, June through August except July 4 and July 5. Call ahead (© **907/474-7581**) to confirm the time and any weather cancellations. A shuttle bus is provided in case of rain or visitor need. More campus attractions are listed below; for a complete list, go to **www.uaf.edu/uaf/community/ visiting.html**. The university's ski trails are covered later under "Winter Activities."

UA Museum of the North ★★★   This rich, interdisciplinary on-campus museum, long one of Alaska's best, recently added a spectacular expansion. First, the original part of the museum: Alaska's best natural history collection and its most scholarly, with information presented at advanced as well as elementary levels. Some of the objects have a real wow factor, such as Blue Babe, the mummified steppe bison; a 5,400-pound copper nugget; and the state's largest public display of gold. There is an audio tour guide, or in the summer you can join free 20-minute talks offered through the day on various Alaska topics. All this remains, and it already provided enough to keep your interest for much of a day. Now the new part: A swooping combination of grand, graceful shapes, designed by Joan Soranno, a disciple of Frank Gehry, it is reminiscent of moving icebergs, or perhaps of the northern lights. Inside, the towering new gallery is devoted to art, with thematic presentation of contemporary art alongside Native and archaeological objects, sound, crafts, and much more. Visit the auditorium for presentations on the aurora, winter, and other subjects.

907 Yukon Dr. (P.O. Box 756960), Fairbanks, AK 99775-6960. © 907/474-7505. www.uaf.edu/museum. Admission $10 adults; $9 ages 60 and older; $5 ages 7–17; free ages 6 and under. Summer daily 9am–7pm; winter Mon–Fri 9am–5pm, Sat–Sun noon–5pm.

Georgeson Botanical Garden ★   I really enjoy the mix of science and contemplation I find at this relaxed working garden. Plots are laid out to compare seeds and cultivation techniques, usually well posted with explanatory information on the experiment; but at the same time the flowers and vegetables are spectacular and there are peaceful memorials and places to picnic. You don't need a tour to enjoy the garden. Nearby, the barn of the university's experimental farm is open for visitors to wander through and view the reindeer.

117 W. Tanana Dr. © 907/474-1744. www.uaf.edu/salrm/gbg. Admission $2. Summer daily 9am–8pm; store 9am–5pm; free guided tours Fri at 2pm.

Large Animal Research Station ★   The university studies captive musk ox, reindeer, and caribou here on a property often called the musk ox farm. Tours are given daily in the high season, with naturalists bringing animals into an amphitheater for close-up viewing. At any time, on a walk along the fence from the parking lot on Yankovich Road, you can see the animals behaving naturally in the large pastures. Best times are the cool morning or evening hours, and binoculars help.

Yankovich Rd. ✆ 907/474-7207. www.uaf.edu/lars. Half-hour tour $6, free ages 6 and under; 1-hour tour $10 adults, $9 seniors, $6 students, free ages 6 and under. Tours Memorial Day through Labor Day daily each hour 10:30am–4:30pm; hour-long tours at 1:30 and 3:30pm, otherwise, half-hour tours. Call ✆ 907/474-5724 to check on tour times and changes. Drive north from campus, turn left on Ballaine Rd., left again on Yankovich.

COMMERCIAL TOURIST ATTRACTIONS

Three major for-profit attractions around Fairbanks pack in visitors by the hundreds of thousands, most of them on group tours. These places are educational and fun, as I've described below, but I think they all charge excessive prices. Whether they're worth your money depends on how much you've got and your level of interest; however, I doubt most independent budget travelers would feel they got their money's worth.

The Riverboat *Discovery* 🎠🎠   The *Discovery* belongs to the pioneering Binkley family, which has been in the riverboat business since the Klondike gold rush and has run this attraction since 1950. The *Discovery* is a real sternwheeler, a 156-foot steel vessel carrying up to 900 passengers on as many as three trips a day. There's nothing intimate or spontaneous about the 3½-hour ride, which mostly carries package-tour passengers off fleets of buses, but the Binkleys still provide a diverting outing that doesn't feel cheap or phony. After loading at a landing with shops off Dale Road, near the airport, the boat cruises down the Chena and up the Tanana past demonstrations on shore—among others, a bush plane taking off and landing, fish cutting at a Native fish camp, and a musher's dog yard. Finally, the vessel pulls up at the bank for an hour-long tour of a mock Athabascan village.

1975 Discovery Dr., Fairbanks, AK 99709. ✆ 866/479-6673 or 907/479-6673. www.riverboatdiscovery.com. Tours $50 adults, $35 ages 3–13, free ages 2 and under. Sailings mid-May to mid-Sept daily at 8:45am and 2pm.

The El Dorado Gold Mine 🎠   A train such as you would find at an amusement park carries visitors though an impressively staged educational tour, including a trip through a tunnel in the permafrost. This is like a land version of the riverboat tour that's operated by the same family, the Binkleys. But the gold miners who act as hosts are the real attraction here. Visitors gather around a sluice to hear the amusing and authentic Dexter and Lynette (aka Yukon Yonda) Clark and watch a swoosh of water and gold-bearing gravel rush by. You pan the resulting pay dirt, and everyone goes home with enough gold dust to fill a plastic locket—typically $5 to $35 worth. Drive out to the mine after making reservations, or take a $4 shuttle.

Off the Elliott Hwy., 9 miles north of town. ✆ 866/479-6673 or 907/479-6673. www.eldoradogoldmine.com. Tours $35 adults, $23 ages 3–12, free ages 2 and under. Tours mid-May to mid-Sept daily; call for times.

Gold Dredge Number 8 🎠   Authenticity makes this is the area's best historic gold-mining site. The centerpiece is a 1927 gold dredge, similar to machines in Dawson City and Nome, standing five stories tall on a barge in a pond it created. When it operated, huge scoops would dig from one end, the mechanism inside would digest the gold from the gravel, and then it would dump the tailings out the back—in this way, the pond and the dredge it supports crept 4½ miles across the frozen ground north of Fairbanks. Many sterile areas you see in this area were created by these earth-eaters, for nothing grows on their leavings for decades after. The tour company that bought the historic site added to the dredge with museums housed in relocated gold camp buildings, showing the harsh, colorless life lived by the miners. A 90-minute tour includes a film, mine tours, and the dredge, and ends with a chance to pan for gold yourself, with success assured.

1755 Old Steese Hwy., Fairbanks, AK 99712. (C) 907/457-6058. www.golddredgeno8.com. Admission $21 tour only, $25 with gold panning, $35 with lunch of stew. Mid-May to mid-Sept tours start hourly 9:30am–3:30pm. To get there, go north on the Steese Expressway from town, turn left on Goldstream Rd., turn left again on the Old Steese Hwy.

GETTING OUTSIDE

In this section, I've described the outdoor opportunities local to Fairbanks, but some other choices are barely farther afield: Check out section 3 of this chapter, on Chena Hot Springs Road, and the later feature, "The Steese Highway: Drive into the Wild." The **Alaska Public Lands Information Center,** 250 Cushman St. (at 3rd Ave.), ((C) **907/ 456-0527**; www.nps.gov/aplic), is a great resource. The staff will advise you on outings, outfitters, and where to find rental equipment. The center also sells the *Fairbanks Area Wildlife Watching Guide,* a $6 booklet that contains thorough descriptions of the best places to go and tips for success. You can also buy it in area bookstores.

GEARING UP

You can rent most of what you need for outdoor explorations around Fairbanks and along the region's extraordinary rural highways from a set of local businesses that have grown up around the needs of adventurers. Some of the outdoor opportunities I describe require a drive on unpaved roads, including portions of the Steese Highway. Two businesses that rent vehicles you can take on these roads are listed in the feature "Equipped for the Back Roads," on p. 395. One of those, GoNorth Alaska Adventure Travel Center, also rents canoes, bikes, and camping gear and offers a shuttle for canoeists and hikers. For ski rentals, see the appropriate sections below.

   Alaska Outdoor Rentals & Guides, owned by the knowledgeable Larry Katkin, has its main location on the riverbank at Pioneer Park ((C) **907/457-2453**; www. akbike.com or www.2paddle1.com). The company rents canoes, kayaks, and bikes and offers pickup or drop off for paddlers in town or far afield—even for trips on the great Yukon River. For an easy in-town paddle, say from the park to Pike's Landing, you would pay $33 for the canoe and $17 for the pickup. If you want to go beyond the road system, Larry also carries foldable canoes that will fit in a bush plane. He also offers lessons. This is a good place to start a mountain-biking outing, too. Bikes rent for $27 for an 8-hour day in summer. You can also rent from the long-established **7 Bridges Boats and Bikes,** at 7 Gables Inn, 4312 Birch Lane ((C) **907/479-0751**; www.7gablesinn.com/7bbb) for $35 per day or $100 per week, and they will drop you off at the river and pick you up at your destination for $2 per mile out of town, with a $15 minimum. Guests at the inn get free rentals (same phone; www.7gables inn.com). Street and mountain bikes go for $20 a day.

SPECIAL PLACES

CREAMER'S FIELD   At 1300 College Rd., right in Fairbanks, this 2,000-acre migratory waterfowl refuge is a former dairy farm that was saved from development in 1966 by a community fund drive. The pastures are a prime stopover point for Canada geese, pintails, and golden plovers in the spring and fall. We've seen many swans there in the spring. Sandhill cranes, shovelers, and mallards show up all summer. The **Friends of Creamers Field** ((C) **907/459-7307**; www.creamersfield.org)

Tips **Equipped for the Back Roads**

Exploring Alaska's gravel highways—camping and fishing along the way, per-haps launching a canoe in a remote lake—can be tough for visitors to arrange because of the policies of most rental car agencies, which don't allow clients to drive off pavement. An exception is the **Alamo/National** franchise in Fairbanks, with locations at the airport and at 4960 Dale Rd. (© **800/227-7368** or 907/451-7368). They rent four-door, four-wheel-drive pickup trucks for travel on gravel roads such as the Dalton, Steese, and Denali highways. Be sure to call the local franchise, not the national reservation number. **GoNorth Alaska Adventure Travel Center,** at 3500 Davis Rd. (© **866/236-7272** or 907/479-7272, www.gonorthalaska.com) goes a step further, renting not only SUVs and trucks, but also campers on four-wheel-drive pickups, perfect for exploring gravel roads. The firm also runs a tent-camp hostel; arranges self-guided outdoor trips; rents canoes, bikes, and camping gear; and drives a shuttle for canoeists and hikers. With unlimited mileage, a pickup camper is $125 to $220 a day; insurance of $18 to $24 a day is required unless you present proof of your own coverage, so be sure to ask about what paperwork you will need when you reserve.

operates a small visitor center in the old farmhouse with displays on birds, wildlife, and history, open June through August daily from 10am to 5pm. They offer guided nature walks in summer Monday, Wednesday, and Friday at 2pm; Wednesday at 9am; and Tuesday and Thursday at 7pm. You don't need a guide, however: During migrations, use the blinds around the edge of the field; other times, explore the 3 miles of trails through forest, field, and wetland. I especially enjoy the boreal forest nature walk, interpreted by an excellent booklet you can pick up at the visitor center or from a kiosk at the trail head when the visitor center is closed. The **Alaska Bird Observatory** (© **907/451-7159,** www.alaskabird.org) conducts research and educational programs on the Creamer's Field refuge, including bird walks and bird banding that visitors can observe (call for times). It is the farthest north facility of its kind in North America. The organization's building has interpretive displays, a nature store, and a library. Located just west of the refuge on the grounds of the Wedgewood Resort (see "Wedgewood Resort," below), the observatory can be hard to find—look for the signs.

CHENA LAKE RECREATION AREA   This is a wonderful and unique place for a family camping trip. A birch-rimmed lake created for a flood-control project has been developed by the local government to provide lots of recreational possibilities: flat walking and bike trails; a swimming beach; fishing; a place to rent canoes and paddle-boats; a self-guided 2.5-mile nature trail; a playground; big lawns; and the terrific campground, with 80 camping sites, from pull-throughs for RVs to tent sites on a lit-tle island you can reach only by boat. In the winter, it's a popular area for cross-country skiing, ice fishing, dog mushing, and snowmobiling. Use of the area requires a $4 fee per vehicle. Tent sites are $10 per night and RV sites are $12. Drive 17 miles east of Fairbanks on the Richardson Highway and turn left on Laurance Road as you leave North Pole. For information, contact Fairbanks North Star Borough Chena Lake Recreation Area (© **907/488-1655;** www.co.fairbanks.ak.us, click on "Parks and Recreation" then "Chena Lake Recreation Area"). Follow the same directions (drive along the dam past the recreation area) to the **Moose Creek Dam Salmon Watch,** a picnic and viewing area built by the U.S. Army Corps of Engineers atop the flood-control project, to watch spawning salmon in crystal-clear water from late June to the end of July. Use of the salmon watch is free, so tell the recreation-area gatehouse you are going there.

SUMMER ACTIVITIES

CANOEING   The rivers in and around Fairbanks are best seen by floating slowly along in a canoe. Paddling is as popular as hiking around here. See "Gearing Up," on p. 394, for companies that rent equipment and offer shuttle services. The Chena River is slow and meandering as it flows through Fairbanks, and you have your pick of restaurants on the bank. Farther upriver, the canoeing passes wilder shores, and near the headwaters becomes more challenging (see "Chena Hot Springs Road," later). For beginners, try the wilderness section from the Chena Lake Recreation Area downstream (see "Chena Lake Recreation Area," above). It's 12 to 16 hours from there all the way into town, or you can take out at one of the roads crossing the river along the way (see "Gearing Up" on p. 394 for businesses that rent canoes and provide drop-off and pick-up service along the area's waterways). The **U.S. Army Corp of Engineers** (© 907/488-2748) produces the "Chena River Float Guide," with put-in and take-out points and float times, available at the Alaska Public Lands Information Center (see "Visitor Information," earlier).

For something a bit more challenging but still manageable, the clear, Class I water of the Chatanika River is perfect for day trips or relaxed expeditions of a week or more, if you know how to handle river hazards such as sweepers and snags that show up on any Alaska stream. Alaska State Parks produces a brochure covering the float from the Upper Chatanika River Campground, at mile 39 of the Steese Highway, to another campground on the Elliot Highway. Low water and logjams requiring portages can slow down the trip so that it takes a long day; in better conditions, expert canoeists can do it in a few hours.

The Steese Highway also meets two National Wild and Scenic Rivers: Beaver Creek, for trips of a week or more over easy Class I water, and Birch Creek, for more expert paddlers. For detailed guidance check with the Alaska Public Lands Information Center in Fairbanks. Also see "The Steese Highway: Drive into the Wild," p. 412.

BIKING & HIKING   Traffic goes fast in Fairbanks and the separated bike trails are few, but strong cyclists can get by. Mountain biking is good on many dirt roads and byways within and beyond Fairbanks and on the ski trails at Birch Hill Recreation Area and the University of Alaska Fairbanks (see "Winter Activities," below). The ski trails are also good for easy summer hikes, or go farther afield for more ambitious trail hikes off Chena Hot Springs Road (see section 3 of this chapter) or the Steese Highway (p. 412). Inquire about all the options or other ideas at the Alaska Public Lands Information Center (p. 387).

FISHING   Salmon season here is brief and the fish, this far inland, have turned spawning colors and have softer, less palatable flesh compared to coastal salmon. Most fishing is in the streams for Arctic grayling, Northern pike, and burbot, and in stocked lakes for rainbow trout, Arctic char, and silver salmon. You can fish right in the Chena as it flows through town, although getting out of town and hiking away from a road yields better results. Fly-in fishing will further increase your chances and add sheefish and Dolly Varden char to your list, but the expense of around $300 a day is easier to justify from Anchorage or another coastal community, where you can find better salmon fishing to go along with the freshwater fish. The Alaska Public Lands Information Center (p. 387) offers guidance, or contact the **Alaska Department of Fish and Game,** at Creamer's Field, 1300 College Rd., Fairbanks, AK 99701 (© **907/459-7228;** sport-fish information recording 907/459-7385; www.alaska.gov/adfg, click on "Sport Fisheries," then on the Interior region on the map, and then "Lower Tanana River Drainage").

WINTER ACTIVITIES

Fairbanks has real Jack London winters. The visitor bureau guarantees it. For the growing number of visitors who want to experience real cold, see the aurora borealis, and ride a dog sled, Fairbanks is the place. Chena Hot Springs Resort (p. 410) and A Taste of Alaska Lodge (p. 400) are the best destinations for winter immersion, but you can also have a good time in town, especially in March, when the days lighten up, the temperatures are moderate, and the town gets busy with dog mushing and the ice carving contest (see "Special Events," earlier).

DOG MUSHING   The long winters and vast wild lands make the Fairbanks area a center of dog sledding, both for racers and recreationists, and there are plenty of people willing to take you for a lift, which is really an experience not to be missed. I've heard good things about **Sun Dog Express Dog Sled Tours** (© **907/479-6983;** www.mosquitonet.com/~sleddog), which charges as little as $15 for a quick spin, up to $250 to learn to drive a team in a half-day. They also have summer cart tours.

During the summer, learn about mushing by taking a wonderfully intimate tour with Mary Shields, the first woman to finish the Iditarod Trail Sled Dog Race. Rather than a tour, a visit to Mary's home on the outskirts of Fairbanks feels more like a chat with a fascinating new friend. You'll meet and pet Mary's dogs, talk about dog mushing, and hear tales of her extraordinary experiences as a musher. The tour, called **Alaskan Tails of the Trails** (© **907/455-6469;** www.maryshields.com), happens every evening in the summer. It costs $28 and lasts 2 hours.

CROSS-COUNTRY SKIING   The **Birch Hill Recreation Area,** off the Steese Expressway just north of town, has about 25km of good cross-country ski trails, most groomed for classical or skate skiing, and two warm-up buildings in which to change clothes. Several loops of a few kilometers each offer advanced skiing on the steep southern side of the hill; loops of up to 10km provide more level terrain to the north. Some trails are lighted. The **University of Alaska Fairbanks** offers a trail network of roughly the same length, two-thirds of it groomed for skate technique. Although I prefer Birch Hill, with its mix of ability levels, the university trails pass through lovely lands and have the advantage of a nearby source of rental equipment, the **Outdoor Adventures Program** at the Wood Student Center (© **907/474-6027;** www.uaf. edu/outdoor). You can rent skis, poles, and boots for a mere $10 a day. One trail head is at the west end of campus, near the satellite dishes at the top of Tanana Loop. Another is off Farmers Loop Road at Ballaine Lake.

DOWNHILL SKIING   Fairbanks has several community-size downhill skiing areas, including the relatively large **Moose Mountain Ski Resort** (© **907/479-4732;** snow report 907/459-8132; www.shredthemoose.com), with 1,300 vertical feet of skiing. Instead of freezing on a lift, you ride back up the hill and socialize in heated buses.

SHOPPING

Fairbanks has a few good shops downtown. **New Horizons Gallery,** at 519 1st Ave. (© **907/456-2063;** www.newhorizonsgallery.com), occupies a large space with the work of some of Alaska's best in oils, inexpensive prints, and sculpture, and also carries gifts. It is open every day. The **Arctic Travelers Gift Shop,** at 201 Cushman St. (© **907/456-7080**), specializes in Native art and crafts, carrying both valuable art and affordable but authentically Alaskan gifts. The staff is knowledgeable about what they sell. Right next door, at 215 Cushman, **If Only...** (© **907/457-6659**) is a charming gift and stationary shop with items to hold locals' as well as visitors' interest—not just tourist stuff.

Near the airport, at 4630 Old Airport Rd., the **Great Alaskan Bowl Company** (© **800/770-4222** or 907/474-9663; www.woodbowl.com) makes and sells bowls of native birch—salad bowls, of course, but also bowls for many other purposes. Some of these bowls are simply amazing. They can carve up to eight nested bowls from one piece of wood and even laser-engrave a photo inside one. Through a glass wall looking into the shop, you can see workers cutting the bowls from raw logs. It's hard to depart without buying a bowl. The shop is open daily all year.

WHERE TO STAY

Going the bed-and-breakfast route is a good choice in Fairbanks. At the B&Bs I've listed below, you can save money over a hotel and get a private room just as good while staying in a unique place with interesting people. The **Fairbanks Association of Bed and Breakfasts** lists about 20 more on its website at **www.ptialaska.net/~fabb**. You also can get B&B information and up-to-date vacancy data at the Fairbanks Log Cabin Visitor Information Center (p. 386).

EXPENSIVE

There are many more hotels in the expensive category than there is any need to describe here, so I have followed my usual practice of including one for each taste. The enormous **Fairbanks Princess Riverside Lodge** (© **800/426-0500** or 907/455-4477; fax 907/455-4476; www.princessalaskalodges.com) also merits a mention as a luxurious and well-run hotel in a pleasant setting near the airport (it's quite similar to Pike's Waterfront). However, in summer the Princess usually books fully with the owner's cruise-line clients. Rooms are most often available Friday, Saturday, or Sunday.

Pike's Waterfront Lodge ★★   When Pike's appeared on the Chena River next to the Pike's Landing restaurant (discussed later) it initially looked like a big rectangle the size and shape of innumerable chain hotels along interstates, but the local owner kept adding features until it became utterly unique, including a greenhouse, an ice cream parlor with an airplane sticking out of it, an extraordinary wildlife art collection, and 28 cabins. The main building is decorated in a mix of modern and faux rustic, with lots of log work. Rooms, while not large, are well equipped, and many look out on the river. The location is a stone's throw from the airport. The place fills on certain days in the summer with package tour guests—as of this writing, Monday through Wednesday—but usually has room the rest of the week. Summer only, a steak-and-seafood restaurant operates on-site. The bar also serves casual meals.

1850 Hoselton Dr., Fairbanks, AK 99709. © 877/774-2400 or 907/456-4500. Fax 907/456-4515. www.pikeslodge. com. 208 units. High season $149–$210 double, $114–$465 suite; low season $69–$99 double, $89–$235 suite. Extra person age 13 and over $10. AE, DC, DISC, MC, V. **Amenities:** Restaurant (summer); bar; exercise room; steam

ACCOMMODATIONS ■
All Seasons Inn **4**
Bridgewater Hotel **5**
Westmark Fairbanks Hotel &
   Conference Center **12**

DINING ◆
Gambardella's Pasta Bella **6**
Lavelle's Bistro **9**
Thai House **11**

ATTRACTIONS ●
Church of the
   Immaculate Conception **1**
Fairbanks Community Museum **7**
Golden Heart Park **8**
Historic Hall **3**
Ice Museum **10**
St. Matthew's Episcopal Church **2**

0 _____ 1/8 mi
0 _____ 1/8 km

room; sauna; tour desk; courtesy van; business center; laundry service; coin-op laundry. *In room:* A/C, TV, dataport, hair dryer, iron, coffeemaker, Wi-Fi, pay movies.

River's Edge Resort Cottages ✶✶ *Kids*   An afternoon on a sunny riverbank exemplifies the best of Interior Alaska; this place is built around that knowledge. Trim little cottages stand in a grassy compound along the gentle Chena River, where guests can fish for grayling. Inside, each light, airy cottage is an excellent standard hotel room, with high ceilings and two queen beds. Outside, they're like a little village, where guests can sit on the patio, watch the river go by, and socialize. The owners got the idea for the place from their RV park next door, when they noticed how their guests enjoyed visiting together in the open with their own private units to retreat to. It's perfect for families, as the outdoor areas are safe for playing and noise inside won't bother the neighbors. A large, summer-only restaurant sits at river's edge, with dining on a deck or inside at round, oak tables. Dinner entrees—steak, seafood, and down-home cooking—range up to $30; a burger is $8.

4200 Boat St., Fairbanks, AK 99709. ℂ 800/770-3343 or 907/474-0286. Fax 907/474-3665. www.riversedge.net. 94 units (86 cottages, 8 suites). High season $205 double; low season $149 double. Extra person over age 11 $10. AE, DISC, MC, V. Closed Oct–Apr. Take Sportsman Way off Airport Way to Boat St. **Amenities:** Restaurant; bar; tour desk; courtesy van; laundry service; ATM. *In room:* TV, dataport, coffeemaker, hair dryer.

Sophie Station Hotel This all-suite hotel, near the university and airport, is well equipped for business travelers or longer stays, with full kitchens, sitting rooms, and separate bedrooms in every suite. The decoration in the rooms is pleasantly muted. Everything is very clean, well maintained, and comfortable. Bathrooms and closets are quite large. The lobby contains a free Internet workstation and all rooms have Wi-Fi. I was startled by the quality of the food and service in the hotel restaurant, called **Zach's**. Each dish I selected was perfectly seasoned and done to a turn, servers were attentive without being annoying, and the meals came quickly. The cuisine includes Alaska seafood and familiar American dishes. Dinner main courses top out at $32. They're open year-round.

1717 University Ave., Fairbanks, Alaska 99709. **©** **800/528-4916** reservations or 907/479-3650 and 907/456-3642. Fax 907/479-7951. www.fountainheadhotels.com. 148 units. High season $169–$205 double; low season $89–$120. Extra person $10. AE, DC, DISC, MC, V. **Amenities:** Restaurant; exercise room; courtesy van; coin-op laundry. *In room:* A/C, TV, kitchen, hair dryer, iron, Wi-Fi.

A Taste of Alaska Lodge Situated atop a grassy slope on 280 acres, facing Mount McKinley, the handcrafted log main building feels like a wilderness lodge but is less than half an hour from Fairbanks. The family that originally homesteaded this property still lives here and runs the lodge, with the third generation now training to take over. Each family member I've met is an Alaskan original. A nearby musher offers dog-team rides in winter (but make sure that's available when you reserve if it's a priority). During the dark months visitors come for exceptional aurora viewing. In summer visitors can enjoy the hot tub and peer at goldfish in a manmade pond set amid a large field of hay. Rooms are decorated with handmade quilts, brass beds, and other reproductions, and an incredible array of knickknacks, collectibles, and pictures of Elizabeth Taylor (some will love all this, some may find it a little corny). Each room has a door straight onto the grounds, where moose often wander. The cabins are large and especially luxurious. They are reasonably priced, while the standard rooms are a bit dear. Breakfast is served at 8am on the dot, and guests have to remove their shoes at the door.

551 Eberhardt Rd. (turn right 5½ miles out Chena Hot Springs Rd.), Fairbanks, AK 99712. **©** **907/488-7855.** Fax 907/488-3772. www.atasteofalaska.com. 8 units, including 2 cabins. $175 double; $195–$225 cabin. Extra person $25. Rates include full breakfast. AE, MC, V. **Amenities:** Hot tub. *In room:* TV, Wi-Fi ($10).

Wedgewood Resort Off College Road near the Creamer's Field Refuge, this well-kept hotel sprawls across a grassy, 23-acre complex in eight large buildings. Seven of them are three-story apartment buildings converted into suites, regularly refitted, without elevators but with large living rooms, separate dining areas, fully equipped kitchens, air conditioners, two TVs, balconies, and phones with voice mail in both the living room and bedroom. The main difference from home is that someone else cleans up after you. Another 157 units are large standard hotel rooms in the 3-story Bear Lodge, which has its own lobby; however, those are closed mid-September to mid-May. A scheduled courtesy van runs to the airport and train depot and various tourist sites in the summer. A footbridge connects the hotel to Creamer's Field and the Alaska Bird Observatory has its research and educational center on the grounds (p. 395). The resort is also building a new trail system that loops around a former gravel pit, hosting waterfowl, shorebirds, and beavers.

212 Wedgewood Dr., Fairbanks, AK 99701. **©** **800/528-4916** reservations or 907/452-1442 and 907/456-3642. Fax 907/451-6376. www.fountainheadhotels.com. 462 units (157 rooms, 305 suites). High season $185 double; $154–$225 suite for 2; low season standard double rooms not offered, $75–$120 suite for 2. Extra person in suite $10. AE, DC, DISC, MC, V. **Amenities:** 2 restaurants (summer only); bar; tour desk; courtesy van; coin-op laundry; dry cleaning; computers in each lobby. *In room:* A/C, TV, dataport, coffeemaker, hair dryer, iron, Wi-Fi (in some).

Tips   Going with the Flow

Many of the large, top quality hotels in Fairbanks, including the Princess, Westmark, Pike's Waterfront Lodge, Sophie Station, River's Edge Resort, and Wedgewood Resort cater to enormous escorted tours, which flow through town on a rhythm set by the arrival of cruise ships hundreds of miles away. As a result, certain nights are booked up every week many months in advance, while others are wide open. Fortunately, this flow alternates on different nights for different companies, so when one hotel is full another is empty. If you find your first choice is booked, just call one of the others. If they have rooms, ask for a discount, as they may have a lot of empty rooms.

Westmark Fairbanks Hotel & Conference Center ★★★   This Fairbanks landmark, the town's grand meeting place, declined until a few years ago, when the owner, Holland America Lines, demolished most of it and built a showplace and the city's tallest tower (not exactly a skyscraper, but you don't need to be very high for good views in Fairbanks). The decor leaped 30 years forward and now the hotel is the city's most stylish, with a post-mod pastiche that includes fabrics and lamps from the Jetsons along with colonial woodwork, big, manly furniture and lots of color. I like it. The rooms are packed with all the latest amenities, including, in many, little shelves for the coffeemakers so they're not down with your toothpaste. Downstairs, the hotel has a cafe with a dining room that's a work of art (open summer only) and a comfortable steakhouse, as well as a large fitness center, large guest laundry, and small business center. A complimentary breakfast is served in the winter months. The company has made a good choice in eschewing the phony Alaskan motif you get so sick of if you spend much time touring here. Instead, they made a cool hotel, a fun place to stay.

813 Noble St., Fairbanks, AK 99701. © **800/544-0970** reservations or 907/456-7722. Fax 907/451-7478. www.westmark hotels.com. 400 units. Summer $200 double, $220–$500 suite; winter $69 double, $79–$500 suite. Extra person over age 18 $15. AE, DC, DISC, MC, V. **Amenities:** 2 restaurants; bar; fitness center; tour desk (seasonal); courtesy van; laundry service; coin-op laundry. *In room:* A/C, TV, dataport, coffeemaker, hair dryer, iron, Wi-Fi (in some).

MODERATE

All Seasons Inn ★★   This charming and comfortable country inn on a pleasant residential street a couple of blocks from the downtown core is the creation of Mary Richards, a longtime transplant from the southern United States who retains, along with a slight accent, the gentle hospitality and refined style she brought with her. Each cozy room has its own inspired decorative details in bold colors, and the housekeeping has always been perfect on our many visits. For visiting with Mary or other guests a series of large, elegant common rooms connect downstairs, where you'll find a bar with hot drinks and a sun porch with books and games. Complimentary newspapers come with the full breakfast and wireless Internet reaches all the rooms. Shoes are removed at the front door in winter. Smoking is not allowed.

763 7th Ave., Fairbanks, AK 99701. © **888/451-6649** or 907/451-6649. Fax 907/474-8448. www.allseasonsinn.com. 8 units. High season $135–$160 double; low season $75–$90 double. Extra person $35. Rates include full breakfast. DC, DISC, MC, V. Nonsmoking. **Amenities:** Coin-op laundry; computer center. *In room:* A/C, TV, hair dryer, iron, Wi-Fi.

Aurora Express Bed and Breakfast ★★ *Finds*   Susan Wilson's late grandmother appeared to her in a dream and told her there would be a train on a bank below her house, on the family's 15 acres high in the hills south of Fairbanks. So Wilson went out and got a train—a collection that includes a pair of 1956 Pullman sleepers, a dining car, a locomotive, a caboose, and a World War II hospital car—and her husband, Mike, brought it all up the mountain to install below the house, right in the spot indicated. Some cars are close to their original form, and Susan says older guests sometimes weep over the memories they bring back. Others were elaborately remodeled into small rooms on themes related to Fairbanks history. A full breakfast is served in the dining car, which also houses the common area, TV, and phone. A screened train car/gazebo is for barbecues. An 85-foot-long car is good for families (children 7 and older only), with railroad-theme decor, puzzles, and toy trains. Then there's the incredible caboose, dedicated to Grandma. They're located 6½ miles out of town, so you will need your own car if you stay here. Smoking is prohibited.

1540 Chena Ridge Rd. (P.O. Box 80128), Fairbanks, AK 99708. ✆ 800/221-0073 or 907/474-0949. www.fairbanks alaskabedandbreakfast.com. 7 units. $135–$150 double. Extra person $25–$50. Rates include full breakfast. MC, V. Closed mid-Sept to mid-May. *In room:* No phone.

Bridgewater Hotel ✿ (Value) This older building in a prime downtown location near the river contains comfortable, immaculate rooms that sacrifice little of substance to places charging as much as $40 a night more. Decoration in pastels creates a feminine, boutique tone in common areas. Rooms are bright and airy and those on the corners have exceptional views. Most have shower stalls only, not tubs. A cafe serves breakfast and one of Fairbanks' best restaurants, Gambardella's, is just steps away and allows guests to charge meals to the rooms. A great choice for summertime travelers who like staying in a traditional downtown hotel but don't need luxury hotel trappings. Weekends have the most vacancies and best bargains.

723 1st Ave., Fairbanks, AK 99701. ✆ 800/528-4916 or 907/452-6661 and 907/456-3642. Fax 907/452-6126. www.fountainheadhotels.com. 94 units. $129–$149 double. Extra person $10. AE, DC, DISC, MC, V. Closed mid-Sept to mid-May. **Amenities:** Tour desk; courtesy van; laundry service; computer and Wi-Fi in lobby. *In room:* A/C, TV, dataport, coffeemaker, hair dryer.

Minnie Street Bed & Breakfast Inn ✿✿ Across the river from the downtown center, four buildings around a garden courtyard contain large, clean, brightly decorated rooms with stylish furniture and many amenities. The inn reflects the personality of its serene but exacting hosts, managing to feel both homey and polished. A full breakfast is served in a dining room with a high-vaulted ceiling and continental breakfasts in some rooms. Huge one- and two-bedroom suites have kitchens and Jacuzzi tubs. There's an Internet-connected computer for guests in the common room as well as Wi-Fi throughout. A Jacuzzi in the courtyard is available to all guests. It's an excellent place, if the rates are a bit higher than expected at a B&B.

345 Minnie St., Fairbanks, AK 99701. ✆ 888/456-1849 or 907/456-1802. Fax 907/451-1751. www.minniestreet bandb.com. 13 units, 9 with private bathroom. High season $129–$179 double, $229 suite; low season $69–$89 double, $150 suite. Extra person $35. Rates include full breakfast. AE, DISC, MC, V. **Amenities:** Business center; massage; coin-op laundry. *In room:* TV, hair dryer, Wi-Fi.

INEXPENSIVE

Besides the other inexpensive places listed below, **Cloudberry Lookout Bed and Breakfast,** off Goldhill Rd. at 351 Cloudberry Lane, Fairbanks, AK 99709 (✆ 907/479-7334; fax 907/479-7134; www.mosquitonet.com/~cloudberry), is an exceptional place, a handcrafted house with a spiral staircase leading up to a 60-foot tower in the woods west of town and an eco-couple as hosts.

Crestmont Manor Bed and Breakfast ⚐ Phil and Connie Horton built this masterpiece of pale custom woodwork to be their home and inn (Phil is a builder), and filled it with handmade quilts (Connie is a quilter), splashes of bright colors, warm decorative themes, and huge impressionistic oil paintings (their son is an artist). The feel is crisp and airy, but the house is traditional, furnished with antiques and reproductions, like an old-fashioned home but more perfect. It sits on the side of Chena Ridge, overlooking the west side of town, near the university and some good restaurants. One small room with two twin beds and a separated bathroom rents for $100 in summer; the rest are typically sized with attached bathrooms with shower stalls.

510 Crestmont Dr., Fairbanks, AK 99709. (ℂ **907/456-3831.** Fax 907/456-3841. www.mosquitonet.com/~crestmnt. 5 units. High season $100–$135; low season $65–$75. Rates include continental breakfast. AE, DISC, MC, V. *In room:* TV.

Golden North Motel *Value* The Baer family, owners since 1971, are constantly improving the rooms in this two-story motel, making it the best bargain in town for those seeking a basic budget room. They make their money on return business from Alaskans who know this secret. The Baers are always replacing something, and where carpets and furniture are worn they're still quite clean. You have a choice of small rooms and units that combine two of the smaller rooms; although strictly functional, they're very reasonably priced and have extras such as voice mail and VCR/DVD players free to borrow, and many with microwaves and refrigerators. The building, on a side street near the airport, is a nondescript brown rectangle brightened by flower boxes on the outdoor walkways. Family members greet guests warmly with free pastries and coffee in the small lobby, which adjoins a business center with a broadband-connected computer and other business machines, free for guest use.

4888 Old Airport Rd., Fairbanks, AK 99709. (ℂ **800/447-1910** or 907/479-6201. Fax 907/479-5766. www.golden northmotel.com. 62 units. Summer $90–$106 double; winter $55–$59 double. Extra person 13 or older $10. Rates include continental breakfast. AE, DC, DISC, MC, V. **Amenities:** Courtesy van; business center. *In room:* TV, VCR/DVD (available from office), Wi-Fi.

A HOSTEL & CAMPING

There are several hostels in Fairbanks. Among the best is the homey **Billie's Backpackers Hostel,** near the university, at 2895 Mack Blvd. (ℂ **907/479-2034;** www. alaskahostel.com). It's a charming place with a charming owner—a real home, but quirky and fun. Billie assigns bunks as people arrive, and you could luck into a private room for the same $28 a night she charges everyone. The price includes all linens, coffee and tea, the Internet, and much else. The Alaska/Yukon Trails shuttle stops out front (see "Getting There," p. 386). To find the hostel, turn south off College Road on Westwood Way and look for the first house on the left just past Mack Boulevard.

Tent camping is a good way to go in Fairbanks, with its mild summers and ample public lands, but stock up on the mosquito repellent. Right in town, the **Chena River Wayside** (ℂ **907/452-7275;** www.chenawayside.com) is located where University Avenue crosses the river. (The campground is also known as the Chena River State Recreation Site and should not be confused with the recreation "area" of the same name described in the next section of this chapter.) Sites are surrounded by birch and spruce, some are near the river, and there are flush toilets. Arrive early to camp close to the river instead of at one of the noisier sites nearer the road. Eleven sites have water and power hookups for RVs and cost $25 a night; another 45 drive-in sites for tent campers or RVs, without hookups, are $17; and 5 tent-only walk-in sites are $10. Getting a bit out of town, there are superb public campgrounds at Chena Lake Recreation

Area (see "Special Places," earlier in this chapter) and along Chena Hot Springs Road (see section 3 of this chapter).

Fairbanks has plenty of commercial RV parks, some with full service and then some. Pick up a list at the visitor center. Among the best is **River's Edge RV Park and Campground,** at a riverside bend of the Chena at 4140 Boat St., off Airport Way and Sportsman Way (© **800/770-3343** or 907/474-0286; www.riversedge.net), with lots of services, including free shuttles. Full hookups are $30 and tent camping is $19. The same people operate the cottage resort and restaurant next door.

WHERE TO DINE
DOWNTOWN
Gambardella's Pasta Bella ★★ ITALIAN   This warm, charming restaurant is right in the center of things. The chicken rustico (which sits on polenta) is tasty, they serve seafood in interesting ways, and the lasagna, made with sausage, thin noodles and a rich, dusky tomato sauce, will improve your opinion of this abused dish. Dining rooms are narrow and segmented, so you always seem to be sitting with just a few other people, with elaborate decoration that adds to a pleasingly busy feeling. The restaurant added more space with a second story dining room and patio while keeping the cozy ambience. Unlike the synthetic ambience of some of Fairbanks's other fine dining places, Gambardella's feels real, a place where a family shares its cuisine. Perfect, no—but pleasant and satisfying. They serve beer and wine.

706 2nd Ave. © **907/456-3417.** www.nvo.com/gambardellas. Lunch $7–$12; dinner main courses $11–$22. 15% gratuity added for parties of 5 or more, or for split checks. AE, MC, V. Mon–Sat 11am–10pm; Sun 4:30–10pm; closing an hour earlier off season.

Lavelle's Bistro ★★★ ECLECTIC   In a big room of chrome, stone, and glass right downtown (at the base of the Marriott SpringHill Suites), Lavelle's has a grown-up, cosmopolitan feel that is quite welcome when you weary of the Alaskan rustic or gold-rush themes of many of the area's restaurants. It's also got the advantage of consistently superb food, ambitious in conception and fine in execution, and expert service. The cuisine is difficult to categorize, as southwest and Italian influences might be brought to a single dish, and Northwest, Asian, and French influences turn up variously. Dinner main courses are mostly over $20, but you can dine economically on the ample appetizers and salads, or choose a vegetarian lasagna that for only $16 comes with soup or a salad and side dishes. The wine list is impressive and the 3,000-bottle cellar is behind glass in the middle of the dining room; the owners are on a mission to educate Fairbanks about wine, as they've already done with food by creating one of Alaska's best restaurants.

575 1st Ave. © 907/450-0555. www.lavellesbistro.com. Reservations recommended. Lunch $11–$16; dinner $16–$40. AE, DC, DISC, MC, V. Summer Mon–Sat 11am–2pm and 4:30–10pm, Sun 4:30–9pm; winter Tues–Sat 4:30–10pm, Sun–Mon 4:30–9pm.

Thai House ★★ THAI   In a small, brightly lit dining room in the downtown area, this is a simple, family-run restaurant with authentic Thai cuisine. Every time we've dined here the food came quickly and was deftly seasoned and cooked to a turn. You can rely on the servers, beautifully attired in national costumes, to help you order; just believe that when they say "hot" they really mean it. The first time I ate here, I rechecked the bill because it seemed too small. Thanks to this terrific restaurant and others, Fairbanks has gone a bit Thai crazy, and now, incongruously for such a provincial town, has at least five Thai restaurants. This one is the most centrally located and among the best, although that debate is part of the fun.

Quick Treats Unique to Fairbanks

A shop that makes its own delicious, natural ice cream started near the university, spread to North Pole, Denali, and Anchorage, and (who knows?) may soon be spread all over the planet, if the way people around here feel is an indicator. **Hot Licks Homemade Ice Cream,** at 3453 College Rd. (© **907/479-7813;** www.hotlicks.net), has all the standard flavors, plus some of their own, including blueberry and cranberry made in season with local wild berries. If you have children, their joy will be completed by a visit to the playground behind the Radio Shack next door. Right across from Hot Licks on College Road, summer only, a travel trailer in the parking lot of a sporting goods store contains a bakery called **Bun on the Run** which turns out fantastic cinnamon rolls and other baked treats, as well as hearty sandwiches.

---

526 5th Ave. © **907/452-6123.** Lunch items $7–$9; dinner main courses $10–$14. MC, V. Mon–Sat 11am–4pm and 5–10pm.

WITHIN DRIVING DISTANCE

Besides the restaurants listed here, there's the salmon bake at Pioneer Park, described earlier, and the excellent restaurant at Sophie Station Hotel (p. 400). Also, in town, near the university at 3702 Cameron St. off University Ave., **Sam's Sourdough Cafe** (© **907/479-0523**) is a masterpiece in the art of the greasy spoon, with quick, friendly service, good burgers, great milkshakes, and breakfast all day. They're open from 6am to 10pm.

Some of the best pizza in town comes from **College Town Pizzeria,** near the intersection of College and University roads (© **907/457-2200**), an East Coast, order-at-the-counter, family place. The crust is wonderful—crisp yet chewy—and they prepare it either in the American style or as Italian gourmet pizza with pesto, spinach, and the like and without tomato sauce. A large combo is $22. They deliver within Fairbanks between noon and 5pm and are closed Sunday.

The Bakery *Finds* DINER There are an infinite number of old-fashioned coffee shops in and around Fairbanks—the kind of place where a truck driver or gold miner can find a hearty, down-home meal, a bottomless cup of coffee, and a motherly waitress. This is one of the better versions. The sourdough pancakes are good, the menu is long and inexpensive, portions are huge (sometimes they require two plates), and the service is fast and friendly. The proverbial motherly waitress called me "Sweetie" on my last visit. Of course, you can get breakfast all day. They have no liquor license.

69 College Rd. © **907/456-8600.** Lunch items $7–$10; dinner main courses $9–$20. MC, V. Mon–Sat 6am–9pm (closing 8pm in winter); Sun 7am–4pm.

Pike's Landing ☆ STEAK/SEAFOOD The dining room of the fine dining section overlooks the Chena River near the airport from a series of tiered levels, each with tables well separated and covered with linens. The menu includes a nice range of simple to more ambitious selections; highlights I have found include the appetizer of spicy crab-stuffed mushrooms with a thick, chowder-like sauce, and a lunch of halibut and chips. Portions are quite large. Sunday brunch is big and delicious. Service, in my experience, is not always perfect, however, and the entire restaurant is a bit dated. For an inexpensive meal, the bar serves basic food on the deck over the river from 2:30to 10pm. It's a pleasant choice on a sunny day, less so in cool or rainy weather, when it remains in operation behind plastic.

The Roster of Rural Roads

Like frayed strands extending from the thicker rope of the main highways, these minor roads reach beyond the settled lines through Alaska into places where visitors can have real adventures. Due to the size of the state, I cannot cover everything to be found on these byways, but I have covered some highlights and enough information for you to explore on your own. You will find few other cars or tourists, lots of open land, friendly rural people, and limitless opportunities for solitude and discovery.

Unpaved highways can be hazardous. Plan on driving only 40 to 45 mph on gravel highways and be aware of the risks of bouncing off the road or damaging your vehicle with rocks. Check road conditions, construction, and weather with the Alaska Department of Transportation (© **511;** http://511. alaska.gov). Bring at least one full-size spare tire and consider carrying extra gasoline in jugs. Most vehicles can make it from one gas station to the next, but what if the station is closed or you have to turn around short of a refill? Insect repellent is an absolute necessity. Drive with your headlights on at all times and wipe the dust off them and your tail lights periodically. Keep an eye on your rear-view mirror, slowing down or even stopping to allow vehicles to pass; to save your windshield from rocks, it's wise to slow down even for vehicles going the opposite direction. Also, pull off for views or pictures—don't just stop on bridges or in the middle of the road, as some people do. (Further safety and packing suggestions for rural highways are in "Driving Safety," p. 50).

Chena Hot Springs Road   A relatively civilized road into the outdoors, this paved 57-mile highway east of Fairbanks meets hiking and river routes on the way to Chena Hot Springs. See section 3 in this chapter.

4438 Airport Way. © **907/479-6500.** Lunch items $9–$14, dinner main courses $10–$38. AE, DC, DISC, MC, V. Mon–Sat 11am–2pm and 5–9pm; Sun 10am–2pm and 5–9pm.

The Pump House Restaurant and Saloon ★★ STEAK/SEAFOOD   The historic, rambling, corrugated tin building on the National Register of Historic Places is elaborately decorated and landscaped with authentic gold-rush relics. Sitting on the deck over the Chena, you can watch the riverboat paddle by or a group in canoes stop for appetizers and drinks from the full bar. For dinner, the cuisine is a cut above the area's typical steaks and seafood and includes game you may not have tried, including reindeer and musk ox. Dishes such as the halibut Florentine and the fish chowder—hearty, creamy, and flavorful—make the most of the regional ingredients without trying to get too fancy. The food is award winning, and we were delighted on our last visit. Many of the side dishes are a la carte, so, although main courses are generous, it's expensive to order a large meal. Besides, you'll want to save room for one of the exceptional desserts. They serve a big Sunday brunch, too.

1.3 Mile, Chena Pump Rd. © **907/479-8452.** www.pumphouse.com. Main courses $18–$36. AE, DISC, MC, V. Summer Mon–Sat 11:30am–11pm, Sun 10am–11pm; winter Mon–Sat 5–9pm, Sun 10am–2pm and 5–9pm.

Dalton Highway (Rte. 11)   Built to haul equipment to the Prudhoe Bay oil fields, about 500 miles north of Fairbanks, the supremely scenic Dalton reaches the heart of the wilderness, crossing the Brooks Range and the North Slope. Services are as much as a day's drive apart. See section 4 in this chapter.

Denali Highway (Rte. 8)   This 133-mile gravel road connects the midpoints of the Parks and Richardson highways, passing stunning alpine vistas high in the Alaska Range that rival those within Denali National Park. Along the way are a rich network of trails and mountain lakes and a good chance to see caribou, bear, moose, and waterfowl. See p. 346.

Edgerton Highway & McCarthy Road (Rte. 10)   Running east from the Richardson Highway south of Glennallen, the Edgerton leads to the tiny town of Chitina, where the McCarthy Road, a one-lane track, penetrates Wrangell–St. Elias National Park to the historic sites at McCarthy and Kennecott. The journey of 98 miles takes half a day. See p. 428.

Steese Highway (Rte. 6)   This road, paved for the first 52 miles, climbs the rounded tundra mountains 162 miles east of Fairbanks to the Native village of Circle, on the Yukon River. It's a rare road deep into Bush Alaska. See p. 412.

Taylor Highway (Rte. 5)   At times rough, narrow, and a little scary, this dirt road leads 161 miles from a junction on the Alaska Highway east of Tok to the fascinating Yukon River village of Eagle, an island in time. See p. 418.

Top of the World Highway (Yukon Rte. 9)   Connecting to the Taylor Highway and crossing the Canadian border to Dawson City, a distance of 79 miles, the road rides mountaintop to mountaintop, above the tree line nearly the entire way. See p. 418.

The Turtle Club *Finds* BEEF/SEAFOOD   Locals pack into this squat, windowless building, with its vinyl tablecloths and stackable metal chairs, for a menu with just a few famous selections: prime rib, lobster, king crab, and prawns. These are simple, burly meals with roadhouse-style service; the menu is printed on the placemat and vegetables are an afterthought from an indifferent salad bar. But when the beef comes, you know it—the middle-size prime-rib cut is over an inch thick and covers a large plate, an insanely large portion—and the meat is tender and cooked right. The atmosphere is noisy and super casual; people laugh loud and don't worry about putting their elbows on the table or spilling a little beer. You won't run into many other tourists here, north of the city in Fox, but you do need reservations, and even with them you often wait half an hour in the smoky bar or a narrow corridor. If this doesn't sound like fun, don't go; but if you get it, the place is energizing.

10 Mile, Old Steese Hwy., Fox. © 907/457-3883. Reservations recommended. Main courses $20–$31. AE, DISC, MC, V. Mon–Sat 6–10pm; Sun 5–9pm.

FAIRBANKS NIGHTLIFE

Fairbanks has a lot of tourist-oriented evening activities, as well as entertainment also attended by locals. Call the 24-hour event recording of what's playing currently

(© 907/456-INFO) or get a copy of the *Fairbanks Daily News-Miner*. A large multiplex **movie theater** is located on Airport Way. The evening show at the **Palace Theatre** is discussed earlier under "Pioneer Park."

There are places to go out in the evening without having to hear about the gold rush (in other words, places real locals go). Check out the "What's Happening" Web page of the Downtown Association of Fairbanks (© 907/452-8671; www.downtown fairbanks.com) for an updated list of entertainment in that part of town. In the university area, hear local and imported folk music live at the **College Coffeehouse**, at 3677 College Rd. (© 907/374-0468; www.collegecoffeehousefairbanks.com). The website lists upcoming acts. Three miles south of town on the Parks Highway, **The Blue Loon** (© 907/457-5666; www.theblueloon.com) has live music, many beers on tap, and good burgers. They even show movies and call themselves the "cultural epicenter of Fairbanks." For something a bit wilder the **Howling Dog Saloon** out in Fox, 2160 Old Steese Hwy. (© 907/456-4695; www.howlingdogsaloon.com), has been the place to cut loose in the summer. Besides a bar, "The Dog" offers live music Wednesday to Saturday, a cafe, and volleyball out back. It is open from May to September.

3 Chena Hot Springs Road

The 57-mile paved road east from Fairbanks is an avenue to an enjoyable day trip or a destination for up to a week's outdoor activities and hot-spring swimming. Of all the roads radiating from Fairbanks, this short highway will be most rewarding to outdoors people, and there is a funky and relaxing resort at the end.

The road travels through the Chena River State Recreation Area, with spectacular hikes and float trips and well-maintained riverside campgrounds, and leads to the Chena Hot Springs, where there's a year-round resort perfect for soaking in hot mineral springs and for use as a base for summer or winter wilderness day trips. The resort is open to people who want to rent one of the comfortable rooms or to campers and day-trippers, and it's even more popular in the winter than in the summer (the slow seasons are spring and fall).

The paved road leads through a forest of birch, spruce, and cottonwood, first passing an area of scattered roadside development and then following the Chena River through the state recreation area. On a sunny summer weekend, the people of Fairbanks migrate to the riverside and the hiking trails; on a sunny winter weekend, they take to the hills on snowmobiles, cross-country skis, or dog sleds. It's a pleasant drive at any time, around 1¼ hours each way from Fairbanks, but not particularly scenic.

A pair of prospectors, the Swan brothers, discovered the hot springs in 1905, having heard that a U.S. Geological Survey crew had seen steam in a valley of the upper Chena. Thomas Swan suffered from rheumatism; incredibly, he and his brother poled up the Chena River from Fairbanks, found the hot springs, built a cabin and rock-floored pool, and spent the summer soaking. He was cured! More visitors followed, drawn by stories that whole groups of cripples were able to dance all night after soaking in the pools—by 1915 a resort was in operation, drawing worn-out miners and gold-rush stampeders and many others as well. It has been in constant use ever since.

ESSENTIALS

GETTING THERE The Chena Hot Springs Road meets the Steese Expressway about 5 miles north of downtown Fairbanks. (Details on renting a car in Fairbanks can be found at the beginning of section 2 of this chapter.) The resort offers rides from anywhere in Fairbanks for $90 round-trip for one or two people, $45 for each additional person. Arrange for this at least 72 hours in advance.

VISITOR INFORMATION   For outdoors information, check the Fairbanks **Alaska Public Lands Information Center,** 250 Cushman St. (at 3rd Ave.), (✆ **907/ 456-0527;** www.nps.gov/aplic).

The **Alaska Division of Parks,** at 3700 Airport Way, Fairbanks, AK 99709 (✆ **907/ 451-2695;** www.alaskastateparks.org, click on "Individual Parks" and choose the recreation area—not the "site"), manages the recreation area and produces trail, river, and road guides, which are also available at trail-head kiosks, from the public lands center, on the website, or in the area's *Chena Trailmarker* brochure. You can also contact the parks office with questions about the public cabins in the area (see "State Parks Cabin Reservations," p. 265, for how to reserve).

THE CHENA RIVER STATE RECREATION AREA

The recreation area takes in 254,000 acres along the river valley and over the rolling mountains of heather around it. Some of Interior Alaska's best hiking and floating are found here. As everywhere in the Interior, the mosquitoes are brutal.

ACTIVITIES

HIKING & BACKPACKING   The best trail hikes in the Fairbanks area are in the Chena Hot Springs State Recreation Area. Backcountry camping requires no permit, and many of the trails go above the tree line, so it's a good area for backpackers to get into the wilderness.

The **Angel Rocks Trail** is a sometimes steep hike of around 4 miles, round-trip, to a group of large granite outcroppings, an impressive destination with good views of the valley below. The trail mostly stays below the tree line; the blackened areas you see are from major fires that burned through the area in 2002 and 2004. Officially a 3.5-mile loop, the trail is better hiked as an out-and-back, because the back part of the loop is in poor shape. A good destination is the top of the main outcroppings, about 2 miles in. The trail head is well marked at mile 48.9 of the road. A side trail heads from the top of the main outcroppings up to the ridgeline and goes all the way to Chena Hot Springs, a one-way hike of 8.3 miles.

The 15-mile loop of the **Granite Tors Trail,** starting at mile 39 of the road, is a challenging day hike, rising through forest to rolling alpine terrain, but the towering tors on top more than reward the effort. (A short-cut loop reduces the hike to 3 miles, but stays in the trees and doesn't make it near the tors.) Like surrealist experiments in perspective, these monolithic granite sentinels stand at random spots on the broad Plain of Monuments, at first confounding the eye's attempts to gauge their distance and size. Like the Angel Rocks, they were created when upwelling rock solidified in cracks in the surrounding earth, which then eroded away. Water is scarce, so bring along plenty. This is an excellent overnight hike, with the driest ground for camping right around the tors. There is a rough public shelter halfway along the trail (first come, first served). Massive fires in 2004 burned over much of the trail but it remains passable and the Plain of Monuments was practically unscathed.

For a longer backpacking trip, the **Chena Dome Trail** makes a 29-mile loop, beginning at mile 50.5 and ending at mile 49. The 3 miles nearest the road at either end pass through forest, but the remaining 23 miles are above the tree line, marked with cairns and with expansive views. The trail summits 4,421-foot Chena Dome after the 10-mile mark. The trail can be quite wet and muddy in parts and steep and rocky elsewhere and it's wise to bring your water with you. A rough public shelter (first come, first served) is near mile 17.

RIVER FLOATING The Chena is a lovely river, growing from a clear, frothy creek near the end of the road to a lazy, brown Class I river as it flows off toward Fairbanks, several days downstream. Where you choose to start depends on your expertise. Easier water is downstream from Rosehip Campground (mile 27), with the slowest of all nearer Fairbanks, but the upper portion is more popular if you are up for something a bit more challenging. The road crosses the river several times, and the state park system has developed other access points, so it's possible to plan a float that exactly matches your time and abilities. Choose your route with the help of the river guide produced by the Alaska Division of Parks (see "Visitor Information," above).

Canoe Alaska (✆ 907/883-2628; www.canoealaska.net) specializes in whitewater canoe instruction for beginners and intermediate paddlers and leads guided canoe and raft outings and expeditions; a guided trip is around $100 a day. They also rent canoes and offer shuttle service.

Other agencies offering such services are covered in section 2, earlier in this chapter (see "Gearing Up," p. 394 and "Equipped for the Back Roads," p. 395).

FISHING Several of the ponds in the recreation area are stocked with rainbow trout, which you can keep subject to harvest limits. Signs along the road mark access points to the ponds and river. You can catch and release Arctic grayling in the Chena, but check current regulations and bait restrictions. Contact with the **Alaska Department of Fish & Game,** 1300 College Rd., Fairbanks, AK 99701 (✆ 907/459-7207; www.alaska.gov/adfg, click on "Sport Fisheries," then on the Interior region on the map, and then "Lower Tanana River Drainage").

CAMPING & CABINS

Three beautiful campgrounds with water and pit toilets lie along the road by the Chena River, managed by the Alaska Division of Parks (see "Visitor Information," above). Although they can't be reserved ahead, the campgrounds are unlikely to be full except on a sunny holiday weekend. The **Rosehip Campground,** at mile 27, has 37 sites, well separated by spruce and birch, with six suitable for RVs. Some sites are right on the river, and some are set up for more private tent camping, in the woods. The **Granite Tors Campground** is across from the trail head at mile 39; it has 24 sites, 7 suitable for RVs. Some sites front on a river slough, and, as at Rosehip, float trips can start or end here. The **Red Squirrel Campground,** at mile 42.8, has 12 sites and a pleasant picnic area on the grassy edge of a small, placid pond, where swimming is permitted. Camping is $10 a night at each of these campgrounds.

There are several public-use cabins in the recreation area, two of them easily accessible to summer visitors and not hard to book a month or two ahead. (See "State Parks Cabin Reservations," p. 265, for how to get one.) These are primitive cabins; you must bring your own sleeping bags, lights, fuel, and cooking gear. The **North Fork Cabin** is at mile 47.7 of the road, and the **Chena River Cabin** faces the river at mile 32.2. You can get to either by car or canoe, and each costs $50 a night in the summer, $40 off season. Other public cabins in the area primarily serve winter users and are difficult to reach when the ground thaws.

THE HOT SPRINGS

Chena Hot Springs Resort ★★ Several years ago, Bernie Karl, a Fairbanks recycling entrepreneur, bought the hot springs, the 440-acre valley they lie in, and the old resort there, which had perennially struggled to stay out of the red. As I walked around the grounds with him he waved his hand here and there while outlining his audacious plans. I admit I nodded patronizingly. Each time I've gone back, however, more of his dream has been realized: an outdoor, boulder-rimmed swimming pond of hot mineral water, without chlorine or treatment; big buildings for large, modern rooms and for recreational activities; geothermal greenhouses growing produce for the restaurant year-round; an innovative geothermal power plant supplying the resort's electricity; and, incredibly, a large arched building made of ice. Bernie built the ice hotel and filled it with expertly carved ice sculptures and got international publicity—then building inspectors shut it down, citing, of all things, the lack of fire extinguishers. (Their real concern was the complete lack of engineering.) Bernie hired an engineer, got the disagreement worked out (in part by renaming it an ice museum rather than a hotel), and operated it for a winter. That building melted the next summer, but Bernie rebuilt it and has kept it going year-round with a unique refrigeration system that uses heated water from the hot springs. Whatever he says he will do next, I will believe him. Tours of the museum are $15 per person ($7.50 ages 4–12) and you can still rent it for a night. (For the price, $575, you also get Arctic clothing and an indoor room, in case you weary of the cold.) The resort also offers tours of the power plant and greenhouses, if you're interested in renewable energy. Two vehicles run on used vegetable oil from the kitchen.

Unfortunately, Bernie is not as good at maintaining as he is at dreaming and building, and those expecting the standards of service and polish of a corporate resort will be disappointed. If you stay, I would recommend renting the newest, most expensive rooms. Or camp out. Our family has enjoyed wonderful days here swimming and exploring. Soak in the pools, hike through the woods, and enjoy the sound of the wind in the trees.

The hot springs supply an indoor pool, a series of indoor and outdoor hot tubs and spas, and the outdoor hot pond (100°–110°F/38°–44°C). Kids are limited to the indoor swimming pool, which is kept cool enough to swim, allowing adults to escape from the noise by swimming outside. The locker rooms are tiny, so guests will want to change in their rooms (a long-promised expansion is supposedly coming by 2008). The swimming facility is open daily from 7am to midnight. Swim passes come with your room if you're staying at the resort; for campers or day-trippers, a day pass is $10 adults, $8 age 60 and older, $7 ages 6 to 17, free ages 5 and under.

Winter is the high season, when the aurora viewing is exceptional, away from city lights, and you can enjoy Nordic skiing groomed for classical or skating techniques, Sno-Cat and snow-machine tours, dog-sled rides, and more. An aurora viewing station, with a warm-up lodge, is established on a hilltop, where guests can flop back in the snow under a dizzying dome of stars and colors. In the summer, you can go horseback riding, rafting, canoeing, hiking, gold panning, mountain biking, or flightseeing (for guests only). Many activities are guided and carry extra fees. Some rental equipment is available.

The accommodations range from simple yurts to the large hotel rooms with televisions, phones, and coffeemakers. The newest rooms, in the Moose building, are solidly built, nicely done up, and scheduled for remodeling in 2007. Noise can be a problem winter nights as guests come and go to look at the aurora. The yurts are basic but adequate if you want inexpensive lodgings and don't mind not having indoor plumbing. The intermediate rooms got new paint, carpet, and furniture in 2005 and 2006, but were cheaply built to start with. They have shower stalls, not tubs. The main lodge building contains the restaurant and bar. The menu and staff change fairly frequently. Over all, this is a good place to have fun in the real Alaska, but be ready for some rough spots.

The Steese Highway: Drive into the Wild

Driving the Steese Highway north from Fairbanks is like following a river upstream as it diminishes into its headwaters. First it's a four-lane freeway, then a two-lane highway, then the pavement gives out (at mile 52), and then the gravel gives out. The road climbs over round tundra mountains, leaves behind the last tiny town, and then drifts through uninhabited woods before ending on the banks of the Yukon River at a tiny Athabascan village, Circle (named for the Arctic Circle, which it isn't on). It's a rough 162-mile drive to nowhere. But if nowhere is where you want to go, the Steese Highway may be the right adventure for you. Just don't forget the mosquito repellent.

Most of the land surrounding the Steese is controlled by the federal **Bureau of Land Management (BLM),** 1150 University Ave., Fairbanks, AK 99709 (© **800/ 437-7021** or 907/474-2200). Small- and large-scale gold mining takes place in the area, but most of the land is managed for recreation, with several campgrounds, some popular river floats, and a couple of beautiful hikes. The BLM website was undergoing a redesign as we went to press, but it still contains a lot of good information. Start at www.blm.gov/ak and do a search for the Steese National Conservation Area and the White Mountains National Recreation Area, among other topics. In addition, state parks manages the **Upper Chatanika River Campground,** at mile 39, with 25 sites, pit toilets, a hand pump for water, and a $10 fee. This is the starting point for the most popular river float on the highway (covered, with others, under "Canoeing," p. 396).

Without driving to the bitter end at Circle (where the only attraction is the Yukon River itself), you can make a goal of **Eagle Summit,** at mile 107, the highest place on the highway (3,624 ft.), and a good spot to be on June 21 each year, the summer solstice. Although it's still a degree of latitude below the Arctic Circle, the sun never sets here on the longest day because of the elevation and atmospheric refraction. People come out from Fairbanks and make a celebration of it. The midnight sun is visible for about 3 days before and after the solstice, too, assuming the sky is clear. The BLM has installed a toilet and a viewing deck on a 750-foot loop trail at the trail head to the 27-mile **Pinnell Mountain National Recreation Trail.** This is a challenging 3-day hike over amazing terrain of rounded, windblown, tundra-clothed mountaintops. To hike it downhill, start at Eagle Summit and end at Twelvemile Summit, mile 86. Two emergency shelters along the trail provide protection from the ferocious weather that can sweep the mountains. Get the free BLM trail brochure before going.

The next sensible destination is the tiny town of Central, 128 miles along the highway. It's a real, old-fashioned gold-mining community where the current price of gold is posted in the bar and you can use gold dust to pay for your drinks. There are a couple of simple diners, lodgings and a campground, and a small community museum.

Mile 56.5, Chena Hot Springs Rd. (P.O. Box 58740), Fairbanks, AK 99711. © **800/478-4681** or 907/451-8104. Fax 907/451-8151. www.chenahotsprings.com. 80 units. $160–$220 double, $65 cabins and yurts. Extra person $20. AE, DC, DISC, MC, V. **Amenities:** Restaurant; bar; indoor and outdoor pools; hot tubs; Jacuzzis; guided activities; tour desk; massage; coin-op laundry. *In room:* TV, coffeemaker.

4 The Dalton Highway

The original purpose was utilitarian: to haul equipment north from Fairbanks for the trans-Alaska oil pipeline, which runs from Prudhoe Bay, on the Arctic Ocean, to Valdez, on the Pacific. But the experience of the Dalton Highway for a traveler is so far beyond the ordinary as to require a whole new frame of reference to take it all in. The road is so very long, so remote, and free of traffic, and the scenery is so mind-boggling in its grandeur and repetition, that after a time it feels like you're living in a dream. At some point you have to swallow and say to yourself, "I guess I didn't know that much about the world after all."

Part of the wonder comes in the difficulty of the drive. There are extreme sports—throwing yourself off the side of a mountain and so forth—and this is an extreme road trip, one that dives into deep wilderness as far from help as most people ever get. In 500 miles there are only two service stations. The road averages only 250 vehicles a day over its entire length. Driving the Dalton is not to be taken lightly or done on a whim. You need to prepare and you need to know you want to do it, because you will be rumbling over gravel for many, many hours, breathing dust, and beating the crud out of your car.

The drive starts in Fairbanks (officially, you drive parts of the Steese Highway and Elliot Highway before the real Dalton Highway begins), crossing the rounded hills and low forest of that region before crossing the Yukon River on a high, wood-decked bridge. Over the miles that follow trees grow sparser and the road crosses some spectacular alpine plateaus until, entering the Brooks Range, Arctic vegetation, and the mountains' rocky ferocity take over. Beyond towering Atigun Pass, the Arctic Slope extends 170 miles, first through sensuous tundra foothills, then over the broad, lake-dotted flatlands that extend to the Arctic Ocean. Arrival at the oil facilities can be a let down, especially if you haven't made arrangements for the tour that is the only way through to the shore. More on that below.

Wildlife shows up all along the road: moose, caribou, and grizzly bears, and sport fish and songbirds. Animals far outnumber people. Two highway businesses are near the Yukon; in Coldfoot there is a truck stop; and Wiseman is 15 miles up the road from Coldfoot, where the 2000 census counted 21 people. And that's it for another 240 miles of gravel to Prudhoe Bay. There are no ATMs, no grocery stores, no cellphone coverage, no medical facilities—civilization just isn't there. Drive carefully.

DALTON HIGHWAY ESSENTIALS

PRACTICAL TIPS   You can drive the highway yourself, staying in the few motels along the way or in a tent or motor home. From Fairbanks take the Steese Highway north to the Elliot Highway. The total road distance from Fairbanks to the Arctic Ocean is 497 miles. Road conditions are notorious on the gravel-and-dirt Dalton, but now much of it is kept in good condition with pavement working its way steadily north. Speeds of 50 mph are possible on some parts of the road, while doing 35 mph will keep you in one piece on rougher spots. The drive takes 12 hours each way, without stops. It's dusty, shoulders are soft, and flat tires are common. In section 2 earlier in this chapter I listed a business that rents four-wheel-drive pickup trucks and campers (see "Equipped for the Back Roads," p. 395). Generally, other rental companies don't allow their vehicles on the Dalton.

Preparing for the drive is essential. Pick up the road guide produced by the BLM and get first-hand, personal advice (see "Visitor Information," below). Read up on the safety advice under "The Roster of Rural Roads," p. 406. For those who want to let someone else do the driving, a bus package is listed in section 9 of chapter 10, on Prudhoe Bay.

VISITOR INFORMATION   Getting up-to-date advice is critical before heading off on the Dalton Highway, and the best place to do that is the Fairbanks **Alaska Public Lands Information Center,** at 250 Cushman St. (at 3rd Ave.), Fairbanks, AK 99701 (© **907/456-0527;** www.nps.gov/aplic). Staffers there drive the road annually to stay on top of current conditions.

Much of the road runs through land managed by the **Bureau of Land Management (BLM),** 1150 University Ave., Fairbanks, AK 99709 (© **800/437-7021** or 907/474-2200; www.blm.gov/ak/dalton). The handy *Dalton Highway Visitor Guide* is a 24-page booklet, free at the public lands information center or from any BLM information center, or by mail by calling the number above; or read it on the website along with other information on the drive.

Two information stops are along the highway, both open summer only. A **contact station** at the Yukon River crossing is staffed by BLM volunteers and open daily in summer from 9am to 6pm. It has no phone. The recently constructed **Arctic Interagency Visitor Center** is at mile 175 on the west side of the highway in Coldfoot (© **907/678-5209** or 907/678-2014), open late May to early September from 10am to 10pm daily. The free center has exhibits about the North, a theater for nightly educational programs, a trip-planning room, a bookstore, and knowledgeable staff. Even if you don't have any questions, it's hard to imagine not stopping at this one real tourist attraction in your many hours of driving.

ON THE ROAD

The bridge over the Yukon River at mile 56 is the only crossing of the river in Alaska, and many people drive the Dalton just to get to the **Arctic Circle** at mile 115, where you'll find a sign for pictures as well as a crude camping area. Many, many places along the highway have incredible views; among the most famous are Finger Mountain at mile 98; Gobbler's Knob at mile 132, which offers the first view of the Brooks Range; and 4,739-foot Atigun Pass at mile 245, where the road crosses the Brooks Range, winding through impossibly rugged country. The pass is the highest point on the Alaska road system, and you may find summer snow. All along the highway are opportunities to see birds and animals, including rabbits, foxes, moose, Dall sheep, bears, and caribou. Sit still if you want to see the skittish caribou, as they may wander closer to an unmoving vehicle. Beware of wolves, which attacked Dalton travelers in 2006. Keep pets under control, and if a wolf approaches yell and throw rocks at it.

The road parallels the 4-foot-wide **trans-Alaska pipeline.** The line, completed in 1977, serves America's largest and second-largest oil fields, Prudhoe Bay and Kuparuk, carrying the hot crude 900 miles from the Arctic Ocean to docks in Valdez, where tankers pick it up for shipment primarily to the West Coast. The public road ends before reaching the Prudhoe Bay complex and the Arctic Ocean. The only way through the gate is with a tour operator, and you must make arrangements at least 24 hours ahead to clear security. Call the **Arctic Caribou Inn** (© **877/659-2368** or 907/659-2368). See section 8 of chapter 10, on Prudhoe Bay, for more details.

HIGHWAY SERVICES: FOOD, FUEL & LODGINGS

Among the three places offering services along the 414 miles of the Dalton you won't find anything luxurious, or even approaching budget chains. Near the spectacular suspended bridge over the Yukon River, at mile 56, is a decidedly unspectacular motel, restaurant, and gas station. **Yukon River Camp** (© 907/474-3557), has a gift shop, fuel, and tire repair as well as food, gas, and lodging, and is open mid-May to mid-September. The motel is a former pipeline construction camp. Just 4 miles up the road from the river, the **Hot Spot Café** (© 907/451-7543) offers dining, lodging, a gift shop, gas, and tire repair.

The **Coldfoot Camp** truck stop at mile 175 (© 866/474-3400 or 907/474-3500; www.coldfootcamp.com) is the one big stopping place along the road. After the endless wilderness miles on the road, no one could stand to pass it by. The year-round camp includes several buildings on a large gravel pad. Most important are the gas pumps and the 24-hour restaurant where you pay for the fuel—a typical but friendly highway diner. Across the lot, the camp's inn is built of leftover construction camp modular units. The small rooms with low ceilings are perfectly comfortable, with private bathrooms, but far from grand. The camp also offers minor vehicle repairs, towing, RV hookup, laundry, a post office, a gift shop, and a saloon. They guide rafting on the Middle Fork Koyukuk River and offer flight tours to the village of Anaktuvuk Pass and shuttles for hiking. In the winter the camp offers dog-sled rides. An air taxi, **Coyote Air** (© 800/252-0603 or 907/678-5995; www.flycoyote.com), offers flightseeing of this amazing country from the air. There are other activities farther afield offered by **Northern Alaska Tour Company** (© 800/474-1986 or 907/474-8600; www.northernalaska.com). Don't miss the new interagency visitor center, described above. The pleasant BLM Marion Creek Campground is 5 miles north of Coldfoot.

After Coldfoot, the next service area is **Deadhorse,** at the end of the road another 240 miles north, with rooms, fuel, restaurants, a post office, vehicle maintenance, a general store, and an airport. See section 8 in chapter 10.

GETTING OUT OF THE CAR
ACTIVITIES

FISHING The streams and lakes of the Arctic are cold, poor in nutrients, and frozen much of the year; fishing is not a good reason to drive the Dalton. However, if you are taking the adventure anyway, there are fish in streams from July to mid-September and in lakes that don't freeze to the bottom. Many of the streams have Arctic grayling, but you'll want to hike farther than a quarter mile from the road to increase your chances (off-road vehicles are not allowed). A good bet is the **Jim River area** between miles 140 and 144, where the river follows the road and fishing pressure is more spread out. Most North Slope rivers have good Dolly Varden fishing in late August and early September. Many of the lakes along the road have grayling, and the deeper ones north of the Brooks Range have lake trout. Check current regulations. Contact the **Alaska Department of Fish & Game,** 1300 College Rd., Fairbanks, AK 99701 (© 907/459-7207; www.alaska.gov/adfg); they produce a booklet called *Sportfishing Along the Dalton Highway,* which you can get on paper or from the website (click on "Sport Fish Publications," and then "Interior.")

HIKING The road has no established hiking trails, but most of the area is open to self-reliant hikers who know how to pick their own route. Hiking brushy or marshy Interior country isn't fun, but the dry tundra of the ridgetops and mountains creates a wonderful sense of freedom. The country opens up north of the Chandalar Shelf at mile 237. The best hiking area is the zone of dry tundra in the foothills north of the Brooks Range. But even at upper elevations you still run into tussocks, wet ground, and stream crossings. Topographical maps and advice on hiking the Brooks Range are available at the sources listed under "Visitor Information," above. Remember, this is remote wilderness; do your research, be prepared, and tell someone where you're going and when you'll be back.

CAMPING

The Bureau of Land Management (BLM) has a few campgrounds along the road, but there seems little reason to wait to reach them, as there are any number of places to pull off the road on a spot of gravel and spend the night, often in places of stunning beauty. The only requirements are for safety and the environment: get far enough off the road to avoid the fast-moving truck spewing rocks as far as 30 feet; read up on bear avoidance on p. 46; don't leave toilet paper or anything else behind; and stay no longer than 14 days in one spot. Parking on pipeline access roads is OK if you don't block the road. I have listed the BLM's developed areas along the Dalton, which include campgrounds and spots where you can park for a while and obtain water. Unless the description mentions a formal campground, these are just pullouts where you can park and camp or sleep in your car. Add 83 miles to the mileposts to get the distance from Fairbanks.

- **Mile 60** (Five Mile): Artesian well with potable water, outhouses, and free public dump station (this is the last dump station on the highway).
- **Mile 98** (Finger Mountain): Nice views, outhouse, and wheelchair-accessible trail with interpretive signs.
- **Mile 115** (Arctic Circle): Outhouses, picnic tables, and an interpretive display; camp only in the undeveloped campground up the hill, which has an outhouse but no water.
- **Mile 150** (Grayling Lake): Wayside with an outhouse.
- **Mile 175** (Coldfoot): A private campground with hookups is part of the truck stop described above.
- **Mile 180** (Marion Creek): A developed BLM campground with 27 campsites, 11 of them for large RVs (no hookups). The campground has a potable well and outhouses; the fee is $8.
- **Mile 235** (Arctic tree line): Outhouse; not an attractive camping site due to truck traffic on a steep grade.
- **Mile 275** (Galbraith Lake): Undeveloped campground with an outhouse about 4 miles off road; follow the access road past the state-operated landing strip, and then continue 2½ miles on an unimproved road. Filter or boil water from the nearby creek before use.
- **Mile 301** (Slope Mountain): Land north of this point is managed by the Alaska Department of Natural Resources, not the BLM; however, you can use the same visitor information sources mentioned above.
- **Mile 355** (on the North Slope): Wayside with an outhouse.
- **Mile 414** (Deadhorse): The end of the road. Deadhorse has a post office, general store, hotel, and other services, and an operator offers tours through to the Arctic Ocean, which must be arranged in advance. See p. 464.

5 The Alaska Highway

Detailed coverage of the entire 2,400-mile drive to Alaska is beyond our scope, but chapter 2's "Getting There" section provides the planning basics. Here I've covered the Alaska portion of the road, the 200 miles of the Alaska Highway that run from the border with Canada to the terminus in Delta Junction. This is mostly boring driving, miles of stunted black spruce and brush, either living or burned out. It's a relief when you hit the first major town, **Tok** (rhymes with Coke), 100 miles along. But don't get your hopes up. This is the only place where I've ever walked into a visitor center and asked what there is to do in town, only to have the host hold up her fingers in the shape of a goose egg and say, "Nothing." Another 100 miles (I hope you brought plenty of music, because no radio station reaches out here) and you've made it to **Delta Junction.** There's a little more to do here, but it's still not a destination. Another 100 miles and you're in Fairbanks.

The main sources of information for the drive are based in Tok, the first town you hit after you cross the border. It acts as a threshold for the entire state. To plan the journey ahead, contact them, and see "Exploring the Interior," at the beginning of this chapter. If you're headed to Anchorage or other points south, see the sections on the Glenn and Richardson highways later in this chapter; those roads branch from the Alaska Highway at Tok and Delta, respectively.

I've arranged this section in order from the border with Canada heading west.

CROSSING THE BORDER

Remember to set your watch back an hour when crossing the border in Alaska—it's an hour later in Yukon Territory. Also, if you make significant purchases or rent rooms in Canada, you may be able to get a refund on the 7% goods and services tax (GST). Ask for the form at a Canadian border station.

CUSTOMS   Crossing the U.S./Canadian border requires a preparation even for U.S. citizens. Starting in 2008, U.S. citizens will need **passports** to re-enter the country over the road or water and Canadians will need passports but not visas (check for changes at www.travel.state.gov, as the implementation of this change may be delayed). See chapter 2 to learn more about passports and entry requirements for international visitors. Besides a passport, **children** with their parents should have a birth certificate; children or youths under 18 unaccompanied by parents need a notarized letter from a parent or guardian; and children with a single parent should carry such a letter from the other parent. There are no duties on products made in the United States or Canada. For duties on items that you buy that originated in other countries or on alcohol or smoking supplies, see chapter 2. Products you buy in Alaska made of **wildlife** will probably require special permits to be taken out of the United States, and most marine mammal products cannot be exported. (See "What You Can Take Home," in section 7 of chapter 2.) If you are a U.S. resident, send the item home by mail without trying to take it through Canada. U.S. authorities no longer let noncitizens into the country with firearms except for permanent resident aliens or foreigners holding both a special permit from the Bureau of Alcohol, Tobacco, Firearms and Explosives and a nonresident hunting license (p. 43). It's complicated for U.S. residents to travel through Canada with **firearms** as well. Guns other than hunting rifles or shotguns generally are not allowed, and you need to fill out a form and pay a $25 fee for guns that are allowed; contact the Canadian Firearms Center (© **800/731-4000;** www.cfc-cafc.gc.ca) before you go to avoid problems. You should also register your firearms with U.S. Customs and Border Patrol before entering Canada to ease your return to the United States. **Dogs** more than 3 months old require a rabies certificate with an expiration date before entering the U.S., which should have the signature of a licensed veterinarian that is dated at least 30 days prior to crossing the border. A certificate without an expiration date is honored only 12 months from the date signed. **Beef** from Canada is not allowed to enter into the U.S., even as ingredients in pet food, nor are **citrus fruits** (except fruit

Dawson City & Eagle: Detour into History

Instead of taking the Alaska Highway directly from Whitehorse, Yukon, to Tok, consider driving north on the Klondike Highway (Yukon Hwy. 2) to Dawson City, then west and south over the Top of the World Highway and partially unpaved Taylor Highway to rejoin the Alaska Highway just east of Tok. This represents 502 miles of driving, about 127 miles more than if you just stay on the Alaska Highway, and includes 43 miles of sometimes rough dirt road, but it's worth doing at least one way to see historic Dawson City and the fabulous mountain scenery of the Top of the World Highway. Dawson was the destination of the 1898 Klondike gold rush; the bed of the Klondike River near here contained thick veins of gold. The town maintains the look of those days, when it was the second largest city on the West Coast, after San Francisco. Many buildings, a gold dredge, and a river boat were restored as part of the Klondike National Historic Sites, managed by **Parks Canada.** Besides the buildings and their setting, there are museums, a working not-for-profit casino, a center of indigenous culture, and other attractions, easily enough for 2 days of sightseeing. The **Klondike Visitor Association,** P.O. Box 389, Dawson City, YT, Canada Y0B 1G0; ℂ **867/ 993-5575;** fax 867/993-6415; www.dawsoncity.ca), offers information on local businesses, accommodations, and community events. For information on the historic sites, contact **Parks Canada** at P.O. Box 390, Dawson City, YT, Canada Y0B 1G0 (ℂ 867/993-7200; www.parkscanada.gc.ca, click on "National Historic Sites," then "Yukon"). For information on the **Han Nation people** here and their cultural center, call ℂ 867/993-7100 (www. trondek.com).

clearly identified as being of U.S. origin). If in doubt about any of these issues call before you go, as the border is a long way from anywhere: **Canadian Customs** in Whitehorse (ℂ **867/667-3943**) or **U.S. Customs and Border Protection** on the highway (ℂ **907/774-2252**) or in Skagway (ℂ **907/983-2325**).

FROM THE BORDER TO TOK

The first 65 miles after entering the United States the road borders the Tetlin National Wildlife Refuge. These broad wetlands and low forests are a migratory stopover in May and in the fall for thousands of songbirds, birds of prey, and waterfowl, and the summer home of trumpeter swans and lesser sandhill cranes, among 143 other species. Caribou show up along the road, especially in the early spring and late fall. The Fish & Wildlife Service's **Tetlin Refuge Visitor Center,** 8 miles past the border, at mile 1,229, is open May 15 to September 15 daily from 8am to 4:30pm, longer when staffing allows. There are exhibits and the observation deck has a great view. The refuge also has two small lakeside campgrounds: Deadman Lake, at mile 1,249, with 16 sites, some OK for RVs; and Lakeview, at mile 1,256, with eight (no RVs over 30 ft.). Rangers give evening campground programs in the summer at Deadman Lake. The campgrounds do not have drinking water. The refuge headquarters is in Tok (ℂ **907/883-5312** headquarters, http://tetlin.fws.gov).

After passing into the United States on the Top of the World Highway (*Note:* this border crossing is open only during the day, and only during the summer), a further detour leads north on the Taylor Highway to the forgotten town of Eagle on the bank of the Yukon River (going south on the Taylor leads you back to the Alaska Hwy.). The trip to Eagle adds 66 miles each way on a winding, narrow dirt road; allow 2 hours each way. But, if you have the time, the destination more than rewards the effort. Eagle is lost in time, a treasure of a gold-rush river town with many original buildings full of original artifacts from a century ago. It's entirely authentic and noncommercial, with few businesses other than the store, cafe, motel, and a B&B. The **Eagle Historical Society and Museums** (✆ **907/547-2325;** www.eagleak.org) shows off the buildings and several museums of materials left behind in this eddy in the stream of history. Their 3-hour walking tour starts once a day at 9am daily Memorial Day to Labor Day and costs $5.

To plan a float trip on the Yukon River from Eagle, or for other outdoor information, contact the Eagle Field Office of the **Yukon–Charley Rivers National Preserve,** P.O. Box 167, Eagle, AK 99738 (✆ **907/547-2233;** www.nps. gov/yuch). The office lies on the far side of the airstrip from the main part of town.

The funny little village of Chicken is the other stop on this drive (the old joke is that they wanted to name the town Ptarmigan but didn't know how to spell it). There are a couple of businesses worth a stop for gold panning, for a meal, or to shop for gifts. Chicken, too, is mixed up in the area's time warp: The town has never had phone service, but has free Wi-Fi.

TOK

Born as a construction station on the highway, Tok's role in the world has never expanded much beyond being a stop on the road. With its location at the intersection of the Alaska Highway and the Glenn Highway (see section 6) to Anchorage and Prince William Sound, the town has built an economy of gas stations, gift stores, cafes, and hotels to serve highway travelers. It brags of being the coldest community in North America, a dubious distinction made possible by both the latitude and the distance from the moderating influence of the ocean.

ESSENTIALS

GETTING THERE You're surely passing through Tok with your own set of wheels. If you get stuck for some reason, one shuttle service or another can get you on your way. **Alaska Trails/Yukon** (✆ **800/770-7275;** www.alaskashuttle.com) runs through Tok between Fairbanks and Dawson City.

VISITOR INFORMATION Public land agencies jointly operate an informative visitor center to introduce highway travelers to Alaska's outdoors. The **Alaska Public Lands Information Center,** P.O. Box 359, Tok, AK 99780 (✆ **907/883-5667;** www. nps.gov/aplic), is on the right (north) side of the road coming from the direction of Canada on the Alaska Highway. It is open daily from 8am to 7pm in summer and from 8am to 4:30pm in winter. You can make ferry reservations on the Alaska Marine Highway System here, too.

A few doors down at the intersection of the Alaska Highway and Tok Cut-Off (also known as the Glenn Highway), the town's **Main Street Visitor Center** is operated by the Tok Chamber of Commerce, P.O. Box 389, Tok, AK 99780 (© **907/883-5775;** www.tokalaskainfo.com). The center provides information on Tok and anywhere else you may be bound on the highway. They're open from May 1 to September 15 daily from 8am to 7pm.

FAST FACTS: Tok

Bank **Denali State Bank** is in the Three Bears Store and has an ATM.

Hospital **Tok Clinic** is on the Tok Cut-Off across from the fire station (© **907/ 883-5855**).

Police Contact the **Alaska State Troopers** (© **907/883-5111**), near the intersection of the Alaska Highway and Glenn Highway.

Post Office At the highway junction next to the Westmark Hotel.

Taxes There are none in the region.

WHERE TO STAY

The motels are numerous and competitive in Tok. There also are many B&Bs. Check at the visitor center. Be sure to get the 50¢ state highway and campground map from the public lands center (see "Visitor Information," above), which includes all the public campgrounds in Alaska. Three attractive state park campgrounds lie near Tok on the three highway links that radiate from the town. Each has a $15 self-service fee.

There are lots of competitive RV parks in Tok, too. One that has wooded sites suitable for tent camping as well is the **Sourdough Campground,** 1½ miles south of town on the Glenn Highway (© **800/789-5543** Alaska and Yukon only, or 907/883-5543; www.sourdoughcampground.com). They charge $30 for full hookups, $17 dry. The campground offers some unusual free services, including Wi-Fi and nightly comedic and musical entertainment. You can buy meals here, too: In the morning, pancake breakfasts and in the evening beef stew or reindeer chili in sourdough bread bowls.

Snowshoe Motel & Fine Arts and Gifts *(Value)*   The motel is behind the gift shop. The best units are the newer nonsmoking rooms near the front, and all are reasonably priced. Each is divided into two sections by the bathroom, providing two separate bedrooms—great for families. They have phones. Outside walkways are decorated with flowers. The gift shop carries some authentic Native art as well as highway kitsch.

Across the highway from the information center (P.O. Box 559), Tok, AK 99780. © **800/478-4511** in Alaska, Yukon, and part of B.C. or 907/883-4511. Fax 907/883-4512. snowshoe@aptalaska.net. 24 units. High season $85 double; low season $67 double. Extra person $5. MC, V. *In room:* TV, fridge, coffeemaker, microwave.

Westmark Tok   The central hotel in town is closed in the winter, as its clientele is primarily the package tour bus trade. It's made up of several buildings connected by boardwalks. Rooms are comfortable and are regularly updated. After several years of hot summers, they have installed air-conditioning throughout. The newer section has larger rooms for the same price. The company offers significant discounts for booking on their website. The restaurant serves breakfast and dinner of Mexican and standard American fare, with dinners from $14 to $23.

Intersection of Alaska and Glenn hwy. (P.O. Box 130), Tok, AK 99780-0130. ℂ 800/544-0970 (reservations) or 907/883-5174. Fax 907/883-5178. www.westmarkhotels.com. 92 units. $139 double. AE, DC, DISC, MC, V. Closed mid-Sept to mid-May. **Amenities:** Restaurant; bar; coin-op laundry; Internet access and Wi-Fi in lobby. *In room:* A/C, TV, coffeemaker, hair dryer, iron.

Young's Motel   Good standard motel rooms occupy three one-story structures on the parking lot behind Fast Eddy's restaurant (described below), where you check in. Eighteen newer, smoke-free rooms are the pick of the litter, but all are acceptable.

Behind Fast Eddy's restaurant on the Alaska Hwy. (P.O. Box 482), Tok, AK 99780. ℂ 907/883-4411. Fax 907/883-5023. 43 units. High season $85 double; low season $62 double. Extra person $5. AE, DISC, MC, V. **Amenities:** Restaurant (Fast Eddy's). *In room:* TV, Wi-Fi.

WHERE TO DINE

A reliable restaurant of many years tenure, **Fast Eddy's** (ℂ **907/883-4411**), is on the right as you enter town from the east. Begun as a typical roadside cafe, it has developed into a place where a wine list and fine-dining entrees don't seem out of place. Yet the proprietor knows that most highway travelers just want a simple, relaxing meal, and the varied menu offers anything they might have in mind. I relish the salad bar and light dishes that offer a break from the usually carnivorous greasy-spoon choices found elsewhere along the highway. The dining room is decorated in maroon, dark wood, and brass. They're open in summer from 6am to 11pm, in winter from 6am to 10pm. Wine and beer are available with meals, but there is no bar.

DELTA JUNCTION

This intersection with the Richardson Highway, which runs from Valdez to Fairbanks (see section 7), is the official end of the Alaska Highway. It's an earnest little roadside town set in a broad plain between the Delta and Tanana rivers. People make their livings from farming and tourism, by working at a trans-Alaska pipeline pump station south of town, and at Fort Greely, where President Bush's missile defense system is based. For visitors, there are two historic roadhouse museums, several good campgrounds, and an unpredictable chance to spy a herd of bison—but not enough to hold most for more than a few hours.

ESSENTIALS

VISITOR INFORMATION   A helpful **visitor center** run by the Delta Chamber of Commerce, P.O. Box 987, Delta Junction, AK 99737 (ℂ **877/895-5068** or 907/895-5068, 907/895-5069 summer only; www.deltachamber.org), stands at the intersection of the Alaska and Richardson highways, in the middle of town; it's open from mid-May to mid-September.

FAST FACTS: Delta Junction

Bank **Wells Fargo,** with an ATM, is next door to the IGA Food Cache on the Richardson Highway at the center of town.

Hospital The **Family Medical Center** is at Mile 267.2 Richardson Hwy., 2 miles north of the visitor center (ℂ **907/895-4879** or 907/895-5100).

Police For nonemergency calls, call the **Alaska State Troopers** at © 907/895-4344.
Post Office On the Richardson, 2 blocks north of the visitor center.
Taxes None of any kind.

EXPLORING THE AREA

Before construction of the first road to Fairbanks in 1917 (today's Richardson Hwy.), travelers to the Interior followed a trail on basically the same route by horse in summer and dog sled in winter, stopping at roadhouses that provided food and shelter a day apart on the 2-week trip. Two well-preserved examples of the roadhouse system survive near Delta Junction.

In 1996, the army saved the 1905 **Sullivan Roadhouse** (© 907/895-4415), which had stood abandoned since 1922 on what became an army bombing range. Today the log building stands near the town visitor center and is open free of charge in summer Monday through Friday 9am to 5pm. Many of the Sullivan's original belongings have been set back in their original places, giving a strong feel for frontier life, but the heart of the restoration is the authentic hospitality of the local volunteers who show off the place with great pride.

The next stop on the trail beyond Sullivan's Roadhouse was 16 miles toward Fairbanks. **Rika's Roadhouse and Landing,** 10 miles northwest of Delta at mile 275 on the Richardson Highway (© 907/895-4201; www.rikas.com), still makes a pleasant stop on your drive. This roadhouse lasted later than the Sullivans' because drivers had to board a ferry here to cross the Tanana River until the 1940s, and the landing was the end of the line for Tanana sternwheelers. The 1906 log building, on the National Register of Historic Places, has been altered too much by its gift shop to feel authentic, but the grassy 10-acre compound completes a vivid scene of Alaska pioneer life with surviving outbuildings, including telegraph cabins, a museum, a barn, a gorgeous vegetable garden, and livestock pens. The entire site overlooks the riverbank and an impressive suspension bridge carries the trans-Alaska pipeline over the Tanana just beyond the park. A private operator does a good job of managing the site for the state of Alaska, including operating a restaurant that serves soups, salads, sandwiches, and pie, and a few hot breakfast choices, daily from 9am to 5pm; the grounds and museum are open from 8am to 8pm from May 15 to September 15.

WHERE TO STAY

Check at the visitor center for a referral to one of the many B&Bs. The cute, funny, and hospitable **Kelly's Alaska Country Inn,** at the intersection of Richardson and Alaska highways (© 907/895-4667; www.kellysalaskacountryinn.com), has rooms for $109 double in summer, $99 winter, right in the middle of town. The 20 rooms have TVs, telephones, microwave ovens, refrigerators, and coffee machines; most are small and ordinary, but a funky few are in an old Quonset hut and have arched wood ceilings. This is a family-run business going way, way back.

Alaska 7 Motel, 3548 Richardson Hwy. (© 907/895-4848; www.alaska7motel. com), is a small, low-slung building containing standard rooms with lots of amenities, including refrigerators, microwave ovens, coffee, Wi-Fi, and satellite TV, for $80 double.

CAMPING

Alaska State Parks maintains five campgrounds on the rivers and lakes in and around Delta Junction and a couple of public cabins. Right on the highway near town, the

Delta State Recreation Area campground lies among large spruce and birch trees, the sites well separated, some with walk-in privacy. It is among the most attractive campgrounds on the highway. The **Quartz Lake State Recreation Area,** 11 miles northwest of town on the Richardson Highway and down a 3-mile turnoff, has an 80-site campground on the shallow fishing lake. The camping fee at each is $10. For information, contact the **Department of Natural Resources Public Information Center,** 3700 Airport Way, Fairbanks, AK 99709 (© **907/451-2705;** www.alaskastate parks.org, click on "Individual Parks").

To park an RV, or if you're tent camping and need a shower, **Smith's Green Acres RV Park and Campground,** 1½ miles north on the Richardson Highway from the visitor center (© **800/895-4369** or 907/895-4369), has grassy RV sites and tent sites among the trees. The place also has cabins, a small playground, and laundry facilities. Full hookup sites are $29, tent sites $16.

WHERE TO DINE

For a picnic or quick, simple meal on your drive, try the **IGA Food Cache** (© **907/ 895-4653**), on the south side of the highway in Delta. The deli counter sells fried food, subs, and ice cream, and the store also has a bakery counter and coffee stand. You can eat in as well as carry out. They're open daily 6:30am to 9pm.

Buffalo Center Diner DINER   The locals eat here, for good reason. The dining room is light and clean, decorated with wood and plants, and the menu covers everything you would hope for in a simple family restaurant—plus buffalo burgers and sausage in honor of the Delta herd. Each time I've stopped the food has been good and the atmosphere relaxing. Service has always been friendly and quick and the waitress called me "Hon."

1680 Richardson Hwy. © **907/895-5089.** Lunch $6–$12; dinner $8–$22. MC, V. Summer daily 6am–10pm, winter daily 7am–8pm.

6 The Glenn Highway

The Glenn Highway, Alaska Route 1, leads from the Alaska Highway at Tok to Anchorage (the section from Tok to Glennallen is also called the Tok Cut-Off). It connects the most populous part of the state to the outside world, a 328-mile strip of blacktop that grows from two lanes in Tok to six or more in urban downtown Anchorage. In this section, I cover the stretch from Glennallen to Palmer. From Tok to Glennallen, the road passes through wilderness. The portion from Palmer to downtown Anchorage is all part of the greater city and encompassed in chapter 6.

GLENNALLEN

It may look like just a wide place in the road, but this little town is the commercial hub for the Copper River Country, a great, thinly settled region. Much of the public land in the Copper River Country is managed by the **Bureau of Land Management (BLM) Glennallen Field Office,** with a log cabin office in town on the north side of the Glenn Highway at mile 186.5 (P.O. Box 147), Glennallen, AK 99588 (© **907/ 822-3217;** www.blm.gov/ak/st/en.html), open Monday through Friday from 8am to 4:30pm. Information also is available from the public land information centers in Anchorage, Fairbanks, and Tok. This huge area, about as large as a midsize eastern U.S. state, is more accessible than Wrangell–St. Elias National Park, an advantage for outdoor recreation, but it's still a rough, remote land with few high-quality visitor facilities. There are several large alpine lakes, two National Wild Rivers, several hiking trails, and four campgrounds (including the state park campground just north of Glennallen), all reached on the Richardson, Glenn, and Denali highways. Guides are available for **rafting** and **fishing** in the rivers. Check at the visitor center or BLM office for a list of operators.

For commercial information, the **Copper Valley Chamber of Commerce and Visitor Center** is in a gray building at the intersection of the highways next to the Hub gas station and store (P.O. Box 469, Glennallen, AK 99588; ☎ **907/822-5555;** www.traveltoalaska.com). The center operates from May 15 to September 15 daily 9am to 7pm. Besides the hotel and restaurant listed below, Glennallen has two banks with ATMs, a post office, groceries, a medical center, and government offices, all centered along a strip of the Glenn Highway around mile 187.

Good standard accommodations are at the **New Caribou Hotel,** in town at mile 187 of the Glenn Highway (☎ **800/478-3302** or 907/822-3302; www.caribouhotel.com). The rooms have the amenities of a roadside chain, but the hotel as a whole has the character of its place. They book up in the summer, so reservations are important. The summer rate is $144 double. Budget rooms are in an annex building, a former construction camp, for $79 double. Their **Caribou Restaurant** is inexpensive but quite fancy inside, with lots of brass and booths. Choices include burgers, fish, and steak.

THE MATANUSKA GLACIER AREA

From Glennallen, the highway traverses a broad tundra area where there's a good chance of seeing caribou and other wildlife from a distance. Next, the road climbs between two mountain ranges—the coastal Chugach Mountains that hold the glaciers around Prince William Sound, and the craggy old Talkeetna Mountains to the north. The road winds through steep, rocky terrain with wonderful, scary views, including a good look at the Matanuska Glacier. In the fall, when the tundra and the birches, aspens, and cottonwoods turn yellow and red, this drive is dizzying in its beauty.

The Matanuska Glacier State Recreation Site overlooks the glacier and has a 1-mile interpretive nature trail and a good, 12-site campground ($15 per site or $10 to park overnight in a paved lot). To get closer to the glacier, you have to take a rough side road and pay a fee to the people who own the land in front of it, doing business as **Glacier Park** (☎ **888/253-4480;** www.matanuskaglacier.com). The cost for the self-guided hike is $15 for adults; $13 for seniors; $10 for students and military; $5 for children 6 to 12. They also offer camping for $15 a night. Turn at mile 102. The side road is 3 miles, followed by a 15-minute walk to the glacier's face. I think they charge too much, especially considering the glaciers you can get to for free described throughout this book.

Two exceptional remote lodges lie along the highway near the Matanuska Glacier, about 70 miles from Glennallen or 115 miles from Anchorage. In this remote area there is no TV and phones are in common rooms.

Majestic Valley Wilderness Lodge ❀ *Finds*   This friendly lodge offers basic rooms with private bathrooms and serves excellent family-style meals to guests and others who reserve in advance. Dining is in an extraordinary log lodge building with a towering ceiling and wonderful mountain views—a quintessentially Alaskan space that is understandably popular for weddings and the like. While most of the rooms are small and basic, they're set in a gorgeous, quiet spot out of sight of the highway. A 20km network of superb cross-country skiing trails in spectacular terrain is groomed with quality equipment for diagonal or skate skiing. Anchorage families, such as ours, come here for fun winter or spring weekends, skiing and sledding all day before cooking in the wood-fired sauna, playing games and cards in the evening, and generally being rambunctious. In the summer, the hiking here, mostly above the tree line, is exceptional.

Mile 114.9, Glenn Hwy. (16162 W. Glenn Hwy., Sutton, AK 99674). © **907/746-2930.** Fax 907/746-2931. www. majesticvalleylodge.com. 12 units, including 2 cabins. $115 double; $140 cabin double. Extra adult $10; extra child ages 4–12 $5. MC, V. **Amenities:** Restaurant; free-standing wood-fired sauna. *In room:* No phone.

Sheep Mountain Lodge ⚐   On a mountainside above the road, a well-loved couple, Zack and Anjanette Steer, preside at this historic log lodge. Zack is a top competitive dog musher, so the operation is mostly oriented to the summer. Guests hike and mountain bike over spectacular trails on the tundra-covered mountains. Cabins are large and stylishly decorated, with high ceilings and walls of rough wood to remind you of the rural location. A few have kitchenettes. The sitting porches have wonderful views down the mountainside. They rent a sleeping-bag bunkhouse too and have a guest sauna and indoor hot tub. The little cafe serves simple, healthy food in the summer. Service is very friendly.

Mile 113.5, Glenn Hwy., (17701 West Glenn Hwy., Sutton, AK 99674). © **877/645-5121** or 907/745-5121. Fax 907/745-5120. www.sheepmountain.com. 11 units (10 cabins and 1 bunkhouse). Summer $149 double cabin, $189 double cabin with kitchenette; winter $99–$149 double; extra person in cabin $10; summer bunkhouse $60 for 4, extra person in bunkhouse $5. MC, V. Closed 1 month each in spring and fall (call ahead). **Amenities:** Restaurant; Jacuzzi; sauna. *In room:* No phone.

CHICKALOON & SUTTON

Be ready for construction delays of up to an hour, slow driving, and nighttime closures in the summer of 2008 between miles 92 and 97. Closures are scheduled between midnight to 6am. Contact © 511 or check http://511.alaska.gov for the latest. Despite the roadwork, the scenery remains attractive, with country-style development cropping up along the road as you approach urban Alaska. Chickaloon is the base of Nova Raft and Adventure Tours, the river-riding company listed in chapter 6; if you're already passing through here, you may want to arrange a float. Sutton is a little town left behind by a coal mine that once operated in these mountains. The charming little historic park there is worthy of a stop to stretch your legs.

7 The Richardson Highway & Copper Center

The 364-mile drive from Fairbanks to Valdez unfolds as a grand cross-section of Alaska. It begins in the broad Interior valleys at the north, rises to the tundra and lakes of the Alaska Range, descends back down to the Copper River Country, and finally climbs over the steep coastal mountains into the Prince William Sound fjord where Valdez resides. This was the first route into Alaska, but today it is little traveled and mostly free of development, an opportunity to see real wilderness by car on paved road.

Delta Junction is covered in section 5 earlier. The intersection with the Denali Highway (see chapter 8) comes 81 miles south of there. This section has the most extraordinary scenery—broad vistas, the Delta River, amazing alpine lakes including long Summit Lake, and many views of the trans-Alaska pipeline. Don't plan on stops or services, although there are a few widely scattered campgrounds and seasonal businesses. The spot on the map known as Paxson, the intersection with the Denali Highway, has a business called the Paxson Inn. You can fill your tanks there (summer 7am–10pm, winter 8am–8pm) or buy a snack, but I wouldn't recommend the restaurant or the rooms.

South from Paxson the views remain lovely, with more lakes, increasingly surrounded by trees, as latitude and elevation decrease going into the Copper River Valley. After 15 miles you reach the only noteworthy business on this 70-mile section of road from Paxson to Glennallen: the **Meiers Lake Roadhouse and Atwater Chateau Motel,** at mile 170 (© **907/822-3151**). Way out here, where they have to make their own electricity, the owners have made a comfortable motel of 16 cozy rooms with satellite TVs and private bathrooms. They charge $100 double, $150 for three or more in a room. The same owners have a restaurant, bar, laundromat, and hardware store.

The next town on the Richardson is Glennallen, which is covered above, in section 6. Fourteen miles south of Glennallen, **Copper Center** is a tiny Athabascan community on the old Richardson Highway. Its historic roadhouse, the **Copper Center Lodge** (© **866/330-3245** or 907/822-3245; www.coppercenterlodge.com) has long been worthy of a stop for dinner or even overnight. The history of the lodge dates from the bizarre gold-rush origins of Copper Center and Valdez, when about 4,000 stampeders to the Klondike tried a virtually impossible all-American route from Valdez over the glaciers of the Wrangell–St. Elias region. Few made it, and the hundreds who died are buried in Copper Center. The original lodge was built of the stuff they left behind. The existing building dates from 1932. Double rooms are $136 to $156 and they're open year-round.

Copper River Princess Wilderness Lodge ☆☆   This first-class lodge built by the Princess Cruise Line brings the comforts of the outside world to this rough and isolated corner of the planet. Where once a room with its own toilet was a rarity, now you can get one with a hair dryer and with a fine restaurant down the hall. Princess has tried to capture the trim, red-and-white look of the historic Kennecott mining district. Inside, common areas are spacious and warm, with a big slate fireplace in the lobby. On clear days, the eastward views of Mounts Drum, Wrangell, and Blackburn are incredible. The hotel has its own walking paths to enjoy the setting. Rooms are in earth tones, with faux-rustic furniture and art reflecting mining history, and have king- and queen-size beds. The restaurant serves three meals a day, including sophisticated cuisine for dinner; those meals are not just in another league, but a completely different game than anything else found on the highway. The smoked salmon benedict, eggs benedict with smoked salmon in place of Canadian bacon, was terrific. Dinner main courses are $16 to $29.

1 Brenwick-Craig Rd. (P.O. Box 422), Copper Center, AK 99573 (turn at mile 102 Richardson Hwy.). © **800/426-0500** reservations or 907/822-4000. Fax 907/822-4044. www.princesslodges.com. 85 units. High season $179 double; low season $139 double. AE, DISC, MC, V. **Amenities:** Restaurant; tour desk; courtesy van to Gulkana airport and national park visitor center. *In room:* TV, hair dryer.

8 Wrangell–St. Elias National Park & Kennecott

Looking at a relief map of Alaska, you'd think the portion drained by the Copper River was so overweighted with mountains that it might topple the whole state into the Pacific. The Alaska Range, in the center of the state, has the tallest mountain, but this Gulf of Alaska region, straddling the Alaska-Yukon border, has more mass—the second- and fourth-tallest mountains in North America (Logan and St. Elias), plus 9 of the tallest 16 peaks in the United States. Four mountain ranges intersect, creating a mad jumble of terrain covering tens of millions of acres, a trackless chaos of unnamed, unconquered peaks. The Copper River and its raging tributaries slice through it all, swallowing the gray melt of innumerable glaciers that flow from the largest ice field in North America. Everything here is the largest, most rugged, most remote; words quickly fall short of the measure. But where words fail, commerce gives a little help: These mountains are so numerous and remote that one guide service makes a business of taking visitors to mountains and valleys that no one has ever explored before.

Ironically for such a wild land, the area's main attraction for visitors is its history. The richest copper deposit in the world was found here in 1900 by a group of prospectors who mistook a green mountaintop for a patch of green grass where they could feed their horses. It was a mountain of almost pure copper, with metallic nuggets the size of desks (one is at the UA Museum of the North in Fairbanks). The deposit produced trainloads of 70% pure copper. The first ore was so rich it required no processing before shipping, and then came lots more copper that did need minimal processing. Much more lower-grade ore still lies underground. The Alaska Syndicate, an investment group that included J. P. Morgan and Daniel Guggenheim, built the Kennecott Copper Corporation from this wealth (its name was a misspelling of the Kennicott River and Glacier, where the copper was found). To get the copper out, they paid for an incredible 196-mile rail line up from Cordova (see chapter 7), and created a self-contained company town deep in the wilderness, called **Kennecott.** When the high-grade ore was gone, in 1938, they pulled the plug, leaving a ghost town of extraordinary beauty that still contains machinery and even documents they left behind.

Wrangell–St. Elias National Park and Preserve now owns Kennecott and more than 13 million acres across this region of Alaska. It's the largest national park in the United States by a long shot, six times the size of Yellowstone and about 25% larger than the entire country of Switzerland. The protected land continues across the border in Canada, in **Kluane National Park,** which is similarly massive. Most of that land is impossibly remote, but Wrangell–St. Elias has two rough gravel roads that allow access to see the mountains from a car. The main route is the abandoned roadbed of the Copper River and Northwestern Railroad leading to Kennecott and the historic sites there. It's an arduous but rewarding journey by car, requiring at least 2 days to do it right. Air taxis, river guides, and remote lodges offer other ways into the park's untouched wilderness, mostly starting from **McCarthy,** a historic village near Kennecott. There are a few trails near Kennecott, but only for day hikes. This is a country where experienced outdoors people can get away from any trace of humans for weeks on end.

THE KENNECOTT & MCCARTHY AREA

This historic copper area is the only part of the park most visitors see, as it's the most accessible and has the most services, interesting sites, and paths to explore. It's still not easy to get to, however—that's why it's still so appealing—and there's little point in going without adequate time. You can hit the highlights at Kennecott and McCarthy in 1 full day, but just getting there takes time. My family and I spent 3 nights and could have stayed longer.

The main event is the ghost town at **Kennecott,** whose red buildings gaze from a mountainside across the Kennicott Glacier in the valley below. Now owned by the park service, the buildings made up an isolated company town until 1938, when it abruptly shut down. Tourists coming here as late as the 1960s saw it as if frozen in time, with breakfast dishes still on the tables from the day the last train left. Most of that was looted and destroyed in the 1970s, but when I toured the company store a few years ago, old documents still remained, and the powerhouse and 14-story mill buildings still had their heavy iron and wood equipment. Besides the buildings, there are excellent hiking trails, including one that traverses the glacier. The town now has only a few year-round residents, but in summer is busy with a lodge, a couple of bed-and-breakfasts, guide services, and park rangers.

Five miles down the road, Kennecott's twin town of **McCarthy** served the miners as a place to drink, gamble, and hire prostitutes on rare days off—the company didn't allow any frivolity in Kennecott or in the bunkhouses high up on the mountain. McCarthy retains the relaxed atmosphere of its past, with businesses and residents living in false-front buildings not much changed from Wild West days. More of a year-round community, McCarthy has a restaurant, lodging, flight services, and other businesses.

Yet even this most populous part of the park is isolated and sparsely inhabited, with few services. Only about 65 people live in the greater area year-round. You will find no banking services, general stores, gas stations, clinics, police, or anything else you're used to relying on. Phones came to McCarthy and Kennecott only in the late 1990s and still are few. Bring what you need.

ESSENTIALS

GETTING THERE   By Car   The paved **Edgerton Highway** starts 17 miles south of Copper Center on the Richardson Highway, and then runs east for 33 miles to the tiny, dried-up former railroad town of **Chitina** (*chit*-na), the last reliable stop for groceries, gas, and other necessities until you return here. Do fill your tank; prudence also demands a full-size spare tire. Heading east, into the park, the **McCarthy Road** continues along the roadbed of the Copper River and Northwestern Railway. This is 60 miles of narrow dirt road, muddy in wet weather and clouded with dust when it's dry. Each year it has been improved a little, and two-wheel-drive cars can normally make it. The drive is a fun adventure, passing through tunnels of alders and crossing rivers on some of the original wooden railroad trestles; one wood-decked bridge spans a canyon more than 200 feet deep. There are virtually no services, very few buildings, and little traffic on the 3-hour drive. If you are driving a rented car, consider using the van or air options mentioned below, leaving the car in Chitina.

The road ends at a parking lot and collection of temporary businesses on the banks of the Kennicott River. You can drive no farther. A fee applies to park at the riverside lot, but you can park free for the day ($6 overnight) a little way off at Glacier View Campground (see "Camping & Hostelling," below). Next, you walk across a footbridge or two. Late in the summer the Kennicott Glacier releases a flood from a glacier-dammed lake, but at other times the second channel is a dry wash and the second bridge isn't needed. Handcarts are available to move your luggage across, and on the other side you can catch a van. The place where you are staying will send one, or you can ride the **van** operated by **Wrangell Mountain Air** (© **907/554-4411**), $2 to McCarthy or $5 per person, one-way, to Kennecott. It runs every half-hour. A public telephone is near the bridge you can use to call your lodgings.

By Van   The **Backcountry Connection** (© **866/582-5292** in Alaska only, or 907/822-5292; www.kennicottshuttle.com) runs vans from Glennallen and Chitina to the Kennicott River footbridge daily in summer. The van leaves Glennallen at 7am and Chitina at 8:30am, arriving at the footbridge around 11am. The trip departs from the footbridge at 4:30pm, getting back to Chitina around 6:30pm and Glennallen at 8:30pm. The same-day round-trip fare is $99, $10 more to return on a different day.

By Air   A simple way to Kennecott and McCarthy is to drive to Chitna—as far as you can go on pavement—and fly the rest of the way on one of the air taxis. Once there, get around in the vans that shuttle back and forth over 5 miles of dirt road. **Wrangell Mountain Air** (© 800/478-1160 or 907/554-4411; www.wrangellmountainair.com) offers three flights daily from Chitina to McCarthy for $199 round-trip. Using their day-trip option, you can have plenty of time at Kennecott without having to spend the night there. A reputable service operating between Chitina and McCarthy on an on-demand basis is **McCarthy Air** (© 888/989-9891 or 907/554-4440; www.mccarthy air.com). Flightseeing over the national park and charters to remote valleys and lakes for backcountry trips are covered below under "Hiking & Backpacking."

Wednesday or Friday, it's possible to fly in a small prop plane all the way from Anchorage. A couple of flight services team up to do this: You fly on one from Anchorage to Gulkana and then on the mail plane from Gulkana to McCarthy. The fare is about $300 one-way. Contact **Ellis Air Taxi** (© 800/478-3368 in Alaska only or 907/822-3368; www.ellisair.com), which handles all the booking and flies the Gulkana to McCarthy leg.

VISITOR INFORMATION   The main park visitor center is on the Richardson Highway near Copper Center (© 907/822-5234; www.nps.gov/wrst). Stop in to buy maps and publications, watch a movie, or to get advice from a ranger on outdoor treks. Hours are Memorial Day to Labor Day, daily from 8am to 6pm; in winter, Monday through Friday from 8am to 4:30pm. You can write for information to P.O. Box 439, Copper Center, AK 99573. The park service is restoring buildings and developing visitor services in Kennecott itself. A former train depot has become a visitor center, a good place to stop with questions for rangers, plan a backcountry trip, or to join one of the daily guided activities. A ranger station for the less-visited northern area of the park is on Nabesna Road near its intersection with the Glenn Highway, about 80 miles north of Glennallen. That's an area for solitary roadside camping among broad views.

EXPLORING THE TOWNS

CHITINA   Chitina lost its reason to exist in 1938, when the last train ran on the Copper River line, but it lives on with 120 residents supporting themselves largely with salmon from the river, produce from their gardens, berries from the forests, and the few tourists who stop. There's a general store and a couple of gas stations (the last gas for many a mile), a wayside interpretive area at the site of the old depot, a pond where you can often see trumpeter swans, and, down by the river, lazily rotating fish wheels plucking salmon from the river. The Copper River is too turbid for angling, but clear water tributaries and stocked lakes in the area have fish. You can also explore south on the old Copper River rail line and even through the tunnels; check with a local or the park headquarters for advice and current conditions before trying it, as landslides sometimes block the way. Chitina has one business worth a special stop: **Spirit Mountain Artworks** (© 907/823-2222, or 907/235-1014 winter; www.spiritmountainalaska.com). Art Koeninger bought a remarkable 1910 structure in 1977, restored it over the next 9 years and listed it on the National Register of Historic Places, using the storefront to create a renowned gallery out here in the boonies. Incredibly, it survives still, although Art manages it now from Homer, where he creates his own artwork.

MCCARTHY   McCarthy feels authentic as soon as you walk down the dirt main street between the false fronts. There are flight service offices to arrange a trip out, a lodge, and a hotel. Then, a street beyond, unbroken wilderness for hundreds and perhaps thousands of miles. On a summer evening young backpackers and locals stand in the road—there is no traffic, since there are almost no vehicles—meeting and talking, laughing loudly, walking around dogs having their own party. Visitors quickly mix in, as everyone seems eager to talk about the town and its history and their own peculiar wilderness lives. The people here know it's unique, and everyone hopes it doesn't change much.

KENNECOTT　This has got to be one of the world's greatest ghost towns, with some 40 buildings, mostly in good enough condition to be reused today—indeed, until the current park service restoration project began, the community still played basketball in one structure. Some historic buildings have become lodgings, and the park service is using others. Locals still pick rhubarb and chives from the company garden. History has the same kind of immediacy here that you get from holding an old diary in your hand, quite different from the sanitized history-through-glass that you're used to at more accessible sites.

The park service bought most of the buildings a few years ago. When we walked through, on the eve of the takeover, items remained out on the ground or on store shelves that would be in museums in many places. If Kennecott were an ordinary industrial site, that would be interesting enough, but this place was something well out of the ordinary: an outpost beyond the edge of the world where men built a self-contained city a century ago. The hardship of the miners' lives and the ease of the managerial families' lives also present a fascinating contrast.

You can take in some of the story by wandering around with a walking tour booklet available from the park service and reading signs, but it would be a big mistake to miss going inside the buildings, and to do that you need to join a **guided tour** with **St. Elias Alpine Guides** (© **888/933-5427** or 907/554-4445; full listing below under "Hiking & Backpacking"). They have an office in the old Chinese laundry right in the ghost town. Tours, which happen three times daily, last 2½ hours and go into real depth on the geology and history, climbing to the perilous 14th floor of the mill building. I've never been on another tour like it: fascinating, challenging, and even exciting; I cannot recommend it strongly enough. They operate mid-May to mid-September and charge $25 per person. Consider making a day of it by adding a glacier hiking trip with the same company, which offers a discount if you do both (see "Hiking & Backpacking," below). The guides will arrange a custom tour, too.

GETTING OUTSIDE
HIKING & BACKPACKING　There are a few trails radiating from Kennecott, for which crude maps are available from the rangers and others around town; or buy the **Trails Illustrated** topographic map, printed on plastic, for sale from some local businesses, or order ahead (see "Fast Facts: Alaska," in chapter 2). An impressive walk continues through the ghost town up the valley, paralleling the Kennicott Glacier and then its tributary, the Root Glacier. You can climb along the Root's edge to a towering ice fall, but a much better outing is to be had by joining a group to walk on the glacier itself. St. Elias Alpine Guides, listed below, accepts walk-ins for daily glacier day hikes and other hikes and tours. A half-day on the glacier goes for $60 a person, while all-day hikes are $100 and ice-climbing lessons $120. We combined the half-day hike with the company's ghost town tour for one of the best days of Alaska tourism we've ever spent. Another fascinating hike you can do on your own leads straight up the mountain behind the Kennecott buildings to the old Bonanza Mine and bunkhouses, 3,000 feet higher on the alpine tundra.

Beyond the trails, the park is endless miles of trackless wilderness—one of Earth's last few places that really deserves that name. Fit hikers without the backcountry experience to mount their own expedition should join one of the guides who work in the area. **St. Elias Alpine Guides** (*©* **888/933-5427** or 907/554-4445; www.stelias guides.com) offers day hikes, rafting, backpacking trips, and alpine ascents, but specializes in guiding extended trips to unexplored territory. Bob Jacobs, the company's founder, stopped guiding on Mount McKinley years ago because of the crowds. At Wrangell–St. Elias it's rare to encounter another party and peaks remain that have never been climbed by anyone: The firm offers the chance to be one of the first. A 2-week trek and climb, including 4 days of mountaineering instruction, is a big commitment and costs $3,000 and up, but then, first ascents are a finite resource. The St. Elias catalog will make anyone who loves backpacking drool. Trips begin at $799 for a 4-day Donoho Peak trek. They are all-inclusive, but not without hardship and risk—nothing can take away from the severity of this wild country.

Hiking on your own in a wilderness largely without trails is a whole new kind of experience for experienced backpackers and outdoors people who are used to more crowded parts of the planet. You feel like an explorer rather than a follower. At times, there's a fairy-tale sense of the world unfolding around you, as fresh as creation. If you're not prepared to select your own route—a task only for those already experienced in trackless, backcountry traveling—there are various established ways through the park you can follow with a topographic map. You can get a trip synopsis from the visitor center or ranger station, or download it from their website (www.nps.gov/wrst). Rangers can help you choose a route to suit your party, although none are easy.

Some routes start from the roads, but a better way to go is to charter a flight into a remote valley from one of the two **air services** in McCarthy, Wrangell Mountain Air or McCarthy Air (p. 429 and 429 respectively). The planes land on gravel strips, river bars, glaciers, alpine tundra, or any other flat place the pilots know about. These companies make a business of flying out backpackers, and so have established rates for different landing sites and can help you determine a route that's right for you, as well as provide a list of supplies. Wrangell Mountain Air rents bear-proof containers and two-way radios, and McCarthy Air and the park service lend the containers. You can charter a flight for $200 to $600 per person, with at least two passengers. Or fly in to a lake for fishing or an alpine area for exploring from a base camp, reducing the worry about how much you pack.

Note: I wouldn't want to scare off anyone who could manage one of these trips, but people do get into trouble in the Alaska wilderness every year, and some of them don't come back. Before you head out into the backcountry, you must know how to take care of yourself where help is unavailable; this includes handling river crossings, bear avoidance, preventing hypothermia, basic first aid, and other issues. Unless you have plenty of backpacking experience in less remote areas, I don't recommend starting here.

MOUNTAIN BIKING   Anywhere else, the 60-mile road that leads to this area would be considered a mountain-biking trail. You also can make good use of bikes between McCarthy, Kennecott, and the footbridge. An old **wagon road** parallels the main road that connects the two towns, 4½ miles each way; the road itself is a one-lane dirt track. Advanced cyclists can also ride the trails around Kennecott described above under "Hiking & Backpacking."

RAFTING   Many great, wild rivers drain these huge mountains, which are still being carved by enormous glaciers. The **Kennicott River,** starting at the glacier of the same name, boils with Class III rapids for some 40 minutes starting right from the footbridge at the end of the McCarthy Road. As the area lacks roads, however, most trips must include a plane ride at least one-way, and that makes whitewater rafting day trips here more expensive than outings near Anchorage or Valdez. At Wrangell–St. Elias, floats punch deep into the backcountry. The Kennicott River meets the Nizina, passing through a deep, dramatic canyon; then the Nizina River flows into the Chitina River, which meets the Copper River near the town of Chitina, 60 miles from the starting point. The Copper River flows to the ocean. A float from the footbridge through the Nizina Canyon takes all day, with lunch and bush plane flightseeing back, which could include a glacier fly-over. St. Elias Alpine Guides (see "Hiking & Back-packing," above) charges $275. Other trips continue for 3 or 4 days to Chitina, for $990 to $1,250 per person; or for 10 to 13 days, 180 miles all the way to the Copper River Delta and the sea (see "Cordova: Hidden Treasure," in chapter 7), for $3,600 per person. This is Alaska on its largest and most grandiose scale, accessible only from the banks of these great rivers.

WHERE TO STAY AND DINE

The closest standard hotel rooms are in Copper Center (see section 7, earlier). In the Kennecott-McCarthy area itself there are several attractive places to stay, all thick with the history the towns represent, but not ordinary American lodgings. Dining is mainly at the lodges. If you're not staying there, it is a good idea to check ahead to make sure they will be ready for you for a meal.

CAMPING & HOSTELLING   There is no campground on the Kennecott-McCarthy side of the Kennicott River footbridge. The park service allows camping anywhere in the park without a permit, but there are few handy spots on public land (remember, much of the land along the roads is private), except on the Nabesna Road, which is several hours away from the historic zone.

A couple of primitive private campgrounds, and a hostel, are at the end of the McCarthy Road. **Glacier View Campground** (© **907/554-4490,** 907/243-6677 off season; www.glacierviewcampground.com) charges $18 a night for camping and has a cabin for rent. The owners also rent mountain bikes and offer showers and free day parking. Their cafe offers barbecue for lunch and dinner and serves beer and wine.

Besides the backpacker's hotel mentioned in the review of the McCarthy Lodge on p. 433, **Kennicott River Lodge and Hostel** (© **907/554-4441** summer, 941/447-4252 winter; www.kennicottriverlodge.com), located at the end of the road 400 feet from the footbridge, offers bunks for $28 per person. Sheets and pillows are included; other bedding is extra. The lodge also rents cabins for $100 double plus $25 for each additional person. They have a common kitchen, lounge, sauna, and showers.

There are three campgrounds on the way to the footbridge. The most attractive is the state parks' **Liberty Falls Campground,** at mile 23 on the Edgerton Highway, which is set among big trees at the foot of a crashing waterfall. Many of the sites are walk-ins, with wooden tent platforms and lots of privacy. The self-service camping fee is $10 per vehicle; the day-use fee is $1. There are pit toilets and no running water.

Kennicott Glacier Lodge 𝒦𝒦   This is the largest and most comfortable accom-modation in the Kennecott-McCarthy area, taking the edges off the isolation. The lodge accurately re-creates an old Kennecott building, with the same red-and-white color scheme, and stands among the historic structures of the ghost town. You can't get any closer to what you want to see. Guests can sip drinks on a long, flower-hung front porch overlooking the glacier, or relax on a lawn with play equipment and the same view. Rooms in the main lodge building are not large and have bathrooms down the hall (six shower rooms and eight bathrooms, all clean but small). The 10 rooms in a newer south wing are larger, with two queen-size beds and private bathrooms. All the bedrooms are remarkably clean and decorated with interesting mine artifacts and papers—telegrams, blueprints, and the like. All but eight overlook the glacier and ghost town, and those on the main floor have second entrances on the veranda. A brief evening tour of the ghost town is included.

Filling dinners are served family style at 7pm on long tables, with a fixed menu in the $28 to $35 range, available to nonguests by prior reservation. The food is excellent and portions are generous: One night we had Copper River salmon with sun-dried tomatoes and pine nuts, the next night prime rib; both those evenings, the bill was $30 per person. Guests linger long after dessert; it's a friendly social occasion. A large breakfast buffet is $16, continental breakfast $10. Lunch is by menu service, with sandwiches, salads, and specials ranging from $9 to $15. Sack lunches are available, too. There's nowhere else to eat right in Kennecott, so it makes sense to book the inclusive meal package, which is $295 double in the shared-bathroom units, $355 in the newer units; a third person is $80 with the meal package, children ages 4 to 12 half price.

P.O. Box 103940, Anchorage, AK 99510. ⓒ **800/582-5128** or 907/258-2350; in season only, 907/554-4477. Fax 907/248-7975. www.kennicottlodge.com. 35 units, 10 with private bathroom. $189 double shared bathroom, $249 double private bathroom; additional adult $30; additional child ages 4–12 $15; free ages 3 and under. AE, DISC, MC, V. Closed mid-Sept to mid-May. **Amenities:** Restaurant; tour desk; courtesy van.

McCarthy Lodge ⓐ   The lodge is the center of the relaxed village of McCarthy, 5 miles from the historically more buttoned-up Kennecott. Although you are not among the mining ruins when you stay here, you are in a real community where you can meet year-round residents and the many interesting characters who spend the summer here among historic buildings. The owners of the lodge also own Ma Johnson's Hotel across the street, a saloon, art shop, store, Internet cafe, and backpacker lodgings. They treasure the history and take great pains with the old buildings and food, having invested $1.25 million in the project. Rooms are full of period charm, with antiques, quilts, and memorabilia. They call it a living museum. Even the soap is authentic, made by hand. The bedrooms—which are small, as always in a historic building—are in a false-front structure that you might see in an old Western movie. Every two rooms share a bathroom. In a separate building, Lancaster's Backpacker's Hotel charges $48 single, plus $20 for each additional person up to four.

The eight-table restaurant is an authentic Bush roadhouse in an unmistakably backwoods structure that was moved here from Cordova in 1916. The dining room is decorated with artifacts, early photographs, and heavy drapes. Our meals were all perfectly prepared: chicken alfredo, Cajun halibut, and, best of all, semolina encrusted Copper River red salmon. The price range for dinner is $15 to $24. Or order from the casual and reasonably priced bar menu of pizza and the like. The McCarthy Store and Erie Internet Cafe serves coffee, sandwiches, and baked goods, and has a shower and laundry.

P.O. Box MXY, McCarthy, AK 99588. ⓒ **907/554-4402**. Fax 877/811-6172. www.mccarthylodge.com. 20 units, none with private bathroom. $159 double. MC, V. **Amenities:** Restaurant; bar; courtesy van. Closed Oct to mid-May.

10

The Bush

The Bush is most of Alaska. On a map of the state, the portion with roads and cities is a smallish corner. Yet most visitors—and, indeed, most Alaskans—never make it beyond that relatively populated corner. Several years ago a lifelong Anchorage resident was elected to the legislature and appointed chair of its rural issues committee, only to admit he had never been to the Bush. It's common for children to grow to adulthood in Anchorage, Fairbanks, or Southeast Alaska without traveling to the Arctic, the Aleutians, or the vast wetlands of western Alaska. It happens for the same reason most tourists don't go to Bush Alaska—getting there is expensive, and there's not much in the way of human activity once you arrive. Bush Alaska is one of the planet's last barely inhabited areas. But that's a reason to go, not a reason to stay away. You can meet indigenous people who still interact with the environment in their traditional way and see virgin places that remain to be explored by self-reliant outdoors people.

Although there are few people in the Bush, the hospitality of those you do meet is special and warming. In Bush Alaska, where the population is overwhelmingly Alaska Native, it's not uncommon to be befriended by total strangers simply because you've taken the trouble to come to their community and are, therefore, an honored guest. Even in the larger towns, people smile as you pass in the street. If you have a questioning look on your face, they'll stop to help. Living in a small place where people know each other and have to work together against the elements makes for a tight, friendly community.

Alaska Native culture is based more on cooperative than competitive impulses. Respect and consensus carry greater weight than in individualistic white society. Cooperation requires slowing down, listening, not taking the lead. People from our fast-paced culture can leave a village after a visit wondering why no one spoke to them, not realizing that they never shut up long enough to give anyone a chance. The cultural differences here are real, unlike the shadows of past differences we celebrate in most regions of the homogenous United States. Long pauses in conversation are normal, looking down while addressing a person demonstrates respect, punctuality is highly relative, child care is a community function, and when gifts are offered, people really mean it—turning down even a cup of coffee is gauche. (For more on the culture of Alaska's Native peoples, see the appendix, "Alaska in Depth.")

The Native people of the Bush also have terrible problems trying to live in two worlds. There's too much alcohol and too many drugs in the Bush, too much TV, but not enough of an economic base to provide for basic services in many villages. Even in some of the relatively prosperous village hubs described in this chapter, visitors will glimpse a kind of rural poverty they may not have seen before—where prices are extremely high and steady jobs scarce and difficult to hold while pursuing traditional hunting and food gathering. But if you ask why Natives stay, you're missing something. In a world where so few indigenous cultures survive, people here are working to retain traditions that give their lives meaning—a sense of place and a depth of belonging that most of us can only envy. It's a work in progress, this combination of tradition and modernity, but there's no question they're slowly succeeding. They control their own land, they're building an economic base, and Native ways are being passed on to younger generations.

The Natives' physical environment is extreme in every respect—the weather, the land, even the geography. There's a special feeling to walking along or upon the Arctic Ocean, the virtual edge of the earth. The quantity and accessibility of wildlife are extreme, too, as are the solitude and the uniqueness of what you can do. Unfortunately, the prices also are extreme. Getting to a Bush hub from Anchorage costs more than getting to Anchorage from Seattle; it's often cheaper to get to Europe from Anchorage than to the Aleutians. And once you're at the rural hub, you're not done. Getting into the outdoors can cost as much again. Many travelers can't afford a Bush sojourn, instead satisfying their curiosity about the state's unpopulated areas on Alaska's rural highways (covered in chapter 9). Most who can afford the trip usually make the most of their time and money with brief prearranged tours or trips directly to wilderness lodges. Only a few explorers head for the Bush unguided, although there are some good places to go that way—Nome, Barrow, Kodiak, and Unalaska among them.

Covering the Bush is a challenge as well for the writer of a book like this one. There are more than 200 Alaska villages; many more lodges, camps, and guides; and a vast, undefined territory to describe. All that information would fill a larger book than this one. I've chosen to provide sections on those few Bush hubs that are most accessible and popular with visitors, those that have modern facilities and can be used as gateways to more of the state for visitors who want to venture beyond the fringe of civilization.

1 Exploring the Bush

Alaska's Bush is better defined by what it's like than by where it is. The most common and convenient conception says the Bush is everything beyond the road system. On a map, everything north and west of Fairbanks obviously meets that definition, but many Bush villages lie elsewhere in the Interior, in Southcentral, and in Southeast Alaska. In fact, there are some Bush villages you can drive to. No simple definition works. You know a Bush community by how it feels. It's a place where the wilderness is closer than civilization, where people still live off the land and age-old traditions survive, and where you have to make a particular effort to get in or out.

THE REGIONS

THE ARCTIC   The Arctic Circle is the official boundary of the Arctic. The line, at 66° 33' north latitude, is the southern limit of true midnight sun—south of it, at sea level, the sun rises and sets, at least a little, every day of the year. But in Alaska, people think of the Arctic as beginning at the **Brooks Range,** which is a bit north of the circle, including **Barrow** and **Prudhoe Bay.** The northwest Alaska region, which includes, **Kotzebue** and, slightly south of the Arctic Circle, **Nome,** also is Arctic in climate, culture, and topography. The biggest geographic feature in Alaska's Arctic is the broad **North Slope,** the plain of tundra that stretches from the northern side of the Brooks Range to the Arctic Ocean. It's a swampy desert, with little rain or snowfall, frozen solid all but a few months a year.

WESTERN ALASKA This is the land of the massive, wet **Yukon-Kuskokwim Delta** and the fish-rich waters of Bristol Bay. The Y-K Delta, as it's known, was never really exploited by white explorers, and its Yup'ik people live in some of Alaska's most culturally traditional villages. In places, Yup'ik is still the dominant language. **Bethel** is the main hub city of the delta but holds little attraction for visitors. **Bristol Bay** is known for massive salmon runs, and avid anglers may be interested in its wilderness lodges, using **Dillingham** as a hub.

Map Pointer

To locate these towns and regions, refer to the "Alaska" map in the color section.

SOUTHWEST ALASKA Stretching from the Aleutians—really a region of their own—to the Alaska Peninsula, Kodiak Island, and the southern part of the mountainous west side of Cook Inlet, this is a maritime region, like Southeast, but far more remote. The hub of the wet, windy **Aleutians** is **Unalaska** and its port of **Dutch Harbor. Katmai National Park** and the adjoining wild lands are the main attraction of the Alaska Peninsula, although there also are fishing lodges on the salmon-rich rivers and on the lakes to the north, including areas in **Lake Clark National Park** and **Iliamna Lake.** The lakes and west side of **Cook Inlet** are accessed primarily by Kenai, Homer, and Anchorage flight services for fishermen and hunters. **Kodiak** is hardly a Bush community, but it fits better in this chapter than anywhere else, and the town is a hub for villages and bear viewing on Kodiak Island.

GETTING AROUND

With a few exceptions for strongly motivated travelers, who might take the ferry to Kodiak and Unalaska or drive to Prudhoe Bay, getting to each town in this chapter will require flying. **Alaska Airlines** (© **800/252-7522;** www.alaskaair.com) offers the only jet service to Bush hubs. Other, smaller operators serve these towns with prop aircraft. Throughout the chapter, I've listed the plane fare to various communities from Anchorage, based on flying coach and getting a significant discount for advance purchase and some restrictions. Full fares cost more. With the way airfares fluctuate, it would be unwise to use these numbers as anything more than rough guides. To get the current best fare, use a travel agent or the Internet.

Kodiak, which barely fits in a chapter on the Bush, is the most accessible of the communities in this chapter, but it still requires either a 10-hour ferry ride from Homer or a $300 round-trip plane ticket from Anchorage. This charming, historic town is similar to towns in Southeast Alaska or Prince William Sound, but it is also a hub for Native villages on the island and remote wilderness. **Unalaska/Dutch Harbor,** in the Aleutian Islands is an interesting place to go way off the beaten path while staying in complete comfort. From Anchorage a visit requires a 3-hour flight on a turbo prop aircraft, and fares of less than $900 are rarely seen. **Barrow,** the **Pribilof Islands, Kotzebue,** and **Kaktovik** are the most purely Native of the communities in the chapter. **Nome** has the advantages of Arctic surroundings easily accessible on gravel roads, but is more of a gold-rush town than a Native village. **Prudhoe Bay,** at the end of the Dalton Highway, is an industrial complex without a real town associated with it. Fares from Anchorage range from $450 to $850 for these communities. Buying an **Alaska Airlines package tour** saves money to Nome or Barrow, and gives you something to do when you arrive.

2 Kodiak: Wild Island

The habitat that makes Kodiak Island a perfect place for bears also makes it perfect for people. Runs of salmon clog unpopulated bays and innumerable, little-fished rivers; the rounded green mountains seem to beg for someone to cross them; the gravel beaches and protected rocky inlets are free of people, but full of promise. But, in this respect, bears are smarter than people. Brown bears own the island, growing to prodigious size and abundant numbers, but Kodiak is as yet undiscovered by human visitors. That's part of the wonder of the place. I'll never forget flying over the luxuriant verdure of Kodiak's mountains and the narrow string of glassy Raspberry Strait on a rare sunny day, seeing no sign of human presence in the most beautiful landscape I had ever beheld.

The narrow streets of the town of Kodiak are a discovery, too. Twisting over the hills in little discernible order, they were the original stomping grounds of **Lord Alexander Baranof,** the first Russian ruler of Alaska, who arrived here in 1790. Kodiak has the oldest Russian building in North America. It was nearly lost in the 1964 Good Friday earthquake, which destroyed most of the town, explaining the general lack of old buildings. The quake brought a 30-foot wave that washed to the building's doorstep. A marker near the police station on Mill Bay Road shows the wave's incredible high-water point. Before the Russians, the **Alutiiq** people lived off the incomparable riches of the island. They're still here, recovering their past in a fascinating little research museum.

The town looks to the sea. Along with the Coast Guard base, fishing makes Kodiak prosperous, creating a friendly, energetic, unpolished community. Kodiak is separate from the rest of Alaska, living its own commercial fishing life without often thinking of what's going on in Anchorage or anywhere else. It's off the beaten path because it doesn't really need anything the path provides.

For the visitor, Kodiak is an undiscovered gem. A few days just scratch the surface of the charming, vibrant town and the easily accessible wild places around it, yet, even in midsummer, you will see few if any other tourists.

There are six **Native villages** on the island. A flight to one of them and back on a clear day is a wonderful, low-cost way to see remote areas of the island and to get a taste of how Alaska Natives live. It's also popular to fly out to see the famous bears on a day trip, or stay at one of several **wilderness lodges** for wildlife-watching, fishing, sea kayaking, or hunting.

ESSENTIALS

GETTING THERE   It's a 1-hour flight from Anchorage to Kodiak on **Alaska Airlines** (© **800/252-7522;** www.alaskaair.com). **ERA Aviation** (© **800/866-8394;** www.flyera.com) also serves the route with prop aircraft, which may save a little money. A round-trip ticket from Anchorage costs $300 or more. A **cab,** from **A&B Taxi** (© **907/486-4343**), runs about $20 from the airport to downtown.

The ferries *Tustumena* and *Kennicott,* of the **Alaska Marine Highway System** (© **800/642-0066** or 907/486-3800; www.ferryalaska.com), serve Kodiak from Homer, the closest port with a road. The run takes 10 hours, but it is truly memorable. The vessels leave land behind and thread through the strange and exposed Barren Islands. The ocean can be quite rough, and when it is, lots of passengers get seasick; read and follow the advice on p. 49. A cabin is a good idea for an overnight run. Without a cabin, the adult passenger fare from Homer is $74. The adult passenger fare for a cabin is $129. Fares for children ages 6 to 12 are half price on all ferries, free if under 6. The U.S. Fish & Wildlife Service staffs the ferry with a naturalist on runs to Kodiak.

VISITOR INFORMATION   The **Kodiak Island Convention and Visitors Bureau,** 100 E. Marine Way, Suite 200, Kodiak, AK 99615 (© **800/789-4782** or 907/486-4782; fax 907/486-6545; www.kodiak.org), occupies a small building on the ferry dock. Hours vary according to the ferry schedule, but essentially follow this pattern: summer Monday from 8am to 8:30pm, Tuesday through Friday 8am to 5pm, Saturday from 11am to 8pm, Sunday from 10am to 5pm; winter Monday through Friday from 8am to 5pm.

The **Kodiak National Wildlife Refuge Visitor Center,** is planning a move to a site near the ferry terminal at Mission Road and Center Avenue around the time this book hits shelves; currently it is located on Buskin River Road, near the airport 4 miles south of town (© **888/408-3514** or 907/487-2600; http://kodiak.fws.gov). The center provides information on a 1.9-million-acre refuge that covers two-thirds of Kodiak island and parts of other islands, the home of the famous Kodiak brown bear. There are seven remote public-use cabins around the refuge, reachable by chartered plane. Permits are $30 a night, available though a quarterly drawing of names (Jan 2 for Apr–June, Apr 1 for July–Sept). The new building will have a complete gray whale skeleton and a full-size replica of a Kodiak brown bear. The center is open from mid-June to August daily from 8am to 4:30pm; the balance of the year Monday through Friday only.

ORIENTATION   The Kodiak Archipelago contains Kodiak, Shuyak, and Afognak islands, and many other, smaller islands. Kodiak is the nation's second-largest island (after Hawaii's Big Island). The city of Kodiak is on a narrow point on the northeast side of Kodiak Island, surrounded by tiny islands. There are six Native villages on other parts of the island. The airport and Coast Guard base are several miles southwest of town on **Rezanof Drive,** which runs through town and comes out on the other side. The center of Kodiak is a hopeless tangle of steep, narrow streets—you need the excellent map given away by the visitor center, but it's all walkable. The ferry dock is on **Marine Way,** and most of the in-town sights are right nearby. Several paved and gravel roads, totaling 100 miles, make wonderful exploring from Kodiak to deserted shorelines, gorgeous views, pastures, recreation areas, and salmon streams. The visitors guide contains a mile-by-mile guide to each drive.

GETTING AROUND   Several companies offer cars for rent, including **Budget** (© **800/527-0700** or 907/487-2220; www.budget.com), which has offices at the airport and downtown. **Avis** is at the Kodiak airport (© **800/331-1212** or 907/487-2264; www.avis.com).

FAST FACTS: Kodiak

Banks Several banks downtown have ATMs, including **Key Bank** and **Wells Fargo** on the mall at the waterfront.

Hospital **Providence Kodiak Island Medical Center** is at 1915 E. Rezanof Dr. (© **907/486-3281**).

Internet Access **Harborside Fly by Coffee,** 1715 Mill Bay Rd. (© **907/486-5864**), has a pay terminal and free Wi-Fi; or try the **A. Holmes Johnson Public Library,** 319 Lower Mill Bay Rd. (© **907/486-8686**).

Police Contact the **Kodiak Police Department** at © **907/486-8000.**

Post Office 419 Lower Mill Bay Rd., at Hemlock Street.

Taxes **Sales tax** is 6% within city limits and the **room tax** is 5% everywhere on the island; rooms are thus taxed 11% in Kodiak city, 5% elsewhere.

SPECIAL EVENTS **Russian Orthodox Christmas,** January 7, includes the evening **Starring Ceremony.** A choir follows a parishioner carrying a star to sing at the homes of church members.

The 5-day **Kodiak Crab Festival** (© **907/486-5557**), over Memorial Day weekend (May 22–26, 2008), is a big event, including a king crab feed, a carnival, many fun community events, the solemn blessing of the fleet and a memorial service for fishermen and mariners lost at sea.

On Labor Day weekend, the **Kodiak State Fair and Rodeo** has all kinds of small-town contests and family entertainment including bull riding, a horse show, and a wild cow-milking contest, in which pairs of amateur cowboys and cowgirls pulled from the audience chase down and milk small cows unleashed in a ring. Call the visitor bureau for information. The bureau also maintains an extensive community calendar online at **www.kodiak.org**.

EXPLORING THE TOWN

The highlights downtown include the **Fishermen's Memorial,** near the harbor master's office at the head of the St. Paul Harbor, where a soberingly long list of Kodiak fishermen who have lost their lives at sea is posted on plaques. The warship set in concrete on Mission Way is the *Kodiak Star,* the last World War II Liberty Ship built. It came here as a fish processor after the 1964 earthquake destroyed the canneries and is still in use. Along Shelikof Avenue, overlooking St. Paul Harbor, the **Kodiak Maritime Museum** has mounted 12 attractive and interesting signs explaining the parts of a boat, North Pacific crabbing and geography, and other nautical topics.

In the same area, stop in at **Kodiak Island Brewing Co.,** 338 Shelikof St., where Ben Millstein brews beer that's mostly organic. You can buy a pint to drink on-site, or order the brew in any of the local restaurants.

At Kashevarof and Mission streets is the **Holy Resurrection Russian Orthodox Church,** founded in 1794, although the present building dates only to 1945, when the original church burned.

Alutiiq Museum ✦ This exceptional museum, governed by Natives, seeks to document and revitalize Kodiak's Alutiiq culture, which the Russians virtually wiped out in the 18th century. Besides teaching about Alutiiq culture in a single gallery, the museum manages its own archaeological digs and repatriates Native remains and artifacts, which researchers removed by the thousands in the 1930s. The archaeological repository now includes 100,000 objects.

215 Mission Rd. © **907/486-7004.** www.alutiiqmuseum.org. Admission $3 adults; free for children under 12. Summer Mon–Fri 9am–5pm, Sat 10am–5pm; winter Tues–Fri 9am–5pm, Sat 10:30am–4:30pm.

The Baranov Museum ⭐ The museum occupies the oldest Russian building of only a few left standing in North America, which is Alaska's oldest building of any kind. Alexander Baranof, who ruled Alaska as manager of the Russian-American Company, built the log structure in 1808 as a magazine and strong house for valuable sea otter pelts—the treasure that motivated the Russians' interest here—his headquarters for the invasion he extended across Alaska and down the Pacific Northwest coast. The museum stands in a grassy park overlooking the water across from the ferry dock. Inside is a little museum rich with Russian and early Native artifacts. The guides know a lot of history and show educational photo albums on various topics. The gift store is exceptional, selling antique Russian items and authentic Native crafts.

101 Marine Way. ℂ 907/486-5920. www.baranov.us. Admission $3; free for children under 12. Summer Mon–Sat 10am–4pm; winter Tues–Sat 10am–3pm. Closed Feb.

GETTING OUTSIDE
TWO RECREATION AREAS

A couple of miles north of town on Rezanof Drive, the **Fort Abercrombie State Historical Park** encompasses World War II ruins set on coastal cliffs amid huge trees. Paths lead to the beaches and good tide-pool walking, a swimming lake, and lots of other discoveries. The gun emplacements, bunkers, and other concrete buildings defended against the Japanese, who had seized islands in the outer Aleutians and were expected to come this way. A group of local World War II buffs have built a museum of war artifacts from the Alaska fighting in the ammunition bunker at Miller Point. Hours change annually, but will be posted at www.kadiak.org (yes, kadiak) or call ℂ **907/486-7015.** The website is extensive. A wonderful 13-site campground sits atop the cliffs among the trees and ruins. Camping is $15. The **Alaska Division of State Parks,** Kodiak District Office, 1400 Abercrombie Dr., Kodiak, AK 99615 (ℂ **907/486-6339;** fax 907/486-3320; www.alaskastateparks.org, click on "Individual Parks," then "Kodiak Islands"), maintains an office here where you can pick up a walking-tour b   office r, during the summer, join the Saturday-night interpretive program or a guided t. pool walk, scheduled to coincide with low tides. Or investigate the tide pools on your own, picking up an identification guide at the park's natural history bookstore.

The **Buskin River State Recreation Site,** 4 miles south of town off Rezanof Drive near the Fish & Wildlife Service visitor center, has 15 campsites, a hiking trail, and access to fishing. Camping is $15. Day-use fees are under consideration for both of these sites.

OUTDOOR ACTIVITIES

BROWN BEAR VIEWING To count on seeing Kodiak's famous bears you need to get out on a plane or boat and visit at the right time of year. The easiest way is a Kodiak-based floatplane; expect to pay $425 to $440 per person, with a two- or three-person minimum for a guided half-day trip. Landing on the water, you don rubber boots (provided) and walk up to half an hour to get to where bears congregate. In early July to early August, depending on salmon runs, flights land on Frazer Lake for viewing at Frazer fish pass. A .75-mile walk on a dirt lane leads to the viewing area. The Kodiak National Wildlife Refuge (ℂ **888/408-3514** or 907/487-2600; http://kodiak.fws.gov; see "Visitor Information," above) controls the viewing area. Flights also sometimes visit Ayakulik and Karluk rivers when fish are present. At any of these sites, binoculars and telephoto camera lenses are essential, as no responsible guide would crowd Kodiak brown bears so closely that such lenses become unnecessary (although the bears could choose to approach within 50 yards of you). Bears congregate only when salmon are running, so the timing of your visit is critical. From early July to mid-August you have a good chance of seeing bears fishing in streams on Kodiak, sometimes in numbers. Contact the refuge for more information on timing and bear activity.

When fish aren't running on Kodiak, such as in June or after mid-August, air services concentrate on flights to the east coast of the Alaska Peninsula, often in Katmai National Park, to watch bears digging clams from the tidal flats and eating grass and greens on the coastal meadows or catching fish in August. It's interesting and the flight is spectacular, but the viewing may be from a greater distance than on the streams and the bears will more likely be on their own.

Generally, the flight services charge their standard bear viewing seat rate regardless of how far they have to fly to find bears; if you charter, it may cost much more, but you will have freedom to determine where the plane goes for added sightseeing.

Several small flight services offer bear viewing, including **Sea Hawk Air** (✆ **800/ 770-4295** or 907/486-8282; www.seahawkair.com).

If a bear viewing day trip is the whole reason you're going to Kodiak, compare your options. You can use Homer as your base (see chapter 7), or spend more money to go to Katmai National Park to see bears really close (see section 3 of this chapter).

For additional money, you can see more of Kodiak's bears on a longer outing: A flight service can leave you at a lodge for an extended stay in bear habitat. Check the visitor center for a referral. Harry and Brigid Dodge host small groups at their rustic, solar-powered Aleut Island Lodge in Uyak Bay, taking an environmentally sensitive approach while spending the time to know the bears and their habitat. The business is called Kodiak Treks (✆ **907/487-2122;** www.kodiaktreks.com). Rates are $300 per person per night, double, including food and activities such as kayaking and fishing, but not including the cost of getting there (about $275 per person round-trip from Kodiak). See "Sea Kayaking," below, for another option.

FISHING   The 70 miles of road leading from Kodiak reach eight good-size rivers with productive fishing for salmon and Dolly Varden char. At times you can drive to places with fishing pressure as light as some fly-in locations on the mainland. Going beyond the road network puts you on some of the best and least used fishing opportunities in Alaska. The visitor center provides a list of where to fish and the names and addresses of guides for remote fishing. You can also seek advice and regulations from the **Alaska Department of Fish & Game,** 211 Mission Rd., Kodiak, AK 99615 (✆ **907/486-1880;** www.adfg.state.ak.us; click on "Sport Fisheries," then on the Southcentral region, then on "Kodiak/Aleutians"). To fish the remote areas, you'll need to charter a plane, going for a day or staying at a remote public-use cabin or wilderness lodge.

About 50 boats are available in the boat harbors for ocean fishing. An advantage of coming to Kodiak is that it puts you near rich halibut grounds—you don't have to take a long boat ride for excellent fishing. Trolling for silvers is good in August. Check with the visitor center for a referral.

HIKING & BIRD-WATCHING   There are good day hikes in Kodiak, some starting from downtown. The local Audubon Society publishes a Kodiak Hiking & Birding Guide that you can pick up at the visitor center. Audubon's guided hikes go to a different place every Saturday and Sunday of the summer, meeting at the visitor center parking lot at 9:30am for car pooling. Again, the center is the best source of information.

SEA KAYAKING   The Kodiak Archipelago, with its many folded, rocky shorelines and abundant marine life, is a perfect place for sea kayaking. Kayaks were invented here and on the Aleutian Islands to the west. For beginners it is best to start with a day trip, and the waters around the town of Kodiak are lovely for such a paddle. Several operators can arrange an outing, although most concentrate on more ambitious trips. For a half-day expect to pay around $100 per person, for a full day $200. One day-trip guide with a strong environmental ethic is Andy Schroeder, whose business is called **Orcas Unlimited Charters** (© 907/539-1979; www.orcasunlimited.com). Schroeder specializes in day trips, but also takes clients on extended outings using a converted fishing boat as a base. Guests paddle by day and sleep and eat onboard. Others operate using the same mother-ship concept. **Mythos Expeditions** (© 907/486-5536; www.thewildcoast.com) has for years housed kayakers on a former fishing vessel for multi-day bear- and whale-watching trips on the coasts of Kodiak and Afognak islands and the Alaska Peninsula's Katmai coast. They do day trips as well.

Shuyak Island State Park, 54 miles north of Kodiak, is famously appealing for sea kayaking expeditions. The park is a honeycomb of islands and narrow passages in virgin Sitka spruce coastal forest. The Division of State Parks (see addresses under "Two Recreation Areas," above) distributes a free kayaking guide with route descriptions and maintains four public-use cabins, which rent for $75 a night in the summer season. These cabins can be quite hard to get in August. See "State Parks Cabin Reservations," in section 1 of chapter 7. Mythos Expeditions, mentioned in the previous paragraph, leads trips to Shuyak Island State Park and rents kayaks there for self-guided paddlers.

WHERE TO STAY

I've listed good places in town and nearby on the roads, but Kodiak has many other B&Bs. Beyond the roads, some of Alaska's best wilderness lodges are on Kodiak Island in remote areas and near Native villages. The visitor center posts links to many B&Bs and lodges on its website at www.kodiak.org.

Best Western Kodiak Inn ⊀ This is the best hotel in downtown Kodiak, with attractive rooms perched on the hill overlooking the boat harbor, right in the center of things. Rooms in the wooden building vary in size and view, but all are acceptable standard rooms with good amenities, including pillow top beds and wireless Internet.

The hotel's restaurant, the **Chart Room,** specializes in seafood and with a great view of the water, is a good choice for a nice dinner out, with entrees in the $15 to $25 range.

236 W. Rezanof Dr., Kodiak, AK 99615. © 888/563-4254 or 907/486-5712. Fax 907/486-3430. www.kodiakinn.com. 81 units. High season $159 double; low season $109 double. Extra person over age 17 $15. AE, DC, DISC, MC, V. **Amenities:** Restaurant; bar; outdoor Jacuzzi; tour desk; courtesy van. *In room:* TV, fridge, coffeemaker, hair dryer, iron, microwave, Wi-Fi.

Comfort Inn Kodiak ⊀ A 50-room hotel facing the airport parking lot offers some of the area's best standard accommodations. All rooms were remodeled in 2006 and 2007 and are equipped with many amenities. Suites are simply larger rooms. The location is distant from Kodiak's downtown or historic sites, but that won't matter much if you rent a car. Those planning remote outdoor activities may prefer it for the close access to air services.

1395 Airport Way, Kodiak, AK 99615. © 800/544-2202 or 907/487-2700. www.choicehotels.com/hotel/ak025. 50 units. High season $160 double, $210 suite; low season $110 double, $130 suite. Extra person over 17 $10. Rates include continental breakfast. AE, DC, DISC, MC, V. **Amenities:** Exercise room; business center. *In room:* TV, fridge, coffeemaker, hair dryer, iron, microwave, Wi-Fi.

Eider House Bed & Breakfast ⊀ This attractive B&B 9 miles south of town is a perfect choice for anglers or anyone who prefers a natural setting. It sits near Sargent

Creek and fishing is within a short walk, with more hot spots not far off. With this in mind, owners Robin and Mike Haight have installed a dedicated fish butchering facility for visitor use that includes vacuum-packing equipment and a freezer. The seaside surroundings are inviting for hiking—despite being on the road system, the B&B has aspects of a wilderness lodge. The exceptionally clean bedrooms, all with their own bathrooms, are attractively decorated with reproductions and comforters. A full breakfast is served at convenient hours and they'll pack a lunch for your charter fishing outing free; however, check-in isn't until 5pm except by special arrangement.

782 Sargent Creek Rd., Kodiak, AK 99615. ℂ 907/487-4315. www.eiderhouse.com. 4 units. High season $145 double; low season $85 double. Extra person $25. AE, MC, V. **Amenities:** Guest kitchen; laundry machines or service; fish processing facility. *In room:* TV, coffeemaker, hair dryer, iron, Wi-Fi.

A Smiling Bear Bed & Breakfast, near Fort Abercrombie (ℂ **907/481-6390**), has suites with Jacuzzis and serves gourmet breakfasts for $150 double in the high season.

WHERE TO DINE

Besides the restaurant listed above at the Best Western Kodiak Inn, Kodiak has several restaurants catering to locals.

The best restaurant in town is a coffee shop. **Mill Bay Coffee & Pastries,** about 2 miles out of downtown at 3833 Rezanof Dr. (ℂ **907/486-4411;** www.millbaycoffee.com), is where award-winning, Paris-trained chef Joel Chenet produces wonderful pastries and, for lunch, brilliant combinations of local seafood and international seasonings brought to inexpensive sandwiches—the Kodiak sea burger is made of salmon, crab, shrimp, and cream cheese, among other ingredients, and costs only $10. The comfortable, casual dining room, managed by Chenet's wife, Martine, is a local hub and has Wi-Fi.

Another unique place to eat, this time for dinner, could be a highlight of your trip. Marty and Marion Owen serve dinner for six on their 42-foot yacht the *Sea Breeze.* The meals from **Galley Gourmet** (ℂ **800/253-6331** or 907/486-5079; www.kodiak-alaska-dinner-cruises.com) are usually elaborate seafood creations. The evening starts at 6pm with a 45-minute cruise in the picturesque waters near Kodiak's harbor, where guests may see puffins, sea lions, and whales. Dinner is served at anchor in a quiet lagoon and you're back at the dock at 9:30pm. The price is $120 per person. The couple offers day-long whale-watching and 3-day cruises, too.

Harborside Coffee and Goods, at 210 Shelikof St., #B (ℂ **907/486-5862**), on the south side of the boat harbor, is a comfortable coffeehouse with soup, bagels, and fresh pastries, popular with young people and fishermen.

Henry's Great Alaskan Restaurant, at 512 Marine Way (ℂ **907/486-8844**), on the waterfront mall, is a bar and grill where you will meet many commercial fishermen and other locals. The menu includes daily specials, local seafood, and good halibut sandwiches. The smoked salmon chowder is excellent. Visitors from the outside world may be surprised to find people smoking in the dining room (yes, Sunny, I do remember the day when that was common). The restaurant has powerful air cleaners and separate seating areas, but nonsmokers still may be bothered.

3 Katmai National Park

Most of the land of the Alaska Peninsula, pointing out to the Aleutian Archipelago, is in one federally protected status or another, centering on Katmai National Park. The park, pronounced "*cat*-my," lies just west of Kodiak Island, across the storm-infested Shelikof Strait. Bear and salmon are the main attractions. **Brooks Camp,** with a campground and lodge within Katmai, is probably the most comfortable place for foolproof bear viewing in Alaska during its peak season. Bears congregate thickly at the falls on the Brooks River when red salmon try to pass up the falls at the beginning of July (for more on the seasons see "Exploring the Park," below). At times, you can sit back on a deck and watch 900-pound brown bears walk by, going about their business of devouring the fish that contribute to their awesome size. (A brown bear is the genetic twin of the grizzly, but generally larger due to its coastal diet of salmon.) Staying the night will require you to reserve a place in the 16-space campground the previous winter or stay in the pricey lodge, where rooms can book up over a year ahead for the bear season. You can go for a day trip with less planning if you can stand to pay around $600 round-trip airfare from Anchorage for 2 or 3 hours at the camp (see "Getting There," below). Bear viewing on the Katmai Coast is covered in the Kodiak section (p. 440), where flight services and charter boats offers trips. If you're comparing, also look at the flight operators in Homer and Anchorage (p. 316 and 245).

Katmai was set aside in 1918 for reasons unrelated to bears. The area exploded into world consciousness in 1912 with the most destructive volcanic eruption to shake the earth in 3,400 years. When Katmai's Novarupta blew, it released 10 times more energy than Mount St. Helen's eruption of 1980 and displaced twice as much matter as 1883s Krakatoa. In Kodiak, the sky was black for 3 days and 2 feet of ash crushed houses and choked rivers. People could clearly hear the blast in Juneau; acid rain melted fabric in Vancouver, British Columbia; and the skies darkened over most of the Northern Hemisphere. At the blast site all life within a 40-square-mile area was wiped out and buried as deep as 700 feet. But so remote was the area, then still unnamed, that not a single human being was killed. The **Valley of Ten Thousand Smokes,** the vast wasteland created by the blast, belched steam for decades after. Today Novarupta is dormant and the steam is gone, but the area is still a barren moonscape, making a fascinating day tour or hiking trip.

ESSENTIALS

GETTING THERE   Most people fly to Katmai from Anchorage by way of the village of **King Salmon,** which lies just west of the park. **Alaska Airlines** (© **800/ 252-7522;** www.alaskaair.com) flies to King Salmon daily in the summer, charging at least $450 round-trip. For more flight options, you can use their prop partner, **PenAir** (© **800/448-4226;** www.penair.com), which can be booked through Alaska Airlines. Air taxis carry visitors the last leg from King Salmon to **Brooks Camp** for a fare of around $170, round-trip. **Katmai Air,** operated by park concessionaire Katmailand (© **800/544-0551** or 907/243-5448; www.katmaiair.com), does these flights and offers round-trip airfare packages from Anchorage that can save a little money (total around $585) and add simplicity to your planning.

As an alternative to Brooks Camp, more and more visitors are exploring the supremely rugged wilderness on the east side of the park from the beaches along **Shelikof Strait.** Air-taxi operators make drop-offs and do bear-viewing day trips from Kodiak or Homer (see section 2 of this chapter or see section 10 in chapter 7), and boats out of Kodiak go across for extended cruising and kayak expeditions (p. 441). In this park, with more than 2,000 brown bears resident (the world's largest protected population), it's easy for pilots to find them digging clams on the tidal marshes, then land on floats for a good, close look.

RESERVATIONS & FEES   No entry fee or permit applies for day trips to Katmai, but once you're there you have to sign up for an hour on the bear-viewing platforms (see "Exploring the Park," below). Camping costs $8 per person per night. Campground capacity is allocated by person, not by site, and the limit of 60 people per night is far lower than the many visitors who want to stay during the bear season in July. The crowds are smaller in September, but the bears are not quite as numerous. Camping reservations become available for the entire summer on January 5. To reserve, contact the **National Recreation Reservation Service** (© 877/444-6777 or 518/885-3639; www.recreation.gov).

VISITOR INFORMATION   For advance planning, contact **Katmai National Park Headquarters** at P.O. Box 7, King Salmon, AK 99613 (© **907/246-3305;** www.nps.gov/katm). At Brooks Camp the park service has a center where all visitors are required to attend a 20-minute orientation called "The Brooks Camp School of Bear Etiquette," designed to train visitors (not bears) and keep them out of trouble. In Anchorage, you can get information at the **Alaska Public Lands Information Center,** at 4th Avenue and F Street (© **907/271-2737;** see "Visitor Information" in section 1 of chapter 6). The King Salmon **Visitor Center** is next door to the airport (© **907/246-4250**), staffed jointly by the U.S. Fish & Wildlife Service, National Park Service, and Alaska Natural History Association. It is open 8am to 5pm daily in high season, Monday through Saturday in winter.

GETTING AROUND   Once you've made it to Brooks Camp, a **bus** carries visitors to the Valley of Ten Thousand Smokes, 23 miles by gravel road from the camp. The park concessionaire, **Katmailand,** charges $88 per person, round-trip, for the all-day guided excursion, plus $8 more for lunch. A ranger leads a walk down into the valley. One-way transfers for hikers are $51.

FAST FACTS: Katmai and Region

Bank **Wells Fargo,** with an ATM, is in the King Salmon Mall adjacent to the airport on the Peninsula Highway in King Salmon.

Hospital The **Camai Clinic,** in Naknek (© **907/246-6155**), is open during normal business hours; calls to the number go to emergency dispatchers after hours.

Police In **King Salmon,** call © **907/246-4222;** elsewhere, call **Alaska State Troopers** at © **907/246-3346** or 907/246-3464. There are no phones or cellular service out in the park.

Shopping The park is remote and other wild lands in the region are without businesses other than remote lodges, such as Brooks Camp. King Salmon is the last stop for basic supplies or groceries. Here you must buy fuel for a camp stove, matches, or other needs you cannot carry on the jet from Anchorage.

EXPLORING THE PARK

Katmai's famous bear viewing occurs at **Brooks Camp** when the bears congregate near the Brooks River to catch salmon. Viewing peaks in early July, but can begin in late June and last through July, with a smaller congregation in September. This is when you're assured of seeing bears from the elevated platforms near the Brooks River falls, half a mile from Brooks Camp, even on a day trip. Forty to sixty bears feed here. Indeed, bears are seen all along the trail to the falls and elsewhere—the falls are just the most concentrated spot. Rangers don't guide visitors, but are on hand to manage the foot traffic. The platforms allow a good view of the bears and just enough separation. The park service recommends that people with mobility problems avoid this trail when bears are present. Considering the expense and potential difficulty, I'd advise those with trouble getting around to choose another venue for bear viewing. Due to the popularity of the experience, there is a 1-hour limit on the falls platform during the peak season (another platform is unlimited). After your turn is up, you can sign up on a waiting list to get another chance. The falls platform and trail are closed 10pm to 7am. Outside of the short salmon runs, there are better places to see bears, so don't spend the money to come here. Bears feed all summer on clams on Katmai's east shore. See "Getting There," above.

The Brooks Camp area has a small park service campground, visitor center, and lodge, located where the Brooks River flows into Naknek Lake. When the area was first developed for fishing in the 1950s the camp was built in the middle of a major bear corridor, where it never would be allowed today, creating a unique opportunity to stay right in some of the most concentrated bear habitat on the globe. The most comfortable way is to stay at the **Brooks Lodge,** operated by Katmailand (© **800/544-0551** or 907/243-5448; www.brookslodge.com). The lodge has 16 units, with private bathrooms with shower stalls. To save money, book the lodge rooms as packages with air travel from Anchorage. The least expensive, 1-night visit is $844 per person, double occupancy, meals not included; 3 nights is $1,447. A double room without airfare is $668. Peak dates (when the bears are around) book up 12 months out or earlier; for your choice, call as soon as the reservation system opens 18 months ahead, January of the year before the visit. Three buffet-style meals are served daily for guests and visitors who aren't staying in the lodge. Breakfast is $13, lunch $19, and dinner $29. For food, they take MasterCard and Visa at the lodge. Also at Brooks Camp, there's a small store, the park service visitor center, and campground. See "Reservations & Fees," above, for info on campground reservations, which should be made 6 months in advance. The rangers require special precautions to keep bears away from campers.

The rivers and lakes of Katmai lure human anglers as well as ursine ones. Katmailand operates two lodges within the park other than Brooks Lodge for remote fishing, the **Kulik** and **Grosvenor lodges.** Check their website at www.katmailand.com for fishing details. The park service also has a list of dozens of fishing, hiking, and air guides. There is no central clearinghouse for remote fishing, but you can find and book a good place through an agency such as **Sport Fishing Alaska,** 9310 Shorecrest Dr., Anchorage, AK 99502 (© **888/552-8674** or 907/344-8674; www.alaskatripplanners.com), listed in full under "Planning an Outdoor Vacation" in chapter 2.

Backcountry hiking in Katmai means crossing a wilderness without trails, including the hazards of river crossings. Only experienced backpackers should plan extended trips. The park service asks hikers to obtain a voluntary permit for backcountry travel, thereby clueing them in to your plans in case you need to be rescued. You will also need to store food and items with odors in bear-resistant containers, which you can check out from the park. Anyone can walk for the day without such precautions in the desolate **Valley of Ten Thousand Smokes.** This 40-square-mile plain remains a moonscape 90 years after the titanic volcanic blast that buried it, little changed except that the famous plumes of smoke are gone and rivers have sliced through the debris in places to create narrow, white-walled canyons. Although it looks like a desert and is subject to dust storms, rain is common and temperatures rarely go higher than 65°F

(18°C). Katmailand operates a tour bus from Brooks Camp, mentioned above under "Getting Around." The visitors on those tours usually stay on a short trail on the valley's rim, where a visitor center is located, but a 3-mile round-trip hike descends 800 feet to the valley floor, where you can get a better look at the ash that helps create the bizarre landforms here.

4 Unalaska/Dutch Harbor: Aleutian Boomtown

After a lifetime of hearing how desolate the Aleutians (uh-*loo*-shens) were, I felt like I was leaving the edge of the earth the first time I traveled to Unalaska (oon-ah-*las*-ka). Shortly after I arrived, a storm started slinging huge raindrops horizontally through the air so hard that they stung as they splattered on my face. People went on about their business as if nothing special was happening—stormy weather constantly batters these rocks that pop up from the empty North Pacific. My expectations seemed justified.

But the next day, the storm cleared like a curtain opening on a rich operatic scene—simultaneously opening the curtain of my dark expectations. Unalaska may lack trees, but it's not a barren rock. The island is covered with heather and wildflowers. Rounded mountains that invite wandering exploration rise from the ocean like the backs of huge beasts. For sightseeing, it has barely a day's attractions, but for outdoor exploring, bird-watching, and halibut fishing, few places come close.

With the protected port of Dutch Harbor so far out in a ferocious ocean habitat rich in crab and bottom fish, Unalaska has grown in 3 decades from a tiny, forgotten Native village to the nation's largest fishing port. The pattern of growth followed the form of the early gold rushes. There was a wild, lawless time in the 1970s when crab fishermen got rich quick and partied like Old West cowboys. Then the overfished crab stocks crashed, only to be replaced, starting in the mid-1980s, by an even bigger boom, when waters within 200 miles of the U.S. shore were rid of foreign vessels and American bottom fishing took off. Big factory ships began unloading here and huge fish plants were built on flat ground chipped from the rock. Today that expansion has reached a steady state and women and families have come to town—another part of the gold-rush pattern. But domestication isn't done yet. Most of the population lives in bunkhouses and flies back to Seattle when the processing plants close for the season. Unalaska may be the best current example of the American cultural phenomenon of the frontier boomtown.

Ironically, Unalaska is Alaska's oldest town as well as its newest city. The value of a good port out in the middle of the ocean was recognized from the beginning by the Aleuts. In 1759, the Russians began trading here and fought a war with the Aleuts from 1763 to 1766, the outcome of which was slavery for the Aleut hunters and the massacre of their people. The Russians built a permanent settlement here in 1792, their first in Alaska. Unalaska also was a key refueling stop for steamers carrying gold-rush stampeders to Nome a century ago, which brought an epidemic that killed a third of the indigenous population. In 1940, Dutch Harbor—the seaport on Amaknak Island associated with the town and island of Unalaska—was taken over by the U.S. Navy to defend against Japanese attack. That attack came: In June 1942, Japanese planes bombed Unalaska, killing 43. The Aleut people were removed from the islands for the duration of the war and interned in inadequate housing in Southeast Alaska, where many died of disease. The military pulled out in 1947, but the remains of their defenses are interesting to explore, part of a unique unit of the national park system. Thanks to a 1971 act of Congress settling Native claims, the Aleut-owned Ounalashka Corporation owns much of the land around town. But the National Park Service protects and interprets the World War II historic sites on Native-owned land.

ESSENTIALS

GETTING THERE   PenAir (© 800/448-4226; www.penair.com) serves Dutch Harbor with 30-passenger turbo props. You can book directly, or through Alaska Airlines. When a squall is hitting Dutch, planes land on a different island and wait for it to clear. The flight from Anchorage takes 3 hours and a ticket is $900 or more round-trip.

The **Alaska Marine Highway System** ferry *Tustumena* (© 800/642-0066; www.ferryalaska.com) makes a 5-day trip from Homer to Unalaska once a month, stopping in Kodiak and the villages along the way. The one-way passenger fare is over $350, and a two-berth outside (with windows) cabin with facilities is more than $300 more. Several travelers who have done this open sea adventure have given me glowing reports of incomparable scenery and wonderful encounters with the people of the villages along the way. Since the ship is in the open ocean, sea sickness is a real concern; read the advice on p. 49. Unless you want to spend half a day in Unalaska and then make the long return trip, you'll need to fly back.

VISITOR INFORMATION   The **Unalaska/Port of Dutch Harbor Convention and Visitors Bureau,** P.O. Box 545, Unalaska, AK 99685 (© 877/581-2612 or 907/581-2612; www.unalaska.info), is at 5th Street and Broadway, in the old part of town.

A visitor center for the **Aleutian World War II National Historic Area** (© 907/581-9944; www.nps.gov/aleu) occupies a war-era building at the airport. The historic area encompasses World War II ruins on the island that stand on Native-owned lands. The National Park Service helped fund the improvements and interpret the history. A $4 entry fee at the visitor center also covers the permit to hike to the ruins (see "Exploring the Town," below). The website is interesting, too.

GETTING AROUND   The main historic part of the town is a tiny street grid on a narrow peninsula facing Iliuliuk Bay. The **Bridge to the Other Side** (that's the official name) leads to Amaknak Island, the site of the airport, the Grand Aleutian Hotel, and the fishing industrial area of Dutch Harbor. Traveling down the road in the other direction leads a little way up into the mountains, a starting point for walks. Van taxis are the main way of getting around town for the hordes of fishermen. One company is **Blue Checker Taxi** (© 907/581-2186). You can rent a car or truck from **North Port Rentals** (© 907/581-3880). Small cars rent for $40 a day.

FAST FACTS: Unalaska/Dutch Harbor

Bank   **Key Bank** is attached to the Alaska Commercial Store and has an ATM.

Hospital   **Iliuliuk Family and Health Services** (© 907/581-1202) offers clinic services.

Internet Access   Free at the **public library** (© 907/581-5060).

Police   **Unalaska Department of Public Safety** (© 907/581-1233) is just above the bridge on the Unalaska side.

Taxes   **Sales tax** is 3%; the total **tax on rooms** is 8%.

EXPLORING THE TOWN

Unalaska's most significant historic site is the **Holy Ascension Cathedral.** Completed in 1896 on the site of churches that had stood since 1808, the white church with green onion-shaped domes contains 697 icons, artifacts, and artworks—a significant collection that has been continuously in use by the Aleut congregation. The congregation was founded by Father Ivan Veniaminov, who translated the gospel into Aleut and has been canonized as Saint Innocent. A $1.3-million restoration saved the church from collapse in 1996. It is a dignified, geometric counterpoint to the soft edge of sparkling Iliuliuk Bay.

The professionally curated **Museum of the Aleutians,** next door to the Ounalashka Corporation on Margaret Bay in Dutch Harbor (© **907/581-5150;** www.aleutians.org), contains some of the region's best artifacts, including some from North America's oldest coastal sites on Umnak and Unalaska islands. Exhibits also cover the region's 9,000-year history. Admission is $5. It's open summer Tuesday through Saturday from 9am to 5pm, Sunday from noon to 5pm; in winter Tuesday through Saturday from 11am to 5pm.

There are several **World War II military ruins** around town, including some that are still in use, such as the submarine dry dock that today fixes fishing boats. Trails lead over the island to other sites included in the Aleutian World War II National Historic Area, which preserves this evidence of war on American soil and helps tell the story of the Native people who were interned by both the Japanese and Americans during the war (see "The Aleutians: The Quiet after War," below). U.S. Army Fort Schwatka, on Mount Ballyhoo, is about an hour's hike from the airport. The fort once had over 100 buildings. Many remain, including the best-preserved gun mounts and lookouts of all the nation's coastal defenses from the war. Besides, it's a spectacular site where you can see ships returning. Stop by the historic site visitor center at the airport first; besides learning the context of the park, your $4 admission fee is your permit for access to the ruins, which belong to the Native-owned Ounalashka Corp. (All use on their land requires a permit; see "Hiking," below).

That's about it for sightseeing in Unalaska, unless you take a walk in the port. The activity there is interesting for the size of the vessels and harvest and the incredible investment in buildings and equipment.

GETTING OUTSIDE

BIRD-WATCHING Flip through the crisp, unused pages of your bird book to find out what you may see in the Aleutians. Several rare bird species nest in the area, and Asian birds occasionally drop in as accidentals. The whiskered auklet and red-legged kittiwake are among the birds commonly found around Unalaska that you probably haven't seen. You'll have the greatest success taking a boat to a seabird colony. The Grand Aleutian Hotel (see "Where to Stay & Dine," below) offers packages; it's also possible to combine halibut fishing and bird-watching on your own chartered boat (see "Fishing," below). You're also likely to encounter sea lions and other marine mammals.

FISHING You can fly out for salmon fishing from black-sand beaches, but Unalaska has become more famous for huge **halibut.** In 1995, a local sport fisherman caught a 395-pound halibut from an 18-foot skiff within a half-mile of town; to kill the behemoth he had to beach it and beat it over the head with a rock. The next year, Fairbanks angler Jack Tragis landed the world's record halibut here, which weighed 459 pounds. If you're having trouble imagining a fish that big, drop by City Hall, where a replica hangs stuffed in the lobby. The convention and visitor bureau can refer

The Aleutians: The Quiet after War

Once thousands of men died for the rocky islands of the Aleutians. What began as a Japanese military diversion became a ferocious fight for honor, one of the worst of World War II's Pacific Theater. Yet when the fighting was done most of the islands were abandoned and left uninhabited, littered with military ruins, for half a century. Finally, with the construction of a new National Park Service visitor center in Unalaska, the battle for the Aleutians is just beginning to enter national consciousness.

The Japanese attacked the islands of **Kiska** and **Attu** at the start of the war in the Pacific to divert the main core of the American navy away from what became the Battle of Midway. But the Americans had intercepted and decoded Japanese transmissions and weren't fooled. Meanwhile, the Japanese had sent 24 ships, including two aircraft carriers, on a fool's errand to bomb the new American naval base at Dutch Harbor and occupy islands in the western Aleutians. Those ships could have tipped the balance at Midway, among the most important battles of the war. Instead, the Japanese met stiff antiaircraft fire in 2 days of bombing at Dutch Harbor; although 43 Americans were killed, the defensive function of the base was not greatly impaired.

The Japanese then took Kiska and Attu, meeting no resistance from 10 Americans staffing a weather station or from an Aleut village whose 43 inhabitants were all—even the children—sent to a prison camp in Japan to mine clay for the duration of the war. About half the prisoners survived to return to Alaska.

The Americans had their own plan to remove the Aleuts, but the idea of depopulating all the islands had been turned down. Now, with the Japanese attack, it was swiftly put into effect. All the Aleuts were rounded up and put on ships. Their villages were burned or trashed by weather and vandalism. With little thought given to their living conditions, the Aleuts were interned in abandoned summer camps and similarly inadequate facilities in Southeast Alaska. Shunned by the local communities and without the basic necessities of life or proper sanitation, 10% died. The U.S. Fish & Wildlife Service took Aleut hunters to hunt furs as virtual slaves, much as the Russians had done 200 years before.

Although the Aleutians quickly became irrelevant to the rest of the war, significant resources were committed to a largely futile air and sea battle in the fog and endless storms. The Americans couldn't spare a land invasion force at first and had to rely on bombing Kiska and Attu to punish the Japanese and try to deter a further advance up the chain. To that end, they built a large base at Adak, among others, so shorter-range fighter escorts could accompany the bombers. Construction in the spongy tundra was difficult in any case, made more so by the length of supply lines.

The Japanese high command never had any intention of advancing up the chain, but also saw no reason to abandon their new Kiska air base when it was causing the Americans to exert such effort. The Japanese concentrated on fortifying Kiska, which became a honeycomb of underground bunkers and heavy antiaircraft guns and withstood constant bombing raids by the Americans.

Finally, on May 11, 1943, almost a year after the Japanese took the islands, Americans landed on Attu and a brutal 18-day battle for the rugged island began. The Japanese were massively outnumbered but heavily dug in. Finally, with only 800 soldiers left from an original force of 2,600, the Japanese mounted a banzai attack. Only 28 were taken prisoner—the rest were killed in battle or committed suicide. The Americans suffered 549 killed, 1,148 wounded, and 2,132 injured. In the end, it was the second most costly island battle in the Pacific, after Iwo Jima.

The battle for Kiska was less dramatic. The Japanese withdrew under cover of fog. After a massive bombardment and the rallying of heavy reinforcements, the Americans landed to find no one there. Still, 105 American soldiers died in accidents and fire from their own forces.

After the Aleutian battle was over, American forces in Alaska declined drastically, but never went away altogether. Before the war, the absurd little Fort William Seward, in Haines, had been the totality of Alaska's defenses. Afterward there were large bases in several areas of the state. Military spending became the biggest economic boom the territory had ever seen, connecting it by a new road to the Lower 48 and bringing precious year-round jobs. The advent of the Cold War, and Alaska's prime strategic location in defense against the Soviet Union, brought ever-greater increases in military spending in Alaska.

The end of the war was bitter for the Aleuts. Returning to villages they had departed hastily 3 years before, they found homes and subsistence gear ruined and even historic Russian Orthodox churches and icons severely damaged. Many who had survived the terrible period of internment never returned. Some of the ancient villages never revived; bureaucrats managing the evacuation wiped them off the map as a cost-saving measure.

Awareness of this injustice began to resurface in the 1980s, and in 1988 Congress and President Reagan formally apologized to the Aleuts and paid compensation of $12,000 to each survivor, then about half the 900 who were evacuated. That act also helped fund restoration of the five historic churches, including the beautiful church in Unalaska, and construction of one replacement. That work has been completed.

Today, the Aleuts own their islands. It's fitting that the National Park Service's Aleutian World War II National Historic Area is their guest, on their land, and the new visitor center belongs to a Native corporation. Stop in to learn about the lives sacrificed here and to wonder why.

To learn more, see Brian Garfield's readable *The Thousand-Mile War: World War II in Alaska and the Aleutians* (University of Alaska Press, $25).

you to a charter boat operator and has a few links to them on its website (see "Visitor Information," above).

HIKING   The island's green heather and rounded mountains of wildflowers are inviting for a walk. You can walk pretty much in any direction. Explore the abandoned World War II defenses; make a goal of a beach or one of the small peaks around the town; or, for the ambitious, head to the top of an active volcano, Mount Makushin. There are no bears and not many bugs, but there's great berry picking and beachcombing. The weather can be a threat, however, and fox holes can trip you up. As always in remote outdoor areas, you must be suitably dressed and leave word of where you're going and when you'll be back. Hikers beyond the World War II historic area have to pay a slightly higher fee to the **Ounalashka Corp.** (© 907/581-1276; www.ounalashka. com), the Native village corporation that owns much of the land around town. A one-day hiking permit is $6 per person or $10 per family; permits for longer periods are available, too. Buy permits from the historic area visitor center (p. 448) or the corporation's office at 400 Salmon Way.

WHERE TO STAY & DINE

Grand Aleutian Hotel ★★   It's almost unreal to arrive at this big, luxurious hotel in a hard-driving Alaska Bush community. The Grand Aleutian is the best hotel in the Alaska Bush, with rooms just as good as you find in Anchorage, but minutes away from some of the best halibut fishing and bird-watching anywhere. The accommodations are well designed and comfortable, many with good water views; the lobby is grand, with a huge stone fireplace; and there's a piano bar. As you walk outside into a driving gale, it's like teleporting from a big city hotel back to an exposed rock out in the North Pacific.

The **Chart Room** restaurant, on the second floor, allows bird-watchers to see waterfowl in the bay while dining on steak, seafood, or pasta. The menu, although brief, is Unalaska's most sophisticated. Dinner entrees range from $15 to $45. The **Margaret Bay Cafe,** downstairs, also has a good view, with grilled sandwiches and some lighter fare.

The hotel sometimes puts together birding or fishing packages or workshops. Check for current offerings.

498 Salmon Way (P.O. Box 921169), Dutch Harbor, AK 99692. © 866/581-3844 or 907/581-3844. Fax 907/581-7150. www.grandaleutian.com. 112 units. $179 double; $249 suite. Extra person $20. Packages available. AE, DC, DISC, MC, V. **Amenities:** 2 restaurants; 2 bars; activities desk; courtesy van; limited room service; laundry service. *In room:* TV, coffeemaker, hair dryer.

5 The Pribilof Islands: Birder's Paradise

The Pribilof Islands of St. Paul and St. George sit out in the middle of the Bering Sea, due north of Unalaska, teeming with marine mammals and seabirds. Some 600,000 fur seals meet at the breeding rookeries in the summer, and two million birds of more than 200 species use the rocks. Bird-watchers visit St. Paul for one of the most exotic and productive birding and wildlife-viewing opportunities anywhere. It's best during the spring migration, from mid-May to mid-June, when great numbers of birds show up, including rare Asian accidental species; the fall migration comes in late July and August. You can count on making rare sightings any time during the summer. Indeed, the National Audubon Society's *Field Guide to North American Birds* calls this "perhaps the most spectacular seabird colony in the world."

The islands are extremely remote, however, and the accommodations simple; if you're not interested in birding or in spending a lot of time watching wildlife, it's probably too much money and trouble. The **King Eider Hotel,** at the airport, has basic rooms and shared bathrooms. Guests eat at the airport kitchen facilities, where each meal is served buffet style: breakfast is $10, lunch $14, dinner $18. There are no other dining choices. The island also has a grocery store, the AC Value Store, with an ATM.

Visitors generally come on tours, which are sold as a package with airfare and guiding by expert birders. With the guides' help and radio communication, your chances of seeing exotic species are much enhanced. The tours are offered by **Tanadguix Corp.,** 4300 B St., Suite 402, Anchorage, AK 99503 (© **877/424-5637;** www.alaska birding.com; e-mail pribilof@tdx.alaska.com). Check the website for a wealth of birding news and species details. Packages from Anchorage start at $1,406 for a 2-night visit and operate from mid-May through August. Travelers can choose to ride on a bus as a group or hike on their own. Permanent blinds are in place for watching birds and seals. Count on cool, damp weather.

6 Nome: Arctic Frontier Town

The accidents of history deposited the streets and buildings of this lusty little town on the shore of Norton Sound, just south of the Arctic Circle in Northwest Alaska, and gave it qualities that make Nome an exceptionally attractive place for a visitor. For once, the local boosters' motto—in this case, "There's no place like Nome"—is entirely accurate, and that's because Nome, although itself nothing special to look at, combines a sense of history, a hospitable and somewhat silly attitude, and an exceptional location on the water in front of a tundra wilderness that's crossed by 250 miles of road. Those roads are the truly unique thing, for Nome is the best place (really, the only place) in Arctic Alaska for a visitor to drive or bike deep into the open country, coming across musk oxen, reindeer, rarely seen birds, Native villages, undeveloped hot springs, and even an abandoned 1881 elevated train from New York City. Elsewhere, you're obliged to fly from rural hubs to get so far into the Bush or drive the endless Dalton Highway, either of which is a more ambitious undertaking for casual explorers.

The accidents of history have been rather frequent in Nome. History has been downright sloppy. Start with the name. It's essentially a clerical error, caused by a British naval officer who, in 1850, was presumably in a creative dry spell when he wrote "? Name" on a diagram rather than name the cape he was sailing past. A mapmaker interpreted that as "Cape Nome." Or so goes one widely accepted explanation. The original gold rush of 1898 was caused by prospectors in the usual way, but a much larger 1899 population explosion happened after one of the '98 stampeders, left behind in a camp on the beach because of an injury, panned the sand outside his tent—and found that it was full of gold dust. By 1900, a fourth of Alaska's white population was in Nome sifting the sand. Small-time operators and tourists are still at it. A huge floating gold dredge of the kind that makes for major historic sites in Fairbanks and Dawson City sits idle on the edge of town. In Nome, it stopped operation only in recent years. There are two other, smaller dredges in town, too. Historic structures are few, however, as fires and storms have destroyed the town several times since the gold rush.

Nome has a particular, broad sense of humor. It shows up in the *Nome Nugget* newspaper and in silly traditions like the Labor Day bathtub race, the sea ice golf tournament, and the polar bear swim. The population is half white and half Native, and the town is run largely by the white group. Some see Nome as a tolerant mixing place of different peoples, while the town strikes others as a bit colonial. Selling booze is outlawed in Kotzebue and Barrow, the Native-dominated cities to the north; but in Nome there is still a sloppy, gold-rush-style saloon scene. That sort of thing is prettier as historic kitsch than when it shows up in the form of drunks staggering down Front Street.

But you can ignore that, instead taking advantage of the great bargains to be had on Iñupiaq arts and crafts. And, most important, you can use a pleasant little inn or bed-and-breakfast as a base to get into the countryside that beckons you down one of the gravel roads. Nome is popular with bird-watchers, who find the roads especially useful.

ESSENTIALS

GETTING THERE   Flying is the only way to get to Nome. **Alaska Airlines** (© 800/252-7522; www.alaskaair.com) flies 90 minutes by jet direct from Anchorage or with a brief hop from Kotzebue. Prices are around $400 round-trip and up. Many visitors come on escorted tour packages sold by **Alaska Airlines Vacations** (© 800/468-2248); as a day trip a tour package costs $474; staying overnight on the package costs $558 per person, double occupancy. Despite those savings, however, I think Nome is a better destination to be on your own, especially if you rent a car. All taxis operate according to a standard price schedule you can get from the visitor center. A ride to town from the airport is $5. There are three companies, including **Louie's Cab** (© 907/443-6000).

VISITOR INFORMATION   The **Nome Convention and Visitors Bureau,** Front and Division streets (P.O. Box 240), Nome, AK 99762 (© 907/443-6624; www.nome alaska.org/vc), provides maps and detailed information for diverse interests. The office is open from late May to mid-September daily from 9am to 9pm, the balance of the year Monday through Friday from 9am to 6pm.

The **Bering Land Bridge National Preserve Headquarters,** 214 Front St. (P.O. Box 220), Nome, AK 99762 (© 907/443-2522; www.nps.gov/bela), is a good source of outdoors information from the rangers who staff a desk and are responsible for a rarely visited 2.8-million-acre national park unit, which covers much of the Seward Peninsula north of the Nome road system.

GETTING AROUND   The town is a street grid along the ocean. **Front Street** follows the sea wall, **First Avenue** is a block back, and so on. A harbor is at the north end of town, and the gold-bearing beach is to the south. You can mostly walk to see this area. Three roads branch out from Nome. I've described them below, under "Venturing Beyond Town by Road." To get out on the roads, you need to take a tour or rent a car, or bring a bike with you. Several local car-rental agencies operate in town; the visitor center maintains a list, with rates. **Stampede Rent-A-Car,** 302 E. Front St. (© 800/354-4606 or 907/443-3838), charges $95 to $150 for SUVs and vans. The same people operate the Aurora Inn (see "Where to Stay," below).

FAST FACTS: Nome

Bank **Wells Fargo,** with an ATM, is at 250 Front St.

Hospital **Norton Sound Regional** is at 5th Avenue and Bering Street (© 907/443-3311).

Internet Access **Nome Public Library** is at 200 Front St. (© 907/443-6626).

Police At Bering Street and 4th Avenue (© 907/443-5262).

Post Office At Front Street and Federal Way.

Taxes The **sales tax** is 5%; the tax on **rooms** totals 8%.

SPECIAL EVENTS The biggest event of the year is the **Iditarod Trail Sled Dog Race** (℃ **907/376-5155;** www.iditarod.com), a marathon of more than 1,000 miles that ends in Nome in mid-March. The sled dog racers, world media, and international visitors descend on the town for a few days of madness, with lots of community events planned. The activities last most of the month; contact the Nome visitor center, or download the calendar from www.nomealaska.org/vc. See p. 40 for information about the exciting option of volunteering for the race; see p. 482 for an article on the emotional issue of the animal rights attack on the sport.

One of the March Iditarod events, showcasing Nome's well-developed sense of humor, is the **Bering Sea Ice Golf Classic** (℃ **907/443-6624**). Six holes are set up on the sea ice. Various similar silly events take place all year (see www.nome alaska.org/vc), including the **Polar Bear Swim** which happens around June 21 (ice permitting) as part of the **Midnight Sun Festival** (℃ **907/443-5535**). The festival celebrates the summer solstice, when Nome gets more than 22 hours of direct sunlight. A parade, a handmade raft race, a folk festival, a bank holdup, and other events headline the festival. Winners of the raft race get possession for a year of the fur-lined honey bucket (known in some places as a chamber pot).

EXPLORING THE TOWN

Most of Nome's original buildings were wiped out by fires or by storms off Norton Sound that tore across the beach and washed away major portions of the business district. A sea wall, completed in 1951, now protects the town. Among the few historic sites that survive are the gold-rush-era Board of Trade Saloon, a church, and a bust of Roald Amundsen, who landed near Nome, in Teller, after crossing the North Pole from Norway in a dirigible in 1926. Below the library, at Front Street and Lanes Way, the small **Carrie M. McLain Memorial Museum** (℃ **907/443-6630**) contains an exhibit on the town's gold rush. The museum is free and open summer daily from noon to 8pm, winter Tuesday through Saturday from noon to 6pm.

In good weather, a pleasant walk is to be had southeast of town, along the **beach.** Small-time miners may be camped there, but the gold-bearing sand extends for miles more of solitary walking. You can buy a gold pan in town and try your luck, but the sand has been sifted for nearly 100 years, so don't expect to gather any significant amount of gold. The **Swanberg Dredge** you can see from here operated until the 1950s; a large dredge north of town worked into the mid-1990s. The 38 gold dredges that once operated on the Seward Peninsula crept across the tundra, creating their own ponds to float in as they went. The **cemetery,** with white wooden crosses on top of a little hill just out of town, also is worth a look.

If you're in the market for walrus ivory carvings and other **Iñupiaq arts and crafts,** you'll find low prices and an extraordinary selection on Front Street in Nome. Jim West has a legendary collection for sale, assembled in the bar room of the historic **Board of Trade Saloon** that is attached to a shop on Front Street. The **Arctic Trading Post** is more of a traditional gift shop and also has a good ivory collection, as does **Maruskiyas of Nome. Chukotka-Alaska,** at 514 Lomen St., is an importer of art and other goods from the Russian Far East. Alaska Native art you find in Nome is likely to be authentic, but still ask (see "Native Art: Finding the Real Thing," p. 24). International visitors should see chapter 2 to find out about the special permit you need to carry ivory out of the United States.

VENTURING BEYOND TOWN BY ROAD

The modest attractions downtown would hardly justify a trip to Nome, but the city's surroundings do. The roads provide unique access to a large stretch of the Seward Peninsula. Unlike other Arctic Bush areas, where someone has to take you into the wilderness, in Nome all you have to do is rent a car and go. There are few cars in Nome (they have to be flown in or shipped by barge), so you won't see many other vehicles on this huge expanse of spectacular territory, with wildlife-viewing opportunities as good as anywhere in the state. The **Alaska Department of Transportation** (① **907/ 443-3444**) can provide current information on road conditions around Nome.

You have a good chance of seeing moose, reindeer, owls, foxes, bears, and musk oxen anywhere you drive, but check in with the visitor center or the **Alaska Department of Fish & Game,** at Front and Steadman streets (① **907/443-5796**), to find out the best locales to see animals. They can also give you guidance on fishing along the roads and a "Nome Roadside Fishing Guide," or you can download it from www.adfg.state.ak.us (click on "Sport Fisheries," then "Interior," then "Northwest"). Check "Getting Around," above, to find a mode of transportation.

ROAD HIGHLIGHTS   None of the three roads radiating from Nome has services of any kind—just small Native villages, a few dwellings, and some reindeer herders—so you must be prepared and bring what you need with you, including insect repellent and a good spare tire. The visitor center provides a road guide. Here are some highlights:

The **Nome-Council road** heads 72 miles to the east, about half of that on the shoreline. It turns inland at the ghost town of Solomon, an old mining town with an abandoned railroad train known locally as the Last Train to Nowhere. The engines were originally used on the New York City elevated lines in 1881, then were shipped to Alaska in 1903 to serve the miners along this line to Nome. This is a scenic spot for bird-watching, and fishing is good in the Solomon River, all along the road. Council, near the end of the road, has a couple of dozen families in the summer. A 3-foot-deep river separates the road from the village.

The **Nome-Taylor road,** also known as the Kougarok Road, runs north of town into the Kigluaik Mountains, 85 miles from Nome, eventually petering out and becoming impassable. About 40 miles out, you reach lovely Salmon Lake, with a lakeshore campground with picnic tables, grills, and outhouses. A few miles farther, a road to the left leads to the 125° Pilgrim Hot Springs, near a Catholic church. Access is limited to when the caretaker is on hand, so check with the visitor center before going.

The **Nome-Teller road** leads 73 miles to the village of Teller, which has 266 residents and a store. It's an opportunity to see an authentic Arctic Native village.

MOUNTAIN-BIKING   The roads of Nome are one of the world's great, undiscovered mountain-biking destinations—where else can you bike past musk oxen and reindeer? There is no bike rental in town, but for bike enthusiasts it may be worth renting a bike in Anchorage or bringing yours from home.

BIRD-WATCHING   Bird-watchers will make many discoveries out on the Nome roads, turning to previously unused pages of their bird books. A bird list is available at the visitor center, and they can tell you where to look—each of the three roads has a different habitat. The best times to visit for birding are right around Memorial Day, and from July to mid-August. There's a chance to see Siberian birds, and you can count on bluethroats, yellow wagtails, wheatears, Arctic warblers, and Aleutian and Arctic terns. Nome is the only place to see a bristle-thighed curlew without chartering a plane. You don't need a guide, although guided field trips do come to Nome (see "Bird-Watching" in chapter 2).

SEEING THE SIGHTS IN THE AIR

Nome is a hub for Bush plane operators. Flightseeing charters are available, or you can fly on one of the scheduled routes out to the villages and spend a couple of hours touring. The way to do it is to contact a flight service, explain what you have in mind, and follow their advice. Expect to pay $175 or more. Don't plan to stay overnight in a village without advance arrangements and don't go in bad weather—you'll see little and may get stuck in a tiny village. **Bering Air** (© 800/478-5422 in Alaska only, or 907/443-5464; www.beringair.com) has a long and illustrious reputation and serves 32 villages from Nome and Kotzebue. They offer flightseeing trips by fixed-wing aircraft or helicopter on hourly charter rates (expensive if there are just one or two of you along). Or they will sell you a seat on a scheduled loop flight that visits various villages, charging the fare only to the closest village on the trip while you enjoy the entire round-trip. They even offer charters across the Bering Strait to the Russian towns of Provideniya and Anadyr.

WHERE TO STAY

There are several good B&Bs and motel rooms besides those listed in full below, including the **Nugget Inn** (© 877/443-2323 or 907/443-2323). Staying at a B&B makes sense, as your host can introduce you to the community in a less contrived way than a formal tour company. The visitor center and their website can provide information on them.

Aurora Inn Suites ⚐   Look here for the best traditional hotel rooms in town in a mock country inn on the town's main street. They're nicely furnished and even have some style, a remarkable contrast to the other hotels in Nome. Another plus in this smoky town, there are lots of nonsmoking rooms here. The same company owns a car rental operation, which is on-site.

302 E. Front St. (P.O. Box 1008), Nome, AK 99762. © 800/354-4606 or 907/443-3838. Fax 907/443-6380. www.aurorainnnome.com. 56 units. $145–$245 double. Extra person over age 15 $10. AE, MC, V. **Amenities:** Sauna; car rental; coin-op laundry. *In room:* TV, dataport, hair dryer.

Sweet Dreams B&B   The B&B is convenient, near the Iditarod finish line, but the hosts make it special: Erna and Leo Rasmussen are deep wells of Nome history and local knowledge. Leo is a former mayor and a personable and funny man. The two-story house has a rustic, old-fashioned feel, with lots of Alaskan memorabilia and a sun room on top. A full breakfast is served when Erna has time to prepare it, and they pick up and deliver to the airport.

406 W. 4th St. (P.O. Box 2), Nome, AK 99762. © 907/443-2919. 3 units, shared bathroom. $120 double. Rate includes full breakfast. MC, V.

WHERE TO DINE

You wouldn't go out of your way to dine at any of the restaurants in Nome, but you can find an adequate family meal at various establishments along Front Street. Several are operated by immigrant families, who offer their national cuisine along with standard American-style fare. There sometimes is a language barrier with the servers.

   Milano's Pizzeria (© 907/443-2924), on 503 Front St. in the Old Federal Building, serves Italian and Japanese meals; its pizza is recommended by the locals. The restaurant accepts Visa and MasterCard.

The Kotzebue Option

The Northwest Arctic's authentic Iñupiaq center of Kotzebue (*kotz*-eh-biew) isn't my first choice for most visitors. Those interested in Iñupiaq culture should go to Barrow, while those looking for bird-watching or self-guided outdoor sightseeing should go to Nome. I used to recommend an Alaska Airlines Vacation tour to Kotzebue, but that stopped running when the NANA Native Corporation closed its museum for demolition and replacement. It is too early to write about resumption of tours or the quality of that future offering.

Intrepid travelers seeking real adventure can still use Kotzebue as a hub for a vast, spectacular area. The National Park Service staffs the **Iññaigvik Education and Information Center** at 2nd Avenue and Lake Street (P.O. Box 1029), Kotzebue, AK 99752 ((C) **907/442-3760;** www.alaskanha.org/innaigvik-education-and-information-center.htm), providing information and displays on the immense area of protected land in the region and offering classes on traditional Native crafts and medicinal plants. Employees will answer questions about the town as well. Hours are changeable, so call prior to your visit to verify when they will be open. The local headquarters of the National Park Service, open during normal business hours all year, is in the Eskimo Building with the post office on Shore Avenue ((C) **907/442-3890).**

There are several remote rivers near Kotzebue with easy self-guided floating for experienced outdoors people. This is the best chance to get deep into the Arctic on your own. The great Noatak River originates in the Brooks Range and flows 450 miles through America's largest undisturbed wilderness in the impressive scenery of the Noatak National Preserve. The Selawik, Squirrel, and Kobuk rivers all have long sections of easy water. **Alaska Discovery,** and **Equinox Wilderness Expeditions,** (see "Planning an Outdoor Vacation," under section 6 in chapter 2) have float trips in the area, although not necessarily every year. Expect to pay $4,000 per person. Most

Twin Dragons, on Front Street near Steadman Street ((C) **907/443-5552**), serves Chinese food good enough to have kept them in business for many years, and pizza too. It also takes Visa and MasterCard.

The other flavor of restaurant in Nome, and the most popular locally, is the classic American greasy spoon.

Fat Freddie's Restaurant, attached to the Nugget Inn ((C) **907/443-5899**) and right next to the Iditarod Trail finish line, is a local favorite. Open three meals a day, the restaurant serves the usual diner fare, plus more elaborate meals in the evening, such as steaks, prime rib, crab, or halibut. They take Visa and MasterCard.

7 Barrow: Way North

Half-liquid land comes to an arbitrary point at the northern tip of Alaska, Point Barrow, a long tendril reaching into the Arctic Ocean where bowhead whales pass close to shore during their annual migrations. The Iñupiat settled here more than a thousand river running in the region is self-guided. Get details from *The Alaska River Guide,* by Karen Jettmar, director of Equinox (Alaska Northwest Books). Obviously you should be experienced in the outdoors and in river floating before heading out for a multiday trip in the Arctic. And plan ahead, arranging details well in advance with the park service and your pilot. **Bering Air** (© 800/478-5422 in Alaska only, or 907/443-5464; www.beringair. com) is one good operator in Kotzebue. A popular way to do a float trip is to charter to your put-in point and then fly a scheduled service from a river village at your take-out point.

Kotzebue also offers curious travelers a chance to dig deep into the Iñupiat way of life with **Arctic Circle Educational Adventures** (© 907/442-6013 in summer, 907/276-0976 in winter; www.fishcamp.org). The adventure takes place at a fish camp similar to those where Native people spend the summer gathering food for the winter—and to participate in set-net fishing, fish cutting, food gathering, and other traditional subsistence activities as well as hiking, town tours, and bird-watching. You are a participant rather than an observer and spend real, unmediated time with Native people. The camp on the beach 5 miles south of town is as simple as Bush life, but with a modern kitchen, dining room, shower, and sauna. Guests sleep in plywood cabins without plumbing. Elderhostel groups sometimes come for a week. Rates are $125 per person per day for lodging and meals and an additional $100 per day for tour activities. The season is from late June to mid-August.

Alaska Airlines (© 800/252-7522; www.alaskaair.com) offers daily jet service to Kotzebue. Lodging is at the **Nullagvik Hotel** (© 907/442-3331; www.nullagvik.com), a comfortable, modern hotel on the beachfront owned by the Iñupiat's NANA corporation. High season rates are $189 double. I am told the hotel is in for major reconstruction, but my informant couldn't predict the date of that work.

years ago because it is such a good whale-hunting spot, and that is still why they live here, dragging their skin boats miles out on the frozen ocean to wait for whales along the cracks in the ice pack. And, according to age-old tradition, here they still share the whales they catch among the entire community. Indeed, even visitors who show up on a Saturday in late June, during the Nalukataq, may be offered a piece of maktak (whale blubber and skin) and a chance to bounce high in the air in the blanket toss.

Barrow is the northernmost settlement on the North American continent, above the 71st parallel, but that's not all that makes it unique. The town of 4,417 is a cultural treasure. It's ancient, but it's also the seat of the North Slope Borough, a county government encompassing an area larger than the state of Nebraska, in which lies North America's largest oil field. The borough has everything money can buy for a local government, yet the people still must contend with crushing ice, snooping polar bears, and utter isolation. From these ingredients, they have concocted an extraordinary mixture of sophisticated modernity and wise tradition. Alaska's largest corporation is based here;

its top executives are also subsistence hunters. At the Iñupiat Heritage Center it has been possible to see, on successive nights, traditional dance in the Iñupiaq language and avant-garde theater in the same language.

Geography and the natural environment also make the place interesting. This is the most heavily instrumented and intensively studied scientific site anywhere in the Arctic. At the labs north of town, cutting-edge work on climate change takes place that could affect the whole world. The tundra around Barrow is dotted with lakes divided by tendrils of swampy tundra no more substantial than the edges of fine lace. On this haven for migratory waterfowl, the flat, wet land and the ocean seem to merge. Indeed, for all but a few months, it's a flat, frozen plain of ocean and land. For 65 days in the winter, the sun never rises. In the summer, it doesn't set. Ice recedes from the shore only for a few brief months. Such extreme geography is a magnet for visitors.

ESSENTIALS

GETTING THERE   Alaska Airlines (© 800/252-7522; www.alaskaair.com) flies a couple of times daily to Barrow from Anchorage, by way of Fairbanks. The fare from Anchorage is $550 and up. You can save by booking their 1-day and overnight tour packages, described in "Exploring the Town & Getting Outside," below. Book them through **Alaska Airlines Vacations** (© 800/468-2248).

VISITOR INFORMATION   The City of Barrow's **visitor center,** at Momegana and Ahkovak streets, near the airport and Wiley Post & Will Rogers Monument, operates in the summer only from 10am to 4:30pm, with a guide to talk to, maps (including a numbered walking tour map), and other publications. To obtain advance information, contact the City of Barrow, Office of the Mayor, P.O. Box 629, Barrow, AK 99723 (© 907/852-5211, ext. 221; www.cityofbarrow.org).

GETTING AROUND   Facing the Chukchi Sea, Barrow has two sections, lying on each side of Isatkoak Lagoon. **Browerville,** to the east, has the Iñupiat Heritage Center and the Stuaqpak, or big store, which contains a small food court and many services. The old part of **Barrow,** with the hotels and airport, is to the west. The northern tip of Alaska, **Point Barrow,** is north of the town on a spit. The road leads 6 miles in that direction, but the absolute end is farther out, beyond the road. Other gravel roads lead about 10 miles out of town on the tundra.

Taxis are handy and come quickly, charging a flat $5 anywhere in town, $10 beyond town, plus $1 for each additional passenger. **Arcticab** (© 907/852-2227) is one of the four cab companies.

Fun Fact **Eskimo Football**

The Barrow High School Whalers fielded their first football team in recent years, despite the impossibility of growing a grass field at this latitude. They played home games on bare gravel. The story of Eskimo football players so interested the national media, however, that the team's plight reached the ears of sympathetic Floridians who set to work in 2007 raising the money for an Astroturf field in Barrow. The Barrow players got to visit Florida, too, trading in whaling on May sea ice in 10-degree temperatures for sand, body surfing, and celebrity.

SPECIAL EVENTS   The return of the sun after 2 months below the horizon is met by traditional celebrations on **January 21.** The **Piuraagiaqta,** a spring festival, takes place in mid-April and includes many fun events, such as a tug-of-war on the lagoon pitting white men against Eskimo women. The women won so many years in a row that in 2006 the white men didn't even show up. In the tea-making contest couples race to set up a camp stove and melt ice to make tea. If the traditional bowhead whaling season is a success, the **Nalukataq** takes place in late June, usually on a Saturday, but the actual date depends on the preference of the successful captain. It is his responsibility to feed the entire community. The Eskimo blanket toss is also a traditional element of the event (injuries are common, so don't take it lightly). In the fall, generally from early to mid-October, the whale hunt launches from the beaches of town (rather than the ice, as in spring). If you're lucky, you can be on hand as a whale is pulled ashore and butchered by the community. This usually occurs at the NARL (Navy Arctic Research Laboratory) runway, north of town; ask around, as everyone will know if a whale has been landed.

FAST FACTS: Barrow

Alcohol Legality The sale of alcohol is illegal in Barrow and importation for personal use in your luggage is limited and controlled by a permit system. Without going through the permit process, you can bring in 1 gallon of beer, *or* 1 liter of distilled spirits, *or* 2 liters wine. Violating these laws is bootlegging, a serious crime. For more information, call ahead to the Barrow Alcohol Distribution (© **907/852-3788**) or the Office of the Mayor (© **907/852-5211** ext. 221) or check the website (www.cityofbarrow.org). I simply don't drink when I go to Barrow.

Bank **Wells Fargo** is at 1078 Kiogak St., with an ATM.

Hospital **Samuel Simmonds Memorial Hospital** is at 1296 Agvik St. (© **907/852-4611**).

Internet Access Free at the **Tuzzy Library,** at the Iñupiat Heritage Center in Browerville.

Police Contact the **North Slope Borough Police Department,** 1068 Kiogak St. (© **907/852-6111**).

Taxes There is no sales or bed tax in Barrow.

EXPLORING THE TOWN & GETTING OUTSIDE

The **Iñupiat Heritage Center** (© 907/852-0422) is the town's main attraction, and one of Alaska's most remarkable cultural institutions. It is part museum, part gathering center, and part venue for living culture. Inside is a workshop for craftspeople where hunters build the traditional boats and tools they use and where drummers build their drums; during the summer, an artist is usually in residence for visitors. There is a performance space for storytellers and dancers and conference rooms where elders tell old stories or identify a rich store of artifacts. In the museum area, displays of artifacts change regularly, while a permanent exhibit covers Eskimo whaling and the influence of Yankee whaling on it (the quiet pride here carries a real emotional wallop). Iñupiaq dancing and drumming demonstrations, a blanket toss, games, and a craft sale happen every afternoon in the summer from 1:30 to 3:30pm; these are the same programs that are the highlight of the escorted tours. Admission, including the program, is $15. The center is open Monday through Friday from 8:30am to 5pm (to see the program on weekends, call ahead). Regular admission is $5 for adults, $2 for students and adults over age 55, free for children age 14 or younger.

The other site that's worthy of a special trip is **NARL,** as the former Navy Arctic Research Laboratory is known. This was once the world's largest Arctic research site, with scores of buildings on the narrow spit of land north of town. Today the navy is long gone but Barrow's Native corporation took over the buildings and nurtured scientific research here. Once again the facilities are the nation's busiest year-round Arctic research site. It's interesting just to walk around, and the cafeteria in the Iligsavik College building serves three good meals a day. The **UIC Science Center** (© 907/ 852-3050), at the north end of the complex, has interesting displays about Arctic science and anthropology that are open to the public. The daily escorted tours come here, or independent travelers can usually find it open Monday through Friday 8:30am to 5pm, closed during the lunch hour of noon to 1pm; however, the two-person staff may not be handy at times, so it could pay to call ahead.

The main tourism business in town is **Tundra Tours** (© 800/882-8478 or 907/ 852-3900; www.tundratoursinc.com). Arctic Slope Regional Corp., a corporation representing the Iñupiat, owns the company and the Top of the World Hotel. Their tour (the same one sold through Alaska Airlines Vacations) introduces the town to visitors who arrive with little idea of what to expect. The 6-hour summer tour, in a small bus, drives around the town to visit an Eskimo skin boat, the cemetery, the UIC Science Center, and the Arctic Ocean, for a dip of toes. The highlight is a visit to the Iñupiat Heritage Center with a cultural presentation, including Eskimo dance and a chance to buy crafts made by Native artists. The day-trip tour is $469 from Fairbanks, or $569 per person, double occupancy, for the tour and a night in Barrow at the Top of the World Hotel, giving you time on your own without the tour group; both prices include airfare and can save over buying a plane ticket alone. The price from Anchorage is $200 more. Book the tour through Alaska Airlines Vacations or with Tundra Tours at the numbers listed above. If you buy the tour separately when you are already in Barrow, it's $85. They also offer a winter tour for seeing the aurora ($99 separately), which does not include the cultural elements.

In season, Barrow is a good place to see polar bears. The bears are always around when the ice is in; they're dangerous and people take extreme care to avoid them. Barrow and other North Slope communities have minimized the danger of bears in town by setting up sites outside of the villages to dispose of gut piles and other hunting waste. It's a way of bribing the bears to leave the town alone. In Barrow, heavy equipment hauls the leftovers from fall whale butchering—bones and a few nonedible organs—out to the very end of the point. Polar bears come for an easy meal whenever the pack ice is close to shore, which is October through June. Commercial tours take visitors out to the point in all-terrain vans or Humvees that can drive on the beach gravel. Arrangements change annually and these are casual home businesses, so if polar bear viewing is your goal be sure to make firm arrangements with someone before you go. **Arctic Tours** (© 907/852-4512 or 907/852-1462 cell) takes visitors out in a

Humvee May through September on a 2-hour tour that costs $60 per person, with a two-person minimum. Go only in May, June, or earlier, when the sea ice is in; you stand little chance of seeing a bear during times of open water, in the summer or fall.

WHERE TO STAY

King Eider Inn ✦✦   The best rooms in town—indeed, some of the best in the Bush—are found in this like-new building near the airport. They're crisp and airy, with faux rustic furniture, and kept up well. It surely helps that shoes are not allowed in the hotel—you have to take them off at the front door every time you come in. The halls and rooms are decorated with Native art and a teddy bear greets you in bed. A room with a kitchenette is $10 more, and the enormous and luxurious Presidential Suite (where Barrow's honeymooners and visiting celebrities stay) is $310 in summer, $285 in winter. The lobby is comfortable, with a stone fireplace and free Internet terminal, and good free coffee and other hot beverages are offered there around the clock. Bathrooms have large shower stalls, not tubs.

1752 Ahkovak St. (P.O. Box 1283), Barrow, AK 99723. ℰ 888/303-4337 reservations or 907/852-4700. Fax 907/852-2025. www.kingeider.net. 19 units. Summer $205 double; winter $185 double. Extra person $25. AE, MC, V. Nonsmoking. **Amenities:** Sauna; car rental. *In room:* TV.

Top of the World Hotel ✦   This is a good hotel with familiar standard rooms, worn in places but perfectly comfortable. The staff works to keep the place clean and quiet. Rooms have light furniture and blue carpet, desks and refrigerators. Those on the water side have wonderful views of the Arctic Ocean, and it's only a few steps to the beach and the heart of Barrow. The lobby is a place where people pass time, somewhat cluttered with a TV and a stuffed polar bear. The hotel is owned by the Native corporation that also operates Tundra Tours, and you stay here if you come on the package tour.

Agvik St. (P.O. Box 189), Barrow, AK 99723. ℰ 907/852-3900. www.tundratoursinc.com. 44 units. Summer $150–$220; winter $125–$155. AE, DC, DISC, MC, V. *In room:* TV, fridge.

WHERE TO DINE

There are several decent restaurants in Barrow. Generally, they stay open very late, always have a TV on, offer free delivery, and don't brew decaffeinated coffee—people around here run on lots of caffeine and sugar.

Adjoining the Top of the World Hotel, **Pepe's North of the Border,** 1204 Agvik St. (ℰ **907/852-8200**), is the most famous place in town thanks to an appearance owner Fran Tate made with Johnny Carson on *The Tonight Show* some 20 years ago. They serve large portions of familiar American-style Mexican food, steak, and seafood. The bus tours come here for lunch and Tate hands out souvenirs.

Brower's Restaurant, 3220 Brower's Hill (ℰ **907/852-3456**), occupies the most historic building in town, the 19th-century whaling station and store built by Charles Brower, who introduced Yankee whaling techniques to the Iñupiat and sired one of its most illustrious families. The restaurant serves a long menu of American and Korean dishes. Big windows look out on the beach and a famous whalebone arch is just outside.

Northern Lights Restaurant, in Browerville at 5122 Herman St. (ℰ **907/852-3300**), has a very comfortable, clean dining room and is operated by a charming family. Their menu goes on and on, with the owner's own Chinese food, plus deli selections and burgers, and the best pizza in town.

8 Prudhoe Bay: Arctic Industry

The Prudhoe (*prew*-dough) Bay complex is more than a huge oil field, it's an amazing achievement. Massive, complex machinery must operate in winter's deep, dark cold and in summer must avoid harm to a critical habitat for migrating caribou and waterfowl, on wet, fragile tundra that permanently shows any mark made by vehicles. Workers are forbidden even to set foot on the tundra. Most places, as you look from the edge of one of the gravel pads, the heathery ground looks as undisturbed as a calm sea.

But that doesn't make it a good place to go on your vacation. The grim town of **Deadhorse**, which serves the oil facility, is really more of an industrial yard; it certainly isn't anything you'd travel to see. To get beyond it to see Prudhoe Bay, you have to sign up for a tour. The tour has never gone inside the buildings, and under post–September 11, 2001, security measures it doesn't even go close to the most interesting areas. Visitors do get to stop at the Arctic Ocean, the only way to get to the water when driving up on the Dalton Highway. That hardly justifies the trip, however, unless you are bent on driving the highway anyway (see section 4 of chapter 9). Frankly, I can't recommend the time and expense required for a Prudhoe tour. If you're curious about the Arctic, a trip to Barrow or Nome makes more sense.

If you do go, you must reserve at least 24 hours ahead to clear security for the oil field tour or the ride to the ocean. Tours are operated by the **Arctic Caribou Inn,** P.O. Box 340111, Prudhoe Bay, AK 99734 (℃ **907/659-2368**). They will need your name and an identification number that British Petroleum can use to run a background check before allowing you on the oil field: a driver's license, passport, or Social Security number will work. The inn also offers the area's visitor services, including a hotel and

Seeing ANWR for Yourself

The decades-old national controversy about whether to open the Arctic National Wildlife Refuge (ANWR) to oil exploration created strong interest in seeing that extraordinarily remote northeast corner of Alaska, which is done best in summer on a float trip. While these floats may have started for political reasons, however, their reputation of beauty and adventure have made them an attraction in their own right. The best time to see caribou is in June. **Alaska Discovery** (p. 38) is famous for ANWR expeditions down from the Brooks Range on either the Kongakut or Hulahula River, and also offers float-supported hikes. Expect to pay as much as $5,000 per person for a trip of up to 2 weeks. Fairbanks-based **Arctic Treks,** operated for 25 years by Jim Campbell and Carol Kasza (℃ **907/455-6502**; www.arctictreksadventures.com), is a smaller company and offers shorter base camp trips in ANWR as well as the long river floats and other arctic journeys. For those who simply want to see ANWR without a wilderness trip, it's possible to visit the Iñupiaq village of Kaktovik, which lies within the boundaries of the refuge. While I wouldn't recommend the journey for most visitors, those with strong interest in a Bush village sojourn may enjoy it. Lodging and meals in Kaktovik are available from the **Waldo Arms Hotel** (℃ **907/640-6513**) a community center known for warm hospitality. Kaktovik is served from Fairbanks by **Frontier Flying Service** (℃ **800/478-6779** or 907-450-7200; www.frontierflying.com).

cafeteria; though tours operate only in the summer, the hotel and restaurant are open year-round. Rooms have two twin beds, and all rent for $235. The restaurant has a buffet for breakfast ($12) and dinner ($20). The town is dry: Sale of alcohol is illegal, and it isn't allowed in the inn. The hotel is near the airport in Deadhorse and serves as the tour's starting point. The tour itself lasts 2 hours, including a 20-minute video. Visitors are carried by bus to the perimeter of the oil field but no farther. The focus instead is on a 15-minute stop at the Arctic Ocean. The tour costs $36 per adult, $17 per child under 12. There's no other way to get from the end of the road to the water.

Alaska Airlines (© 800/252-7522; www.alaskaair.com) has a couple of flights daily to Prudhoe Bay from Anchorage or by way of Barrow. A round-trip ticket costs $750 or more from Anchorage. Several companies drive bus tours up the Dalton Highway all the way to Prudhoe, flying the other way. **Northern Alaska Tour Company** (© 800/474-1986 or 907/474-8600; www.northernalaska.com) offers these trips, with add-ons to make it more interesting: flightseeing stops, day hikes, village visits, and other choices. The basic 3-day, 2-night tour is $789.

Appendix:
Alaska in Depth

An old photo album opens, emitting a scent of dust and dried glue. Inside, pale images speak wanly of shrunken mountains and glaciers, a huge blue sky, water, trees, and a moose standing way off in the background. No family photographer can resist trying to capture Alaska's vastness in the little box of a camera, and none, it seems, has ever managed it. Then, turning the page, there it is—not in another picture of the landscape, but reflected in a small face at the bottom of the frame: my own face, as a child. For anyone who hasn't experienced that moment, the expression is merely enigmatic—slightly dazed, happy, but abstracted. But if you've been to Alaska, that photograph captures something familiar: It's an image of discovery. I've seen it on the fresh, pale faces in photographs stamped with the dates of my family's first explorations of Alaska 40 years ago. And then, when I began researching this book, I got to see it once again, on my own young son's face. And I knew that, like me, he had discovered something important.

So what, exactly, am I talking about? Like anything worth experiencing, it's not simple to explain.

Tour guides try to get it across with statistics. Not much hope of that, although some of the numbers do give you a general idea of scale. Once you've driven across the continental United States and know how big that is, seeing a map of Alaska placed on top of the area you crossed, just about spanning it, provides some notion of size. Alaska has 627,000 residents. If you placed them an equal distance apart, each would be almost a mile from any other. Of course, that couldn't happen. No one has ever been to some parts of Alaska.

But none of that expresses what really matters. It's not just a matter of how big Alaska is or how few people it contains. It's not an intellectual conception at all. None of that crosses your mind when you see a chunk of ice the size of a building fall from a glacier and send up a huge splash and a wave surging outward, or when you feel a wave lift your sea kayak from the fall of a breaching humpback whale. Or when you hike for a couple of days to stand on top of a mountain, and from there see more mountaintops, layered off as far as the horizon, in unnamed, seemingly infinite multiplicity. A realization of what Alaska means can also come in a simple moment. It can come at the end of a long day driving an Interior Alaska highway, as your car climbs into yet another mountain range, the sun still hanging high in what should be night, storm systems arranged across the landscape before you, when you realize that you haven't seen another car in an hour. Or standing on an Arctic Ocean beach, it can happen when you look around at the sea of empty tundra behind you, the sea of green water before you, and your own place on what seems to be the edge of the world.

What's the soul alchemy of such a moment? I suppose it's different for each person, but for me it has something to do with realizing my actual size in the world, how I fit in, what it means to be just another medium-size mammal, no longer armed with the illusions supplied by civilization. On returning to the city from the wilderness, there's a reentry process, like walking from a vivid movie to the mundane, gray street outside—it's the movie that seems more real. For a while, it's hard to take human institutions seriously after you've been deep into Alaska.

Some people never do step back across that boundary. They live their lives out in the wilderness, away from people. Others compromise, living in Alaskan cities and walking out into the mountains when they can, the rest of the time just maintaining a prickly notion of their own independence.

Anyone with the courage to come to Alaska—and the time to let the place sink in—can make the same discovery. You don't have to be an outdoors enthusiast or a young person. You only have to be open to wonder and able to slow down long enough to see it. Then, in a quiet moment when you least expect it, things may suddenly seem very clear and all that you left behind oddly irrelevant.

How you find your way back to where you started is your affair.

1 Natural History: Rough Drafts & Erasures

THE SURGING ICE

In 1986, Hubbard Glacier, north of Yakutat, suddenly decided to surge forward, cutting off Russell Fjord from the rest of the Pacific Ocean. A group of warmhearted but ill-advised wildlife lovers set out to save the marine mammals that had been trapped behind the glacier. Catching a dolphin from an inflatable boat isn't that easy—they didn't accomplish much, but they provided a lot of entertainment for the locals. Then the water burst through the dam of ice and the lake became a fjord again, releasing the animals anyway. In 2002 it happened again (no rescue this time). Ships were warned away as the 70-square-mile lake, having risen 61 feet above sea level, quickly drained through a 300-foot-wide channel with a whoosh. Geologists say it could happen again any time.

Bering Glacier, the largest in North America (about 30 by 145 miles in area), can't decide which way to go. Surging and retreating on a 20-year cycle, it reversed course in 1995 after bulldozing a wetland migratory bird stopover, and speedily contracted back up toward the mountains. Yanert Glacier surged 100 yards a day in 2000 after moving 100 yards a year since 1942. The next year Tokositna Glacier

started galloping after 50 years of quiet. In 1937, surging Black Rapids Glacier almost ate the Richardson Highway. In Prince William Sound, Meares Glacier plowed through old-growth forest. On a larger scale, all the land of Glacier Bay—mountains, forests, sea floor—is rising 1½ inches a year as it rebounds from the weight of melted glaciers that 100 years ago were a mile thick and 65 miles longer.

Yet these new and erased lands are just small corrections around the margins compared to all the earth has done in setting down, wiping out, and rewriting the natural history of Alaska. In the last ice age, 15,000 years ago, much of what is Alaska today was a huge glacier. Looking up at the tops of granite mountains in Southeast Alaska, especially in the Lynn Canal, you can see a sort of high-water mark—the highest point to which the glaciers came in the ice age.

Some 7-year-old children worry about the bogeyman or being caught in a house fire. When I was that age, living with my family in Juneau, I was worried about glacier ice. I had learned how Gastineau Channel was formed, I had seen Mendenhall Glacier, and I had heard how it was really a river of ice, advancing and retreating. I came to fear that while I slept another ice age would come and grind away the city of Juneau.

It's possible that a glacier *could* get Juneau—the city fronts on the huge Juneau Ice Field—but there would be at least a few centuries' warning before it hit. Glaciers are essentially just snow that doesn't get a chance to melt. The snow accumulates at higher elevations until it gets deep enough to compress into ice and starts oozing down the mountainside. When the ice reaches the ocean, or before, the melt and calving of icebergs at the leading edge reaches equilibrium with the snow that's still being added at the top. The glacier stops advancing, becoming a true river of ice, moving a snowflake from the top of the mountain to the bottom in a few hundred years. When conditions change—more snow or colder long-term weather, for example—the glacier gets bigger; that's called advancing, and the opposite is retreating. Sometimes something strange will happen under the glacier and it will surge. Bering Glacier started to float on a cushion of water, and Yanert Glacier slid on a cushion of mud. But most of the time, the advance or retreat is measured in inches or feet a year.

It took some time to figure out how glaciers work. The living glaciers of Alaska, like living fossils from the last ice age, helped show the way. In the 1830s, scientists in Switzerland found huge rocks (now called glacial erratics) that appeared to have moved miles from where they had once been a part of similar bedrock. Scientists theorized that ancient glaciers shaping the Alps must have moved the rocks. John Muir, the famous writer and naturalist, maintained in the 1870s that the granite mountains of Yosemite National Park had been rounded and polished by the passing of glaciers that melted long ago (he was only partly right). He traveled to Alaska to prove it. Here, glaciers were still carving the land—they had never finished melting at the end of the last glacial period—and Muir could see shapes like those at Yosemite in

the act of being created. Glacier Bay, which Muir "discovered" when guided there by his Alaska Native friends, was a glacial work in progress, as it still is today.

When you visit, you can see for yourself how the heavy blue ice and white snow are streaked with black rock and dust that were obviously gouged from mountains and left in hills at the faces and along the flanks of the glaciers, in debris piles called moraines. At Exit Glacier, in Kenai Fjords National Park, you can stand on a moraine that wraps the leading edge of the glacier like a scarf and feel the cold streaming off spires of clicking ice—like standing in front of a freezer with the door open. Find another hill like that, no matter where it is, and you can be pretty sure a glacier once came that way. Likewise, you can see today's glaciers scooping out valleys in the mountains.

Today, Alaska's 100,000 glaciers cover about 5% of its landmass, mostly on the southern coast. There are no glaciers in the Arctic—the climate is too dry to produce enough snow. The northernmost large glaciers are in the Alaska Range, such as those carving great chasms in the side of Mount McKinley. At that height, the mountain creates its own weather, wringing moisture out of the atmosphere and feeding its glaciers. The Kahiltna Glacier flows 45 miles from the mountain, descending 15,000 feet over its course. The Ruth Glacier has dug a canyon twice as deep as the Grand Canyon, half filled with mile-deep ice. Similarly, fjords and valleys all over Alaska were formed by the glaciers of 50 ice ages that covered North America in the last 2.5 million years.

THE TREMBLING EARTH

Despite my early glacier phobia, I never had a similar fear of earthquakes. Living in Anchorage, I'd been through enough of them that, as early as I can remember, I generally didn't bother to get out of bed when they hit. Alaska has an average of 13 earthquakes a day, or 11% of all the earthquakes in the world, including 3 of the 10 largest ever recorded. On November 3, 2002, Alaska felt the world's largest earthquake of the year and one of the largest ever in the United States. My car rocked as I drove in Anchorage. Waves slopped across the bayous of Louisiana, and geysers at Yellowstone changed their size and period of eruptions. No one died and few people were injured because the quake occurred in such a sparsely populated area, the region between Anchorage and Fairbanks in the Alaska Range east of Mount McKinley. A 140-mile-long crack appeared right across that region, running over mountains and through glaciers. The land on each side moved laterally as much as 22 feet and vertically up to 6 feet. The Glenn Highway section known as the Tok Cut-off, between Glennallen to Tok, broke into many deep cracks. A tractor-trailer fell into one of them. Where the Interior highways crossed the big fault-line crack, lanes no longer lined up and the road got a new jog where it used to be straight.

It's all part of living in a place that isn't quite done yet. Any part of Alaska could have an earthquake, but the Pacific Rim from Southcentral Alaska to the Aleutians is the shakiest. This is where Alaska is still under construction. The very rocks that make up the state are something of an ad hoc conglomeration, still in the process of being assembled. The floor of the Pacific Ocean is moving north, and as it moves, it carries islands and mountains with it. When they hit the Alaska plate, these pieces of land, called terranes, dock like ships arriving, but slowly—an island moving an inch a year takes a long time to travel thousands of miles. Geologists studying rocks near Mount McKinley found a terrane that used to be tropical islands. In Kenai Fjords National Park, fossils have turned up that are otherwise found only in Afghanistan and China. The slowly moving crust of the earth brought them here on a terrane that makes up a large part of the south coast of Alaska.

The earth's crust is paper thin compared to the globe's forces, and, like paper, it folds where two edges meet. Alaska's coast is bending down; farther inshore, where McKinley stands, it is bowing up. At Kenai Fjords National Park, you can see steep little rock islands flocked with birds: They are old mountaintops, shrinking down into the earth. The monolith of McKinley is a brand-new one growing higher.

Here's how it works: Near the center of the Pacific, underwater volcanoes and cracks that constantly ooze molten new rock are adding to the tectonic plate that forms the ocean floor. As it grows from the middle, the existing sea floor spreads at a rate of perhaps an inch a year. At the other side of the Pacific plate, where it bumps up against Alaska, there's not enough room for more crust, so it's forced, bending and cracking, downward into the planet's great, molten, recycling mill of magma. Landmasses that are along for the ride smash into the continent that's already there. When one hits—the so-called Yakutat block is still in the process of docking—a mountain range gets shoved up. Earthquakes and volcanoes are byproducts.

Living in such an unsettled land is a matter of more than abstract interest. The Mount Spurr volcano, which erupted most recently in 1992, turned day to night in Anchorage, dropping a blanket of ash all over the region. A Boeing 747 full of passengers flew into the plume and lost power in all its engines, falling in darkness for several minutes before pilots were able to restart the clogged jets. After that incident, the airport was closed until aviation authorities could find a way to keep volcanic plumes and planes apart. In the winter of 2005–06, the Anchorage airport repeatedly closed due to minor eruptions of Augustine Volcano, west of Homer. More than 80 volcanoes have been active in Alaska in the last 200 years. Earthquakes between 7 and 8 on the Richter scale—larger than the 1994 Los Angeles quake—occur once a year on average, and huge quakes over 8 averaged every 13 years over the last century. The worst of the quakes, on March 27, 1964, was the strongest ever to hit North America. It ranked 9.2 on the Richter scale, twisting an entire region of the state so land to the west sank 12 feet while on the east it rose 30 feet. More land moved laterally than in any other recorded earthquake as well. The earthquake destroyed much of Anchorage and several smaller towns, and killed about 131 people, mostly in sea waves created by underwater landslides. In Valdez, the waterfront was swept clean of people. In the Prince William Sound village of Chenega, built on a hill along the water, people started running for higher ground when the wave came. About half made it.

But even that huge earthquake wasn't an unusual occurrence, at least in the earth's terms. Geologists believe the same Alaska coast sank 6 feet in an earthquake in the year 1090.

THE FROZEN TUNDRA

The northern Interior and Arctic parts of the state are less susceptible to earthquakes and, since they receive little precipitation, they don't have glaciers, either. But there's still a sense of living on a land that's not permanent, since most of northern Alaska is solid only by virtue of being frozen. When it thaws, it turns to mush. The phenomenon is caused by permafrost, a layer of earth a little below the surface that never thaws—or at least, you'd better hope it doesn't. Buildings erected on permafrost without some mechanism for dispersing their own heat—pilings, a gravel pad, or even refrigerator coils—can thaw the ground below and sink into a self-made quicksand. With the climate warming, sections of the trans-Alaska pipeline are leaning, and many miles of highway in Interior Alaska are being rebuilt each year because the ground they traverse has turned to mush due to increased average temperatures (more on this below).

The Arctic and much of the Interior are a swampy desert. Annual precipitation measured in Barrow is the same as in Las Vegas. Most of the time, the tundra is frozen in white; snow blows around, but not much falls. It melts in the summer, but the water can't sink into the ground, which remains frozen. Liquid water on top of the permafrost layer creates huge, shallow ponds. Alaska is a land of 10 million lakes, with 3 million larger than 20 acres. Birds arrive to feed and paddle around those circles and polygons of deep green and sky blue.

Permafrost makes the land do other strange things. On a steep slope, the thawed earth on top of the ice can begin to slowly slide downhill like a blanket sliding off the side of a bed, setting the trees at crazy angles. These groves of black spruce—the only conifer that grows in this kind of ground—are called drunken forests, and you can see them in Denali National Park and elsewhere in the Interior. Permafrost also can create weird tundra, with shaky tussocks the size of basketballs that sit a foot or two apart on a wet, muddy flat. From a distance it looks smooth, but walking on real basketballs might be easier. In other places, freezing and thawing processes create ponds with straight sides and sharp corners, polygons that appear manmade.

The permafrost also preserves many things. Although few and far between, tractor tracks remain clearly delineated for decades after they're made, appearing as narrow, parallel ponds reaching from one horizon to the other. The meat of prehistoric mastodons, still intact, has been unearthed from the frozen ground. On the Arctic Coast, the sea eroded ground near Barrow that contained ancient ancestors of the Eskimos who still inhabit the same neighborhood. In 1982, a family was found that apparently had been crushed by sea ice up to 500 years ago. Two of the bodies were well preserved, sitting in the home they had occupied and wearing the clothes they had worn the day of the disaster, perhaps around the time Columbus was sailing to America.

Sea ice is the frozen ocean that extends from northern Alaska to the other side of the world. For a few months of summer, it pulls away from the shore. Then, in October, icebergs floating toward land are cemented together by new ice forming along the beach. But even when the ice covers the whole ocean, it still moves under the immense pressure of wind and current. The clash creates towering pressure ridges—piles of broken ice that look like small mountain ranges and are about as difficult to cross.

The National Weather Service keeps track of the ice pack and issues maps and predictions you can find on the Internet (www.arh.noaa.gov). Eskimo hunters traveling on the ice by snowmobile need this information, as do crabbers who tempt disaster by fishing the south-moving ice edge in the fall, and shippers looking for the right moment in the summer to venture north with barges of fuel and other supplies for the coast of the Arctic Ocean. Sometimes there is barely time in the summer to get there and back before the ice closes in again in the fall.

THE RAINFOREST

By comparison, southern coastal Alaska is warm and biologically rich. Temperate rainforest ranges up the coast from Southeast Alaska into Prince William Sound, with bears, deer, moose, wolves, and even big cats living among the massive western hemlock, Sitka spruce, and cedar. This old-growth forest, too wet to burn in forest fires, is the last vestige of the virgin, primeval woods that seemed so limitless to the first white settlers who arrived on the east coast of the continent in the 17th century. The trees grow on and on, sometimes rising more than 200 feet high, with diameters up to 10 feet, and falling only after hundreds or even thousands of years. When they fall, the trees rot on the damp

moss of the forest floor and return to soil to feed more trees, which grow in rows upon their nursery trunks.

Here at least, Alaska *does* seem permanent. That sense helps explain why logging the rainforest is so controversial. Just one of these trees contains thousands of dollars' worth of wood. Vast Southeast lands owned by Alaska Native corporations were stripped of their old trees for the money they brought to their owners. But the great majority of this rainforest land belongs to the federal government, and a combination of environmental campaigns and economics put a stop to large-scale logging on that land while most of it remained virgin. When the Southeast Alaska logging economy died in the 1990s, the towns there suffered heavy economic blows. Tourism is taking the place of logging (with its own environmental and cultural impacts), but deep antipathy remains against logging opponents.

The rivers of the great coastal forests bring home runs of big salmon, clogging in spawning season like a busy sidewalk at rush hour. The fish spawn only once, returning by a precisely tuned sense of smell to the streams where they were hatched as many as 7 years before. When the fertilized eggs have been left in the stream gravel, the fish conveniently die on the beach, making a smorgasbord for bears and other forest animals. The huge Kodiak brown bear, sometimes topping 1,000 pounds, owes everything to the millions of salmon that return to the island each summer. By comparison, the grizzly bears of the Interior—the same species as browns, but living on grass, berries, and an occasional ground squirrel—are mere midgets, their weight counted in the hundreds of pounds. Forest-dwelling black bears grow to only a few hundred pounds.

FORESTS OF FIRE

Rainforest covers only a small fraction of Alaska. In fact, only a third of Alaska is forested at all, and most of this is the boreal forest that covers the central part of the state, behind the rain shadow of coastal mountains that intercept moist clouds off the oceans. Ranging from the Kenai Peninsula, south of Anchorage, to the Brooks Range, where the Arctic begins, this is a taiga—a moist, subarctic forest of smaller, slower-growing, hardier trees that leave plenty of open sky between their branches. In well-drained areas, on hillsides and southern land less susceptible to permafrost, the boreal forest is a lovely, broadly spaced combination of straight, proud white spruce and pale, spectral paper birch. Along the rivers, cottonwoods grow, with deep-grained bark and branches that spread in an oaklike matrix—if they could speak, it would be as wise old men.

Forest fires tear through Alaska's boreal forest each summer. In the newly warmed climate, million-acre years have become common, and in 2004, a record 6.5 million acres burned—an area the size of Massachusetts. It's impossible to fight that much fire. Alaska has always allowed fire to take its course unless structures or certain resources are at risk. In most cases, forest managers do no more than note the occurrence on a map. Unlike the rainforest, there's little commercially valuable timber in these thin stands, and, anyway, trying to halt the process of nature's self-immolation would be like trying to hold back a river with your hands. The boreal forest regenerates through fire—it was made to burn. The wildlife that lives in and eats it needs new growth from the burns as well as the shelter of older trees. When the forest is healthiest and most productive, the dark green of the spruce is broken by streaks and patches of light-green brush in an ever-changing succession.

This is the land of the moose. They're as big as large horses, with a long, bulbous nose and huge eyes that seem to know, somehow, just how ugly they are. Their flanks look like a worn-out shag carpet draped over a sawhorse. But moose are survivors. They thrive in land that no

one else wants. In the summer, they wade out into the swampy tundra ponds to eat green muck. In the winter, they like nothing better than an old burn, where summer lightning has peeled back the forest and allowed a tangle of willows to grow— a moose's all-time favorite food. Eaten by wolves, hunted and run over by man, stranded in the snows of a hard winter, the moose always come back.

In the summer, moose disperse and are not easily seen in thick vegetation. In the winter, they gather where walking is easy, along roads and in lowlands where people also like to live. Encounters happen often in the city, until, as a resident, you begin to take the moose for granted, or see them as a pest that eats decorative plantings and blocks bike trails. Then, skiing on a Nordic trail one day, you round a corner and come face to face with an animal that stands 2 feet over you. You can smell the beast's foul scent and see his stress, the ears pulled back on the head and the whites of the eyes showing, and you know that this wild creature, fighting to live till summer, could easily kill you.

LIGHT & DARKNESS

There's no escaping the stress of winter in Alaska—not for moose or people—nor any shield from the exhilaration of the summer. In summer, it never really gets dark at night. In Fairbanks in June, the sun sets in the north around midnight, but it doesn't go down far enough for real darkness to settle, instead rising again 2 hours later. It's always light enough to keep hiking or fishing, and, in clear weather, it's always light enough to read. You may not see the stars from early May until sometime in August (the climate chart in chapter 2 gives seasonal daylight for various towns). Visitors have trouble getting used to it: Falling asleep in broad daylight can be hard. Alaskans deal with it by staying up late and being active outdoors.

In the winter, on the other hand, you forget what the sun looks like. Kids go to school in the dark and come home in the dark. The sun rises in the middle of the morning and sets after lunch. At high noon in December, the sun hangs just above the southern horizon with a weak, orange light, a constant sunset. Animals and people go into hibernation.

As you go north, the change in the length of the days gets bigger. In Ketchikan, the longest day of the year, on the June 21 summer solstice, is about 17 hours, 20 minutes; in Fairbanks, 22 hours; and in Barrow, the longest day is more than 2 months. In contrast, in Seattle, the longest day is 16 hours, 15 minutes; and in Los Angeles, 14 hours, 30 minutes. On the equator, days are always the same length, 12 hours. At the North Pole and South Pole, the sun is up half the year and down the other half.

The best way to understand this is to model it with a ball and a lamp. The earth spins on its axis, the North and South poles, once a day around. When the axis is upright, one spin of the ball puts light on each point on the ball equally—that's the spring and fall equinox, March 21 and September 21, when the day is 12 hours long everywhere. In the summer, the North Pole leans toward the light and the Northern Hemisphere gets more light than darkness, so during the course of one rotation, each northern spot is lighted more than half the time. In winter, the Southern Hemisphere gets its turn, and more than half the Northern Hemisphere is in shadow, meaning shorter days. As you go farther north in winter, the shadow gets larger, and the day in any one spot shorter. But no matter how the axis leans, the equator is always half light and half dark, like the entire globe as a whole.

In the North, on a long summer evening, you can almost feel the planet leaning toward the sun. The world lies under a bright, endless dome. In the winter, darkness falls as deep as space, and you can almost feel the earth's warmth wafting away into the universe as the freeze sinks

ever deeper in the land. Now the rainforest rivers and permafrost lakes are hard ice, the salmon are away at sea, and the bears are asleep. The moose and other wintering animals burn their summer fat, a finite store of provisions that may or may not last. Up in the mountains, the glaciers grow.

THE WARMING CLIMATE

In the past 2 decades, winters have warmed and shortened and summers have gotten hotter. Individual years are sometimes closer to the long-term norm, but the trend is for warming. Years of bizarrely warm weather have become common and records have been broken so often they are hardly noted. In Anchorage, where I live, that has meant ski seasons ruined by rainy weather, massive insect kills of trees, and extraordinary forest fire danger, among many other changes. My friends and I, who grew up in Anchorage, never heard thunder until our teens; now it's commonplace, even early in the summer. Starting in the summer of 2004, the ocean warmed so much we were able to swim in it in places. That's never been possible before in my 44-year life. Alaska didn't even smell like Alaska that summer. Something about how the sun heated the ground and the plants created an odor I remember from travels in the Lower 48, not here.

In Arctic Alaska, the changes are much more pronounced: Sea ice is withdrawing from shore, catastrophic erosion washing away bluffs and villages, permafrost softening and giving way, winters warming and shortening, and ecosystems becoming disrupted as plant and animal life is stressed by the new conditions. A team of 300 scientists from all the Arctic nations, including the United States, completed a 4-year *Arctic Climate Impact Assessment* in 2004 and 2005. The report documents the changes and says they were largely driven by human carbon dioxide emissions. It predicts more changes, most of them negative. For example, if the sea ice continues to melt at the current rate, this century will see the end of the ecosystem that lives upon it, including the likely extinction of the polar bear.

Carbon dioxide warms the earth by trapping the heat of the sun in the atmosphere, a phenomenon understood since the late 1800s. Climate records reconstructed from ancient ice show the amount of carbon dioxide in the atmosphere has closely matched average temperature and climate conditions for more than 400,000 years. Due to human burning of fossil fuels, the carbon dioxide level in the atmosphere now is higher than at any time in that period. And now Arctic temperatures are rising at a rate that appears unprecedented in thousands of years.

Does this mean adjusting your plans as a visitor? Yes and no. Tourists in recent years have enjoyed sunny weather, but also suffered through forest fire smoke and rainy skiing. But how the changes will play out in any particular year cannot be predicted, just as you cannot set your vacation dates based on a TV weather forecast. On the other hand, we may all need to adjust our plans. The amount of carbon dioxide each of us is responsible for emitting relates directly to the nonrenewable energy we use. You can help save Alaska by carpooling or turning off an extra light.

I've written a book on this subject, *The Whale and the Supercomputer; On the Northern Front of Climate Change* (North Point Press, $14), which tells the story of how Alaska's Iñupiat and scientists are experiencing and learning about the changing climate. You can read more about it on my website, at www.wohlforth.net.

2 Politics & History: Living a Frontier Myth

The occupations of prospector, trapper, and homesteader—rugged individualists relying only on themselves in a limitless land—would dominate Alaska's economy if the state's image of itself were accurate. Alaskans talk a lot about the Alaskan spirit of independence, yearn for freedom from government, and declare that people from "Outside" just don't understand Alaskans when they insist on locking up Alaska's lands in parks and wilderness status. A bumper sticker says, simply, "We don't give a damn how they do it Outside." A state full of self-reliant frontiersmen can't be tied down and deterred from their manifest destiny by a bunch of Washington bureaucrats. At the extreme, there has even been a movement to declare independence as a separate nation so Alaskans can extend the frontier,

Dateline

- **Approximately 15,000 years ago** First human explorers arrive in Alaska from Asia.
- **1741** Vitus Bering, on a mission originally chartered by Peter the Great, finds Alaska; ship's surgeon and naturalist Georg Steller goes ashore for a few hours on Kayak Island, the first white man to set foot in Alaska.

- **1743** Russian fur traders enter the Aleutian Islands; Aleuts are enslaved to hunt sea otter and are massacred when they try to revolt; Aleut cultural traditions are eliminated, and over the coming decades they are relocated as far south as California for their hunting skills.
- **1772** Unalaska, in the Aleutian Islands, becomes a permanent Russian settlement.

- **1778** British Capt. James Cook makes voyages of exploration to Alaska, seeking the Northwest Passage from the Pacific to the Atlantic, and draws charts of the coast.
- **1784** Russians build a settlement at Kodiak.
- **1799** Russians establish a fort near present-day Sitka, which will later become their capital; Tlingits attack and

extracting its natural resources unfettered by bunny-hugging Easterners.

But just because you wear a cowboy hat doesn't mean you know how to ride a horse. In Las Vegas you find a lot more hats than horsemen, and Alaska is full of self-reliant pioneers who spend rush hour in traffic jams and worry more about urban drug dealing and air pollution than where to catch their next meal or dig the mother lode. As for self-reliance and independence from government, Alaska has the highest per-capita state spending of any state in the nation, with no state income or sales taxes and an annual payment that has ranged in the last decade from $845 to almost $2,000 a year to every man, woman, and child just for living here. The state government provides retirement homes; it owns various businesses, including a dairy, a railroad, and a subsidized mortgage lender; it has built schools in the smallest communities; it operates a state ferry system and a radio and television network; and it owns nearly a third of the landmass of Alaska. The state government relies on the oil industry; when oil prices are high, the state spends a lot, but when they go down, budget cuts can go deep.

That conflict between perception and reality grows out of the story of a century of development of Alaska. The state is a great storehouse of minerals, oil, timber, and fish. A lot of wealth has been extracted, and many people have gotten rich. But it has always been because the federal government let them do it. Every acre of Alaska has belonged to the U.S. government from the day Secretary of State William Seward bought Alaska from Russia in 1867. Since then, the frontier has never been broader than Uncle Sam made it.

Yet the whole concept of ownership didn't fit Alaska well from the start. Did the Russians really own what they sold? Alaska Natives didn't think so. They'd been living on this land for more than 100 centuries, and at the time of the purchase, most had never seen a white face. How could Russia hold title to land that no Russian had so much as explored? As Americans flooded into Alaska to search for gold at the turn of the 20th century, this conflict became obvious. Alaska Natives, never conquered by war or treaty, soon began their legal and political fight to recover their land—a fight they would eventually win.

The concept of ownership has changed in other ways, too. For the first 100 years after the United States bought Alaska, it maintained the vast majority of the territory as "public domain," with federal land and its mineral resources free for the

---

destroy the fort, but are later driven off in a counterattack; the Russian-American Company receives a 20-year exclusive franchise to govern and exploit Alaska.

■ 1821 Russian naval officers are placed in control of the Russian-American Company, which begins to decline in profitability.

■ 1824 Boundaries roughly matching Alaska's current borders are set by treaty between Russia, Britain, and the United States.

■ 1839 The British Hudson's Bay Company, surpassing Russia in trade, begins leasing parts of Southeast Alaska and subsequently extends trading outposts into the Interior.

■ 1843 First overtures are made by American officials interested in buying Alaska from the Russians so U.S. instead of British power could expand there.

■ 1848 New England whalers begin to exploit rich Arctic stocks; over the next 60 years, they transform Native cultures and severely reduce marine mammal numbers.

■ 1865 A Confederate navy ship attacks the whaling fleet, destroying 20 ships and capturing 4 more.

continues

taking, as in the Old West of frontier lore. Each piece of Alaska belonged to everyone until someone showed up to lay private claim. Today, amid deep conflict over whether to develop such areas as the Arctic National Wildlife Refuge (known as ANWR), federal control stands out far more clearly than it did during the gold rush, when the land's wealth was free to anyone with strength enough to take it. Alaskans who want to keep receiving the good things that a rich state government brings equate the frontier spirit of the past with their own financial well-being, whether that means working at a mining claim or at a desk in a glass office tower. But other Americans feel they own Alaska, too, and they don't necessarily believe in exploiting its resource treasure. They may want the frontier to stay alive in another sense—unconquered and still wild.

White colonization of the territory came in boom-and-bust waves of migrants arriving with the goal of making a quick buck and then clearing out—without worrying about the people who already lived there. Although the gold-rush pioneers are celebrated today, the Klondike rush of 1898 that opened up and populated the territory was motivated by greed and was a mass importer of crime, inhumanity, and, for the Native people, terrible epidemics of new diseases that killed off whole villages. Like the Russians 150 years before, who had made slaves of the Natives, the new white population behaved as if the indigenous people were less than human. Until Franklin Roosevelt became president, federal policy was to suppress Alaska Native cultures. Protestant missionaries had the authority of law to forbid Native people from telling their old stories or even speaking their own languages. Segregation ended only after World War II. Meanwhile, the salmon that fed the people of the territory were overfished by a powerful Outside-owned canning industry with friends in Washington, D.C. Their abuses destroyed salmon runs. Formerly rich Native villages faced famine when their primary food source was taken away.

It was only with World War II, and the Japanese invasion of the Aleutian Islands, that Alaska developed an industry that was not based on exploitation of natural resources: the military industry. The war brought the construction of the territory's first road to the outside world, the Alaska Highway. After the war, military activity dropped off, but only briefly. By the late 1940s, Alaska was on the front line of the Cold War. Huge air force and army bases were built, and remote radar stations were

- **1867** In need of money and fearful that Russia couldn't hold on to Alaska anyway, Czar Alexander II sells Alaska to the United States; Secretary of State William Seward negotiates the deal for a price of $7.2 million, roughly 2¢ an acre; the American flag is raised in Sitka, and the U.S. military assumes government of Alaska.

- **1870** The Alaska Commercial Company receives a monopoly on harvesting seals in the Pribilof Islands and soon expands across the territory (the company remains a presence in the Alaska Bush today).

- **1879** Naturalist and writer John Muir explores Southeast Alaska by canoe, discovering Glacier Bay with Native guides.

- **1880** Joe Juneau and Richard Harris, guided by local Natives, find gold on Gastineau Channel and found the city of Juneau; gold strikes begin to come every few years across the state.

- **1884** Military rule ends in Alaska, but residents still have no right to elect a legislature, governor, or congressional representative, or to make laws.

installed to detect and repel Soviet bombers and missiles. To this day, the federal government remains a key industry whose removal would deal the economy a grievous blow.

The fight for Alaska statehood also began after World War II. Alaskans argued that they needed local, independent control of natural resources, pointing to the example of overfishing in the federally managed salmon industry. Opponents said that Alaska would never be able to support itself, would always require large subsidies from the federal government, and therefore should not be a state. But the advocates pointed out that Alaska's lack of self-sufficiency came about because its citizens did not control the resources— Alaska was a colony, with decisions and profits taken away by the mother country. If Alaskans could control their own land, they could use the resources to fund government. The discovery of oil on the Swanson River on the Kenai Peninsula in 1957 helped win that argument. Here was real money that could fund a state government. In 1959, Alaska finally became the 49th state. Along with the rights of entering the Union, Alaska received a dowry, an endowment of land to develop and pay for future government. The Statehood Act gave the new state the right to select 103 million acres from a total landmass of 365 million acres. Indeed, that land does pay for state government in Alaska, in the form of oil royalties and taxes—but, to this day, the federal government still spends a lot more in Alaska than it receives.

Oil revenues supported the new state as it began to extend services to the vast, undeveloped expanse of Alaska. Anchorage boomed in the 1960s in a period of buoyant optimism. Leaders believed that the age-old problems of the wide-open frontier—poverty, lack of basic services, impenetrable remoteness—would succumb to the new government and new money, while the land would remain wide open. The pace of change redoubled in 1968 with the discovery of the largest oil field in North America at Prudhoe Bay on land that had been a wise state selection in the federal land-grant entitlement. The state government received as much money in a one-day oil lease auction as it had spent in total for the previous 6 years. This was going to be the boom of all booms.

The oil bonanza on the North Slope would change Alaska more than any other event since the gold rush. Once, opening the frontier meant letting a few prospectors scratch the dirt in search of a poke of gold. But getting this immense pool of oil to market from one of the most remote spots on the globe would require allowing the world's largest companies to build

- **1885** Protestant missionaries meet to divide up the territory, parceling out each region to a different religion; they begin to fan out across Alaska to convert Native peoples, largely suppressing their traditional ways.
- **1898** After prospectors arrive in Seattle with a ton of gold, the Klondike gold rush begins; gold rushes in Nome and Fairbanks follow within a few years; Americans begin to populate Alaska.
- **1906** Alaska's first (nonvoting) delegate in Congress takes office; the capital moves from Sitka to Juneau.
- **1908** The Iditarod Trail, a sled dog mail route, is completed, linking trails continuously from Seward to Nome.
- **1913** The first territorial legislature convenes, although it has few powers; the first automobile drives the Richardson Highway route, from Valdez to Fairbanks.
- **1914** Federal construction of the Alaska Railroad begins; the first tents go up in the river bottom that will be Anchorage, along the rail line.
- **1917** Mount McKinley National Park is established.
- **1920** The first flights connect Alaska to the rest of the United States; aviation

continues

across Alaska a pipeline that, when completed, could credibly claim to be the largest privately financed construction project in world history. With the stakes suddenly so much higher, it came time to figure out exactly who owned which parts of Alaska. The land couldn't just be public domain any longer.

That division wouldn't be easy. Much of the state had never even been mapped, much less surveyed, and there were some large outstanding claims that had to be settled. Alaska Natives, who had lost land, culture, and health in 2 centuries of white invasion, finally saw their luck start to turn. It wouldn't be possible to resolve the land issues surrounding the pipeline until their claims to land and compensation were answered. Native leaders cannily used that leverage to ensure that they got what they wanted.

In the early 1970s, America had a new awareness of the way its first people had been treated in the settlement of the West. When white frontiers expanded, Native traditional homelands were stolen. In Alaska, with the powerful lure of all that oil providing the impetus, Native people were able to insist on a fairer resolution. In 1971, with the support of white Alaskans, the oil companies, and President Richard Nixon, Congress passed the Alaska Native Claims Settlement Act, called ANCSA.

The act transferred 44 million acres of land and $962.5 million to corporations whose shareholders were all the Native people of Alaska. The new Native corporations would be able to exploit their own land for their shareholders' profit. In later legislation, Natives also won guaranteed subsistence hunting and fishing rights on federal land. Some Natives complained that they'd received only an eighth of the land they had owned before white contact, but it was still by far the richest settlement any of the world's indigenous people had received at that time. Today the Native corporations are Alaska's largest and most powerful homegrown businesses.

It was a political deal on a grand scale. It's unlikely that Natives would have gotten their land at all but for the desire of whites to get at the oil and their need for Native support. Nor could the pipeline have overcome environmental challenges without the Natives dropping their objections. Even with Native support in place, legislation authorizing the pipeline passed the U.S. Senate by only one vote, cast by Vice President Spiro Agnew.

But there were other side effects of the deal that white Alaskans didn't like so much. The state still hadn't received a large portion of its land entitlement, and now the Native corporations also had a

---

quickly becomes the most important means of transportation in the territory.

■ **1923** President Warren Harding drives the final spike on the Alaska Railroad at Nenana and then dies on the way home, purportedly from eating bad Alaska seafood.

■ **1925** Leonhard Seppala and other dog mushers relay diphtheria serum on the Iditarod Trail to fight an epidemic in Nome; Seppala and a lead dog, Balto, become national heroes.

■ **1934** Federal policy of forced assimilation of Native cultures is officially discarded and New Deal efforts to preserve Native cultures begin.

■ **1935** New Deal "colonists," broke farmers from all over the United States, settle in the Matanuska Valley north of Anchorage.

■ **1940** A military buildup begins in Alaska; bases built in Anchorage accelerate the city's growth into a major population center.

■ **1942** Japanese invade the Aleutians, taking Attu and Kiska islands and bombing Unalaska/Dutch Harbor (a U.S. counterattack the next year drives out the Japanese); the Alaska Highway links Alaska to the rest of the right to select the land they wanted. There still remained the question of who would get what, and the question of the wild lands that Congress, influenced by a strong new environmental movement, wanted to maintain as national parks and wilderness and not give away. That issue wasn't settled until 1980, when the Alaska National Interest Lands Conservation Act passed, setting aside an additional 106 million acres for conservation, an area larger than California. Alaska's frontier-minded population screamed bloody murder over "the lockup of Alaska," but the act was only the last tangible step in a process started by the coming of big oil and the need its arrival created to draw lines on the map, tying up the frontier.

When construction of the $9 billion pipeline finally got underway in 1974, a huge influx of new people chasing the high-paying jobs put any previous gold rush to shame. The newcomers were from a different part of the country than previously, too. Alaska had been a predominantly Democratic state, but oil workers from Texas, Oklahoma, and other Bible Belt states helped shift the balance of Alaska's politics, and now it's solidly Republican. In its frontier days, Alaska had a strong Libertarian streak, but now it became more influenced by Christian conservatism. A hippie-infested legislature of the early 1970s legalized marijuana for home use. Conservatives at the time, who thought the government shouldn't butt into its citizens' private lives, went along with them. After the pipeline, times changed, and Alaska developed tough antidrug laws.

Growth also brought urban problems. As the pipeline construction boom waned in 1977, the boomtown atmosphere of gambling and street prostitution disappeared with it, but other big-city problems remained. No longer could residents of Anchorage and Fairbanks go to bed without locking their doors. Both cities were declared "nonattainment" areas by the Environmental Protection Agency because of air pollution near the ground in cold winter weather, when people leave their cars running during the day to keep them from freezing.

But the pipeline seemed to provide limitless wealth to solve these problems. For fear that too much money would be wasted, the voters altered the state constitution to bank a large portion of the new riches. The new Permanent Fund would be off-limits to the politicians in Juneau, with half the annual earnings paid out to citizens as dividends. The fund now contains nearly $40 billion in savings and has become one of the largest sectors of the economy simply

country overland for the first time but is open to civilians only after the war.

- **1949** Massive Cold War military buildup feeds fast economic growth.
- **1957** Oil is found on Kenai Peninsula's Swanson River.
- **1959** Alaska becomes a state.
- **1964** The largest earthquake ever to strike North America shakes Southcentral Alaska,

killing 131 people, primarily in tsunami waves.

- **1968** Largest oil field in American history is found at Prudhoe Bay, on Alaska's North Slope.
- **1970** Environmental lawsuits tie up work to build the Alaska pipeline, which is needed to link the North Slope oil field to markets.
- **1971** Congress acknowledges and pays the federal

government's debt to Alaska's indigenous people with the Alaska Native Claims Settlement Act, which transfers 44 million acres of land and almost $1 billion to new Native-owned corporations.

- **1973** The first Iditarod Trail Sled Dog Race runs more than 1,000 miles from Anchorage to Nome.
- **1974** Congress clears away legal barriers to construction

continues

by virtue of paying out as much as $1 billion a year in dividends to everyone who lives at least a year in the state. All major state taxes on individuals were canceled, and people got used to receiving everything free from the government.

Then, in 1985, oil prices dropped, deflating the overextended economy. Housing prices crashed and thousands of people simply walked away from their mortgages. All but a few of the banks in the state went broke. Condominiums that had sold for $100,000 went for $20,000 or less a year later. It was the bust that always goes with the boom, but it still came as a shock to many. The spending associated with the clean-up of the *Exxon Valdez* oil spill in 1989 restarted the economy, and it continues on an even keel today, but the extreme wealth of the earlier oil years never returned.

Meanwhile, the oil from Prudhoe Bay started running out. Oil revenues, an irreplaceable 85% of the state budget, started an inexorable downward trend in the early 1990s. The oil companies downsized. Without another boom on the horizon, the question became how to avoid, or at least soften, the next bust. At this writing, that question remains unanswered. Ironically, polls show that Alaskans would support a personal income tax, but so far they haven't been given the choice. Politically, it's more expedient to hope high oil prices hold until the next big project gets the good times rolling again, such as a natural gas pipeline from the North Slope to middle America or oil development in ANWR.

Culture moves slower than politics or economics, and Alaskans still see themselves as gold-rush prospectors or wildcat oil drillers, adventuring in an open land and striking it rich by their own devices. Even as the economy blends ever more smoothly into the American corporate landscape, Alaskans' myth of themselves remains strong. Today the state's future is as little in its own hands as it has ever been. Big petroleum projects will be decided in Congress and in distant corporate boardrooms, not here. Ultimately, an economy based on exploiting natural resources is anything but independent.

3 The People: Three Ways to Win an Argument in Alaska

NUMBER 1: WAIT FOR SPRING

A small town in Alaska in March. Each time it snows, you have to throw shovels of it higher over your head to dig out. The air in the house is stale and the view out the window is black, white, and gray. Everyone's going nuts with winter. It's time for a good political ruckus. No one

---

of the trans-Alaska pipeline; Vice President Spiro Agnew casts the deciding vote in the U.S. Senate.

■ 1977 The trans-Alaska pipeline is completed and begins providing up to 25% of the U.S. domestic supply of oil.

■ 1980 Congress sets aside almost a third of Alaska in new parks and other land-conservation units; awash in new oil wealth, the state legislature abolishes all taxes paid by individuals to state government.

■ 1982 Alaskans receive their first Alaska Permanent Fund dividends, interest paid on an oil-wealth savings account.

■ 1985 Declining oil prices send the Alaska economy into a tailspin; tens of thousands leave the state and most of the banks collapse.

■ 1989 The tanker *Exxon Valdez* hits Bligh Reef in Prince William Sound, spilling 11 million gallons of North Slope crude in the worst oil spill ever in North America.

■ 1994 A federal jury in Anchorage awards $5 billion to 10,000 fishermen, Natives, and others hurt by the Exxon oil spill; Exxon appeals continue today.

can predict exactly what will set it off—it could just be an ill-considered letter to the editor in the local newspaper, or it could be something juicier, like a controversial development proposal. At some point, when the cabin fever gets bad enough, it almost doesn't matter what sparks the inferno. Alaskans can generate outrage about almost anything, with a ritual of charges and countercharges, conspiracy theories, and impassioned public testimony.

It's particularly amusing when some outsider is involved, thinking he's at the town council meeting in a normal political process to get some project approved, only to wind up on the receiving end of a public hearing from hell. I'll never forget a sorry businessman who was trying to lease some land from the town of Homer. He endured hours of angry public testimony one night. He was sweating, the only person in the packed city hall meeting room wearing a tie, surrounded by flannel shirts, blue jeans, and angry faces. Finally, he stood up at his chair and, in a plaintive tone of frustration near tears, declared, "You're not very professional as a community!" For once, no one could disagree.

He gave up. He didn't know that if he had only waited a couple of months, the opposition would dry up when the salmon started running. Then most of the city council meetings are canceled, and the rest are brief and sparsely attended. If anything really important comes up, the council is smart enough to postpone it till fall. In the summer, Alaskans have more important things to attend to than government.

The sun shines deep into the night so you can catch fish and tourists, not sit inside. It's the season when the money is made. The streets are full of new people, like a bird rookery refreshed by migrants. Everyone stays awake late pounding nails, playing softball, and fly-casting for reds. Office workers in Anchorage depart straight from work for a 3-hour drive down to the Kenai Peninsula, fish through the night, catch a quick nap in the car in the wee hours, and make it to work on time the next morning, with fish stories to share. Sleep is expendable—you don't seem to need it that much when the sky is light all night.

In the Native villages of the Bush, everyone has gone to fish camp. Families load everything in an aluminum riverboat and leave town, headed upriver. On the banks and beaches, they set up wall tents and spruce-log fish-drying racks, maybe a basketball hoop and campfire, too. Extended families work as a unit. Men gather in the salmon and the women gut them with a few lightning strokes of a knife and hang them to dry on the racks. Children run around in a countryside paradise, watched by whichever adults are handiest.

Suddenly, August comes. For the first time in months, you can see the stars. It comes as a shock the first time you have to use your car headlights. The mood gets even more frantic. There's never enough time in the summer to do everything that needs to get done. Construction crews can count the days now till snow and cold will shut them down. Anything that's not done now won't be done until next May. Labor Day approaches as fast as 5pm on a busy business day.

As September turns to October, the last tourists are gone and T-shirt shops are closed for the season. The commercial fishing boats are tied up back in the harbor and the fishermen prepare for vacation. Cannery workers are already back at college. For the first time in months, people can slow down long enough to look at each other and remember where they left off in the spring. It's time to catch up on sleep and make big decisions. The hills of birch turn bright yellow, the tundra goes brick red, and the sky turns gray—there's the smell of wood smoke in the air—and then, one day, it starts to snow.

The Iditarod

The Iditarod Trail Sled Dog Race, a 1,000-mile run from Anchorage to Nome that takes place over 2 weeks in mid-March, is the biggest event of Alaska's year, not only in terms of sports, but also culturally and as a unifying event. The race is big news—TV anchors speculate on the mushers' strategies at the top of the evening news and break away live to cover the top finishers, regardless of the time of day or night. Schoolchildren plot the progress of their favorite teams on maps and over the Internet. Increasingly, the world is joining in. Visitors, especially Europeans, fill hotels in Anchorage and Nome for the Iditarod. Voices speaking French and German waft through the restaurants. It's a wonderful time of year to visit, with light skies, excellent late-season skiing, and winter festivals enlivening many towns. Nome goes crazy when the mushers hit. Even if the first team crosses the finish line at 3am in −30°F (−34°C) weather, a huge crowd turns out to congratulate the winner. And crowds keep turning out for the also-rans, too.

Given all this, it's difficult for me to report objectively on the activities of animal rights opponents to the race, currently led by People for the Ethical Treatment of Animals (PETA)—but my editors insist that I try. While PETA opposes all human use of animals, some mainstream animal welfare advocates also criticize the race. They charge that dogs can suffer and die on the trail and, while not racing, are inhumanely tethered in dog lots. Organized boycotts against race sponsors have peeled off some national companies, but the campaign doesn't seem to be affecting the race, which grows every year. Iditarod supporters—the universal view in Alaska—claim the critics exaggerate and distort their charges. Iditarod mushers insist that the dogs, which are worth thousands of dollars, receive veterinary care superior to the doctoring that most people get. Sick dogs have been evacuated from the trail by helicopter. Mushers who abuse dogs are kicked out of the sport.

But framing the debate by focusing on the sport's marquee event probably skews the facts in the mushers' favor. Harmful practices do occur in the lower ranks of mushing. For example, uncontrolled breeding by amateurs or careless professionals produces too many pups that end up being killed. Sadly, that problem isn't unique to mushing—it happens to pets in cities all over the U.S. It's also true that sled dogs can be tethered excessively or otherwise abused. Successful mushers—including Iditarod competitors—must give their dogs thorough exercise, as only that way can the animals perform as athletes, but there's no law limiting how many dogs an irresponsible musher or pet owner can acquire or how often they must be run.

Our society is inhumane to animals in many ways. The question for visitors to consider is if the Iditarod is a fit symbol of that inhumanity, or the opposite.

It's not the velvet darkness of midwinter that gets you. December is bearable, even if the sun rises after the kids get to school, barely cruises along the horizon, and sinks before they start for home. Nowhere is Christmas more real than in Alaska, where carolers sing with cheeks tingling from the cold. January isn't so hard. You're still excited about the skiing. The phone rings in the middle of the night—it's a friend telling you to put on your boots and go outside to see the northern lights. February is a bit harder to take, but most towns have a winter carnival to divert your attention from the cold.

March is when bizarre things start to happen. People are just holding on for the end of winter, and you never know what will set them off. That's when you hunker down and lay low, watch what you say, and bite your tongue when your spouse lets hang a comment you'd like to jump on like a coho hitting fresh bait. Hold on—just until the icicles start to melt, the mud shows around the snowbanks, and the cycle starts fresh.

NUMBER 2: BE HERE FIRST

There's a simple and effective way to win an argument in Alaska—state how long you've lived here. If it's longer than your adversary, he'll find it difficult to put up a fight. This is why, when speaking in public, people will often begin their remarks by stating how many years they've been in Alaska. It's a badge of authenticity and status in a place with a young, transient population that's grown fast. No one cares where you came from or who you were back there, and there's no such thing as class in Alaska—anyone who tries to act superior will quickly find that no one else notices. But if you haven't made it through a few winters, you probably don't know what you're talking about.

It's also traditional—although, sadly, a fading tradition—to treat strangers as friends until they prove otherwise. The

smaller the town you visit, the more strongly you'll find that hospitality still alive. Visitors find it pleasantly disorienting to arrive in a small town and have everyone in the street greet them with a smile. These traditions of hospitality run deep in Alaska's Native people. (Alaskans use the word *Native* to mean all the indigenous peoples of Alaska.) But instead of beginning a conversation by stating how long they've lived here, Natives—who've always been here—try to find a relation with a new person by talking about where their families are from.

Theories differ about how North America was originally populated. The traditional notion is that the first people walked across a land bridge from Asia over the dry Bering Sea around 15,000 years ago, when glacial ice sequestered enough of the earth's water to lower the sea level. The bridge, up to 1,000 miles wide, included the entire west coast of Alaska at its largest size and lasted longest in the area between Nome and Kotzebue.

But new archaeology and geology throw doubt on that theory, suggesting a migration story that's much more complex. People who know the Arctic know the land bridge simply wasn't necessary for migration: In the winter, you can sometimes walk between Siberia and Alaska even today, and the seafaring skills of Alaska's Aleuts and Eskimos would have enabled them to travel back and forth to Asia at any time. Siberian and Alaskan Natives share language, stories, and kin. Perhaps the connection across the north was continuous and followed many routes after northern people learned to sew skin boats and clothing about 15,000 years ago. Certainly, the idea that they walked seems increasingly questionable. Geologists now believe the route south was largely impassable during the last glacial period; if migrants did use it, they must have used boats to connect coastal pockets that remained free of glacial ice.

However and whenever the first people arrived, they quickly spread through the Americas, creating cultures of incredible complexity and diversity. Most scientists believe migrants through Alaska were the ancestors of all the indigenous peoples of the hemisphere, from the Inca to the Algonquin. Those who stayed in Alaska became the Eskimos, who include the Iñupiat of the Arctic, the Yup'ik of the Southwest, and the Alutiiq of the Gulf of Alaska coastline. They also became Indians: the Athabascan of the Interior and the Tlingits, Haida, and Tsimshians of Southeast Alaska and British Columbia.

The Native groups of Alaska have a lot in common culturally, but before the white invasion they had well-defined boundaries and didn't mix much. They didn't farm, and the only animal they domesticated was the dog—dog teams and boats were the primary means of transportation and commerce. But they generally were not nomadic, and no one in Alaska lived in ice igloos (farther east, in Canada, igloos were used as winter dwellings on the ice pack). On the treeless Arctic coast, houses were built of sod atop supports of whalebone and driftwood; where wood was plentiful, in the rainforests, large and intricately carved houses sheltered entire villages. Typically, a family-connected tribal group would have a winter village and a summer fish camp for gathering and laying up food. Elders guided the community in important decisions. A gifted shaman led the people in religious matters, relating to the spirits of ancestors, animals, trees, and even the ice that populated their world. Stories passed on through generations explained the universe.

Those oral traditions kept Native cultures alive. Twenty distinct Native languages were spoken. A few elders still speak only their Native language today, and only one language, Eyak, is essentially extinct. The languages break into four major families: Eskimo-Aleut, Athabascan-Eyak-Tlingit, Haida, and Tsimshian (the last two are primarily Canadian). The Eskimo-Aleut language group includes languages spoken by coastal people from the Arctic Ocean to the Gulf of Alaska, including Iñupiat in the Arctic; Yup'ik in the Yukon-Kuskokwim and Bristol Bay region; Aleuts in the Aleutian Islands; and Alutiiq on the Alaska Peninsula, Kodiak, and Prince William Sound. There are 12 Athabascan and Eyak languages in Alaska, and more Outside, including Apache and Navajo. In Southeast Alaska, Tlingit was spoken across most of the Panhandle. Haida was spoken on southern Prince of Wales Island and southward into what's now British Columbia, where Tsimshian also was spoken.

The first arrival of whites was often violent and destructive, spanning a 100-year period that started in the 1740s with the coming of the Russian fur traders, who enslaved the Aleuts, and continued to the 1840s, when New England whalers first met the Iñupiat of the Arctic. There were pitched battles, but disease and nonviolent destruction of oral traditions were more influential. Protestant missionaries, backed by government assimilation policy, drove the old stories and even Native languages underground. Lela Kiana Oman, who has published traditional Iñupiaq stories to preserve them, told me of her memories of her father secretly telling the ancient tales at night to his children. She was forbidden to speak Iñupiaq in school and did not see her first traditional Native dance until age 18.

Oman's work is part of today's Native cultural renaissance. It's not a moment too soon. In some villages, children know as much about Beverly Hills, which they see on television, as they do about their own culture. A few don't share a language with their own grandparents. But schools in many areas now require Native language classes, or even teach using language-immersion techniques. For the Aleut, whose cultural traditions were almost completely wiped out, the process of renewal involves a certain amount of invention. On the other hand, some traditional villages remain, especially deep in the country of the Yukon-Kuskokwim Delta, where Yup'ik is still the dominant language and most of the food comes from traditional subsistence hunting and gathering, altered only by the use of modern materials and guns.

Alaska Natives also are fighting destruction fueled by alcohol and other substance-abuse problems. Rates of suicide, accidents, and domestic violence are high in the Bush. Statistically, nearly every Alaska Native in prison is there because of alcohol. A sobriety movement is attacking the problem one person at a time. One of its goals is to use traditional Native culture to fill a void of rural despair where alcohol flows in. Politically, a "local option" law provides communities the choice of partial or total alcohol prohibition; it has been successfully used in many towns but remains controversial in others.

There are social and political tensions between Natives and whites on many levels and over many issues. The Alaskan city and Alaskan village have less in common than do most different nations. Although village Natives come to the city to shop, get health care, or attend meetings, urban Alaskans have no reason to go to the villages, and most never have made the trip.

The most contentious rural-urban issue concerns allocation of fish and game. Some urban outdoorsmen feel they should have the same rights to hunt and fish that the Natives do, and the state supreme court has interpreted Alaska's constitution to say they're correct. But rural Natives have federal law on their side, which overrules the state. A decade of political stalemate over the issue divided Alaskans until, in 2000, the feds finally stepped in and took over fish and game management in the majority of the state to protect Native subsistence. Many Natives were glad to see it happen, as humiliating as the move was for independent-minded Alaskans. Natives feel subsistence hunting and fishing are an integral part of their cultural heritage, far more important than sport, and should take priority. Darker conflicts exist, too, and it's impossible to discount the charges of racism that Native Alaskans raise in issues as diverse as school funding and public safety.

Alaska Natives have essentially become a minority in their own land. In 1880, Alaska contained 33,000 Natives and 430 whites. By 1900, with the gold rush, the numbers were roughly equal. Since then, whites have generally outnumbered Natives in ever greater numbers. Today there are about 98,000 Alaska Natives—27,000 of whom live in the cities of Anchorage and Fairbanks—out of a total state population of 627,000 people of all races. Consequently, Alaska Natives must learn to walk in two worlds. The North Slope's Iñupiat, who hunt the bowhead whale from open boats as their forefathers did, must also know how to negotiate for their take in international diplomatic meetings. And they have to use the levers of government to protect the whale's environment from potential damage by the oil industry. The Alaska Native Claims Settlement Act created a new class, the corporate Native, responsible for representing rural needs but also obliged to function as an executive for large, far-reaching business concerns.

Non-Natives traveling to the Bush also walk in two worlds, but they may not even know it. In a Native village, a newly met friend will ask you in for a cup of coffee; it can be rude not to accept. Too much eye contact in conversation also can be rude—that's how Native elders look at younger people who owe them respect. If a Native person looks down, speaks slowly, and

An Alaska Glossary

If Alaska feels like a different country from the rest of the United States, one reason may be the odd local usage that makes English slightly different here—different enough, in fact, that the Associated Press publishes a separate style-book dictionary just for Alaska. Here are some Alaskan words you may run into:

breakup   When God set up the seasons in Alaska, he forgot one: spring. While the rest of the United States enjoys new flowers and baseball, Alaskans are looking at melting snowbanks and mud. Then, in May, summer miraculously arrives. Breakup officially occurs when the ice goes out in the Interior's rivers, but it stands for the time period of winter's demise and summer's initiation.

bunny boots   If you see people wearing huge bulbous white rubber boots in Alaska's winter, it's not necessarily because they have enormous feet. Those are bunny boots, superinsulated footwear originally designed for Arctic air force operations—and they're the warmest things in the world.

cheechako   A newcomer or greenhorn. Not used much anymore because almost everyone is one.

dry or damp   Many towns and villages have invoked a state law that allows them to outlaw alcohol completely (to go dry) or to outlaw sale but not possession (to go damp).

Lower 48   The contiguous United States.

Native   When capitalized, the word refers to Alaska's indigenous people. "American Indian" isn't used much in Alaska, "Alaska Native" being the preferred term.

seems to mumble, that's not disrespect, but the reverse. Fast-talking non-Natives have to make a conscious effort to slow down and leave pauses in conversation because Natives usually don't jump in or interrupt—they listen, consider, and then respond. Of course, most Native people won't take offense at your bad manners. They're used to spanning cultures. When I was in a village a few years ago, I looked in confusion at a clock that didn't seem right. "That's Indian time," my Athabascan companion said. Then, pointing to a clock that was working he said, "White man time is over there."

Urban visitors who miss cultural nuances rarely overlook the apparent poverty of many villages. Out on a remote landscape of windswept tundra, swampy in summer and frozen in winter, they may secretly wonder why Natives endure the hardships of rural Alaskan life when even the most remote villager can see on television how easy it is in Southern California. Save your pity. As Yup'ik social observer Harold Napoleon once said, "We're poor, all right, but we've got more than most people. Our most important asset is our land and our culture, and we want to protect it, come hell or high water."

NUMBER 3: BE A REAL ALASKAN

Alaska's history books are full of the stories of economic booms, the people who came, what kind of wealth they were after, and how they populated and developed the land. In a largely empty place, you can

Native corporation   In 1971, Congress settled land claims with Alaska's Natives by turning over land and money; corporations were set up, with the Natives then alive as shareholders, to receive the property. Most of the corporations still thrive.

oosik   The huge penile bone of a walrus. Knowing this word could save you from being the butt of any of a number of practical jokes people like to play on cheechakos.

Outside   Anywhere that isn't Alaska. This is a widely used term in print and is capitalized, like any other proper noun.

PFD   No, not personal flotation device; it stands for Permanent Fund Dividend. When Alaska's oil riches started flowing in the late 1970s, the voters set up a savings account called the Permanent Fund. Half the interest is paid annually to every man, woman, and child in the state. With nearly $40 billion in investments, the fund now yields from $900 to $2,000 in dividends to each Alaskan annually.

pioneer   A white settler of Alaska who has been here longer than most other people can remember—25 or 30 years usually does it.

Southeast   Most people don't bother to say "Southeast Alaska." The region may be to the northwest of everyone else in the country, but it's southeast of most Alaskans, and that's all they care about.

village   A small Alaska Native settlement in the Bush, usually tightly bound by family and cultural tradition. The word *village* is roughly analogous to *tribe* elsewhere in the U.S.

make it into history just by showing up. But every wave is followed by a trough, the bust that comes after the boom when those who came just for the money go back where they came from. Those are the times when the real Alaskans—those who live here for the love of the place, not only the money—are divided from the rest. The real Alaskans stay; the others leave. It's the perfect way to settle an argument.

Other people have other definitions of what it takes to be a real Alaskan. One definition, which I once read on a place mat in a diner in Soldotna, holds that to be a real Alaskan, you have to know how to fix a Caterpillar tractor. Similar definitions require various feats in the outdoors—hunting, fishing, or shooting—and even acts in the barroom or the bedroom. They

all assume that a real Alaskan is a big, tough, white, male, bulldozer-driving type of guy. But those can be the first to leave when the economy goes down the tubes.

The first to leave were the Russians sent by the czar and the Russian-American Company. On October 18, 1867, their flag came down over Castle Hill in Sitka in a solemn ceremony, got stuck, and had to be untangled by a soldier sent up the pole. The territory was virtually empty of Russians before the check was even signed, as Congress didn't much like the idea of the purchase and took a while to pay. The gold-rush stampeders were the next to leave. The population of Nome went from 12,500 to 852 after the stampede was over. The oil years have seen the same phenomenon.

But each time the boom went bust, enough stayed that Alaska ended up with more people than before. Over the long term, the population has kept growing dramatically. And each set of migrants has been similar: young, transplanted mostly from the West, but from other parts of the United States, too. Most people who came to Alaska prior to 1990 were white, but that's changed, and strong minority communities have grown in Anchorage and some other towns. In Kodiak and some other coastal towns the canneries are run by tight Filipino communities started by just a few pioneer immigrants.

The non-Native part of Alaska, 100 years old with the anniversary of the gold rush in 1998, hasn't had time to develop an Alaskan accent. It's a melting pot of the melting pot, with a population made up of odds and ends from all over the United States. Everyone arrives with a clean slate and a chance to reinvent himself or herself. On occasion, that ability to start from scratch has created some embarrassing discoveries when the past does become relevant. A series of political scandals erupted when reporters checked the resumes of well-known politicians, only to find out they had concocted their previous lives out of thin air. One leading legislative candidate's husband found out about his wife's real background from such a news story.

Alaska's population is as mismatched and haphazard as a thrift store clothing rack, but we do have some cultural traditions, or at least accepted ways of thinking: tolerance and equality, hospitality, independence—and a propensity for violence. In the late 1980s in Homer, a gunfight over a horse left a man lying dead on a dirt road. In the newspaper the next week, the editorial called for people not to settle their differences with guns. A couple of letters to the editor shot back on the theme, "Don't you tell *us* how to settle our differences." Guns are necessary tools in Alaska. They're also a religion. I have friends who actually exchanged handguns instead of rings when they got married.

The tradition of tolerance of newcomers has made Alaska a destination for oddballs, religious cults, hippies, and people who just can't make it in the mainstream. Perhaps the most interesting of the religious groups that formed its own community is the Old Believers, who in recent decades have built villages of brightly painted houses around Kachemak Bay, near Homer. Their resistance to convention dates from Peter the Great's reforms to Russian Orthodoxy in the 18th century, which they reject. In Alaska they've found a place where they can live without interference—in fact, they've thrived as fishermen and boat builders. You see them around town in their 18th-century Russian peasant dress. Until a few years ago, even the girls' high-school basketball team wore long dresses, with their numbers stitched to the bodice.

Nikolaevsk was the first of the Russian Old Believer villages. In the public school there, they didn't teach about dinosaurs or men landing on the moon—that was considered heresy. Yet other Old Believers rebelled, convinced that Nikolaevsk was making too many compromises and was bound to lose the next generation to decadent American ways. They broke off and formed another village, farther up the bay, unreachable except by all-terrain vehicle, and adhered to stricter rules. That village, in turn, suffered another schism and yet another village was formed, farther up the bay, virtually inaccessible and with even stricter rules. The process continues. The fight against assimilation may be hopeless, as children will ultimately do as they please, but it's the Old Believers' own struggle. No one in Homer pushes them to change. No one pays any attention at all, except to buy their fish and their top-quality boats.

After several decades, it looks as if the Old Believers are here to stay. Whether they speak English or not, I'd say they're real Alaskans.

Index

FROMMER'S® COMPLETE TRAVEL GUIDES

FROMMER'S® DAY BY DAY GUIDES

PAULINE FROMMER'S GUIDES! SEE MORE. SPEND LESS.

FROMMER'S® PORTABLE GUIDES

FROMMER'S® CRUISE GUIDES

Alaska Cruises & Ports of Call   Cruises & Ports of Call   European Cruises & Ports of Call

FROMMER'S® NATIONAL PARK GUIDES

Algonquin Provincial Park	National Parks of the American West	Yosemite and Sequoia & Kings
Banff & Jasper	Rocky Mountain	Canyon
Grand Canyon	Yellowstone & Grand Teton	Zion & Bryce Canyon

FROMMER'S® MEMORABLE WALKS

London	Paris	San Francisco
New York	Rome	

FROMMER'S® WITH KIDS GUIDES

Chicago	National Parks	Toronto
Hawaii	New York City	Walt Disney World® & Orlando
Las Vegas	San Francisco	Washington, D.C.
London		

SUZY GERSHMAN'S BORN TO SHOP GUIDES

France	London	Paris
Hong Kong, Shanghai & Beijing	New York	San Francisco
Italy		

FROMMER'S® IRREVERENT GUIDES

Amsterdam	London	Rome
Boston	Los Angeles	San Francisco
Chicago	Manhattan	Walt Disney World®
Las Vegas	Paris	Washington, D.C.

FROMMER'S® BEST-LOVED DRIVING TOURS

Austria	Germany	Northern Italy
Britain	Ireland	Scotland
California	Italy	Spain
France	New England	Tuscany & Umbria

THE UNOFFICIAL GUIDES®

Adventure Travel in Alaska	Hawaii	Paris
Beyond Disney	Ireland	San Francisco
California with Kids	Las Vegas	South Florida including Miami &
Central Italy	London	the Keys
Chicago	Maui	Walt Disney World®
Cruises	Mexico's Best Beach Resorts	Walt Disney World® for
Disneyland®	Mini Mickey	Grown-ups
England	New Orleans	Walt Disney World® with Kids
Florida	New York City	Washington, D.C.
Florida with Kids		

SPECIAL-INTEREST TITLES

Athens Past & Present	Frommer's Exploring America by RV
Best Places to Raise Your Family	Frommer's NYC Free & Dirt Cheap
Cities Ranked & Rated	Frommer's Road Atlas Europe
500 Places to Take Your Kids Before They Grow Up	Frommer's Road Atlas Ireland
Frommer's Best Day Trips from London	Great Escapes From NYC Without Wheels
Frommer's Best RV & Tent Campgrounds	Retirement Places Rated
in the U.S.A.	

FROMMER'S® PHRASEFINDER DICTIONARY GUIDES

French   Italian   Spanish